Gerry Frank's

WHERE TO FIND IT, BUY IT, EAT IT IN NEW YORK

Gerry Frank's

WHERE TO FIND IT, BUY IT, EAT IT
IN
NEW YORK

GERRY'S FRANKLY SPEAKING, INC.
PO Box 2225
Salem, OR 97308
503/585-8411
800/NYC-BOOK (800/692-2665)
Email: gerry@teleport.com
newyorkcityguidebook.net

Gerry Frank's
Where to Find It, Buy It, Eat It in New York

Copyright © 2015
by Gerry Frank

Printed in the United States of America
Library of Congress Catalog Card Number 80-7802

ISBN (13): 978-1879333-26-0

First Edition, 1980
Second Edition, 1981
Third Edition, 1983
Fourth Edition, 1985
Fifth Edition, 1987
Sixth Edition, 1989
Seventh Edition, 1991
Eighth Edition, 1993
Ninth Edition, 1995
Tenth Edition, 1997
Eleventh Edition, 1999
Twelfth Edition, 2001
Thirteenth Edition, 2003
Fourteenth Edition, 2005
Fifteenth Edition, 2007
Sixteenth Edition, 2009
Seventeenth Edition, 2011
Eighteenth Edition, 2013
Nineteenth Edition, 2015

No fees were paid or services rendered in exchange for inclusion in this book. Although every effort was made to ensure that all information was accurate and up-to-date at the time of publication, neither the publisher nor the author can be held responsible for any errors, omissions or adverse consequences resulting from the use of such information.

It is recommended that you call before your visit to verify the information contained in individual business listings.

CONTENTS

Chapter 4
Where to Find It: New York's Best Food Shops 219

Chapter 5
Where to Find It: New York's Best Services 271

VIII   CONTENTS

Chapter 6
Where to Buy It: New York's Best Stores 351

FROM THE AUTHOR

This book all started over 35 years ago with friends encouraging me to write a book about my experiences in New York City.

Since the first edition in 1980, I have concentrated on Manhattan (often synonymous with the whole of New York City), which offers residents and tourists a powerful experience. Still in love with my adopted city, I remain insatiably curious about the latest worthwhile retail stores, accommodations, services, restaurants and museums since my soul was first stirred during childhood visits.

Growing up in a retail family led me to New York and provided me with invaluable training. Through marital liaisons, the Frank family joined with the Meiers to build a major department-store chain that is historic in the annals of retailing history. The first Meier & Frank department store was established in 1857 by my great-grandfather on the banks of the Willamette River in Portland, Oregon. Meier & Frank had its own New York City buying office—an anomaly among retailers and one reason I made so many personal trips to this great city. Today the Meier & Frank stores of old fly under the fine Macy's insignia.

Because the family business was sold, I found myself as a young man without the career I had assumed would be my life's work; so began a second vocation in the political world. I chaired the campaigns for Mark Hatfield, who served Oregon as secretary of state and a two-term governor, and then went on to serve five terms in the U.S. Senate. For 26 years my role was helping with state and federal elections and serving as Hatfield's chief of staff during his lengthy tenure in the Senate. Being in Washington, D.C. with a powerful senator was stimulating beyond anything I could have imagined. However, for me, the downside to living in our nation's capital was the round-the-clock clamor, solely focused on politics. I found this confining, if not unhealthy, so I alternated weekends in Oregon and New York.

Those weekends in the city led to accumulating a wealth of knowledge about Manhattan, from the familiar to the esoteric. Back in the Senate or at home in Oregon, people would ask me where to go or stay in New York, what to do and how to find particular items. Finally, they said, "Gerry, you should write a book."

Initially I knew nothing about writing a book but felt confident that I could do the job. Proud of my finished manuscript, I made the rounds of publishing houses in New York. All of them categorically slammed the door in my face. There was no desire for another Manhattan guidebook (especially one written by an Oregonian) or appreciation of my unique expertise. Not to be denied, I decided to self-publish, which left me with several thousand books but no distribution. Off I went, like a door-to-door salesman, to bookstores, hotel gift shops and anywhere else I thought might benefit from having my book on their shelves.

My efforts have been rewarded through a record sale of over 1.2 million copies of **Where to Find It, Buy It, Eat It in New York**. Publishers have since come calling with offers to publish, to which I happily say, "No thanks."

Native New Yorkers have told me over the years how much they rely on this book (the most complete guide to Manhattan), often referring to it as their Big Apple "bible." One-time tourists and frequent visitors alike also relate how much they depend on it. I hear from readers who ask when the next edition will be published! It is gratifying to have faithful readers who purchase every edition, not only for themselves, but for friends heading to Manhattan.

Where to Find It, Buy It, Eat It in New York is a compendium of information and opinions. I mix facts with subjective commentary based on my lifelong interest and expertise in retailing, eating and travel. No one pays to be listed in my book; these are all my honest choices and appraisals.

I must give credit where credit is due, as I could not have finished the first edition, let alone the 19th, without my team. Cheryl Johnson has been with me since the beginning (33 years) and has been involved in nearly every aspect of the editorial production. Linda Chase (now retired) made order out of my ideas and stacks of notes and clippings; she was also my executive assistant who kept my personal life running smoothly. Jan Boutin and Bryan Miller each had a hand in content and fact-checking; graphic artist Nancy Chamberlain created another winning cover and Randy Mishler masterfully manipulated the drafts to create the finished product.

It's my honor having you among my readers. I hope you enjoy using **Where to Find It, Buy It, Eat It in New York** to help navigate the stimulating streets and eclectic sights of the greatest city in the world.

Gerry Frank

CHAPTER 1

IN AND AROUND THE **WORLD'S GREATEST CITY**

GETTING TO NEW YORK

New York is a popular destination for tourists from around the world. Whether you are a first-time tourist or a regular visitor, you're in for a wonderful treat. Planes, trains and automobiles bring over 50 million visitors a year to Manhattan.

Three major airports serve New York City, and 112 million passengers annually pass through them on about 100 carriers. LaGuardia Airport is most frequently used for domestic flights. John F. Kennedy International Airport has both domestic and international flights, as does Newark Liberty International Airport, located across the Hudson River in New Jersey. I don't recommend landing at Newark if you are going to the city; it is an expensive hassle.

The most common means of traveling between these airports and Manhattan are by taxicab, shuttle bus and car or limousine service. Ground transportation representatives at each airport are pros at recommending the best way to reach your destination. Public transportation is usually the least expensive alternative but may take the longest time. Moreover, you will have to load and unload your own luggage and may have to make one or more transfers. Shared-ride vans, such as SuperShuttle and Go Airlink NYC, offer door-to-door service, but may make for a lengthy trip into the city. Taxicabs are readily available, and if there are two or more in your party, they can be a good deal. To avoid the chaos of taxicabs and mass transit (but pay a bit more), arrange for a private car or limousine. You'll arrive in style and someone else will schlep your luggage.

Amtrak runs in and out of Pennsylvania Station (commonly referred to as Penn Station), a major subway hub located beneath Madison Square Garden between 31st and 33rd streets and Seventh and Eighth avenues. While Amtrak's passenger train service is concentrated between Washington, D.C. and Boston on the Acela Express, long- and short-distance trains from all across the country and some Canadian cities also make stops at Penn Station.

The station is open 24/7 and tickets can be purchased anytime from the Quik-Trak kiosks. Hours for the staffed ticket office and checked baggage are from 5:10 a.m. until 9:50 p.m. An enclosed waiting area for ticketed Amtrak passengers is located in the middle of the main concourse. Be prepared! This is the busiest train station in North America, and you will not want to spend more time here than is necessary. (Call Amtrak at 800/872-7245 or go to amtrak.com for fare and schedule information.)

Metro-North Railroad operates frequent train service in and out of Grand Central Terminal, serving 122 stations as far away as Poughkeepsie and Brewster in New York state and New Haven and Waterbury in Connecticut. For schedule information, call 511, visit mta.info/mnr, or stop by a ticket window at Grand Central Terminal, 42nd Street and Park Avenue.

MANHATTAN'S RIVERS

From its origin in upstate New York, the Hudson River flows along the west side of Manhattan. On the northern tip of the island, the eight-mile long Harlem River empties into the East River. The East and Hudson rivers converge to form Upper New York Bay, also referred to as New York Harbor, near Battery Park.

The Long Island Rail Road (LIRR) operates frequent train service in and out of Penn Station in Manhattan and Atlantic Terminal in downtown Brooklyn. It serves 124 stations in New York City and throughout the length of Long Island. For schedule information, call 511, go to mta.info/lirr, or stop by a ticket window at Penn Station.

While traveling is expensive, bus travel remains a relative bargain. In addition to Greyhound, several express bus companies operate regularly between New York City and Washington, Boston, Philadelphia and other cities on the East Coast and beyond. Bus fares remain more economical than air or train fares. Amenities vary by operator. Some offer reserved seats, discounts for frequent riders, Wi-Fi and TVs, but you're on your own for food and beverage. Be sure to check details carefully.

Many buses depart from Port Authority Bus Terminal (between Eighth and Ninth avenues from 40th to 42nd streets), others provide scheduled pickups around town. Among the operators: BestBus, 202/332-2691, bestbus.com; BoltBus, 877/265-8287, boltbus.com; Greyhound, 800/231-2222, greyhound.com; LimoLiner, 888/546-5469, limoliner.com and Peter Pan Bus, 800/343-9999, peterpanbus.com.

AREA AIRPORTS

Information on airport parking, ground transportation, nearby hotels, driving directions to the airports, flight status, airline information, passenger paging and lost items is only a phone call away.

John F. Kennedy International Airport (718/244-4444, panynj.gov/airports/jfk.html)

LaGuardia Airport (718/533-3400, panynj.gov/airports/laguardia. html)

Newark Liberty International Airport (973/961-6000, panynj.gov/airports/newark-liberty.html)

If you don't have to drive in New York, then don't! The fact that most New Yorkers don't own cars should tell you something. Traffic congestion, extremely aggressive drivers, unbelievably complicated on-street parking regulations — not to mention pricey towing charges and parking fines — are among the reasons to avoid driving. If you must get behind the wheel, then consult a good map or use an app, GPS, MapQuest or some other means to get a clear indication of where you're heading. Don't forget to buckle up!

GETTING AROUND NEW YORK

Compared to most of the world's large cities, Manhattan is much easier to navigate, mainly because it is confined to an island and is therefore relatively compact. Here are some tips on getting around:

WALKING — Moving under one's own power is still my favorite mode of travel in the city. For one thing, the people watching is great! By walking, you will also feel less guilty about indulging in the tempting eats everywhere you go. Traveling in a north-south direction, 20 blocks are the equivalent of one mile. Most east-west blocks are much longer. Walking is fast, cheap and the most interesting way to explore the diverse neighborhoods. If you need directions along the way, duck into a shop or ask one of New York's finest. Many New Yorkers are also willing to aid a perplexed tourist pondering a map, but exercise common sense when talking to strangers.

SUBWAY — Newcomers are sure to get confused with the **Metropolitan Transportation Authority**'s (MTA) 24 subway lines traveling along 659 miles of track and stopping at 468 stations throughout the systems, but over six million people ride the subway every day. It's relatively inexpensive, and it's the fastest way to travel between Upper and Lower Manhattan. With the MetroCard fare card, you can buy a single ride or a seven- or 30-day unlimited ride card, which is accepted on both the subway and local bus systems. Cards can be purchased in subway stations in booths and MetroCard vending machines and at many neighborhood merchants. All machines accept credit cards and ATM/debit cards, and larger machines also accept currency. Station booths take cash only. Up to three children under 44 inches tall can ride free with a fare-paying adult on buses and subways.

Spend a bit of time familiarizing yourself with the map for subway routes, and don't be afraid to ask where to catch a subway and which train to take. Once in the station, digital displays and audio announcements at many stations will provide the length of time until a train is expected to arrive. Visit MTA's TripPlanner (tripplanner.mta.info), an online travel itinerary service for subway, rail, bus and walking directions.

Manhattan's subway stations are nearly all underground, and almost all are on a corner marked by signs with a big "M," "MTA" or an illuminated green globe. Although the subway system operates 24 hours a day, not all station entrances are accessible at all times or have full-time agents. Trains generally run every two to five minutes during rush hours, every five to ten minutes during midday, every five to 15 minutes in the evening, about every 20 minutes between midnight and 6:30 a.m. and on weekends. (Check the schedule for night service.) As you might guess, subway cars can be very crowded during rush hours.

A GEM OF A SUBWAY HUB

Fulton Center, the city's newest and largest subway hub, is capped with a glass and steel dome allowing daylight into two below-ground levels with shops and kiosks. The complex was built at a cost of $1.4 billion to replace the one destroyed in 2001. About 300,000 passengers a day pass through this Fulton Street and Broadway hub where nine subway lines converge.

Once you've passed through the turnstiles and are inside a station, you can transfer between lines or ride for as long as you like. With a MetroCard, you can transfer for free onto a local bus within two hours — or anytime you want if you're using an unlimited-ride card. Station names are printed on the walls of the stations and announced inside subway cars. Pay close attention at all times so you don't miss your stop. Subway cars usually have at least one map posted. The newest cars have strip maps that show stops along the line, with a digital readout of the upcoming stop and an announcement of the current and next stations.

The MTA has a full list of Rules of Conduct, and I'd like to add some common-sense suggestions to make your subway journey safe and pleasant:

■ Don't ride in an empty car. At times of low ridership, move to the car with the conductor — usually in the middle of the train.

■ Don't wear flashy jewelry or display expensive electronics like personal music devices, smartphones, laptops or tablets.

■ Don't wander around aimlessly.

■ Don't stand too close to the tracks; always wait behind the yellow line.

■ Do watch your wallet or purse, particularly in crowded cars, and don't flash cash when purchasing a MetroCard or at any time.

If you have questions or problems regarding the subway or bus systems, contact the **Metropolitan Transportation Authority** at 511

TAXI! TAXI!

Some locations are more popular than others for hailing cabs at certain times of day. Penn Station is the best place to flag one down. If you're going in or near the Port Authority or Grand Central terminals, plenty of rides are nearby, too. Above 96th Street, however, taxis are less plentiful. Cabbies hang around Columbus Circle at 59th Street or Broadway (the southwest boundary of Central Park) to accommodate shoppers and visitors to Central Park. Drivers also know that late-night revelers need lifts home, so look for them around nightclubs and hot spots. One last tip: if you're downtown, stand on the uptown side; if you're uptown, stand on the downtown side.

between 6 a.m. and 10 p.m. every day or consult the MTA website (mta. info). You'll find schedules, locate the nearest bus stops or subway stations, be informed of travel advisories and determine fares. There's also an automated "plan a route" option. Follow the prompts, provide your starting and ending locations, answer a couple of questions and bus and/or subway lines will be suggested, as well as estimated travel times.

BUSES — Buses operate above ground with bus stops at street corners. Look for a round blue sign with a white bus outline. Many signs are accompanied by a "Guide-A-Ride" information box with a route map and schedule. Not all stops have bus shelters. As you board a bus, double-check the destination and be ready to dip your MetroCard into the fare reader. If you don't have a MetroCard, deposit coins for the fare and ask the driver for a transfer to another bus. Since buses do not accept paper currency, be prepared to carry quarters; otherwise, you might be begging your fellow passengers for change to pay your fare. Follow the route map on the bus or check with the bus operator if you have questions about your destination. You'll have a better opportunity to check out the city on a bus, as they offer a slower ride.

A number of buses run on express routes with limited stops, mainly during weekday rush hours. For safety, late-night and early-morning riders can request a drop-off at non-scheduled bus stops. Many museums, attractions and major stores include the nearest bus stops and subway lines with their address information. Maps are readily available throughout the area. Buses are wheelchair accessible and friendly to those who have problems navigating stairs. The MTA's live bus-tracking service, MTA Bus Time™ (bustime.mta. info) can be used to track the current locations of upcoming buses.

TAXIS —Officially licensed medallion taxicabs in New York are yellow, have the words "NYC Taxi" or "NYC" and a big "T" with base information written on the side doors and post their medallion numbers in a box on the roof. Also, color-coded decals are affixed to the rear passenger window, and the driver's credentials are posted. There are many "cars for hire" (known as gypsy cabs).

The **Taxi and Limousine Commission** (TLC) has mandated that all drivers be required to accept major credit and debit cards and that cabs be equipped to process such transactions. A word of warning: scrutinize your credit card receipt before leaving a taxi. If you want to register a compliment or complaint, or report lost or found items, make note of the driver's name and medallion number and contact the Taxi and Limousine Commission at 33 Beaver Street, New York, NY 10004; 212/NEW-YORK (212/639-9675) or 311 (locally); or nyc.gov/taxi.

Your first encounter with a New York taxi may be at an airport. Legitimate taxi lines form in front of most terminals; follow signs to ground transportation. Cab rides into Manhattan are a flat rate from Kennedy and metered fares from LaGuardia and Newark. Allow about an hour between Kennedy and anywhere in Manhattan and expect to pay about $52, plus bridge or tunnel toll and tip. A cab ride between LaGuardia and midtown will take about half an hour and cost about $35, plus bridge toll and tip. Allow as long as an hour between Newark and Manhattan and plan to pay more — as much as $70, plus a $15 surcharge and tolls. Cab fares begin at $3 the moment you get in, and then you're charged 40 cents for each additional unit, which is each one-fifth of a mile while traveling or each minute while stopped in traffic or at stoplights. There are also late-evening and early-morning surcharges and a weekday evening peak-hour surcharge. Standard tipping is 15% to 20% of the price of the trip, and debit and credit cards, as well as cash, are accepted.

Enlist the aid of employees at your hotel, restaurant or other accommodating business to call a cab. If you're on your own, look for the lighted middle number on the roof of the cab, which indicates availability. If the light is off, the cabbie already has a fare or is off-duty. Stand on a street corner and raise your arm to flag a taxi. You may observe the creative lengths to which some New Yorkers will go to hail a cab. When giving an address or destination to your driver, it's helpful to also provide the cross street. The familiar yellow taxis operate 24/7 and generally accommodate no more than four passengers. For safety's sake, always enter and exit curbside.

CAR SERVICES — The countless number of black Lincoln Town Cars and other distinctive black vehicles are not reserved for just the elite; it may be cost-effective to book a stretch limo or passenger van for families (child safety seats available on request) and groups. Unlike yellow taxis, for-hire car services are by reservation only and generally charge by the hour or trip plus tolls and gratuities. Fares are not regulated by the Taxi and Limousine Commission and vary among the many companies. Be sure to agree on a price and method of payment before settling in for a ride.

To forgo the chaos of taxicabs and mass transit, prearrange for a private car or limousine to transport you from the airport. Last-minute reservations can also be made at the ground transportation desks or self-service kiosks, but you might have to wait awhile. Your hotel concierge or bellman will also be able to arrange for a car to drive you around the city for business or pleasure or back to the airport. See the Services section (Chapter V) of this book for my recommendations.

Uber rides are a popular alternative to taxis and car services. Passengers subscribe to Uber service and request a ride through a phone app. Confirmation is sent via text or email and fares are charged to an on-file credit card. There is a choice of budget to high-end luxury vehicles. Costs are either flat rate or calculated on base fare, time and distance.

TWO WHEELING

For exercise and seeing the sights, biking is a fun mode of transportation. Places to rent bikes, helmets and accessories are conveniently located.

Champion Bikes (896 Amsterdam Ave, 212/662-2690, championbicycles.com): repair work

Citi Bike (855/2453-311, citibikenyc.com): operated by NYC Bike Share. Docking stations are accessible 24/7 at more than 300 locations throughout town; daily and weekly access passes and annual memberships

Loeb Central Park Boathouse Bike Rental (Central Park, 212/517-2233, thecentralparkboathouse.com): April-November; for use in Central Park only

Pedal Pusher Bike Shop (1306 Second Ave, 212/288-5592, pedalpusherbikeshop.com): largest rental fleet in the city; road racing bikes

Toga Bikes (110 West End Ave, 212/799-9625, togabikes.com) and Gotham Bikes (112 West Broadway, 212/732-2453, togabikes.com): New York's oldest bike retailer; two shops

DRIVING — If you're driving in or through New York City, know where you're going and plan an alternate route. Be patient and try to avoid daily rush hours, a city-declared "gridlock day warning," Sunday afternoons and holidays.

Tune in to an all-news format radio station or consult an app for timely traffic updates. Using hand-held mobile devices (talking, texting or otherwise) while driving is prohibited, and fines are levied on violators. Obey directional signs and be aware that streets are often closed for special events or construction. Speaking of signs, pay heed to those mandating no turn on red, no parking, no turning during certain hours and fire hydrant and crosswalk zones, or you may wind up paying steep fines. Pedestrians do not always confine their crossing to crosswalks, so keep an eye open for jaywalkers and fearless bike messengers, who often go against the traffic flow.

PARKING — Parking a car in Manhattan can be very costly. Hotel parking fees are sky high, if available, and on-street metered parking spots are rarely empty. Before you claim a spot, look for red-and-white parking signs listing restrictions, which are located on both sides of a street. Be aware of tow-away zones; no parking, no standing and no stopping signs. Street cleaning rules ban parking on alternate sides of streets on certain days. Meters accept quarters; "Muni-meters" control several parking spots and, in addition to quarters, accept the NYC Parking Card.

Municipal and private parking garages are plentiful, and the rules are confusing. Read the fine print and verify rates, accessibility after hours and form of payment before leaving your car or keys. It's possible to search for a parking garage near your destination and compare rates by visiting bestparking.com. Calling 311 or using 311 Online will yield information on public parking and towed vehicles.

BICYCLING — Every day thousands of people ride bicycles to work in New York City. The city has designated bicycle lanes that move in the same direction as traffic. If there is no separate lane, use extreme caution when sharing the roadway with cars and trucks. Bikes are not permitted on city buses, but are permitted on subway trains at all times. However, avoid crowded rush-hour trains and do not block doors.

Some buildings provide bike storage, and some employers allow riders to store bikes in their offices. Avoid chaining your bike to anything (sign posts, parking meters, fences, railings and grates) except bike racks, as you may rack up a fine. Invest in a heavy-duty, theft-deterrent lock, as New York City bike thieves are notoriously quick and nimble. Wear a helmet!

GETTING TO KNOW NEW YORK

References to New York can mean several different things. New York state is the third most populated state in the country. New York County is the most populated county in New York state. New York City, comprised of five boroughs, is the most populous city in the United States. In this book, New York City, "the city" and Manhattan are used interchangeably and all mean the same thing: the borough of Manhattan. Manhattan is one of four New York City boroughs that are islands. The fifth borough, The Bronx, is attached to the mainland.

A LITTLE HISTORY

Native Americans were the first known inhabitants of this area. Italian explorer Giovanni da Verrazano (for whom the Verrazano Narrows Bridge was named) sailed into New York Harbor in 1524 and discovered Manhattan for his French patron, King Francis I. In 1609, Henry Hudson, a trader for the Dutch East India Company, entered the harbor and navigated the river that now bears his name. The first permanent European settlement in Manhattan, a Dutch trading post called Nieuw Amsterdam, was established at the southern tip of the island, where Battery Park is today.

It's true that the Dutch East India Company bought the area from local Indians for inexpensive beads, cloth and other trinkets, but the two sides had vastly different understandings of what the agreement meant.

It was renamed New York in 1664 after the British gained control. In the early 1800s, 60,000 New Yorkers lived mainly on the southern tip of Manhattan, with the rest of the island made up of country estates, fertile farmland, thick forests and wilderness.

New York's historical museums depict life on the island from the days before skyscrapers, subways and millions of people.

John Randall, Jr. implemented an organizational plan for New York City's

COMMON NEW YORK TERMS

Many places in America have their own special words and phrases that people from elsewhere don't understand. Here are some terms commonly heard in New York:

Bridge and tunnel crowd: a disparaging term for visitors from New Jersey; also "B&T crowd"

The City: shorthand for New York City

Coffee regular: coffee with milk and sugar

The FDR: Franklin Roosevelt Drive, an expressway running the length of Manhattan's East Side along the East River

Fuhgeddaboudit: "Forget about it," as in "Don't mention it." It can also mean "No way."

The Garden: Madison Square Garden

Houston: a street in lower Manhattan, pronounced HOUSE-ton

The Island: Long Island

The Met: the Metropolitan Opera or Metropolitan Museum of Art

Schmear: a smear of cream cheese, usually on a bagel

Slice: a piece of pizza

Soda: any sweet carbonated beverage; short for "soda pop"

Straphanger: a subway rider, named for the long-gone leather straps that standing passengers held onto in subway cars

undeveloped land. The system is referred to as the Commissioners Plan of 1811 and encompasses the area from about present-day 14th Street north to 155th Street. Take a look at the map at the front of this book and you'll see a neatly aligned north-south, east-west grid. Below 14th, many streets take off in different directions — a remnant of Manhattan's rural past. Broadway heads northwest from 14th Street. It was once a footpath and is actually one of our nation's longest streets, reaching all the way to the state capital of Albany, some 160 miles north. Though the Plan proved efficient, one major drawback ultimately cost the city millions of dollars, since little space was set aside for public parks.

KEY TO ADDRESSES

All of Manhattan's east-west streets are numbered, as are many of its north-south avenues. In general, most avenues are one-way and alternately northbound and southbound. Most streets are one-way as well; the even-numbered ones tend to be eastbound, and the odd-numbered ones are westbound. Some major east-west thoroughfares accommodate two-way traffic.

Thanks to the Internet and high-tech information devices and apps, pinpointing an address in Manhattan can be a snap. Phone directories and other publications generally include cross-street information as part of an address listing. If you're stuck finding a location with only the street address, here's a reliable system for figuring it out.

AVENUES — If you have a numerical address on one of the north-south avenues, drop the last number, divide the remainder by two and add or subtract the number indicated to find the corresponding cross street.

For example, to find 620 Avenue of the Americas:

$62 \div 2 = 31\text{-}12 = 19\text{th Street}$

Avenue A, B, C, or D . . . . Add 3
First Avenue . . . . Add 3
Second Avenue . . . . Add 3
Third Avenue . . . . Add 10
Lexington Avenue . . . . Add 22
Fourth Avenue/Park Avenue South . . . . Add 8
Park Avenue . . . . Add 35
Madison Avenue . . . . Add 26
Fifth Avenue
  • addresses up to 200 . . . . Add 13
  • between 201 and 400 . . . . Add 16
  • between 401 and 600 . . . . Add 18
  • between 601 and 774 . . . . Add 20
  • between 775 and 1288 . . . . Subtract 18
  • between 1289 and 1500 . . . . Add 45
  • addresses up to 2000 . . . . Add 24
Avenue of the Americas/Sixth Avenue . . . . Subtract 12
Lenox Avenue/Malcolm X Boulevard . . . . Add 110
Seventh Avenue . . . . Add 12
Adam Clayton Powell, Jr. Boulevard . . . . Add 20
Broadway
  • addresses up to 754 are below 8th Street
  • between 755 and 858 . . . . Subtract 29
  • between 859 and 958 . . . . Subtract 25
  • addresses above 958 . . . . Subtract 31
Eighth Avenue . . . . Add 10
Ninth Avenue . . . . Add 13
Columbus Avenue . . . . Add 60
Tenth Avenue . . . . Add 14
Amsterdam Avenue . . . . Add 60
Eleventh Avenue . . . . Add 15
West End Avenue . . . . Add 60
Convent Avenue . . . . Add 127
St. Nicholas Avenue . . . . Add 110
Manhattan Avenue . . . . Add 100
Edgecombe Avenue . . . . Add 134
Fort Washington Avenue . . . . Add 158

CENTERS OF TRADE

Crystal District — The five-block stretch of Madison Avenue between 58th and 63rd streets is home to luxury crystal boutiques: Swarovski, Baccarat, Daum-Haviland and Lalique.

Diamond District — Dozens of jewelers and gem-cutters are located on 47th Street between Fifth Avenue and Avenue of the Americas.

Financial District — Banks, investment firms and stock markets are headquartered south of City Hall down to Exchange Place. The heart is the corner of Wall and Broad streets.

Flower District — 28th Street between Avenue of the Americas and Seventh Avenue.

Garment District — Fifth to Ninth avenues between 34th and 42nd streets is the fashion center. Since the early 1900s, this has been the hub of fashion design, production facilities and fabric and notion suppliers.

Museum Mile — Some of New York's finest museums are strung along Fifth Avenue from 82nd Street to 105th Street.

Music Row — The highest concentration of music instrument stores is on West 48th Street.

Theater District — Renowned on- and off-Broadway theaters are scattered from Avenue of the Americas to Tenth Avenue between 42nd and 54th streets.

Central Park West and Riverside Drive have formulas of their own. To find the cross street for a building on Central Park West, divide the address by 10 and add 60. To find the cross street for a building on Riverside Drive up to 165th Street, divide the address by 10 and add 72.

Because certain addresses (particularly those on Fifth, Madison and Park avenues) are thought to be prestigious, many buildings use them even if the entrances are actually on a side street. This is most common in midtown and along Fifth Avenue on the Upper East Side. Remember, if you can't find an address, look around the corner.

CROSS STREETS — Numbered cross streets run east-west. Addresses on them are easy to find. Allow for a little variation below 23rd Street (because Madison, Eleventh and Twelfth avenues have yet to begin) and throughout the city wherever Broadway is involved.

EAST SIDE

1 to 49	between Fifth Avenue and Madison Avenue
50 to 99	between Madison Avenue and Park Avenue
100 to 149	between Park Avenue and Lexington Avenue
150 to 199	between Lexington Avenue and Third Avenue

200 to 299 . . . . between Third Avenue and Second Avenue
300 to 399 . . . . .between Second Avenue and First Avenue
400 to 499 . . . . between First Avenue and York Avenue
500 to 599 . . . . between Avenue A and Avenue B
WEST SIDE BELOW 59th STREET . . . .
1 to 99 . . . . between Fifth Avenue and Avenue of the Americas
100 to 199 . . . . . between Avenue of the Americas and Seventh Avenue
200 to 299 . . . . between Seventh Avenue and Eighth Avenue
300 to 399 . . . . .between Eighth Avenue and Ninth Avenue
400 to 499 . . . . .between Ninth Avenue and Tenth Avenue
500 to 599 . . . . between Tenth Avenue and Eleventh Avenue
600 and up . . . . between Eleventh Avenue and Twelfth Avenue
WEST SIDE ABOVE 59th STREET . . . .
1 to 99 . . . . .between Central Park West and Columbus Avenue
100 to 199 . . . . . . between Columbus Avenue and Amsterdam Avenue
200 to 299 . . . . . . between Amsterdam Avenue and West End Avenue
300 and up . . . . .between West End Avenue and Riverside Drive

Odd-numbered addresses on east-west streets are on the north (uptown) side, while even-numbered ones are on the south (downtown) side.

NEIGHBORHOODS

Manhattan is composed of over 40 diverse neighborhoods whose names and boundaries change from time to time. There are usually no hard and fast borders defining neighborhoods, which are influenced by economics and demographics. Upper Manhattan refers to the area above 59th Street, which runs along the southern border of Central Park. Midtown refers to the area between 34th and 59th streets. The West Side refers to everything west of Fifth Avenue. Likewise, the East Side refers to the area east of Fifth Avenue. Downtown and Lower Manhattan refer to everything below 14th Street. (The map at the front of this book is a quick guide to these areas.) I encourage you to visit as many neighborhoods as possible to experience the city's exhilarating sights, sounds, flavors and people.

INWOOD AND WASHINGTON HEIGHTS — This racially and ethnically mixed residential neighborhood in northernmost Manhattan is now primarily Dominican. In 1776, this was the site of the last Revolutionary War Battle in New York City, necessitating George Washington's retreat across the Hudson to New Jersey. The Morris-Jumel Mansion, now on 160th Street, served as Washington's headquarters. There are several beautiful parks up here, including Fort Tryon Park (which boasts The Cloisters Museum and Gardens), Inwood Hill Park and Isham Park. Other points of interest are the Dyckman Farmhouse Museum (the last remaining Dutch Colonial-era farmhouse in Manhattan), Audubon Terrace Historic District, Children's Cultural Center of Native America, USA Track and Field Hall of Fame and the Little Red Lighthouse (made famous in a 1940s children's book). The Dominican populace is reflected in bodegas, clubs, street vendors, food carts and distinctive music. Life in this area was depicted in the Broadway musical *In the Heights*.

Marble Hill is actually the northernmost neighborhood of Manhattan, but it is no longer on Manhattan Island, due to the construction of the Harlem River Ship Channel. For this reason, it is now considered part of The Bronx.

HARLEM — The neighborhoods of Hamilton Heights, Astor Row, Sugar Hill, East Harlem and Central Harlem all fall within the area known as Harlem. Residents of East Harlem are predominantly Latino, and the remaining Harlem population is mainly African-American. Harlem is known worldwide as a center of African-American music, politics and culture. It has experienced a renaissance over time, with much to offer residents and visitors. Because of the neighborhood diversity, there are equally assorted dining, shopping and entertainment venues; Harlem Shake is a fun spot for burgers. You'll find the City College of New York, Hamilton Grange National Memorial, St. Nicholas Park, the impressive Museum of the City of New York, the Schomburg Center for Research in Black Culture, the world-famous Apollo Theater, the Classical Theatre of Harlem and the Dance Theatre of Harlem. Former President Bill Clinton's personal office is located on West 125th Street. Many notable figures have resided here, including George and Ira Gershwin, F. Scott Fitzgerald, Thurgood Marshall, Kareem Abdul-Jabbar, Harry Houdini and Adam Clayton Powell, Jr. (for whom a boulevard is named).

HIGHBRIDGE PARK

Highbridge Park is somewhat off the radar, stretching along the Harlem River between 155th and Dyckman streets. The gem of this greenspace, the High Bridge (originally the Old Croton Aqueduct), has been rehabilitated to allow pedestrian and bicycle traffic to cross the 130-foot high span into The Bronx. Dating back to 1847, this is New York City's oldest remaining bridge. Other park highlights include playgrounds, a pool, recreation centers, ball fields and recreational trails.

MORNINGSIDE HEIGHTS — Since the 1890s, a small and vibrant area along the Hudson River has been known as Morningside Heights. Some people now consider Morningside Heights an extension of the Upper West Side, and a few refer to this area as SoHa (South of Harlem) and incorporate SoHa into their business names. Tom's Restaurant (112th and Broadway) gained notoriety from the popular Seinfield television series. (The exterior was shown as Monk's Cafe.) Colleges and institutions proliferate: Barnard College, Columbia University, the Manhattan School of Music, The Cathedral Church of Saint John the Divine, The Riverside Church, St. Luke's Roosevelt Hospital and The Jewish Theological Seminary of America. Riverside Park stretches for four glorious miles along the river and offers abundant recreational opportunities and interesting monuments, the most famous of which is Grant's Tomb. Kids are entertained on the Hippo Playground and the popular winter sledding hill. Check out the variety of convenient neighborhood dining options: Max SoHa (trattoria), Kitchenette Uptown (home cooking) and The Hungarian Pastry Shop (Old World bakery).

UPPER WEST SIDE — This is a largely residential area crowded with families and children. The Upper West Side is ethnically and racially mixed. The apartment buildings facing Central Park have long been considered some of the most desirable in the city for the breathtaking views and coveted location. This area is frequently seen on TV shows and in movies; the magnificent Dakota and Ansonia apartment buildings, as well as the area's unique restaurants and shops, have had recognizable roles.

To say there are lots of quirky and nationally known shops on the Upper West Side is an understatement. Restaurants for every taste, budget and ethnicity abound, some of them open around the clock. Everything is accessible: banks, gyms, cleaners, museums, churches and schools. Bordering Central Park West is the green expanse of Central Park. Some other notable destinations are Zabar's (among my favorite gourmet shops), ABC Studios, Trump International Hotel and Tower, the New-York Historical Society and the American Museum of Natural History. Lincoln Center encompasses more than a square block and is the cultural gem of this area. Midtown Manhattan and the Upper West Side share Columbus Circle. The Shops at Columbus Circle draw people to the Time Warner Center for upscale shopping and award-winning dining; the huge Whole Foods Market is first-class. Below ground, the Columbus Circle subway hub is getting a makeover to include a shopping center and food and dining options.

UPPER EAST SIDE — The Upper East Side is directly east of Central Park. This is a prestigious old-money residential neighborhood with more than its share of sophisticated art museums and galleries, posh boutiques and fine restaurants and cafes. This area has been home to the Vanderbilts, Rockefellers, Carnegies and Kennedys, and has rightfully earned such monikers as "Millionaires Row" and the "Silk Stocking District." It is still home to expensive apartment buildings, former mansions and foreign consulates. Affluent luxury shoppers enjoy superb selections of fine jewelry, multi-carat baubles, furs and other high-end goods on nearly every street. Exclusive private schools reflect the desire for superior education (and status). New York-Presbyterian/Weill Cornell Medical College and the Mount Sinai Icahn School of Medicine call this prominent neighborhood home.

Many chic international designers have boutiques in the area. Bloomingdale's and Barneys New York have been fixtures on the retail front for decades. The Upper East Side has the greatest concentration of museums and galleries in the city, including the Cooper-Hewitt, Smithsonian Design Museum, the Metropolitan Museum of Art and the Solomon R. Guggenheim Museum. The Asia Society is headquartered here, as is the mayor's official abode, Gracie Mansion. This is an area to stroll for fascinating architecture, celebrity spotting and colorful window and patio gardens.

MIDTOWN — Many people associate midtown Manhattan with Times Square's convergence of bright lights and towering buildings, but there's much more. The core of midtown comprises theaters, hotels, offices, restaurants and retailers of every ilk. Famous names include Tiffany's, F.A.O. Schwarz, Saks Fifth Avenue, Macy's, Lord & Taylor, Bergdorf Goodman and Niketown New York, which share the avenues with smaller stores and sidewalk vendors. Midtown landmarks worth visiting are Carnegie Hall, Rockefeller Center, St. Patrick's Cathedral, Trump Tower, the Chrysler Building, New York Public Library, Grand Central Terminal, Radio City

COMMERCE IN HARLEM

This area is rich in culture, history, architecture and unique shopping.

Bébénoir (2164 Frederick Douglass Blvd, 212/828-5775): local designer clothing

The Brownstone Boutique (24 E 125th St, 212/996-7980): women's boutique with local designers

Carol's Daughter (24 W 125th St, 212/828-6757): skin-care, hair and body products

Champs Sports (208 W 125th St, 212/280-0296): sporting goods

Demolition Depot & Irreplaceable Artifacts (216 E 125th St, 212/860-1138): antiques, architectural items; four floors

Duke Ellington Circle (110th St at Fifth Ave): a statue of Sir Duke posed beside a grand piano

Grandma's Place (84 W 120th St, 212/360-6776): books and toys

Harlem Flo (2276 Frederick Douglass Blvd, 212/316-3031): florist

Harlem Haberdashery (245 Malcolm X Blvd, 646/707-0070): classy menswear with style

Harlem Underground (20 E 125th St, 212/987-9385): Harlem-themed T-shirts

Hats by Bunn (2283 Seventh Ave, 212/694-3590): stylish head toppers

Malcolm Shabazz Harlem Market, a.k.a. "African Market" (52 W 116th St, 212/987-8131): traditional crafts and textiles; open 365 days a year

Studio Museum (144 W 125th St, 212/864-4500): emerging and established artists of African descent

The Winery (257 W 116th St, 212/222-4866): wine boutique; spirits and liquor

---

Music Hall and bustling Bryant Park. Closer to the East River is Turtle Bay, home to the United Nations and luxurious residences. Well-appointed and spacious environs are constructed in the Sutton Place and Beekman Place areas, with abundant greenspaces and parks. The area is teeming with great restaurants, cafes, specialty eateries and nightclubs. Greenacre Park on 51st Street is an urban oasis with a waterfall, reflecting pool and seating area.

CLINTON — Some folks still refer to this area as Hell's Kitchen, while others prefer the newer and more descriptive alternative Midtown West. It is no longer the dangerous and violent region of the past, but instead is an upscale neighborhood of diverse residents. Many actors live here because of its close proximity to Broadway theaters. Restaurant Row, on 46th Street, has a profusion of appealing dining options and Ninth Avenue has attracted quite a number of Thai restaurants. Ethnic grocers, bakers, butchers and other food shops coexist with offices, car dealerships, horse stables and myriad small shops. Each day tens of thousands of people pass through the Port Authority Bus Terminal (and past the larger-than-life statue of Jackie Gleason's TV character, bus driver Ralph Kramden) and the Lincoln Tunnel. Passenger ship terminals, Circle Line Cruises and the Intrepid Sea, Air & Space Museum are on the west side of the Henry Hudson Parkway.

MURRAY HILL AND KIPS BAY — These are primarily residential areas with essential businesses that cater to apartment complexes and institutions. Rents are a bit lower here than in surrounding neighborhoods. Several blocks along the East River are dominated by New York University Medical Center and its associated schools, Bellevue Hospital (the oldest continuously operating public hospital in America) and the Veterans Administration Medical Center. The 69th Armory building on Lexington between 25th and 26th streets was completed in 1906 and continues to house the Fighting 69th Army Regiment and special events.

CHELSEA — Big-box stores have made their mark in this largely residential multicultural neighborhood, noted for art galleries, clothing boutiques, small hotels, rocking nightclubs and extraordinary restaurants. The former noisy, grimy industrial buildings have morphed into luxury lofts mixed with apartment complexes. The Fashion Institute of Technology and the High School of Fashion Industries are convenient to the nearby Garment District. The Chelsea Piers development and the Hudson River Park Waterfront Promenade occupy the western border of Chelsea and offer abundant recreational activities; the majority of the elevated High Line Park is in west Chelsea. Foodies are attracted to the Chelsea Market, which has over 40 food-related shops. The offices of TV's Food Network are also in this complex. The General Theological Seminary of the Episcopal Church, the Rubin Museum of Art, the Chelsea Art Museum and The Joyce Theater also call Chelsea home. Madison Square Garden, built atop Penn Station, draws thousands to concerts and sporting events.

COLUMBUS CIRCLE

This traffic circle at the southwest corner of Central Park has the distinction of being the point from which all official distances from New York City are measured. The monument consists of a marble statue of Christopher Columbus and bronze reliefs depicting Columbus' ships.

FLATIRON DISTRICT — The flatiron-shaped building on Fifth Avenue at Broadway is the inspiration for the name of this district. Over the years it has also been referred to as Ladies' Mile, the Photo District and the Toy District. Notable buildings include the MetLife Tower, the Woolworth Building and the New York State Supreme Court building. Brightly illuminated big box retailers, contemporary residential condominiums, the Ace and NoMad hotels and Mario Batali's Eataly have changed the face of the neighborhood. Madison Square (not to be confused with Madison Square Garden) is in the shadow of the Flatiron Building. The Shake Shack and outdoor concerts in the park are warm weather favorites.

GRAMERCY — This area has long been one of the city's most elegant, with some streets reminiscent of old London. Gramercy Park is a small private park accessible only to key-holding tenants of apartment buildings facing the gated Eden. A few blocks away is the very public Union Square; look for the Metronome artwork, which is actually a timepiece. Definitely don't miss the Greenmarket, a favorite farmers market, open seasonally. To the east, Stuyvesant Town and Peter Cooper Village are very large private planned communities with multistory residential buildings.

MEATPACKING DISTRICT — This neighborhood now incorporates high-end boutiques, romantic restaurants and fascinating nightlife along its crooked streets where many illicit activities once defined this 20-square-block area. In the early 1900s, cattle were barged from New Jersey and transported through underground cattle tunnels to slaughterhouses and meatpacking plants. West 14th Street has morphed into a destination for high-end designer boutiques and trendy hotels. A former elevated freight railroad has been transformed into High Line Park, with various activities for the entire family. The Whitney Museum of American Art has recently located to a spectacular building between the Hudson River and the High Line.

GREENWICH VILLAGE — Beatniks, jazz clubs and folk artists in the 1950s and 1960s brought Greenwich Village into the public eye. Coffeehouses, experimental theaters, underground jazz clubs and comedy clubs are still popular, and now small specialty stores share the premises. Many middle-class families reside in mid-rise apartments, 19th-century row houses and walkups. Streets are generally named rather than numbered, and the grid layout found throughout the city basically doesn't exist here. Washington Square Park is a well-known gathering spot, and its impressive stone arch and central water fountain are often photographed. It has also been the site of numerous riots and rallies. Families and students from adjacent New York University use the park for rest and relaxation and play chess, checkers or other games. Not surprisingly, the Village has been home to many artists and political figures, such as Edgar Allan Poe, Allen Ginsberg, Bob Dylan and Abbie Hoffman.

EAST VILLAGE — Within the East Village are Alphabet City, The Bowery, St. Mark's Place and Loisaida. Similar to Greenwich Village, the East Village is made up of offbeat and colorful nightclubs, commerce and interesting people. Outdoor activities come to life in Tompkins Square, the East River Park (along FDR Drive) and the Toyota East Children's Learning Garden. The East Village is also home to some notable off-Broadway productions and boasts the city's highest concentration of bars and taverns.

SOHO — Soho offers energy and charisma and is named for the area South of Houston Street. Old buildings are embellished with cast-iron works in intricate patterns. Tourists and assertive vendors interact on the sidewalks, haggling over jewelry and souvenir prices. Other folks patronize the eclectic mix of trendy shops, boutiques, art galleries and eating places. Businesses stay open late to cater to the weekend and after-work crowds. Buildings are shorter and streets are narrower compared to uptown; some streets are paved with Belgian blocks.

TRIBECA — Thousands of cars pass through Tribeca each day via the Holland Tunnel. The name of this neighborhood is an acronym for its shape (the Triangle Below Canal Street). Former industrial buildings are now trendy residences and the neighborhood is a favorite for on-location filming. Enjoy a tranquil respite at Washington Market Park. The Tribeca Film Center, founded by Robert DeNiro, mixes well with resident artists, local entertainment and antique stores.

CHINATOWN — The periphery of Chinatown continues to creep into surrounding neighborhoods, including Little Italy, expanding this bustling area. Various dialects of Chinese are spoken freely. Just about any consumer product made in China is sold here. Prices are noisily negotiated in jam-packed shops along overcrowded Canal Street. Authentic restaurants and food stuffs are everywhere. To learn more about this culture, visit the Museum of Chinese in America. Beware of vendors offering to sell the latest DVDs, brand-name watches or handbags. This infamous underground economy of copyright-infringed knockoff merchandise attracts both bargain-seeking shoppers and law enforcement.

NOLITA — Short for North of Little Italy, Nolita is one of New York's smaller neighborhoods, sandwiched between Soho, Noho and Little Italy. Vibrant restaurants, galleries and boutiques delight residents and visitors. The gilded figure of Puck (Shakespeare's mischievous sprite) keeps watch on the Puck Building, above Lafayette Street. Torisi Italian Specialties and adjacent Parm offer outstanding Italian fare.

LOWER EAST SIDE — This large area encompasses the Cooperative Village and abuts The Bowery and Chinatown. Again, the perimeters change, but there are still vestiges of Jewish heritage, as demonstrated in the Lower East Side Tenement Museum, the Eldridge Street Synagogue and the Bailystoker Synagogue. Some businesses are closed for Shabbat on Friday afternoon and Saturday, and Sunday remains the primary Jewish shopping day. Visit famous Katz's Delicatessen for an authentic kosher meal to experience this unique local flavor. The area redevelopment has brought high-rise housing, new markets, hip nightclubs, a wide range of new restaurants and fashionable boutiques. Under the Williamsburg Bridge, the East River Park provides a long, green swath with outdoor recreation opportunities and a view of Brooklyn and Manhattan bridges.

LOWER MANHATTAN — The southernmost and oldest part of Manhattan includes the Financial District, the Civic Center, downtown and Battery Park City — just about everything south of Chambers Street. From the canyons and skyscrapers of Wall Street, this area is hectic. The *Charging Bull* statue, symbolic of Wall Street, is in Bowling Green Park, New York City's oldest park. Small family-owned shops are nestled next to major chain stores and intimate restaurants. The lineup of imposing structures and museums is impressive: the World Trade Center and National September 11 Memorial and Museum, the beautifully restored and landscaped City Hall, the Federal Reserve Bank, the Vietnam Veterans Memorial Plaza, the Skyscraper Museum, the National Museum of the American Indian, Trinity Church, the Federal Hall National Memorial, Fraunces Tavern Museum and the Museum of American Finance. The South Street Seaport complex extends alongside the East River, just south of the Brooklyn Bridge. If the weather is nice, take a stroll, walk or ride a bike over the bridge. Battery Park City is yet another planned residential area of high-rise apartment buildings whose residents are treated to fabulous views of Battery Park and Castle Clinton National Monument, the Statue of Liberty, Ellis Island and the Staten Island Ferry.

NEW YORK CITY TAXI AND LIMOUSINE COMMISSION'S TAXI RIDERS' BILL OF RIGHTS

As a taxi rider, you have the right to:

- go to any destination in New York City, Westchester County, Nassau County or Newark Airport.
- decide the route taken, be it the most direct route or one of your choice.
- a safe and courteous driver who obeys all traffic laws.
- a knowledgeable driver who speaks English and knows city geography.
- air conditioning or heat upon request.
- a noise-free trip without gratuitous horn-honking or radio.
- clean, smoke- and scent-free air.
- working seatbelts for all passengers.
- a taxicab with a clean interior, exterior and partition.
- accompaniment by a service animal.
- a driver who does not use a cell phone (hand-held or hands-free) while driving.
- decline to tip for poor service.
- pay by credit or debit card.

WHAT TO EXPECT

THE EXPERIENCE

New York is surprisingly clean and safe and much easier to navigate than most people expect. The good news is that it is remarkably livable for its size, and the crime rate has plummeted since the early 1990s. The New York Police Department has a strong 24/7 presence on the streets, on the water and in the air. Anytime there is a gathering (and there is always something going on in the city) the NYPD is visible. Feel comfortable about approaching officers with questions. A call to 911 will aid you in an emergency, while 311 is the source for New York City government information and non-emergency issues.

That being said, keep in mind these common sense "don'ts":

- Don't display wads of money, flashy watches, jewelry or electronics. Leave most of your cash and all of your valuables at home or in the hotel safe.
- Don't use ATMs when no one else is around.
- Don't leave an ATM until you've put your money in a wallet and then put the wallet in your pocket or purse.

■ Don't keep your wallet in your back pocket unless it's buttoned. Better yet, carry your wallet in a front pocket, along with keys and other important items.

■ Don't wear your purse slung over one shoulder. Instead, put the strap over your head and keep your purse in front of you or to the side.

■ Don't doze off on the subway or bus.

■ Don't jog in Central Park or anywhere else after dark.

■ Don't let yourself believe that staying in "good" neighborhoods protects you from crime.

■ Don't let anybody into your hotel room, even if they claim to work for the hotel, unless you've specifically asked them to come or have checked with the front desk to verify their authenticity.

■ Don't talk to strangers who try to strike up a conversation unless you're sure of their motivation.

■ Don't ever leave bags unattended. If you're going to put a bag or backpack on the floor at a restaurant or bathroom stall, put your foot or a leg of your chair through the strap.

■ Don't hang your purse or anything else on the back of the door in a public bathroom stall.

■ Don't walk around with your mouth open and your camera and map visible while saying things like, "Gee, we sure don't have buildings this tall back home!"

■ Don't be afraid to cross the street if a situation doesn't feel right. Shout for help or approach a policeman or store worker if you are being bothered.

■ Don't make eye contact with panhandlers, and never give them money.

■ Move away from unattended packages and immediately report any suspicious items or behavior to authorities.

A final word of warning: watch where you walk. Manhattan has an incredible amount of traffic, and the struggle among cars, taxis, trucks, buses, bicycles and pedestrians is constant. It may seem silly to repeat a warning from childhood, but look both ways before stepping into the street.

If you're traveling with a group, it's always a good idea to plan a meeting place and contact strategy (be sure to share cell-phone numbers) in case you get separated. If there's an emergency, call 911.

Average temperatures range from highs in the 30s and 40s in December, January and February (snow is always a possibility) to highs in the 80s and 90s in June, July and August (when the humidity can be stifling).

TIPPING AND OTHER EXPENSES

No doubt about it: New York can be expensive. Basic hotels start at about $200 a night, while upscale ones often run upwards of twice that. An average dinner at a respectable restaurant will run about $30 (without cocktails or wine). Theater tickets are at least $125. Look for discounts and coupons in publications, on the Internet and through membership benefits. Elsewhere in this book you'll discover less expensive alternatives and suggestions for free events and activities.

Tipping is expected in many instances. Keep small bills handy, as you'll

TIPS FOR TIPPING

AIRPORTS

Skycap—$1 to $2 a bag (more if the bag is big and/or heavy)

Taxi drivers—15% to 20% of the fare

Shuttle drivers—$2 per person

HOTELS

Doorman—1 to $2 a bag; $1 to $2 per person for hailing a taxi

Bellhop—$1 to $2 a bag, depending on size and weight; $1 to $2 for deliveries to your room

Concierge—$5 to $20 for special services, like securing hard-to-get theater tickets and restaurant reservations

Housekeeper —$3 to $4 a night; for extra service, an additional $1 to $2

Room service—15% to 20% of the bill (before taxes), if not included

Parking valet—$2 to $5

RESTAURANTS

Check your bill carefully, as a tip may already have been included!

Coat check —$1 an item

Maitre d'—$10 to $100 (depending on the occasion, restaurant and level of service you wish to receive, given before being seated)

Wait staff—15% to 20% of the bill before taxes

Sommelier—10% to 15% of the wine bill, lesser amounts for very expensive bottles

Bartender/server—$1 to $2 per drink, or 15% to 20% of tab

Restroom attendant—50 cents to $1 for handing you a towel or if you use any products or cosmetics

Buffet server—$1 per person or 10% to 20% of the bill, according to the level of service

burn through them. You won't be exposing all of your cash if you keep singles separated from larger bills. An easy way to figure out the tip on a restaurant tab is to double the tax, which is 8.875%.

CHECKLISTS

Planning ahead for your trip will help alleviate stress. Read the relevant sections of this book, call ahead and order tickets well in advance when appropriate. Bear in mind some activities and events are seasonal.

When traveling remember these essentials:

▇ a government-issued picture ID card

▇ student ID card, if applicable (to obtain student discounts)

■ AARP or similar identification, if you qualify for a senior discount

■ emergency contact information

■ medications

■ tickets for travel and events

■ comfortable walking shoes

■ umbrella and raincoat (or warm coat, scarf, boots and gloves)

■ opera glasses, if you're heading to the theater

■ electronics and chargers

Most hotels provide in-room coffeemakers (with coffee), irons and hair-dryers, and they also supply toiletries and mending kits. In-room Internet connections are generally available (sometimes at a cost), as are in-room safes. Organize your credit cards and cash before leaving the room. Use a secure pocket or money belt. Ladies, be especially mindful of your handbag and do not wear gaudy jewelry. Carry a small bag or tote with these daily essentials:

■ mobile phone

■ address and phone numbers of places you plan to visit and directions to get there

■ maps of the bus and subway systems and an unlimited-ride MetroCard

■ tissues

■ list of public bathrooms in the areas you'll be visiting

■ loose change and small bills

■ small notepad and pen

■ weather-appropriate accessories: sunglasses, sunscreen, water bottle, umbrella or gloves

Most important of all, don't forget this book!

TAXI NEWS

After much ballyhoo, New York City's iconic yellow cabs will be replaced with a fleet of Nissan NV200 vans as existing cabs are retired or replaced. The new, more comfortable rides are outfitted with skylights, USB ports and 12-volt outlets, retractable steps, passenger airbags and low-annoyance horns. A wheelchair accessible model features a fold-flat ramp and a restraint system.

You may see green-colored taxis. Boro Taxis can pick up passengers in northern Manhattan and other areas of the five boroughs not served by medallion cabs for any destination including the airports. They are, however, prohibited from picking up passengers in the Manhattan exclusionary zone.

CHAPTER 2

WHERE TO EAT
IT NEW YORK'S
BEST RESTAURANTS

IT IS POSSIBLE

to get whatever kind of meal you want, at almost any price you want — and often at any hour you want — in this great "eating out" city. Lower Manhattan is no exception with an abundance of interesting and varied eateries.

To the delight of restaurants, more people are eating out for daily meals and special occasions. However, we are seeing prices escalate mainly, but not exclusively, due to rising food and labor costs.

In my opinion, several areas in the restaurant business need attention. Many chefs have become "celebrities" and some spend more time polishing their image than working and training in the kitchen.

The biggest complaints from diners continue to be due to shoddy treatment by reservation agents and front-door personnel resulting in unnecessary difficulty getting a table on the day and time you want. Don't let the lack of a reservation deter you from a spot you really want to visit; instead, walk in and in most cases they will take care of you. It is totally unacceptable to be shuffled off to the bar if the dining room is not full.

Too many hosts and hostesses are haughty, self-important and more interested in projecting their personal "style" than greeting diners and setting a proper tone for the dining experience. Restaurateurs need to properly train and supervise their employees to provide the best customer service experience for their patrons; otherwise, they will likely go to one of the many other dining options in the city.

Following are some observations that I hope will be helpful:

■ Dining hours: Tables are usually available early, up to about 6 p.m. Most restaurants fill up around 8 p.m., especially the more "in" establishments.

■ It is very inconsiderate and costly to an establishment if you are a no-show for your reservation. Taking into account Manhattan traffic, most places will give 20 to 30 minutes of leeway to tardy diners. Try not to give a credit card number when making reservations, but if you do, be aware of the restaurant's cancellation policy. If possible, make a reservation at least a week ahead of time.

■ Most restaurants (exceptions noted elsewhere) do not have a strict dress code. Dress neatly and comfortably; business casual is always a safe bet. Unlike the old days, it is rare to see a gentleman in a suit and tie at a nice restaurant or at the theater.

■ Some of the best dining spots in New York are the old-time, tried-and-true establishments. They wouldn't be around today if they were not very special. Just because a place is new does not necessarily mean that it is better than those that have taken proper care of patrons for years.

■ New York tap water is among the best in the country, so don't waste your dollars on expensive bottled water.

■ Study the wine list carefully or enlist a knowledgeable member of your party to do so. Markups on wine can be outrageous.

■ Try eating in the bar at some of the pricier establishments. It is quicker and often prices are lower.

■ Regarding tipping, a good rule of thumb is to double the tax. If someone gives really special service or attention, a little extra is always appropriate. Before paying your tab, review your bill for unexpected charges; in some instances, especially for parties of six or more, the tip is added to the bill.

This book is not a directory of Manhattan restaurants. I have selected places where I have personally dined, providing listings in every price range, every neighborhood and encompassing almost every type of food. The evaluations are mine alone. No one pays to be listed or receives special favors in a review. Please remember that these write-ups are up to date at the time this volume goes to press, although a given restaurant's situation can change at any time.

If you have a particularly good or bad dining experience, don't hesitate to talk with the owner or manager. Please let me know, too, as your feedback and suggestions are very important. Bon appétit!

PRICE RANGES

In the following pages, you'll find lists of restaurants categorized by neighborhood and specialties. In addition, I've written almost 300 full-length reviews, beginning on page 71. Those restaurants fall into four price ranges, based on the combined cost of an appetizer and entree (not including drinks):

Inexpensive	up to $25 per person
Moderate	$26 to $40 per person
Moderately expensive	$41 to $54 per person
Expensive	$55 and up per person

RESTAURANTS
QUICK REFERENCE
GUIDE

Note: Restaurants receiving full write-ups in this chapter are listed by neighborhood in this reference guide. The type of cuisine and the word "Sunday" (if a given restaurant is open that day) follow each address.

BATTERY PARK CITY/FINANCIAL DISTRICT/TRIBECA
Acappella (1 Hudson St): Italian
American Cut (363 Greenwich St): steak
Bâtard (239 West Broadway): American/European
Blaue Gans (139 Duane St): Austrian/German, Sunday
Blue Smoke (255 Vesey St): barbecue, Sunday
Bouley (163 Duane St): French/American
Bouley Test Kitchen (88 West Broadway, 5th floor): cooking classes/test kitchen, by appointment
Brushstroke (30 Hudson St): Japanese
Capital Grille (120 Broadway): steak
Delmonico's (56 Beaver St): steak
Landmarc (179 West Broadway): French, Sunday
Les Halles (15 John St): French, Sunday
Locanda Verde (The Greenwich Hotel, 377 Greenwich St): Italian, Sunday
Luke's Lobster (26 S William St): seafood, Sunday
MarkJoseph Steakhouse (261 Water St): steak, Sunday
Morton's The Steakhouse (136 Washington St): steak, Sunday
Ninja New York (25 Hudson St): Japanese, Sunday
Nobu New York/Nobu Next Door (105 Hudson St): Japanese, Sunday
North End Grill (104 North End Ave): American/seafood, Sunday
P.J. Clarke's on the Hudson (4 World Financial Center): pub food, Sunday
The Palm (206 West St): steak, Sunday
Sarabeth's (339 Greenwich St): American, Sunday
Scalini Fedeli (165 Duane St): Italian
Tres Carnes (101 Maiden Ln): Tex-Mex, Sunday
Tribeca Grill (375 Greenwich St): American, Sunday
Wolfgang's Steakhouse (409 Greenwich St): steak, Sunday

CENTRAL PARK AREA
A Voce (Time Warner Center, 10 Columbus Cir, 3rd floor): Italian, Sunday
Jean Georges (Trump International Hotel and Tower, 1 Central Park W): French
Landmarc (Time Warner Center, 10 Columbus Cir, 3rd floor): French, Sunday
Luke's Lobster (Plaza Food Hall, 1 W 59th St, lower level): seafood, Sunday
Nougatine at Jean Georges (Trump International Hotel and Tower, 1

Central Park W): French, Sunday
Plaza Food Hall (The Plaza, 1 W 59th St, lower level): eclectic, Sunday
Sarabeth's (40 Central Park S): American, Sunday

CHELSEA/WEST CHELSEA

Colicchio & Sons (85 Tenth Ave): American, Sunday
Cookshop (156 Tenth Ave): American, Sunday
Del Posto (85 Tenth Ave): Italian, Sunday
Gigi Cafe (307 Seventh Ave): health food, Sunday
La Lunchonette (130 Tenth Ave): French, Sunday
Rare Bar & Grill (Hilton New York Fashion District, 152 W 26th St): burgers, Sunday
Scarpetta (355 W 14th St): Italian, Sunday
Tao Downtown (Maritime Hotel, 92 Ninth Ave): Asian, Sunday
Tipsy Parson (156 Ninth Ave): Southern, Sunday
Toro (85 Tenth Ave): Spanish
Trestle on Tenth (242 Tenth Ave): American, Sunday

CHINATOWN

Golden Unicorn (18 East Broadway): Chinese, Sunday

EAST SIDE/UPPER EAST SIDE

2nd Ave Deli (1442 First Ave): deli/kosher, Sunday
Arlington Club (1032 Lexington Ave): steak, Sunday
Café Boulud (20 E 76th St): French, Sunday
Cafe d'Alsace (1695 Second Ave): French, Sunday
Cafe Sabarsky (Neue Galerie New York, 1048 Fifth Ave): Austrian, Sunday
Cucina Vivolo (138 E 74th St): Italian
Daniel (60 E 65th St): French
Elio's (1621 Second Ave): Italian, Sunday
Eli's Table (1413 Third Ave): American, Sunday
Fig & Olive (808 Lexington Ave): Mediterranean, Sunday
Freds at Barneys New York (660 Madison Ave, 9th floor): American, Sunday

FOOD TRUCKS

Not that long ago the only trucks roaming the streets with things to eat were the summertime ice-cream vendors. Times have changed! Contemporary New York food trucks are large, artfully decorated and outfitted with kitchens to prepare and serve pastries, sandwiches, soups, full meals and even freshly cooked French fries. Some have become so successful that they have led to bricks-and-mortar restaurants. The bottom line is that food trucks now offer an easy option for a quick snack anywhere in the city. There are websites to help you choose a truck by location and cuisine (findnycfoodtrucks.com).

Il Mulino Uptown (37 E 60th St): Italian, Sunday
Il Vagabondo (351 E 62nd St): Italian, Sunday
Jackson Hole Burgers (232 E 64th St): burgers, Sunday
Jacques Brasserie (204-206 E 85th St): French, Sunday
King's Carriage House (251 E 82nd St): American, Sunday
Luke's Lobster (242 E 81st St): seafood, Sunday
The Mark Restaurant by Jean-Georges (The Mark, 25 E 77th St): American, Sunday
Nicola's (146 E 84th St): Italian, Sunday
Paola's (Hotel Wales, 1295 Madison Ave): Italian, Sunday
Rotisserie Georgette (14 E 60th St): French, Sunday
Sarabeth's (Hotel Wales, 1295 Madison Ave): American, Sunday
Serendipity 3 (225 E 60th St): dessert, Sunday
Sette Mezzo (969 Lexington Ave): Italian, Sunday
Sfoglia (1302 Lexington Ave): Italian, Sunday
Shake Shack (154 E 86th St): burgers, Sunday
The Simone (151 E 82nd St): French
Sirio Ristorante (The Pierre, 795 Fifth Ave): Italian, Sunday
Sistina (1555 Second Ave): Italian, Sunday
Spigolo (1561 Second Ave): Italian, Sunday
Texas de Brazil (1011 Third Ave): Brazilian/steak, Sunday
Vivolo (140 E 74th St): Italian

EAST VILLAGE/NOLITA

Balaboosta (214 Mulberry St): Mediterranean/Mideastern, Sunday
Bar Primi (325 Bowery): Italian, Sunday
Cherche Midi (282 Bowery): French, Sunday
DBGB Kitchen and Bar (299 Bowery): French, Sunday
Feast (102 Third Ave): American, Sunday
Huertas (107 First Ave): Spanish, Sunday
Jacques 1534 (20 Prince St): French/gastropub, Sunday
King Bee (424 E 9th St): Canadian/Cajun, Sunday
Luke's Lobster (93 E 7th St): seafood, Sunday
Miss Lily's 7A Cafe (109 Ave A): Caribbean/diner, Sunday
The Musket Room (265 Elizabeth St): New Zealand, Sunday
Shuko (47 E 12th St): Japanese

FLATIRON DISTRICT/GRAMERCY PARK/ LOWER BROADWAY/UNION SQUARE

A Voce (41 Madison Ave): Italian
ABC Kitchen (ABC Carpet & Home, 35 E 18th St): American, Sunday
Aldea (31 W 17th St): Mediterranean
Blue Water Grill (31 Union Square W): seafood, Sunday
The Breslin (Ace Hotel, 16 W 29th St): British/gastropub, Sunday
City Bakery (3 W 18 St): bakery/cafe, Sunday
Craft (43 E 19th St): American, Sunday

Da Umberto (107 W 17th St): Italian
Dévi (8 E 18th St): Indian, Sunday
Eleven Madison Park (11 Madison Ave): American/French, Sunday
Gramercy Tavern (42 E 20th St): American, Sunday
Hanjan (36 W 26th St): Chinese
Hill Country (30 W 26th St): barbecue, Sunday
Hill Country Chicken (1123 Broadway): Southern, Sunday
The John Dory Oyster Bar (Ace Hotel, 1196 Broadway): seafood, Sunday
L'Express (249 Park Ave S): French, Sunday
Maialino (Gramercy Park Hotel, 2 Lexington Ave): Italian, Sunday
Marta (Martha Washington Hotel, 29 E 29th St): Italian/pizza, Sunday
Millesime (The Carlton Hotel, 92 Madison Ave): French/seafood, Sunday
NoMad (NoMad Hotel, 1170 Broadway): American/European, Sunday
Rosa Mexicano (9 E 18th St): Mexican, Sunday
Sarabeth's (381 Park Ave S): American, Sunday
Shake Shack (Madison Square Park, 23rd St bet Madison Ave and Broadway):
   burgers, Sunday
Tocqueville Restaurant (1 E 15th St): American
Tres Carnes (688 Ave of the Americas): Tex-Mex, Sunday
Union Square Cafe (21 E 16th St): American, Sunday

GARMENT DISTRICT/KIPS BAY/MURRAY HILL

2nd Ave Deli (162 E 33rd St): deli/kosher, Sunday
Blue Smoke (116 E 27th St): barbecue, Sunday
Docks Oyster Bar and Seafood Grill (633 Third Ave): seafood, Sunday
El Parador Cafe (325 E 34th St): Mexican, Sunday
Jackson Hole Burgers (521 Third Ave): burgers, Sunday
Les Halles (411 Park Ave S): French, Sunday
Marchi's (251 E 31st St): Italian
The Morgan Dining Room (The Morgan Library & Museum, 225 Madison
   Ave): American, Sunday
Rare Bar & Grill (Affina Shelburne, 303 Lexington Ave): American, Sunday
Resto (111 E 29th St): Belgian, Sunday
Rose Bakery (160 Lexington Ave): English/bakery, Sunday
Sarabeth's (381 Park Ave S): American, Sunday
Turkish Kitchen (386 Third Ave): Turkish, Sunday

GREENWICH VILLAGE/WEST VILLAGE

Annisa (13 Barrow St): American, Sunday
Babbo (110 Waverly Pl): Italian, Sunday
Bar Six (502 Ave of the Americas): French, Sunday
Blue Hill (75 Washington Pl): American, Sunday
Blue Ribbon Bakery (35 Downing St): American, Sunday
bobo (181 W 10th St): French, Sunday
Buvette (42 Grove St): French, Sunday

THEME RESTAURANTS

Check out these splashy operations, which are good, kid-friendly party venues.

Barking Dog Luncheonette (1678 Third Ave, 212/831-1800 and other locations): canine themed; dogs welcome

Hard Rock Cafe (1501 Broadway, 212/489-6565): Elvis has not left the building.

Jekyll and Hyde (91 Seventh Ave S, 212/989-7701): Haunted!

Ninja New York (25 Hudson St, 212/274-8500): subterranean, secret paths

Planet Hollywood (1540 Broadway, 212/333-7827): memorabilia galore

Cafe Cluny (284 W 12th St): American/French, Sunday
Camaje (85 MacDougal St): French, Sunday
Chez Jacqueline (72 MacDougal St): French, Sunday
Good (89 Greenwich Ave): American, Sunday
Gotham Bar & Grill (12 E 12th St): American, Sunday
Gyu-Kaku (34 Cooper Sq): Japanese/barbecue, Sunday
Han Dynasty (90 Third Ave): Chinese, Sunday
Il Mulino New York (86 W 3rd St): Italian
Jeffrey's Grocery (172 Waverly Pl): American, Sunday
Joseph Leonard (170 Waverly Pl): American, Sunday
La Ripaille (605 Hudson St): French, Sunday
Le Gigot (18 Cornelia St): French, Sunday
Little Owl (90 Bedford St): American, Sunday
Market Table (54 Carmine St): American, Sunday
Minetta Tavern (113 MacDougal St): French, Sunday
Miss Lily's (132 W Houston St): Caribbean/diner, Sunday
Morandi (211 Waverly Pl): Italian, Sunday
One if by Land, Two if by Sea (17 Barrow St): American, Sunday
Perilla (9 Jones St): American, Sunday
Piora (430 Hudson St): American, Sunday
Pó (31 Cornelia St): Italian, Sunday
Recette (328 W 12th St): American, Sunday
RedFarm (529 Hudson St): Chinese, Sunday
Rosemary's Enoteca & Trattoria (18 Greenwich Ave): Italian, Sunday
The Spotted Pig (314 W 11th St): European/gastropub, Sunday
Strip House (13 E 12th St): steak, Sunday
Tartine (253 W 11th St): French, Sunday
Wallsé (344 W 11th St): Austrian, Sunday
Waverly Inn (16 Bank St): American, Sunday

HARLEM/EAST HARLEM/MORNINGSIDE HEIGHTS
Dinosaur Bar-B-Que (700 W 125th St): barbecue, Sunday
Rao's (455 E 114th St): Italian
Red Rooster Harlem (310 Lenox Ave): American/Southern, Sunday

LOWER EAST SIDE
Clinton St. Baking Co. & Restaurant (4 Clinton St): American, Sunday
Dirty French (The Ludlow Hotel, 180 Ludlow St): French/Moroccan, Sunday
Freemans (Freeman Alley off Rivington St): American, Sunday
Ivan Ramen (25 Clinton St): Japanese/noodle shop, Sunday
Katz's Delicatessen (205 E Houston St): deli, Sunday
Russ & Daughters Cafe (127 Orchard St): Jewish, Sunday
Schiller's (131 Rivington St): eclectic, Sunday
Yunan Kitchen (79 Clinton St): Chinese, Sunday

MEATPACKING DISTRICT
Fig & Olive (420 W 13th St): Mediterranean, Sunday
Macelleria (48 Gansevoort St): Italian/steak, Sunday
Spice Market (403 W 13th St): Asian, Sunday
The Standard Grill (Standard Hotel, 848 Washington St): American, Sunday
Valbella (421 W 13th St): Italian

MIDTOWN EAST
Aquavit (65 E 55th St): Scandinavian
Artisanal Fromagerie, Bistro and Wine Bar (2 Park Ave): French, Sunday
BLT Steak (106 E 57th St): steak, Sunday
Bottega del Vino (7 E 59th St): Italian, Sunday
Brasserie (100 E 53rd St): French, Sunday
Café Centro (MetLife Building, 200 Park Ave): Mediterranean
Capital Grille (Chrysler Center, 155 E 42nd St): steak, Sunday
Casa Lever (390 Park Ave): Italian
Cucina & Co. (MetLife Building, 200 Park Ave, lobby): Italian

INCREASED FOOD PRICES
A bit of information to avoid sticker-shock when ordering at restaurants these days: retail prices for steak will average around $8 a pound this year, which is nearly double what it cost in 2000. This huge increase will be reflected in the menu prices at quality dining venues. Prices for hamburger meat is up even more! One of the reasons for this is that the U.S. cattle herd has been at an all-time low. And for breakfast-lovers, bacon, at about $6 a pound, is about double what it was 15 years ago. Savvy shoppers will note that overall grocery prices will increase nearly 3% this year (2015).

Cucina Vivolo (222 E 58th St): Italian
Felidia (243 E 58th St): Italian, Sunday
Fig & Olive (10 E 52nd St): Mediterranean, Sunday
Four Seasons (99 E 52nd St): American
Fresco by Scotto (34 E 52nd St): Italian
Gigi Cafe (958 Third Ave): health food, Sunday
Grand Central Oyster Bar Restaurant (Grand Central Terminal, 42nd
St at Vanderbilt Ave, lower level): seafood
Gyu-Kaku (805 Third Ave, 2nd floor): Japanese/barbecue, Sunday
Hatsuhana (17 E 48th St): Japanese
Il Postino (337 E 49th St): Italian, Sunday
La Grenouille (3 E 52nd St): French
Lavo (39 E 58th St): Italian, Sunday
Le Cirque (1 Beacon Ct, 151 E 58th St): French
Le Périgord (405 E 52nd St): French, Sunday
Maloney & Porcelli (37 E 50th St): American, Sunday
Morton's The Steakhouse (551 Fifth Ave): steak, Sunday
Mr. K's (570 Lexington Ave): Chinese, Sunday
Naples 45 (MetLife Building, 200 Park Ave): Italian
P.J. Clarke's (915 Third Ave): pub food, Sunday
The Palm (837 Second Ave and 840 Second Ave): steak, Sunday (only at 840
Second Ave)
Pietro's (232 E 43rd St): Italian
The Polo Bar (1 E 55th St): American, Sunday
Rosa Mexicano (1063 First Ave): Mexican, Sunday
San Pietro (18 E 54th St): Italian
Shun Lee Palace (155 E 55th St): Chinese, Sunday
Smith & Wollensky (797 Third Ave): steak, Sunday
Sparks Steak House (210 E 46th St): steak
Tao (42 E 58th St): Asian, Sunday
Totto Ramen (248 E 52nd St): Japanese/noodle shop, Sunday
Tres Carnes (954 Third Ave): Tex-Mex, Sunday
Valbella (11 E 53rd St): Italian
Wolfgang's Steakhouse (4 Park Ave and 200 E 54th St): steak, Sunday

MIDTOWN WEST
Abboccato Italian Kitchen (136 W 55th St): Italian, Sunday
Bar Americain (152 W 52nd St): American, Sunday
Benoit (60 W 55th St): French, Sunday
Betony (41 W 57th St): American
Brasserie 8½ (9 W 57th St): French, Sunday
Brasserie Ruhlmann (45 Rockefeller Plaza): French, Sunday
Brooklyn Diner USA (212 W 57th St): eclectic/diner, Sunday
Capital Grille (Time-Life Building, 120 W 51st St): steak, Sunday
Carmine's (200 W 44th St): Italian, Sunday
Casa Nonna (310 W 38th St): Italian, Sunday

Gigi Cafe (64 E 34th St): health food, Sunday
Circo NYC (120 W 55th St): Italian, Sunday
Del Frisco's Double Eagle Steak House (McGraw-Hill Building, 1221 Ave of the Americas): steak, Sunday
Del Frisco's Grille (50 Rockefeller Plaza): steak, Sunday
Gotham West Market (600 Eleventh Ave): food market, Sunday
Il Gattopardo (13-15 W 54th St): Italian, Sunday
Keens Steakhouse (72 W 36th St): American, Sunday
Le Bernardin (155 W 51st St): French
Madangsui (35 W 35th St): Korean/barbecue, Sunday
Marea (240 Central Park S): Italian/seafood, Sunday
Michael's (24 W 55th St): California
The Modern (Museum of Modern Art, 9 W 53rd St): American/French
Nobu 57 (40 W 57th St): Japanese, Sunday
Oceana (McGraw-Hill Building, 120 W 49th St): American/seafood, Sunday
The Palm (250 W 50th St): steak, Sunday
Patsy's Italian Restaurant (236 W 56th St): Italian, Sunday
Print (Ink48, 653 Eleventh Ave): American, Sunday
Quality Meats (57 W 58th St): American/steak, Sunday
Rainbow Room (30 Rockefeller Plaza, 65th floor): American, Sunday
Redeye Grill (890 Seventh Ave): American/seafood, Sunday
Remi (145 W 53rd St): Italian, Sunday
Rue 57 (60 W 57th St): French, Sunday
The Russian Tea Room (150 W 57th St): Continental/Russian, Sunday
Sarabeth's (Lord & Taylor, 424 Fifth Ave, 5th floor): American, Sunday
The Sea Grill (Rockefeller Center, 19 W 49th St): seafood
Shabu Shabu Kobe (3 W 36th St): Japanese, Sunday
Strip House (15 W 44th St and 464 W 51st St): steak, Sunday
Totto Ramen (366 W 52nd St): Japanese/noodle shop, Sunday
Tout va Bien (311 W 51st St): French, Sunday
Trattoria dell'Arte (900 Seventh Ave): Italian, Sunday
Uncle Jack's Steakhouse (440 Ninth Ave and 44 W 56th St): steak, Sunday

NOHO/SOHO/LITTLE ITALY

Acme (9 Great Jones St): American, Sunday
Balthazar (80 Spring St): French, Sunday
Bistro les Amis (180 Spring St): French, Sunday
Blue Ribbon (97 Sullivan St): eclectic, Sunday
David Burke Kitchen (The James Hotel, 23 Grand St): American, Sunday
The Dutch (131 Sullivan St): American, Sunday
Giorgione (307 Spring St): Italian, Sunday
Hundred Acres (38 MacDougal St): American, Sunday
Il Buco Alimentari e Vineria (53 Great Jones St): Italian/Mediterranean, Sunday
Il Cortile (125 Mulberry St): Italian, Sunday
Il Mulino Prime (331 West Broadway): Italian/steak, Sunday

Lafayette (380 Lafayette St): French, Sunday
Onieal's Grand Street (174 Grand St): American, Sunday
Osteria Morini (218 Lafayette St): Italian, Sunday
Raoul's (180 Prince St): French, Sunday
Spring Street Natural (62 Spring St): health food, Sunday
Vic's (31 Great Jones St): Italian/Mediterranean, Sunday

THEATER DISTRICT/TIMES SQUARE
Barbetta (321 W 46th St): Italian
Bond 45 (154 W 45th St): Italian/steak, Sunday
Brooklyn Diner USA (155 W 43rd St): eclectic/diner, Sunday
Bryant Park Grill (25 W 40th St): American, Sunday
Carnegie Deli (854 Seventh Ave): deli, Sunday
db Bistro Moderne (City Club Hotel, 55 W 44th St): French, Sunday
Ellen's Stardust Diner (1650 Broadway): diner, Sunday
Gyu-Kaku (321 W 44th St): Japanese/barbecue, Sunday
John's of Times Square (260 W 44th St): pizza, Sunday
Le Rivage (340 W 46th St): French, Sunday
Orso (322 W 46th St): Italian, Sunday
Ruby Foo's (1626 Broadway): Chinese, Sunday
Shake Shack (691 Eighth Ave): burgers, Sunday
Wolfgang's Steakhouse (New York Times Building, 250 W 41st St): steak, Sunday

WEST SIDE/UPPER WEST SIDE/LINCOLN CENTER
Awadh (2588 Broadway): North Indian, Sunday
Bar Boulud (1900 Broadway): French, Sunday
Boulud Sud (20 W 64th St): Mediterranean, Sunday
Cafe Lalo (201 W 83rd St): coffeehouse/dessert, Sunday
Carmine's (2450 Broadway): Italian, Sunday
'Cesca (164 W 75th St): Italian, Sunday
Ed's Chowder House (Empire Hotel, 44 W 63rd St): seafood, Sunday
Gabriel's Bar & Restaurant (11 W 60th St): Italian
Gigi Cafe (2067 Broadway): health food, Sunday
Good Enough to Eat (520 Columbus Ave): American, Sunday
Jackson Hole Burgers (517 Columbus Ave): burgers, Sunday
La Boite en Bois (75 W 68th St): French, Sunday
Land Thai Kitchen (450 Amsterdam Ave): Thai, Sunday
Luke's Lobster (426 Amsterdam Ave): seafood, Sunday
Ocean Grill (384 Columbus Ave): seafood, Sunday
Ouest (2315 Broadway): American, Sunday
P.J. Clarke's at Lincoln Square (44 W 63rd St): pub food, Sunday
Picholine (35 W 64th St): French/Mediterranean, Sunday
RedFarm (2170 Broadway): Chinese, Sunday
Rosa Mexicano (61 Columbus Ave): Mexican, Sunday
Sarabeth's (423 Amsterdam Ave): American, Sunday

Shake Shack (366 Columbus Ave): burgers, Sunday
Shun Lee Cafe/Shun Lee West (43 W 65th St): Chinese, Sunday
Spring Natural Kitchen (474 Columbus Ave): health food, Sunday
Telepan (72 W 69th St): American, Sunday

OUTSIDE MANHATTAN

Brooklyn
The Commodore (366 Metropolitan Ave, at Havemeyer St): Southern,
   Sunday
Peter Luger Steak House (178 Broadway, at Driggs Ave): steak, Sunday
River Café (1 Water St): American, Sunday

Queens
Park Side (107-01 Corona Ave, at 51st Ave): Italian, Sunday
Uncle Jack's Steakhouse (39-40 Bell Blvd): steak, Sunday

FINDING NEW YORK'S SECRET RESTAURANTS

There are some lesser known special restaurant spaces which are worthy of consideration:

Bohemian (57 Great Jones St, no phone): This hidden gem is located at the end of a long, narrow hallway behind the counter of specialty butcher shop, Japanese Premium Beef. You can only get a reservation by calling a secret number, at which point you'll be asked who referred you; they keep it strictly for their customer base. In other words, it is *who you know* that gets you in this place. Once inside the small, intimate room you can have a $60 six-course tasting menu of Japanese small plates or order a la carte.

The Brasserie at La Esquina (106 Kenmare St, 646/613-1333): Lots of people know that there is a restaurant deeply buried below La Esquina, accessible only by an unmarked door in the taqueria on Kenmare Street, but very few know how to actually get a table there. The staff will tell you to call for a reservation three weeks in advance, but often the trouble is that no one picks up the phone. Probably the only way that you're going to get a reservation at Akhtar Nawab's brasserie is if you know someone on the inside.

Hudson Clearwater (447 Hudson St, 212/989-3255): This new West Village restaurant is one of two new big speakeasies in New York, and it's a bit difficult to find; there won't be a line of people waiting to get past a bouncer out front. If you go to the restaurant's address, look for a storefront that might be under construction. If you head west down Moore Street, you can enter the restaurant by the patio. Once inside, you'll find a rustic dining room with an intimate and romantic atmosphere; full bar and good service included.

The Mulberry Project (149 Mulberry St, 646/448-4536): The Mulberry Project is the other new speakeasy in New York. You can get to it through an underground door beneath a Little Italy souvenir shop. It is part club, part restaurant and puts on a delicious weekend brunch if you get there early. There is usually a long line of people waiting to get past the person at the door with a clipboard.

The Naked Lady Room at Bell, Book and Candle (141 W 10th St, 212/414-2355): You will find this secret room right behind a fake wall near the end of a bar in the main dining room. The space seats two to six people and features naked lady wallpaper, exposed brick, high ceilings and a big chandelier. There's no chance you'll sit here as a walk-in, but you can reserve the room if you call far enough in advance.

The Taqueria inside of Tehuitzingo (578 Ninth Ave, 646/707-3916): If you head to the back of this Hell's Kitchen shop, past the snack display and soda refrigerators, there's a tiny taqueria serving some of the best Mexican food in the area, very inexpensively. Get the tacos – absolutely delicious!

The Third Floor at the Spotted Pig (314 W 11th St, 212/620-0393): This great little pub has a third floor accessible through its own entrance on Greenwich Street or an unmarked door in the second floor dining room. This third floor space resembles an apartment and is frequently used for events and parties. It can also be rented for the evening, otherwise it is not accessible to guests. Walk-in guests are taken care of downstairs only.

The Third Floor at Tiny's (135 West Broadway, 212/374-1135): This family-run restaurant is located in an historic 1810 building. The building's antique details are interesting; look for the original tin ceiling. You might try finding a mystery room here at Matt Abramcyk's new casual Tribeca bar and restaurant. The third floor is only accessible by a secret, ground-floor door.

The Wine Cellar Room at 21 Club (21 W 52nd St, 212/582-7200): Walk to the back of the 21 Club kitchen and down a long flight of stairs. Here you'll find a fake wall with a secret keyhole that looks like a crack in the cement. On the other side is a prohibition-style wine cellar and a VIP dining room which can be rented for private events. The wine cellar also holds bottles from famous guests, including Richard Nixon. More than 2,000 other bottles are still waiting for famous guests like Sammy Davis Jr. and Elizabeth Taylor.

GERRY'S EXCLUSIVE LIST

THE BEST PLACES TO FIND SPECIFIC FOOD ITEMS AND
SETTINGS IN NEW YORK'S KALEIDOSCOPIC RESTAURANT SCENE

BAGELS

Absolute Bagels (2788 Broadway)
Bagels on the Square (7 Carmine St)
BagelWorks (1229 First Ave)
Barney Greengrass (541 Amsterdam Ave)
Black Seed Bagels (170 Elizabeth St)
Ess-a-Bagel (359 First Ave and 831 Third Ave)
H&H Midtown Bagels East (1551 Second Ave)
Kossar's Bagels and Bialys (367 Grand St)
Lenny's Bagels (2601 Broadway)
Murray's Bagels (500 Ave of the Americas)

BARBECUE

Big Wong (67 Mott St): Chinese style
Blue Smoke (116 E 27th St and 255 Vesey St)
Daisy May's BBQ USA (623 Eleventh Ave)
Dallas BBQ (1265 Third Ave, 27 W 72nd St, 132 Second Ave and other
   locations): big and busy
Dinosaur Bar-B-Que (700 W 125th St)
Great NY Noodletown (28 Bowery St): Order a whole pig in advance.
Hill Country (30 W 26th St): live music
Kang Suh (1250 Broadway)
Mighty Quinn's Barbecue (103 Second Ave, 200 Vesey St and 75 Greenwich
   Ave): "Texalina" barbecue
New Kam Man (200 Canal St): Chinese barbecue
Shun Lee Cafe/Shun Lee West (43 W 65th St): classy Chinese
Southern Hospitality (645 Ninth Ave): messy comfort food
Sylvia's (328 Lenox Ave): reputation better than the food
Virgil's Real Barbecue (152 W 44th St): big, brassy, mass production

BARS AND PUBS

Ace Bar (531 E 5th St): boozy rec room vibe
Alphabet City Beer Co. (96 Avenue C): a.k.a. ABC, small production beer
   and cider
B Flat Bar (277 Church St): low lights and live jazz
The Bar at Four Seasons Hotel (57 E 57th St)
Baraonda (1439 Second Ave): Italian
Bemelmans Bar at the Carlyle Hotel (35 E 76th St): old-school
   hotel bar
Birdland (315 W 44th St): jazz
Blarney Rock Pub (137 W 33rd St): Irish all the way
Blind Barber (339 E 10th St): complimentary cocktail while getting a shave
   or haircut

Blue Note (131 W 3rd St): lots of talent
Blue Ribbon Downing Street Bar (34 Downing St): sip and be seen
bobo (181 W 10th St)
Boqueria Soho (171 Spring St) and **Boqueria Flatiron** (53 W 19th St): tapas bar
Bourbon Street Cafe (407 Amsterdam Ave): year-round Mardi Gras
Bourgeois Pig (111 E 7th St and 127 McDougal St): romantic Victorian opulence
Brandy Library (25 N Moore St): fine liquor
Brass Monkey (55 Little West 12th St): Hudson River views from roof deck
Brinkley's Station (153 E 60th St): wood-burning hearth
Bull & Bear (Waldorf Astoria New York, 301 Park Ave)
Burp Castle (41 E 7th St): 100 international bottles and a dozen taps focusing on Belgian beers
Butterfield 8 (5 E 38th St): unassuming pub and lounge
Campbell Apartment (Grand Central Terminal, 42nd St at Vanderbilt Ave, off West Balcony): unique
Carnegie Club (156 W 56th St): smoking lounge
Cellar Bar (Bryant Park Hotel, 40 W 40th St): hotel bar
Corner Bistro (331 W 4th St)
d.b.a. (41 First Ave): a relaxed place with an expanded bar list, including 130 single-malt Scotches and 50 tequilas
Dempsey's Pub (61 Second Ave): live Irish music Tuesday evenings
El Quinto Pino (401 W 24th St): tapas bar
Eleven Madison Park (11 Madison Ave)
Employees Only (510 Hudson St): focus on fresh ingredients and rejuvenated classics
Flatiron Lounge (37 W 19th St): plush banquettes, Manhattan's best Manhattans
Freemans (Freeman Alley, off Rivington St bet Bowery and Chrystie St)
Gramercy Tavern (42 E 20th St)
Great Hall Balcony Bar (The Metropolitan Museum of Art, 1000 Fifth Ave): culture
Hudson Bar & Books (636 Hudson St): reading
Jeremy's Ale House (228 Front St): quart-size cups; a favorite of cops
Keens Steakhouse (72 W 36th St)
King Cole Bar (St. Regis New York, 2 E 55th St): delicious Red Snapper (alias Bloody Mary)
Landmark Tavern (626 Eleventh Ave): 19th-century decor
Little Branch (20 Seventh Ave S): perfectly calibrated cocktails in subterranean venue
Living Room (W New York Times Square, 1567 Broadway): tourists
Lobby Lounge (Mandarin Oriental New York, 80 Columbus Cir, 35th floor): phenomenal Central Park views
Macao Trading Co. (311 Church St)
McQuaid's Public House (589 Eleventh Ave)
Mercer Kitchen (99 Prince St): celebrity watching
Minus5 Ice Bar (New York Hilton, 1335 Ave of the Americas)
Molly's Pub and Shebeen (287 Third Ave): Irish

Monkey Bar (Hotel Elysée, 60 E 54th St)
Mustang Sally's (324 Seventh Ave): basketball
No Idea (30 E 20th St)
P.J. Clarke's (915 Third Ave, 44 W 63rd St and 4 World Financial Center)
The Park (118 Tenth Ave): people watching
Peacock Alley (Waldorf Astoria New York, 301 Park Ave): old-school cocktail
  menu
Peculier Pub (145 Bleecker St): 350 bottles, 27 draft beers!
Pegu Club (77 W Houston St): inventive twists on cocktails
Peter McManus Cafe (152 Seventh Ave)
Rao's (455 E 114th St)
Rattle N Hum (14 E 33rd St): 40 taps, sizable space
Rock Center Cafe (Rockefeller Plaza, 20 W 50th St): Watch the ice skaters.
Rose Bar (Gramercy Park Hotel, 2 Lexington Ave)
Sakagura (211 E 43rd St): Japanese restaurant bar
Session 73 (1359 First Ave): live music
Slaughtered Lamb Pub (182 W 4th St): Drink and dine by the fire.
Smoke Jazz and Supper Club (2751 Broadway): best jazz bar
The Spotted Pig (314 W 11th St): gastropub
Standings (43 E 7th St): cozy sports bar
Stone Street Tavern (52 Stone St): relaxed spot for beers after the market
  closes
Swift Hibernian Lounge (34 E 4th St): 26 beers on tap
Tonic and the Met Lounge and **Tonic East** (727 Ave and 411 Third Ave):
  boxing
Trailer Park Lounge (271 W 23rd St): turkey burgers
The View (New York Marriott Marquis, 1535 Broadway): rotating rooftop
  views
Walker's (16 N Moore St): frequented by local firefighters
Waterfront Ale House (540 Second Ave): great Belgian beer, good food
West 79th Street Boat Basin Cafe (79th St at Hudson River, Riverside
  Park; seasonal): view with a bar
Whitman & Bloom Liquor Company (384 Third Ave): sit fireside
Wollensky's Grill (201 E 49th St)
Zinc Bar (82 W 3rd St): good music

BARS AND PUBS WITH GOOD EATS

Alder (157 Second Ave): impressive bar food
Aquagrill (210 Spring St)
Aretsky's Patroon (160 E 46th St)
Babbo (110 Waverly Pl)
Bar Primi (325 Bowery): antipasto and pastas
Boomer Esiason's Stadium Grill (at Bowlmor Times Square, 222 W 44th
  St)
China Grill (60 W 53rd St)
Cipriani Dolci (Grand Central Terminal, 89 Vanderbilt Ave)
Crimson & Rye (198 E 54th St): Charlie Palmer
Del Posto (85 Tenth Ave)
Delmonico's (56 Beaver St)
Distilled (211 West Broadway): refined comfort food
El Colmado (Gotham West Market, 600 Eleventh Ave)

Fanelli's Cafe (94 Prince St)
The Gilroy (1561 Second Ave)
Gotham Bar & Grill (12 E 12th St)
Gramercy Tavern (42 E 20th St)
Hallo Berlin (626 Tenth Ave)
Hanjan (36 W 26th St): Korean gastropub
Harrington's Bar & Grill (370 Seventh Ave)
Huertas (107 First Ave)
Keens Steakhouse (72 W 36th St)
McSorley's Old Ale House (15 E 7th St): Irish pub since 1854
Monkey Bar (Hotel Elysée, 60 E 54th St)
NoMad Bar (10 W 28th St): gourmet bar food
Old Town Bar and Restaurant (45 E 18th St)
Pearl & Ash (220 Bowery)
Picholine (35 W 64th St)
Plaza Food Hall (The Plaza, 1 W 59th St, lower level)
Redeye Grill (890 Seventh Ave)
Union Square Cafe (21 E 16th St)
Wollensky's Grill (201 E 49th St)
Yopparai (151 Rivington St): saké bar, plates of yakitori and sashimi
Zutto Japanese American Pub (77 Hudson St)

BARS FOR QUIET CONVERSATION

Bar Pleiades (The Surrey, 20 E 76th St)
Bar Room at the Modern (Museum of Modern Art, 9 W 53rd St)
Bemelmans Bar at the Carlyle Hotel (35 E 76th St)
Blue Bar (Algonquin Hotel, 59 W 44th St)
Burp Castle (41 E 7th St)
Cafe Luxembourg (200 W 70th St)
Carnegie Club (156 W 56th St)
King Cole Bar (St. Regis New York, 2 E 55th St)
The Third Man (116 Ave C)
Vero (1004 Second Ave and 1483 Second Ave)

BREAD

Arcade Bakery (220 Church St)
Bouchon Bakery (1 Rockefeller Plaza and 10 Columbus Cir)
Breads Bakery (18 E 16th St)
City Bakery (3 W 18th St)
Clinton St. Baking Company & Restaurant (4 Clinton St)
Dominique Ansel Bakery (189 Spring St)
Eataly (200 Fifth Ave)
Eli's Bread (Grand Central Market, 89 E 42nd St)
Le Pain Quotidien (42 Ninth Ave, 833 Lexington Ave and 1270 First Ave)
Sullivan Street Bakery (236 Ninth Ave)
Whole Foods Market (250 Seventh Ave, 226 E 57th St, 270 Greenwich St
and other locations)

BREAKFAST

2nd Ave Deli (162 E 33rd St and 1442 First Ave)

Amy Ruth's (113 W 116th St)
Balthazar (80 Spring St)
Big Wong (67 Mott St): Chinese breakfast
Brasserie (100 E 53rd St)
The Breslin (Ace Hotel, 16 W 29th St)
Brooklyn Diner USA (155 W 43rd St and 212 W 57th St)
Bubby's (120 Hudson St and 71 Gansevoort St)
Burger Heaven (9 E 53rd St, 20 E 49th St and 804 Lexington Ave)
Buvette (42 Grove St)
Cafe Cluny (284 W 12th St)
Carnegie Deli (854 Seventh Ave)
City Bakery (3 W 18th St)
Cucina & Co. (Macy's, 151 W 34th St; MetLife Building, 200 Park Ave; and 30 Rockefeller Center, concourse level)
Dishes (48 Grand Central Terminal, 42nd St at Vanderbilt Ave, lower level)
E.A.T. (1064 Madison Ave)
El Malecon (764 Amsterdam Ave and 4141 Broadway): Latin American
Ellen's Stardust Diner (1650 Broadway)
Fairway Cafe & Steakhouse (Fairway Market, 2127 Broadway)
The Fitz (Fitzpatrick Manhattan Hotel, 687 Lexington Ave)
Friend of a Farmer (77 Irving Pl)
Grey Dog's Coffee (90 University Pl, 244 Mulberry St, 49 Carmine St and 242 W 16th St)
Heartbeat (W New York, 541 Lexington Ave)
Hill Country Chicken (1123 Broadway)
Joseph Leonard (170 Waverly Pl)
Katz's Delicatessen (205 E Houston St)
Kitchenette (156 Chambers St and 1272 Amsterdam Ave)
Lafayette (380 Lafayette St)
Locanda Verde (The Greenwich Hotel, 377 Greenwich St): one of the best breakfasts in the city
Maialino (Gramercy Park Hotel, 2 Lexington Ave): a Danny Meyer operation
The Mark Restaurant by Jean-Georges (The Mark, 25 E 77th St): Vongerichten's spacious, chic dining
Mezzanine (Paramount Hotel, 235 W 46th St)
Michael's (24 W 55th St)
Morandi (211 Waverly Pl): Italian breakfast
New York Luncheonette (135 E 50th St)
Nice Matin (201 W 79th St)
Nios (Muse Hotel, 130 W 46th St)
NoHo Star (330 Lafayette St)
Norma's (Le Parker Meridien New York, 118 W 57th St): best breakfast in town
Once Upon a Tart (135 Sullivan St)
Pigalle (790 Eighth Ave)
Rue 57 (60 W 57th St)
Sarabeth's (423 Amsterdam Ave; Hotel Wales, 1295 Madison Ave; 40 Central Park S; 381 Park Ave S and 339 Greenwich St), **Sarabeth's at Lord & Taylor** (324 Fifth Ave) and **Sarabeth's Bakery** (Chelsea Market, 75 Ninth Ave)
The Standard Grill (848 Washington St)

Sugar Cafe (200 Allen St): open 24/7
Veselka (144 Second Ave)
Viand Coffee Shop (673 Madison Ave, 2130 Broadway and 1011 Madison Ave): crowded, but great value
Whole Foods Market (270 Greenwich St, 4 Union Square S, 95 E Houston St, 226 E 57th St and other locations)

BRUNCH

Acme (9 Great Jones St)
Aquagrill (210 Spring St)
Aquavit (65 E 55th St): all-you-can-eat Sunday Swedish brunch
Awadh (2588 Broadway)
Balthazar (80 Spring St)
Bar Primi (325 Bowery)
Barney Greengrass (541 Amsterdam Ave)
Blue Ribbon Bakery (35 Downing St)
Cafe Gitane (Jane Hotel, 113 Jane St)
Cafe Habana (17 Prince St)
Cafe Lalo (201 W 83rd St)
Candle 79 (154 E 79th St)
Church Lounge (2 Ave of the Americas)
Clinton St. Baking Company & Restaurant (4 Clinton St)
Colicchio & Sons (85 Tenth Ave)
Cookshop (156 Tenth Ave)
Cupping Room Cafe (359 West Broadway)
Edi & the Wolf (102 Avenue C)
Eli's Vinegar Factory (431 E 91st St)
Eli's Table (1413 Third Ave)
Freemans (Freeman Alley, at Rivington St)
Friend of a Farmer (77 Irving Pl)
Good (89 Greenwich Ave)
Good Enough to Eat (520 Columbus Ave)
Hundred Acres (38 MacDougal St)
Isabella's (359 Columbus Ave)
La Ripaille (605 Hudson St)
Minetta Tavern (113 MacDougal St): Keith McNally offers Old World breakfast treats like shirred eggs with black truffles.
Miss Lily's (132 W Houston St) and **Miss Lily's 7A Cafe** (109 Ave A): Jamaican
Morandi (211 Waverly Pl)
Nice Matin (201 W 79th St)
NoMad (NoMad Hotel, 1170 Broadway)
North End Grill (104 North End Ave): a Danny Meyer production
The Odeon (145 West Broadway)
Peacock Alley (301 Park Ave)
Pig 'n' Whistle (922 Third Ave and 951 Second Ave): traditional Irish breakfast
Prune (54 E 1st St): inspired weekend brunch
Quantum Leap Natural Food (226 Thompson St)

Rainbow Room (30 Rockefeller Plaza, 65th floor): Sunday only
Rosemary's Enoteca & Trattoria (18 Greenwich Ave)
Sarabeth's (423 Amsterdam Ave; Hotel Wales, 1295 Madison Ave; 40 Central Park S; 381 Park Ave S and 339 Greenwich St), **Sarabeth's at Lord & Taylor** (324 Fifth Ave) and **Sarabeth's Bakery** (Chelsea Market, 75 Ninth Ave)
Schiller's (131 Rivington St)
Spring Street Natural (62 Spring St)
Sylvia's (328 Lenox Ave)
Tartine (253 W 11th St)
Tribeca Grill (375 Greenwich St)
Vic's (31 Great Jones St)
Wallsé (344 W 11th St)
The Wren (344 Bowery): bargain, Irish-style gastropub

BURGERS

5 Napkin Burger (630 Ninth Ave, 2315 Broadway and 150 E 14th St)
21 Club (21 W 52nd St)
Ai Fiori (400 Fifth Ave)
Bar Six (502 Ave of the Americas)
Bill's Bar & Burger (22 Ninth Ave, 85 West St and 16 W 51st St): short-rib blend
Black Iron Burger Shop (540 E 5th St): kitchen open late
Black Market (110 Ave A): excellent house cheeseburger
Blue Ribbon Bakery (35 Downing St)
Blue Smoke (116 E 27th St)
Brgr (287 Seventh Ave and 1026 Third Ave)
Brindle Room (277 E 10th St)
Burger & Barrel (25 W Houston St): white truffles
Burger Heaven (536 Madison Ave, 9 E 53rd St and 804 Lexington Ave)
Burger Joint at Le Parker Meridien New York (119 W 56th St)
Burgers and Cupcakes (458 Ninth Ave)
Chelsea Grill (675 Ninth Ave)
Cherche Midi (282 Bowery)
Coppelia (207 W 14th St): Latin-style
Corner Bistro (331 W 4th St)
db Bistro Moderne (City Club Hotel, 55 W 44th St)
Dram Shop (339 9th St)
Eats on Lex (1055 Lexington Ave)
Fanelli's Cafe (94 Prince St)
Five Guys (296 Bleecker St, 316 W 34th St, 36 W 48th St, 690 Third Ave, 43 W 55th St and 2847 Broadway): worth the calories; a Virginia-based chain
Flip (Bloomingdale's, 1000 Third Ave): choose your own combination
The Garrett (296 Bleecker St)
Great Jones Cafe (54 Great Jones St)
Half King (505 W 23rd St): one of the best budget burgers
Hard Rock Cafe (1501 Broadway)
Home Restaurant (20 Cornelia St)
J.G. Melon (1291 Third Ave)
Jackson Hole Burgers (232 E 64th St, 521 Third Ave and 517 Columbus Ave)

Jeepney (201 First Ave)
Keens Steakhouse (72 W 36th St)
Knickerbocker Bar and Grill (33 University Pl)
The Lion (62 W 9th St): with pork belly
Little Owl (90 Bedford St): sliders
Mark (33 St. Mark's Pl): lively little burger bar
Market Table (54 Carmine St)
Minetta Tavern (113 MacDougal St): Black Label hamburger
The Odeon (145 West Broadway)
Old Town Bar and Restaurant (45 E 18th St)
P.J. Clarke's (915 Third Ave, 44 W 63rd St and 4 World Financial Center)
Patroon (160 E 46th St)
Paul's da Burger Joint (131 Second Ave)
Rare Bar & Grill (Affinia Shelburne, 303 Lexington Ave and Hilton New York Fashion District, 152 W 26th St)
Resto (111 E 29th St)
Royale (157 Ave C)
Rue 57 (60 W 57th St)
Shake Shack (Madison Square Park, Madison Ave at 23rd St; 366 Columbus Ave; 154 E 86th St; 691 Eighth Ave and other locations): a New York City experience brought to you by the extraordinary Danny Meyer
The Spotted Pig (314 W 11th St)
Steak 'n Shake (1695 Broadway)
Trading Post (170 John St)
Txikito (240 Ninth Ave): Basque-inspired ingredients
Umami Burger (432 Ave of the Americas)
Union Square Cafe (21 E 16th St)
Waverly Inn (16 Bank St)
White Horse Tavern (567 Hudson St)
Whitehall Bar & Kitchen (19 Greenwich Ave)
Whitmans (406 E 9th St): Try the Juicy Lucy!
Wollensky's Grill (201 E 49th St)

CHEAP EATS

107 West (2787 Broadway)
Beyoglu (1431 Third Ave)
Black Seed Bagels (170 Elizabeth St)
Boqueria Soho (171 Spring St)
Bouchon Bakery (1 Rockefeller Center and Time Warner Center, 10 Columbus Cir, 3rd floor)
Buddakan (Chelsea Market, 75 Ninth Ave)
Burger Joint at Le Parker Meridien New York (119 W 56th St)
Buvette (42 Grove St)
Cafe Lalo (201 W 83rd St)
Carmine's (2450 Broadway and 200 W 44th St)
Cascabel Taqueria (1556 Second Ave)
City Bakery (3 W 18th St)
Corner Bistro (331 W 4th St)
David Burke at Bloomingdale's (150 E 59th St)

Degustation (239 E 5th St)
Earl's Beer & Cheese (1259 Park Ave)
Egg Shop (151 Elizabeth St)
Frank (88 Second Ave)
Frankie's Spuntino (570 Hudson St and 457 Court St)
Gigi Cafe (64 E 34th St, 958 Third Ave, 2067 Broadway and 307 Seventh Ave)
Golden Unicorn (18 East Broadway)
Gotham West Market (600 Eleventh Ave)
Grand Sichuan (15 Seventh Ave, 23 St. Mark's Pl and 368 W 46th St)
Gray's Papaya (2090 Broadway)
Han Dynasty (90 Third Ave)
Ivan Ramen (25 Clinton St)
Ivan Ramen Slurp Shop (Gotham West Market, 600 Eleventh Ave)
John's of Times Square (260 W 44th St)
Katz's Delicatessen (205 E Houston St)
Kitchenette (156 Chambers St and 1272 Amsterdam Ave)
Lil' Frankie's Pizza (19 First Ave)
Parm (248 Mulberry St)
Paul's da Burger Joint (131 Second Ave)
The Redhead (349 E 13th St)
Sapporo (152 W 49th St)
The Smith (55 Third Ave, 1900 Broadway and 956 Second Ave)
Soba-ya (229 E 9th St)
Spot Dessert Bar (13 St. Mark's Pl and 11 W 32nd St)
Spring Natural Kitchen (474 Columbus Ave)
Spring Street Natural (62 Spring St)
Supper (156 E 2nd St)
Sylvia's (328 Lenox Ave)
Tartine (253 W 11th St)
Tea & Sympathy (108 Greenwich Ave)
Turkish Cuisine (631 Ninth Ave)
Vanessa's Dumpling House (118 Eldridge St, 220 E 14th St and 310 Bedford St)
Veselka (144 Second Ave)
'wichcraft (555 Fifth Ave and other locations)
Xi'an Famous Foods (81 St. Mark's Pl, 67 Bayard St and 24 W 45th St)
Yakitori Totto (251 W 55th St)
Yonah Schimmel Knish Bakery (137 E Houston St)

CHEESE PLATES

Artisanal Fromagerie, Bistro and Wine Bar (2 Park Ave)
Circo NYC (120 W 55th St)
Craftbar (900 Broadway)
Daniel (60 E 65th St)
Eleven Madison Park (11 Madison Ave)
Gramercy Tavern (42 E 20th St)
Jean Georges (Trump International Hotel and Tower, 1 Central Park W)
La Grenouille (3 E 52nd St)
Le Cirque (1 Beacon Ct, 151 E 58th St)
The Morgan Dining Room (The Morgan Library & Museum, 225 Madison Ave)

Picholine (35 W 64th St)
Solera (216 E 53rd St)
Telepan (72 W 69th St)
Wallsé (344 W 11th St)

COFFEE BARS

71 Irving Place (71 Irving Pl)
Aroma Espresso Bar (145 Greene St, 161 W 72nd Ave and 205 E 42nd St)
Cafe Grumpy (224 W 20th St and 13 Essex St)
Cafe Lalo (201 W 83rd St)
Caffe Dante (79-81 MacDougal St)
Caffe Roma (385 Broome St)
City Bakery (3 W 18th St)
Cupcake Cafe (545 Ninth Ave)
Cupping Room Cafe (359 West Broadway)
El Rey Coffee Bar & Luncheonette (100 Stanton St)
Ferrara Bakery and Cafe (195 Grand St)
French Roast (78 W 11th St and 2340 Broadway)
Hungarian Pastry Shop (1030 Amsterdam Ave)
Jack's Stir Brew Coffee (138 W 10th St and 222 Front St)
Joe The Art of Coffee (141 Waverly Pl, 9 E 13th St, 405 W 23rd St and
    other locations)
Kaffe 1668 (275 Greenwich St and 401 Greenwich St)
La Colombe Torrefaction (319 Church St, 270 Lafayette St and 400
    Lafayette St)
Laughing Man Coffee & Tea (184 Duane St): organic brews
Le Pain Quotidien (1131 Madison Ave; ABC Carpet & Home, 38 E 19th St
    and other locations)
Little Collins (667 Lexington Ave)
Once Upon a Tart (135 Sullivan St)
Oren's Daily Roast (1144 Lexington Ave and other locations)
The Roasting Plant (81 Orchard St and 75 Greenwich Ave)
Sarabeth's (423 Amsterdam Ave; Hotel Wales, 1295 Madison Ave; 40 Central
    Park S; 381 Park Ave S and 339 Greenwich St), **Sarabeth's at Lord &
    Taylor** (324 Fifth Ave) and **Sarabeth's Bakery** (Chelsea Market, 75
    Ninth Ave)
Sensuous Bean (66 W 70th St)
Starbucks (numerous locations)
Stumptown Coffee Roasters (Ace Hotel, 18 W 29th St)
Third Rail Coffee (240 Sullivan St)
Two Hands (164 Mott St)
Veselka (144 Second Ave)
Zabar's (2245 Broadway)

DELIS AND QUICK LUNCHES

2nd Ave Deli (162 E 33rd St and 1442 First Ave)
Amy's Bread (Chelsea Market, 75 Ninth Ave; 672 Ninth Ave and 250 Bleecker
    St)
Artie's Delicatessen (2290 Broadway)
Balthazar (80 Spring St)

Barney Greengrass (541 Amsterdam Ave)
Ben's Kosher Deli (209 W 38th St)
Bread (20 Spring St)
Carnegie Deli (854 Seventh Ave)
City Bakery (3 W 18th St)
City Market Cafe (178 Fifth Ave, 551 Madison Ave and 1100 Madison Ave)
Clinton St. Baking Company & Restaurant (4 Clinton St)
Dil-E Punjab (170 Ninth Ave)
Dishes (6 E 45th St; 399 Park Ave and Grand Central Terminal, 42nd St at Vanderbilt Ave)
E.A.T. (1064 Madison Ave)
Ess-a-Bagel (831 Third Ave and 359 First Ave)
Fine & Schapiro (138 W 72nd St)
Garden of Eden (7 E 14th St, 162 W 23rd St and 2780 Broadway)
Grace's Marketplace (1299 Second Ave)
Juice Generation (171 W 4th St, 644 Ninth Ave, 117 W 72nd St and other locations)
Junior's (1515 Broadway; Grand Central Terminal, 42nd St at Vanderbilt Ave, lower level and West 45th St, Broadway at Eighth Ave)
Just Salad (320 Park Ave, 134 W 37th St, 600 Third Ave and other locations)
Katz's Delicatessen (205 E Houston St)
M&O Market and Deli (124 Thompson St)
Samad's (2867 Broadway)
Sarabeth's (423 Amsterdam Ave; Hotel Wales, 1295 Madison Ave; 40 Central Park S; 381 Park Ave S and 339 Greenwich St), **Sarabeth's at Lord & Taylor** (324 Fifth Ave) and **Sarabeth's Bakery** (Chelsea Market, 75 Ninth Ave)
Zabar's (2245 Broadway)

DESSERTS

Acme (9 Great Jones St)
Asiate (Mandarin Oriental New York, 80 Columbus Cir, 35th floor)
BabyCakes (248 Broome St): vegan
Bouley (163 Duane St)
Cafe Lalo (201 W 83rd St)
Cafe Sabarsky (Neue Galerie New York, 1048 Fifth Ave)
ChikaLicious (203 E 10th St)
Cupcake Cafe (545 Ninth Ave)
Dirty French (Ludlow Hotel, 180 Ludlow St)
Ferrara Bakery and Cafe (195 Grand St)
Gramercy Tavern (42 E 20th St)
Hearth (403 E 12th St)
Il Laboratorio del Gelato (188 Ludlow St)
Jacques Torres Chocolate (350 Hudson St, 285 Amsterdam Ave, 30 Rockefeller Plaza and other locations)
Jean Georges (Trump International Hotel and Tower, 1 Central Park W)
Lady M Cake Boutique (41 E 78th St and Plaza Food Hall, 1 W 59th St)
Magnolia Bakery (401 Bleecker St, 200 Columbus Ave, 1240 Ave of the Americas and other locations)
Once Upon a Tart (135 Sullivan St)

Petrossian Restaurant (182 W 58th St)
Schiller's (131 Rivington St)
Serendipity 3 (225 E 60th St)
Veniero's (342 E 11th St)
Zabar's Cafe (2245 Broadway)

DIM SUM

The serving of small tea pastries called dim sum originated in Hong Kong and has become a delicious Chinatown institution. Although dim sum is usually eaten for brunch, some restaurants also serve it as an appetizer. Dim sum items are rolled over to your table on carts, and you simply point at whatever looks good. This eliminates the language barrier and encourages experimentation. When you're finished, the accumulated small plates are counted and the bill is calculated accordingly.

Here are some of the most popular dim sum dishes:
Cha Siu Bow (steamed barbecued pork buns)
Cha Siu So (flaky buns)
Chun Guen (spring rolls)
Dai Tze Gau (steamed scallop and shrimp dumplings)
Don Ta (baked custard tarts)
Dow Sah Bow (sweet-bean-paste-filled buns)
Fancy Fans (meat-filled pot sticker triangles)
Four-Color Siu Mai (meat-and-vegetable-filled dumplings)
Gau Choi Gau (pan-browned chive and shrimp dumplings)
Gee Cheung Fun (steamed rice-noodle rolls)
Gee Yoke Go (savory pork triangles)
Ha Gau (shrimp dumplings)
Jow Ha Gok (shrimp turnovers)
Pot Sticker Kou The (meat-filled dumplings)
Satay Gai Tran (chicken satay)
Siu Mai (steamed pork dumplings)
Tzay Ha (fried shrimp ball on sugarcane)

For the most authentic and delicious dim sum in New York, try these places:
Dim Sum Go Go (5 East Broadway)
Golden Mandarin Court (61 Mott St)
Golden Unicorn (18 East Broadway): an especially fine selection
Jing Fong (20 Elizabeth St)
Oriental Garden (14 Elizabeth St)
Our Place (242 E 79th St)
Ping's Seafood (22 Mott St)
RedFarm (529 Hudson St and 2170 Broadway)
Shun Lee Cafe/Shun Lee West (43 W 65th St)

DINERS

Brooklyn Diner USA (212 W 57th St and 155 W 43rd St): outstanding
City Diner (2441 Broadway): retro-elegant
The Diner (44 Ninth Ave): Meatpacking District

Ellen's Stardust Diner (1650 Broadway)
Empire Diner (210 Tenth Ave)
Hudson Diner (468 Hudson St)
Miss Lily's (132 W Houston St)
Skylight Diner (402 W 34th St)
Tick Tock Diner (481 Eighth Ave): open 24 hours
Westway Diner (614 Ninth Ave)

DINING SOLO

Some of these restaurants have dining counters, while others are tranquil and suitable for single diners.

Aquavit (65 E 55th St)
Babbo (110 Waverly Pl)
Cafe S.F.A. (Saks Fifth Avenue, 611 Fifth Ave, 8th floor)
Carnegie Deli (854 Seventh Ave)
Caviar Russe (538 Madison Ave)
Chez Napoléon (365 W 50th St)
Cupcake Cafe (545 Ninth Ave)
Elephant & Castle (68 Greenwich Ave)
Eleven Madison Park (11 Madison Ave)
Gotham Bar & Grill (12 E 12th St)
Grand Central Oyster Bar Restaurant (Grand Central Terminal, 42nd St at Vanderbilt Ave, lower level)
J.G. Melon (1291 Third Ave)
Jackson Hole Burgers (232 E 64th St, 521 Third Ave and 517 Columbus Ave)
Joe's Shanghai (9 Pell St and 24 W 56th St)
Joseph Leonard (170 Waverly Pl)
Kitchenette (156 Chambers St and 1272 Amsterdam Ave)
La Bonne Soupe (48 W 55th St)
La Caridad 78 (2199 Broadway)
Locanda Verde (The Greenwich Hotel, 377 Greenwich St)
Naples 45 (MetLife Building, 200 Park Ave)
Pepolino (281 West Broadway)
Perry St. (176 Perry St
Raoul's (180 Prince St)
Republic (37 Union Square W)
Sarabeth's (Hotel Wales, 1295 Madison Ave; 423 Amsterdam Ave and 40 Central Park S), **Sarabeth's at Lord & Taylor** (424 Fifth Ave) and **Sarabeth's Bakery** (Chelsea Market, 75 Ninth Ave)
Trattoria dell'Arte (900 Seventh Ave)
Union Square Cafe (21 E 16th St)
Viand Coffee Shop (673 Madison Ave, 1011 Madison Ave, 300 E 86th St and 2130 Broadway)

DOUGHNUTS, PASTRIES AND OTHER SWEETS

BabyCakes (248 Broome St)
Butterfield Express (1102 Lexington Ave)
Cafe Lalo (201 W 83rd St)
Dough Loco (1261 Park Ave): seven glazes, including miso-maple

Doughnut Plant (379 Grand St and other locations)
Doughnuttery (Chelsea Market, 425 W 15th St)
Grace Street (17 W 32nd St)
Holey Donuts (101 Seventh Ave S)
Magnolia Bakery (1240 Ave of the Americas, 200 Columbus Ave, 401 Bleecker St and other locations)
Momofuku Milk Bar (251 E 13th St, 15 W 56th St and 561 Columbus Ave)
Orwasher's Bakery (308 E 78th St)
Sarabeth's Bakery (Chelsea Market, 75 Ninth Ave)
Sugar Sweet Sunshine (126 Rivington St)
Sullivan Street Bakery (236 Ninth Ave and 533 W 47th St)

FAMILY-STYLE DINING

Carmine's (2450 Broadway and 200 W 44th St)
China Grill (60 W 53rd St)
Phoenix Garden (242 E 40th St)
Piccolo Angolo (621 Hudson St)
Ruby Foo's (1626 Broadway)
Tao (42 E 58th St)
Tao Downtown (Maritime Hotel, 92 Ninth Ave)

FIRESIDE

21 Club (21 W 52nd St): cocktail lounge
Alta (64 W 10th St)
Bouley (163 Duane St)
Cornelia Street Cafe (29 Cornelia St)
The Dutch (131 Sullivan St)
Employees Only (510 Hudson St)
The House (121 E 17th St)
I Trulli (122 E 27th St)
Keens Steakhouse (72 W 36th St)
Lobby Bar (The Bowery Hotel, 335 Bowery)
Locanda Verde (The Greenwich Hotel, 377 Greenwich St)
Molly's Pub and Shebeen (287 Third Ave)
Moran's Chelsea (146 Tenth Ave)
NoMad (1170 Broadway)
One if by Land, Two if by Sea (17 Barrow St)
Quality Meats (57 W 58th St)
Vivolo (140 E 74th St)
Water's Edge (401 44th Dr at East River, Queens)
Waverly Inn (16 Bank St)

FOREIGN FLAVORS

Some of these commendable ethnic establishments do not have full write-ups in this chapter. Here are the best of the more exotic eateries, arranged by cuisine:

AFGHAN | **Afghan Kebab House** (1345 Second Ave and 764 Ninth Ave)

AFRICAN, NORTH | **NoMad** (78 Second Ave)

ARGENTINEAN | **Chimichurri Grill** (609 Ninth Ave)

ASIAN | **Chopshop** (254 Tenth Ave), **The General** (199 Bowery), **Tao** (42 E 58th St), **Tao Downtown** (Maritime Hotel, 92 Ninth Ave) and **Toy** (Gansevoort Meatpacking NYC, 18 Ninth Ave)

AUSTRALIAN | **Burke & Wills** (226 W 79th St), **Holyland Market** (122 St. Marks Pl), **Public** (210 Elizabeth St) and **Tuck Shop** (68 E 1st St; 115 St. Mark's Pl and Chelsea Market, 75 Ninth Ave)

AUSTRIAN | **Cafe Sabarsky** (Neue Galerie New York, 1048 Fifth Ave), **Seäsonal Restaurant & Weinbar** (132 W 58th St) and **Wallsé** (344 W 11th St)

BELGIAN | **The Cannibal** (113 E 29th St) and **Resto** (111 E 29th St)

BRAZILIAN | **Churrascaria Plataforma** (Belvedere Hotel, 316 W 49th St), **Churrascaria Tribeca** (221 West Broadway), **Circus** (132 E 61st St) and **Emporium Brazil** (15 W 46th St)

BRITISH | **Jones Wood Foundry** (401 E 76th St) and **The Peacock** and **The Shakespeare Pub** (The William Hotel, 24 E 39th St)

CHINESE | **Big Wong** (67 Mott St), **Bo Ky** (80 Bayard St), **Flor de Mayo** (484 Amsterdam Ave and 2651 Broadway), **Golden Unicorn** (18 East Broadway), **Grand Sichuan** (15 Seventh Ave, 368 W 46th St and 23 St. Mark's Pl), **Han Dynasty** (90 Third Ave), **Hop Lee** (16 Mott St), **Jing Fong** (20 Elizabeth St), **Joe's Ginger** (25 Pell St), **Joe's Shanghai** (9 Pell St and 24 W 56th St), **Mr. K's** (570 Lexington Ave), **Nice Green Bo** (66 Bayard St), **Oriental Garden** (14 Elizabeth St), **Ping's Seafood** (22 Mott St), **Red Egg** (202 Centre St), **RedFarm** (529 Hudson St and 2170 Broadway), **Shanghai Cuisine** (89-91 Bayard St), **Shun Lee Palace** (155 E 55th St), **Shun Lee Cafe/Shun Lee West** (43 W 65th St), **Tang Pavilion** (65 W 55th St), **Wu Liang Ye** (36 W 48th St) and **Yunnan Kitchen** (79 Clinton St)

CUBAN | **Cabana** (1022 Third Ave), **Cafecito** (185 Ave C), **Cafe Con Leche** (424 Amsterdam Ave), **Cafe Habana** (17 Prince St), **Coppelia** (207 W 14th St) and **Victor's Cafe** (236 W 52nd St)

EAST EUROPEAN | **Petrossian Restaurant** (182 W 58th St), **Sammy's Roumanian Steak House** (157 Chrystie St) and **Veselka** (144 Second Ave)

ETHIOPIAN | **Meskerem** (468 W 47th St and 124 MacDougal St) and **Queen of Sheba** (650 Tenth Ave)

FILIPINO | **Jeepney** (201 First Ave) and **Pig and Khao** (68 Clinton St)

FRENCH | see restaurant write-ups (beginning on page 71)

GERMAN | **Blaue Gans** (139 Duane St), **Hallo Berlin** (626 Tenth Ave), **Loreley** (7 Rivington St) and **Zum Schneider** (107 Ave C)

GREEK | **Ammos** (52 Vanderbilt Ave), **Avra** (141 E 48th St), **Estiatorio Milos** (125 W 55th St), **Ithaka** (308 E 86th St), **Kellari Taverna** (19 W 44th St), **Molyvos** (871 Seventh Ave), **Periyali** (35 W 20th St), **Pylos** (128 E 7th St), **Snack** (105 Thompson St), **Thalassa** (179 Franklin St) and **Uncle Nick's** (747 Ninth Ave)

INDIAN | **Awadh** (2588 Broadway), **Brick Lane Curry House** (99 Second Ave), **Bukhara Grill** (217 E 49th St), **Chola** (232 E 58th St), **Darbar** (152 E 46th St), **Dawat** (210 E 58th St), **Dévi** (8 E 18th St), **Haandi** (113 Lexington Ave), **Haveli** (100 Second Ave), **Indus Valley** (2636 Broadway), **Minar** (5 W 31st St and 138 W 46th St), **Moti Mahal**

Delux (1149 First Ave), **Salaam Bombay** (319 Greenwich St), **Tamarind** (99 Hudson St), **Tulsi** (211 E 46th St), **Utsav** (1185 Ave of the Americas) and **Yuva** (230 E 58th St)

INDONESIAN | **Bali Nusa Indah** (651 Ninth Ave)

IRISH | **Eamonn's Bar & Grill** (9 E 45th St), **The Fitz** (Fitzpatrick Manhattan Hotel, 687 Lexington Ave) and **Molly's Pub and Shebeen** (287 Third Ave)

ISRAELI | **Bar Bolonat** (611 Hudson St)

ITALIAN | see restaurant write-ups (beginning on page 71)

JAMAICAN | **Miss Lily's** (132 W Houston St) and **Miss Lily's 7A Cafe** (109 Ave A)

JAPANESE | **Benihana** (47 W 56th St), **Bond Street** (6 Bond St), **Curry Ya** (214 E 10th St), **Donguri** (309 E 83rd St), **EN Japanese Brasserie** (435 Hudson St), **Hakata Tonton** (61 Grove St), **Hakubai** (The Kitano New York, 66 Park Ave), **Ippudo** (65 Fourth Ave), **Japonica** (90 University Pl), **Jewel Bako** (239 E 5th St), **Kurumazushi** (7 E 47th St), **Kyo Ya** (94 E 7th St), **Minamoto Kitchoan** (509 Madison Ave), **Nobu 57** (40 W 57th St), **Nobu New York** and **Nobu Next Door** (105 Hudson St), **Omen** (113 Thompson St), **Ozu** (566 Amsterdam Ave), **Sakagura** (211 E 43rd St), **Seo** (249 E 49th St), **Shabu Shabu Kobe** (3 W 36th St), **Soto** (357 Ave of the Americas), **Sugiyama** (251 W 55th St), **SushiSamba** (87 Seventh Ave S), **Sushi Yasuda** (204 E 43rd St), **Torishin** (1193 First Ave) and **Yakitori Totto** (261 W 55th St)

KOREAN | **Cho Dang Gol** (55 W 35th St), **Danji** (346 W 52nd St), **Do Hwa** (55 Carmine St), **Gahm Mi Oak** (43 W 32nd St), **Gaonnuri** (1250 Broadway, 39th floor), **Hangawi** (12 E 32nd St), **Kang Suh** (1250 Broadway), **Kori** (253 Church St), **Kum Gang San** (49 W 32nd St), **New WonJo** (23 W 32nd St), **Seoul Garden** (34 W 32nd St) and **Shilla Restaurant** (37 W 32nd St)

LEBANESE | **Al Bustan** (319 E 53rd St), **Ilili** (236 Fifth Ave), **Naya** (1057 Second Ave) and **Naya Express** (688 Third Ave)

MALAYSIAN | **Laut** (15 E 17th St)

MEDITERRANEAN | **Antique Garage** (41 Mercer St), **Balaboosta** (214 Mulberry St), **Boulud Sud** (20 W 64th St), **Il Buco Alimentari e Vineria** (53 Great Jones St) and **Vic's** (31 Great Jones St)

MEXICAN | **Cascabel Taqueria** (1556 Second Ave), **Cosme** (35 E 21st St), **Dos Caminos** (825 Third Ave, 373 Park Ave S and 475 West Broadway), **El Parador Cafe** (325 E 34th St), **Empellón Cocina** (105 First Ave), **Empellón Taqueria** (230 W 4th St), **Fresco Tortillas** (819 Second Ave), **Hechoen Dumbo** (354 Bowery), **Itzocan Cafe** (438 E 9th St), **La Esquina** (114 Kenmare St), **Maya** (1191 First Ave), **Mexican Radio** (19 Cleveland Pl), **Pampano** (209 E 49th St), **Rosa Mexicano** (1063 First Ave, 9 E 18th St and 61 Columbus Ave), **Toloache** (251 W 50th St, 166 E 82nd St and 83 Maiden Lane) and **Tortilla Flats** (767 Washington St)

MIDDLE EASTERN | **Balaboosta** (214 Mulberry St), **Bar Six** (502 Ave of the Americas), **Cleopatra's Needle** (2485 Broadway) and **Moustache** (90 Bedford St, 265 E 10th St and 1621 Lexington Ave)

MOROCCAN | **Cafe Mogador** (101 St. Mark's Pl) and **Zerza** (320 E 6th St)

NEW ZEALAND | **Musket Room** (265 Elizabeth St)
PERSIAN | **Café Nadery** (16 W 8th St) and **Persepolis** (1407 Second Ave)
PORTUGUESE | **Aldea** (31 W 17th St), **Macao Trading Co.** (311 Church St) and **Pao** (322 Spring St)
PUERTO RICAN | **Cuchifritos** (168 E 116th St) and **La Taza de Oro** (96 Eighth Ave)
RUSSIAN | **Russian Samovar** (256 W 52nd St) and **Uncle Vanya Cafe** (315 W 54th St)
SCANDINAVIAN | **Aquavit** (65 E 55th St) and **Smörgås Chef** (Scandinavia House: The Nordic Center in America, 58 Park Ave; 53 Stone St and 283 W 12th St)
SCOTTISH | **Highlands** (150 W 10th St) and **St. Andrew's** (140 W 46th St)
SOUTHWESTERN | **Agave** (140 Seventh Ave S)
SPANISH AND SOUTH AMERICAN | **Alcala** (342 E 46th St), **Boqueria Flatiron** (53 W 19th St), **Boqueria Soho** (171 Spring St), **Cafe Español** (172 Bleecker St), **Cafe Riazor** (245 W 16th St), **Huertas** (107 First Ave), **La Fonda del Sol** (MetLife Building, 200 Park Ave), **Rayuela** (165 Allen St), **Solera** (216 E 53rd St), **Tio Pepe** (168 W 4th St), **Toledo** (6 E 36th St) and **Toro** (85 Tenth Ave)
TEX-MEX | **Tres Carnes** (954 Third Ave and 101 Maiden Lane)
THAI | **Kin Shop** (469 Ave of the Americas), **Peep** (177 Prince St), **Pongsri Thai** (106 Bayard St, 165 W 23rd St and 244 W 48th St), **Royal Siam** (240 Eighth Ave) and **Topaz** (127 W 56th St)
TIBETAN | **Tsampa** (212 E 9th St)
TURKISH | **Ali Baba** (212 E 34th St and 862 Second Ave), **Beyoglu** (1431 Third Ave), **Pasha** (70 W 71st St), **Pera Mediterranean Brasserie** (303 Madison Ave), **Sip Sak** (928 Second Ave), **Turkish Cuisine** (631 Ninth Ave), **Turkish Kitchen** (386 Third Ave) and **Üsküdar** (1405 Second Ave)
UKRAINIAN | **Veselka** (144 Second Ave)
VIETNAMESE | **Le Colonial** (149 E 57th St), **Mekong** (18 King St), **NhaTrang** (87 Baxter St and 148 Centre St), **Omai** (158 Ninth Ave) and **Pho Viet Huong** (73 Mulberry St)

FRENCH BISTROS

Balthazar (80 Spring St)
Café Boulud (The Surrey, 20 E 76th St)
Cafe Luxembourg (200 W 70th St)
Cherche Midi (282 Bowery)
Deux Amis Restaurant (356 E 51st St)
JoJo (160 E 64th St)
Lafayette (380 Lafayette St)
Le Gigot (18 Cornelia St)
Le Philosophe (55 Bond St)
Raoul's (180 Prince St)
Rue 57 (60 W 57th St)

GAME

Game is generally offered at these restaurants in winter months or by special request.

Annisa (13 Barrow St)
Aquavit (65 E 55th St)
Babbo (110 Waverly Pl)
Barbetta (321 W 46th St)
Blue Hill (75 Washington Pl)
Bouley (163 Duane St)
Café Boulud (The Surrey, 20 E 76th St)
Daniel (60 E 65th St)
Eleven Madison Park (11 Madison Ave)
Felidia (243 E 58th St)
Four Seasons (99 E 52nd St)
Il Buco Alimentari e Vineria (53 Great Jones St)
Il Mulino New York (86 W 3rd St)
Jean Georges (Trump International Hotel and Tower, 1 Central Park W)
La Grenouille (3 E 52nd St)
Le Périgord (405 E 52nd St)
Ouest (2315 Broadway)
Pearl & Ash (220 Bowery)
Picholine (35 W 64th St)
Tocqueville Restaurant (1 E 15th St)
Toro (85 Tenth Ave)
Union Square Cafe (21 E 16th St)

HEALTHY FARE

Angelica Kitchen (300 E 12th St): organic and vegan
Calista Superfoods (1217 Lexington Ave): inventive, made from scratch
Candle 79 (154 E 79th St)
Dirt Candy (86 Allen St): best vegetarian
Four Seasons (99 E 52nd St): expensive
Gigi Cafe (64 E 34th St, 958 Third Ave, 2067 Broadway and 307 Seventh Ave)
Hangawi (12 E 32nd St)
Josie's Restaurant (300 Amsterdam Ave)
Little Chef (Gotham West Market, 600 Eleventh Ave)
Narcissa (25 Cooper Sq)
Pure Food and Wine (54 Irving Pl)
Quantum Leap Natural Food (226 Thompson St)
Spring Street Natural (62 Spring St): your best bet
Sweetgreen (1164 Broadway): cafeteria-style salad chain

HOTEL RESTAURANTS AND BARS

Manhattan hotel dining has regained some of its glow of long ago. No longer are on-premises eateries just for the convenience of registered guests. Now they are destinations for those who desire a less trendy scene with an inviting, elegant atmosphere. Noteworthy choices include:

6 Columbus (308 W 58th St): **Blue Ribbon Sushi Bar & Grill**
Ace Hotel (20 W 29th St): **The Breslin, The John Dory Oyster Bar** and **Stumptown Coffee Roasters**
The Algonquin Hotel (59 W 44th St): **Round Table**
Andaz Wall Street (75 Wall St): **Bar Seven Five** (after-hours watering hole)
Archer Hotel (45 W 38th St): **Fabrick**

The Carlton Hotel (92 Madison Ave, 2nd floor): **Millesime** (French treasures from the sea)

The Carlyle (35 E 76th St): **Bemelmans Bar at the Carlyle Hotel** and **The Carlyle** (overpriced)

Chambers Hotel (15 W 56th St): **MáPêche** and **Momofuku Milk Bar**

The Chatwal Hotel (132 W 44th St): **The Lambs Club** (upscale American)

City Club Hotel (55 W 44th St): **db Bistro Moderne** (Daniel Boulud's urbane bar-restaurant)

Dylan Hotel (52 E 41st St): **Benjamin Steak House**

Empire Hotel (44 W 63rd St): **Ed's Chowder House** (raw bar and restaurant)

Gansevoort Meatpacking NYC (18 Ninth Ave): **Plunge** (rooftop)

Gramercy Park Hotel (2 Lexington Ave): **Maialino** (Danny Meyer's house)

The Greenwich Hotel (377 Greenwich St): **Locanda Verde**

Hilton New York Fashion District (152 W 26th St): **Rare Bar & Grill** and **Rare View Rooftop Bar**

Hilton Times Square (234 W 42nd St): **Restaurant Above** and **Pinnacle Bar** (breathtaking views, creative American menu with Italian accents)

Hotel Elysée (60 E 54th St): **Monkey Bar** (great history and eclectic menu with Asian touches)

Hotel Plaza Athenee (37 E 64th St): **Arabelle** (dignified)

Hotel Wales (1295 Madison Ave): **Paola's** (Italian) and **Sarabeth's** (delightful)

Ink48 (653 Eleventh Ave): **PRINT** and **Press Lounge**

Inn at Irving Place (56 Irving Pl): **Cibar Lounge** and **Lady Mendl's Tea Salon** (very proper)

Kimberly Hotel (145 E 50th St): **Ibis** (Mediterranean) and **Upstairs** (rooftop lounge)

The Kitano New York (66 Park Ave): **Hakubai** (Japanese)

Le Parker Meridien New York (119 W 56th St): **Burger Joint at Le Parker Meridien New York** (lobby) and **Norma's** (breakfast, brunch and lunch)

Library Hotel (299 Madison Ave): **Madison and Vine** (American bistro and wine bar)

Loews Regency Hotel (540 Park Ave): **Regency Bar & Grill** (innovative American)

The London NYC (151 W 54th St): **Maze** (casual)

The Lowell (28 E 63rd St): **Pembroke Room**

Mandarin Oriental New York (80 Columbus Cir): **Asiate** (*prix-fixe* only dinner, fabulous views)

Maritime Hotel (92 Ninth Ave): **Tao Downtown** (dramatic Asian bistro)

The Mark (25 E 77th St): **The Mark Restaurant by Jean-Georges** (lavish brunch menu)

Martha Washington Hotel (29 E 29th St): **Marta** (Italian, pizza)

New York Marriott Marquis (1535 Broadway): **The View** (revolving top-floor eatery with New York-centric menu)

NoMad Hotel (1170 Broadway): **NoMad** (Mediterranean)

The Pierre (795 Fifth Ave): **Sirio Ristorante** (Italian) and **Two E Bar** (eclectic)

Ritz-Carlton New York, Battery Park (2 West St): **2 West** (modern American)

St. Regis New York (2 E 55th St): **King Cole Bar & Salon**

Sheraton New York Times Square Hotel (811 Seventh Ave): **Hudson Market Bistro**

Shoreham Hotel (33 W 55th St): **Shoreham Bar and Restaurant** (California cuisine)

Smyth Hotel (85 West Broadway): **Little Park** (veggie-centric)

The Standard High Line (848 Washington St): **The Biergarten** (German fun) and **The Standard Grill** (American)

Standard East Hotel (21 Cooper Square): **Narcissa** (farm-to-table new American)

The Surrey (20 E 76th St): **Bar Pleiades** (Coco Chanel-inspired decor) and **Café Boulud** (French)

Trump International Hotel and Tower (1 Central Park W): **Jean Georges** (The Donald's personal gem) and **Nougatine at Jean George** (casual)

Trump Soho New York (246 Spring St): **Koi** (Japanese)

Viceroy New York (120 W 57th St): **Kingside** (American; Marc Murphy)

W New York (541 Lexington Ave): **Heartbeat** (especially breakfast)

W New York Times Square (1567 Broadway): **Blue Fin** (seafood)

Waldorf Astoria New York (301 Park Ave): **Bull & Bear** (British atmosphere), **Oscar's American Brasserie** (cafeteria) and **Peacock Alley** (sumptuous Sunday brunch)

Washington Square Hotel (103 Waverly Pl): **North Square** (moderately priced American)

Westin New York Grand Central (212 E 42nd St): **The LCL Bar & Kitchen** (a.k.a. The Local; casual, seasonal American menu)

The William Hotel (24 E 39th St): **The Peacock** and **The Shakespeare Pub**

KOSHER

Kosher dining experiences in New York City run the gamut from elegant restaurants with celebrity chefs to the falafel stand outside Rockefeller Center and the kosher hot dog stands. Especially with kosher dining, phone ahead to make sure restaurants are open.

Abigael's on Broadway (1407 Broadway): largest kosher restaurant

Cafe K (8 E 48th St): This may be the busiest lunch spot in New York City.

Cafe Roma Pizzeria (854 Amsterdam Ave)

Caravan of Dreams (405 E 6th St): natural, raw and vegetarian East Village kosher restaurant

Circa (22 W 33rd St): This upscale cafeteria lunch location has everything from sushi to create-your-own salads and hot lasagna—all delicious!

Colbeh (32 W 39th St): Mediterranean

Eden Wok (43 E 34th St): great kosher Chinese restaurant with sushi bar

Jack's Wife Freda (224 Lafayette St): cozy Soho spot that re-imagines (as in tweaks) Jewish dishes

Jerusalem II (35 W 36th St): Crowds keep coming back to one of the first and best pizza, falafel and salad-bar emporiums in town.

Le Marais (150 W 46th St): This French steakhouse, which has a butcher store in the front, sets the kosher standard.

Lox at Cafe Weissman (The Jewish Museum, 1109 Fifth Ave): This museum was the old Felix Warburg mansion, and this intimate spot in the basement is a kosher oasis on Museum Row.

Mendy's (875 Third Ave; 61 E 34th St; 30 Rockefeller Plaza and Grand Central Terminal, 42nd St at Vanderbilt Ave): huge portions, fantastic food and friendly service

My Most Favorite Food (247 W 72nd St): Expensive pasta, fish, salads and desserts are all delectable.

Pongal (110 Lexington Ave): all kosher vegetarian

Russ & Daughters Cafe (127 Orchard St): comfort food

Talia's Steakhouse & Bar (668 Amsterdam Ave): Glatt kosher restaurant

Tevere (155 E 84th St): old family Italian/Jewish recipes and great traditions

Va Bene (1582 and 1583 Second Ave): superb pastas, Sunday brunch

Yonah Schimmel Knish Bakery (137 E Houston St): Schimmel started serving knishes to immigrants 150 years ago, and it is still in business.

LATE HOURS
The city that never sleeps...

69 Chinese Restaurant (69 Bayard St): Chinese
Agozar Cuban Bistro Bar (324 Bowery St)
Balthazar (80 Spring St)
Baraonda (1439 Second Ave)
Big Arc Chicken (233 First Ave)
Black Iron Burger Shop (540 E 5th St)
Blue Ribbon (97 Sullivan St)
Blue Ribbon Sushi (119 Sullivan St)
Cafe Lalo (201 W 83rd St)
Carnegie Deli (854 Seventh Ave)
Corner Social (321 Lenox Ave)
Cozy Soup 'n' Burger (739 Broadway)
dell'anima (38 Eighth Ave)
Employees Only (510 Hudson St)
Frank (88 Second Ave)
French Roast (78 W 11th St and 2340 Broadway)
Fuleen Seafood (11 Division St)
Gray's Papaya (2090 Broadway)
Great NY Noodletown (28 Bowery)
Green Kitchen (1477 First Ave)
Hanbat (53 W 35th St)
Kum Gang San (49 W 32nd St)
Landmarc (Time Warner Center, 10 Columbus Cir and 179 West Broadway)
L'Express (249 Park Ave S)
The Lion (62 W 9th St)
Macao Trading Co. (311 Church St)
The Meatball Shop (84 Stanton St)
Momofuku Ssäm Bar (207 Second Ave)
New WonJo (23 W 32nd St)
P.J. Clarke's (915 Third Ave, 44 W 63rd St and 4 World Financial Center)
Raoul's (180 Prince St)
Remedy Diner (245 E Houston St)
The Spotted Pig (314 W 11th St)
Sushi Seki (1143 First Ave)

Terroir (439 Third Ave): Murray Hill location
Veselka (144 Second Ave)
Viand Coffee Shop (2130 Broadway)
Wollensky's Grill (201 E 49th St)

MUNCHING AT THE MUSEUMS

Even some of the smallest museums have cafes. Often these are upscale spots where you can rest your feet and get a surprisingly good bite to eat. They are usually quite expensive. Some of the best:

Asia Society and Museum (725 Park Ave): **Garden Court Cafe**
The Jewish Museum (1109 Fifth Ave): **Lox at Cafe Weissman**
The Metropolitan Museum of Art (1000 Fifth Ave): **Cafeteria** (basement) and **Petrie Court Cafe and Wine Bar** (looks onto Central Park)
The Morgan Library & Museum (225 Madison Ave): **The Morgan Cafe** and **The Morgan Dining Room**
Museum of Arts and Design (2 Columbus Cir): **Robert** (9th floor)
Museum of Modern Art (9 W 53rd St): **The Modern**
Neue Galerie New York (1048 Fifth Ave): **Cafe Sabarsky**
New-York Historical Society (170 Central Park W): **Caffe Storico**
Rubin Museum of Art (150 W 17th St): **Cafe at the RMA**
Scandinavia House: The Nordic Center in America (58 Park Ave): **Smörgås Chef**
Solomon R. Guggenheim Museum (1071 Fifth Ave): **The Wright**
Whitney Museum of American Art (99 Gansevoort St): **Untitled**

OLD-TIMERS

1783: **Fraunces Tavern** (54 Pearl St)
1864: **Pete's Tavern** (129 E 18th St)
1868: **Old Homestead** (56 Ninth Ave)
1885: **Keens Steakhouse** (72 W 36th St)
1887: **Peter Luger Steak House** (178 Broadway, Brooklyn)
1888: **Katz's Delicatessen** (205 E Houston St)
1890: **P.J. Clarke's** (915 Third Ave)
1906: **Barbetta** (321 W 46th St)
1913: **Grand Central Oyster Bar Restaurant** (Grand Central Terminal, 42nd St at Vanderbilt Ave, lower level)
1920: **Waverly Inn** (16 Bank St)
1926: **Palm One** (837 Second Ave)
1927: **Minetta Tavern** (113 MacDougal St)
1929: **21 Club** (21 W 52nd St)

OUTDOOR DINING AND DRINKS

Aquagrill (210 Spring St)
Barbetta (321 W 46th St): garden
Bello Giardino (71 W 71st St)
The Biergarten (The Standard High Line, 848 Washington St)
Blue Water Grill (31 Union Sq W)
The Boathouse (Central Park at E 72nd St)
Bottino (246 Tenth Ave)

Bryant Park Grill (25 W 40th St)
Bull McCabe's (29 St. Mark's Pl)
Café Centro (MetLife Building, 200 Park Ave)
Caffe Dante (79-81 MacDougal St)
Casimir (103-105 Ave B)
Da Nico (164 Mulberry St)
Da Silvano (260 Ave of the Americas)
Financier Patisserie (3-4 World Financial Center, 1121 Ave of the Americas, 90 Nassau St and other locations)
Finnegan's Wake (1361 First Ave)
Gigino at Wagner Park (20 Battery Pl)
Hallo Berlin (626 Tenth Ave)
Home Restaurant (20 Cornelia St)
I Trulli (122 E 27th St)
Il Gattopardo (13-15 W 54th St)
Jackson Hole Burgers (232 E 64th St, 521 Third Ave and 517 Columbus Ave)
La Lanterna (129 MacDougal St)
Metro Grill Roof Garden (Hotel Metro, 45 W 35th St)
Mezzogiorno (195 Spring St)
New Leaf Cafe (Fort Tryon Park, 1 Margaret Corbin Dr)
Nice Matin (201 W 79th St)
Pampano (209 E 49th St, 2nd floor terrace)
Paradou (8 Little West 12th St)
The Park (118 Tenth Ave)
Patroon (160 E 46th St, 3rd floor)
Pete's Tavern (129 E 18th St)
Pure Food and Wine (54 Irving Pl)
Roc Restaurant (190-A Duane St)
Rock Center Cafe (Rockefeller Center, 20 W 50th St)
San Pietro (18 E 54th St)
Shake Shack (Madison Square Park, 23rd St bet Madison Ave and Broadway; 154 E 86th St; 215 Murray St and 600 Third Ave; seasonal)
Spring Street Natural (62 Spring St)
SushiSamba (87 Seventh Ave S)
Trattoria dell'Arte (900 Seventh Ave)
Waverly Inn (16 Bank St)
White Horse Tavern (567 Hudson St)

PERSONAL FAVORITES

40 Carrots (Bloomingdale's, 1000 Third Ave, 7th floor): nice atmosphere, great name, wonderful coffee frozen yogurt
ABC Kitchen (ABC Carpet & Home, 35 E 18th St)
Arlington Club (1032 Lexington Ave)
Babbo (110 Waverly Pl): fabulous food
Balthazar (80 Spring St): really fun atmosphere
Barbetta (321 W 46th St): a classy operation
Blue Ribbon (97 Sullivan St): great value
Bouley (163 Duane St): none better
Brooklyn Diner USA (212 W 57th St and 155 W 43rd St): satisfying meals all day

Cucina & Co. (MetLife Building, 200 Park Ave, lobby; Macy's, 151 W 34th St and 30 Rockefeller Center, concourse level): great quick meals

Daniel (60 E 65th St)

Del Posto (85 Tenth Ave): very classy service

Forty Four (Royalton Hotel, 44 W 44th St): the cocktail spot

Four Seasons (99 E 52nd St)

Golden Unicorn (18 East Broadway): great Chinese platters

Gotham Bar & Grill (12 E 12th St): all is good

Gramercy Tavern (42 E 20th St): quintessential New York

Il Mulino New York (86 W 3rd St): Italian heaven!

Jackson Hole Burgers (232 E 64th St, 521 Third Ave and 517 Columbus Ave): best burgers

La Grenouille (3 E 52nd St): beautiful

Lavo (39 E 58th St)

Le Périgord (405 E 52nd St): impeccable

Marchi's (251 E 31st St)

Michael's (24 W 55th St)

The Modern (Museum of Modern Art, 9 W 53rd St): great setting

Nobu 57 (40 W 57th St)

Nobu New York (105 Hudson St): Japanese food at its best

One if by Land, Two if by Sea (17 Barrow St): romantic

Peter Luger Steak House (178 Broadway, Brooklyn)

Piccolo Angolo (621 Hudson St): like family

Quality Meats (57 W 58th St)

River Café (1 Water St, Brooklyn)

Sfoglia (1402 Lexington Ave): wonderful bread

Shake Shack (Madison Square Park, 23rd St bet Madison Ave and Broadway; 366 Columbus Ave; 154 E 86th St; 691 Eighth Ave and other locations): delicious shakes

Shun Lee Palace (155 E 55th St)

Smith & Wollensky (797 Third Ave): old-time flavor

Spice Market (403 W 13th St)

Tao (42 E 58th St)

Union Square Cafe (21 E 16th St): justly famous

PIZZA

Adrienne's Pizzabar (54 Stone St)

Angelo's Pizzeria (117 W 57th St, 1043 Second Ave and 1697 Broadway)

apizz (217 Eldridge St): gourmet

Artichoke Basille's Pizza & Brewery (328 E 14th St, 114 Tenth Ave and 111 MacDougal St): really good

Arturo's Coal Oven Pizza (106 W Houston St)

Bella Vita (211 W 43rd St and 158 W 58th St)

Birdbath Bakery (160 Prince St; 200 Church St and New Museum, 235 Bowery)

Circo NYC (120 W 55th St)

Co. (230 Ninth Ave): baker Jim Lahey's restaurant debut

Da Nico (164 Mulberry St)

Emmett's (50 MacDougal St)
Emporio (231 Mott St)
Freds at Barneys New York (660 Madison Ave)
Giorgione (307 Spring St)
Grandaisy Bakery (250 West Broadway and 176 W 72nd St)
Il Corallo Trattoria (176 Prince St)
Joe's Pizza (7 Carmine St)
John's of Times Square (260 W 44th St)
Juliana's Pizza (19 Old Fulton St)
Kesté Pizza & Vino (271 Bleecker St): Margherita
La Pizza Fresca (31 E 20th St): Neapolitan pizza
Lazzara's Pizza Cafe (221 W 38th St, upstairs)
Lil' Frankie's Pizza (19 First Ave)
Lombardi's (32 Spring St)
Luzzo's (211 First Ave)
Marta (Martha Washington Hotel, 29 E 29th St)
Mezzogiorno (195 Spring St)
Motorino (349 E 12th St)
Naples 45 (MetLife Building, 200 Park Ave)
Nick & Toni's Cafe (100 W 67th St)
Nick's Pizza (1814 Second Ave)
Olio Pizza e Più (3 Greenwich Ave): mezzaluna (pizza-calzone hybrid)
Orso (322 W 46th St)
Patsy's Pizzeria (2287 First Ave and other locations)
Pizza Mezzaluna (146 W Houston St)
Pizza 33 (489 Third Ave): by the slice
PizzArte (69 W 55th St): Neapolitan
Rubirosa (235 Mulberry St)
Sal's & Carmine's Pizza (2671 Broadway): Neapolitan
Serafina (29 E 61st St; 38 E 58th St; 1022 Madison Ave; Time Hotel, 224 W 49th St and Dream Midtown, 210 W 55th St)
Trattoria dell'Arte (900 Seventh Ave)
Two Boots (42 Ave A)
Upland (345 Park Ave S)
Vic's (31 Great Jones St)
Vinny Vincenz Pizza (231 First Ave)

POWER MEALS

21 Club (21 W 52nd St)
Balthazar (80 Spring St)
Café Boulud (The Surrey, 20 E 76th St)
The Carlyle (Carlyle Hotel, 35 E 76th St)
Daniel (60 E 65th St)
Da Silvano (260 Ave of the Americas)
Delmonico's (56 Beaver St)
Del Posto (85 Tenth Ave)
Four Seasons (99 E 52nd St)
Gabriel's Bar & Restaurant (11 W 60th St)
Gotham Bar & Grill (12 E 12th St)
Il Mulino New York (86 W 3rd St)

Jean Georges (Trump International Hotel and Tower, 1 Central Park W)
La Grenouille (3 E 52nd St)
Le Bernardin (155 W 51st St)
Maloney & Porcelli (37 E 50th St)
Michael's (24 W 55th St)
Monkey Bar (Hotel Elysée, 60 E 54th St)
Morton's The Steakhouse (551 Fifth Ave)
Nobu 57 (40 W 57th St)
Nobu New York and **Nobu Next Door** (105 Hudson St)
The Palm (837 Second Ave, 840 Second Ave, 206 West St and 250 W 50th St)
Rao's (455 E 114th St)
Sette Mezzo (969 Lexington Ave)
Smith & Wollensky (797 Third Ave)

PRE-THEATER

Let your waiter know when you are first seated that you will be attending the theater so that service can be adjusted accordingly. Some restaurants have specially priced pre-theater dinners. If it is raining, allow extra time for getting a taxi.

Aquavit (65 E 55th St)
Barbetta (321 W 46th St)
Becco (355 W 46th St)
Blue Fin (W New York Times Square, 1567 Broadway)
Cafe Un DeuxTrois (123 W 44th St)
Carmine's (2450 Broadway and 200 W 44th St)
Chez Josephine (414 W 42nd St)
Dawat (210 E 58th St)
Esca (402 W 43rd St)
Four Seasons (99 E 52nd St)
Hearth (403 E 12th St)
Hell's Kitchen (679 Ninth Ave)
Indochine (430 Lafayette St)
La Boite en Bois (75 W 68th St)
Marchi's (251 E 31st St)
Momofuku Noodle Bar (171 First Ave)
Ollie's Noodle Shop and Grill (411 W 42nd St)
Orso (322 W 46th St)
Picholine (35 W 64th St)
Red Cat (227 Tenth Ave)
Spice Market (403 W 13th St)
Telepan (72 W 69th St)
Thalia (828 Eighth Ave)

ROMANTIC

Barbetta (321 W 46th St)
Blue Hill (75 Washington Pl)
Bouley (163 Duane St)
Caffe Reggio (119 MacDougal St)

Caffe Vivaldi (32 Jones St)
Chez Josephine (414 W 42nd St)
Daniel (60 E 65th St)
Eleven Madison Park (11 Madison Ave)
Erminia (250 E 83rd St)
Four Seasons (99 E 52nd St)
I Trulli (122 E 27th St)
Il Buco (47 Bond St)
Il Cortile (125 Mulberry St)
Jean Georges (Trump International Hotel and Tower, 1 Central Park W)
King Cole Bar (St. Regis New York, 2 E 55th St)
Lady Mendl's Tea Salon (Inn at Irving Place, 56 Irving Pl)
La Grenouille (3 E 52nd St)
Le Périgord (405 E 52nd St)
One if by Land, Two if by Sea (17 Barrow St)
Paola's (Hotel Wales, 1295 Madison Ave)
Rainbow Room (30 Rockefeller Plaza, 65th floor)
River Café (1 Water St, Brooklyn)
Scalinatella (201 E 61st St)
Spice Market (403 W 13th St)
Water's Edge (401 44th Dr and East River, Queens)

ROOFTOP DRINKS

230 Fifth Garden Bar (230 Fifth Ave): heated
Above 6 Rooftop Bar (Thompson Hotel, 6 Columbus Cir)
Ava Lounge (Dream New York, 210 W 55th St)
Birreria (Eataly, 200 Fifth Ave)
Bookmarks Lounge (Library Hotel, 299 Madison Ave)
Cantor Roof Garden Cafe (The Metropolitan Museum of Art, 1000 Fifth Ave)
The Delancey (168 Delancey St)
Empire Hotel Bar and Lounge (44 W 63rd St): view of Lincoln Center
Glass Bar (Hotel Indigo, 127 W 28th St)
Gramercy Terrace (Gramercy Park Hotel, 2 Lexington Ave, 18th floor)
Hudson Terrace (621 W 46th St)
La Birreria (200 Fifth Ave, 14th floor)
La Piscine (Hotel Americano, 518 W 27th St): rooftop pool bar via external glass elevator
Lobby Lounge (Mandarin Oriental, 80 Columbus Cir, 35th floor)
Lounge at Pod 39 (Pod 39 Hotel, 145 E 39th St): views of Empire State Building
Plunge (Gansevoort Meatpacking NYC, 18 Ninth Ave)
Press Lounge (Ink48, 653 Eleventh Ave)
Private Rooftop Garden (Surrey Hotel, 20 E 76th St, 17th floor)
Rare View Rooftop Lounge (Affinia Shelburne, 303 Lexington Ave)
The Roof (The Viceroy Hotel, 120 W 57th St)
Roof at Park South (Park South Hotel, 125 E 27th St)
Rooftop Terrace Lounge (Marriott Renaissance New York Hotel, 130 E 57th St)
Salon de Ning (The Peninsula New York, 700 Fifth Ave)
Sky Room (Fairfield Inn & Suites by Marriott Times Square, 330 W 40th St)

Sky Terrace (Hudson Hotel, 356 W 58th St)

The Skylark (200 W 39th St, 30th floor)

Tonic East (411 Third Ave): year-round

Top of the Strand (The Strand Hotel, 33 W 37th St)

Upstairs (Kimberly Hotel, 145 E 50th St)

SANDWICHES

Alidoro (105 Sullivan St)

Amy's Bread (672 Ninth Ave; 250 Bleecker St and Chelsea Market, 75 Ninth Ave)

Bread Market Cafe (1290 Ave of the Americas)

Cafe Gitane (242 Mott St and Jane Hotel, 113 Jane St)

Carnegie Deli (854 Seventh Ave)

City Bakery (3 W 18th St)

Cosi Sandwich Bar (841 Broadway and other locations)

Cucina & Co. (MetLife Building, 200 Park Ave)

Deb's Catering (200 Varick St)

E.A.T. (1064 Madison Ave)

Faicco's Pork Store (260 Bleecker St)

Manganaro's Hero Boy (494 Ninth Ave)

Mile End Sandwich (53 Bond St)

Once Upon a Tart (135 Sullivan St)

Parm (248 Mulberry St)

Piada (601 Lexington Ave): Italian

Porchetta (110 E 7th St)

Potbelly Sandwich Shop (501 Seventh Ave)

Salumeria Biellese (376-378 Eighth Ave)

Shorty's (576 Ninth Ave)

Sullivan Street Bakery (533 W 47th St)

Taboonette (30 E 13th St): hearty flatbread sandwiches

Todaro Bros. (555 Second Ave)

Union Square Cafe (21 E 16th St)

'wichcraft (555 Fifth Ave and other locations)

SEAFOOD

Aquagrill (210 Spring St)

Aquavit (65 E 55th St)

BLT Fish & Fish Shack (21 W 17th St)

Blue Fin (W New York Times Square, 1567 Broadway)

Blue Ribbon (97 Sullivan St): oyster bar

Blue Water Grill (31 Union Square W)

Docks Oyster Bar and Seafood Grill (633 Third Ave)

Ed's Lobster Bar (222 Lafayette St)

Esca (402 W 43rd St)

Estiatorio Milos (125 W 55th St)

Fish Tag (222 W 79th St)

Grand Central Oyster Bar Restaurant (Grand Central Terminal, 42nd St at Vanderbilt Ave, lower level)

The John Dory Oyster Bar (Ace Hotel, 1196 Broadway)
Kurumazushi (7 E 47th St, 2nd floor)
Le Bernardin (155 W 51st St)
Lure Fishbar (142 Mercer St)
Marea (240 Central Park S)
Mary's Fish Camp (64 Charles St)
Mermaid Inn (79 MacDougal St, 96 Second Ave and 568 Amsterdam Ave):
   oyster bar
Millesime (The Carlton Hotel, 92 Madison Ave)
North End Grill (104 North End Ave)
Ocean Grill (384 Columbus Ave)
Oceana (McGraw-Hill Building, 120 W 49th St)
Oriental Garden (14 Elizabeth St)
Pearl Oyster Bar (18 Cornelia St)
Primola (1226 Second Ave)
Remi (145 W 53rd St)
Sea Grill (Rockefeller Center, 19 W 49th St)
Westville (210 W 10th St, 173 Ave A and 246 W 18th St)

SHOPPING BREAKS

To replenish your energy, here are some good places to eat in the major
Manhattan stores:

ABC Carpet & Home (888 Broadway, 212/473-3000): **ABC Cocina** (Latin
   American), **ABC Kitchen** (Jean- Georges Vongerichten's green restaurant)
   and **Le Pain Quotidien** (bakery and cafe)
Barneys New York (660 Madison Ave, 212/833-2200): **Freds at Barneys
   New York** (upscale)
Bergdorf Goodman (men's store, 745 Fifth Ave, 212/753-7300): **Bar III**
Bergdorf Goodman (women's store, 754 Fifth Ave, 212/753-7300): **Bar 5F** (7th
   floor), **BG Restaurant** (7th floor) and **Goodman's** (plaza level)
Bloomingdale's (1000 Third Ave, 212/705-2000): **B Cafe** (6th floor), **David
   Burke** (1st floor), **Flip** (lower level), **40 Carrots** (7th floor), **Le Train
   Bleu** (6th floor) and **Magnolia Bakery** (1st floor)
Lord & Taylor (424 Fifth Ave, 212/391-3344): **Sarabeth's** (5th and 6th floors)
Macy's (151 W 34th St, 212/695-4400): **Au Bon Pain** (street level and 8th
   floor), **Cucina & Co.** (cellar), **Macy's Cellar Bar and Grill** (cellar),
   Starbucks (3rd floor) and **Stella 34 Trattoria** (6th floor, Italian
   eatery)
Saks Fifth Avenue (611 Fifth Ave, 212/753-4000): **Cafe S.F.A.** (8th floor, tasty
   and classy)

SOUTHERN FLAVORS AND SOUL FOOD

107 West (2787 Broadway)
Amy Ruth's (113 W 116th St)
Ashford and Simpson's Sugar Bar (254 W 72nd St): dinner and live
   entertainment Tuesday to Saturday
Bubby's (120 Hudson St and 71 Gansevoort St)
Charles' Country Panfried Chicken (2841 Frederick Douglass Blvd)
Great Jones Cafe (54 Great Jones St)

King Bee (424 E 9th St)
Londel's Supper Club (2620 Frederick Douglass Blvd)
Miss Mamie's Spoonbread Too (366 W 110th St)
Red Rooster Harlem (310 Lenox Ave)
Root & Bone (200 E 3rd St)
Sister's Caribbean Cuisine (47 E 124th St)
Sylvia's (328 Lenox Ave)
Tipsy Parson (156 Ninth Ave)

STEAKS

212 Steakhouse (316 E 53rd St)
American Cut (363 Greenwich St)
Arlington Club (1032 Lexington Ave)
Bistro le Steak (1309 Third Ave): inexpensive and good
BLT Steak (106 E 57th St)
Bowery Meat Company (9 E 1st St)
Bull & Bear (Waldorf Astoria New York, 301 Park Ave)
Capital Grille (Chrysler Center, 155 E 42nd St; Time-Life Building, 120 W 51st St and 120 Broadway)
Churrascaria Plataforma (Belvedere Hotel, 316 W 49th St)
Del Frisco's Double Eagle Steak House (1221 Ave of the Americas)
Donohue's Steak House (845 Lexington Ave)
Frankie and Johnnie's (269 W 45th St and 32 W 37th St)
Harry's Cafe & Steak (1 Hanover Sq)
Keens Steakhouse (72 W 36th St)
Le Marais (150 W 46th St): kosher
Maloney & Porcelli (37 E 50th St)
MarkJoseph Steakhouse (261 Water St)
Mastro's Steakhouse (1285 Ave of the Americas)
Minetta Tavern (113 MacDougal St)
Morton's The Steakhouse (551 Fifth Ave)
The Palm (837 Second Ave, 840 Second Ave, 206 West St and 250 W 50th St)
Patroon (160 E 46th St): outrageously expensive
Peter Luger Steak House (178 Broadway, Brooklyn): a tradition since 1887
Pietro's (232 E 43rd St)
Quality Meats (57 W 58th St)
Ruth's Chris Steak House (148 W 51st St)
Smith & Wollensky (797 Third Ave)
Sparks Steak House (210 E 46th St)
Strip House (13 E 12th St and 15 W 44th St)
Uncle Jack's Steakhouse (440 Ninth Ave; 44 W 56th St and 39-40 Bell Blvd, Queens)
Vic & Anthony's Steakhouse (233 Park Ave S)

SUSHI

In the early 1980s, sushi bars became the trendy haute cuisine of the fashionable set. To this day, New Yorkers love to wrap their chopsticks around succulent slivers of raw or cooked seafood on rice. Although many are content to order assortments concocted by the chef, true aficionados prefer to select by the piece. To tailor your next sushi platter to your own taste, here's what you need to know:

Amaebi (sweet shrimp)
Anago (sea eel)
California roll (avocado and crab)
Hamachi (yellowtail)
Hirame (halibut)
Ika (squid)
Ikura (salmon roe)
Kappa maki (cucumber roll)
Maguro (tuna)
Nizakana (cooked fish)
Saba (mackerel)
Sake (salmon)
Tekkamaki (tuna roll)
Toro (fatty tuna)
Umeshisomaki (plum roll)
Unagi (freshwater eel)
Uni (sea urchin)

Give any of these a try for sushi:
15 East (15 E 15th St)
Blue Ribbon Sushi (119 Sullivan St)
Bond Street (6 Bond St)
Hatsuhana (17 E 48th St)
Japonica (90 University Pl)
Jewel Bako (239 E 5th St)
Kurumazushi (7 E 47th St, 2nd floor)
Kyo Ya (94 E 7th St)
Masa (Time Warner Center, 10 Columbus Cir, 4th floor)
Neta (61 W 8th St)
Nippon (155 E 52nd St)
Nobu 57 (40 W 57th St)
Nobu New York and **Nobu Next Door** (105 Hudson St)
Ruby Foo's (1626 Broadway)
Sasabune (401 E 73rd St)
Shabu-Tatsu (216 E 10th St)
Sugiyama (251 W 55th St)
Sushi-Azabu (428 Greenwich St)
Sushi of Gari (347 W 46th St, 370 Columbus Ave and 402 E 78th St)
Sushi Seki (1143 First Ave)
Sushi Yasuda (204 E 43rd St)
Sushi Zen (108 W 44th St)
Sushiden (19 E 49th St and 123 W 49th St)
SushiSamba (87 Seventh Ave)

Takahachi (85 Ave A and 145 Duane St)
Tomoe Sushi (172 Thompson St)
Yama (38 Carmine St, 122 E 17th St and
   308 E 49th St)

TAKEOUT AND DELIVERY

Balthazar (80 Spring St)
Bread (20 Spring St)
Brick Lane Curry House (99 Second Ave)
Bubby's (120 Hudson St and 71 Gansevoort St)
Cafe Español (172 Bleecker St)
City Market Cafe (178 Fifth Ave)
Cucina Vivolo (138 E 74th St)
Dean & Deluca (560 Broadway and 1150 Madison Ave)
Demarchelier (50 E 86th St)
Food Passion (1200 Lexington Ave)
Gigi Cafe (64 E 34th St, 958 Third Ave, 2067 Broadway and 307 Seventh Ave)
Henry's (2745 Broadway)
Jacques Brasserie (204-206 E 85th St)
Jubilee (948 First Ave)
Just Salad (320 Park Ave, 134 W 37th St, 100 Maiden Lane and other locations)
Kitchenette (156 Chambers St and 1272 Amsterdam Ave)
Lorenzo and Maria's Kitchen (1418 Third Ave)
Maria Pia (319 W 51st St)
Molyvos (871 Seventh Ave)
Murray's Cheese Shop (254 Bleecker St and Grand Central Market,
   Lexington Ave at 43rd St)
Pepe Giallo to Go (253 Tenth Ave)
Sarabeth's Bakery (Chelsea Market, 75 Ninth Ave)
Schiller's (131 Rivington St)
Sushi Zen (108 W 44th St)
Tea & Sympathy (108 Greenwich Ave)
Tio Pepe (168 W 4th St)
Turkuaz Restaurant (2637 Broadway)
Virgil's Real Barbecue (152 W 44th St)
Westville (173 Ave A, 210 W 10th St, 246 W 18th St and 333 Hudson St)
'wichcraft (555 Fifth Ave and other locations)

TEATIME

Alice's Tea Cup (102 W 73rd St, 156 E 64th St and 220 E 81st St)
Bar Seine (Hotel Plaza Athenee, 37 E 64th St)
Betony (41 W 57th St)
Bosie Tea Parlor (10 Morton St)
Cafe S.F.A. (Saks Fifth Avenue, 611 Fifth Ave, 8th floor)
Cha-An (230 E 9th St, 2nd floor): Japanese teahouse
Crosby Bar (Crosby Street Hotel, 79 Crosby St): afternoon tea service
The Gallery (Carlyle Hotel, 35 E 76th St)
Gotham Lounge (The Peninsula New York, 700 Fifth Ave)
Harney & Sons (433 Broome St)
King's Carriage House (251 E 82nd St)

Lady Mendl's Tea Salon (Inn at Irving Place, 56 Irving Pl)
The Morgan Cafe (The Morgan Library & Museum, 225 Madison Ave)
Palm Court (The Plaza, 59th St at Fifth Ave)
Pembroke Room (The Lowell, 28 E 63rd St)
Podunk (231 E 5th St)
Radiance Tea House & Books (158 W 55th St)
Rose Bakery (Dover Street Market, 160 Lexington Ave)
The Russian Tea Room (150 W 57th St)
Sant Ambroeus (1000 Madison Ave and 259 W 4th St)
Sarabeth's (423 Amsterdam Ave; Hotel Wales, 1295 Madison Ave; 40 Central Park S; 381 Park Ave S and 339 Greenwich St)
Tea & Sympathy (108 Greenwich Ave)
Teanissimo (90 Rivington St)
Two E Bar (The Pierre, 2 E 61st St)
Ty Bar (Four Seasons Hotel New York, 57 E 57th St): weekends

TOP-RATED

Aquagrill (210 Spring St)
Babbo (110 Waverly Pl)
Barbetta (321 W 46th St)
Bâtard (239 West Broadway)
Betony (41 W 57th St)
Blue Ribbon Sushi (119 Sullivan St)
Bouley (163 Duane St)
Café Boulud (The Surrey, 20 E 76th St)
Craft (43 E 19th St)
Daniel (60 E 65th St)
db Bistro Moderne (City Club Hotel, 55 W 44th St)
Del Posto (85 Tenth Ave)
Eleven Madison Park (11 Madison Ave)
Four Seasons (99 E 52nd St)
Gotham Bar & Grill (12 E 12th St)
Gramercy Tavern (42 E 20th St)
Il Mulino New York (86 W 3rd St)
Jean Georges (Trump International Hotel and Tower, 1 Central Park W)
Keens Steakhouse (72 W 36th St)
Kyo Ya (94 E 7th St)
La Grenouille (3 E 52nd St)
Le Bernardin (155 W 51st St)
Maialino (Gramercy Park Hotel, 2 Lexington Ave)
The Mark Restaurant by Jean-Georges (The Mark, 25 E 77th St)
Masa (Time Warner Center, 10 Columbus Cir, 4th floor)
The Modern (Museum of Modern Art, 9 W 53rd St)
Nobu 57 (40 W 57th St)
Nobu New York and **Nobu Next Door** (105 Hudson St)
Oceana (McGraw-Hill Building, 120 W 49th St)
Pearl Oyster Bar (18 Cornelia St)
Per Se (Time Warner Center, 10 Columbus Cir, 4th floor)
Peter Luger Steak House (178 Broadway, Brooklyn)
Picholine (35 W 64th St)

The Polo Bar (1 E 55th St)
Public (210 Elizabeth St)
Sasabune (401 E 73rd St)
Scarpetta (355 W 14th St)
Sugiyama (251 W 55th St)
Sushi of Gari (402 E 78th St, 347 W 46th St and 370 Columbus Ave)
Sushi Seki (1143 First Ave)
Sushi Yasuda (204 E 43rd St)
Union Square Cafe (21 E 16th St)

VEGAN AND VEGETARIAN

Angelica Kitchen (300 E 12th St)
Barbetta (321 W 46th St)
Benny's Burritos (113 Greenwich Ave and 93 Avenue A)
Cafe Blossom (507 Columbus Ave, 187 Ninth Ave and 41 Carmine St)
Candle Cafe (1307 Third Ave and 2427 Broadway)
Chennai Garden (129 E 27th St)
Chola (232 E 58th St)
Dévi (8 E 18th St)
Dovetail (103 W 77th St)
EN Japanese Brasserie (435 Hudson St)
Green Table (Chelsea Market, 75 Ninth Ave)
Hangawi (12 E 32nd St)
Maoz Vegetarian (59 E 8th St and 558 Seventh Ave)
Monte's Trattoria (97 MacDougal St)
Peacefood Cafe (460 Amsterdam Ave)
Piora (430 Hudson St)
Pure Food and Wine (54 Irving Pl)
Quantum Leap Natural Food (226 Thompson St)
Quintessence (263 E 10th St)
Snack (105 Thompson St)
Soomsoom Vegetarian Bar (166 W 72nd St)
Souen (28 E 13th St, 210 Ave of the Americas and 326 E 6th St)
Spring Street Natural (62 Spring St)
Two Boots (42 Ave A and other locations)
V-Note (1522 First Ave)
Vatan (409 Third Ave)
Vegetarian's Paradise 2 (144 W 4th St)
Village Natural (46 Greenwich Ave)

VIEW RESTAURANTS

These are restaurants with a view, beyond the bars and lounges listed in "Rooftop Drinks" (see page 62).

A Voce (Time Warner Center, 10 Columbus Cir, 3rd floor): Central Park view
Asiate (Mandarin Oriental New York, Time Warner Center, 80 Columbus Cir, 35th floor)
Gaonnuri (1250 Broadway, 39th floor): stunning high-rise view of cityscape

Gigino at Wagner Park (20 Battery Pl); terrace views of Miss Liberty
The Modern (Museum of Modern Art, 9 W 53rd St): outdoor sculpture garden
Per Se (Time Warner Center, 10 Columbus Cir, 4th floor): Central Park
Rainbow Room (30 Rockefeller Plaza, 65th floor)
River Café (1 Water St, Brooklyn): romantic; sensational Lower Manhattan views
Sea Grill (19 W 49th St): Rockefeller Center view
The View (New York Marriott Marquis, 1535 Broadway): lounge; revolves high above Times Square
World Yacht Cruises (Pier 81, 41st St at Hudson River): Manhattan from the water

WINE BARS

Amélie (22 W 8th St)
Ara (24 Ninth Ave)
Artisanal Fromagerie, Bistro and Wine Bar (2 Park Ave)
Bar Boulud (1900 Broadway)
Blue Ribbon Downing Street Bar (34 Downing St): 300-bottle wine list
Bottegadel Vino (7 E 59th St)
Cafe Katja (79 Orchard St): Austrian wines and nibbles
Casellula Cheese & Wine Cafe (401 W 52nd St): extensive cheeses and superb tasting menu
Drunken Horse (225 Tenth Ave): international selection
Epistrophy (200 Mott St): romantic
Il Buco Alimentari e Vineria (53 Great Jones St)
Il Posto Accanto (190 E 2nd St)
Jadis (42 Rivington St)
Lelabar (422 Hudson St): artsy wine room with good, affordable vino
Morrell Wine Bar & Cafe (1 Rockefeller Plaza)
Paradou (8 Little West 12th St)
Pata Negra (345 E 12th St): Spanish hams and cheeses
Pearl & Ash (220 Bowery)
Pure Food and Wine (54 Irving Pl)
Tangled Vine Wine Bar & Kitchen (434 Amsterdam Ave): eco-friendly
Ten Degrees (121 St. Mark's Pl and 131 Ave A)
Terroir (413 E 12th St): 50 wines by the glass
Turks and Frogs (323 W 11th St)
Wined Up (913 Broadway, 2nd floor)

WHAT TO EXPECT
THE BEST IN EVERY PRICE CATEGORY

2ND AVE DELI

1442 First Ave (at 75th St)   212/737-1700
Daily: Mon-Fri: 11 a.m.-midnight; Sat, Sun: 9 a.m.-midnight
162 E 33rd St (bet Lexington and Third Ave)   212/689-9000
Daily: 6 a.m.-midnight   2ndavedeli.com
Moderate

Both locations of this famous kosher deli and restaurant continue to draw crowds who love the gigantic portions and quality plates. The rather nondescript settings seem unimportant when there's a menu offering up favorite Jewish deli dishes. A plate of delicious crisp dill pickles is placed in front of you at the start. Appetizers include chopped liver, stuffed cabbage and chicken wings; soups include the favorite matzo ball. There are also blintzes, potato pancakes, challah French toast, knishes, kugels, cole slaw, huge open (and closed) sandwiches, burgers, deli platters and many beef entrees. Don't forget the chicken, fish and steaks. I rate 2nd Ave Deli as among the best delis in the city, or anywhere, for that matter.

A VOCE

Time Warner Center
10 Columbus Cir (at Eighth Ave), 3rd floor   212/823-2523
Lunch: Mon-Sat; Dinner: Daily; Brunch: Sun
41 Madison Ave (at 26th St)   212/545-8555
Lunch: Mon-Fri; Dinner: Mon-Sat   avocerestaurant.com
Moderately expensive

An excellent ingredient-driven contemporary Italian menu is offered at A Voce. Both locations are polished and well-appointed. The Columbus Cir house has a stunning Central Park view for those lucky enough to sit by the window; patrons of the Madison Avenue restaurant are treated to an outside dining piazza in nice weather. Menus change frequently, but highlights include Mediterranean sea bass, pan-roasted chicken with root vegetable medley and excellent pasta dishes including ricotta dumplings with braised oxtail. Save room for some really good desserts like chestnut apple tart with chocolate gelato and daily sorbet flavors.

ABBOCCATO ITALIAN KITCHEN

136 W 55th St (bet Ave of the Americas and Seventh Ave)   212/265-4000
Breakfast: Daily; Lunch: Mon-Sat; Dinner: Daily   abboccato.com
Moderately expensive to expensive

Expect big things! The Livanos family, known and respected on the New York restaurant scene, owns this elegant Italian dining spot, which serves authentic regional dishes of Italy. As either a starter or light meal, a great selection of *cicchetti* (small plates) tempt the taste buds. Most of the appetizers, especially the ten varieties of pasta, are excellent and the breadsticks are fabulous! Noteworthy entrees like roasted veal chops and grilled Mediterranean sea bass are very good and the $38 *prix-fixe*, six-course dinner is a great value. A sizeable dessert menu, including homemade gelato, is a dream. However dreamy the dining experience, the sizable tab will wake you up.

ABC KITCHEN

ABC Carpet & Home
35 E 18th St (at Broadway)   212/475-5829
Lunch: Mon-Fri; Dinner: Daily; Brunch: Sat, Sun   abckitchennyc.com
Moderately expensive to expensive

At ABC Kitchen, super-chef Jean-Georges Vongerichten's farm-to-table menu utilizes fresh, organic, local ingredients. Although many of the items are pricey, with careful selection you can do well. The fresh, airy space within ABC Carpet & Home is warm and modern and the front desk personnel and wait staff are exceptionally friendly, informed and efficient. Seasonal soups and a wonderful apple and pear salad are great starters. The variety of pastas and whole-wheat pizzas is excellent; vegetable dishes are particularly appealing. Entrees range from $24 (cheeseburger) to $40 for wood-oven-roasted Maine lobster; seafood dishes are the main attraction. The dessert menu is large and varied. A sundae of salted caramel ice cream with candied peanuts and popcorn, whipped cream and chocolate sauce is almost a meal in itself. ABC offers a one-of-a-kind, noisy, fun atmosphere, great people watching and really delicious platters. A fitting description of this place would be a "haute green cuisine" experience.

ACAPPELLA

1 Hudson St (bet West Broadway and Chambers St)   212/240-0163
Lunch: Mon-Fri; Dinner: Mon-Sat   acappellarestaurant.com
Moderately expensive

Acappella, classy and upscale in atmosphere, food and pricing, provides a very special Tribeca dining experience with a highly professional staff. It's a good place for a romantic interlude, for an important business lunch or to experiment with unique Northern Italian dishes. You'll find wonderful homemade pastas, risotto, fish, veal scaloppine and tasty chicken dishes on the menu; they claim to have the best veal chop in the city. For dessert, splurge on the homemade Italian cheesecake.

ACME

9 Great Jones St (bet Lafayette St and Broadway)   212/203-2121
Dinner: Daily; Brunch: Sat, Sun   acmenyc.com
Moderately expensive

Finding Acme's location might be a bit tricky if you are unfamiliar with Noho; Great Jones Street is a two block section completing West and East Third streets where odd-numbered addresses are uncharacteristically on the south side of the street. Executive chef Mads Refslund describes the fare as American with Nordic twists and divides the menu into raw, cooked, soil, sides and sea/land categories. Depending on the season, you may find interesting items such as duck in a jar, country toast (with cheese and vegetables), hay-roasted vegetables, Arctic char, chicken and eggs and much more. A $65 vegetable tasting menu or a $75 protein selection balance the land and sea

RAMEN

I dare say that struggling college students and young adults remember meal after meal that consisted primarily of ramen noodles in a salty broth. The cheap mealtime staple came in a square cellophane package with a tiny packet of seasoning and could be prepared just about anywhere. Well, ramen noodle soups have reached a new gastronomic height and are now made with rich stocks, gourmet meats, fresh veggies and goodies formerly out of budget during lean times. You're sure to enjoy slurping noodles at these restaurants:

Hanjan (36 W 26th St, 212/206-7226)

Hide-Chan (248 E 52nd St, 212/813-1800)

Ivan Ramen Slurp Shop (Gotham West Market, 600 Eleventh Ave, 212/582-7940)

Ramen.co (100 Maiden Lane, 646/490-8456)

Takashi (456 Hudson St, 212/414-2929): reservations for parties of four or more

Totto Ramen (366 W 52nd St, 212/813-1800 and 464 W 51st St, 646/596-9056)

flights. This tight space is lively and includes dining tables with an eating bar and rail for walk-in customers. A downstairs cocktail bar (open Tuesday through Saturday 7 p.m. to 3 a.m.) has a limited menu from the restaurant.

ALDEA

31 W 17th St (bet Fifth Ave and Ave of the Americas)   212/675-7223
Dinner: Mon-Sat   aldearestaurant.com
Moderately expensive

The best seats at Aldea are at the chef's counter, overlooking the kitchen. Chef George Mendes orchestrates this sleek, contemporary Mediterranean hot spot. The menu reflects the best of the current season from land and sea. Small bites, charcuterie and entrees like farm-raised venison leg, suckling pig, Manila clams and black bass pepper the listings; take note of the $79 four-course *prix-fixe* menu. Cool, housemade sorbet or ice cream is a wonderful finish.

AMERICAN CUT

363 Greenwich St (bet Franklin and Harrison St)   212/226-4736
Dinner: Mon-Sat   americancutsteakhouse.com
Expensive

Tribeca is home to Marc Forgione's most recent venture, American Cut. The grand and modern trappings complement the perfectly executed steakhouse classics. Interesting appetizers include cornflake crab cakes with smoked onion remoulade or Diamond Jim Brady oysters with black truffle sauce and splash of Champagne. As you would expect, the feature here is beef – filet mignon, beef short ribs, ribeye, New York strip, porterhouse and more, but you'll also find lamb, veal, salmon and halibut dishes. Sides include glazed carrot (that's one large carrot), potato puree or baked onions with crème fraiche. To finish, candy bar cake with roasted peanut ice cream or pumpkin cheesecake with cranberries are worthy of your attention. Expect a pretty price!

ANNISA

13 Barrow St (bet Seventh Ave S and 4th St) 212/741-6699
Dinner: Daily annisarestaurant.com
Moderately expensive to expensive

Consider a visit to Annisa for an intimate dinner in the West Village. Award-winning chef Anita Lo creates an impressive American menu with multicultural accents inspired by her Asian roots, the seasons and extensive travel. Start with roasted beet salad with cashew puree or seared foie gras with soup dumplings and jicama, and on to skillfully prepared entrees that may include broiled Spanish mackeral with garlic fried milk, a tasting of lamb with cauliflower, capers and pecorino and seared venison tenderloin with parsnip, black trumpets and berries. Consider the $85 five-course or $115 seven-course tasting menu to maximize your options. The space is tiny and unimpressive, but comfortable; the service is polished and graceful.

AQUAVIT

65 E 55th St (bet Park and Madison Ave) 212/307-7311
Lunch: Mon-Fri; Dinner: Mon-Sat aquavit.org
Expensive

For fresh, yet authentic Scandinavian cuisine, you can't do better than Aquavit. Owner Hakan Swahn has partnered with chef Emma Bengtsson to create a first-class establishment. An exceptional staff serves you in a warm, rustic, light-filled space. Hearty lunch appetites will enjoy the Scandinavian bouillabaisse or Swedish meatballs. A three-course $85 *prix-fixe* and eight-course $135 chef's tasting menu are offered at dinner. Early choices include herring and diver scallops, then on to cod, striped bass, duck and cauliflower and braised brisket as main course offerings. If you are fortunate, dessert might be blonde chocolate ganache over basil sorbet with blackberries.

ARLINGTON CLUB

1032 Lexington Ave (near 74th St) 212/249-5700
Dinner: Daily arlingtonclubny.com
Moderately expensive to expensive

Arlington Club is an U.E.S. destination for excellent steaks, exquisitely presented sushi and contemporary American fare. Offerings include dry-aged prime beef and a Porterhouse for two that is worth the price for very special occasions. You won't go wrong with the potatoes Arlington or mac and cheese alongside the black bass or Dover sole. On-the-job partner Paul Goldstein and his crew run a professional operation. Warm brick walls and ceilings, curved banquettes, comfortable high-back benches and chairs surrounding the tables and arched ceilings, all create a clubby atmosphere. Sorry to say, the place has gone down a bit since opening; the big popovers are no longer!

THE CLASSIC NEW YORK COCKTAIL

There is no more typical New York cocktail than the Old Fashioned and purists will go most anywhere to find the real thing. Here are a few spots:

The 21 Club (21 W 52nd St, 212/582-7200)

Barramundi (67 Clinton St, 212/529-6999)

The Four Seasons (99 E 52nd St)

Jbird Cocktails (339 E 75th Street, 212/288-8033)

Le Cirque (1 Beacon Ct, 151 E 58th St)

Monkey Bar (Hotel Elysée, 60 E 54th St)

ARTISANAL FROMAGERIE, BISTRO AND WINE BAR

2 Park Ave (at 32nd St)   212/725-8585

Lunch: Mon-Fri; Dinner: Daily; Brunch: Sat, Sun   artisanalbistro.com

Moderately expensive to expensive

This midtown Parisian bistro specializes in fondue and artisanal cheeses. Being a cheese lover, I found the menu and stylish retail cheese counter first-rate. Maine lobster and avocado salad is a great way to start, followed by a seafood platter of littleneck clams, east and west coast oysters, jumbo shrimp and more. Several fondues are offered, including the Artisanal blend composed of a classic fusion of three Swiss cheeses, aged Gouda and Stout. House specialties include delicate Dover sole or a casserole of duck, garlic sausage and lamb. For dessert, cruise the cheese counter and load your plate from a selection of 100 handcrafted choices, or try Artisanal's renowned cheesecake with buttery pecan-shortbread crust and a dousing of praline and caramel sauce. Seating is comfortable in the spacious art deco room, and service is highly informed and personable.

AWADH

2588 Broadway (at 98th St)   646/861-3604

Lunch: Mon-Fri; Dinner: Daily; Brunch: Sat, Sun   awadhnyc.com

Inexpensive to moderate

You want to visit Awadh for nouveax North Indian cooking. This small, chic Murray Hill jewel, with a waitstaff that is patient and hardworking, features the ancient Hindu cuisine of Awadhi with its bold flavors and uncommon spices. Chef/owner Gaurav Ahand's training in *dum pukht*, the traditional Indian art of cooking over a slow fire in a sealed heavy pot, results in tender, juicy meats that may then be finished on the grill. Skewers of vegetables, chicken and lamb, coconut shrimp curry, grilled spiced sweet potato with pineapple, mustard marinated lamb chops and carom seed-marinated grilled prawns are some of the choices. To finish, desserts include warm rose syrup dumplings and saffron-infused bread pudding. Whether you come for just a nibble or a meal, Awadh will satisfy. A private upstairs space is available for up to 50 guests.

BABBO

110 Waverly Pl (at Washington Square)   212/777-0303
Lunch: Tues-Sat; Dinner: Daily   babbonyc.com
Moderate to moderately expensive

Surely you have heard about Babbo! For many years 110 Waverly Place has been one of my favorite dining addresses. First it was the legendary Coach House, but now it is the magnificent Babbo, which means "daddy" in the native tongue. It has become one of the most respected houses of fine Italian dining in New York, and this is one of the toughest reservations in Manhattan. The townhouse setting is warm and comfortable, the service is highly professional and an evening at Babbo is one you will savor for a long time! Most everything is good, but I especially recommend sweetbreads, grilled ribeye steak for two and beef cheek ravioli. Wonderful desserts might include chocolate hazelnut cake, saffron panna cotta, pistachio and chocolate *semifreddo* and the ever-popular cheese plate. Best of all is the assortment of homemade gelato and sorbetti.

BALABOOSTA

214 Mulberry St (at Spring St)   212/966-7366
Lunch: Tues-Fri; Dinner: Daily; Brunch: Sat, Sun   balaboostanyc.com
Moderately expensive

Balaboosta is as warm and cozy a place as you'll find in your own neighborhood. The front window is lined with large jars of pickles and preserves and offers a view of the open kitchen where Mediterranean and Middle Eastern cuisine is prepared. Start with small plates, appetizers, daily ceviche or a chalkboard special. Lunch options include a goat cheese-stuffed lamb burger, Tunisian sandwich and crusty chicken schnitzel. Later in the day, grilled fish, steaks, chicken and lamb chops are accompanied by couscous, vegetables and other sides appropriate to the region. Some of these items plus Moroccan baked eggs, breakfast pizza and their rendition of French toast

KOREAN FOOD

Have a hankering for authentic Korean food? Well, the answer, if you are serious, is to take a journey to the last stop on the Flushing local line, which is really the start of the best Korean food in the area. The Queens kimchi presentations are not really that well known, but you can't go wrong in this area. The outlets in the West 30s in Manhattan can't hold a candle to this little-explored region.

Some good bets:

Bonjuk (152-26 Northern Blvd, 718/939-5868)

Debasaki (33-67 Farrington St, 718/886-6878)

Keum Sung Food (40-07 149th Pl, 718/539-4596)

Mapo Korean BBQ (149-24 41st Ave, 718/886-8292)

P.S. Come when you are really hungry.

are tempting brunch dishes. The service is attentive, the food is delicious and the environs are most relaxing.

BALTHAZAR

80 Spring St (at Crosby St)   212/965-1414
Breakfast, Lunch: Mon-Fri; Dinner: Daily; Brunch: Sat, Sun
Moderate   balthazarny.com

This Soho brasserie is a fun, popular destination at any time of the day (or night, as they serve late). The setting at Balthazar — with old mirrors, ceiling fans and a yellow tin ceiling — is unique, and the food is quite good, considering the size of the operation. The bustling personnel are well-trained; you will not wait for your water glass to be filled. At lunch and dinner you can enjoy delicious seasonal salads, sandwiches, cheeses, paninis, fabulous French onion soup, duck confit, steak *frites* and an abundant seafood selection (including a seafood bar). For dessert the tarte tatin is a must. A separate takeout menu is offered in the bakery, which includes breads, pastries (particularly good at breakfast), sandwiches and salads.

BAR AMERICAIN

152 W 52nd St (bet Ave of the Americas and Seventh Ave)   212/265-9700
Lunch: Mon-Fri; Dinner: Daily; Brunch: Sat, Sun   baramericain.com
Moderately expensive to expensive

Bar Americain is indeed almost purely American with some Southern touches. Perhaps best described as an American brasserie, the setting is large with offbeat decor and chef Bobby Flay has made the room come alive. The food quality and attentive, professional service make this a good bet. To start, the cocktails are numerous and interesting and an eye-catching raw bar is stocked with oysters, clams, lobsters and more. One could make a meal on the appetizers: vidalia onion soup with blistered Vermont cheddar cheese is superb and don't pass up a side of hot potato chips with blue cheese sauce. The same holds true for escargot and crawfish served with a side of brioche. Among the entrees, cioppino, steaks, duck with dirty spelt and rack of pork chops are definitely worth a try. You'll want to take extra time to study the excellent dessert menu!

BAR BOULUD

1900 Broadway (bet 63rd and 64th St)   212/595-0303
Lunch: Mon-Fri; Dinner: Daily; Brunch: Sat, Sun   barboulud.com/nyc
Moderate

Conveniently located just steps from Lincoln Center, the sleek wine-cellar-like dining room features a charcuterie bar and communal tables. The rustic French menu features a number of Daniel Boulud's favorites. You'll find signature terrines and patés, hearty soups and seasonal French bistro cooking. The croque monsieur with housemade ham, gruyere cheese and béchamel is delicious. For heartier fare, you'll find coq au vin, steak *frites* and seasonal seafood with a distinctive French flavor. Charcuterie specialties are available daily. Bar Boulud features a good showing of cheese, ice creams, sorbets and rich chocolate treats for dessert. This is an obvious winner for Lincoln Center opera-goers.

BARBETTA

321 W 46th St (bet Eighth and Ninth Ave)   212/246-9171
Lunch, Dinner, Supper: Tues-Sat   barbettarestaurant.com
Moderate to moderately expensive

Barbetta is one of those special places you'll find only in New York! Owner Laura Maioglio is a very special person, as well. This elegant restaurant serves Piemontese cuisine; Piemonte is located in northern Italy, and the cuisine reflects that charming region. You can dine here in European elegance. One of New York's oldest restaurants, Barbetta will celebrate its 109th year in 2015; amazingly, it is still owned by its founding family. A special attraction is dining alfresco in the garden during the summer. The main dining room and private rooms are magnificent! Barbetta offers an extensive a la carte menu at lunch and dinner with numerous fish and seafood dishes. Before theater, Barbetta serves a three-course *prix-fixe* menu with eight choices at each course. Among Barbetta's signature dishes are delicate gnocchetti, light as powder puffs; Bagna Cauda; quail's nest of fonduta; beef braised in Barolo wine and rack of venison. Sixteen desserts are prepared daily including an assortment of cakes, tarts, fruits and one of the best panna cotti in the city. Barbetta's wine list, recipient of many awards, numbers over 1,700 labels. By the way, service is expeditious so that you can make opening curtain if you're headed to the theater.

BAR PRIMI

325 Bowery (at 2nd St)   212/220-9100
Lunch: Mon-Fri; Dinner: Daily; Brunch: Sat, Sun   barprimi.com
Moderate to moderately expensive

Bar Primi is a casual, rustic, walk-in restaurant offering seating on two-levels; reservations are only required for six or more. Andrew Carmellini's marinara-sauced Italian menu is a bit like good old-fashioned Italian home cooking; both traditional and seasonal items of piccolini, antipasti and housemade pasta are listed. Start with delicious meatballs stuffed with melted fontina or roasted beets gorgonzola, then on to small plates of spaghetti and clams, short rib raviolini, ricotta ravioli with swiss chard or pork ragu in red wine. Meaty main entrees make appearances as nightly specials; scallops on Wednesday, duck breast on Thursday, chianti short ribs on Saturday and so on. The beautiful bar is a popular spot for a late snack and cocktails or wine.

BAR SIX

502 Ave of the Americas (bet 12th and 13th St)   212/691-1363
Lunch: Mon-Fri: Dinner: Daily; Brunch: Sat, Sun   barsixny.com
Inexpensive to moderate

For a quiet and casual meal or just meeting for drinks, Bar Six is a great choice. This cutesy French bistro-like space in Greenwich Village allows for easy conversation while enjoying a varied French/Moroccan menu; the offerings change seasonally, but if available, Moroccan chicken is one of their most popular dishes. Mussels Provencale, vegetable couscous, curried chicken salad, croque monsieur sandwich and hanger steak *frites* are possible items, along with an exceptional hamburger. Check out the late-night menu, if dining fashionably late.

LOWER EAST SIDE EATS

For those with long (and pleasant) memories, the Lower East Side is not "the same as it used to be." Gentrification has erased some of the treasures of the area. Now we have only **Katz's Delicatessen** (205 E Houston St), **Yonah Schimmel Knish Bakery** (137 E Houston St), **Russ & Daughters Cafe** (127 Orchard St) and **Economy Candy** (108 Rivington St) as survivors. What a loss! Just shed a few tears for Ratner's, Schapiro Wine and Schmulka Bernstein's (kosher Chinese); they are no more! (And what about all those great old tie stores? My closet is still full of their bargains!)

BÂTARD

239 West Broadway (bet Walker and White St)
Dinner: Mon-Sat
Expensive

212/219-2777
batardtribeca.com

Top restaurateur Drew Nieporent has reinvented this Tribeca real estate into a more casual fine dining restaurant. Warm and minimal with hardwood floors, this house serves up New American tastes with European accents. Two-, three- and four-course *prix-fixe* menu formats feature chef Markus Glocker's ongoing new flavor combinations. Offerings might include cauliflower soup with charred onion, white port and thyme; braised artichokes with barley and poached hen's egg; Canadian lobster with carrot fondue and parsnip and veal tenderloin with trumpet mushrooms, sweetbreads and sauce *diable* (spicy, tangy). Like all Nieporent operations, this one is professional in all aspects. A practiced wait staff adds to the positives.

BENOIT

60 W 55th St (bet Fifth Ave and Ave of the Americas)
Lunch: Mon-Sat; Dinner: Daily; Brunch: Sun
Expensive

646/943-7373
benoitny.com

Master foodie Alain Ducasse has designed a charming bistro with special touches only the French can create. It is like going to heaven by way of France! One immediately notices the warm greeting, very professional service and interesting diners. What to eat? The paté en croute (an 1892 recipe) is fabulous, and a charcuterie and paté selection is varied and filling. "Ladies who lunch" will delight in the quenelles de brochet, and the cassoulet is sensational. At lunch, feast on escargots, ravioli, chocolate soufflé, the flawless onion soup or dishes created with fresh, seasonal ingredients. Portions are huge! Take your time and savor the atmosphere as well as the platters.

BETONY

41 W 57th St (bet Fifth Ave and Ave of the Americas)
Lunch: Mon-Fri; Dinner: Mon-Sat
Expensive

212/465-2400
betony-nyc.com

You'll find it all at Betony — a downstairs bar, a gorgeous upper level dining room, sophisticated yet playful food and ultra-professional service. This midtown space is truly a feast for the senses; executive chef Bryce Shuman's New American menu is outstanding.   Begin with foie gras bonbons with cashews, fried pickles with fennel and yogurt or chickpea panisse with ham. Entrees might include seared duck breast with glazed cabbage and apple, poached lobster with chestnuts and spiced bisque or red oak acorn lasagna with acorn squash and pumpernickel. General manager Eamon Rockey keeps everything clicking; it is definitely worth the tab!

BISTRO LES AMIS

180 Spring St (at Thompson St)   212/226-8645
Lunch, Dinner: Daily; Brunch: Sat, Sun   bistrolesamis.com
Moderate to moderately expensive

Bistro les Amis is a delightful bistro in the middle of Soho shopping and galleries. In the warmer months, the doors open onto the sidewalk, and the passing parade is almost as inviting as the varied menu. French onion soup with gruyere is a must, and salmon marinated with fresh dill and herbs is just as good. Lunch entrees include sandwiches and fresh salads; in the evening, seafood and steak dishes are available. Steak *frites* with herb butter are first-class, and a *prix-fixe* menu is offered to early diners. There's nothing very fancy about this bistro − just comforting food with an extra touch of friendly service.

BLAUE GANS

139 Duane St (bet Church St and West Broadway)

212/571-8880
Lunch, Dinner: Daily; Brunch: Sat, Sun
kg-ny.com
Moderate to moderately expensive

Chef Kurt Gutenbrunner lives up to his heritage with Austro-German bistro Blaue Gans ("Blue Goose"). Delicious platters like red cabbage salad, smoked trout crepes, beef goulash, wiener schnitzel, blood

TO TIP OR NOT TO TIP

Should restaurants simply add a service charge to dining tabs and eliminate tipping, as they do in Europe? Many Manhattan establishments are wrestling with the issue. So far at least two spots have taken the lead: the Midtown Japanese restaurant Sushi Yasuda and Per Se, in the Time Warner Center. Expect this practice to grow.

sausage and *Kavalierspitz* (boiled beef shoulder) served with fabulous creamed spinach are offered. For dessert, go for the Salzburger Nockerl, a warm dessert soufflé with tart huckleberries. The folks here are delightful, which makes the meal even more memorable.

BLT STEAK

106 E 57th St (bet Park and Lexington Ave)   212/752-7470
Lunch: Mon-Fri; Dinner: Daily   bltsteak.com
Moderately expensive to expensive

A professional team has made this modern American steakhouse one of the best in Manhattan. The delicious popovers served at the start absolutely melt in your mouth! Most of the pricey salads are big and healthy, but save room for the main show: hanger steak, Wagyu ribeye steak, filet mignon, New York strip steak and more; the rack of lamb is superb. You have your choice of eight great sauces to accompany the meat entree. Also on the menu: fish, shellfish and potatoes done six different ways. (I could make an entire meal of BLT's potato choices!) Chocolate tart smothered with creamy pistachio ice cream is one of the best desserts in Manhattan (or anywhere).

BLUE HILL

75 Washington Pl (bet Ave of the Americas and MacDougal St)   212/539-1776
Dinner: Daily   bluehillfarm.com
Moderate to moderately expensive

If you're looking for a great Village dinner location, try Blue Hill. This standout restaurant is named for a farm that is owned and operated by Dan and David Barber. The vision here is fresh, local sourcing for creative American food. Their James Beard award-winning chef has created a standout menu that changes daily and might include diver scallops with pickled squash and red cabbage borscht, Halloran Farm venison with radicchio and black trumpet mushrooms or Berkshire pig with stewed carrots and curry. The Farmers Feast, a six-course tasting menu, is a great way to sample Blue Hill's unique offerings.

BLUE RIBBON

97 Sullivan St (bet Spring and Prince St)   212/274-0404
Daily: 4 p.m.-4 a.m.   blueribbonrestaurants.com
Moderate

Blue Ribbon is one of the most popular spots in Soho, with a bustling bar scene and people lining up for its limited number of tables; don't come for a relaxed evening. Regulars savor the exceptional food in this unpretentious restaurant which is strictly an all-American culinary experience. There is a raw bar to attract seafood lovers, along with clams, lobster, crab, boiled crawfish and the house special "Blue Ribbon Royale" appetizer platter. One can choose from two dozen appetizers, including barbecued ribs, smoked trout, caviar and chicken wings. Entrees are just as wide-ranging: sweetbreads, catfish, tofu ravioli, fried chicken and mashed potatoes, burgers and more. How the smallish kitchen can turn out so many dishes is amazing, but they certainly do it well. Those who experience hunger pangs after midnight will appreciate the late hours. Try the excellent sushi at their nearby **Blue Ribbon Sushi** (119 Sullivan St, 212/343-0404). Then there is the **Blue Ribbon Sushi Bar & Grill** (308 W 58th St, 212/397-0404), in the 6 Columbus hotel. The sushi menu is expanded, with a wide variety of popular cold and hot dishes, all expectedly very good. This hotel location also offers traditional or Asian breakfast and Sunday brunch.

BLUE RIBBON BAKERY

35 Downing St (at Bedford St)   212/337-0404
Lunch, Dinner: Daily; Brunch: Sat, Sun   blueribbonrestaurants.com
Moderate

The rustic breads at this cafe and bakery are excellent, but there is so much more. Downstairs, customers dine in a fantastic brick oven atmosphere, complete with a wine cellar and family dining room, and wonderful fresh-bread aroma. The menu features signature brick-oven breads, sandwiches, steaks, seafood, cheeses, seasonal salads, local fish, veggies and yummy desserts (including profiteroles).

BLUE SMOKE

255 Vesey St (bet North End Ave and West St)   212/889-2005
116 E 27th St (bet Lexington Ave and Park Ave S)   212/447-7733
Lunch, Dinner: Daily   bluesmoke.com
Moderate

And then there were two! Danny Meyer has filled a real void in the Manhattan dining scene with Blue Smoke, satisfying legions of Southern food aficionados. Now there are locations in Murray Hill and the Financial District! In addition to baby back ribs, you'll find fried chicken and biscuits, smoked beef brisket, tasty sandwiches, collard greens with *potlikker* (the cooking liquid from collard greens) and a combo of ribs, pulled pork, chicken and sausage. Blue Smoke is not just a Southern restaurant, but a full-fledged scene, with an ultra-busy bar attracting fun-loving trendsetters. A variety of delicious homestyle desserts, from award-winning key lime pie to sticky toffee pudding, rhubarb crisp and chocolate layer cake served with a glass of cold milk. Call ahead for large orders.

BLUE WATER GRILL

31 Union Sq W (at 16th St)   212/675-9500
Lunch: Mon-Sat; Dinner: Daily; Brunch: Sun   bluewatergrillnyc.com
Moderate to moderately expensive

In a building that was once the Metropolitan Bank, this historic space was reinvented into a bustling seafood restaurant.   Blue Water Grill is a "see and be seen" kind of place where superbly-trained personnel serve classic seafood dishes and innovative sushi. Wonderful appetizers may include lobster cocktail, shrimp dumplings and tuna ceviche. Tuna, salmon, swordfish and other fish are prepared "simply grilled." Lobsters and oysters (several dozen varieties) are fresh and tasty as are the extensive sushi offerings. For those who want to stick to shore foods, roasted chicken, blue cheese-crusted filet mignon and pork chops are available. Flourless chocolate layer cake with vanilla bean gelato or warm apple crisp with rum raisin gelato make a sweet finish. Check out the live music in the Jazz Room.

CARNIVORE ALERT

It's pretty hard to foul up short ribs at home—they are so moist and succulent that even overcooking fails to diminish their allure. Some New York City restaurants have elevated them to celestial heights:

Balthazar (80 Spring St, 212/965-1414)

Buddakan (Chelsea Market, 75 Ninth Ave, 212/989-6699)

Craft (43 E 19th St, 212/780-0880)

Daniel (60 E 65th St, 212/288-0033)

Ouest (2315 Broadway, 212/580-8700)

Scarpetta (355 W 14th St, 212/691-0555)

DINING AT THE BAR

Solo diners have a wealth of restaurants where they can relax at a convivial bar and have first-rate food. Among them:

China Grill (60 W 53rd St)

Circo NYC (120 W 55th St)

Gotham Bar and Grill (12 E 12th St)

Gramercy Tavern (42 E 20th St)

Grand Central Oyster Bar (Grand Central Terminal, 42nd St at Vanderbilt Ave, lower level)

Hearth (403 E 12th St)

L'Artusi (228 W 10th St, 212/255-5757)

Plaza Food Hall (The Plaza, 1 W 59th St, lower level)

BOBO

181 W 10th St (at Seventh Ave)   212/488-2626
Dinner: Daily; Brunch: Sat, Sun   bobonyc.com
Moderately expensive

Tucked away in a restored 1839 building just off Seventh Avenue, Bobo is a warm and charming place to dine. Attentive service, sizeable portions and quite good French fare make this a rather romantic dining spot. A fully heated glassed-in garden area offers additional seating. Menu favorites include Long Island crescent duck duo, steak au poivre, bouillabaisse and sea scallop risotto as well as seafood dishes with bass, cod and skate. Eight cheeses are listed at reasonable prices, or finish with the housemade sorbet and ice cream.

BOND 45

154 W 45th St (bet Ave of the Americas and Seventh Ave)   212/869-4545
Breakfast: Mon-Sat; Lunch, Dinner: Daily; Brunch: Sat, Sun   bond45.com
Moderate to moderately expensive

In the middle of the Theater District, busy restaurateur Shelly Fireman has created a huge dining hall. Billed as an Italian steak room, Bond 45 is named for the old Bond men's store that used to occupy this site. If it's Italian, Bond 45 has it! The antipasto bar at the entrance makes a mouth-watering beginning. Beyond that, there are salads, mozzarella, carpaccio dishes, cured meats, pastas, steaks and so on. An abundance of wait personnel ensures prompt service. The dessert selection doesn't live up to the rest of the fare.

BOTTEGA DEL VINO

7 E 59th St (bet Fifth and Madison Ave)   212/223-2724
Breakfast, Lunch, Dinner: Daily   bottegadelvinonyc.com
Moderately expensive

The midtown location of Bottega Del Vino is a replica of the Verona original, pampering guests with Northern Italian cuisine combined with fresh and seasonal ingredients. Service is professional and buoyant. All the dishes are tasty, especially the steaks. If risotto with shrimp and asparagus tips is on the menu, go for it! Grilled Australian lamb chops, veal scaloppine and oven-roasted sea bass are typical entrees. Desserts such as a cheese selection with sweet marmalades, fresh fruit tarts and chocolate *semifreddo* with mixed berry sauce – all are delicious and filling.

BOULEY

163 Duane St (at Hudson St)   212/964-2525
Lunch, Dinner: Mon-Sat
Expensive

BRUSHSTROKE

30 Hudson St (bet Duane and Reade St)   212/791-3771
Lunch: Tues-Sat; Dinner: Mon-Sat   davidbouley.com
Expensive

The culinary genius of David Bouley is unmatched and it can be experienced in multiple venues, including both Bouley and Brushstroke. Flagship Tribeca restaurant, Bouley, features a state-of-the art kitchen in one of Manhattan's finest dining venues, with superb French fare and professional service. Offerings on an ever-changing dinner menu include such delights as a forager's treasure of wild mushrooms with sweet garlic, special spices and grilled toro; all-natural Pennsylvania chicken baked *en cocotte* (in a pot) with alfalfa and clover hay, organic butter beans, chanterelles, Brussels sprouts and Napa cabbage. Finish with Chocolate Frivolous, a warm chocolate tart with Valrhona sorbet and prune Armagnac ice cream or chocolate crème brûlée and sweet pleasure. Besides Bouley's main dining room, private dining spaces for special events include the versatile Red Room which seats up to 50 guests; the space is reminiscent of the South of France where eating and drinking are of primary importance. Nestled between the kitchen and main dining room, Chef's Pass seats from eight to 13 guests; here chef personally familiarizes guests with the beautiful ingredients that compose his dishes, and via Skype, brings in the artisans who had something to do with the ingredients being served, be it the farmer, winemaker or cheese ager. At Brushstroke, a joint effort with the Tsuji Culinary Institute, *kaiseki* cuisine (traditional Japanese menus) is featured on a seasonal tasting menu. Ichimura at Brushstroke is an eight-seat sushi bar serving an *omakase* menu. Additional Bouley enterprises include **Bouley Test Kitchen** (88 West Broadway, 5th floor, 212/964-2505), a venue for visiting chefs, catering special event space, cooking classes and testing ground for recipe development; **Bouley Botanical** (281 Church St, 917-237-3205) is a downtown Eden-like private event space where planters of herbs, flowers and vegetables bring inspiration for chef Bouley's newly imagined dishes. All of David Bouley's operations are first-class!

BOULUD SUD

20 W 64th St (bet Central Park West and Broadway)   212/595-1313
Lunch: Mon-Fri; Dinner: Daily; Brunch: Sat, Sun   bouludsud.com
Moderately expensive

Boulud Sud is one of Daniel Boulud's Manhattan wonders. It is just around the corner from popular Bar Boulud and Épicerie Boulud, an eat-in, takeout market. The menu features flavors that travel the entire Mediterranean region from the shores of Southern France to the coast of North Africa and beyond, plus the full selection of wines offered at Bar Boulud. There is an emphasis on grilled fish and lamb as well as an abundance of fresh vegetables on the menu. An octopus appetizer with marcona almonds is outstanding, so is the robust main course chicken tagine. Desserts, ice cream and sorbets are all homemade, with grapefruit givré (sorbet) the number one pick. Lincoln Center patrons will appreciate a $60 three-course *prix-fixe* menu before the evening performance. Boulud's corner is a comfy-chic addition to the neighborhood.

BRASSERIE

100 E 53rd St (bet Park and Lexington Ave)   212/751-4840
Breakfast, Lunch: Mon-Fri; Dinner: Daily; Brunch: Sat, Sun   patinagroup.com
Moderate

Brasserie is a New York tradition for those who like big, brassy, fun dining spots that serve very good food. What was once a round-the-clock operation now keeps handy late hours (Mon-Thurs till 11 p.m.; Fri, Sat till midnight; Sun till 10 p.m.). The sleek, attractive quarters include a grand staircase fit for a fashion show with sexy lighting and a bar that offers all manner of goodies. Much of the food has a French flair, but there are also well-prepared grill dishes, short ribs, grilled fish, scallops, crab cakes, *pot-au-feu*, steamed mussels with *frites* and daily specials. Favorites include good old-fashioned onion soup gratinée, burgers and chicken chop chop salad. For dessert, try the chocolate beignets.

BRASSERIE 8½

9 W 57th St (bet Fifth Ave and Ave of the Americas)   212/829-0812
Lunch: Mon-Fri; Dinner: Daily; Brunch: Sun   patinagroup.com
Moderately expensive

Dramatic best describes both the interior and the dining at Brasserie 8½. Descending a long spiral staircase, you enter a spectacular room filled with comfy chairs, an attractive bar, a wall of Léger stained glass and a collection of signed Matisse prints; even the tableware is pleasing. With a French menu that features the best of the season, veggies, lamb, veal and fish may be roasted or grilled in appealing combinations, some with a lighter point of view. Daily specials are offered along with a $38 three-course *prix-fixe* menu. Great desserts might include warm molten chocolate cake with espresso ice cream or the day's selection of sorbet. Sunday buffet brunch is definitely worth a visit.

BRASSERIE RUHLMANN

45 Rockefeller Plaza (enter on 50th St, bet Fifth Ave and Ave of the Americas)
Lunch, Dinner: Mon-Sat: Brunch: Sun   212/974-2020
Moderate to moderately expensive   brasserieruhlmann.com

The big attraction is the location – right in the heart of the midtown shopping area. The large room (232 seats) at Brasserie Ruhlmann is bold and classy, the service is highly professional and you are greeted with genuine enthusiasm. Some signature dishes: roasted free-range chicken, hanger steak *frites* and a shrimp and lobster roll served with hand cut fries. Top the meal off with a yummy profiterole drizzled in chocolate sauce. You will also appreciate designer Emile-Jacques Ruhlmann's red art-deco interior.

THE BRESLIN

Ace Hotel
16 W 29th St (at Broadway)   212/679-1939
Breakfast, Lunch: Mon-Fri; Dinner: Daily; Brunch: Sat, Sun   thebreslin.com
Moderately expensive

Things here are pretty hot! This area is hot, the hotel is hot, the bar is hot and the restaurant is especially hot! In an old-time atmosphere, The Breslin is a very comfortable place to dine, with friendly and efficient service. As you might expect in a cool, gastropub atmosphere, the snack choices are unusual: caramel popcorn, scotch eggs and scrumpets with mint vinegar; all fall in the $5 to $9 range. Terrine boards offer rustic pork, rabbit with prunes and more for $34; the chargrilled lamb burger is a bargain at $21. For a group of eight or more, make reservations for the very popular fried chicken feast which includes delicious fried buttermilk chicken with habanero and gorgonzola sauces, four accompanying sides and strawberry balsamic pie. The bars are cozy and crowded, and the whole experience is unique. Diets are out the window here!

BROOKLYN DINER USA

212 W 57th St (bet Broadway and Seventh Ave)   212/977-1957
155 W 43rd St (bet Broadway and Ave of the Americas)   212/265-5400
Breakfast, Lunch, Dinner, Late Supper: Daily   brooklyndiner.com
Moderate

Brooklyn Diner USA (which is really located in Manhattan) is worth a visit. With all-day dining, an expansive menu, pleasant personnel, better-than-average diner food and reasonable prices, these places are winners. A tile floor and comfortable booths add to the authentic diner ambience. You can find just about anything your heart desires: breakfast fare, chicken soup, baked mac and cheese, sandwiches (the pastrami reuben is a must), salads (Chinese chicken salad is a favorite), hearty lunch and dinner plates of comfort food (chicken pot pie), homemade desserts and good drinks. Their muffins are moist, flavorful and outrageously good; pastrami and corned beef are made on-site and carved to order.

BRYANT PARK GRILL

25 W 40th St (bet Fifth Ave and Ave of the Americas)   212/840-6500
Lunch: Mon-Fri; Dinner: Daily; Brunch: Sat, Sun   arkrestaurants.com
Moderate

Enjoy a refreshing view of Bryant Park at one of Manhattan's most charming American grills, Bryant Park Grill. In a Parisian-style garden setting, the space is covered and heated in the winter, open in the summer and festive all year round. This popular destination offers a family-friendly menu that changes with the seasons; count on a good selection of soups, salads and steak and seafood items at lunch and dinner; country salad, lamb kabobs and crusted sea bass are excellent choices. A weekend *prix-fixe* brunch is served alongside the regular lunch menu. Adjacent is the **Bryant Park Cafe** which serves small and large plates of wonderfully delicious fare; personnel at both the cafe and grill are friendly and child-oriented.

MODERN JAPANESE

If you have a yen for modern Japanese cuisine, **Haru Sushi** has plenty to offer. Of course you'll find sushi and sashimi on the menu plus appetizers, lunch boxes, entrees, sushi rolls, hand rolls and special rolls. Attractive locations are conveniently located around town and they also provide pick-up and delivery services. Please note that the Saké Bar serves the same menu and is the only locale with a full bar.

221 W 43rd St, 212/398-9810: Lunch, Dinner: Daily

433 Amsterdam Ave, 212/579-5655: Lunch: Sat, Sun; Dinner: Daily

220 Park Ave S, 646/428-0989: Lunch: Mon-Fri; Dinner: Daily

1 Wall Street Ct, 212/785-6850: Lunch: Mon-Fri; Dinner: Daily

1329 Third Ave, 212/452-2230: Dinner: Daily

Saké Bar: 1329 Third Ave, 212/452-1028: Lunch, Dinner: Daily (full bar)

BUVETTE

42 Grove St (bet Bedford and Bleecker St)   212/255-3590
Breakfast, lunch, dinner: Daily   ilovebuvette.com
Moderate

Here's a find in the West Village: a tiny (50-seat) French gastrothèque which is open until the wee hours. For breakfast, chef Jody Williams whips up wonderful steamed eggs, fresh pastries and espresso with hot chocolate. In addition to traditional croque monsieur and madame sandwiches for lunch, Buvette serves croque forestier, a vegetarian variety containing roasted mushrooms. Cassoulet, coq au vin, octopus salad, charcuterie and other choices are on the dinner menu along with small plates of tartinettes and cheeses. The ambience is delightful and the outdoor garden is charming, especially with a glass of wine; reservations not required. Note that they do not have a land line, so communicate via the email mentioned on their website.

CAFÉ BOULUD

20 E 76th St (at Madison Ave)   212/772-2600
Lunch: Mon-Sat; Dinner: Daily; Brunch: Sun   cafeboulud.com/nyc
Moderately expensive

Café Boulud is a famous name in Manhattan food circles. The food is quite good, though the room is rather drab and I sometimes find the attitude haughty; once seated, however, you'll enjoy the innovative menu. There are always vegetarian selections, world cuisines (every season highlights a different area), traditional French classics and country cooking, and menu items inspired by the "rhythm of the seasons." A three-course *prix-fixe* menu is available at lunch and brunch. Evening prices are higher, but remember this place belongs to *the* Daniel Boulud, one of the nation's best chefs. Unfortunately he isn't in the kitchen at Café Boulud, because he is busy doing great things at his flagship restaurant, Daniel, but you can hopefully count on the talents of chef Aaron Bludorn.

CAFÉ CENTRO

MetLife Building
200 Park Ave (45th St at Vanderbilt Ave)   212/818-1222
Breakfast, Lunch: Mon-Fri; Dinner: Mon-Sat   patinagroup.com
Moderate to moderately expensive

A grand cafe reminiscent of 1930s Paris, New York's Café Centro offers a classic Parisian brasserie menu. Guests are greeted with a gas-fired rotisserie and a beautiful open kitchen that's spotlessly clean and efficient. Service that is prompt helps keep this a busy lunch scene. For starters, crusty French bread is laid out in front of you. Specialties include a hefty seafood platter, excellent steaks and French fries, sea bass and moist, flavorful rotisserie chicken. The pastry chef turns out a variety of changing desserts: pecan tartlet with Riesling poached pear, apple crisp with maple ice cream, molten chocolate cake and a sampler plate of cookies and petit fours. Adjoining the dining room is a busy beer bar that serves sandwiches and appetizers. You'll feel like you are really in Paris dining al fresco in warm weather.

CAFE CLUNY

284 W 12th St (at 4th St)   212/255-6900
Breakfast, Lunch: Mon-Fri; Dinner: Daily; Brunch: Sat, Sun   cafecluny.com
Moderate to moderately expensive

Located on hard-to-find West 12th Street in the West Village, Cafe Cluny is worth tracking down. You can drop by anytime (the neighboring regulars do) and be assured of very good French-American food at sensible prices. Interesting sandwiches and salads are the order of the day at noon. A pricier dinner menu features rabbit, beef and fish entrees accompanied with savory sides like red Russian kale gratin with aged Gouda and horseradish. Brunch is very popular and can be especially busy, so plan to arrive early.

CAFE D'ALSACE

1695 Second Ave (at 88th St)   212/722-5133
Lunch: Mon-Fri; Dinner: Daily; Brunch: Sat, Sun   cafedalsace.com
Moderate

If bistro ambience appeals to you, then check out this casual, sometimes noisy charmer on the Upper East Side. The menu is large and varied with many dishes prepared Alsatian-style: quiches (excellent!), sandwiches, homemade sausages served with sauerkraut, substantial salads, sirloin or lamb burgers, trout, steaks, choucroute (pork, duck or seafood) and an extensive brunch selection. Young helpers provide informed service. Desserts may list sugar cookies, chocolate and fruit tarts, fruit soufflé and an assortment of French cheeses. Cafe d'Alsace stocks over 100 varieties of beer, and a beer sommelier is on hand to help with selections.

CAFE LALO

201 W 83rd St (bet Amsterdam Ave and Broadway)   212/496-6031
Mon-Thurs: 8 a.m.-2 a.m.; Fri: 8 a.m.-4 a.m.; Sat: 9 a.m.-4 a.m.; Sun: 9 a.m-2 a.m.
Moderate   cafelalo.com

This place can be busy, but in my opinion, this is the best dessert shop

FAMOUS EGG CREAM

A New York invention, the egg cream, is generally credited to Louis Auster, a Jewish immigrant who owned a candy store at Stanton and Cannon streets in the early 20th century. Mostly to amuse himself, he started mixing carbonated water, sugar and cocoa until he concocted a drink he liked. It was such a hit that Schraft's reportedly offered him $20,000 for the recipe. Auster wouldn't sell and secretly continued making his own syrup in the back room of his store. When he died, his recipe went with him. Some years later, Herman Fox created another chocolate syrup, which he called Fox's U-Bet. To this day Fox's brand is regarded as the definitive egg cream syrup.

in town. You will be reminded of a fine European pastry shop as you enjoy delicious desserts with cappuccino, espresso, cordials or other libations from the well-stocked bar. Cafe Lalo offers more than a hundred decadent choices, including cakes, cheesecakes, tarts, pies and connoisseur cheese platters. Yogurt and ice cream are also available and breakfasts and brunches are also a treat. Soothing music makes every calorie go down sweetly! Delivery is offered throughout Manhattan.

CAFE SABARSKY

Neue Galerie New York
1048 Fifth Ave (at 86th St)
Breakfast, Lunch: Wed-Mon; Dinner: Thurs-Sun
Moderate

212/288-0665
cafesabarsky.com

The U.E.S. setting is quaint, the personnel are gracious, the prices are right and the German-Austrian food is delicious. For breakfast, try Sabarsky Frühstück (Viennese mélange, orange juice, soft-boiled eggs and Bavarian ham). Lunch and dinner selections include pea soup with mint, paprika sausage salad, crepes with smoked trout, Bavarian sausage, späetzle with mushrooms and peas and Hungarian beef goulash. Cafe Sabarsky also serves sandwiches, sensational sweets (like Viennese dark chocolate cake and traditional apple strudel), Viennese coffees and much more. Cafe Sabarsky is often crowded, so come early and expect to wait. Music is offered for special events, such as the spring and fall cabaret series. The same lunch and dinner menu is served in the lower level of the Neue Galerie, at **Cafe Fledermaus** (Thursday through Sunday).

CAMAJE

85 MacDougal St (bet Bleecker and Houston St)
Daily: Daily; Brunch: Sat, Sun
Inexpensive to moderate

212/673-8184
camaje.com

In tiny Village quarters with a capacity of about two dozen, this cozy French bistro may evoke memories of some wonderful little place you discovered in Paris. Camaje is one of those New York restaurants relatively few know about, yet those who do, return often. Abigail Hitchcock knows how to cook a great meal. From the moment delicious, crusty bread arrives through the serving of excellent homemade desserts, everything is wholesome and tasty. There's onion soup gratinee, crostini, small plates, burgers, meat and fish entrees and vegetable side dishes. You can create your own three-ingredient crepe with a light cream sauce. Try one of their crepe sucrées for dessert; my favorite is a chocolate ice-cream crepe with caramel sauce. Other pluses are the large selection of quality teas and cooking classes which are offered several times a week. Reservations are recommended.

CAPITAL GRILLE

Time-Life Building	
120 W 51st St (at Seventh Ave)	212/246-0154
Chrysler Center, Trylon Towers	
155 E 42nd St (bet Lexington and Third Ave)	212/953-2000
Lunch: Mon-Fri; Dinner: Daily	
120 Broadway (at Nassau St)	212/374-1811
Lunch: Mon-Fri; Dinner: Mon-Sat	thecapitalgrille.com
Moderately expensive	

With all the top-drawer steakhouses in Manhattan, it's amazing they are all so busy. The Chrysler Center location is stunning, having been designed by Philip Johnson with glass and steel pyramids. The room exudes comfort and congeniality underscored by a welcoming, efficient and informed wait staff. The midtown location is handy and popular; the Broadway house in the financial district is equally appealing. The menu is full of the usual appetizers, soups (a wonderful lobster bisque) and salads, and dry-aged steaks, chops and fresh, creative seafood dishes are fabulous; desserts are good – I liked the flourless chocolate espresso cake. The bar is popular, which might have something to do with the award-winning wine list at this topnotch steakhouse.

JACKET REQUIRED

The more exclusive restaurants still impose a "business casual" dress code that requires men to wear jackets. If you show up without one, don't be surprised if they discreetly loan one to you.

21 Club: jacket required; no jeans or sneakers

Bouley: jacket requested, no sneakers

Daniel: jacket required, no sneakers

Four Seasons: jacket preferred

Jean Georges: jacket required, tie optional; no jeans, sneakers and T-shirts

La Grenouille: jacket required

Le Bernardin: jacket required, no sneakers

Le Cirque: jacket required; no shorts and open-toe shoes

Le Périgord: jacket preferred

Picholine: jacket preferred; no jeans or sneakers

River Café: jacket required

DINING WITH A WATER VIEW

If a romantic dinner with a water view is on your agenda, make reservations at one of these restaurants.

Battery Gardens (Battery Park at State St, 212/809-5508): New York Harbor view

The Boathouse (Central Park Lake, 212/517-2233): picturesque lake view

Gigino (Wagner Park, 20 Battery Pl, 212/528-2228): Statue of Liberty scene

River Café (1 Water St, Brooklyn, 718/522-5200): great views of the Lower Manhattan skyline and East River

Riverpark (450 E 29th St, 212/729-9790): East River views; alfresco dining

Water Club (500 E 30th St, 212/683-3333): Long Island City landscape

CARMINE'S

2450 Broadway (bet 90th and 91st St)	212/362-2200
200 W 44th St (bet Seventh and Eighth Ave)	212/221-3800
Lunch, Dinner: Daily	carminesnyc.com
Moderate	

Want to treat the gang or the whole family to a meal out? Go online or call Carmine's for reservations and be sure to show up famished. Wall signs explain the offerings: Southern Italian-style family dining with huge portions and zesty seasonings; the platters (for four to six people) are delicious and filling. Menu choices run the gamut of pastas, chicken, veal, seafood and Italian appetizers (such as calamari); all tasty. Arrive early if your party numbers less than six, as they will not reserve tables for smaller parties between 7 p.m. and 9:30 p.m. This fun, face-paced, family-style restaurant is a great value.

CARNEGIE DELI

854 Seventh Ave (at 55th St)	212/757-2245, 800/334-5606
Breakfast, Lunch, Dinner: Daily	carnegiedeli.com
Moderate	

There's no city on earth with delis that compare to New York's, and Carnegie Deli is one of the best. Located in the middle of a busy hotel district, it is perfect for midnight snacks. Everything is made on-premises, with free delivery between 6:30 a.m. and 2 a.m. within a five-block radius. Making your food choice is difficult, but I dare say your favorite Jewish mother didn't make chicken soup better than Carnegie's homemade variety. Order it with matzo balls, golden noodles, rice, kreplach or kasha. Beyond soup, there are great blintzes, potato knishes and gargantuan sandwiches galore, including Reuben, pastrami and corned beef, a very juicy burger with all the trimmings as well as salmon and gefilte fish entrees. There is an unequaled choice of egg dishes, salads and numerous side orders of everything from hot baked potatoes to potato pancakes. Desserts cover everything from A to Z; an outrageous New

York cheesecake is served plain or topped with strawberries, blueberries or cherries.

CASA LEVER

390 Park Ave (at 53rd St)   212/888-2700
Breakfast, Lunch: Mon-Fri; Dinner: Mon-Sat   casalever.com
Expensive

Milanese-influenced cuisine, Warhol-adorned walls and a modernist dining room set the stage for a good dining experience, but this Lever Building restaurant comes with a high price. A-list types dine here on classic dishes like veal Milanese, carpaccio, veal shank gremolata, homemade pastas and a limited raw bar, all prepared with premium ingredients. Another option is the $39 three-course dinner menu offered on Friday and Saturday nights. The dessert menu features Italian cheeses, Gianduia (Italian hazelnut spread) and other regional sweets. Enjoy the outdoor lounge during the warmer months.

CASA NONNA

310 W 38th St (bet Eighth and Ninth Ave)   212/736-3000
Lunch: Mon-Fri; Dinner: Daily   casanonna.com
Moderate

As you would expect from a restaurant with this name, great Italian food comes from the kitchen; Casa Nonna literally means "Grandmother's House" in Italian. Executive chef Julio Genao has crafted a menu which includes a long list of antipasto, pizzas baked in a wood-fired oven, paninis served with mixed greens or caponata, salads such as tuna Tuscan bread, homemade pasta dishes and authentic meat and fish entrees. This roomy, attractive Hell's Kitchen restaurant is near Penn Station and is good for a romantic dinner for two, pizza and beer after work or a family dinner with the kids; takeout and delivery are also available.

'CESCA

164 W 75th St (at Amsterdam Ave)   212/787-6300
Dinner: Daily; Brunch: Sun   cescanyc.com
Moderate to moderately expensive

You'll love 'Cesca's atmosphere, situated in a former hotel lobby that is both intimate and elegant. The wait staff is efficient and accommodating, and the food is deliciously Italian from start to finish. Perennial favorites like dry aged ribeye, slow-roasted duck and lamb and veal ragu are uniformly well done and skillfully delivered from an open kitchen. You'll also find delicious pasta and seafood offerings; superb Italian bread adds to the meal. If you are heading to the Beacon Theater this would be an excellent pre-show choice.

CHERCHE MIDI

282 Bowery (bet Houston and Prince St)   212/226-3055
Lunch, Dinner, Brunch: Daily   cherchemidi.com
Moderate to moderately expensive

This charming Paris room is complete with globe lighting, mirrors, pressed tin ceiling and red banquettes. A patient, pleasant staff greets you as you enter and chefs Daniel Parilla and Shane McBride painstakingly prepare tasty French comfort fare. Start with parmesan custard or pan-roasted foie gras with green apple and brioche, then on to homemade lobster ravioli, bouchot mussels with caramelized fennel and dry-aged prime rib with cider-braised onions and pommes soufflé. Chocolate espresso *pot de crème* or raspberry soufflé are excellent finales to your visit to this complete French package from legendary Keith McNally.

CHEZ JACQUELINE

72 MacDougal St (bet Bleecker and Houston St)   212/505-0727
Dinner: Daily; Brunch: Sat, Sun   chezjacquelinerestaurant.com
Moderate

It's no wonder that Chez Jacqueline is a very popular neighborhood French bistro; the atmosphere and service are appealingly relaxed and unassuming. Whether you are hand-holding lovers or seasoned seniors, everyone has a good time on a special evening here. Popular appetizers are fish soup, escargots and chicory goat-cheese salad. Roasted loin of lamb and braised pork shoulder are frequent entrees; my favorite is hearty beef stew. If you like mussels or steak, take note: Tuesday features about a half dozen mussel preparations and various steaks are the Wednesday special. Any day of the week try the caramelized apple tart anglaise for dessert. This place is charming.

CIRCO NYC

120 W 55th St (bet Ave of the Americas and Seventh Ave)   212/265-3636
Lunch: Mon-Fri; Dinner: Daily   circonyc.com
Moderately expensive

Mauro Maccioni (son of the legendary restaurateur Sirio Maccioni of Le Cirque fame) operates a classy establishment with a friendly, circus-themed ambience, deliciously authentic Tuscan menu and a touch of Le Cirque's magic. The tastiest items include housemade pizzas and pastas, including Mamma Egi's famous ravioli with ricotta, spinach, butter and sage. Satisfying soups, excellent seafood and veal dishes and outstanding desserts round out the menu. You'll enjoy an Italian favorite called bomboloncini: small vanilla-, chocolate- and marmalade-filled doughnuts. A three-course *prix-fixe* menu ($28 lunch, $48 dinner) as well as pre- and post-theater dinners ($42) make this a real Italian gem in midtown.

CITY BAKERY

3 W 18th St (at Fifth Ave)   212/366-1414
Breakfast, Lunch: Daily; Brunch: Sat, Sun   thecitybakery.com
Moderate

Your taste buds will begin to tingle the moment you walk into bustling City Bakery. It is really not a bakery but a buffet operation. Your eyes and stomach will savor the fresh-looking salad bar, tempting hot entrees, hearty sandwiches, yummy pastries and much more. Treat yourself to their "so good" hot chocolate, made from melted candy bars and a sweet and salty pretzel croissant; or go for something healthier from the juice bar. I am impressed with the well-trained personnel, who keep displays well stocked, tables clean and checkout counters running efficiently. For a casual, moderately priced meal in plain surroundings, this is a good deal.

CLINTON ST. BAKING COMPANY & RESTAURANT

4 Clinton St (at Houston St)   646/602-6263
Breakfast, Lunch, Dinner: Daily; Brunch: Sat, Sun   clintonstreetbaking.com
Moderate

Come here for New York's best pancakes and waffles! Their hot buttered cider is famous, too. Clinton Street may be a bit out of the way – it's on the Lower East Side – but the trip is worth it if you want wholesome food at very reasonable prices in a humble setting. Homemade breakfast selections include granola, French toast, great pancakes, biscuit sandwiches, omelets and more with soups, salads, eggs and sandwiches featured for lunch. The evening menu includes eclectic twists to the American menu as well as award-winning fried chicken and waffles. Homemade cakes and pastries are available all day and extra thick shakes, sundaes and sodas are a feature of their fountain. A large takeout menu is also available.

COLICCHIO & SONS

85 Tenth Ave (at 15th St)   212/400-6699
Lunch: Wed-Fri; Dinner: daily; Brunch: Sat, Sun (Tap Room);
Dinner: Daily (Dining Room)   craftrestaurantsinc.com
Tap Room: Moderately expensive; Dining Room: Very expensive

Colicchio & Sons is a "wow" dining destination guaranteed to create memories. Award-winning chef Tom Colicchio prepares spectacular American fare that is served up in two rooms; the Tap Room is more affordable, relatively speaking. From the Tap Room listings try prosciutto, black garlic and arugla pizza; the namesake TC burger with drunk onions or spice-rubbed brisket sandwich with horseradish. Complete your meal with an unusual daily ice cream or sorbet selection like candied ginger or persimmon. Dinner in the more refined dining room offers meats, seafood and fish from around the country. Choose from selections like black truffle Amish chicken with Brussels sprouts and wheat berries or apple-fed lamb loin with butternut squash and chestnuts, all given the Colicchio touch.

COOKSHOP

156 Tenth Ave (at 20th St)   212/924-4440
Breakfast, Lunch: Mon-Fri; Dinner: Daily; Brunch: Sat, Sun   cookshopny.com
Moderate to moderately expensive

This place is always packed, and that's no surprise! The Cookshop is one of the most pleasant dining venues on the far West Side, with really great food (featuring mainly organic seasonal items from local farms), efficient service and a fun atmosphere. Meats, fish, poultry and seasonal game entrees are prepared on the grill, in the wood-burning oven or on the rotisserie; oysters by the piece are also available. Unique side flavors include buttery sunchoke mash and roasted potatoes with fried herbs. There is a nice selection of cheeses and an interesting changing dessert menu with sweets like pumpkin monkey bread with pumpkin ice cream. When the place gets loud and crowded, you might want to opt for outside seating.

BREAD IS HOT

Whereas in the past bread baskets were an afterthought, loaded with commercial, bland selections, today's bread is an art form. Among the best:

Balthazar (80 Spring St, 212/965-1414)

Blue Ribbon Bakery (35 Downing St, 212/337-0404)

Calle Ocho (Excelsior Hotel, 45 W 81st St, 212/873-5025)

Commerce (50 Commerce St, 212/524-2301)

Daniel (60 E 65th St, 212/288-0033)

Del Posto (85 Tenth Ave, 212/497-8090)

Scarpetta (355 W 14th St, 212/691-0555)

Butter is much better today as well.

CRAFT

43 E 19th St (bet Broadway and Park Ave S)   212/780-0880
Dinner: Daily   craftrestaurant.com
Expensive

There are a number of reasons why Craft is utterly unique and worth visiting for a splurge. The atmosphere is conducive to good eating and the help is particularly friendly and accommodating. Even the way you order is unique; everything is a la carte. The menu is divided into sections: fish and shellfish, meats, pasta, vegetables, mushrooms, potatoes and grains. You can put together any combination you find appealing, and the classic farm-to-table plates prepared by chef/owner Tom Colicchio won't overwhelm your appetite. The dessert selection includes wonderful cheeses, pastries, chocolate soufflé, ice creams and sorbets. **Craftbar** (900 Broadway, 212/461-4300), a sister operation, is more casual with a contemporary New American menu and composed dinner plates.

CUCINA & CO.

MetLife Building
200 Park Ave (45th St at Vanderbilt Ave), lobby   212/682-2700
Breakfast, Lunch, Dinner: Mon-Fri   patinagroup.com
Takeout: Mon-Fri (7 a.m.-9 p.m.)
Moderate

This treasure is hidden away inside of the huge MetLife Building. The Cucina & Co. takeout counter is one of the best in mid-Manhattan, displaying all sorts of prepared foods, sandwiches, salads, great cookies, cakes, breads and whatever else you might want to take home or to the office. Adjoining is a bustling, crowded cafe that serves first-class food at reasonable prices for such a prime location. You will find delicious burgers (served on sesame brioche rolls), baked pastas, quiches, seafood, health-food dishes and a good selection of dessert items. The service is fast and the personnel highly professional; they have to be in order to serve so many people during rush hours! I heartily recommend this place, especially for lunch. Two other Cucina & Co. locations (30 Rockefeller Center, 212/332-7630 and Macy's Cellar, 151 W 34th St, 212/868-2388) occupy similarly prime Manhattan locales and offer the same quality of food and service. Unlike the MetLife location, the other two are also open on weekends.

DA UMBERTO

107 W 17th St (bet Ave of the Americas and Seventh Ave)   212/989-0303
Lunch: Mon-Fri; Dinner: Mon-Sat   daumbertonyc.com
Moderate to moderately expensive

This Tuscan trattoria appeals to the senses of serious Italian diners. At Da Umberto a groaning table of inviting antipasto dishes greets guests; one could easily make an entire meal just from this selection. All of the platters look so fresh and healthy! Owner Vittorio Assante is around much of the time, ensuring that the service is as good as the food. Look into the glass-framed kitchen at the rear to see how the professionals prepare pastas, fish, veal, game (in season) and chicken; your waiter will have many specials to detail. If you have room, chocolate truffle cake and tiramisu are the best of the dessert selections.

DANIEL

60 E 65th St (bet Madison and Park Ave)   212/288-0033
Dinner: Mon-Sat   danielnyc.com
Expensive

Every detail at Daniel is a work of art, especially the dishes placed in front of you. If you are ready to have an absolutely superb dining experience and money is no object, then join the normally long waiting list for a table. The appealing U.E.S. space is a treat for the eyes as well as the stomach. Daniel Boulud deserves to feel immensely proud of his strikingly contemporary four-star restaurant with a wait staff that is highly professional and knowledgeable.

DINER LINGO

Small restaurants, diners and delis are usually colorful places to take a meal. Since the quarters are generally quite close, it's inevitable to eavesdrop on the staff's dialogue. They seem to have a language all their own. Here are some examples, along with their meanings:

Axle grease: butter
Bossy in a bowl: beef stew
Bullets: baked beans
In the alley: served as a side dish
Italian perfume: garlic
On the hoof: meat cooked rare
Vermont: maple syrup
Wreck 'em: scramble the eggs

Signature dishes change seasonally on the contemporary French *prix-fixe* menu. It might be a duo of roasted beef tenderloin and braised short ribs (the best I have ever tasted), suckling pig with crispy polenta or roasted turbot – each dish infused with a dose of comfort. Desserts are delicious and beautiful, especially the chocolate creations. Don't miss the cheese selection! Every time I visit this restaurant I don't want the meal to end, and I can't think of a higher compliment. Note: an a la carte menu is available in the bar and lounge. Jackets required.

DAVID BURKE KITCHEN

The James Hotel
23 Grand St (bet Ave of the Americas and Thompson St)   212/201-9119
Breakfast, Lunch: Mon-Fri; Dinner: Daily; Brunch: Sat, Sun
Moderately expensive to expensive   davidburkekitchen.com

This David Burke winner serves delicious, inventive American fare in the Soho neighborhood. You can sip and snack at the upstairs Treehouse Bar or eat in the attractive, airy dining room, complete with a carving station right in the center; meats, fish, lobster and casseroles are plated here. Order the duck toast or lobster dumpling soup for a starter, then braised short ribs with Swiss chard and egg ravioli in a horseradish parsnip emulsion. Definitely do not skip the desserts; fudge brownie casserole, toffee monkey bread and cheesecake lollipop tree are designed for sharing. At brunch, the buttermilk fried chicken is satisfying.

DB BISTRO MODERNE

City Club Hotel
55 W 44th St (bet Fifth Ave and Ave of the Americas)   212/391-2400
Breakfast: Daily; Lunch: Mon-Fri; Dinner: Daily; Brunch: Sat, Sun
Moderate to moderately expensive   dbbistro.com/nyc

Renowned restaurant impresario Daniel Boulud's db Bistro Moderne is, for him, a more casual dining experience. Even burgers are served, and they are very good; at $35, they should be! Of course, this is no ordinary hamburger. It is ground sirloin filled with red wine-braised short ribs, foie gras and black truffles, served on a parmesan bun and accompanied by delicious, light pommes *frites* in a silver cup. Diners have their choice of two rooms with a communal table that is comfortable for singles. The menu offers several items in each category of fish, charcuterie and meats. For dessert, the cheese selection is a real winner, as are any of Daniel's specialties that use berries and other fresh fruit. The location makes db Bistro Moderne ideal for Broadway theatergoers.

DBGB KITCHEN AND BAR

299 Bowery (bet 1st and Houston St)   212/933-5300
Lunch: Fri; Dinner: Daily; Brunch: Sat, Sun   dbgb.com/nyc
Moderate

Daniel Boulud has created a lively winner with DBGB Kitchen and Bar. This is a fun place and noisy, too. Designed with the influence of the Bowery neighborhood's restaurant-supply businesses in mind, bottles, gleaming copper pots and dishes are stored on open shelving in the dining area. The kitchen is also open and part of the ambience. The Kitchen Table, the private dining section, overlooks the kitchen. The French brasserie menu is varied: sausages, meats, salads and burgers (order the ménage a trios, a platter of three burgers and trimmings – Yankee, Piggie and Frenchie) or go whole hog and order the roasted pig feast for up to eight guests (72 hours notice is required). Whatever you order, set your sights on a dessert of Baked Alaska for two and plan your meal accordingly.

DEL FRISCO'S DOUBLE EAGLE STEAK HOUSE

McGraw-Hill Building
1221 Ave of the Americas (at 49th St)   212/575-5129
Lunch: Mon-Fri; Dinner: Daily   delfriscos.com
Expensive

DEL FRISCO'S GRILLE

50 Rockefeller Plaza (51st St, bet Fifth Ave and Ave of the Americas)
                                                         212/767-0371
Lunch, Dinner: Daily   delfriscosgrille.com
Moderately expensive

Del Frisco's offers a good meal with accommodating service in two different settings. At the McGraw-Hill location, where corporate types fill the room, both the ceiling and prices are high. Fresh, warm bread is brought to the table as you enjoy a seafood appetizer or beefsteak tomato and sliced onion salad. Savory steaks, veal dishes and tuna with large accompanying side dishes are all first-rate. A $36 three-course *prix-fixe* lunch is a good value here. The location at Rock Plaza has an upscale bar and grill with wood-burning oven and large patio. Here you'll find some of the same steaks and seafood, but the menu is less "fussy" and equally delicious. Beef stroganoff, truffled macaroni and cheese, veal meatloaf, burgers and sandwiches are all available.   In-house desserts include warm chocolate cake and a six-layer lemon buttercream cake; all are winners.

DEL POSTO

85 Tenth Ave (bet 15th and 16th St)   212/497-8090
Lunch: Mon-Fri; Dinner: Daily   delposto.com
Expensive

Del Posto is big and bold and yet refined! No question about it, this is an "occasion" restaurant. Mario Batali has shown what can be done with good taste. Afterward, diners may notice that their wallets have become a bit thinner, but they will long remember the experience of dining here. The room is warm and opulent, with adequate space between tables, a huge staff, informed service and beautiful china. Some dishes are prepared tableside. Soothing piano music will calm those who arrive after a harried day. All of these touches speak to this class operation. The menu is constantly changing and all offerings are *prix-fixe*; $49 lunch; $126 five-course dinner and should you feel a bit self-indulgent, order the $179 eight-course Captain's Menu. Offerings? Veal agnolotti with cauliflower, sliced lamb with warm figs and pistachio gremolata, slow-cooked chicken with cranberries and root vegetables or interesting vegan dishes; the accompanying bread basket is superb. Leave room for the fine selection of complimentary after-dinner cookies.

DELMONICO'S

56 Beaver St (at William St)   212/509-1144
Lunch: Mon-Fri; Dinner: Mon-Sat   delmonicosny.com
Moderately expensive

You've heard and read about Manhattan's Financial District, but if you really want a feel for the area and the people who make it tick, have a meal at Delmonico's. It is truly a New York institution dating from 1837; the atmosphere is old-time New York, but with a very appropriate renovated flair. As you might imagine, service is highly professional and the wine cellar is filled with a huge selection of the world's best vintages. The Delmonico steak (a boneless ribeye that originated here) and other prime meat cuts are house specialties, with accompaniments like famous Delmonico potatoes (the recipe was created here many years ago). Delmonico steaks may be served elsewhere, but the authentic item is found only at the namesake restaurant. Don't be afraid to try chicken, duck, eggs Benedict, lobster Newberg, rack of lamb or tuna; all are made from tried and true recipes. The adjoining Grill Room offers more casual dining, including a less costly bar menu. And private dining is also offered. By all means try Baked Alaska, the signature dessert or superb cheese selection. After over a century of presenting gourmet plates, Delmonico's is still on top! **Delmonico's Kitchen** (207 W 36th St, 212/695-5220) offers an updated twist on Delmonico's original menu.

> # FOR SAKÉ LOVERS!
>
> **Sakagura** (211 E 43rd, 212/953-7253) is a very popular destination for saké (over 200 choices) and Japanese small plates. This basement hangout, with the ambience of Tokyo, is known as one of the top saké bars in the U.S. Most small plates are priced well under $10. Sakagura is open weekdays for lunch and daily for dinner.

DÉVI

8 E 18th St (bet Broadway and Fifth Ave)   212/691-2100
Lunch, Dinner: Daily   devinyc.com
Moderate to moderately expensive

You can't do better than Dévi for Indian food. The setting is attractive – colorful, yet understated, and small enough to be inviting. A full vegetarian selection is offered and seafood, poultry and meat dishes are also featured; signature tandoor grilled lamb chops are a flavorful entree. For those who really know Indian food, the side dishes (crispy okra salad, spiced spinach sauce with mushrooms and wonderful Indian bread) are very special. A full menu of unusual desserts is presented: Indian ice cream, crispy saffron bread pudding and much more. The staff is attentive, polite and helpful and the excellent food lives up to the setting.

DINOSAUR BAR-B-QUE

700 W 125th St (at 12th St)   212/694-1777
Lunch, Dinner: Daily   dinosaurbarbque.com
Moderate

Dinosaur ribs are not on the menu! Instead, it's dry-rubbed and slow pit-smoked pork, beef and chicken entrees – plus the obligatory fried catfish – that satisfy hungry carnivores. Choose from freshly made beans, rice, greens, salads, mac and cheese, deviled eggs and more as side dishes. Combination platters are a convenient solution to the ordering dilemma. Sandwiches include the aforementioned meats, or you can choose a ground beef, turkey or portobello mushroom burger. Long lines are the norm at this bustling, bare bones ribs-and-more joint. Order the party package to go if you're hosting that big game party.

DIRTY FRENCH

The Ludlow Hotel
180 Ludlow St (bet Houston and Stanton St)   212/254-3000
Lunch, Dinner: Daily   dirtyfrench.com
Moderately expensive to expensive

Expect the unexpected when you enter Dirty French where the decor of mismatched bric-a-brac, contemporary art and pink neon accents, as well as a modernized French menu with bold flavors will surprise you. Chefs Rich Torrisi and Mario Carbone create French fare with Moroccan and Cajun accents. To start, instead of the traditional basket of French baguettes, an attentive server brings buttery flatbread with herbed fromage blanc for schmearing. Delicious! Equally tasty are lamb carpaccio with a Moroccan kick and a $72 chicken feast that is served in two stagings, each with unique flavorings and presentation. Pastry chef, Heather Bertinetti, offers unusual, yet delicious treats like coconut-passionfruit Napoleon and pineapple tart served with rum raisin ice cream.

DOCKS OYSTER BAR AND SEAFOOD GRILL

633 Third Ave (at 40th St)   212/986-8080
Lunch: Mon-Fri; Dinner: Daily; Brunch: Sat, Sun   docksoysterbar.com
Moderate to moderately expensive

Fresh seafood is just waiting for you at Docks Oyster Bar, but it is also a raw bar, sushi restaurant and cocktail bar. You'll find maki rolls, sushi and sashimi, swordfish, lobster, tuna, Norwegian salmon, red snapper and stone crab claws depending on the season; the raw bar offers oyster and clam selections at dinner. For a lighter meal, try steamers in beer broth or mussels in tomato and garlic. Delicious smoked sturgeon and whitefish are available, as are great beef

TABLE TIME

What is the appropriate amount of time to spend at a restaurant during the dinner hour? If it is just two of you, an hour and a half is about right. If your party numbers four, two hours would be fair to the establishment. Remember, however, that when foreigners are involved, the meal is far more leisurely.

entrees. Docks has a special New England clambake on Sunday and Monday nights. The atmosphere and waiters are always congenial.

THE DUTCH

131 Sullivan St (at Prince St)   212/677-6200
Lunch: Mon-Fri; Dinner: Daily; Brunch: Sat, Sun   thedutchnyc.com
Moderate to moderately expensive

At the corner of Prince and Sullivan is The Dutch, chef Andrew Carmellini's welcoming and tastefully appointed house. The menu is regional American; for lunch or dinner starters, the Oyster Room offers Louisiana crawfish, American caviar and tantalizing seafood platters; salads or assorted vegetable appetizers are good alternatives. The lunch menu features sandwiches, fried chicken and snacks. About a dozen dinner selections include dry-aged meats, fresh fish and seasonal game dishes; the 40-ounce beef ribeye dinner for two is excellent. For dessert, I recommend the freshly made pies (cherry-buttermilk or caramel apple – a la mode, of course) or the dark chocolate sponge cake with sesame mousse and chocolate sorbet. Linger over brunch with the Dutch's version of iced tea (a boozy concoction of gin, Pimm's, curacao and iced tea) and select from savory egg dishes made with local organic eggs, housemade bologna sandwiches, muffins and scones, steak tartare and aforementioned seafood.

ED'S CHOWDER HOUSE

Empire Hotel
44 W 63rd St (bet Broadway and Columbus Ave)   212/956-1288
Breakfast, Lunch, Dinner: Daily   Facebook
Moderate to moderately expensive

To show your out-of-town guests what Manhattan life is really like, then a stop at the Empire Hotel (near Lincoln Center) should be on the schedule. First, move to the rooftop bar for a pre-dinner drink. The place is literally jumping, noisy, crowded, and full of folks making all kinds of deals. Besides a complete array of drinks (including really unique cocktails), a bar menu of tasty items like crudités, crispy calamari and sliders is available. When your ears begin to ache, it's time to go downstairs to Ed's Chowder House for a step into the New England atmosphere and a vast array of delicacies from the deep. Chowders? Four of them, from clam to crab. Raw bar? Atlantic oysters, littleneck clams and lobster. The main bill of fare presents a wide variety of seafood to choose from: tuna, branzino, salmon, lobster, scallops and such; non-seafood diners will find limited offerings like filet mignon. For dessert, try apple cobbler a la mode or chocolate ganache tart with coffee ice cream.

EL PARADOR CAFE

325 E 34th St (bet First and Second Ave)   212/679-6812
Lunch, Dinner: Daily   elparadorcafe.com
Moderate

Having been in business since 1959, El Parador is considered the granddaddy of New York's Mexican restaurants. Delicious Mexican food is served in a fun atmosphere at down-to-earth prices, moreover, these are some of the nicest folks in the city. Warm tortilla chips arrive at your table while you study the list of specialties. There are quesadillas, ceviche and black bean soup to start;

delicious shrimp, pork, beef and chicken dishes follow. Create your own tacos and fajitas or try wonderful seafood-loaded paella with rice. El Parador has an impressive number of premium tequilas, and they concoct what many consider the best margaritas in New York.

ELEVEN MADISON PARK

11 Madison Ave (at 24th St)	212/889-0905
Lunch: Thurs-Sat; Dinner: Daily	elevenmadisonpark.com
Expensive	

Treat yourself to impressive French-influenced cuisine prepared by Swiss chef Daniel Humm inside this gorgeous parkside location. The classy environs, an exceptional staff and the whimsical tasting menu make this an extra special event, so be prepared for an equally impressive tab. Both lunch and dinner are multicourse affairs; lunch is an $88 three-course meal, with offerings like poached lobster and a roulade of prawns. The 14-course dinner will set you back $225; you choose the first three courses and chef will select the remaining eleven. Don't expect to rush through your meal, instead, plan about three hours for this amazing dining experience. I would suggest that you be sure to dress to impress.

ELIO'S

1621 Second Ave (at 84th St)	212/772-2242
Dinner: Daily	
Moderately expensive	

For years Elio's has been the classic clubby Upper East Side dining room for those who are recognizable, as well as those who aspire to be. In not so fancy surroundings, with waiters who greet regulars as if they are part of the family, tasty Italian platters of beef carpaccio, clams, mussels, stuffed mushrooms and minestrone are offered as starters. Lots of spaghetti and risotto dishes follow, along with seafood (their specialty), liver, scaloppine and more of the usual Italian assortment. For dessert, try the delicious sorbets. Although half the fun is watching the not-so-subtle eye contact among diners, the food is excellent and it is easy to see why Elio's remains a neighborhood favorite.

ELI'S TABLE

1413 Third Ave (bet 80th and 81st St)	212/717-9798
Dinner: Daily; Brunch: Sat, Sun	elizabar.com
Moderate to moderately expensive	

Hats off to Eli! Fine dining at Eli's Table is the natural culmination of Eli

YOU WENT WHERE?

In many ways, real estate dictates the taste of New York—or at least where you find it. A number of high profile restaurants hit the road last year because of extravagant rents: **wd-50** and **Pastis** among them. Other major restaurant closings in 2014 include **Telepan Local**, **Heartwood**, **General Assembly**, **Crif Dogs**, **La Cenita Steakhouse** and **Apres**. A reminder to call ahead.

ESSEX STREET EATERY

Shopsin's (120 Essex St, 212/312-3603) is a small, very casual 20-seat eatery in the Essex Street Market open Wednesday through Sunday for breakfast and lunch. Kenny Shopsin and crew are a bit irreverent, highly opinionated and a tad quirky which makes this a unique New York City food experience. Reading the staggering menu may cause you to readjust your eyeglasses, although alphabetical entries of pancakes, burgers and breakfast dishes bring a sense of order to the listings. Where else can you order a pig newton (eggs, grits, pork and fig gravy sandwich), Capt J (fried chicken, eggs, two mac 'n jack pancakes) or other politically incorrect-named dishes?

Zabar's longtime efforts. The large space is located next door to his famous gourmet market and wine shops, from which ingredients are conveniently gathered – baked bread, freshly roasted coffee, fresh produce and a wonderful selection of wines. The menu includes interesting salads with veggies from Eli's rooftop garden. Housemade tagliatelle with Dungeness crab and chives, braised veal ravioli with chanterelles and parmigiana or wild halibut with kale, rutabaga and apple cider are possible main courses. Impressive small plates are available from the bar menu and brunch will satisfy your cravings for pancakes, slathered bagels, meatloaf on an onion roll and much more.

ELLEN'S STARDUST DINER

1650 Broadway (at 51st St)   212/956-5151
Breakfast, Lunch, Dinner: Daily   ellensstardustdiner.com
Inexpensive to moderate

This is one of those "only in New York" experiences. With its singing wait staff, most hoping to be discovered as the next movie or Broadway star, Ellen's Stardust Diner fits right into the theater neighborhood. This 50s diner is a fun and noisy spot that serves satisfying food the traditional American way. The breakfast menu includes bagels and biscuits, along with tasty buttermilk pancakes, French toast and omelets. For the rest of the day, comfort foods are in order: salads and sandwiches, burgers, chicken pot pie, chili and meatloaf. Don't forget the egg creams, shakes, malts and a nice selection of caloric desserts; be sure to ask that your shake be made "thick!" Delivery is available.

FEAST

102 Third Ave (at 13th St)   212/529-8880
Lunch: Mon-Fri; Dinner: Mon-Sat; Brunch: Sat, Sun   eatfeastnyc.com
Moderate to moderately expensive

At Feast, enjoy a feast of modern American cuisine in a rustic, warm setting. The seasonal menu offers two *prix-fixe* feasts ($58 and $68 per person), each offering eight dishes; full table participation is required. For example, a poultry feast included chicken soup with rice; buttermilk fried quail salad; duck egg scramble of potato, onion and brioche; duck breast with rutabaga; rotolo house pasta; braised cabbage; roasted garlic tabais beans and twinkies with duck fat buttercream. Crafted by chef Christopher Meenan, the feast is delivered in groups of four plates to the center of the table, like a buffet. A less expensive a la carte menu with shared plates is also listed. Try to snag the communal table in the back for some privacy.

FELIDIA

243 E 58th St (bet Second and Third Ave)	212/758-1479
Lunch: Mon-Fri; Dinner: Daily	felidia-nyc.com
Expensive	

Chef/owner Lidia Bastianich has made her mark in New York's Italian food circles. She's a well-respected restaurateur, cookbook author, TV chef, purveyor of her own line of sauces and tabletop items and wine producer. Lidia has personally greeted diners at Felidia, her warm and cozy midtown east townhouse, since 1981. Choices are either a la carte or from the chef's tasting menus, including a gluten-free option. Offerings include a half dozen fresh pastas with tantalizing combinations of seasonal ingredients, as well as entrees of bass, veal, calves liver, tripe and other delectables from land and sea. A $32 three-course *prix-fixe* lunch offers a good value for the more budget-conscious. The mascarpone, chocolate and coffee tiramisu is a sweet ending.

FIG & OLIVE

808 Lexington Ave (bet 62nd and 63rd St)	212/207-4555
10 E 52nd St (bet Fifth and Madison Ave)	212/319-2002
420 W 13th St (bet Ninth Ave and Washington St)	212/924-1200
Lunch: Mon-Fri; Dinner: Daily; Brunch: Sat, Sun	figandolive.com
Moderately expensive	

Fig & Olive is all about passion for the best olive oils, flavors and cuisine of the Mediterranean area. Small plates are enhanced with delicate or robust flavors of extra virgin olive oils that are selected as the perfect match for each dish. For example: the appetizer truffle mushroom croquette is served with

FRENCH FARE

Bouillabaisse: French seafood stew

Confit: goose, duck or pork that has been salted, cooked and preserved in its own fat

Coulis: a thick, smooth sauce, usually made from vegetables but sometimes from fruit

Croque madame: grilled ham-and-cheese sandwich, topped with a cooked egg

En croute: anything baked in a buttery pastry crust or hollowed-out slice of toast

Foie gras: duck or goose liver, usually made into paté

Tartare: finely chopped and seasoned raw beef, often served as an appetizer

Terrine: finely minced ingredients or paté prepared in a loaf shape

truffle olive oil aioli and a salad of figs, apples, cheeses and walnuts is tossed with a fig balsamic and aromatic arbequina olive oil dressing. Similarly, rosemary garlic olive oil and fresh herbs are a delicious addition to lamb chops. A large variety of olive oils are offered for tasting at the beginning of each meal and they can be purchased at each location. For dessert, crème brûlée cheesecake and chocolate *pot de crème* are outstanding choices.

FOUR SEASONS

99 E 52nd St (bet Lexington and Park Ave)   212/754-9494
Lunch: Mon-Fri; Dinner: Mon-Sat   fourseasonsrestaurant.com
Expensive

The elegant Four Seasons is awe-inspiring in its simplicity and charm. Two separate dining areas, the Grill Room and the Pool Room, have different menus and appeal. *Prix-fixe* and a la carte menus are available in both rooms. Business and media heavy hitters in dark suits congregate at noon in the Grill Room, where the waiters know them by name and menu preferences. The Pool Room is more romantic; tables surround a bubbling marble pool. Society mavens and couples who want to dine with the stars are made to feel at home with superb service. A special for two might include crispy farmhouse duck with roasted figs and the dessert menu can only be described as obscene; individual soufflés are a splendid treat.

FREDS AT BARNEYS NEW YORK

660 Madison Ave (at 60th St), 9th floor   212/833-2200
Lunch, Dinner: Daily; Brunch: Sat, Sun   barneys.com
Moderate to moderately expensive

It would be a tossup as to which is better at Freds – the Italian/American food or the people watching – where the "beautiful" people definitely like to see and be seen. You'll find the dishes ample and delicious (and they should be, at the prices charged). Selections include beef, chicken and lamb entrées; seafood dishes; pastas; salads; pizzas and sandwiches with French fries that are served Belgian-style. There's no shortage of selections or calories on the dessert menu.

FREEMANS

Freeman Alley (off Rivington St, bet Bowery and Christie St)   212/420-0012
Lunch: Mon-Fri; Dinner: Daily; Brunch: Sat, Sun   freemansrestaurant.com
Moderate to moderately expensive

Freemans is almost impossible to locate, and you don't want to miss the hipster scene in this colonial-like tavern. Crowded, noisy and unpretentious, it has a nice kitchen, extra-friendly service personnel, clean restrooms and a great bar and bartender. But most of all, it has really delicious rustic, American food. You must start with "Devils on Horseback" (Stilton-stuffed prunes wrapped in bacon and served piping hot) or try Freemans signature cocktail made with pomegranate molasses. Cassoulet with pork belly, pork sausage, pork loin, white beans and buttery croutons is unusual and filling; all the breads are excellent. Desserts are just okay, but a visit here is so unique you can overlook your sweet tooth! Reservations can only be made for parties of six or more.

FRESCO BY SCOTTO
34 E 52nd St (bet Madison and Park Ave)   212/935-3434
Lunch: Mon-Fri; Dinner: Mon-Sat   frescobyscotto.com
Moderate to moderately expensive

For the past several decades, Fresco by Scotto has become a midtown Manhattan tradition for lunch and dinner. Owned and operated by the hospitable Scotto family, the restaurant is often referred to as the "NBC Commissary." Potato and zucchini chips with gorgonzola cheese; eggplant and zucchini pie with ricotta, mozzarella and tomato sauce and pappardelle with duck and wild mushroom ragu are menu items worth noting. Fresco offers countless meat and fish dishes, scrumptious pastas and homemade *bomboloni* for dessert. **Fresco on the Go** (40 E 52nd St, 212/754-2700) offers homemade muffins and pancakes, sticky buns and eggs-to-order for breakfast; at noon, delicious sandwiches, pizzas, soups, salads and homemade pastas are available to order.

GABRIEL'S BAR & RESTAURANT
11 W 60th St (bet Broadway and Columbus Ave)   212/956-4600
Lunch, Dinner: Mon-Sat   gabrielsbarandrest.com
Moderate to moderately expensive

For dining in the Lincoln Center area, Gabriel's is a winner; you are greeted by Gabriel Aiello, an extremely friendly host. And what good food and drink; delicious bread and a fine assortment of Italian appetizers. Then it's on to first-class pastas (like tortellini with lamb garlic filling), wood-grilled chicken, steaks, seafood dishes and a daily risotto special. The in-house gelato creations are among New York's best, as is the warm chocolate truffle cake. Gabriel doesn't have to blow his own horn; his satisfied customers are happy to do it for him!

GIGI CAFE
64 E 34th St (bet Park and Madison Ave)   212/686-1900
958 Third Ave (bet 57th and 58th St)   212/319-0400
2067 Broadway (bet 71st and 72nd St)   212/501-7500
307 Seventh Ave (bet 27th and 28th St)   212/807-8500
Breakfast, lunch, dinner: Daily   gigicafe.com
Inexpensive

Wanting something quick, casual and healthy at any time of the day? Gigi Cafe locations are friendly and clean and have an amazing number of flavorful, fresh food selections. And there really is something for everyone here: fresh salads with homemade dressings, hearty soups, quiche and sandwiches from roast beef to wraps and melts; the bakery selections include breads, cookies and pastries. You can order sides or select from the buffet; eat in or takeout; catering, too. The fresh-made juices and smoothies are worthy of a visit!

GIORGIONE
307 Spring St (bet Greenwich and Hudson St)   212/352-2269
Lunch: Mon-Fri; Dinner: Daily   giorgionenyc.com
Moderate to moderately expensive

Giorgio Deluca (as in Dean & Deluca) is the proprietor of this neighborhood

BARS FOR SMOKING

Nowadays, you will get the boot in most New York bars if you try to have a smoke. However, there are a few places left where you can legally light up, toss back a drink and grab a meal.

Carnegie Club (156 W 56th St, 212/957-9676): cigar bar and jazz

Circa Tabac (32 Watts St, 212/941-1781): over 70 brands of cigarettes; cigars

Club Macanudo (26 E 63rd St, 212/752-8200): private humidors

Hudson Bar & Books (636 Hudson St, 212/229-2642): Monday is ladies' night.

Lexington Bar & Books (1020 Lexington Ave, 212/717-3902): collars required, jackets preferred

---

trattoria in Hudson Square, so you know it is a quality operation. The space features shiny metal-top tables and an inviting pizza oven that turns out remarkable pies. This is a very personal restaurant, with Italian dishes like you'd find in mother's kitchen in the Old Country: carpaccio, prosciutto, ravioli, risotto and linguine. The minestrone is as good as I have ever tasted. Pizzas come in eight presentations and a raw bar is also available. Finish with a platter of exquisite Italian cheeses or pick from the appealing desserts.

GOLDEN UNICORN

18 East Broadway (at Catherine St) 212/941-0911
Lunch, Dinner, Dim Sum: Daily; Dim Sum Breakfast: Sat, Sun
Inexpensive to moderate goldenunicornrestaurant.com

Golden Unicorn prepares the best dim sum outside of Peking! This bustling, two-floor, Hong Kong-style Chinese restaurant serves delicious dim sum every day of the week (until 4 p.m.; 5 p.m. on the weekend). Besides the nearly 100 delicacies from the rolling carts, diners may choose from a wide variety of Cantonese dishes off the regular menu. Pan-fried noodle dishes; Peking duck with pancake, scallions and cucumbers; rice noodles and noodles in soup are all house specialties. Despite the size of the establishment (they can accommodate over 500 diners), you will be amazed at the fast service, cleanliness and prices. This is one of the best values in Chinatown.

GOOD

89 Greenwich Ave (bet Bank and 12th St) 212/691-8080
Lunch: Tues-Fri; Dinner: Daily; Brunch: Sat, Sun goodrestaurantnyc.com
Moderate

This popular destination for locals is a casual, take-your-time establishment. Chef/owner Steven Picker creates hearty, rustic American fare that is served by friendly personnel. Expect to wait in line for brunch; a menu highlight is the "Good Breakfast:" two eggs with a choice of pancakes, home fries and bacon or sausage. Lamb burgers and green-chile mac and cheese are full of flavor and pork tenderloin or rainbow trout are good bets for dinner. All menu items are available for takeout and delivery.

GOOD ENOUGH TO EAT

520 Columbus Ave (at 85th St)   212/496-0163
Breakfast: Daily; Lunch: Mon-Fri; Dinner: Daily; Brunch: Sat, Sun
Inexpensive to moderate   goodenoughtoeat.com

New York is a weekend breakfast and brunch town, and you cannot do better than Good Enough to Eat in both categories. Savor the apple pancakes, four-grain pancakes with walnuts and fresh bananas and chocolate and coconut pancakes. Additional offerings include French toast, waffles, a half dozen of omelets, scrambled-egg dishes, corned beef hash, real Irish oatmeal, fresh-squeezed orange juice and homemade sausage. Lunches feature inexpensive and delicious salads, burgers (juicy and delicious) and sandwiches. More of the same is served for dinner, plus meatloaf, turkey, pork chops, fish and roast chicken plates. This is comfort food at its finest, all the way through wonderful homemade peach pie.

GOTHAM BAR & GRILL

12 E 12th St (bet Fifth Ave and University Pl)   212/620-4020
Lunch: Mon-Fri; Dinner: Daily   gothambarandgrill.com
Moderately expensive to expensive

The Gotham is a must! Since 1984 it has been recognized as one of New York's best. Dining here can be summed up in one word: exciting! The modern, high-ceilinged space is broken by direct spot lighting on the tables; fresh plants and floral arrangements lend a bit of color. It is not inexpensive, but every meal I have had has been worth the tab – and there is a really good $35 *prix-fixe* lunch deal; you may also eat at the bar. Alfred Portale is one of the most talented chefs in the city and his new American menu is devoted to seasonality. For starters try the seafood salad or striped bass ceviche, excellent free-range chicken and superior dry-aged New York steak; rack of lamb is one of the tastiest in town. Each entree is well seasoned and attractively presented. For dessert try the peanut butter sundae with chocolate cookie crumbles or the excellent artisanal cheese selection. A sophisticated wait staff will take good care of you.

GOTHAM WEST MARKET

600 Eleventh Ave (bet 44th and 45th St)   212/582-7940
Mon-Fri: 7 a.m. -11 p.m.; Sat, Sun: 8 a.m. – 11 p.m.   gothamwestmarket.com
Inexpensive

Gotham West Market is a collection of vendors on the ground level of a luxury high-rise apartment building. This industrial-chic market and food hall is recognized as one of the hottest culinary outposts in Manhattan. Within the 15,000-square-foot space are restaurants, a cookware grocery store and a coffee shop; highly regarded chefs, including Ivan Orkin and Seamus Mullen, can be found cooking here. Current restaurants include: **Blue Bottle Coffee** (fresh roasted coffee), **The Cannibal** (small meat plates and on-tap drinks), **Choza Taqueria** (fresh Mexican food), **Court Street Grocers Sandwich Shop** (handcrafted sandwiches), **El Colmado** (Spanish tapas bar), **Genuine Roadside** (burgers, salads, tacos) and **Ivan Ramen Slurp Shop** (classic ramen and rice bowls). Casual counter and communal seating or takeout is available.

GRAMERCY TAVERN

42 E 20th St (bet Park Ave S and Broadway)   212/477-0777
Lunch, Dinner: Daily (Tavern)   gramercytavern.com
Lunch: Mon-Fri; Dinner: Daily (Dining Room)
Moderate (Tavern)
Expensive (Dining Room)

Gramercy Tavern is a very busy place, both in the rustic tavern (where meals are prepared on a wood-burning grill) and the fine dining area in the back. The landmark space is unusually attractive; the ceiling is a work of art, the private party room is magnificent and there is not a bad seat in the house. Chef Michael Anthony's fiercely seasonal American cuisine can be sampled with both regular and vegetarian tasting menus; a la carte items are offered at lunch and in the front tavern. Unique dishes might include celery root chowder with halibut, clams and trout roe; duck breast and bacon with mushrooms and Brussels sprouts and to finish, superior offerings of cheese, sorbet and ice cream. The food and servers are excellent.

GRAND CENTRAL OYSTER BAR RESTAURANT

Grand Central Terminal (42nd St at Vanderbilt Ave), lower level   212/490-6650
Lunch, Dinner: Mon-Sat   oysterbarny.com
Moderate

Native New Yorkers are familiar with the 1913 institution that is the Oyster Bar at Grand Central, but this iconic midtown destination is also popular with tourists, commuters and residents; over 2,000 visitors are served daily! The young help are accommodating, and the drain on the pocketbook is reasonable. The menu boasts more than 72 seafood items (with special daily entrees), about 25 varieties of oysters, a superb oyster stew, clam chowder (Manhattan and New England styles), bouillabaisse, Maine lobsters, marvelous homemade desserts and other listings. Be sure to look up at the high-vaulted ceiling and notice the other beautiful architectural features of this landmark location.

GYU-KAKU

805 Third Ave (bet 49th and 50th St), 2nd floor   212/702-8816
321 W 44th St (bet Eighth and Ninth Ave)   646/692-9115
34 Cooper Sq (bet 5th and 6th St)   212/475-2989
Lunch: Mon-Fri; Dinner: Daily; Brunch: Sat, Sun   gyu-kaku.com
Moderate to moderately expensive

Gyu-Kaku is a Japanese barbecue restaurant that is best described as a fun experience with good tasting food. After a gracious greeting, you are seated at tables with a charcoal grill in the center. Then you choose from a lengthy menu of items to grill: short ribs, ribeye, filet mignon, hanger steak, shrimp, chicken and fish. Accommodating servers will give instructions on how to cook the various items. Non-grill items include soups, salads, noodles, rice and dumplings. The Kobe beef slices and lobster tail are marvelous, as are the lamb and seafood dishes. Japanese restaurants are generally not great for desserts, but it's worth getting your hands and face gooey with the s'mores dish at Gyu-Kaku. It really makes for a memorable meal.

HAN DYNASTY

90 Third Ave (bet 12th and 13th St)   212/390-8685
Lunch: Mon-Fri; Dinner: Daily   handynasty.net
Inexpensive to moderate

For a taste of Sichuan in the Village, Han Dynasty is a busy and affordable option.   Contemporary art hangs on the bright mustard walls of this neighborhood choice. Owner Han Chiang employs a friendly staff adept in guiding guests through the many spice levels, from meek and mild to fierce and spicy. You can move from dumplings and won tons to braised-beef noodle soup; Han's version of the Sichuan standby, dan dan noodles (with minced pork) or sesame noodles; then on to dry-pot-style fish or lamb or one of the specials like three-cup chicken. Tasting menus starting at $25 per person (for parties of eight or more) are available.

HANJAN

36 W 26th St (bet Broadway and Avenue of the Americas)   212/206-7226
Lunch: Mon-Fri; Dinner: Mon-Sat   hanjan26.com
Moderate to moderately expensive

Hanjan is a popular Korean gastropub where waits are not uncommon. That being said, expect to order several small items from the traditional, modern and skewer categories for your meal. Popular selections include scallion pancakes (with or without squid), pork belly skewers and fried chicken skin, gizzards and hearts. For a late-night snack, ramen (nowhere near the college-student staple) is served after 10 p.m. The drink choices are nearly global: saké and soju, Asian beers, cocktails with Korean flavors, wines from around the world and champagne. The atmosphere is relaxed with a long, communal table in the center of the room, which encourages guests to intermingle.

HATSUHANA

17 E 48th St (bet Fifth and Madison Ave)   212/355-3345
Lunch, Dinner: Mon-Sat   hatsuhana.com
Moderate to moderately expensive

Hatsuhana has a longstanding reputation as one of the best sushi houses in Manhattan inspite of rather uninteresting trappings. One can sit at a table or the sushi bar and get equal attention from the informed help. There are several dozen appetizers, including broiled eel in cucumber wrap; next try salmon or chicken teriyaki or any number of savory sushi dishes. Forget about desserts and concentrate on the exotic appetizer and main-dish offerings.

HILL COUNTRY

30 W 26th St (bet Broadway and Ave of the Americas)   212/255-4544
Lunch, Dinner: Daily   hillcountryny.com
Moderate

Hill Country is an unusual, very informal spot, modeled after the old-

CELEBRITY CHEFS AND OWNERS

New York has many world-class restaurants with world-class chefs. They have not only made their mark in the kitchen, but as television hosts, cookbook authors and designers of kitchenware and food product lines. Here are some of the big-name personalities:

Nick Anderer: pizza creations, Marta

Mario Batali: Italian empire, Eataly and more

David Bouley: genius in the kitchen, Bouley

Daniel Boulud: namesake eateries around town, Daniel

David Burke: creative, David Burke Kitchen

Andrew Carmellini: of Italian fame

David Chang: Momofuku empire

Tom Colicchio: the man behind Craft

Todd English: Plaza Food Hall

Marc Forgione: American Cut

Danny Meyer: Marta (and much more) impresario

Drew Nieporent: Nobu and other unique houses

Marcus Samuelsson: Red Rooster Harlem

Jean-Georges Vongerichten: master of French cuisine, Jean Georges

Michael White: Marea and other Italian spots

fashioned meat markets of Central Texas. Order from counter stations that offer meat dishes (like brisket, pork spare ribs, whole chicken and Texas sausage), beans, macaroni and cheese, corn pudding and salads. Heavenly PB&J cupcakes, banana cream pudding and seasonal crisps are popular desserts. Choose a seat at one of the long tables, revisit the food and drink counters (if you wish), and enjoy live country music (Wednesday through Saturday). This is cafeteria-style; the more you eat, the more you pay! New York may not be a great barbecue town, but this place does its best to bring Texas flavors to the Big Apple.

HILL COUNTRY CHICKEN

1123 Broadway (at 25th St)   212/257-6446
Lunch, Dinner: Daily   hillcountrychicken.com
Inexpensive to moderate

It is easy to see why Hill Country Chicken is so busy with both sit-down customers and takeout orders. The all-natural, hormone-free chicken is moist, flavorful and very fresh. Pick your favorites: breasts, thighs, legs or wings; all priced by the piece, with or without the skin. As a crispy fried chicken fan, I was in seventh heaven. Also available are Texas tenders, sandwiches, salads, fries, biscuits, cheesy fried mashed potatoes, cole slaw, pies and homemade ice cream. I found the biscuits disappointing, but the pies are excellent.

HUERTAS

107 First Ave (bet 6th and 7th St)   212/228-4490
Dinner: Daily; Brunch: Sat, Sun   huertasnyc.com
Expensive (Back Dining Room)
Inexpensive to Moderate (Pintxos Bar)

Huertas, in the East Village, is a casual Basque-inspired restaurant led by a team of young up-and-comers. The word *huertas* means orchards in Northern Spain, and executive chef Jonah Miller creatively captures the fresh flavors of that area. Up front at the walk-in Pintxos Bar, the menu offers unique tapas (small bites) of meats, seafood and cheese combinations passed dim sum-style on trays. In the 24-seat Back Dining Room, a changing $55 five-course dinner might include swordfish, goat cheese, lamb and scallion bites, citrus and mustard greens with Spanish mackerel, housemade chorizo, eggs with cabbage and ham, beef shank with carrots, and lastly, goat cheese mousse with cranberries and sweet crumbs; $30 beverage pairings are available. Wednesdays bring two Cider Dinner seatings which recreate the communal eating and drinking dinners of Northern Spain traditions. The menus include Spanish cider and run $150 for up to six people; reservations required.

HUNDRED ACRES

38 MacDougal St (at Prince St)   212/475-7500
Lunch: Mon-Fri; Dinner: Daily; Brunch: Sat, Sun   hundredacresnyc.com
Moderately expensive

The weekend brunch crowd likes to linger at this convivial Soho eating place, especially on a warm day when the expansive front French doors are opened wide. It doesn't hurt, either, that brunch cocktails and Bloody Marys

RESTAURANTS NEAR CARNEGIE HALL

Just as there are a wide variety of performances staged at Carnegie Hall, there are varied opportunities to indulge the appetite. Here are some great choices in the neighborhood.

Brasserie 8½ (9 W 57th St, 212/829-0812): French brasserie

Burger Joint at Le Parker Meridien New York (119 W 56th St, 212/708-7414): burgers, shakes

Great American Health Bar (35 W 57th St, 212/355-5177): breakfast, lunch, dinner

Le Pain Quotidien (922 Seventh Ave, 212/757-0775): European; breakfast, lunch, dinner

Mangia (50 W 57th St, 212/582-5882): breakfast and lunch; pizza, salads, sandwiches, entrees, sweets

Nobu 57 (40 W 57th St, 212/757-3000): Japanese; celebrities

The Russian Tea Room (150 W 57th St, 212/581-7100): The well-known name says it all!

Trattoria dell'Arte (900 Seventh Ave, 212/245-9800): Italian; celebrities

are available both by the glass and by the pitcher. The ever-changing farm-fresh menu focuses on local and all-natural foods; there are sweets, savories, egg dishes, sandwiches and other kitchen inspirations for brunch. Similarly, the dinner menu is market driven, changes frequently and encompasses small nibbles, sharable plates and heartier choices of seafood, meat and poultry. For lunch, the three-course market menu offers appetizer and entree choices, plus dessert; a good deal at $24. Hundred Acres has a notable selection of American whiskeys and house cocktails.

IL BUCO ALIMENTARI E VINERIA

53 Great Jones St (bet Bowery and Lafayette St)   212/837-2622
Breakfast, Lunch, Dinner: Daily   ilbucovineria.com
Moderately expensive

One of the most fun places I have visited in a long time has a long name to remember: Il Buco Alimentari e Vineria, located on busy Great Jones Street in downtown Manhattan. This is a market restaurant, with a dry goods section along with a very appetizing butcher case; all manner of spectacular cured meats tempt you as you come and go. (The curing equipment is located in the basement of the restaurant.) You may look into the open kitchen, but the fun is just to sit back and enjoy some of the best Italian pastas you can imagine. Get started with a super bread basket; I almost ate so much that I didn't have room for the slow-roasted short ribs! What a dish! There is much more: seared Vermont quail, grilled chicken, roasted lamb ribs and on and on to Italian heaven. There are lots of good choices for dessert including semolina cake, panna cotta and first-rate gelati and sorbets. For a lunch or evening of true Italian joy, I would highly recommend this delightful establishment.

IL CORTILE

125 Mulberry St (bet Canal and Hester St)   212/226-6060
Lunch, Dinner: Daily   ilcortile.com
Moderate to moderately expensive

Il Cortile is a good reason to visit Little Italy! While the area is more for tourists than serious diners, there are some exceptions. This eatery is an oasis of tasty Italian fare in an attractive and romantic setting with waiters who have been here forever. A bright, airy garden atrium in the rear is the most pleasant part of the restaurant. The menu is typically Italian, with main listings that include fish, chicken and veal dishes, plus excellent spaghetti, fettuccine and ravioli. Sauteed vegetables like bitter broccoli, hot peppers, mushrooms, spinach and green beans are specialties of the house. There is a daily *prix-fixe* menu as well as extensive a la carte offerings. Service is excellent and expeditious, and the waiters zip around like they are on roller skates. If you can fight your way through the gawking visitors, you will find Il Cortile worth the effort!

IL GATTOPARDO

13-15 W 54th St (bet Fifth Ave and Ave of the Americas)   212/246-0412
Lunch, Dinner: Daily   ilgattopardonyc.com
Expensive

This midtown restaurant is set in a simple and elegant Manhattan townhouse, a space that once was Aquavit. The restaurant and bar occupy the ground floor; a downstairs room with atrium is reserved for special events. The interesting and varying appetizers may include beef and veal meatballs wrapped in cabbage leaves, braised octopus with eggplant and buffalo ricotta cakes with spicy tomato sauce. Among the many pastas, homemade scialatielli is delicious. Main-course highlights include herb-crusted rack of lamb, traditional Neapolitan meatloaf, fish and shellfish stew and much more. If your favorite dish is not on the menu, ask in advance and they'll probably make it for you. For dessert, chocolate mousse cake with coffee gelato and tableside *zabaglione* are sinfully good.

IL MULINO NEW YORK
86 W 3rd St (bet Sullivan and Thompson St)   212/673-3783
Lunch: Mon-Fri; Dinner: Mon-Sat
Moderately expensive

IL MULINO PRIME
331 West Broadway (at Grand St)   212/226-0020
Lunch, Dinner: Daily
Moderately expensive

IL MULINO UPTOWN
37 E 60th St (bet Madison and Park Ave)   212/750-3270
Lunch, Dinner: Daily   ilmulino.com
Moderately expensive

For three decades, Il Mulino has produced the authentic cuisine of the Abruzzo coastal region of Italy.   Known for turning fresh, simple ingredients into sumptuous feasts, you'll taste the vibrant, Italian flavors in fresh homemade pastas, chicken braised in wine, sea bass and scallops wrapped in pancetta. Exemplary service, one-of-a-kind fare and a stunning atmosphere combine to make this an exceptional experience! The newest Soho offshoot on West Broadway offers prime cuts of beef alongside the signature Italian classics.

TRATTORIA IL MULINO
Without a doubt, a meal at the original **Il Mulino** is an experience, unequalled most anywhere in the country. The atmosphere is a bit mafia-like, the food is extraordinary and the service memorable. Alas, an offspring, **Trattoria Il Mulino** (336 E 20th St, 212/777-8448), is nothing like its parent. This place is cold and uninviting, with very mediocre food and is sparsely populated during meal hours. Trying to duplicate what has been a success story for many years obviously is very disappointing.

IL POSTINO
337 E 49th St (bet First and Second Ave)   212/688-0033
Lunch: Mon-Sat; Dinner: Daily   ilpostinony.com
Expensive

It is nice to splurge on occasion, if what you get is worth the extra bucks.

LINCOLN RISTORANTE

Dinner at the very expensive Italian fine-dining hot spot **Lincoln Ristorante at Lincoln Center** (142 W 65th St, 212/359-6500) offers more than just the impressive modern Italian cuisine of chef Jonathan Benno. The Hearst Plaza setting is spectacular. A reflecting pool is viewed through soaring windows, and a pedestrian-friendly grass-covered geometric roof envelops the restaurant. There is much to enjoy at Lincoln Ristorante, although your pocketbook will take a beating.

Il Postino does have rather hefty prices, but the offerings rival the best in Manhattan! The intimate setting is comfortable and not showy. You'll be impressed by the captains, who can recite a lengthy list of specials without hesitation. You have your choice of ground-level tables or a slightly raised balcony; the latter feels more comfortable to me. An extraordinarily tasty bread dish and assorted small appetizer plates get things off to a good start. Pastas like linguine with three kinds of clams or the signature pasta dish, Agnolotti (pasta stuffed with ricotta cheese and spinach in a light cream sauce), are sensational. Chicken in a baked crust is very satisfying and roasted loin of veal for two is also top-grade. Authentic Italian sorbets finish a memorable gourmet experience; incidentally, lunch is equally delicious and easier on the wallet.

IL VAGABONDO

351 E 62nd St (bet First and Second Ave)   212/832-9221
Lunch: Mon-Fri; Dinner: Daily   ilvagabondo.com
Moderate to moderately expensive

Il Vagabondo is a great spot to recommend to your visiting friends, and many old school Italian fans consider it their favorite restaurant! This bustling house has been popular with New Yorkers in the know since 1965. The atmosphere is strictly old-time, complete with white tablecloths, four busy rooms and an even busier bar. Spaghetti, ravioli and absolutely marvelous veal, chicken and eggplant parmigiana are popular dishes. There is no pretense at this place, which is a terrific spot for office parties. You will see happy faces, compliments of a delicious meal and reasonable bill. Save room for the bocce ball dessert (tartufo). Il Vagabondo is the only restaurant in New York with an indoor bocce court!

IVAN RAMEN

25 Clinton St (bet Houston and Stanton St)   646/678-3859
Lunch: Mon-Fri; Dinner: Daily; Brunch: Sat, Sun   ivanramen.com
Inexpensive to Moderate

When you walk into Ivan Ramen's colorful space you enter the ramen revolution that has taken over New York. Chef Ivan Orkin dishes up delicious and creative Japanese noodles as well as izakaya-style small plates; he was named one of the best new chefs for 2014 by *New York* magazine. His spicy chile ramen is a popular menu item, but don't stop there. Double-dredged chicken hearts; triple-pork, triple-garlic mazemen; pork meatballs and braised beef tongue are all winners. Chances are you will have a wait to get a table, so on a nice day seek out the mosaic-walled backyard patio. A more casual location with counter seating and communal tables is **Ivan Ramen Slurp Shop** located at the Gotham West Market (600 Eleventh Ave, 212/582-7940).

JACKSON HOLE BURGERS

232 E 64th St (bet Second and Third Ave)	212/371-7187
521 Third Ave (at 35th St)	212/679-3264
517 Columbus Ave (at 85th St)	212/362-5177
Breakfast, Brunch, Lunch, Dinner: Daily	jacksonholeburgers.com
Inexpensive	

Jackson Hole is my favorite burger destination! You might think that a burger is a burger, but having tried hamburgers all over the city, I can attest that this chain has some of the best. Each one weighs at least seven juicy, delicious ounces. You can get all kind of burgers: pizza, English or the Baldouni burger (mushrooms, fried onions and American cheese), including chicken, turkey and vegetable options. They have appetizers, omelets, salads, soup, sandwiches and wraps, plus breakfast and brunch items. The atmosphere isn't fancy, but once you sink your teeth into a Jackson Hole burger, accompanied by great onion rings or French fries, you'll see why I'm so enthusiastic. Check with each location, as hours vary.

JACQUES 1534

20 Prince St (bet Mott and Elizabeth St)	212/966-8888
Lunch: Mon-Fri; Dinner: Daily; Brunch: Sat, Sun	jacques1534.com
Moderate	

Just steps from the bustling streets of Nolita is Jacques 1534, one part French gastropub and one part sexy underground cocktail lounge. Jacques 1534 brings a fresh and creative approach to the traditional French fare with a locally-sourced menu and expertly crafted cocktails. The a la carte menu is basically the same for lunch, dinner and brunch. The $18 business lunch (soup or salad, sandwich or mussel and coffee or tea) is an excellent value. The brunch menu includes a variety of egg dishes and up to five brunch cocktails with your meal. The downstairs lounge, which features cocktails from the colonial settlements, encourages mingling, laughter and imbibing; after all, it is the reason you're there.

JACQUES BRASSERIE

204-206 E 85th St (bet Second and Third Ave)	212/327-2272
Lunch, Dinner: Daily; Brunch: Sat, Sun	jacquesbrasserie.com
Moderate	

Jacques Brasserie is the sister operation to Jacques 1534. And there are just so many reasons why this bistro is popular with folks in the neighborhood. It is cozy, friendly, moderately priced and they serve great food. In addition, Jacques himself is one of the friendliest proprietors in town. All of the classic French dishes are available: French onion soup, steak *frites*, bouillabaisse, crème brûlée, cheeses and a wonderful bittersweet chocolate soufflé. There also are outstanding seafood dishes, including mussels prepared six ways.

JEAN GEORGES

Trump International Hotel and Tower
1 Central Park W (bet 60th and 61st St)   212/299-3900
Lunch, Dinner: Mon-Fri
Very expensive

NOUGATINE AT JEAN GEORGES

Front room at Jean Georges
Breakfast, Lunch, Dinner: Daily   jean-georges.com
Moderately expensive

Jean-Georges Vongerichten is the master of the cool, calm, formal and très French dining hall that bears his name. The understated elegance of the room and uninterrupted service set the tone for a fine dining experience. Lunch and dinner are *prix-fixe*; at $48, lunch is a bargain. Dinner starts at $128 for three courses; tasting menus are $208. The more casual cafe, Nougatine, offers many of the same menu items at a slightly lower price and serves both a la carte and *prix-fixe* meals. Where to start? Foie gras brûlée with pineapple-Meyer lemon jam and rose salt, or in contrast, crab fritters with chipotle emulsion; either would be a pleasing choice. Rack of lamb is outstanding, as are the fish dishes from the seasonal menu. The chocolate dessert tasting, especially if it includes the decadent chocolate cake, is wonderful. You can't do better than Jean Georges, especially if price is unimportant!

JEFFREY'S GROCERY

172 Waverly Pl (at Christopher St)   646/398-7630
Breakfast, Lunch: Mon-Fri; Dinner: Daily; Brunch: Sat, Sun   jeffreysgrocery.com
Moderate to moderately expensive

Jeffrey's Grocery may seem like a vintage 1930s mom-and-pop grocery, but the menu and tantalizing aromas tell otherwise. Cozy seating, a communal table and bar stools accommodate about 40 folks. Don't be surprised if you're asked to scoot down a seat to make room for another diner. Fans of traditional soups, salads and sandwiches will discover intriguing contemporary twists on Jeffrey's somewhat limited menu. The braised brisket sandwich is tender and satisfying. Dinner plates feature fresh local seafood, meats and vegetables and you could make a meal out of the cheese, charcuterie or raw bar offerings. It's a "feel good" kind of place!

THE JOHN DORY OYSTER BAR

Ace Hotel
1196 Broadway (at 29th St)   212/792-9000
Lunch, Dinner: Daily   thejohndory.com
Moderate

The John Dory at the Ace Hotel is another of the city's hot spots. The corner space is light and bright, thanks to spacious floor-to-ceiling windows. A raw bar and small plates dominate the menu; a separate bar serves over a dozen signature cocktails. Be prepared to wait for a table and just relax and enjoy the scene at this Friedman and Bloomfield property. It's very casual, with bar tables and stools (no white-cloth draped tables) or you can also join the crowd standing at the bar late into the night.

JOHN'S OF TIMES SQUARE

260 W 44th St (bet Eighth Ave and Broadway)   212/391-7560
Daily: 11:30 to 11:30   johnspizzerianyc.com
Moderate

John's of Times Square prepares some of the best coal-fired brick-oven handmade pizzas in the city. Mouthwatering thin-crust varieties are made-to-order and include cheese and tomatoes to a gut-busting extravaganza of anchovies, sausage, peppers, meatballs, onions, mushrooms and fresh herbs. John's also does appetizers, salads, sandwiches and pastas well. The enormous pizzeria occupies the former Gospel Tabernacle Church in Times Square and can seat groups of any size (seating for 400) in a New York minute. Interestingly, the church was built in 1888 and has all of its original stained glass.

JOSEPH LEONARD

170 Waverly Pl (at Grove St)   646/429-8383
Breakfast: Tues-Fri; Lunch: Mon-Fri; Dinner: Daily; Brunch: Sat, Sun
                                                            josephleonard.com
Moderate to moderately expensive

Chef Jim McDuffee has a winner! Joseph Leonard is a small, rustic place with an exceedingly busy small bar and a no-reservations policy that can mean quite a wait later in the evening. Wait or not, the New York strip steak is worth a visit in itself. Feast upon soups, salads and paté, and if they have the butternut squash soup, go for it. Fish, shellfish, chicken and lamb shank make great main courses. Two bits of advice before venturing to this place for dinner – come early and don't come here if you want a slow, quiet meal!

KATZ'S DELICATESSEN

205 E Houston St (at Ludlow St)   212/254-2246
Mon-Wed: 8 a.m.-10:45 p.m.; Thurs: 8 a.m.-2:45 a.m.; Fri: 8 a.m. - all night; Sat: all
day; Sun: till 10:45 p.m.   katzdelicatessen.com
Inexpensive to moderate

This one is truly a New York institution. Going strong since 1888, Katz's Delicatessen is the oldest and largest deli in Manhattan. If you're experiencing hunger pangs on the Lower East Side, then try Katz's hand-carved and overstuffed sandwiches, which are among the best in town. Mainstays include pastrami and corned beef sandwiches, hot dogs and potato pancakes. When you order at the counter it is fun to watch the no-nonsense operators slicing and fixing; or sit at a table where a seasoned waiter will take care of you. Incidentally, Katz's is a perfect place to sample the unique (and disappearing) lowbrow "charm" of the Lower East Side. While you wait for a table or discover that the salt and pepper containers are empty and the catsup is missing, you'll know what I mean. Catering at attractive rates and private party facilities are available. Be sure to get dill pickles and sauerkraut with your sandwich.

KEENS STEAKHOUSE

72 W 36th St (bet Fifth Ave and Ave of the Americas)   212/947-3636
Lunch: Mon-Fri; Dinner: Daily   keens.com
Moderate

Keens Steakhouse is one of the most reliable longtime Manhattan restaurants;

BEYOND BACON AND EGGS PLUS

Forget your usual breakfast of cold cereal and dry toast and try some of these great morning choices:

Bacon: **Jack's Wife Freda** (224 Lafayette St, 212/510-8550): house-cured duck bacon

Belgian waffles: **Le Pain Quotidien** (100 Grand St, 212/625-9009; 1131 Madison Ave, 212/327-4900 and other locations)

Corned beef hash: **Carnegie Deli** (854 Seventh Ave, 212/757-2245)

English-style breakfast: **The Breslin** (Ace Hotel, 16 W 29th St, 212/679-1939)

Pancakes: **Clinton St. Baking Company & Restaurant** (4 Clinton St, 646/602-6263), **Friend of a Farmer** (77 Irving Pl, 212/477-2188) and **Veselka** (144 Second Ave, 212/229-9682): raspberry

Roast beef hash and poached eggs: **Wollensky's Grill** (201 E 49th St, 212/753-0444): weekend brunch

---

a truly unique New York institution. I can remember coming here decades ago, when those in the garment trade made Keens their lunch headquarters; this has not changed. Keens still has the same attractions: the bar reeks of atmosphere, and there are great party facilities and fine food to match. Keens has been a fixture in the Herald Square area since 1885. For some time it was for "gentlemen only," and although it still has a masculine atmosphere, ladies are made to feel comfortable and welcome. The "powerhouse porterhouse" and famous mutton chop with mint are house specialties, but other delicious dishes include steak, lamb, fish and lobster. They do single-malt scotch tastings from fall through spring and stock one of the largest collections in New York. If you have a meat-and-potato lover in your party, this is the place to come. Save room for the fantastic key lime pie.

KING BEE

424 E 9th St (bet First Ave and Ave A)   646/755-8088
Dinner: Daily   kingbeenyc.com
Moderate

For unique Southern food, visit King Bee in the East Village where chef Jeremie Tomczak specializes in Acadian cuisine. What's Acadian, you ask? This dates back to 17th-century French colonists, or Acadians, who migrated to the South where Cajun culture was developed. At King Bee the old Acadian comfort recipes are given a modern twist; starters include pork cracklings with peanuts, cane caramel and malt-vinegar powder and grilled oysters in cabbage garlic butter. The more ambitious entrees include Poutine Rapée which are potato dumplings stuffed with lamb's neck and partridgeberries, rabbit rillettes with crispy leeks and buckwheat pappardelle with wild mushrooms, Jerusalem artichoke and soft-poached egg. The room has a warm farmhouse feel complete with reclaimed barn wood accents; select tables look out onto the backyard garden.

KING'S CARRIAGE HOUSE

251 E 82nd St (bet Second and Third Ave)   212/734-5490
Lunch, Dinner: Tues-Sat; Tea: Tues-Sun (3-5); Brunch: Sun
Moderately expensive   kingscarriagehouse.com

King's is indeed an old carriage house, remade into a charming two-story dining salon that your mother-in-law would love. The ambience is Irish manor house. In a quaint setting with real wooden floors, you dine by candlelight in a very civilized atmosphere. Even some folks in the immediate neighborhood are unaware of this sleeper. The luncheon menu stays the same: salads, sandwiches and lighter fare and afternoon tea that is a real treat. The continental menu changes nightly and may feature grilled items like prime rib, rack of lamb and filet mignon; while the $49 *prix-fixe* menu is a really good value. I found the Stilton cheese with a nightcap of ruby port absolutely perfect for dessert, but there are also carrot macadamia cake and other good finishers.

LA BOITE EN BOIS

75 W 68th St (at Columbus Ave)   212/874-2705
Lunch: Mon-Sat; Dinner: Daily; Brunch: Sat, Sun   laboitenyc.com
Moderate

La Boite en Bois is ideal for pre-theater or pre-Lincoln Center diners. It packs them in every evening for obvious reasons: delicious food, personal service and moderate prices. Salads are unusual, and the country paté is a great beginner. For an entree, I recommend filet of snapper, roast chicken with herbs or *pot-au-feu*; desserts include sorbet and are made in-house. The weekend brunch menu includes egg dishes, hors d'oeuvres and entrees. The atmosphere is intimate, and all the niceties of service are operative from start to finish. La Boite en Bois is small and popular, so call ahead for reservations.

RESTAURANTS FOR A CROWD

The Big Apple boasts some big restaurants. Top chefs and restaurateurs keep pumping up the square footage of their newest outposts. Bigger is not necessarily better, but at these operations, size and quality coexist just fine, along with the hum of hundreds of conversations.

Buddakan (Chelsea Market, 75 Ninth Ave, 212/989-6699): Asian hot spot

Daniel (60 E 65th St, 212/288-0033): exquisite space

Del Posto (85 Tenth Ave, 212/497-8090): palatial

John's of Times Square (260 W 44th St, 212/391-7560)

Morimoto (88 Tenth Ave, 212/989-8883): modern space

Nobu 57 (40 W 57th St, 212/757-3000): done with style and grace

Rosa Mexicano (9 E 18th St, 212/533-3350): festive south-of-the-border treats

Spice Market (403 W 13th St, 212/675-2322): family-style Asian street cuisine

Tao (42 E 58th St, 212/888-2288) and **Tao Downtown** (Maritime Hotel, 92 Ninth Ave, 212/888-2724): impressive Asian bistros

LA GRENOUILLE

3 E 52nd St (bet Fifth and Madison Ave)   212/752-1495
Lunch, Dinner: Tues-Sat   la-grenouille.com
Expensive

Put on your finest clothes to dine at La Grenouille, a special place that must be seen to be believed. Beautiful fresh-cut flowers herald a unique, not-to-be-forgotten dining experience, complete with a professional staff. The haute French food is as great as the atmosphere, and although prices are high, La Grenouille is worth every penny. Meals are *prix-fixe*; $110 for lunch and $195 for dinner. Celebrity-watching adds to the fun and you'll see most of the famous faces at the front of the room. Be sure to try the cold hors d'oeuvres, which are a specialty of the house, as are the lobster dishes, sea bass and poached chicken. Nowhere in New York are sauces any better or the dessert soufflés more superb. The tables are close together, but what difference does it make when the people at your elbows are so interesting?

LA LUNCHONETTE

130 Tenth Ave (at 18th St)   212/675-0342
Lunch: Tues-Sun; Dinner: Daily
Inexpensive to moderate

La Lunchonette proves that you don't have to be fancy to succeed, as long as you serve good food at reasonable prices. In an unlikely Chelsea location, this popular spot offers some of the tastiest French dishes around: snails, sauteed portobello mushrooms and lobster bisque to start, and omelets, grilled lamb sausage, sauteed calves liver and more for entrees. On Sunday evening, live accordion music is featured.

LA RIPAILLE

605 Hudson St (bet 12th and Bethune St)   212/255-4406
Lunch, Dinner: Daily; Brunch: Sat, Sun   laripailleny.com
Moderate

Since 1980 this small, bright, Parisian-style bistro in the West Village has made a cozy spot for informal, intimate meals. Depending on the season you might want to enjoy a cocktail on the lovely outdoor terrace or fireside. Owner Alain Laurent seeks out the freshest produce for the daily specials. The chef puts his heart into every dish for weekend brunch, lunch and dinner where the seafood is always fresh and classic French desserts are delicious.

LAFAYETTE

380 Lafayette St (at Great Jones St)   212/533-3000
Breakfast, Lunch: Mon-Fri; Dinner: Daily; Brunch: Sat, Sun   lafayetteny.com
Expensive

A beautiful, bustling brasserie describes this Andrew Carmellini production in Noho, with a retail bakery up front showcasing fresh-baked croissants, baguettes and other pastries. The spacious and lavish cafe is complete with picture windows, tiled columns, a long zinc bar and caramel-hued banquets. Excellent French starters might include homemade country patés, fussy salads, foie gras terrine and tartines topped with duck-liver mousse. Black macaroni with rock shrimp, cuttlefish and roasted garlic; duck au poivre dressed with kumquats and prime rib roast with wild mushrooms and potato cakes are satisfying entrees. For a fabulous finish save room for a rustic seasonal fruit tart with pistachio cream or fromage blanc cheesecake with warm poached cranberries and fresh thyme. Bring along your rich French uncle.

LAND THAI KITCHEN

450 Amsterdam Ave (at 82nd St)   212/501-8121
Lunch, Dinner: Daily   landthaikitchen.com
Moderate

Land Thai Kitchen has become a neighborhood favorite for well-prepared and -presented Thai food and reasonable prices. The menu offers about a dozen noodle and rice dishes and combinations from the wok. Other main offerings are fish, steak and chicken, all served with jasmine rice. Appetizers, salads and side dishes round out the menu. The chef is known for spicy sauces; ask your server to have the heat of the dish turned up or down to suit your taste. Because this is a busy place you may want to avoid peak times or may opt to take advantage of delivery and takeout.

LANDMARC

Time Warner Center
10 Columbus Cir (at 60th St), 3rd floor   212/823-6123
Daily: 7 a.m.-2 a.m.
179 West Broadway (bet Leonard and Worth St)   212/343-3883
Daily: 11 a.m.-11 p.m.   landmarc-restaurant.com
Moderate to moderately expensive

Landmarc offers a big menu, very tasty food and accommodating staff – what more could you want? Seafood entrees include roasted branzino, grilled salmon and tuna. Lamb chops, roasted chicken and burgers are excellent and steaks with French fries are a specialty. Delicious fresh salads like the niçoise are a lunch favorite and pasta specials are offered each day. For a novel dish try the crispy sweetbreads or the popular mussels with a selection of sauces like rosemary and bacon or pesto and tomato. Both locations are neighborhood favorites and offer crowded, high-energy dining.

LAVO

39 E 58th St (bet Park and Madison Ave)   212/750-5588
Lunch: Mon-Fri; Dinner: Daily; Brunch: Sat, Sun;   lavony.com
Nightclub: Thurs-Sat
Moderately expensive

Talk about a scene! New York's noteworthy young set have descended on the place. A bar, restaurant and nightclub make up the operation; it is noisy but amazingly efficient for such a mob scene. The menu is full of good-tasting Italian fare, sensational Wagyu-stuffed rice balls, Caesar salad and raw bar items. Steaks and chops, pizzas and pastas are popular dishes for the throngs, who seem to enjoy an atmosphere that is not conducive for people with hearing problems! The Oreo *zeppole* (deep-fried, double-stuffed Oreos) served with a malted vanilla shake chaser) completes a rather unique experience.

HISTORIC WATERING HOLE

Here's a bar that is both an attraction and a thriving watering hole. The story of the **Campbell Apartment**, located off the West Balcony of Grand Central Terminal (42nd St at Vanderbilt Ave, 212/953-0409), is a fascinating one. The space was once the private office of John Campbell, a very wealthy financier. In its heyday, these classy digs had a butler and some of the most expensive furnishings available. Even jaded New Yorkers like to tell stories about this fellow and that room. It is surely worth a visit!

LE BERNARDIN

155 W 51st St (bet Ave of the Americas and Seventh Ave) 212/554-1515
Lunch: Mon-Fri; Dinner: Mon-Sat   le-bernardin.com
Expensive

This is an award-winning seafood palace with seamless, Old World service! There has to be one restaurant that tops every list, and for seafood Le Bernardin holds that spot. Co-owner Maguy LeCoze and executive chef Eric Ripert make this house extremely attractive to the eye and very satisfying to the stomach. Wonderfully fresh oysters and clams make a great start and whatever your heart desires from the ocean is represented on the menu. Signature dishes change seasonally and might include yellowfin tuna, Hamachi, bay scallops, monkfish, halibut and skate; duck, lamb and short ribs are available on request. The dessert menu usually includes a cheese assortment, superb chocolate dishes and unusual flavors of ice cream and sorbet. What truly distinguishes La Bernardin is presentation and you'll pay accordingly: *prix-fixe* lunch is $76; dinner is $135 and the tasting menu is $155.

LE CIRQUE

1 Beacon Ct
151 E 58th St (bet Lexington and Third Ave)   212/644-0202
Lunch: Mon-Fri; Dinner: Mon-Sat   lecirque.com
Expensive

Probably no one on the Manhattan restaurant scene has more devoted followers than Sirio Maccioni! His difficult-to-find retreat at Le Cirque is frequented by fans looking for such dishes as quenelle of artichoke, morel risotto, rack of lamb, duck breast and foie gras. Choose a decadent finish with the signature chocolate passion mousse or pistachio soufflé. The food is absolutely superb, but more than that, diners want to be seen and get a kiss from Sirio himself, the epitome of what a restaurateur should be. The atmosphere is what you would expect (classy, subdued, jackets required), as are the prices (expensive). If you want the same great food in a more relaxed setting, head to the cafe and wine lounge.

LE GIGOT

18 Cornelia St (bet Bleecker and 4th St)   212/627-3737
Lunch: Tues-Fri; Dinner: Tues-Sun; Brunch: Sat, Sun   legigotrestaurant.com
Moderate

Le Gigot is a charming, romantic 28-seat bistro in the Village; most taxi drivers have never heard of Cornelia Street, so allow extra time if you come by cab. Once you're here, the cozy atmosphere and warm hospitality of the gentlemen who greet and serve combines with hearty dishes to please the most discerning diner. Snails and patés make delicious starters. My suggestion for a memorable meal: bouillabaisse or, in winter, le boeuf bourguignonne (beef stew in red wine with shallots, bacon, carrots, mushrooms and potatoes). Tasty desserts like upside-down apple tart and flambé bananas with cognac are offered, and weekend brunches are a specialty. Le Gigot is a lot less expensive than its counterpart in Paris, but just as appealing. Note that only cash and American Express are accepted for payment.

LE PÉRIGORD

405 E 52nd St (bet First Ave and East River)   212/755-6244
Lunch: Mon-Fri; Dinner: Daily   leperigord.com
Expensive

Superb! I love this place, which has been charming diners since 1964. Civilized is the word to describe Le Périgord. It is like dining in one of the great rooms of Manhattan in the "good old days," but with a distinctively modern presence. From gracious host Georges Briguet to the talented chef, everything is class personified. Every captain and waiter has been trained to perfection. Fresh roses and Limoges dinner plates adorn each table, but this is just half the pleasure of the experience. Every dish – from the magnificent cold appetizer buffet that greets guests to the spectacular pastry trolley – is tasty and memorable. You may order a la carte, of course. Soups are outstanding. Dover sole melts in your mouth. A fine selection of game is available in winter. Roasted free-range chicken, served with the best potato dish I have ever tasted (bleu de gex potato gratin), is spectacular. Finish your meal with a selection of cheeses. The luxurious setting of Le Périgord makes one appreciate what gracious dining on a special night out is all about. Gentlemen should wear jackets.

BUFFET LINES

Savvy New Yorkers line up to fill their plates with items from a number of attractive and well-stocked buffets. The assortment is staggering, with salad bars, breads, hot and cold entrees and desserts. At the bigger operations there are stations for carving meats, preparing omelets and ordering pasta dishes. Service is quick, prices are generally reasonable and you select only what you want to eat.

Brasserie 8½ (9 W 57th St, 212/829-0812): Sunday brunch

The Carlyle (Carlyle Hotel, 35 E 76th St, 212/570-7192): Sunday brunch, expensive

Chola (232 E 58th St, 212/688-4619): Indian lunch extravaganza

Dhaba (108 Lexington Ave, 212/679-1284): Indian lunch

Palm Court (The Plaza, 768 Fifth Ave, 212/546-5302): weekend brunch

Turkish Kitchen (386 Third Ave, 212/679-6633): Sunday brunch

LE RIVAGE

340 W 46th St (bet Eighth and Ninth Ave)   212/765-7374
Lunch, Dinner: Daily   lerivagenyc.com
Moderate

A great choice for pre- or post-theater, Le Rivage is one of the survivors along the highly competitive "restaurant row" of 46th Street. In business since 1958, three generations of the Denamiel family have served French food that's well-prepared and reasonably priced. Escargots, onion soup, quiche, coq au vin rouge, roast duck with orange sauce and peach melba are all delectable and well-presented. The atmosphere and pleasant attitude of the servers will put you in the proper frame of mind to enjoy that Broadway show.

LES HALLES

411 Park Ave S (bet 28th and 29th St)   212/679-4111
15 John St (at Broadway)   212/285-8585
Daily: 8 a.m. to midnight   leshalles.net
Moderate

Come here anytime you are hungry! These popular brasseries provide flavorful food in an appealing atmosphere at reasonable prices. Specialties like blood sausage with apples, choucrote garnie (sauerkraut with sausage and pork) and filet of beef are served in hefty portions with fresh salad and delicious French fries. Harried waiters try their best to be polite and helpful, but they are not always successful, as tables turn over rapidly. If a week in Paris is more of a dream than a reality, then you might settle for mussels, snails, onion soup and classic cassoulet at this busy establishment. About a dozen dessert items include chocolate-banana cake with chocolate sauce and crepes Suzette, prepared tableside.

L'EXPRESS

249 Park Ave S (at 20th St)   212/254-5858
Open 24/7   lexpressnyc.com
Moderate to moderately expensive

You can eat well in Gramercy without any consideration for time at L'Express as this Lyonnaise-style bistro is open 24/7. This quaint, full-service restaurant and bar prepares delicious French food that celebrates the meat and dairy products of the Lyon area. You'll find several different menu listings depending on the time of day: omelets, French toast, croissant sandwiches and more for breakfast; onion soup gratinée, warm goat cheese salad and quiche Lorraine at lunch; savory onion tart, pike or perch quenelles with spinach and rice pilaf and calf's liver with sautéed onions and bacon for dinner. Lamb burgers are a favorite item for either lunch or dinner. If there is a downside, it might be the somewhat inconsistent service. Takeout is available around the clock and delivery hours are 8 a.m. to 11:30 p.m.

LITTLE OWL

90 Bedford St (at Grove St)   212/741-4695
Lunch: Mon-Fri; Dinner: Daily; Brunch: Sat, Sun   thelittleowlnyc.com
Moderate

With tiny tables and a capacity of only 30 diners, this corner establishment is a very personal place with a wait staff that is warm and eager to please. Every seasonal Mediterranean-influenced dish I've tasted is excellent and reasonably priced. They are famous for their signature gravy meatball sliders and juicy, thick cut pork chops served with creamy butterbeans; lobster ravioli or seafood fritters are also good. The brunch menu is particularly attractive, with dishes like whole-wheat pancakes, surf and turf tacos and a bacon cheeseburger with spiced fries. Just one drawback: Little Owl is very popular, so reservations are a must.

LOCANDA VERDE

The Greenwich Hotel
377 Greenwich St (at N Moore St)   212/925-3797
Breakfast, Dinner: Daily; Lunch: Mon-Fri; Brunch: Sat, Sun
Moderate   locandaverdenyc.com

Comfortable, energetic and Italian – all that describes this Greenwich Hotel taverna. Chef Andrew Carmellini has created an enticing menu. Start the day with a combination of pomegranate, blood-orange and Valencia-orange juices;

DAVID CHANG'S EMPIRE

What is momofuku? It translates into "lucky peach," but in the dining arena it is the domain of chef David Chang. His original **Momofuku Noodle Bar** (171 First Ave, 212/475-7899) is open daily for lunch and dinner. You'll find noodles, small dishes and a large variety of small plates, with items changing by the season, plus heritage pork and shellfish offerings.

Momofuku Ssäm Bar (207 Second Ave, 212/254-3500) is open daily for lunch and dinner. This noisy place first offers a choice of ssäm (a kind of wrap) or bowl, pork shoulder steak, roasted scallops, shanghai noodles and cranberry beans. You won't go away hungry. Best description: earthy, Asian-accented New American. Reserve ahead for their feast!

Momofuku Milk Bar (72 Wooster St, 251 E 13th St, 15 W 56th St and 561 Columbus Ave; 347/577-9504 for all locations) does justice to pies, cakes, breads, cookies and croissants. Many are their own concoctions, with names like dream girl pie and compost cookie. But where's the peach?

Inside Chambers Hotel, **Má Pêche** (15 W 56th St, 212/757-5878; online reservations only) presents a New American menu of small plates like trout Sichuan, shrimp balls and pork buns. Changing entrees include tasty roasted lamb brisket or fried rice with duck and sweet potato. Delicious bakery goods from the Momofuku Milk Bar delight the neighborhood crowd.

The 12-seat **Momofuku Ko** (8 Extra Pl, 212/203-8095) is one of the hardest restaurants in town to score a lunch or dinner reservation. Prices hover around $125 to $175 per plate for the multicourse, three-hour meal. This is superb eclectic dining, if you have the patience to wait for a seat. There are no walk-ins, and reservations are accepted only online (momofuku.com) seven days in advance. Good luck!

GOOD EATING AT JFK

There is something to satisfy every palate and wallet at Kennedy Airport. There are plenty of places for a quick bite on the run, as well as full-service restaurants where you can enjoy a nice meal. Some of Manhattan's better restaurants have set up satellite kitchens at JFK.

5ive Steak: Terminal 5
Au Bon Pain: Terminals 4, 8
Balducci's: Terminals 2, 3, 7
Bobby Van's Steakhouse: Terminal 8
Deep Blue Sushi: Terminal 5
The Palm Bar & Grille: Terminal 4
Shake Shack: Terminal 4 (two locations)
Todd English's Bonfire Bar and Bonfire Steakhouse: Terminals 2, 7

whole grain waffles with strawberries and mascarpone cream and pastry chef Kierin Baldwin's fresh pastries. It's hard to pass up the lunch and dinner pasta dishes with duck sausage; or flavorful, succulent leg of lamb and other entrees from the wood-burning oven. Desserts such as apple and concord grape crostada with cider caramel or chocolate budino with hot fudge pose real dietary dilemmas. Though cozy inside, the casual dining atmosphere extends to the outdoors in summer.

LUKE'S LOBSTER

93 E 7th St (at First Ave)	212/387-8487
242 E 81st St (at Second Ave)	212/249-4241
426 Amsterdam Ave (bet 80th and 81st St)	212/877-8800
26 S William St (at Stone St)	212/747-1700
Plaza Food Hall, 1 W 59th St (at Fifth Ave), lower level	646/755-3227
Hours vary	lukeslobster.com
Moderate	

A trip to Luke's Lobster is reminiscent of a summer visit to Maine. Seafood is the signature at these small eateries where tasty lobster rolls are piled high with fresh lobster; lemon butter and secret spices ensure that this is a tasty treat (mayo is optional). Crab and shrimp rolls, chowders, soups and a limited number of other sides round out the menu. The atmosphere and size of each "shack" is somewhat different and seating may be limited at some locations; or simply stop by and take your order to go.

MACELLERIA

48 Gansevoort St (bet Washington and Greenwich St)	212/741-2555
Lunch: Mon-Fri; Dinner: Daily; Brunch: Sat, Sun	macelleria.com
Moderate	

Macelleria (Italian for butcher shop) is a bright spot in the Meatpacking

District, and is essentially a Northern Italian steakhouse with added attractions. The setting is what you might expect: masculine and unpretentious, with outside tables for nice-weather dining. Friendly and welcoming help make an excellent first impression. The menu is traditional, with some pleasant additions: fresh and filling salads, a number of pastas, chicken, seafood, chops and veal. Prime, dry-aged steaks are the primary draw. I highly recommend this spot for dinner with business partners after consummating a big deal, and for private events, try the wine cellar or the chef's table — located in the meat locker! Their special steaks and homemade fresh sausage are available for take home at Gansevoort Market.

MADANGSUI

35 W 35th St (bet Fifth Ave and Ave of the Americas)   212/564-9333
Lunch, Dinner: Daily   madangsui.com
Moderate

I got hooked on Korean barbecue while in South Korea, so it was only natural that I've been trying out various places in Manhattan that duplicate those authentic tastes. Madangsui surely qualifies. The menu literally covers over a hundred dishes, with combinations sure to please. The place is usually crowded with Korean folks and their families — an indication that Madangsui knows what it is doing! Personally, I get a big kick out of fixing my own dishes on the hot plate in the middle of the table. The fresh, butterflied short rib with Korean red pepper sauce is absolutely first-rate; you'll also find an extensive array of rice, chowder and vegetarian dishes.

MAIALINO

Gramercy Park Hotel
2 Lexington Ave (at 21st St)   212/777-2410
Breakfast, Lunch: Mon-Fri; Dinner: Daily; Brunch: Sat, Sun   maialinonyc.com
Moderately expensive

I have the utmost respect for Danny Meyer; this gentleman knows what pleases the American diner, and his operations exude this in spades. This trattoria is bright and cheery, with food stations placed between the bar and crowded dining room; come early if you want a table. Chef Nick Anderer's menu is as big in size as it is in variety. Perhaps start with fried pork terrine and charred scallions or an assorted plate of salami; then on to savory seafood stew or roasted suckling pig and roasted carrots. If you can, save room for vanilla cheesecake with sour cherry sauce or spiced apple cake. What a feast; everything at Maialino is served with the Meyer heritage of superb service.

MALONEY & PORCELLI

37 E 50th St (bet Park and Madison Ave)   212/750-2233
Breakfast, Lunch, Dinner: Daily   maloneyandporcelli.com
Moderately expensive

Alan and Michael Stillman have continually found ways to reenergize this midtown steakhouse, whether it is freshening up the clubby space or adding new items to the menu. But regulars will still be given a warm welcome and can rest assured they will find their favorite listings. Fabulous steaks from

RAW BARS

Connoisseurs of raw-bar delicacies will find these spots to be some of the best in the city. The assortment depends on market availability.

Aquagrill (210 Spring St, 212/274-0505)

Atlantic Grill (1341 Third Ave, 212/988-9200 and 49 W 64th St, 212/787-4663)

Balthazar (80 Spring St, 212/965-1414)

Blue Ribbon (97 Sullivan St, 212/274-0404)

Grand Central Oyster Bar Restaurant (Grand Central Terminal, 42nd St at Vanderbilt Ave, lower level, 212/490-6650)

Marea (240 Central Park S, 212/582-5100)

The Mark Restaurant by Jean-Georges (The Mark, 25 E 77th St, 212/606-3030)

Momofuku Ssäm Bar (207 Second Ave, 212/254-3500)

Ocean Grill (384 Columbus Ave, 212/579-2300)

Oceana (McGraw-Hill Building, 120 W 49th St, 212/759-5941)

Pearl Oyster Bar (18 Cornelia St, 212/691-8211)

beef butchered on premises to pork, veal or lamb shank — are all wonderful. Lobster dishes are another specialty and wine dinners are offered nightly. It is tempting to fill up on the housemade warm pretzel sticks served with mustard butter, but leave room for first-rate appetizers like veal meatballs, crab cakes and lobster bisque. A tempting dessert selection is also available, including icebox chocolate cake with mocha-rum sauce. Inviting private dining rooms would make a special event indeed special.

MARCHI'S

251 E 31st St (at Second Ave)   212/679-2494
Dinner: Mon-Sat   marchirestaurant.com
Moderate

Marchi's has been a New York fixture since 1930, when it was established by the Marchi family in an attractive brownstone townhouse. Three sons are on hand, lending a homey flavor to the restaurant's three dining rooms. It's almost like eating at your favorite Italian family's home, especially since there are no menus. Bring a hearty appetite to take full advantage of a superb five-course feast for a reasonable tab. The first course is a platter of antipasto — including radishes, *finocchio* (Italian winter celery) and Genoa salami — plus a salad of tuna, olives and red cabbage. The second is an absolutely delicious homemade lasagna — the recipe is a family secret. The third is crispy deep-fried fish, light and tempting, served with beets and string beans. The entree is delicious roasted chicken and veal served with fresh mushrooms and tossed salad. Dessert consists of fresh fruit, cheese, lemon fritters and sensational *crostoli* (crisp fried twists sprinkled with powdered sugar). Outside seating in a garden setting provides a little taste of Italy.

MAREA

240 Central Park S (bet Broadway and Seventh Ave)   212/582-5100
Lunch: Mon-Fri; Dinner: Daily; Brunch: Sat, Sun   marea-nyc.com
Expensive

Suitable to its name (Marea means tides in Italian), dinner at this regional Italian seafood restaurant will soothe frazzled nerves. Flawless service, a sleek and classy contemporary setting and beautifully presented coastal cuisine from chef Michael White add to the contentment. Fresh seafood dominates the menu, but a couple of meat and poultry selections are also offered. Lunch and brunch have a *prix-fixe* menu only and a la carte and tasting menus are offered at dinner. Especially notable are the caviar, handmade pasta and *budino di cioccolato* (chocolate pudding) with pomegranate ginger gelato. Bring along a gold credit card!

THE MARK RESTAURANT BY JEAN-GEORGES

The Mark
25 E 77th St (at Madison Ave)   212/606-3030
Breakfast: Daily; Lunch: Mon-Fri; Dinner: Daily; Brunch: Sat, Sun
Moderately expensive   themarkrestaurantnyc.com

Jean-Georges Vongerichten chose a good location at the Mark, and just as you would expect in this classy hotel, you get a very classy restaurant with the added bonus of great people watching. The ladies who lunch. The big-time power brokers. The couples from the society lists. All of them (and you, too) will be enjoying the excellent food: wonderful butternut squash soup, shrimp salad with avocado, veal Milanese and roasted lobster. You will even find a superb burger and a fantastic black-truffle pizza! Save room for the Grand Marnier chocolate chip soufflé. I found the folks who serve to be down to earth, with none of the attitude you might expect at a place like this.

MARKET TABLE

54 Carmine St (at Bedford St)   212/255-2100
Lunch: Mon-Fri; Dinner: Daily; Brunch: Sat, Sun   markettablenyc.com
Moderate

This farm-to-table place is always packed, and it is easy to see why. The food is excellent, the personnel polite and helpful, the prices moderate and the atmosphere inviting (and sometimes loud). It's all about comfort food: nice salads, crispy chicken, lamb shank with crunchy gratin and braised greens and more. The hamburgers alone are worth a visit — huge, juicy and served with delicious fries. An inventive brunch menu includes ham flannel hash and poached eggs with ham biscuits. With great food, good value and a friendly neighborhood location, Market Table is a winner.

MARKJOSEPH STEAKHOUSE

261 Water St (at Peck Slip)   212/277-0020
Lunch: Mon-Fri; Dinner: Daily   markjosephsteakhouse.com
Moderately expensive to expensive

If the trendy uptown steakhouses turn you off, then head downtown — with good directions, as Water Street turns into Pearl Street near this location.

GASTROPUBS

Head to one of these drinking establishments, which also serve really good pub grub:

The Breslin (20 W 29th St, 212/679-1939): casual; British

The Cannibal (113 E 29th St, 212/686-5480 and 600 Eleventh Ave, 212/582-7947): Belgian small plates

DBGB Kitchen and Bar (299 Bowery, 212/933-5300): a Daniel Boulud operation; over a dozen sausage varieties

The Half Pint (76 W 3rd St, 212/260-1088): over 200 types of beers; build-your-own sandwiches

Resto (111 E 29th St, 212/685-5585): meat-heavy Belgian eats

The Spotted Pig (314 W 11th St, 212/620-0393): NYC's first gastropub

This comfortable, homey neighborhood room is high on quality meat (USDA prime dry-aged) and low on attitude. The room is filled with folks in casual garb who are more intent on delving into huge, juicy steaks than wondering who's at the next table. If you're dining with a group, the hot seafood platter (lobster, shrimp, clams, calamari and mussels) is a great place to start. T-bone steak and filet mignon are highly recommended and baked and hash brown potatoes are great side dishes. At lunch, the burgers are big and wonderful, as is the signature steak sandwich. If there's still room for dessert, opt for tartufo or the MarkJoseph special. You'll be surprised at its contents! A private area for larger parties requires reservations.

MARTA

Martha Washington Hotel
29 E 29th St (bet Madison and Park Ave)   212/651-3800
Breakfast, Lunch: Mon-Fri: Dinner: Daily; Brunch: Sat, Sun   martamanhattan.com
Moderate

Danny Meyer has designed an airy space with a copper bar and open kitchen for Marta; just off the lobby of the revamped Martha Washington Hotel. You'll immediately notice two wood-burning ovens and an open-fire grill where chef Nick Anderer creates your meal. There are interesting dishes any time of day: open-fired frittata, rabbit meatballs, fried vegetables and seafood, flash-fired Spanish mackerel, beer-brined chicken, beef short ribs and other trout, lamb and beef dishes. But the star here is the dressed-up pizza — Roman-style; paper-thin crust becomes the landing for delicious 11-inch pies. There are breakfast-inspired pies with lots of mozzarella cheese, ribbons of prosciutto, artichoke hearts and Kalamata olives all surrounding a yolky egg; or try a somewhat healthier choice of Brussels sprouts, cauliflower, pickled chili and parmigiano. Counter seats facing the open kitchen guarantee dinner plus a dough-slinging show.

MICHAEL'S

24 W 55th St (bet Fifth Ave and Ave of the Americas)   212/767-0555
Breakfast, Lunch: Mon-Fri; Dinner: Mon-Sat   michaelsnewyork.com
Moderately expensive

Located conveniently for shoppers, business types, hotel visitors and the like, this very attractive restaurant would best be described as "a midtown scene." Its several rooms are filled with modern art treasures and fresh flowers; you'll see some familiar media faces, society types, important-looking business execs and ordinary fat-walleted gawkers. While items on the classic, contemporary California menu can be pricey, there is no question about the quality or presentation. Appetizers and small plates include clams, oysters and tacos made with duck confit or Korean steak. Lobster risotto and crab gnocchi are tasty offerings, but perhaps the real treat is the fabulous Cobb salad, one of the best in New York. Prepare to splurge!

MILLESIME

The Carlton Hotel
92 Madison Ave (bet 28th and 29th St)   212/889-7100
Breakfast: Daily; Lunch: Mon-Fri; Dinner: Mon-Sat; Brunch: Sun
Moderately expensive   millesimenyc.com

Millesime is a charming, beautiful brasserie with tile floors, soaring walls and a Tiffany skylight dome. This French seafood restaurant offers the old and the new — like wonderful fresh bread, a really good Caesar salad and the almost forgotten quenelles (a seasoned dumpling of fish, meat and poultry) with rich lobster sauce. Expertly prepared shellfish platters for two, four or six people will certainly satisfy. Breakfasts will appease American and French palates alike, with cold cereal, fresh fruit and berries, eggs en cocotte, a salmon plate and many other choices.

MINETTA TAVERN

113 MacDougal St (at Bleecker St)   212/475-3850
Lunch: Wed-Fri; Dinner: Daily; Brunch: Sat, Sun   minettatavernny.com
Moderate

Run by Keith McNally and his team, this longtime Greenwich Village favorite

BAR SNACKS

No need to worry about finding some real goodies when you go out for a drink. Some of the better snacks, along with tasty cocktails, can be found at **Ardesia** (510 W 52nd St, 212-247-9191), **Cicco** (190 Ave of the Americas, 646/476-9498), **Fung Tu** (22 Orchard St, 212/219-8785), **The Gander** (15 W 18th St, 212/229-9500) and **Hanjan** (36 W 26th St, 212/206-7226)— depending on what you have a hankering for at cocktail time. **Alder** (157 Second Ave, 212/539-1900) is also a special place for chicken wings and onion rings. All of these places give one time for pleasant conversation, as well as good dining at the bar.

LA SAVANE

This place is different! For a delicious taste of authentic Ivory Coast-style African food, make your way for lunch or dinner to **La Savane** (239 W 116th St, 646/490-4644) in Harlem. Be forewarned that communication may be a problem unless you speak some French. There may only be a few worn menus available. The small room has limited tables and is rather nondescript (except for the mural of an African village scene), but the pan-African cuisine makes up for it. Generous servings of lamb stew in a creamy peanut sauce, whole guinea fowl that is split and deep-fried or melt-in-your mouth lamb shanks with tomatoes, peppers and onions are more than satisfying. Watch out for the Ivorian Coast hot sauce! You can cool the palate with half-moons of sweet plantain or a punch made of hibiscus blossoms and pineapple juice.

can be a magnet for celebrities. "Parisian steakhouse meets classic New York City tavern" best describes this house. Minetta's ambience: a vintage wall mural, red-leather banquettes, a photo gallery and a long mahogany bar up front have all been preserved. Located where Minetta Brook wandered through Manhattan in the early days, this tavern was made famous by Eddie "Minetta" Sieveri, a friend of many sports and stage stars of yesteryear. Comfort dishes like great burgers, pastas and grilled meats with tasty sides are featured. Everyone is made to feel comfortable here. Night owls will appreciate the supper menu, offered from midnight to 1 a.m.

MISS LILY'S

132 W Houston St (at Sullivan St)   646/588-5375
Lunch, Dinner: Daily; Brunch: Sat, Sun

MISS LILY'S 7A CAFE

109 Ave A (at 7th St)   212/812-1482
Lunch, Dinner: Daily   misslilysnyc.com
Inexpensive to moderate

Wanting a Caribbean getaway? The bright colors and wild patterns of the decor and the cheerful reggae tunes will certainly give you an island vibe at Miss Lily's. Offerings include crispy cod fritters, mac and cheese pie, West Indian curry vegetable stew, curried goat and gravy-doused jerk turkey with roasted yams. The theme continues at brunch with jerk pork belly hash and grilled jerk corn. Signature jerk and jerk barbecue sauce and kettle-style potato chips in curry are available for purchase. Next door to the Soho location, **Melvin's Juice Box** (130 W Houston St, 646/588-5375) specializes in made-to-order fresh juices. The lively bar in the Village cafe focuses on Caribbean rum spirits to add to your tropical escape.

THE MODERN

Museum of Modern Art
9 W 53rd St (bet Fifth Ave and Ave of the Americas)   212/333-1220
Lunch: Mon-Fri; Dinner: Mon-Sat (Dining Room)   themodernnyc.com
Lunch, Dinner: Daily (Bar Room)
Museum hours (Cafe 2 and Terrace 5)
Moderate to moderately expensive (The Modern and Bar Room)

Under the expert eye of restaurateur Danny Meyer, the museum features
four unique dining venues. The Modern's stunning and elegant Dining Room has
a grand view of the outdoor sculpture garden and offers *prix-fixe* and tasting
menus of executive chef Abram Bissell's contemporary American cuisine. The
lobster marinated with truffles or the chicken stuffed with pistachios are just
two of the dishes listed. Next door, the more casual and vibrant Bar Room
offers an a la carte menu for guests who want to create their own multicourse
experience. The tarte flambé is worth a visit in itself. Chef Dan Jackson helms
Cafe 2 and Terrace 5 located on the museum's upper floors. An Italian-inspired
menu is meant to restore guests; there is quick service and a kid-friendly menu,
too.

MORANDI

211 Waverly Pl (at Seventh Ave S)   212/627-7575
Breakfast, Lunch: Mon-Fri; Dinner: Daily; Brunch: Sat, Sun   morandiny.com
Moderate

Morandi is the ultimate location for the Italian food lover who wants
authentic dishes without a huge tab. The setting is comfortable and inviting,
the service prompt and the menu unbelievably complete. You'll find every
antipasti, salad and primi and secondi piatti you could imagine. The paninis and
pastas are delicious along with daily specials; I recommend meatballs with pine
nuts and raisins or dry-aged porterhouse with rosemary for two. A hearty
Italian breakfast is served with Morandi's delicious bread; homemade gelato is
excellent.

THE MORGAN DINING ROOM

The Morgan Library & Museum
225 Madison Ave (bet 36th and 37th St)   212/683-2130
Lunch: Tues-Fri; Brunch: Sat, Sun   themorgan.org
Moderate

The Morgan Library & Museum is a grand place to visit, and you can extend

NARCISSA

A great idea for a delicious meal: **Narcissa** (The Standard, East Village,
21 Cooper Sq, 212/228-3344), where veggie-lovers will think they have
gone to heaven when they order the carrots Wellington dish, at just $20.
The hotel proprietor, André Balazs, owns a farm that sends produce to his
outlet that is fresh and delicious. You name the vegetable and it most likely
is on the menu when you arrive!

HARLEM DINING

Harlem has a growing share of respectable dining options.

Amy Ruth's (113 W 116th St, 212/280-8779): soul food; excellent chicken and waffles

Dinosaur Bar-B-Que (700 W 125th St, 212/694-1777): affordable roadhouse barbecue

Melba's (300 W 114th St, 212/864-7777): down south comfort food; live music Tuesdays

Patsy's Pizzeria (2287-2291 First Ave, 212/534-9783): since 1933

Rao's (455 E 114th St, 212/722-6709): famous Italian landmark

Red Rooster Harlem (310 Lenox Ave, 212/792-9001): affordable comfort food

Sylvia's (328 Lenox Ave, 212/996-0660): soul food and Sunday entertainment

the experience by eating in the original dining room where J.P. Morgan himself broke bread. It is a great place to meet friends and the tab is surprisingly friendly. First courses include salads, soups and seasonal gravlax. Among the tasty entrees are large salads, lobster pot pie and braised pork belly; you'll be attended by a welcoming staff.

MORTON'S THE STEAKHOUSE

551 Fifth Ave (at 45th St)   212/972-3315
136 Washington St (at Albany St)   212/608-0171
Lunch: Mon-Fri; Dinner: Daily   mortons.com
Moderately expensive to expensive

The decor is inviting at both of these modern spaces, and every member of the highly efficient staff has been trained in Morton's manner of personalized service! Appetizers are heavy in the seafood department; shrimp, oysters, smoked salmon, sea scallops and salads are attractive and appetizing. The generously-portioned steaks and lamb chops are so tender you can cut them with a fork, and they arrive promptly, too. (Not the case in many steakhouses.) There are several potato choices, including wonderful hash browns, and the sauteed spinach with mushrooms, steamed broccoli and asparagus are fresh and tasty. The busy bar offers Bar Bites, a menu of tasty small plates of salads, sandwiches, pizza, seafood and various other appetizers. Arrive hungry and be prepared for expense-account prices.

MR. K'S

570 Lexington Ave (at 51st St)   212/583-1668
Lunch, Dinner: Daily   mrksny.com
Moderately expensive to expensive

High-powered politicos and famous celebrities come to dine at this upscale, art deco Chinese room. Whet your appetite with Shanghai spring rolls, dumplings and a delicious seafood dish of sauteed lobster, shrimp and scallops. Of course, there is chicken and corn chowder; in my opinion, no Chinese dinner is complete without it. Share an assortment of plates with your table partners: lemon chicken, Peking duck, honey-braised pork ribs and baked Chilean sea bass. If you like spicy dishes, try the firecracker prawns with Szechuan sauce! Check out the *prix-fixe* lunch and dinner options.

THE MUSKET ROOM

265 Elizabeth St (bet Houston and Prince St)   212/219-0764
Dinner: Daily   musketroom.com
Moderate to moderately expensive

Award-winning chef Matt Lambert serves up inventive dishes at the Musket Room, a rustic space with modern touches and a back room offering a garden view. Meals are meant to reflect the early adventures of the chef's native land and are delivered by a patient, informed staff; you can order a la carte or give in to a six-course tasting meal. Composed dishes might include butternut squash custard; quail with blackberries, roasted onion and bread sauce or beets with goat cheese and pistachios and lemongrass custard. Consider an accompanying kiwi wine to accompany the New Zealand fare.

NAPLES 45

MetLife Building
200 Park Ave (45th St at Vanderbilt Ave)   212/972-7001
Breakfast, Lunch, Dinner: Mon-Fri   patinagroup.com
Moderate

Naples 45 may well be the best pizza house in Manhattan! Absolutely delicious, authentic Neapolitan pizzas are made with caputo flour (imported from Southern Italy) and other tasty ingredients. Cooked in a wood-burning oven, the pizzas are a sight to behold and taste. You have your choice of by-the-slice, individual ten-inch pizzas or their "Mezzo Metro," large enough to feed three or four persons. Other offerings include small dishes (like veal meatballs and baked eggplant), pizza-oven sandwiches, soups, seafood, pastas and salads.

BRING YOUR OWN

Bringing your own bottle of wine to a restaurant is a great savings. However, the vast majority of places do not allow it, or they charge corkage fees ranging from $10 to $50 and up. Here are six reliable spots that welcome BYOs:

Afghan Kebab House (1345 Second Ave, 212/517-2776 and 764 Ninth Ave, 212/307-1612)

Angelica Kitchen (300 E 12th St, 212/228-2909)

Golden Mandarin Court (61 Mott St, 212/608-3838)

Ottomanelli's 86th Street Cafe (1626 York Ave, 212/772-0080)

Tartine (253 W 11th St, 212/229-2611): no corkage fee

Tea & Sympathy (108 Greenwich Ave, 212/989-9735)

Takeout and delivery are available, as is patio dining in nice weather. The place can be jammed (closed on weekends)!

NICOLA'S

146 E 84th St (bet Lexington and Third Ave)   212/249-9850
Dinner: Daily   nicolasnyc.com
Moderately expensive

Upper-crust New Yorkers who like a clubby atmosphere and good food — which are not often found together — love this U.E.S. place! In a setting of rich wood with familiar framed faces on the walls, the noise level at times rivals that of a Broadway opening. No-nonsense waiters serve delicious platters of pasta, veal, chicken and fish. The emphasis is Italian, and there are inviting daily specials in every category.

NINJA NEW YORK

25 Hudson St (bet Duane and Reade St)   212/274-8500
Dinner: Daily   ninjanewyork.com
Moderately expensive

Be prepared for loads of fun and the unexpected as you enter a ninja village re-creation — fire, chants, screams, swords, hand signals and costumed ninja servers — all while enjoying a Japanese-style dinner. This is a perfect spot to celebrate with friends in either the Village or Rock Garden dining rooms. Three- and four-course dinners and an a la carte menu offer sushi, sashimi, appetizers, a variety of main courses and desserts, many of which are prepared and served with special effects. The signature dish, Katana, is Angus steak with fried risotto and Alaska king crab with tomato mango sauce. Kids will get a kick out of the ninja antics; beware of ninjas dropping in from the ceiling or appearing out of nowhere.

NOBU 57

40 W 57th St (bet Fifth Ave and Ave of the Americas)   212/757-3000
Lunch: Mon-Sat; Dinner: Daily

NOBU NEW YORK

105 Hudson St (at Franklin St)   212/219-0500
Lunch: Mon-Fri; Dinner: Daily

NOBU NEXT DOOR

105 Hudson St (at Franklin St)   212/334-4445
Dinner: Daily; Brunch: Sat, Sun   noburestaurants.com
Moderately expensive

Nobu Matsuhisa and partners have put together spectacular venues for those who love sushi and great Japanese food that's not too complex and unfailingly tasty. Yes, these places are busy and expensive, but they are worth every penny and any frustrating wait for reservations. Because I like vibrant flavors, this menu appeals to me. The Nobu eateries are classy and crowded, with an unmistakable party atmosphere. Sitting at the sushi bar allows you to watch the well-trained staff perform like a symphony orchestra. The black cod miso is a standout; dozens of sushi and sashimi selections are available. The chef's choice multicourse *omakase* dinner is an excellent pick and fresh, delicious salads abound. Leave room for the Bento Box dessert: warm chocolate soufflé cake with green-tea ice cream. You're going to pay well for all these treats but you'll leave relishing a very special dining experience. Note that Nobu Next Door serves an inventive weekend brunch.

NOMAD

NoMad Hotel
1170 Broadway   347/472-5660
Breakfast, Lunch, Dinner: Daily   thenomadhotel.com
Moderately expensive to expensive

Delectable American-European fare is served up just off the lobby of the NoMad Hotel. Award-winning Daniel Humm has created a somewhat fancy, yet relaxed setting within the several rooms of his restaurant. The Parlour and the glass-enclosed Atrium rooms offer a la carte dining; only snacks and cocktails are available in the Library and stand-up bar areas. Suckling pig, tagliatelle with crab and roast chicken are excellent entrees, while the Milk and Honey dessert is a delicious ending to the meal. Mark this location for your next special occasion.

NORTH END GRILL

104 North End Ave (bet Murray and Vesey St)   646/747-1600
Lunch: Mon-Fri; Dinner: Daily; Brunch: Sat, Sun   northendgrillnyc.com
Moderately expensive

SPANISH FOOD TERMS

In case you're wondering what you're eating in a Spanish or Mexican restaurant, let this list be your guide.

Ajo: garlic

A la plancha: cooked over hot griddle

Bacalao: salt cod

Boquerones: Spanish white anchovies

Calamares en su tinta: squid cooked in its ink

Callos: tripe

Chorizo: smoked pork Spanish sausage

Churros con chocolate: fried dough dipped in rich hot chocolate

Flan: custard dessert

Gambas al ajillo: shrimp cooked with garlic

Jamon serrano: Iberian cured ham

Langostinos: prawns

Merluza: hake

Queso manchego: nutty tasting aged Spanish cheese

LUZZO'S PIZZA

If you can track it down, **Luzzo's** pizza cart dispenses good stuff in less than a minute from a coal-fired oven and at a tiny $7 to $8 price; locations announced on Twitter. A full menu of Italian appetizers, soups, salads and artisanal pizzas is available at the original brick-and-mortar joint (211 First Ave, 212/473-7447).

Danny Meyer has used his magic touch to bring us some of the city's best eating places, seemingly anywhere in Manhattan. North End Grill is situated way downtown at Battery Park City, next to the Conrad Hotel. The kitchen puts out tasty American food with a seafood emphasis; typically, the service is prompt and informative, and a buzz is definitely present. You may enjoy eating at a bar (open for drinks all day) looking into the open kitchen or in the more formal dining room. The market-driven menu features a variety of grilling techniques; for starters, you'll find a unique grilled-clam pizza. Pork chops, lamb chops, steaks and fish — all grilled — are delicious entrees, especially with a side of decadent duck fat fries. Sunday night diners should consider the shellfish bake with lobster, prawns, mussels, clams, new potatoes and corn. For dessert, Almond Joy ice cream cake with passion fruit and warm fudge sauce is a winner. As expected, genial general manager Kevin Richer keeps the place humming in professional Meyer style.

OCEAN GRILL

384 Columbus Ave (at 78th St)   212/579-2300
Lunch: Mon-Sat; Dinner: Daily; Brunch: Sun   oceangrill.com
Moderate

Ocean Grill is one of the few good seafood restaurants on the Upper West Side, white tablecloths and all. Watching the passing parade from an outside sidewalk table is fun. Popular with young professionals, the place is quite noisy. To start, the raw bar offers a selection of oysters and sushi. Mainstay listings of simply grilled fish — salmon, tuna, mahi-mahi, wild striped bass and more — are prepared with your choice of marinades and sauces. For a party, chilled shellfish towers offer a selection of lobster, clams, crab, oysters and shrimp. Other attractions include crab cakes and lobster bisque as well as a *prix-fixe* option for lunch. For brunch, various omelets and Benedicts, as well as buttermilk pancakes and cinnamon raisin French toast are good bets.

OCEANA

McGraw-Hill Building
120 W 49th St (bet Ave of the Americas and Seventh Ave)   212/759-5941
Breakfast: Mon-Fri; Lunch: Mon-Fri; Dinner: Daily   oceanarestaurant.com
Moderately expensive

You'll want to dine at Oceana for the freshest seafood meal. The location is spot-on; so is the 50-foot-long Italian marble bar, featuring innovative small bites and potent drink concoctions. It's all here — cafe and raw bar, private dining and a large expansive dining room — and each menu item is outstandingly prepared to capture the best flavor of the fresh catch. Check the menu for seafood towers (appropriately named the Radio City, the Rock and the Oceana), General Tsao's lobster, seafood charcuterie plate and chocolate layer trifecta. Oceana is also an ideal choice for pre- and post-theater gatherings.

ONE IF BY LAND, TWO IF BY SEA

17 Barrow St (bet Seventh Ave and 4th St)   212/255-8649
Dinner: Daily; Brunch: Sat, Sun   oneifbyland.com
Expensive

One if by Land, Two if by Sea is housed in an 18th-century carriage house once owned by Aaron Burr. Allow extra time to find this place, as Barrow Street (one of the West Village's most charming) is generally unknown to taxi drivers, and there's no sign out front! Candlelight, flowers, a fireplace and background piano music all add to the ambience of this romantic room. Tables at the front of the balcony are particularly appealing. Individual beef Wellington, spice-rubbed lobster and rack of pork chops are excellent choices on the three-course *prix-fixe* menu; a chef's tasting menu is also available. Bourbon and banana French toast served at brunch is quite tasty.

ONIEAL'S GRAND STREET

174 Grand St (bet Lafayette and Mulberry St)   212/941-9119
Dinner, Late Night Menu, Brunch: Daily   onieals.com
Moderate

This legendary and historic former speakeasy, with its secret tunnel to the old police headquarters, evokes memories of days long past. Housed beneath a 150-year-old hand-carved mahogany ceiling, this bar, lounge and restaurant achieved latter-day celebrity as a backdrop on HBO's *Sex and the City*. You'll find marinated grilled yellowfin tuna, Cobb salad, hanger steak au poivre, shitake risotto and one of the best burgers in town. For dessert, try the Four Devils chocolate cake (named after the four devils intricately carved into the ceiling). Service at Onieal's is friendly and efficient.

ORSO

322 W 46th St (bet Eighth and Ninth Ave)   212/489-7212
Lunch: Mon-Fri; Dinner: Daily; Brunch: Sun   orsorestaurant.com
Moderate

This cozy midtown trattoria features the same menu all day long and is an excellent choice for theatergoers. Orso is one of the most popular places on

KALE FATIGUE

Are you tired of the kale craze? Sure it can be tasty and packs lots of nutrients (vitamins A, C and K), but in New York City restaurants it is has become as ubiquitous as pinot grigio. Now cauliflower is becoming the new kale. Expect to find it everywhere, even if is not visible on the plate. But, oh, the smell!

DAIRY QUEEN

Dairy Queen outlets seem much more at home in mid-America than in the canyons of the Big Apple, but, alas, not any more. The first outlet of this place famous for good burgers and the fabulous Blizzards has opened at 54 W 14th Street. The kids will love the famous rich drink (in a number of flavors) served upside down! And this is a great place for kids' birthday parties or to get an ice cream cake for celebrations at home. Prices are very comfortable.

restaurant row, so if you're planning to dine here, be sure to make reservations. The intimate room is watched over by a portrait of Orso, a Venetian street dog who served as the restaurant's inspiration. The changing menu offers many good salads, appetizers and small plates, as well as a variety of pizzas and pasta dishes. Venetian-style sauteed calves liver and oven-roasted quail stuffed with sausage are two popular regional favorites. A three-course *prix-fixe* lunch menu is available weekdays and there is a special Sunday brunch menu as well. Apple crostata with vanilla gelato, one of many homemade desserts, will finish off a great meal.

OSTERIA MORINI

218 Lafayette St (bet Kenmare and Spring St) 212/965-8777
Lunch: Mon-Fri; Dinner: Daily; Brunch: Sat, Sun osteriamorini.com
Moderate to moderately expensive

Osteria Morini, under the capable direction of chef Michael White, is a superb Northern Italian house. This is not just another Italian restaurant! Calorie-counting is out and great taste is the order of each meal. Diners will find a bit of Old World decor, a lot of noise and waiters who can't do enough for their patrons. The handmade pastas, like apple and sweet potato-filled pasta or truffled ricotta ravioli will please any discerning palate. A number of veal, lamb and fish dishes (like grilled sea bass), plus succulent braised beef short ribs round out the delicious menu. Chef White is the consummate host, delighting in personally visiting with his guests. I would hope that he is cooking the night you are there.

OUEST

2315 Broadway (at 84th St) 212/580-8700
Dinner: Daily; Brunch: Sun ouestny.com
Moderate to moderately expensive

This U.W.S. eatery continues to be overflowing with happy locals enjoying one of the best rooms in the city. The comfortable booths, open kitchen, cozy (if dark and noisy) balcony and pleasant serving staff combine to make Tom Valenti's jewel first-class. This is not surprising with Valenti's vast experience. The inventive American fare is inviting, with appetizer choices like jumbo crispy-fried oysters, winter truffle omelet soufflé and several fresh salads. Grilled duck breast, braised lamb shank and roasted stuffed quail melt in your mouth. From delicious warm bread at the start to dense chocolate cake for dessert, the experience at Ouest is pure pleasure.

P.J. CLARKE'S
915 Third Ave (at 55th St)   212/317-1616

P.J. CLARKE'S AT LINCOLN SQUARE
44 W 63rd St (at Columbus Ave)   212/957-9700

P.J. CLARKE'S ON THE HUDSON
4 World Financial Center (at Vesey St)   212/285-1500
Lunch, Dinner: Daily   pjclarkes.com
Moderate

Beginning in 1884 as a saloon, P.J. Clarke's can rightfully be called a Manhattan institution. Every day at lunch and dinner, regulars are joined by hordes of visitors guzzling at the liquor bar, eyeing the raw bar or fighting for a table. No one is disappointed with the sizable platters, great burgers and fresh seafood. Check out the daily blackboard specials and numerous tasty sides. Service is highly professional, and the price is right. Upstairs at the Third Avenue location, you'll be taken with the decor at **The Sidecar** (212/317-2044), which has its own kitchen and entrance. All patrons at P.J. Clarke's on the Hudson have a stunning view of New York Harbor and the Statue of Liberty, and a seasonal cafe alongside the marina is great for leisurely dining. The 63rd Street locale is a stellar place before or after a performance at Lincoln Center.

THE PALM
837 Second Ave (at 44th St)   212/687-2953
Lunch: Mon-Fri; Dinner: Mon-Sat
840 Second Ave (at 44th St)   212/697-5198
206 West St (at Warren St)   646/395-6393
Lunch: Mon-Fri; Dinner: Daily
250 W 50th St (bet Eighth Ave and Broadway)   212/333-7256
Lunch: Mon-Sat; Dinner: Daily   thepalm.com
Moderately expensive

Steak and lobster lovers still hold a special place in their hearts for The Palm, even with the glut of steakhouses in Manhattan. The original location on

WI-FI A LA CARTE
Mobile technology is the wave of the future, even in restaurants. An increasing number of places allow ordering from the menu with your iPhone, paying the bill, calculating the check and tip, even sending real time feedback to owners. And if the restaurant has your phone number, every time you are in the neighborhood it can send you enticements to come in, like a free drink. Open Table has introduced an app that allows this technology... that is a pretty big deal!

Second Avenue started as a speakeasy in 1926. There are now four locations, all with much the same atmosphere — masculine and earthy — so don't get too dressed up. They're noted for huge, delicious steaks, chops and jumbo Nova Scotia lobster. Don't miss the terrific "half and half" — cottage fries and onion rings. Daily specials vary among The Palm locations, and unfortunately, indolent waiters may be a part of the scene.

PAOLA'S

Hotel Wales
1295 Madison Ave (at 92nd St)   212/794-1890
Lunch, Dinner: Daily; Brunch: Sat, Sun   paolasrestaurant.com
Moderately expensive

Paola's is a wonderful and welcoming place for lunch or a romantic evening! The Italian home cooking is first-class, with matriarch Paola overseeing the kitchen. Great filled pastas (like rigatoni with spicy sausage and mushrooms) and superb veal dishes are served with tasty hot vegetables. Top it all off with a slice of rich ricotta cheesecake or lemon tart with cappuccino. Casual sidewalk dining is offered in summer months.

PARK SIDE

107-01 Corona Ave (51st Ave at 108th St), Queens   718/271-9274
Lunch, Dinner: Daily   parksiderestaurantny.com
Moderate

I've included this landmark Italian restaurant because it is exceptional, even though it is outside of Manhattan. Visit Park Side, in Queens, if you want to show someone who claims to know everything about New York a place he or she likely hasn't heard about. Or eat here on your way to or from LaGuardia or Kennedy airports. This first-class, spotlessly clean restaurant serves large portions of wonderful Italian food at reasonable prices. Start with garlic bread and then choose from nearly 20 kinds of pasta and an opulent array of fish, steak, veal and poultry dishes. The meat is all prime-cut and fresh — nothing frozen. Finish with a choice from the extensive dessert menu. You'll find polite, tuxedoed waiters who are very knowledgeable. Get a table in the Garden Room or the Marilyn Monroe Room upstairs.

PATSY'S ITALIAN RESTAURANT

236 W 56th St (bet Broadway and Eighth Ave)   212/247-3491
Lunch, Dinner: Daily   patsys.com
Moderate

Since 1944 the Scognamillo family has operated this popular eatery, specializing in homemade Neapolitan cuisine. The late Patsy Scognamillo and his wife, Concetta, founded the restaurant; at present, son, Joe, is taking care of the front of the house, while grandson, Sal, is following the family tradition in the kitchen. Patsy was an immigrant gentleman chef whose nickname graces this bilevel restaurant. Each floor has its own cozy atmosphere and convenient kitchen. The family makes sure that every party is treated with courtesy and concern, as if they are in a private home. A full Italian menu includes a special soup and seafood entree each day. If you can't find what you like among the more than a dozen pasta choices and the many signature dishes — chicken cacciatore, veal chop siciliano or stuffed calamari — you are in deep trouble! There are also *prix-fixe* lunch and dinner (pre-theater) menus, which are convenient if you are headed to Lincoln Center, Carnegie Hall or the Theater District.

PERILLA

9 Jones St (bet Bleecker and 4th St)   212/929-6868
Dinner: Daily; Brunch: Sat, Sun   perillanyc.com
Moderate

Perilla is a good bet for a leisurely weekend brunch in the Village. With equal quality in both food and service, this neighborhood hideaway offers an ever-changing New American menu of satisfying flavors. For brunch, creamy white grits, vanilla scented doughnuts and French toast are tasty choices. Of course there are nightly dinners, too. Try spicy duck meatballs or the Monday night bourbon barbecue tasting. I found the dessert offerings to be particularly appealing. The cheese selection is excellent and reasonably priced. The milk chocolate malted cake or vanilla panna cotta with grapefruit sorbet are interesting choices. Perilla really packs a lot into a compact, informal space of 18 tables and ten bar seats.

PETER LUGER STEAK HOUSE

178 Broadway (at Driggs Ave), Brooklyn   718/387-7400
Lunch, Dinner: Daily   peterluger.com
Expensive

If it's steak you want, you simply can't do better than Peter Luger Steak House. Their reputation is sometimes larger than the restaurant itself! Folks don't come to this bustling spot for the ambience or service. The menu makes it simple: your choices are steak for one, two, three or four. The creamed spinach and steak sauce (which they sell by the bottle) are out of this world. Daily luncheon specials include pot roast, roast prime rib and chopped steak. Peter Luger is only a stone's throw from Manhattan (take the first right off the Williamsburg Bridge), and the staff is accustomed to ordering cabs. Making reservations well in advance is suggested.

PICHOLINE

35 W 64th St (bet Broadway and Central Park W)   212/724-8585
Dinner: Daily   picholinenyc.com
Moderately expensive to expensive

Picholine is an attractive restaurant near Lincoln Center where Terrance Brennan showcases his culinary expertise. The warm atmosphere is achieved through the use of dusky lavender, shades of purple and crystal chandeliers; a perfect backdrop for the seasonal, Mediterranean-inspired plates. The many positives include outstanding service with superbly prepared fish, game, lamb, beef and more. Choose from a three-course *prix-fixe* dinner or larger course tasting menus. Two private dining options include the intimate wine room (seats four to eight) lined with 2,500 wine bottles and featuring a cheese cave; the elegant L'Olivier Room seats up to 22 guests. I always look forward to the magnificent cheese dessert cart, with more than 60 artisanal cheeses; there is also a separate wine and cheese bar. Jackets are preferred for gentlemen.

PIETRO'S

232 E 43rd St (bet Second and Third Ave)   212/682-9760
Lunch: Mon-Fri; Dinner: Mon-Sat (closed Sat in summer)   pietrosnyc.com
Moderately expensive

Pietro's is a steakhouse featuring Northern Italian cuisine with everything cooked to order. The dining room is not at all fancy, so tell your companions not to bother dressing up; bring an appetite, however, because portions are huge. Regulars come mostly for delicious dry-aged prime steaks, but the extensive menu also lists chicken and veal selections (marsala, cacciatore, scaloppine, piccata, francaise, etc.), seafood, chops, pasta and nine potato dishes. Prices border on expensive, but you'll certainly get your money's worth. By the way, Pietro's is very child-friendly with an accommodating staff.

PIORA

430 Hudson St (bet Morton St and St. Lukes Pl)   212/960-3801
Dinner: Daily   pioranyc.com
Moderately expensive

Vegetarians will especially enjoy dining at Piora in the West Village. Enter past a long bar into a snug, serene dining space brightened by a window wall of lit trees. Here chef Chris Cipollone's American plates show Korean and Italian influences in elegant fruit and vegetable preparations. The signature vegetable salad is playful and flavorful and pasta dishes are popular; rigatoni and duck sausage is a favorite. Other worthy entrees include confit chicken nuggets nestled in pureed potatoes and crisp-skinned ocean trout spiked with pork sausage spread; be sure to taste the monkey bread. For now at least, skip the desserts.

PLAZA FOOD HALL

The Plaza
1 W 59th St (at Fifth Ave), lower level   212/986-9260
Mon-Sat: 8 a.m.-9:30 p.m.; Sun: 11-6   theplazany.com
Varying price ranges

Inspired by European food halls, the concourse of the famed Plaza Hotel is alive with tantalizing aromas, beautiful foods and the bustle of diners and shoppers enjoying an array of edible items (and nonedible) within the stained-glass, mosaic-tiled space. The idea first began with the Todd English Food Hall where nine food stations include a bakery, sushi bar, cheese and charcuterie, fresh seafood and raw bar, grill (sliders, salads and burgers), dumpling bar, brick-oven pizza, wine bar and seasonal marketplace. A demo kitchen features cooking classes, wine tastings and other events; the area can be rented for private parties. With its success the project expanded into the 32,000-square-foot Plaza Food Hall and the addition of another 20 carefully selected eateries:

Billy's Bakery, Chi Noodle Bar, Lady M, La Maison du Chocolat, Luke's Lobster, No. 7 Sub, Piada, Sabi Sushi, William Greenberg Desserts and others. There are counter seats at some kiosks and another 75 seats in a communal area where you can enjoy the offerings from the interesting mix of food shops.

PÓ

31 Cornelia St (bet Bleecker and 4th St)	212/645-2189
Lunch: Wed-Sun; Dinner: Daily	porestaurant.com
Moderate	

Steven Crane has found the formula for a successful eating establishment. The small space is always busy; the service is family-friendly, informed and quick. The food is hearty, imaginative and exceptionally tasty, plus the prices are right. As I have noted before, if the bread is good, chances are what follows will be also. Pó has crusty, fresh Italian bread. The creative pasta dishes — tagliatelle, fettuccine, linguine and a special or two — are huge. Other entrees (like grilled salmon or veal picatta) are available, along with lunch paninis like grilled portobello with roasted peppers. Affogato, an unusual and satisfying dessert, consists of coffee gelato in chilled cappuccino with chocolate caramel sauce.

THE POLO BAR

1 E 55th St (at Fifth Ave)	212/207-8562
Dinner: Daily (Bar opens at 3 p.m.)	ralphlauren.com
Moderately expensive to expensive	

Ralph Lauren's long-awaited Polo Bar occupies the space next door to his flagship store. With burnished wood paneling, hunter green walls, a fireplace, leather banquettes and a brass-topped bar, the room is everything you would expect from his collections — preppy American, the Wild West and stylish sportif. The wait staff are capable and beautifully outfitted in custom grey flannel trousers. At press time Polo Bar is only open for dinner, with the iconic designer's favorite American dishes being served: crab cakes, grilled fish, steaks, burgers, corned beef sandwiches, BLT salads, caviar and fingerling potatoes and more; finish with housemade coffee ice cream or a cup of Polo's custom coffee blend. This is an excellent place to begin a new family tradition.

PRINT

Ink48	
653 Eleventh Ave (at 48th St)	212/757-2224
Breakfast, Lunch: Mon-Fri; Dinner: Daily; Brunch: Sat, Sun	printrestaurant.com
Moderate	

On the far reaches of the West Side, this repurposed printing factory offers attractive dining located off the hotel lobby of Ink48. The mood is modern and comfortable, with pleasant personnel serving farm-to-table dishes that are uniformly tasty. Chef Charles Rodriguez is in the kitchen serving up fresh salads, soups, chicken, steak and whatever else makes a traveler happy. The braised short ribs with smashed rutabaga, seared sea scallops with sunchoke puree and Brussels sprouts with black trumpet mushroom sauce are first-class. The extensive brunch menu features apple confit lemon cake and an excellent fried

IT CAN HAPPEN TO THE BEST OF THEM

Danny Meyer's operations have always been consistently first-rate, but over the last couple of years there have been some cracks in this beautiful façade. Because of a plethora of changing chefs at Mr. Meyer's restaurants, not all have remained at Meyer standards. Happily, it seems that there may now be a charge for renewal as seen at both Blue Smoke and North End Grill. With chef Jean-Paul Bourgeois presently at **Blue Smoke**, the contemporary Southern offerings are now head-of-the-pack; seven-pepper rubbed beef brisket is delicious. And at **North End Grill**, chef Eric Korsh maximizes the wood grill; his charcuterie is worth a visit by itself. So it would seem that even the best of restaurants must continually work to remain at the top of their game, and Danny Meyer's houses are no exception.

chicken sandwich with cabbage jalapeno coleslaw accompanied by exceptional French fries piled high. On a clear day, be sure to visit the rooftop lounge, **Press**, for fantastic panoramic views of the city.

QUALITY MEATS

57 W 58th St (bet Fifth Ave and Ave of the Americas)   212/371-7777
Lunch: Mon-Fri; Dinner: Daily   qualitymeatsnyc.com
Moderately expensive to expensive

This midtown quasi-steakhouse has become popular with younger meat lovers with its butcher-shop like space on several levels; pulleys and meat scales have been creatively transformed into lighting fixtures. Quality Meats has all the basics soundly covered and the kitchen and wait staff really know what they are doing. The beginning course lists extensive oyster selections, ample salads and other tasty appetizers. Entrees include a number of steaks (the filet is fantastic), seared scallops, Cajun short ribs and veal chops. Don't pass up pan-roasted crispy potatoes, gnocchi and cheese, sauteed spinach and grilled asparagus. For dessert, the homemade ice creams are a treat (especially the coffee and doughnuts flavor) as are the red velvet cake and warm apple-plum tart; the Charcuterie Bar offers individual items and a sampler plate as well.

RAINBOW ROOM

30 Rockefeller Plaza, 65th floor   212/632-5000
Dinner: Mon; Brunch: Sun   rainbowroom.com
Expensive

What great memories of wining and dining and dancing halfway to heaven in the Rainbow Room at Rock Center. It was closed for some time, but now it is back in business catering especially to special events. The rooftop setting is glorious, the views magnificent, the food quite good and the prices are in keeping with the location (sky high). If you feel like a special dinner dance, the room is open for dinner with music and all the trimmings on Monday evenings. An international Sunday brunch is also available for the public; check for reservations on special holidays. The former Pavilion, **SixtyFive**, is a cocktail lounge with an outdoor terrace; food is served Monday through Friday evenings.

RAO'S

455 E 114th St (at First Ave)   212/722-6709
Dinner: Mon-Fri   raos.com
Moderately expensive

If you want to go to Rao's — an intimate, old-time (1896) Italian restaurant — it will take a lot of luck and you will need to plan a bit in advance — like a year ahead! The place is crowded all the time for several reasons: the Neapolitan cuisine is great, celebrity-watching is fantastic and there are only ten tables and one seating. If you're lucky enough to score a "rez," don't walk or take a car; hail a taxi and step out in front of the Spanish Harlem restaurant, and when you're ready to leave, they will call a cab. Frankie Pellegrino is a gregarious and charming host who makes guests feel right at home and will even sit at your table while you order. Be prepared for leisurely dining, and while you're waiting, enjoy the excellent bread and warm atmosphere. Believe it or not, besides the luscious, award-winning pasta, the Southern fried chicken (Rao's style) is absolutely superb and would be my number-one choice. No credit cards.

RAOUL'S

180 Prince St (bet Sullivan and Thompson St)   212/966-3518
Dinner: Daily   raouls.com
Moderately expensive

There are dozens of good places to eat in Soho, and Raoul's is certainly one to visit. This long, narrow French bistro used to be an old saloon and three dining areas include a loft and a hidden garden. The lively neighborhood favorite is somewhat of an art gallery with a picture collection lining the walls. House favorites include paté maison, artichokes with vinaigrette and steak au poivre. Whatever your choice, Raoul's is laid-back and friendly and a natural for those whose days begin when the rest of us are ready to hit the sack.

RARE BAR & GRILL

Affinia Shelburne
303 Lexington Ave (at 37th St)   212/481-1999

Hilton New York Fashion District
152 W 26th St (bet Ave of the Americas and Seventh Ave)   212/807-7273
Breakfast, Lunch, Dinner: Daily; Brunch: Sat, Sun   rarebarandgrill.com
Moderate

If noise is your thing, you will be right at home at Rare. At the Lexington Avenue location, tables are filled with yuppies and button-down business types, and this restaurant literally vibrates with energy. The food is almost secondary to the scene, but the burgers are fabulous. You can get a classic burger or order

TIME WARNER CENTER DINING

The exclusive address of the **Time Warner Center** (10 Columbus Cir) is home to upscale shops, markets and restaurants. As you would expect, the variety is wide and prices are generally expensive. **A Voce** (212/823-2523, Italian), **Bouchon Bakery** (212/823-9366, American/ French) and **Landmarc** (212/823-6123, French) are all on the third floor. **Center Bar** (212/823-9482, tapas-style small plates), **Masa** and the more modest **Bar Masa** (212/823-9800, Japanese), **Per Se** (212/823-9335, American/French) and **Porter House New York** (212/823-9500) have stylish dining facilities on the fourth floor. All are open for dinner, and most serve lunch. Call well in advance for reservations. Also on this floor is **Stone Rose Lounge** (212/823-9769), a prime venue for cocktails and small bites.

vegetable. They also serve a tasting basket of French fries (cottage, shoestring, sweet potato and parmesan truffle with three dipping sauces), salads and soups. The more recent Fashion District location is in the hotel lobby. There are some differences in menu offerings, so if you have a favorite item in mind, you might call ahead. Check out the panoramic view from the rooftop lounge, **Rare View**, at each bar and grill location.

RECETTE

328 W 12th St (at Greenwich St)   212/414-3000
Dinner: Daily; Brunch: Sun   recettenyc.com
Moderately expensive

Enter the white-paned doors and you will find yourself ensconced in this casual yet sophisticated Greenwich Village establishment. Chef Jesse Schenker adjusts an inventive, seasonal menu; diners can order from one of three tasting menu options (five-, seven- and ten-course) or a la carte for playful and flavorful American snacks and small plates; scallops, duck breast, venison, pork belly and more are combined in tantalizing and unique flavor combinations. Decadent desserts prepared by pastry chef Christina Lee make a delicious finish.

RED ROOSTER HARLEM

310 Lenox Ave (bet 125th and 126th St)   212/792-9001
Lunch: Mon-Fri; Dinner: Daily; Brunch: Sat, Sun   redroosterharlem.com
Moderate

In Marc Samuelsson's crowded, boisterous house, you will see both old-time and modern Harlem touches that are meant to welcome you into the neighborhood. American fare with heavy Southern accents include shrimp and dirty rice, fried yard bird (chicken), blackened catfish and grits and Helga's meatballs — all worth crowing about. Additional items: cauliflower and oyster soup, sweet potato-filled doughnuts, pineapple upside down cake and black bottom peanut pie with rum-raisin ice cream. Be sure to make a reservation to ensure a seat as Red Rooster has become a popular destination for comfort cooking at its best. Upstairs, **Ginny's Supper Club** (212/421-3821) offers live jazz and blues performances most evenings.

REDEYE GRILL

890 Seventh Ave (at 56th St)   212/541-9000
Lunch: Mon-Fri; Dinner: Daily; Brunch: Sat, Sun   redeyegrill.com
Moderately expensive

Owner Sheldon Fireman has created an eye-appealing, sophisticated house across from Carnegie Hall; the mega room is a bustling place. American and seafood dishes are featured with specialties of the house including all shapes and sizes of shrimp, a huge seafood appetizer platter, grilled fish and pastas. Steaks, burgers, egg dishes, sushi and their famous lobster Cobb salad round out the menu. The personnel are hip and helpful, but the busy scene is the major attraction. Live music is featured nightly, and outdoor terrace dining is available during spring, summer and fall.

REDFARM

2170 Broadway (bet 76th and 77th St)   212/724-9700
Lunch: Mon-Fri; Dinner: Daily; Brunch: Sat, Sun
529 Hudson St (bet Charles and W 10th St)   212/792-9700
Dinner: Mon-Fri; Brunch: Sat, Sun   redfarmnyc.com
Moderate

These noisy and busy eateries are serving up some of the best Chinese cuisine in Manhattan. The inventive menu is full of upscale, creative takes on traditional items, merging Chinese and Western flavors. Start with unusual pastrami egg rolls or shrimp and mango fried wontons. Grilled short ribs with udon noodles, crispy-skin smoked chicken with garlic and delicious dumplings are suggested savory entrees. Servers are pleasant and accommodating within the rustic, yet modern walls. Note that the newer Upper West Side location is much larger than the tiny West Village space and could make a difference as to seating.

WE ARE NOT PULLING YOUR LEG

Feline fans can have their treats and petting, too. **Meow Parlour** (46 Hester Street) is a cheerful cafe where customers can enjoy coffee and snacks while petting all manner of cats (they are available for adoption).

REMI

145 W 53rd St (bet Ave of the Americas and Seventh Ave)   212/581-4242
Lunch: Mon-Fri; Dinner: Daily
Moderate   remi-nyc.com

With a spectacular space in midtown, Remi is handy to hotels and theaters. In an unusually long room dominated by a dramatic 120-foot Venetian wall painting by Paulin Paris, the food soars as high as the setting. In warm weather, the doors open up and diners can enjoy sitting at tables in the adjoining atrium. Waiters' attire, chairs and wall fabrics all match in attractive stripes. Antipasto such as baked eggplant

FAVORITE CHOCOLATE DESSERTS

Bar Room at The Modern (Museum of Modern Art, 9 W 53rd St, 212/333-1220): chocolate and hazelnut dacquoise

Bouley (163 Duane St, 212/964-2525): the Chocolate Frivolous

Cafe Lalo (201 W 83rd St, 212/496-6031): Chocolate Madness

Craft (43 E 19th St, 212/780-0880): chocolate soufflé

Jean Georges (Trump International Hotel and Tower, 1 Central Park W, 212/299-3900): warm, soft chocolate cake

La Grenouille (3 E 52nd St, 212/752-1495): chocolate soufflé

The Spotted Pig (314 W 11th St, 212/620-0393): flourless chocolate cake

and mozzarella gratinée will get you off to a delicious start. Come here for the best seafood risotto in town! The spaghetti, taglioni and ravioli can match any house in Venice; of course there are fish and meat dishes for more mainstream appetites. The chocolate-raspberry mousse cake is superb. Paddle on down (Remi is Italian for oars) for a first-class experience; private rooms are available or make use of convenient takeout and delivery.

RESTO

111 E 29th St (bet Lexington and Park Ave)	212/685-5585
Lunch: Mon-Fri; Dinner: Daily; Brunch: Sat, Sun	restonyc.com
Moderate	

This Belgian gastropub offers much more than the delicious burgers for which they have become famous. With an emphasis on seasonal, farm-fresh ingredients, you will find small plates (like deviled eggs with pork toast, mustard spaetzle with duck confit and Tuscan kale salad) and a collection of house charcuterie; the housemade bratwurst is exceptional. Larger plates include steak and onions and roasted chicken. With a week's advance notice you can enjoy the Nose to Tail feast of pig, goat, lamb or beef. Resto's extensive list of Belgian beers adds to the attraction at this popular spot.

RIVER CAFÉ

1 Water St (Brooklyn Bridge), Brooklyn	718/522-5200
Lunch: Sat; Dinner: Daily; Brunch: Sun	therivercafe.com
Moderately expensive	

No visit to New York City is complete without a meal at Brooklyn's 40-year-old River Café. Superstorm Sandy did damage to this romantic spot, but thankfully, all is back in order, with the food and setting better than ever. What to eat? Anything! The steak tartare, the rack of lamb or the great seafood are all highly recommended. Chef Brad Steelman has a brand new kitchen in which he prepares dishes that will long be remembered. For a really special occasion, you can't do better!

ROSA MEXICANO

1063 First Ave (at 58th St)   212/753-7407
Lunch: Sat, Sun; Dinner: Daily

61 Columbus Ave (at 62nd St)   212/977-7700
9 E 18th St (bet Fifth Ave and Broadway)   212/533-3350
Lunch, Dinner: Daily   rosamexicano.com
Moderate

Rosa Mexicano offers regionally-authentic Mexican cuisine in a fun, festive atmosphere. Start with the signature tableside guacamole or a pomegranate margarita. There are also great fresh salads, handmade tacos, sandwiches (at lunch) and many chicken, beef and seafood entrees. Ask about the three-course sharing menu which offers some of the best tastes at Rosa Mexicano. Save room for *churros en bolsa* (Mexican doughnut) with three dipping sauces for dessert. The atmosphere at these three locations is friendly, the energy level high and the food is definitely worth the tab.

ROSE BAKERY

160 Lexington Ave (at 30th St)   646/837-7754
Mon-Sat: 11 a.m.-6:30 p.m.; Sun: noon-5:30 p.m.
Inexpensive   newyork.doverstreetmarket.com

If you are shopping in Dover Street Market and need a place to refortify, step into Rose Bakery. The ground-floor space with communal tables is a branch of the original Paris bakery and restaurant. A daily-changing menu is English cuisine with Mediterranean influences and it reflects the best ingredients available. Quiche, sticky toffee pudding, lemon-polenta tea cakes, roasted vegetables, scones and other pastries are available. Chef Rose Carrarini calls the *kedgeree* (basmati rice with smoked fish, hard-boiled eggs and cream) a perfect breakfast; the flavorful fusion is an Anglo-Indian classic that has gained popularity of recent. After 4 p.m. only tea (and other drinks) and pastries are available.

ROSEMARY'S ENOTECA & TRATTORIA

18 Greenwich Ave (at 10th St)   212/647-1818
Breakfast, Lunch: Mon-Fri; Dinner: Daily; Brunch: Sat, Sun   rosemarysnyc.com
Moderate

A good choice for weekend brunch, date night or just because, Rosemary's occupies a casual, open and attractive space across from Jefferson Market Garden. Much of the seasonal produce and many of the herbs are fresh from

COMING AND GOING

Pop-up restaurants and food trucks have taken the country by storm. Pop-ups are restaurants that operate temporarily in various locations, allowing chefs to serve any crazy dishes they want without fear of dining critics. Look for them on local food websites like Eater and Grub Street.

CUP OF SOUP

Not much compares to a bowl of steaming chowder, stew or soup to stave off the chill of New York's notorious wicked, wet and cold winters. Here are my recommendations:

Alfanoose (64 Fulton St, 212/528-4669): lentil soup

Aquagrill (210 Spring St, 212/274-0505): Manhattan clam chowder

Carnegie Deli (854 Seventh Ave, 212/757-2245): chicken noodle soup

Grand Central Oyster Bar Restaurant (Grand Central Terminal, 42nd St at Vanderbilt Ave, 212/490-6650): oyster stew

Kelley and Ping (127 Greene St, 212/228-1212): duck or chicken broth with noodles

La Bonne Soupe (48 W 55th St, 212/586-7650): French onion soup

Pearl Oyster Bar (18 Cornelia St, 212/691-8211): New England-style clam chowder

Union Square Cafe (21 E 16th St, 212/243-4020): black bean soup (seasonal)

the rooftop garden. The housemade pastas, foccacia and mozzarella are equally fresh and delicious on their own or in salads, main dishes or panini sandwiches. The menu includes weekly specials for lunch and dinner, cheeses, salumis and dinners-for-two. A wine bar serves proseco on tap; reservations are accepted for groups of seven or more. The place can be busy, but takeout is an option.

ROTISSERIE GEORGETTE

14 E 60th St (bet Fifth and Madison Ave)   212/390-8060
Lunch: Mon-Sat; Dinner: Daily   rotisserieg.com
Moderately expensive to expensive

Rotisserie Georgette is a stylish U.E.S. bistro with an easy-going ambience where you'll feel welcome in blue jeans or black tie. Chef Chad Brauze executes French rotisserie fare and an abundance of seasonal vegetables. From the open kitchen you can view the meat and poultry cooking on open flames. The contemporary comfort food might include seasonal fruit compotes, roasted artichokes, rotisserie potatoes, generous main course salads, whole roasted fish, baby back ribs, roasted chicken stuffed with wild mushrooms and accompanied with your choice of sauce — all beautifully prepared. For dessert, fresh fruit crumbles and ice cream or decadent chocolate *pot de crème* are excellent choices. Expect a tab to match the excellence!

RUBY FOO'S

1626 Broadway (at 49th St)   212/489-5600
Lunch, Dinner: Daily   rubyfoos.com
Moderate

This mega Pan-Asian house in Times Square is a great pre- or post-theater choice! Busy Ruby Foo's is billed as a dim sum and sushi palace, with the best dishes being in the latter category. However, if you and your tablemates share the roasted Peking duck, you will go home happy. There is a large (changing) selection of maki rolls: spicy tuna, lobster, shrimp tempura and California style. Sushi platters are well-selected and great for a party. Land lovers will find crispy pork and beef udon; dim sum, hand rolls, soups, salads and rice dishes are also featured. The crowd is hip, the noise level high, the food very good and the value outstanding. Takeout and delivery are offered in the Times Square area.

RUE 57

60 W 57th St (at Ave of the Americas)   212/307-5656
Breakfast, Lunch: Mon-Fri; Dinner: Daily; Brunch: Sat, Sun   rue57.com
Moderate (lunch) to moderately expensive (dinner)

This Parisian-style brasserie is one busy place due to its extremely convenient midtown location, friendly service and pleasant atmosphere. The menu encompasses soups and salads, sandwiches, oysters and clams, steaks, varied other entrees (like salmon, chicken and miso bass) and daily specials. Lovers of Japanese cuisine will find sushi, sashimi and Japanese platters to share. Don't pass up the beefsteak-tomato salad with charred onions and Roquefort! The young ones will enjoy the great burgers.

RUSS & DAUGHTERS CAFE

127 Orchard St (bet Delancey and Rivington St)   212/475-4881
Mon-Fri: 10-10; Sat, Sun: 8 a.m.-10 p.m.   russanddaughterscafe.com
Moderate (unless ordering caviar)

Finally, a place to sit! For more than a century the iconic Russ & Daughters has been providing classic Jewish comfort food to faithful legions. To the delight of their regulars, that same food is now also served in a cheery L.E.S. full-service luncheonette just around the corner from the original shop. Knishes, latkes, smoked fish, soups, salads, sandwiches, egg dishes and even caviar. Sweet offerings include blintzes, kugel and challah bread pudding. A white-jacketed bartender makes fresh cucumber soda, cherry shrubs, egg creams and excellent Bloody Marys. Be sure to allow a little extra time as reservations are not accepted.

TOP SECRET RAMEN SHOPS

Looking for a hidden ramen restaurant?

SEO Japanese (249 E 49th St, 212/355-7722): Starting at 11 p.m. each night, this sushi restaurant turns into a ramen shop; salt and soy ramen available. Cash only and just until the broth runs out.

Tsukushi (300 E 41st St, 212/599-8888): Tsukishi serves a regular Japanese *omakase* menu until 10 p.m.; then amazing shoyu ramen is served until 2 a.m.

Tsushima (141 E 47th St, 212/207-1938): In midtown this sushi restaurant serves ramen at noon on Wednesday and Friday; early birds may be lucky enough to get a bowl of Shio ramen, a salad and rice dish for $14.

FRIED CHICKEN

Crispy fried chicken is one of my all-time favorite foods any time of year – especially if it is dipped in buttermilk, fried golden brown and served with potato salad and baked beans. These places will satisfy your poultry craving:

Birds & Bubbles (100-B Forsyth St, 646/368-9240)

Blue Ribbon Fried Chicken (28 E 1st St, 212/228-0404)

Blue Ribbon Sushi Bar & Grill (308 W 58th St, 212/397-0404)

Blue Smoke (116 E 27th St, 212/447-7733)

Bobwhite Lunch and Supper Counter (94 Ave C, 212/228-2972)

Charles' Country Panfried Chicken (2841 Frederick Douglass Blvd, 212/281-1800)

Clinton St. Baking Company & Restaurant (4 Clinton St, 646/602-6263): at dinner only

Georgia's Eastside BBQ (192 Orchard St, 212/253-6280)

Hill Country Chicken (1123 Broadway, 212/257-6446)

Red Rooster Harlem (310 Lenox Ave, 212/792-9001)

The Redhead (349 E 13th St, 212/533-6212)

Root & Bone (200 E 3rd St, 646/682-7080)

THE RUSSIAN TEA ROOM

150 W 57th St (bet Ave of the Americas and Seventh St)   212/581-7100
Breakfast, Lunch, Dinner: Daily   russiantearoomnyc.com
Expensive

Since 1927, the Russian Tea Room has offered a bit of nostalgia and perhaps a taste of caviar, borscht, chicken Kiev or beef Stroganoff. The ambience is A+ and dining is opulent in the dining room and elsewhere. But the Bear Lounge is magical; a 15-foot tall, revolving polar bear aquarium and a golden tree with Venetian glass eggs are as famous as the A-listers who are frequent patrons. Traditional fare is served for breakfast, lunch, dinner and their famous afternoon teas; the vodka menu is ostensibly the best in the city. The place is legendary!

SAN PIETRO

18 E 54th St (bet Fifth and Madison Ave)   212/753-9015
Lunch, Dinner: Mon-Sat   Facebook
Expensive

The Bruno brothers have brought the joys and bounty of Southern Italy to their upscale (and pricey) midtown restaurant. Salads with fresh fruits and vegetables are legendary, as is linguine with anchovies. Spaghetti dishes and scialatielli are special and fish, veal and chicken dishes are well crafted. The signature dish is branzino baked in an aromatic crust of herbs and sea salt. After dinner, finish with a cup of cappuccino and a dessert like tiramisu, crème brûlée or gelato. If you want to enjoy tasty Italian dishes while seeing how the other half lives, San Pietro is the ticket!

SARABETH'S

423 Amsterdam Ave (at 80th St)	212/496-6280
Hotel Wales	
1295 Madison Ave (at 92nd St)	212/410-7335
40 Central Park S (bet Fifth Ave and Ave of the Americas)	212/826-5959
381 Park Ave South (at 27th St)	212/335-0093
339 Greenwich St (at Jay St)	212/966-0421
Breakfast, Lunch, Dinner: Daily; Brunch: Sat, Sun	
Lord & Taylor	
424 Fifth Ave (at 39th St), 5th floor	212/827-5068
Lunch: Mon-Fri; Brunch: Sat, Sun	sarabeth.com
Moderate	

A visit to one of Sarabeth's locations reminds me of the better English tearooms. The creation of Sarabeth Levine, the big draw is the homemade quality of the dishes, including the baked items and excellent desserts. Menu choices include excellent omelets, French toast, pancakes, porridge and fresh fruit for breakfast; a fine assortment of light items for lunch including salads, pot pie and even adult grilled cheese sandwiches; and large salads, burgers, seafood sandwiches, chicken pot pies and fish, game and meat dishes for dinner. The chocolate truffle cake, warm apple-apricot bread pudding and homemade ice cream are splendid desserts. They also make gourmet preserves and sell them nationally, along with their cakes, cookies and soups. Service is rapid and courteous. Look in on **Sarabeth's Bakery** (75 Ninth Ave, 212/989-2424) at the Chelsea Market.

SCALINI FEDELI

165 Duane St (bet Greenwich and Hudson St)	212/528-0400
Dinner: Mon-Sat	scalinifedeli.com
Expensive	

Head to this upscale Italian restaurant for a truly classic meal. Vaulted ceilings, beautiful antiques, white tablecloths and Tuscan details create a romantic setting. Michael Cetrulo's *prix-fixe* and tasting offerings are exotic: chive and Maryland crabmeat napoleon, soft egg-yolk ravioli with ricotta and spinach . . . and that's just to start! Then it's on to delicious braised short ribs with cherry pepper and port wine glaze, slow-roasted duck breast crusted with almonds and wonderful roasted rack of lamb with orange-scented carrots. Desserts are equally fabulous, like almond *semifreddo* with orange-honey sauce and caramelized pear or warm caramelized apple tart in a baked phyllo crust. A private room in the wine cellar is available for parties.

SCARPETTA

355 W 14th St (at Ninth Ave)	212/691-0555
Dinner: Daily	scarpettanyc.com
Moderately expensive	

Chef Scott Conant has created a neighborhood venue that attracts folks

TABLESIDE SERVICE

I am very impressed when there is well-done culinary tableside activity available and these places are not a disappointment:

Eleven Madison Park (11 Madison Ave, 212/889-0905): unique wine presentation

Porter House New York (Time Warner Center, 10 Columbus Cir, 212/823-9500): roasted duck

Quality Italian (57 W 57th St, 212/390-1111): lobster diavolo

from all over the city. At the edge of the Meatpacking District, Scarpetta's townhouse setting is most appealing, with a retractable roof, high rafters, a very busy bar and rows of light bulbs suspended in unique boxes. What you really come here for, though, is savory Italian cooking, and that is exactly what you get. The breads are good enough for an entire meal; in fact, scarpetta refers to the Italian tradition of sopping up great sauces with bread. Pastas are the chef's trademark; his spaghetti is especially marvelous. Other sure bets are black cod and melt-in-your-mouth braised short ribs of beef. Top it all off with wonderful chocolate cake served with salted caramel gelato and chocolate butterscotch. (P.S. I defy you to find the almost hidden outdoor sign!)

SCHILLER'S

131 Rivington St (at Norfolk St)   212/260-4555
Lunch: Mon-Fri; Dinner: Daily (open late Mon-Sat); Brunch: Sat, Sun
Moderate   schillersny.com

There is simply no place quite like Schiller's in Manhattan. Keith McNally has created an unusual, fun and deservedly popular munching and drinking spot in an area not renowned for exciting places. The casual, noisy atmosphere at Schiller's Liquor Bar (that's the full name) is rather Parisian and the service is informal. Tasty comfort food includes excellent salads, an oyster bar, burgers, sandwiches, pasta, chicken pot pie and daily specials. Sticky toffee pudding and key lime pie are two of the better desserts. Takeout and delivery are also offered.

THE SEA GRILL

Rockefeller Center
19 W 49th St (bet Fifth Ave and Ave of the Americas)   212/332-7610
Lunch, Dinner: Mon-Sat   theseagrillnyc.com
Moderately expensive

You'll pay for the setting as well as the food at this Rockefeller Center seafood house, which overlooks ice skaters in winter and features open-air dining in nice weather. Take advantage of the well-stocked raw seafood bar to start. Well-prepared main courses include tasty crab cakes, salmon and sushi and sashimi platters; delicious sides of roasted cauliflower with pine nuts, portobello fries and lobster mac and cheese. I love the desserts, which might include warm chocolate steamed pudding and caramelized apple tart with cranberry puree. The Sea Grill is truly one of Rock Center's gems; now if they could just lighten up on the prices!

SERENDIPITY 3

225 E 60th St (bet Second and Third Ave)   212/838-3531
Daily: 11:30 a.m.-midnight (Fri, Sat till 1 a.m.)   serendipity3.com
Moderate

For the young and young-at-heart, Serendipity 3 rates numero uno on their list of "in" places. In an atmosphere of nostalgia set in a quaint two-floor brownstone (circa 1954), this full-service restaurant offers a complete selection of delicious entrees, crepes, casseroles, sandwiches, soups, salads, burgers and pastas. The real treats are the fabulous desserts, including favorites like hot fudge sundaes and the signature frozen hot chocolate (which can also be purchased in mix form to take home); the Forbidden Broadway ice cream sundae is awesome. If you are planning a special gathering for the kids in your family, make Serendipity 3 the destination!

SETTE MEZZO

969 Lexington Ave (bet 70th and 71st St)   212/472-0400
Lunch, Dinner: Daily   Facebook
Moderately expensive

This spot is a well-kept secret among Manhattan's elite business world. Sette Mezzo is small, professional and busy, and it makes a great place for people watching. There are no affectations in decor, service or food preparation. And don't worry about dressing up, as most diners come casually attired. All of the grilled items are excellent; for some marvelous combinations, ask about the special pasta dishes. More traditional Italian plates include veal paillard, stuffed baked chicken or fried calamari and shrimp. Desserts are homemade with the listings you'd expect at an Italian restaurant; caloric cakes, cheesecakes and lemon tarts. Cash only (unless you are a regular with a house account).

SFOGLIA

1402 Lexington Ave (at 92nd St)   212/831-1402
Lunch: Wed-Sun; Dinner: Daily   sfogliarestaurant.com
Moderate

Most folks would probably never notice this unassuming little trattoria on the Upper East Side, but believe me, you don't want to miss it! Pronounced SFOG-lea, the restaurant name means uncut sheet of pasta. How appropriate for this rustic Italian eatery. The place is rather bare-bones, with several large

COCKTAIL SHOCK

2014 saw the average price of a cocktail in upscale eateries rise to close to the north side of $15 dollars. Put a different way, a couple waiting at the bar who have two drinks apiece have already blown the price of a main course!

SUPERB BREAKFAST

Head straight to **Norma's** (Le Parker Meridien New York, 118 W 57th St, 212/708-7460) for Manhattan's best breakfast. Any day will be a little brighter with beautifully presented blueberry or buttermilk pancakes, breakfast dumplings, barbecue pulled pork hash, breakfast pizza, Norma's granola with fruits and nuts, a gooey four-cheese omelet or chocolate blintz crepes. Enjoy the newspaper while sipping a fresh smoothie, orange juice or French-press coffee or tea. For a big splash, start the morning with the "Zillion Dollar" lobster frittata ($1,000), with a generous serving of sevruga caviar! Just as tasty for lunch, this menu is offered until Norma's 3 p.m. closing. Possible star-spotting as well!

farmhouse tables where you might be seated with folks unknown. No problem! The food is so good you will quickly become best friends with the strangers at your elbows as you exchange bites. The staff couldn't be friendlier. Delicious warm bread arrives at the start. The menu changes every few weeks, but you will always find something good: fish, pappardelle, meat, gnocchi, pork chops, chicken and more. You'll enjoy just gazing upon the bowls of fruit and vegetables and fresh flowers on the tables. Reservations are strongly suggested.

SHABU SHABU KOBE

3 W 36th St (bet Fifth Ave and Ave of the Americas)   212/695-8855
Lunch, Dinner: Daily   shabushabukobe.com
Inexpensive

If you are a *shabu shabu* fan (Japanese dish featuring thinly sliced beef) like your author, Shabu Shabu Kobe is surely the place to visit. Besides being fun and entertaining and adding a small bit of cooking skills to the table, the morsels are really delicious, and not very fattening. The midtown quarters feature additional Japanese-style entrees such as sukiyaki, sashimi and tempura accompanied with veggies and a variety of dipping sauces. Besides, you will be able to have a really leisurely meal, something not so common these days.

SHAKE SHACK

Madison Square Park (23rd St bet Madison Ave and Broadway)   212/889-6600
366 Columbus Ave (at 77th St)   646/747-8770
154 E 86th (bet Lexington and Third Ave)   646/237-5035
691 Eighth Ave (at 44th St)   646/435-0135
Numerous other locations
Lunch, Dinner: Daily   shakeshack.com
Inexpensive

Danny Meyer's Shake Shack started out as a popular seasonal hot dog cart in Madison Square Park. The lines were long and customers clamored for more of the burgers, fries, hot dogs, frozen custards, shakes, floats, beer, wine and such. Now there are seven locations in the city, so this is quite a success story.

Each Shack has its own frozen concrete concoctions. I'll have a ShackBurger, cheese fries and a concrete with chocolate-truffle cookie dough — to go, please! Danny has expanded outside the Big Apple with three locations in Brooklyn and there are more on the way across the country.

SHUKO

47 E 12th St (between University Pl and Broadway)   212/228-6088
Daily: 5:30 p.m. to 10:30 p.m.; Sat till 11:30 p.m.   shukonyc.com
Expensive

If you're lucky enough to claim one of the 20 counter seats at Shuko, you will enjoy impressive, upscale sushi with theatrical flair. From the beautifully-carved wooden counter you'll enjoy watching chefs Nick Kim and Jimmy Lau (previously under Masa Takayama at Masa) work their modern interpretation of a traditional sushi bar. Daily tasting menus reflect the best fish selections and local, seasonal ingredients for both the sushi and sashimi. A $135 sushi-only *omakase* (chef's choice) might include vegetable sushi creations of pickled persimmons, fried sweet potatoes or crunchy matsutake mushrooms wrapped in toasted seaweed; $175 *kaiseki* meals of 12 to 15 courses might list a lobster dish with sunchokes, white truffles and bacon. If you still have room, a surprisingly flavorful apple pie is baked in-house and leavened with a touch of white miso; wash it all down with saké.

SHUN LEE CAFE

43 W 65th St (bet Columbus and Central Park West)   212/595-8895
Lunch: Sat, Sun; Dinner: Daily

SHUN LEE WEST

Lunch, Dinner: Daily   shunleewest.com
Moderate

Shun Lee Cafe serves dim sum and street-food combinations in an informal setting. It's a fun place where you can try some unusual and delicious Chinese dishes. Service is prompt and offers an excellent choice pre-Lincoln Center. A good-natured dim sum server comes to your table with a rolling cart and describes the various goodies. The offerings vary, but don't miss stuffed crab claws if they are available. Go on to the street-food items: delicious barbecued spare ribs, a large selection of noodle and rice dishes, soups and a menu full of mild and spicy entrees. Crispy prawns with ginger and braised duck with

WORLD'S BEST WINE GUY

Eric Ripert, Maguy LeCoze and Aldo Sohm opened their first-ever spinoff of **Le Bernardin** (155 W 51st St, 212/554-1515) in 2014. It is really a wine bar at the same location named **Aldo Sohm**. Austrian-born sommelier Sohm has impressive credentials; he was once named best sommelier in the world! It's much more casual than its upscale sister restaurant, with wines starting at $30 and a moderately priced menu.

seasonal vegetables are great choices. For heartier appetites, Shun Lee West — the excellent Chinese restaurant that adjoins Shun Lee Cafe — is equally good in its more elegant setting. Some of the best Chinese food in Manhattan is served here: tingling curry chicken, lobster Szechuan style and baby eggplant with ginger, garlic and scallions. If you come with a crowd, family-style dining is available. Prices are a bit higher at the restaurant than in the cafe, but it is still a good value.

SHUN LEE PALACE

155 E 55th St (bet Lexington and Third Ave)　　　　　212/371-8844
Lunch, Dinner: Daily　　　　　　　　　　　　　　　shunleepalace.net
Moderate

All manner of Chinese restaurants can be found in Manhattan: colorful Chinatown varieties, the mom-and-pop corner operations, the overly Americanized establishments and the grand Chinese dining rooms. Shun Lee Palace belongs in the last category, possessing a very classy, Asian-chic look. Michael Tong offers a delicious journey into the best of this historic cuisine. You can dine rather reasonably at lunch; a $25 three-course *prix-fixe* experience is available. Ordering from the menu (or through your captain) can be a bit pricier, but the platters are worth it. Specialties include beggar's chicken (24 hours advance notice required), casserole specials and curried prawns, veal, lamb, beef or pork entrees. For an absolutely divine culinary experience, indulge in popular Beijing duck served tableside with pancakes, hoisin sauce and scallion brushes. Yes, this is just about the closest thing Manhattan has to a real Chinese palace.

THE SIMONE

151 E 82nd St (bet Lexington and Third Ave)　　　　212/772-8861
Dinner: Mon-Sat　　　　　　　　　　　　　thesimonerestaurant.com
Moderately expensive to expensive

With less than a dozen tables, a seat at The Simone might be difficult ticket to obtain, but it will be worth the effort. Situated in an Upper East Side townhouse, the room is intimate and elegant, complete with white tablecloths. Tina Vaughn and chef Chip Smith (a husband and wife team) present well-prepared French dishes that are served by a professional and amiable staff. Caramelized onion tart, comforting terrines, goat cheese soufflé, roasted chicken, pan-crusted sea bass and other rabbit, lamb, duck and beef dishes are tasty entrees; classic Lord Baltimore cake is a delicious finale.

SIRIO RISTORANTE

The Pierre
795 Fifth Ave (at 61st St)　　　　　　　　　　　　212/940-8195
Breakfast: Daily; Lunch: Mon-Fri; Dinner: Daily; Brunch: Sat, Sun　　siriony.com
Moderately expensive

The swanky Pierre hotel is home to Sirio Maccioni's namesake restaurant, Sirio. The opening of this elegant house was somewhat of a homecoming for the restaurant impresario who at one time served as maitre d' at the hotel's fine dining establishment. Fast forward to the present where Maccioni's culinary team focuses its talents on contemporary versions of traditional Italian dishes. The superb quality and excellent service are on par with sister properties **Circo NYC** and **Le Cirque**. The cocktail menu lists inventive selections and wines which are produced in Italy especially for this restaurant. Breakfasts are a treat; especially the frittatas and Sirio's high energy juice (apple, carrot, spinach, celery, red beet and ginger). Maybe the juice is the octogenarian's secret to always being at the top of his game?

SISTINA

1555 Second Ave (at 80th St)	212/861-7660
Lunch, Dinner: Daily	sistinany.com
Moderately expensive	

This cheery dining space, with flowers, whimsical decor and white tablecloths, has much to offer. Sistina's seasonal Italian menu emphasizes fresh herbs and vegetables. Chef/host/owner Giuseppe Bruno's plates might include braised rabbit with parsnip puree, housemade pappardelle with wild mushrooms or grilled swordfish with roasted artichokes. Daily specials are offered on the pricey menu. A monumental wine list of 65,000 bottles is equally impressive.

SMITH & WOLLENSKY

797 Third Ave (at 49th St)	212/753-1530
Lunch, Dinner: Daily	smithandwollenskynyc.com
Moderate to moderately expensive	

Smith & Wollensky is a great choice for visitors to the Big Apple wanting a taste of what this great city is all about. There is an abundance of space (two floors) and talented, helpful personnel. I always grade a place on the quality of their bread, and Smith & Wollensky's housemade Parker House rolls are excellent and arrive warm. The lobster cocktail is one of the best in the city. Featured entrees include wonderful steaks (USDA prime, dry-aged and hand-butchered), prime rib, fresh seafood and lamb chops. Every man in the family will love the place, and the ladies will appreciate the special attention paid to them. Come here when you and your guests are really hungry.

SAVE YOUR DINING DOLLARS

- Eat out at lunchtime rather than dinner . . . or eat a Sunday brunch.
- Dine at the bar, where the menu is less expensive.
- Order a few appetizers rather than a main entree.
- Don't order bottled water.
- Don't go for the expensive wines. Some less expensive bottles are just as good!
- Don't go for the entree specials, which are often overpriced.
- Don't feel that you must have a dessert.
- The first main dish listed on a menu is usually the most profitable.
- Be sure to "check your check." Watch for included gratuities.

ICONIC DINING

The iconic **21 Club** (21 W 52nd St, 212/582-7200; 21club.com) has been around since the 1920s, with a reputation as a place to see and be seen. I can remember fascinating lunches here with my uncle, who was a daily diner. Many celebrities, politicians and moguls have laid claim to their usual table in the Bar Room, and the seating chart may read like an A-list of who's who. The atmosphere is still quite special. At one time, patrons dressed to the nines for an evening at the 21 Club. Yes, there is still a gentleman at the door to give you the once-over and men's jackets are required (no jeans or sneakers) in the Bar Room and restaurant. The Bar Room is open for lunch Tuesday through Friday and dinner Monday through Saturday; take note of the ceiling which holds an astounding collection of sports memorabilia and corporate logo items. The more relaxed Bar 21 and Lounge serves lunch Tuesday through Friday and is a watering hole during evening hours. For elegant dining (Tuesday through Saturday) reserve a table in Upstairs at 21, a romantic spot for marriage proposals, anniversaries, birthdays and other memorable special occasions. Oh the secrets this former speakeasy holds!

SPARKS STEAK HOUSE

210 E 46th St (bet Second and Third Ave)   212/687-4855
Lunch: Mon-Fri; Dinner: Mon-Sat   sparkssteakhouse.com
Moderately expensive

You come to Sparks Steak House to eat, period. This well-seasoned and popular beef restaurant is very traditional with its dark wood paneling. Since 1966 businessmen have made an evening at Sparks a must, and the house has not let time erode its reputation. You can choose from veal and lamb chops, beef scaloppine and medallions of beef. There are a half-dozen steak items, like steak fromage (with Roquefort), prime sirloin, sliced steak with fresh mushrooms and top-of-the-line filet mignon. Seafood dishes are another specialty. Rainbow trout, tuna steak and halibut steak are as good as you'll find in most seafood houses; lobsters are enormous, delicious and expensive. Skip the appetizers and desserts, and concentrate on the main dishes. An extensive, award-winning wine list and private party rooms are available.

SPICE MARKET

403 W 13th St (at Ninth Ave)   212/675-2322
Lunch, Dinner: Daily   spicemarketnewyork.com
Moderate to moderately expensive

Located in the trendy Meatpacking District, Spice Market is a Jean-Georges Vongerichten operation. As one of the city's hot dining spots for atmosphere and tasty upscale Asian street food, it is a charming bi-level space with tables surrounding an open area that leads to an inviting downstairs bar. The decor is tasteful with carvings, screens and pagodas, while the food is different and exciting. A la carte and chef's tasting menus list many savory dishes. Vietnamese spring rolls are yummy, the salads are unusual and good and the ribeye skewer with Thai basil dipping sauce is outstanding. Other wonderful dishes: striped bass with wok-fried Napa cabbage, jicama and cucumber; onion- and chili-crusted short ribs that melt in your mouth and a large selection of vegetables, noodles and rice. Desserts are even better; Thai jewels of fruits with fresh coconut ice — one of the most famous street desserts in Thailand — is a must. Other sweet selections: a fabulous Ovaltine kulfi and toasted coconut cake.

SPIGOLO

1561 Second Ave (at 81st St)   212/744-1100
Dinner: Daily   spigolonyc.com
Moderate

Spigolo is a popular dinner house for many Upper East Siders craving traditional Italian fare. The menu is inspired by seasonal bounty from the land and sea; seafood dishes, including clams, oysters and bass or monkfish, are quite flavorful. Pasta dishes are prepared with market-fresh ingredients in delicious combinations that are laced with cheese, garlic and sauces; entrees are hearty and satisfying. Sweet finishes include a half dozen or so Italian desserts and an array of dessert wines and liquors. Reservations can be difficult, so look for first-come, first-serve outside seating.

THE SPOTTED PIG

314 W 11th St (at Greenwich St)   212/620-0393
Lunch, Dinner: Daily; Brunch: Sat, Sun   thespottedpig.com
Moderate

April Bloomfield and Ken Friedman are the driving forces behind this Manhattan gastropub, which has pig statues and porcine likenesses throughout the boisterous scene. The seasonal British and Italian menu is really good. Start with snacks like deviled eggs or a pot of pickles, then move on to lunch staples of delicious burgers and shoestring potatoes, soup or chowder and salads. Dinner is served until 2 a.m. Creative beef, lamb, poultry, fish, seafood and (of course) pork preparations are offered. Vegetarians can make a meal of five side dishes for $27. Beer choices include cask-conditioned ale. This place hops, and in proper gastropub fashion, no reservations are accepted.

CLARKE'S STANDARD

If you crave a juicy hamburger, think of **Clarke's Standard** (636 Lexington Ave, 212/838-6000 and 101 Maiden Lane, 212/797-1700; clarkes-standard.com) where beef is ground according to standards established by the city's classic butcher shops and hot dogs are custom blended. Other choices are limited to turkey and housemade veggie burgers, a couple of chicken sandwiches and sides of fries, tater tots and chili. The vibe is retro: sandwiches are served on a tray in paper and cardboard holders and fries are in handy paper cups. Little Clarke's ice cream cups are akin to the orange and vanilla summertime treats of childhood; flavors reflect present-day tastes for salted caramel, mint chip and more. The midtown locale is small, busy and frequently has a line out the door.

STELLA!

There's one more reason to visit Macy's at Herald Square. **Stella 34 Trattoria** (151 W 34th St, 6th floor, 212/967-9251), an Italian eatery, is a lunch and dinner destination that comes with an eye-popping view of the Empire State Building. The three wood-burning ovens turn out fabulous entrees and pizzas, substantial selections (strip steak and pork chops) and salads of roasted beets or mixed greens. Stella includes a prosecco bar, gelato counter and comfortable lounge area, and is open until 9:30 p.m. most nights. Use the department store's entrance on 35th Street and Broadway and take an express elevator straight to the sixth floor.

SPRING NATURAL KITCHEN

474 Columbus Ave (at 83rd St)   646/596-7434
Lunch: Mon-Fri; Dinner: Daily; Brunch: Sat, Sun   springnaturalkitchen.com

SPRING STREET NATURAL

62 Spring St (at Lafayette St)   212/966-0290
Breakfast: Mon-Fri; Lunch, Dinner: Daily; Brunch: Sat, Sun
Moderate   springstreetnatural.com

Both of these locations are leaders in offering healthy cuisine. From attractive and unfussy surroundings, the kitchen provides seasonal meals prepared with fresh, unprocessed foods and most everything is cooked to order. Neighborhood residents are regular customers, so you know the food is top-quality. Specials are offered every day, with a wide variety of natural and flavorful fresh-squeezed juices, organic salads, pastas, vegetarian meals, free-range poultry and fresh fish and seafood. Try wonderful roasted salmon with cucumber salad and red potatoes. Spring Street also produces great desserts like warm banana-caramel bread pudding and fresh fruit salad with sorbet.

THE STANDARD GRILL

Standard Hotel
848 Washington St (at 13th St)   212/645-4100
Breakfast, Lunch, Dinner: Daily; Brunch: Sat, Sun   thestandardgrill.com
Moderate to moderately expensive

The Standard Grill, a bustling Meatpacking District eatery, is a real winner. Not only does the place literally rock, but it also offers first-class American bites in every category. The wait staff is superbly trained, friendly and competent. The house seats hundreds of guests at both an outside patio and an indoor room. The bread selection is great, and refreshing radishes are a complimentary touch. Menu specialties include patés, oysters, a number of appetizers and delicious soups. Memorable (sometimes seasonal) entrees include lobster thermidor, steaks and marinated lamb T-bone. A bowl of bittersweet chocolate mousse (for two) is rightfully named "The Deal Closer." Reservations are strongly suggested.

STRIP HOUSE

15 W 44th St (bet Fifth Ave and Ave of the Americas) Lunch: Mon-Fri; Dinner: Daily	212/336-5454

13 E 12th St (bet Fifth Ave and University Pl) Dinner: Daily Moderately expensive	212/328-0000 striphouse.com

The Strip House offers a modern twist to the traditional steakhouse experience. Rich leather, plush fabrics and dark red walls lined with photographs of sultry 1920s burlesque stars all create a seductive atmosphere. The innovative menu features signature prime cuts of beef, all charred to perfection with house seasoning. Flavorful sides like black truffle creamed spinach, crisp goose-fat potatoes and garlic-herbed French fries complement the entrees. Decadent desserts include 24-layer chocolate cake and ginger crème brûlée with brandied cherries. **Strip House Next Door** (11 E 12th St, downstairs, 212/838-9197) offers simpler fare, plus items from the original 12th Street menu.

BROOKLYN DINING

Brooklyn has successfully made a mark on the dining scene with a large number of great dining options. Restaurants in all categories have received top ratings by critics and are now drawing customers from the city. Previously only a handful of choices were worth the trip across the East River; now, times have changed, and patrons have even more possibilities to the age old question: "Where shall we go for dinner?"

Bar Corvo (Prospect Heights): Italian

Blanca (Bushwick): New American tasting

Buttermilk Channel (Carrol Gardens): American

Chef's Table at Brooklyn Fare (Downtown): Japanese-influenced French plates

Colonie (Brooklyn Heights): American

Di Fara (Midwood): pizza

Five Leaves (Greenpoint): American

The Grocery Restaurant (Carrol Gardens): American

Locanda Vini e Olii (Clinton Hill): Italian

Mimi's Hummus (Ditmas Park): Middle Eastern

Momo Sushi Shack (Bushwick): sushi

Peter Luger Steak House (Williamsburg): steak

Roberta's (Bushwick): Italian/pizza

Saraghina (Bedford-Stuyvesant): pizza

Saul (Boerum Hill): American

Semilla (Williamsburg): vegetarian-leaning

Tanoreen (Bay Ridge): Mediterranean/Middle Eastern

AUTHENTIC TAPAS

What are called tapas in most New York restaurants are really just small plates, really appetizers. Spanish tapas are rustic tidbits featuring regional ingredients. You can find them at places like:

Bar Jamón (125 E 17th St, 212/253-2773): wine and tapas

Casa Mono (52 Irving Pl, 212/253-253-2773): full dining

Las Ramblas (170 W 4th St, 646/415-7924): small plates, small place

Tertulia (359 Ave of the Americas, 646/559-9909): expensive

Txikito (240 Ninth Ave): moderately priced wine selection

TAO

42 E 58th St (bet Park and Madison Ave)   212/888-2288
Lunch: Mon-Sat; Dinner: Daily; Brunch: Sun   taorestaurant.com

TAO DOWNTOWN

Maritime Hotel
92 Ninth Ave (bet 16th and 17th St)   212/888-2724
Dinner: Daily   taodowntown.com
Moderate to moderately expensive

Tao is billed as an Asian bistro, but it is much more than that. These dramatic dining settings feature a huge Buddha overlooking a large, sexy room as you enjoy wonderful food at reasonable prices. A number of small plates are available to start, including lobster wontons and squab lettuce wraps. Save room for delicious dragon-tail spare ribs or a marvelous wok-seared New York sirloin with shiitake mushrooms that melts in your mouth. A $27.50 *prix-fixe* lunch is offered daily. Reservations are strongly recommended, as thirtysomethings make Tao their hangout.

TARTINE

253 W 11th St (at 4th St)   212/229-2611
Lunch: Mon-Fri; Dinner, Brunch: Daily   tartinecafenyc.com
Bakery: Daily from 9 a.m.
Moderate

This tiny cafe/bakery/French bistro (about 20 chairs) serves some of the tastiest dishes in the Village. There are soups, salads, quiches and omelets, plus chicken, meat, fish entrees and daily specials at pleasing prices; French fries are a treat. Desserts and pastries are baked on-premises in the bakery, and for about half the price of what you would pay uptown, you can finish your meal with splendid custard-filled tarts, meringues, fabulous almond-covered chocolate ganache or warm, thinly sliced cinnamon apples on puff pastry with ice cream. There is always a wait at dinner and brunch — a good sign, since neighborhood folks know the best spots; try for one of the sidewalk tables. If you want wine, you are encouraged to bring your own. Cash only.

TELEPAN

72 W 69th St (at Columbus Ave)   212/580-4300
Lunch: Wed-Fri; Dinner: Daily; Brunch: Sat, Sun   telepan-ny.com
Moderate

After you have overloaded on the flashy dining scene, step back and be Bill Telepan's guest. Everything about this place — surroundings, menu and service — reflects the laid-back personality of chef/owner Telepan. It is a quiet and reliable restaurant enhancing the Upper West Side for more mature diners. Local ingredients are featured on the changing New American menu. There are worthy egg dishes, scallop and sea urchin stew, roasted chicken, lobster Bolognese, house-smoked brook trout and the heritage pork dish. A four-course tasting menu is offered for $85. **Telepan Local** (329 Greenwich St, 212/966-9255) is a much smaller sister operation in Tribeca that offers similar bites.

TEXAS DE BRAZIL

1011 Third Ave (bet 60th and 61st St)   212/537-0060
Dinner: Daily   texasdebrazil.com
Moderately expensive

Meat lovers will appreciate this all-you-can-eat Brazilian steakhouse. Texas de Brazil's colorful, bi-level space has an energetic vibe; the food, service and atmosphere are very good. The $59.99 *prix-fixe* meal begins with a bountiful 50-item salad bar along with soups, roasted vegetables and other sides. Meats are the star and are offered by roaming gaucho waiters who carve your choice of beef, chicken, lamb, pork and sausage; all slow-roasted and grilled over an open flame. Assorted sides like fried bananas and cheese bread are served tableside. An excellent bar offers an amazing selection of wines and cocktails, including the famous Caipirinha, their signature Brazilian lime cocktail. It's doubtful that you saved room, but the desserts include Brazilian flan, key lime pie, pecan pie and more, and are deserving of attention.

TIPSY PARSON

156 Ninth Ave (bet 19th and 20th St)   212/620-4545
Lunch: Mon-Fri; Dinner: Daily; Brunch: Sat, Sun   tipsyparson.com
Moderately expensive

When someone mentions Southern food, I think of warm hospitality and

A SECOND HELPING OF DINER LINGO (USED BY WAITERS)

Burn the British: a toasted English muffin

Cackleberries: eggs

Flop two: two fried eggs over easy

Heart attack on a rack: biscuits and gravy

Houseboat: banana split

Nervous pudding: bowl of Jell-o

Sinkers and suds: doughnuts and coffee

SOMETHING FOR EVERYONE

These dishes may be delicacies to some and revolting to others. You be the judge!

Ceviche (marinated seafood): **Rosa Mexicano** (1063 First Ave, 212/753-7407; 61 Columbus Ave, 212/977-7700 and 9 E 18th St, 212/533-3350)

Haggis (Scotch pudding made of sheep innards): **St. Andrew's** (140 W 46th St, 212/840-8413)

Tripe (edible parts of the cow stomach): **Locanda Verde** (The Greenwich Hotel, 377 Greenwich St, 212/925-3797)

Sweetbreads (thymus gland of veal): **Casa Mono** (52 Irving Place, 212/253-2773)

big helpings of grits, hushpuppies and catfish. All that and more can be found near the High Line at Tipsy Parson in various delicious combinations. Try grits solo or with shrimp, a steakburger, fried green tomatoes or Pennsylvania Amish chicken with black-eyed peas. Plan a return visit for weekend brunch and indulge in pulled pork spoonbread and biscuits with country sausage. Incidentally, the homey restaurant is named for a dessert of brandy-soaked almond cake, custard, fruits and nuts (sometimes on the menu) — not a tippling Southern minister.

TOCQUEVILLE RESTAURANT

1 E 15th St (bet Union Square W and Fifth Ave) 212/647-1515
Lunch, Dinner: Mon-Sat tocquevillerestaurant.com
Moderate

Husband and wife team Marco Moreira and Jo-Ann Makovitzky operate their pride-and-joy posh restaurant in a Flatiron location. Innovative dishes are featured on a constantly changing American-French menu. At lunchtime, a $27 three-course *prix-fixe* menu is offered. Seasonal ingredients from the Union Square Greenmarket are featured. You will enjoy an absolutely fabulous meal made all the more pleasant by a well-trained and accommodating staff. Homemade brioche, rosemary focaccia and sourdough breads are so good you must be careful not to ruin your appetite. At dinner a four-course tasting menu ($85) might include cheddar salad, truffled creamy parmesan grits, seared scallops and foie gras, with chocolate soufflé to finish. The locale affords room for private dining (up to 28 people) and a bar area where you can enjoy drinks and snacks or order from the full menu. This talented pair also operates **Catering by Tocqueville**, a service accessible via the restaurant's phone number. Personal food delivery is a given, but they can also take care of location selection, decor, rental items, photographers and professional service staff.

TORO

85 Tenth Ave (bet 15th and 16th St) 212/691-2360
Daily: Mon-Sat toro-nyc.com
Moderate

Toro occupies a large industrial-chic space in what was the former Nabisco

Factory. The tall-ceilinged setting in Chelsea offers 120 seats at communal tables and some smaller, unshared tables. The place gets quite loud and the wait staff seem a bit harried, but the savory Spanish flavors and techniques on display will make you forget that part. The large menu lists traditional Spanish classics as well as over 50 tapas — hot, cold and grilled — some quite unusual. Dishes might include rabbit and snail paella; tuna tartare; marinated skirt steak with blue cheese butter; stew of lobster, sea urchin and parsnip and griddled garlic shrimp with chilies — all tastefully done. For parties of eight or more, a family-style menu is a great option; check out a separate speakeasy-style lounge, **Backbar**.

TOTTO RAMEN

464 W 51st St (bet Ninth and Tenth Ave)	646/596-9056
248 E 52nd Street (bet Second and Third Ave)	212-421-0052
366 W 52nd St (bet Eighth and Ninth Ave)	212/582-0052
Lunch: Mon-Sat; Dinner: Daily	tottoramen.com
Inexpensive	

Ramen has become a hot commodity and you'll find this delicious Japanese comfort food at Totto Ramen. Noodles are served al dente, are MSG-free and vary in spiciness by the addition of sesame oil. Combinations of chicken or pork and vegetables create different flavors along with more than a dozen toppings including scallions, corn, avocado, bamboo shoots and more. Saké, Japanese beer and a few appetizers round out the menu at these casual, very busy spaces. Note that there are no reservations and no takeout or delivery; cash only.

TOUT VA BIEN

311 W 51st St (bet Eighth and Ninth Ave)	212/265-0190
Lunch, Dinner: Daily	letoutvabien.com
Moderate	

Tout Va Bien has been consistently preparing old school French food at reasonable prices since 1948. The place is hopping every night — there is much noise, hilarity and crowding. This French bistro serves all the things you would expect for hors d'oeuvres: scallops, escargots, fromage and other French traditions. Popular items include boeuf bourguignonne (beef stew), veal scaloppini, frog legs and Chabeaubriand (for two). Come to this vibrant spot to celebrate or when you need cheering up.

L'ATELIER TO RETURN

Celebrated French chef Joël Robuchon has announced the reopening of his restaurant, **L'Atelier de Joël Robuchon** (250 Vesey Street), Spring 2015. Located in Battery Park City, the 11,000-square-foot space will include both counter and table seating. Right in the heart of the city's financial district and across from the World Trade Center, waterside outdoor seating will offer spectacular views of the Hudson River and Statue of Liberty.

SUNNYSIDE UP AND MORE

Not being an egg lover myself, but a man who has lots of egg-loving friends, I direct you to the **Egg Shop** (151 Elizabeth St, 646/666-0810) where eight different egg sandwiches await you. But if you are like me, overlook the eggs and go for the great fried chicken! Any time of the day is a good time to get an egg-fix at this delightful spot.

TRATTORIA DELL'ARTE

900 Seventh Ave (at 57th St)   212/245-9800
Lunch, Dinner: Daily; Brunch: Sun   trattoriadellarte.com
Moderate

Native New Yorkers keep Trattoria dell'Arte bursting at the seams every evening. A casual cafe is at the front, seats are available at the antipasto bar in the center and the dining room is in the rear. One would be hard-pressed to name a place at any price with tastier Italian food. The antipasto selection is large, fresh and inviting; you can choose a platter with various accompaniments. There are daily specials, superb pasta dishes, grilled fish and meats and salads; wonderful pizzas are available every day. The atmosphere and personnel are warm and pleasant. I recommend this place without reservation — although you'd better have one if you want to sit in the dining room. An outdoor sidewalk cafe provides seating in warmer months.

TRES CARNES

954 Third Ave (bet 57th and 58th St)   212/989-8737
101 Maiden Ln (at Pearl St)   (same phone for all locations)
688 Ave of the Americas (at 22nd St)
Lunch, Dinner: Daily   trescarnes.com
Inexpensive

For a quick fix of authentic Tex-Mex, Tres Carnes offers three outposts in Manhattan. Due to a minimum of counter space, most customers choose takeout, and you can also order by phone or online and request delivery. Delicious slow-cooked brisket, chicken and pork fill the made-to-order burritos, tacos, bowls and salads. Sides include green poblano and yellow rice, pinto and black beans, roasted corn, chipotle squash and smoky guacamole. What a great alternative to the usual fast food; be sure to include a sweet churro doughnut on your order!

TRESTLE ON TENTH

242 Tenth Ave (at 24th St)   212/645-5659
Breakfast, Lunch, Dinner: Daily; Brunch: Sat, Sun   trestleontenth.com
Moderate

This house does well with a seasonal menu of farm fresh American entrees, mostly with a Swiss nod. Trestle on Tenth is located just across from High Line Park in the heart of the Chelsea art district. There are chicken and salmon dishes, pork garlic sausage, seared brook trout, a superb *crépinette* (pulled pork shoulder) and delicious sides. I always enjoy a light and tasty butter-lettuce salad to start; here it is made with crispy bacon and delicious buttermilk dressing. Cured meats, aged cheeses and sandwiches are featured at lunch. A roasted, stuffed whole pig feast, served family style, can be requested five days in advance. These folks are down-to-earth and the atmosphere is unpretentious; for more private dining try the garden in the back.

TRIBECA GRILL

375 Greenwich St (at Franklin St)   212/941-3900
Lunch: Mon-Fri; Dinner: Daily; Brunch: Sun   myriadrg.com
Moderate to moderately expensive

Tribeca Grill has been a fine dining destination since 1990, helping to put Tribeca's neighborhood on the map. The setting is a huge old coffee-roasting house that also houses the Tribeca Film Center on the floors above. The bar comes from the historic Jack Dempsey and Maxwell Plum restaurants; the kitchen is first-class. The genius is savvy Drew Nieporent, with actor Robert De Niro as co-owner. Put it all together, and you have a winner; no wonder the people watching is so good here! Guests enjoy a spacious bar and dining area, an engaging collection of paintings by De Niro's father, ample banquet facilities for private parties plus a fabulous private screening room upstairs. The food is stylish and wholesome, and signature dishes include seared sea scallops with carrot risotto and black truffle Madeira vinaigrette and lemon and rosemary roasted Amish chicken with confit fingerling potatoes and broccolini. The desserts, including the signature banana tart and Tribeca chocolate cake, also rate with the best. A world-class wine list (2,200 selections and over 22,000 bottles) perennially wins the Grand Award from Wine Spectator. Please note the address is Greenwich Street, in the heart of Tribeca, not Avenue.

THE BIERGARTEN

Tucked under the High Line is The Standard High Line hotel's **The Biergarten** (848 Washington St, 212/645-4646). Traditional German sausages and pretzels, along with famous mugs of German beer, are served in a great atmosphere. It's an excellent spot for an after-work drink or a fun evening. Biergarten is open until midnight on weekdays and 1 a.m. on weekends. Zum Wohl!

TURKISH KITCHEN

386 Third Ave (bet 27th and 28th St)   212/679-6633
Lunch: Mon-Fri; Dinner: Daily; Brunch: Sun   turkishkitchen.com
Moderate

This family-run Turkish delight in Murray Hill has great food and is absolutely spotless; moreover, the staff exudes charm. There are all kinds of tasty Turkish specialties, like zucchini pancakes, hummus and offerings of chicken, lamb and fish that have been baked, char-grilled, pan-fried, skewered or stuffed with

JAMES BEARD HOUSE

167 W 12th St (bet Ave of the Americas and Seventh Ave)   212/675-4984
jamesbeard.org

Attention, foodies! The legendary James Beard had roots in Oregon, so anything to do with his life is of special interest to this author. He was a familiar personality on the Oregon coast, where he delighted in serving the superb seafood for which the region is famous. When Beard died in 1985, his Greenwich Village brownstone was put on the market and purchased by a group headed by the late Julia Child. Now the home is run by the nonprofit James Beard Foundation and features continuing education and kids' programs, as well as tastings, readings and tours. Notable chefs show off their substantial talents here. This is a great opportunity for a one-on-one with some really interesting folks as an observer or volunteer. Call or check the website for scheduled events. The foundation's private boardroom is a unique, elegant dining space for a special gathering. Schedule a multicourse tasting with a renowned chef (up to 12 guests) for an exceptional epicurean experience!

flavorful herbs, eggplant, cabbage leaves, rice and more. You can wash it all down with sour cherry juice from Turkey or cacik, a homemade yogurt. Locals rave about the all-you-can-eat brunch buffet; a great value at $22.

UNCLE JACK'S STEAKHOUSE

440 Ninth Ave (at 34th St)	212/244-0005
44 W 56th St (bet Fifth Ave and Ave of the Americas)	212/245-1550
39-40 Bell Blvd (at 40th St), Queens	718/229-1100
Lunch, Dinner: Daily; Brunch: Sat, Sun	unclejacks.com
Moderate (lunch) to expensive (dinner)	

Stepping into Uncle Jack's Steakhouse is like going back decades in time. The hand-carved mahogany bar, antique light fixtures, blackboard menu and private Library Room (Ninth Avenue location) create a masculine and comfortable setting. You will be well taken care of, as the wait staff and captains are right on the job. Vegetables and herbs are grown locally and seafood is fresh, local and imported. A dozen impressive sides include mashed sweet potatoes, five-cheese mac and cheese and creamed spinach. Uncle Jack's specializes in dry-aged prime steaks and meats, cooked and seasoned to perfection; you can expect an equally grand price tag. The 56th Street location has a sushi menu.

UNION SQUARE CAFE

21 E 16th St (bet Fifth Ave and Union Square W)	212/243-4020
Lunch, Dinner: Daily; Brunch: Sat, Sun	unionsquarecafe.com
Moderate to moderately expensive	

Union Square Cafe is the flagship restaurant of Danny Meyer. It goes without saying that the place is very popular, with the clientele as varied as the food. The

American menu is creative, the staff unusually down-to-earth and the prices very much within reason. For lunch, try the yellowfin tuna burger with ginger-mustard glaze or one of the great pastas. Chef Carmen Quagliata offers such specialties as whole wheat pappardelle with pork ragu and wonderful soups like cauliflower or sunchoke. Dinner entrees from the grill are always delicious (lamb chops, shell steak and veal). I come just for the warm banana tart with honey-vanilla ice cream and macadamia brittle! There are plans for a move at the end of 2015.

VALBELLA

11 E 53rd St (bet Madison and Fifth Ave)	212/888-8955
	valbellamidtown.com
421 W 13th St (bet Ninth Ave and Washington St)	212/645-7777
Lunch: Mon-Fri; Dinner: Mon-Sat	valbellanyc.com
Moderate to moderately expensive	

Service is key in today's highly competitive marketplace, and at Valbella, it is top-notch. Wait staff are in constant motion and obviously well-trained at both of these elegant locations. The Northern Italian fare is first-rate, featuring a decent selection of typical dishes. The pastas caught my eye: penne alla vodka, cavatelli with broccoli rabe, linguine with seafood, fresh herbs and plum-tomato sauce and a risotto lobster bisque with asparagus; lamb and veal dishes are also worth trying. Beautiful private dining rooms are available at each house.

VIC'S

31 Great Jones St (bet Lafayette St and Bowery)	212/253-5700
Lunch: Mon-Fri; Dinner: Daily; Brunch: Sat, Sun	vicsnewyork.com
Moderate	

Vic's is the new creation of Vicki Freeman and chefs Marc Meyer and Hillary Sterling; it is the same space and the same owner as the former Five Points. The clean, casual and open space offers Italian-Mediterranean dishes at affordable prices. Inventive, market-driven plates are vegetable-heavy and include pastas (available in half portions), and pizzas and entrees cooked in the wood-burning oven; all entrees, including rye rigatoni with braised lamb, oregano, lemon and white wine sauce, are beautifully presented. The same high standard for good food is equally evident in the service; this is a good brunch, lunch and dinner choice in Noho.

WEST VILLAGE FIND

Restaurateur Graydon Carter saw good bones in the derelict **Beatrice Inn** (285 W 12th St, 646/896-1804) in the West Village. Building on that framework, he restored the cozy restaurant and bar to a neighborhood steak and chophouse. The somewhat pricey menu is not large and the house is still determining what works best. That being said, Carter's following and New York's elite have found the place and made it their local see-and-be-seen spot.

NOT YOUR ORDINARY PIZZA

Are you feeling adventuresome when it comes to pizza? Forego pepperoni and try one of these toppings on your Italian pie:

Artichoke Basille's Pizza & Brewery (114 Tenth Ave, 212/792-9200): burnt anchovies (intentional)

Balaboosta (214 Mulberry St, 212/966-7366): fresh carrot puree

The Mark Restaurant by Jean-Georges (The Mark, 25 E 77th St, 212/744-4300): black truffles

Marta (Martha Washington Hotel, 29 E 29th St, 212/651-3800): Roman-style by Nick Anderer

Nino's Positano (890 Second Ave, 212/355-5540): luxury pizza with lobster and caviar

VIVOLO

140 E 74th St (bet Park and Lexington Ave)   212/737-3533
Lunch, Dinner: Mon-Sat
Moderate to moderately expensive

CUCINA VIVOLO

222 E 58th St (bet Second and Third Ave)   212/308-0222
Breakfast, Lunch: Mon-Sat
138 E 74th St (at Lexington Ave)   212/717-4700
Lunch, Dinner: Mon-Sat; Brunch: Sat   vivolonyc.com
Moderate

Angelo Vivolo created a neighborhood classic from an old townhouse back in 1977. Since then, the charming two-story restaurant, with cozy fireplaces and professional service, expanded to the Cucina Vivolo specialty food shops. There are great things to eat at each place. You can sit down and be pampered, have goodies ready for takeout or place an order for delivery. In the restaurant proper, there are pastas, chicken, fish, veal dishes, eggplant parmigiano and daily specials like Italian meatloaf; both lunch and dinner offer a three-course *prix-fixe* listing. The Cucina menu offers wonderful Italian specialty sandwiches made with all kinds of breads, as well as breakfast treats, soups, salads, cheeses, appetizers, homemade desserts, espresso and cappuccino. Note that only the Cucina locations serve breakfast.

WALLSÉ

344 W 11th St (at Washington St)   212/352-2300
Dinner: Daily; Brunch: Sun   kg-ny.com
Moderate to moderately expensive

Vienna it is not, but Kurt Gutenbrunner brings a refined, modern take on Austrian flavors to the West Village. The two dining rooms are sparse but elegant and the staff is pleasant and helpful, adding to the dining experience. Appetizers, like foie gras terrine and späetzle with braised rabbit, are classic favorites. Yes, there is wiener schnitzel with potato-cucumber salad, and you can always hope that crispy cod strudel is on the menu. Great pastries for dessert: chef Kurt's famous apple strudel, crepes with Grand Marnier mousse and Salzburger nockerl; the Austrian cheese selection is first-rate.

WAVERLY INN

16 Bank St (bet 4th and Waverly St)   917/828-1154
Dinner: Daily; Brunch: Sat, Sun   waverlynyc.com
Moderately expensive to expensive

If you are lucky enough to make a reservation at Waverly Inn, you won't be disappointed. Once seated, you'll find the service professional and pleasant and the surroundings (with working fireplace) charming. Small plates include oysters on the half shell, salads, crab cakes and more; you might also choose a Waverly burger, chicken pot pie, truffle mac and cheese or other comforting favorite. If it's on the menu, the Berkshire pork with roasted apple is a sensational entree. By the way, the Waverly Inn is owned by Graydon Carter, publisher and editor of Vanity Fair.

DRUZE CUISINE

Gazala Place (380 Columbus Ave, 212/873-8880 and 709 Ninth Ave, 212/245-0709) is the only place in Manhattan to enjoy Druze cuisine. The Druze are a mixed-race religious community originating in Israel, Jordan, Lebanon and Syria. Hospitality is a hallmark here. The tasty fare is Middle Eastern, influenced by those regions with an emphasis on hummus, falafel, wraps and kabobs.

WOLFGANG'S STEAKHOUSE

409 Greenwich St
(bet Beach and Hubert St)
                                    212/925-0353
4 Park Ave (at 33rd St)   212/889-3369
New York Times Building
250 W 41st St
(bet Seventh and Eighth Ave) 212/921-3720
200 E 54th St (at Third Ave)
                                    212/588-9653
Lunch, Dinner: Daily
Expensive   wolfgangssteakhouse.net

Wolfgang Zwiener heads up these upscale steakhouses in Manhattan. These manly spaces offer just what you would expect — quality red meat. Signature items include Porterhouse, filet mignon, ribeyes, lamb chops and fresh seafood. Portions are huge and should be shared; the German potatoes are tasty. Service is professional and prompt, which it should be for the price. I can recommend these classic American steakhouses for a quality (not outstanding) experience.

YUNNAN KITCHEN

79 Clinton St (bet Delancey and Rivington St)   212/253-2527
Dinner: Tues-Sun   yunnankitchen.com
Inexpensive to moderate

Yunnan Kitchen is a trendy, cozy and very popular Lower East Side restaurant. The menu represents the culture, flavors and cooking techniques of China's Yunnan Province. Flavorful dishes are market-driven and presented on

DON'T BOTHER LIST

Dining out should result in a good meal in a comfortable setting at a fair price. Unfortunately, many restaurants don't meet that criteria and are mediocre at best. Some restaurants on the following list may be well-known, but there are better options elsewhere.

Azuri Cafe: good tastes but unwelcome atmosphere

Bice: very noisy, expensive, unimaginative food

BLT Prime: unlike the sister operations, not ready for prime time

Blue 9 Burger: indifferent service and unexciting digs

BonChon: forever waits, poor service and no decor

Bubba Gump: unclassy tourist trap

Cipriani Downtown: customers are more attractive than the prices

Coffee Shop: attractive wait staff with unattractive attitudes

Crispo: rude service and management

Giorgio's of Gramercy: good if you are in the area, but don't spend the cab fare if you're not

Giovanni VentiCinque: overpriced dinners; affordable *prix-fixe* lunch

Island Burgers & Shakes: soggy fries, cramped quarters

Le Veau d'Or: time-worn French restaurant

Leopard at des Artistes: The only good part of the experience – the murals!

Michael Jordan's The Steak House NYC: no slam dunk here; overrated

Nello: big prices and skimpy portions

Old Homestead: historical only

Philippe: inexcusably bad service, expensive Chinese dishes

Pho Bang: dingy and discourteous

Prosperity Dumpling: cramped quarters and haphazard service

Rothmann's: inconsistent in every way

Shula's Steak House: pass this one up for a real winner

Tavern on the Green: big, beautiful, but not a good place to eat

Triomphe: small in size, with spotty service and high prices

the menu as small and large plates. Interesting small plates include Uncle Ning's chicken salad (peanuts and spicy Sichuan dressing), a lamb dish with Yunnan spices and Pomelo salad (grilled shrimp, mushrooms, chrysanthemum greens and palm vinaigrette). Large plates list a spicy, cumin-beef stir fry, braised pork with fried rice, Chinese eggplant with chili oil and crushed peanuts and more. Some reservations are accepted, but most of the room is kept open for the busy walk-in traffic; takeout is available.

NOTES

CHAPTER 3

WHERE TO FIND IT MUSEUMS, TOURS AND MORE

A WEEK IN NEW YORK

"How can I see and do everything in New York City in a week?" You could spend an entire lifetime in New York and still never see and do everything this fabulous city has to offer. If you're here for a week, you first need to gather information and make choices.

My advice is to pick one or two places you really want to visit each day and build your itinerary around them. Because New York is so big, I suggest limiting your daily itinerary to just one or two neighborhoods. Also check to be sure that places you want to visit will be open on that day before you get too far along in your planning. Many museums and other tourist spots have reduced hours in the winter months. Of course, some activities are seasonal: ice skating in Rockefeller Plaza can be done only in winter, while Shakespeare in the Park is offered only in summer.

Every trip to New York is different, and every writer will have a varying list of favorites. If you have friends who know New York, by all means ask for their recommendations. The following itinerary for a week in New York combines my own favorites with some of the absolute "don't miss" classics. Whether you follow this outline or take a friend's suggestions, remember that part of the pleasure of New York is simply taking it all in at your leisure. Whatever else you do, spend a little time just walking around!

MONDAY | GETTING ORIENTED

■ Buy the current edition of *Time Out New York*, and read the various sections over coffee.

■ Stop by an official New York City information center at Macy's Herald Square, City Hall, Chinatown or South Street Seaport, to pick up maps and brochures and ask questions.

■ Take a **Hop-On Hop-Off Bus Tour** of Manhattan (Gray Line New York Visitor Center, 777 Eighth Ave, 212/445-0848, 800/669-0051) in a bright-red double-decker bus.

■ Walk along Madison Avenue in the 60s and 70s, checking out all the big-name boutiques.

■ Take a walk or carriage ride through Central Park.

■ Lunch at one of the restaurants at **The Shops at Columbus Circle**, Time Warner Center (10 Columbus Circle).

■ Dinner at **Brooklyn Diner USA** (212 W 57th St).

TUESDAY | MUSEUM MILE, UPPER EAST SIDE

■ Breakfast at **Norma's** at Le Parker Meridien Hotel (119 W 57th St).

■ **Cooper Hewitt, Smithsonian Design Museum** (2 E 91st St).

■ **Solomon R. Guggenheim Museum** (1071 Fifth Ave) and lunch in The Wright.

■ **The Metropolitan Museum of Art** (1000 Fifth Ave).

■ Visit the **Apple Store** (767 Fifth Ave).

■ Dinner at **Arlington Club Steakhouse** (1032 Lexington Ave).

■ Take in a show on Broadway or at a comedy club.

WEDNESDAY | MIDTOWN

■ Stroll through **Rockefeller Plaza** (Fifth Ave bet 48th and 51st St).

■ Stop by **St. Patrick's Cathedral** (Fifth Ave bet 50th and 51st St).

■ Visit the **United Nations** (First Ave bet 42nd and 47th St).

■ Lunch at **Stella 34 Trattoria** (Macy's, 151 W 34th St, 35th and Broadway entrance).

■ Take the 12:30 p.m. tour of **Grand Central Terminal,** offered by the Municipal Art Society.

■ Visit the **New York Public Library** (455 Fifth Ave).

■ Spend the afternoon touring the **Museum of Modern Art** (11 W 53rd St).

■ Dinner at **Eataly** (200 Fifth Ave): Eat in one of the restaurants or order take-out from the food shops.

THURSDAY | UPPER WEST SIDE

■ Start the day with a nosh at **Zabar's** (2245 Broadway).

■ Stop by **The Cathedral Church of Saint John the Divine** (1047 Amsterdam Ave).

■ Stock up on sweets at **Mondel Chocolates** (2913 Broadway).

■ Lunch at **Cafe Lalo** (201 W 83rd St).

■ Spend the afternoon at the **American Museum of Natural History** (Central Park W at 79th St).

■ Dinner at **Barbetta** (321 W 46th St).

FRIDAY LOWER MANHATTAN

■ Take the first ferry from Battery Park to the **Statue of Liberty** and **Ellis Island**.

■ Walk up the Battery Park Esplanade.

■ Visit the rebuilt **World Trade Center** complex and the **National September 11 Memorial & Museum** (180 Greenwich St).

■ Lunch at **Balthazar** (80 Spring St).

■ Stop by **St. Paul's Chapel** (209 Broadway).

■ Take a leisurely late-afternoon stroll on the Brooklyn Bridge.

■ Dinner at **Bouley** (163 Duane St).

■ See a Broadway show. Get tickets well in advance from **Americana Tickets,** or try your luck at a **TKTS** booth.

SATURDAY CHELSEA AND SOHO

■ Shop at **ABC Carpet & Home** (881 and 888 Broadway).

■ Browse the **Strand Book Store** (828 Broadway).

■ Go gallery hopping in Chelsea (on and around W 22nd St).

■ Have a late-morning brunch at **Aquagrill** (210 Spring St).

■ Walk along the elevated **High Line Park** (Gansevoort St to West 34th St).

■ Dinner at **Osteria Morini** (218 Lafayette St).

■ Take a late-evening elevator ride up to an observation deck of the **Empire State Building** (350 Fifth Ave).

■ Walk along Fifth Avenue.

SUNDAY LOWER EAST SIDE, MIDTOWN EAST

■ Lunch at **Katz's Delicatessen** (205 E Houston St).

■ Take one of the many scheduled tours at the **Lower East Side Tenement Museum** (103 Orchard St) or an interesting walking tour of the Lower East Side.

■ Visit the remarkable **Eldridge Street Synagogue** (12 Eldridge St).

■ Dinner at **Le Périgord** (405 E 52nd Ave).

Information on all places listed in these itineraries can be found in other sections of this book. Whatever else you do during your visit, I have two final pieces of advice:

■ Get to know the subway system. It is generally safe, reliable, convenient, inexpensive (particularly if you get a seven-day pass) and by far the most efficient way to travel in New York, unless you have mobility issues. If you take cabs everywhere, you'll burn both money and time.

■ Slow down. New Yorkers move very fast. It is fun to get into the flow of things, but it is also good to pause and take a look around. Don't get so focused on your destination that you fail to savor the experience of getting where you're going.

TOP 12 PLACES TO VISIT IN NEW YORK

There are certain places in New York that everyone has on their "must visit" list. I've listed mine here, in alphabetical order, for easy reference.

AMERICAN MUSEUM OF NATURAL HISTORY

Central Park W at 79th St   212/769-5100
Daily: 10-5:45   amnh.org

Founded in 1869, this remarkable museum has taught generations of New York children and out-of-town visitors alike about the remarkable diversity of our planet and the natural world around us. It is hard to overstate the size of this sprawling place: the museum has 45 permanent exhibition halls in 25 interconnected buildings—including the Rose Center for Earth and Space and the Hayden Planetarium—covering almost 20 acres. The museum alone has more than 33 million artifacts and specimens.

Like several other museums of its size in New York, the American Museum of Natural History can seem overwhelming. My advice is to go to the information desk when you first arrive, get a floor plan and then sit down and think about where you would like to go. If you're planning to see an IMAX movie or the Space Show at the Rose Center, be sure to note the time on your ticket and plan the other parts of your visit accordingly. While the constantly changing special exhibits are often fascinating, be aware that they are also often very crowded. So, too, are some of the permanent exhibits, including the Hall of Biodiversity, the Akeley Hall of African Mammals, the Milstein Hall of Ocean Life and the Spitzer Hall of Human Origins. However, exhibits on the Northwest Coast and other Native Americans, as well as Asian, African and Central and South American cultures, are often entirely empty even on busy days and yet full of fascinating items. Between all of the fossils, minerals, skeletons and insects, there's really something for everyone. Plan to stay for at least a half day.

Four eateries, more gift shops than you can count and guided tours are available. Admission fee charged (reasonable).

CENTRAL PARK

Bounded by Central Park W and Fifth Ave from 59th to 110th St
                                                       centralparknyc.org

This urban gem was designed in 1858 by landscape architect Frederick Law Olmsted and architect Calvert Vaux. Olmsted also designed the U.S. Capitol grounds in Washington, D.C. Central Park occupies a rectangle in the heart of Manhattan that's bounded by Fifth Avenue on the East Side and Central Park West on the west side. Its 843 acres of grass, rocky outcroppings, ponds, 19,000 trees and 58 miles of paths stretch from 59th Street to 110th Street.

BEFORE YOU SNAP

Some museums and galleries allow visitors to freely snap photos of famous works on display. Others have strict "no photography" policies enforced by security officers. The same prohibition may apply to sketching. Always check the fine print online before you go or ask at the museum or gallery. Be respectful of the property and other visitors.

Tennis courts, baseball diamonds, playgrounds, restaurants, ice-skating (in winter) and a castle can all be found inside the park. Thanks to the Central Park Conservancy, a nonprofit organization that began managing the park in 1980, it is all clean, safe and wonderfully accessible to the 40 million people who use it every year.

Regardless of season, the best way to experience Central Park is just to walk in it. (If you ever get lost, it helps to know that the first digits of the number plate on the lampposts correspond to the nearest cross street.) There's so much to see and do in the park that it's almost a city within the city. Just about every New Yorker has a favorite spot. Some of my favorites include the **Conservatory Gardens** (just off Fifth Ave and 105th St), the **Loeb Boathouse** (near 72nd St on the east side), **Central Park Zoo** (just off Fifth Ave at 64th St), **Belvedere Castle** (mid-park, near 79th St), **Strawberry Fields** (near Central Park West, between 71st and 74th St) and **Tavern on the Green** (just off Central Park West at 67th St). Alas, the popular polar bear exhibit at the zoo is no longer, but grizzlies are now in residence. You can get one of those quintessential New York photos standing on the rock outcroppings just inside the park near 59th Street at Avenue of the Americas. Originally used to store munitions, the historic Arsenal Building (which predates the park), now houses the NYC Department of Parks and Recreation.

Another great way to experience Central Park is by attending an event there. Particularly in the summer, the **Naumburg Bandshell** and SummerStage are home to free concerts. The Great Lawn is the setting for free outdoor concerts by the New York Philharmonic and the Metropolitan Opera. The **Delacorte Theater** is home to the popular Shakespeare in the Park performances, which are also free. For a complete listing of events, walking tours and other park activities, visit the website.

EMPIRE STATE BUILDING

350 Fifth Ave (bet 33rd and 34th St)   212/736-3100

Daily: 8 a.m.-2 a.m. (last elevator trip at 1:15 a.m.)   empirestatebuilding.com

Often the first image that comes to mind when people think of New York is this 102-story building. Soaring above its neighbors in the heart of NYC, this skyscraper was built in 1931 and has defined the New York City skyline ever since. (In case you're wondering, there are 1,860 steps from street level to the 102nd floor!) The Empire State Building's LED tower lights, illuminated to commemorate holidays, events and special causes are a beloved beacon of light for New York City and the world. They also stage dazzling light shows celebrating holidays and events, often synchronized to music broadcast simultaneously on iHeartMedia radio stations.

Tourists from all over the world and fans of movies like *King Kong*, *An Affair to Remember* and *Sleepless in Seattle* simply can't come to New York without visiting this landmark and its observatories on the 86th and 102nd floors. On a clear day, you can see about 80 miles. It's worth noting that the ticket office and security checkpoint are located on the second floor visitors center. If you really have your heart set on a visit here, consider coming early in the morning or late at night, or buy advance tickets online. Tickets to the 102nd floor observatory cost extra. An ESB Express Pass, although pricey, will put you at the front of all lines. Audio tours, in eight languages, are available with all tickets and guide visitors through the icon's extraordinary exhibits and detail the city's unique skyline. The recently renovated lobby on the first floor was restored to the original architects' art deco vision. **State Grill and Bar** (212/216-9693) is an elegant addition on the ground floor and is open for both lunch and dinner. Three sleek rooms on the concourse level offer exceptional private dining experiences and space for exclusive events. Admission fee charged (reasonable to expensive, depending on tour package).

FIFTH AVENUE

London. Paris. Tokyo. They all have fashionable streets with skyrocketing rents. But nowhere in the world is quite as fashionable or quite as expensive as New York's Fifth Avenue.

Fifth Avenue starts down in Greenwich Village at Washington Square Park. However, when tourists say they want to visit Fifth Avenue, they generally mean midtown and the Upper East Side. Fifth Avenue between 42nd and 59th streets is the heart of New York. It was once lined with mansions and is still home to some of the grandest and most recognizable buildings in the city. They include the midtown branch of the **New York Public Library** (at 42nd St), **Rockefeller Center** (between 48th and 51st St), **Saks Fifth Avenue** (at 50th St), **St. Patrick's Cathedral** (at 51st St), **Tiffany & Co.** (at 57th St) and **The Plaza** (at 59th St). The presence of swanky retailers affirms the reputation that Fifth Avenue has earned as a tourist mecca and pricey shopping district.

The stretch of Fifth Avenue between 59th Street and 110th Street runs along the east side of Central Park. You'll find the **Neue Galerie New York** (at 86th Street), the **National Academy Museum and School** (between 89th and 90th Street), **The Jewish Museum** (at 92nd Street) and the **Museum of the City of New York** (at 103rd Street). Museum Mile extends all the way to the top of Central Park at 110th Street.

Like much of New York, the best way to see Fifth Avenue is on foot. The sidewalks along Central Park are a particular pleasure. There's no subway line running on Fifth Avenue, although there are plenty of buses and cabs. Traffic on Fifth Avenue is one-way heading south. One more tip: Under no circumstances should you shop in a store on Fifth Avenue in midtown with "Going Out of Business" signs in the windows. They have a habit of going out of business regularly and this is likely just a come-on.

LINCOLN CENTER

Columbus Ave bet 62nd and 65th St   212/546-2656
                                                     lincolncenter.org

Just as Museum Mile along Fifth Avenue is the most stunning concentration of art anywhere in the world, the 16-acre Lincoln Center campus may be the world's most amazing grouping of performing-arts institutions. Nearly a dozen resident companies are housed here including **The Julliard School of Music**, the **New York City Ballet**, the **Chamber Music Society of Lincoln Center**, the **New York Philharmonic** and the **Metropolitan Opera**. There is also a branch of the New York Public Library devoted entirely to the performing arts.

If you want to peek inside some of these concert halls and other spaces, daily tours are available (212/875-5350). The campus and concert halls were modernized in 2012 culminating a $1.2 billion project. You're also welcome to wander around and enjoy the fountains, open terraces, restaurants and other public spaces. Each of the several stops is well worth your time. If you're interested in seeing one of the hundreds of performances that take place here every year, then visit the website for the latest information. Seeing a production at Lincoln Center is a special only-in-New-York treat!

LOWER EAST SIDE TENEMENT MUSEUM

103 Orchard St (bet Delancey and Broome St)   212/431-0233
Daily: 10-5   tenement.org

Whether or not you're among the countless millions in this country whose family traces its arrival in America to the Lower East Side, a visit to this living history museum is another one of my "must-sees" in New York.

Building tours start at the visitors center (103 Orchard St) and then go down the block to the tenement building at 97 Orchard Street, where various apartments are frozen in time. Home to as many as 7,000 people from more than 20 nations between 1863 and 1935, this building is a living memorial to the hundreds of thousands who passed through the Lower East Side as immigrants to this country. An interesting guided tour is "The Moores: An Irish Family in America." Depending on the tour, you'll encounter various immigrant families modeled on real people who lived in this building between the 1860s and the 1930s. Walking tours of the Lower East Side are also available on weekends in warmer months. Take time for the excellent 25-minute film about the history of immigration on the Lower East Side, which runs continuously at the visitors center or browse the excellent gift shop. There is no cost to enter the visitors center. Fee charged (reasonable) for tours; reservations strongly suggested.

ADMISSION PRICES

Following each museum or attraction write-up I've noted whether adult admission is free or if the fee charged is nominal ($1 to $5), reasonable ($6 to $19) or expensive ($20 and up). Taxes and add-ons are extra. Be sure to carefully check suggested admission prices.

THE METROPOLITAN MUSEUM OF ART

1000 Fifth Ave (bet 80th and 84th St)   212/535-7710
Sun-Thurs: 10-5:30; Fri, Sat: 10-9   metmuseum.org

Five thousand years of art. That's how The Metropolitan Museum of Art

("The Met," as it's known to New Yorkers and art fans) describes its vast holdings. It's all here: Egyptian tombs. Greek sculptures. African masks. European and Japanese arms and armor. Vases from China. Early American furniture. Tiffany windows. Nineteenth-century costumes. Twentieth-century photography. And no matter how many times you visit or how much time you spend here, there's just no way you'll ever see it all. The depth and breadth of The Met's collection is unparalleled.

There are several ways to approach touring The Met. Arrive early on a weekday morning, get a copy of the floor plan at the information desk and figure out a couple areas of the museum you want to visit over the course of a day. The museum's suggested itineraries highlight artwork saved by the Monument Men, items of interest to families, visitors' favorites and other specialties; foreign language tours are also available. You can always break for lunch at one of the museum's several restaurants or end your weekend day with a drink at the **Great Hall Balcony Bar**. My favorite strategy is simply going where everyone else isn't. Crowds can be overwhelming on weekends and whenever there's a special exhibit. Buying advance admission online is a good way to avoid long lines.

For many people, a favorite part of a Met visit is a trip to one of the museum's many stores. Although you can now visit Met gift stores at Kennedy airport, Rockefeller Center, The Cloisters and elsewhere, it's more fun to browse the shops inside The Met itself. Recommended admission fee (expensive) includes same day entry to the main building and to **The Cloisters Museum and Gardens**, located in northern Manhattan's Fort Tryon Park.

NEW YORK CITY'S TALLEST BUILDINGS

Skyscraper construction is elevating the Manhattan skyline, pushing the **Empire State Building** (1,250 feet) to the third tallest building in the Big Apple (it reigned as the world's tallest for over 40 years). One **World Trade Center** (1,776 feet) has surpassed the Empire State Building as the city's tallest building and when it is completed, **432 Park Avenue**, a residential building (1,396 feet), will be the city's second tallest.

MUSEUM OF MODERN ART

11 W 53rd St (bet Fifth Ave and Ave of the Americas)	212/708-9400
Daily: 10:30-5:30 (Fri till 8)	moma.org

This museum is itself a masterpiece, filled with glass and soaring spaces. Located in midtown, MoMA (pronounced MO-ma) is the leading museum in the world dedicated to modern art. Well over 150,000 pieces of art (paintings, prints, photography and sculpture) are housed here, along with a remarkable archive and film library. From Cezanne, van Gogh, Matisse and Picasso to Jasper Johns, Jeff Koons, Georgia O'Keeffe and Jackson Pollack, just about any 20th-century artist you can imagine is represented. Indeed, MoMA's sleek galleries are a Who's Who of modern art history.

MoMA's curatorial departments include Architecture and Design,

NEW YORK STOCK EXCHANGE

Steeped in history, the world's largest stock exchange originated on Wall Street in 1792. Several locations on Wall and Broad streets were home to the New York Stock Exchange until the erection of the current neoclassical structure on Broad Street in 1903. Home to many of America's greatest companies and its globally recognized trading floor, this National Historic Landmark has been shaped by booms, busts and images of frenetic trading for over 200 years. Alas, this iconic temple of trading (a.k.a. the "Big Board") is no longer open for public tours.

Drawings and Prints, Painting and Sculpture, Photography, Film, Media and Performance Art. Pieces from each department are always on display in various collection galleries. In addition, MoMA has changing exhibitions and often hosts special traveling exhibitions. If you have time, I suggest starting on the sixth floor and working your way down. If you want a quick tour of some of the museum's most famous holdings including van Gogh's *Starry Night*, Picasso's *Guitar*, Matisse's *Dance (I)* and Andy Warhol's *Campbell's Soup Cans*, then stop by the information desk and get a map.

A visit to this amazing place is not complete without a visit to the MoMA Bookstore (just off the foyer on the first floor) and the MoMA Design Store (across the street). Although there is some overlap between the two stores, there are enough differences to make it well worth your time to peruse both, as well as have lunch at either of the two cafes at MoMA or dinner at **The Modern**, a high-end Danny Meyer restaurant. Admission fee charged (expensive); Fri: 4-8, free. Admission to films is free with same-day museum ticket, otherwise film tickets are $12. Admission to MoMA PS 1, an affiliated museum in Long Island City, is free if you show your MoMA ticket stub within 30 days.

SOLOMON R. GUGGENHEIM MUSEUM

1071 Fifth Ave (at 89th St)   212/423-3500
Sun-Wed, Fri: 10-5:45; Sat: 10-7:45   guggenheim.org

The Solomon R. Guggenheim Museum began in 1939 as the Museum of Non-Objective Painting. It was created to house the growing art collection of American industrialist Solomon Guggenheim. His collection included the work of such contemporaries as Vasily Kandinsky, Paul Klee and Marc Chagall, and many of those original pieces form the backbone of this remarkable museum today. Of course the collection has grown tremendously, since it incorporates work from artists ranging from late 19th-century impressionists to contemporary artists.

Although Guggenheim museums in Venice, Italy, and Bilbao, Spain, showcase parts of the collection, the museum on Fifth Avenue is still the Guggenheim. In addition to the works displayed inside, people put this world-famous museum at the top of their itineraries because of its instantly recognizable building. It's an inverted ziggurat that looks a bit like a snail from the outside and allows visitors on the inside to wind their way through the collection rather than roaming in and out of rooms. The Guggenheim was designed by Frank Lloyd Wright and sits at the north end of Museum

Mile, right across Fifth Avenue from Central Park. It opened in 1959 and underwent an extensive renovation for its 50th anniversary. Stand across the street to get the best architectural view.

In some ways, the breadth of the Guggenheim's collection rivals that of the Museum of Modern Art (in midtown) and the Metropolitan Museum of Art (five blocks south on Fifth Ave). But the great pleasure of the Guggenheim is that it's a bit smaller and more intimate than its famous cousins, giving art lovers time to linger. If 20th-century art is your passion, then there's no place you'll rather spend a day! Admission fee charged (reasonable); Sat: 5:45-7:45, pay what you wish.

STATUE OF LIBERTY

New York Harbor (south of Battery Park)   212/363-3200
Daily: 9-5 (adjusted seasonally)   nps.gov/stli

They call her Miss Liberty. This 151-foot copper statue of a woman holding a torch was created by Frederic-Auguste Bartholdi and given to the United States as a gift from France in 1886. Standing on Liberty Island in New York Harbor, it's probably the single most iconic sight in all of New York. For the 12 million immigrants who came through nearby Ellis Island, it was also the first real sight they had of this new land. The words from "The New Colossus," a poem written by Emma Lazarus to help raise money for the completion of the pedestal for this powerful monument, still express basic instincts of our country and symbolism associated with the Statue of Liberty: "Give me your tired, your poor, Your huddled masses yearning to breathe free."

A trip to the Statue of Liberty National Monument will take the better part of a morning or afternoon, so plan accordingly. Both the Statue of Liberty and Ellis Island are administered by the National Park Service. Visiting either destination requires a trip by boat from Battery Park. Head to Castle Clinton in Battery Park for tickets and detailed information, or buy your tickets in advance via Statue Cruises (201/604-2800, 877/523-9849). Tickets to the crown and pedestal are also sold through Statue Cruises; crown tickets are limited to 365 per day and should be reserved well in advance. Climbing to

MUSEUM MEMBERSHIPS AND ADMISSIONS

Check into yearly membership rates if you plan to make multiple visits to your favorite museum. An annual membership may pay for itself in four or five visits. Member perks, such as special or exclusive events and museum-store discounts, are added values. Many institutions list their entry fees as a suggested amount. Translation: offer what you would like to pay. That is especially prudent if you plan to be in a museum for only a short time and the admission charge is steep.

If possible, plan your visit to coincide with free admission hours. Many museums offer free or pay-as-you-wish admission to customers one evening a week. However, a possible tradeoff for going on a free night is a thicker crowd.

TOURING ON TWO WHEELS

The knowledgeable guides at **Bike the Big Apple** (347/878-9809, 877/865-0078, bikethebigapple.com) put a different spin on seeing the sights. Of course you can cruise through Central Park and trendy nearby neighborhoods, but they'll also lead riders down the trails of high finance and Chinatown; on a journey in quest of brews, chocolates and great views; across the East River to Queens and Brooklyn for an ethnic tour; or to check out city lights on a twilight pedal across the Brooklyn Bridge after a swing through Lower Manhattan. Prices include bike and helmet rental fees.

the crown entails ascending (and descending) 377 steps (the equivalent to climbing 20 stories) without air conditioning; high heat factors may close the Statue from time to time. Even if you have tickets, you'll need to wait in line for the next available boat. My advice: go early on a weekday and bring along lots of patience. Crown reservations: nominal fee; pedestal reservations: free. Ferry ticket (reasonable) is required.

The **Ellis Island Immigration Museum** has partially reopened after damage from Superstorm Sandy for visitors to wander the Great Hall. Ranger-led tours of the museum are free but there is a fee for the guided hard-hat tours of the 750-bed Hospital Complex including the laundry building, kitchen, autopsy room, staff housing and more (expensive).

TIMES SQUARE

42nd St at Broadway and surrounding area   timessquarenyc.org

When I first started writing this book, Times Square was synonymous with petty crime, prostitution and filth. Not anymore. In fact, I find it hard to believe that the Times Square of yesteryear and the Times Square of the 21st century are the same place. Named for the original New York Times building and incorporating the neighborhood around 42nd Street and Broadway, Times Square is now a center of New York's burgeoning tourist industry. It's full of family-friendly restaurants, hotels and entertainment venues. A TKTS booth is conveniently located under the ruby-red steps in Father Duffy Square at Broadway and 47th Street. Learn the history of theater in Times Square on an escorted tour with **Walkin' Broadway** (212/997-5004). Personal headsets provide show tunes and interviews with Broadway's greatest. Tours are offered year-round with 48-hour advance reservations (expensive).

All of those changes do not, however, put Times Square at the top of my "Top 12" list of places to visit. The whole area is wildly crowded with out-of-towners. In fact, it's a bit like going to a big mall somewhere in the nondescript suburbs around the winter holidays.

WORLD TRADE CENTER

Bounded by Vesey, Liberty, Church St and the West Side Highway   wtc.com

One World Trade Center rises a symbolic 1,776 feet in height joining 7 World Trade Center in Lower Manhattan. Four other towers will complete the complex on this emotionally-charged site.   When the buildings are completed, they will include observation decks, a performing arts center and vibrant retail and office spaces. Recently completed, the all new Fulton Center subway hub is magnificent. **The National September 11 Memorial & Museum** (180 Greenwich St, 212/266-5211, 911memorial.org) offers a quiet place to remember and reflect upon the tragic losses of September 11, 2001 and February 26, 1996. Five galleries constitute **9/11 Tribute Center** (120 Liberty St, 212/393-9160, tributewtc.org), the official partner and tour provider of the Memorial Museum. **9/11 Tribute Center Memorial Walking Tours** are led by people directly affected by the events of that day. Memorial is free; fee charged for admission and/or tour (reasonable to expensive).

BEST OF THE REST

The previous "Top 12" list includes the museums and sights most everyone wants to see when they come to New York. Although many of the museums and sights on that list are definite "must-sees," they are by no means all there is to New York. In fact, some of my "must-sees" are less well known, smaller or a bit off the beaten path. The following list includes what I consider to be among the crown jewels of this remarkable city.

AMERICAN FOLK ART MUSEUM

2 Lincoln Square (Columbus Ave at 66th St)   212/595-9533
Mon-Sat: 11-7 (Fri till 7:30; Sun: 11-6)   folkartmuseum.org

The museum's collection spans three centuries. Traditional folk art and works by self-taught artists are featured in changing exhibitions that come from the museum's collection and other lenders, public and private. The museum is located in a large two-level space with an excellent gift shop. Live music is featured in the galleries Friday evenings. Admission is free.

BROOKLYN BRIDGE

Broadway at City Hall Park in Lower Manhattan

Spanning the East River, this spectacular suspension bridge links Lower Manhattan to Brooklyn. It took 15 years and two generations to build. After its designer, John Roebling, was killed in an accident, his son Washington and daughter-in-law Emily took over the project. Pedestrians and bicyclists share the bridge's historic 1.3 mile-promenade; bicyclists have the north lane, pedestrians the south. To reach the bridge, go to the east side of City Hall Park, just off Broadway, and follow the signs. For the rest of the story you may want to join a tour or download an iPhone app. Sunset and sunrise are particularly beautiful times to take a stroll on the bridge, although it's open 24 hours a day.

THE CATHEDRAL CHURCH OF SAINT JOHN THE DIVINE

1047 Amsterdam Ave (at 112th St)   212/316-7540
Daily: 7:30-6   stjohndivine.org

Gracing Amsterdam Avenue on the east side of Columbia University, The Cathedral Church of Saint John the Divine is one of the largest Christian houses of worship in the world.   Part Gothic, part Romanesque, this

HIGH LINE PARK

You won't be disappointed by a walk along the very popular High Line (212/206-9922, thehighline.org), a unique public park built on a 1.45-mile-long elevated rail structure with views of New York's magnificent skyline and the Hudson River. The route runs from Gansevoort Street and continues up to 34th Street where it terminates at the West Side Rail Yards. The former freight rail line ceased operation in 1980 and after a decade of efforts by Friends of the High Line, and with support from the City of New York, it was redesigned to accommodate a water feature, sundeck, gathering areas and safe walking surfaces. Areas are designated for educational programs, art installations and performances, but dogs, Frisbees and playing catch are prohibited. Park hours fluctuate according to the season; snow and ice removal keeps the High Line open even in the dead of winter. Come spring, food vendors set up shop between April and October. There are currently eleven access points to the park, and since High Line Park sits above city streets, elevators are located at six of those entry points providing wheelchair accessibility.

magnificent Episcopal cathedral is so enormous that the Statue of Liberty could easily fit inside the main sanctuary. For information about daily tours, call 212/932-7347. Admission is free, but donations are accepted and a minimal fee is charged for tours.

THE CLOISTERS MUSEUM AND GARDENS

Fort Tryon Park (99 Margaret Corbin Dr)   212/923-3700
Daily: 10-5:15 (till 4:45, Nov-Feb)   metmuseum.org/cloisters

Perhaps the finest medieval art museum in the world, this branch of **The Metropolitan Museum of Art** is also one of the quietest and most beautiful places in all of New York. Built at the far north end of the island on land donated by John D. Rockefeller, Jr. in the late 1930s, the museum incorporates large sections of cloisters and other medieval buildings brought from Europe. Tapestries, ivories, paintings, sculptures and other decorative items are part of the spectacular collection on display. From the outdoor terrace, you can look at the Hudson River and the steep cliffs known as the Palisades beyond, easily forgetting that you're in a 21st-century city. Recommended admission fee charged (expensive) includes same-day admission to The Metropolitan Museum of Art.

COOPER HEWITT, SMITHSONIAN DESIGN MUSEUM

2 E 91st St (at Fifth Ave)   212/849-8400
Daily: 10-6 (Sat till 9)   cooperhewitt.org

Founded as the Cooper Union Museum for the Arts of Decoration in 1897, this remarkable institution became part of the Smithsonian Institution in 1967 and now has a new look thanks to a $91 million restoration of the entire Andrew Carnegie Mansion. Previously off limits to the public, the third floor is a signature gallery for temporary exhibitions; the new and improved establishment has nearly 60% more gallery space. The second floor features wallcoverings from the extensive collection with the opportunity to design your own pattern. Visitors are loaned an interactive pen to collect information and create while experiencing the museum. Outside, the Arthur Ross Terrace and Garden were spiffed up as well. Admission fee charged (reasonable).

FRICK COLLECTION

I E 70th St (at Fifth Ave)   212/288-0700
Tues-Sat: 10-6; Sun: 11-5   frick.org

This elegant mansion takes my breath away! Built in 1914 by industrialist Henry Clay Frick to house his growing art collection, the Frick Collection is one of the last great mansions on Fifth Avenue and it is definitely on my "must-see" list. Gilbert Stuart's portrait of George Washington is here, as are works by Vermeer, Rembrandt, El Greco, Goya and masters ranging from the Italian Renaissance to the 19th century. But it isn't just the paintings that dazzle. Frick's collection also includes stunning Oriental rugs, Chinese porcelain, Limoges enamels and a wide range of decorative arts that must be seen to be believed. Take time to wander and look at everything from the paintings to the light fixtures and rugs, to the serene Garden Court. Tour the museum at no additional charge with the purchase of a Sunday concert ticket, otherwise, admission fee charged (reasonable); Sun: 11-1, pay what you wish.

GRAND CENTRAL TERMINAL

42nd St bet Vanderbilt and Lexington Ave   212/340-2345
Daily: 5:30 a.m.-2 a.m.   grandcentralterminal.com

New York's past, present and future come together in this marble palace that was voted "New York's Greatest Building." Opened in 1913, Grand Central is first and foremost a train station, home to hundreds of commuter trains that operate between Manhattan and points north in Westchester County and Connecticut. It also plays host to an upscale food market, dozens

UP IN THE AIR

Some people say the best way to see all of New York City is from the sky. A helicopter tour not only provides a birdseye view, but covers more sights in a short timespan than any other means of sightseeing. Each exhilarating tour departs from the Downtown Manhattan Heliport (Pier 6 and the East River). Tour lengths vary from a quick 12-minute journey to a more-inclusive 30-minute buzz around the Big Apple and beyond; inquire about custom, private and special occasion tours.

Helicopter New York City (212/747-9282, helicopternewyorkcity.com)
Liberty Helicopters (212/967-6464, 800/542-9933; libertyhelicopters. com)
Manhattan Helicopters (212/845-9822, 866/592-9655; flymh.com)

Since inclement weather conditions may cause disruptions to scheduled flights, it might be a good idea to plan your flight at the front end of your trip in case you need to reschedule.

of shops featuring everything from unique toys to fine jewelry and cutting edge technology and a gourmet dining concourse. (Stores and restaurants keep varying hours.) Exciting events and promotions happen daily in historic Vanderbilt Hall and live guided (expensive) and audio tours (reasonable) are available on the main concourse. There's no charge to wander around the terminal and take in its extraordinary century-old beaux-arts architecture.

THE JEWISH MUSEUM

1109 Fifth Ave (at 92nd St)   212/423-3200
Sat-Tues: 11-5:45; Thurs: 11-8; Fri: 11-4   thejewishmuseum.org

The Jewish Museum is housed in yet another grand Fifth Avenue mansion. This one was donated by Felix Warburg's widow in 1945 (Warburg was a Jewish philanthropist). The museum explores 4,000 years of art and Jewish culture and has the largest collection of Jewish-related art and Judaica in the United States, 30,000 works. The heart of the museum is "Culture and Continuity: The Jewish Journey" comprised of 800 objects including paintings, drawings, sculptures, ritual art, archaeology and photography. A visit to the museum's excellent gift shop or Celebrations, a smaller design shop in an adjacent brownstone, is well worth an extra half-hour. The cafe is under renovation and will reopen summer 2015 as **Russ & Daughters** at The Jewish Museum. Admission fee charged (reasonable); Sat: free; Thurs: 5-8, pay what you wish.

THE MORGAN LIBRARY & MUSEUM

225 Madison Ave (at 36th St)   212/685-0008
Tues-Thurs: 10:30-5; Fri: 10:30-9; Sat: 10-6; Sun: 11-6   themorgan.org

Built between 1902 and 1906 to house the astonishing collection of rare items and prized treasures amassed by Pierpont Morgan (an industrialist and financier), the elegant library and study and their contents will transport you to another time and place. Just imagine yourself surrounded by these paintings, sculptures, furniture, books, architectural details and textiles spanning many centuries and several continents! It's hard to believe anyone ever lived like this. Morgan's collection includes historical, artistic, literary and musical works. The spaces in the rest of the museum, including an atrium and other galleries, are often crowded. A center of research, the Drawing Institute, is based at the Morgan and is dedicated to the study of drawings from all periods. **The Morgan Cafe** is a good place for casual midday fare and **The Morgan Dining Room** is open for brunch and lunch. Admission fee charged (reasonable); Fri: 7-9, free.

MUSEUM OF JEWISH HERITAGE:
A LIVING MEMORIAL TO THE HOLOCAUST

36 Battery Pl (in Battery Park City)   646/437-4202
Sun-Tues: 10-5:45; Wed: 10-8; Thurs: 10-5:45; Fri: 10-5 (till 3 during EST)
                                                                        mjhnyc.org

This remarkable and sometimes overlooked museum just north of Battery Park in Lower Manhattan manages to be not only a memorial to those who perished in the Holocaust but also a vibrant, life-affirming celebration of Jewish culture and its endurance. Using first-person narratives, a remarkably diverse collection and special exhibitions, the museum's three-part permanent display tells the unfolding story of Jewish life a century ago, the persecution of Jews and the Holocaust and modern Jewish life and renewal in the decades since. An audio guide is available at no charge, and a free activity book assists families with young children to explore the first and third floors. Both the cafe, which has amazing views of the Statue of Liberty and New York Harbor, and the museum's gift shop merit a visit.   Andy Goldsworthy's *Garden of Stones* outside the museum is a terrific spot to sit and meditate.   Visitors should be prepared to take their time.   Admission fee charged (reasonable); children 12 and under, free; Wed: 4-8, free.

MUSEUM OF THE CITY OF NEW YORK

1220 Fifth Ave (bet 103rd and 104th St)   212/534-1672
Daily: 10-6   mcny.org

Housed in a landmark Georgian-style mansion, this museum is dedicated to preserving the history of New York, starting with its earliest European settlement. A $93 million expansion and modernization project will be completed in 2016 bringing a new energy to the changing and permanent exhibitions, lectures, classes, programs for city school students and other events. Among the 750,000 objects are a room of Duncan Phyfe furniture, Eugene O'Neill's handwritten manuscripts, costumes, paintings, sculptures, theatrical memorabilia and much more. Admission fee charged (reasonable).

NEW YORK PUBLIC LIBRARY

455 Fifth Ave (bet 40th and 42nd St)   917/275-6975
Mon, Thurs-Sat: 10-6; Tues, Wed: 10-8; Sun: 1-5   nypl.org

This main branch of the New York Public Library, the iconic Stephen A. Schwarzman Building, is a leading public research library and home to a wide range of collections, public programs and electronic databases. But this isn't just any library! Located along Fifth Avenue, it's a "must-see" if you're in midtown. Standing guard out front are two stately lions named Patience and Fortitude by former mayor Fiorello LaGuardia. Inside you'll find marble staircases, an excellent gift shop, the dramatic Rose Main Reading Room on the third floor (nearly two city blocks long and enhanced with Wi-Fi and laptop docking), an amazing map collection on the first floor and various reading rooms and gallery spaces. Underground vaults beneath Bryant Park hold research material, rare books and manuscripts. In the Children's Center, kids enjoy visiting the original Winnie the Pooh, Eeyore, Piglet, Kanga and Tigger which were once the play toys of Christopher Robin. Stop by the information desk in the elegant lobby to find out about frequent tours offered by the Friends of the New York Public Library. Free admission. There are over 40 branches of the New York Public Library in Manhattan; during the holidays, the Jefferson Market Library offers tours of its tower which has 360-degree views of Greenwich Village.

ROOSEVELT ISLAND

East River, between Manhattan and Queens

If you're a photographer looking for that perfect shot of the Manhattan skyline, a trip to Roosevelt Island should be at the top of your itinerary. At various times in its history, Roosevelt Island was known as Blackwell's Island and Welfare Island, and it's been home to prisons, hospitals and asylums.

HISTORIC HOUSES OF WORSHIP

Because New York was a British colony for much of its early history, the city's lower half is full of historic Episcopal churches. They include:

Church of the Transfiguration (1 E 29th St): also known as "the Little Church Around the Corner"

Grace Church (Broadway between 10th and 11th St)

St. Mark's Church in-the-Bowery (10th St at Third Ave): constructed on the site of Peter Stuyvesant's personal chapel in 1799

St. Paul's Chapel (Broadway between Fulton and Vesey St): the oldest church building in the city, dating from 1766

Trinity Church (Broadway at Wall St)

Other historic houses of worship in Manhattan include:

Abyssinian Baptist Church (132 Odell Clark Pl)

Bialystoker Synagogue (7-11 Willett St)

Central Synagogue (652 Lexington Ave)

Congregation Shearith Israel (8 W 70th St): also known as the Spanish and Portuguese Synagogue

Eldridge Street Synagogue (12 Eldridge St)

Marble Collegiate Church (1 W 29th St)

Riverside Church (490 Riverside Dr)

Temple Emanu-El (1 E 65th St): largest synagogue in the world

Renwick Ruin, the former Smallpox Hospital, is the only New York City ruin which is also a landmark. Today this two-mile island in the middle of the East River is home to 14,000 residents, many of whom commute into Manhattan each day. Visitors come for the view, particularly from the tram and from the northwest tip of Lighthouse Park. At the southern end, Franklin D. Roosevelt Four Freedoms Park is named for the freedoms (freedom of speech and expression, freedom of religion, freedom from want and freedom from fear) which Roosevelt described in his 1941 State of the Union address. Walking tours of the island are both fun and educational. The three-minute tram ride from Manhattan leaves from a small station at Second Avenue and 59th Street and runs daily from 6 a.m. to 2 a.m. (Fri and Sat till 3:30 a.m.) for a nominal fare of $2.50 (subway MetroCards also accepted).

ST. PATRICK'S CATHEDRAL

Fifth Ave between 50th and 51st St   212/753-2261
Daily: 6:30 a.m.-8:45 p.m.   saintpatrickscathedral.org

Designed in the middle of the 19th century by famed architect James Renwick, Jr., this Gothic cathedral is a much-loved Fifth Avenue landmark and the largest Neo-Gothic Roman Catholic church in the United States. A major project restored the beauty of the interior and exterior and made necessary upgrades and repairs. The main organ has over 9,000 pipes, and the sanctuary can seemingly seat half of Manhattan. Whether you're here for a service or just peeking inside, it's hard to overstate the beauty and elegance of St. Patrick's. Please remember that this is an active church. Mass is said several times each day, eight times on Sunday and even more on Holy Days. You are welcome to come in and light a vigil candle or just sit in silence. Here's a tip: the cathedral's steps along Fifth Avenue are one of the best places in New York for resting your feet and watching the world go by! Free admission.

STATEN ISLAND FERRY

Whitehall Ferry Terminal (at the foot of Whitehall St)   nyc.gov/dot

On a typical weekday, five ferries make a combined 100+ round trips between Staten Island and the Whitehall Ferry Terminal on Manhattan's southern tip. The trip covers just over five miles in less than 30 minutes. And what a trip it is! The Staten Island passenger ferries offer some of the very best views of Lower Manhattan's skyscrapers, the Statue of Liberty and Ellis Island with a comfortable place to sit and take them in. Bicycles are allowed if stored in designated areas, but vehicles are not permitted on the ferries. Best of all, the Staten Island ferry is free 24/7!

TRINITY CHURCH

Broadway at Wall St   212/602-0800
                                                          trinitywallstreet.org

This is the third iteration of Trinity Church to occupy a site on land that was part of a charter granted by King William III of England in 1697. This building, in the heart of Lower Manhattan's Financial District, was completed in 1846, although the headstones in the 2.5-acre graveyard date back to the late 17th century. Believe it or not, Trinity Church was the tallest building in Manhattan for most of the 19th century. Today it offers guided tours (Mon-Fri: 2 p.m.), free concerts and daily worship services. Remember that this is an active house of worship.

UNITED NATIONS

First Ave bet 42nd and 47th St   212/963-4440 (tours)
Mon-Fri: 10:15-4:45 (tours)   visit.un.org

New York is a great American city, but it is also a great international city hosting the United Nations. The flags of 193 member nations fly along First Avenue in front of the UN Headquarters. Many languages are spoken

SOUTH STREET SEAPORT WATER TOURS

The South Street Seaport offers East River departures for water travel.

New York Water Taxi (Pier 16, 212/742-1969, nywatertaxi.com): This company's distinctive boats are painted to resemble yellow checker cabs. Commuter schedules, sightseeing tours and charter boats are offered.

The Pioneer (Pier 16, 212/748-8600, southstreetseaportmuseum. org): Set sail on an authentic 1885 schooner around New York Harbor. Offered in summer only, it can accommodate 35 passengers.

LIGHTS, CAMERA, ACTION!

The Museum of the Moving Image (36-01 35th Ave, Astoria, Queens, 718/777-6888, movingimage.us) is this country's only museum dedicated to anything having to do with films (art, technology, technique and history). Allow several hours to peruse the interesting exhibits and collections (everything from action figures to a zoetrope), fan magazines, TV- and movie-inspired games and products, costumes and equipment used throughout the decades. Check the schedule for film showings in the theater and screening room. This museum is both educational and entertaining! Admission fee charged (reasonable); Fri: 4-8 free.

in this area as staff members and delegates from all over the world come and go. You can visit the beautiful and peaceful grounds of the UN to take guided tours of the renovated Conference Building and General Assembly Hall. Be sure to stop by the UN Bookstore in the new Visitor Centre, as well as the UN's very own post office before or after your guided tour. **The Delegates Dining Room** (917/367-3314) is again open weekdays to the public; global cuisine is featured on a *prix-fixe* luncheon buffet. Admission fee charged for tours (reasonable); children must be at least five years of age.

WHITNEY MUSEUM OF AMERICAN ART

99 Gansevoort St (bet Washington St and 10th Ave)   212/570-3600
Call for days and hours   whitney.org

The biggest news is the museum's move to the Meatpacking District! The new digs welcome visitors into a grand plaza only steps away from the southern entrance to the High Line. The artist and art collector Gertrude Vanderbilt Whitney opened the original museum in 1931 with her personal collection of 20th-century American art. Of course, the Whitney's mission means its remarkable collection now spans more than a century and continues to expand. It includes the world's largest collections of Edward Hopper, Reginald Marsh and Alexander Calder, as well as sculptures, paintings, drawings, media installations and other works by established and emerging artists. Facilities include state-of-the-art classrooms, a multi-use black box theater, a 170-seat theater and study center. Admission fee charged (reasonable). With a May 2015 opening, Danny Meyer's **Untitled** (212/570-3670) offers seasonal American fare daily.

SMALLER MUSEUMS AND SPECIAL SPOTS

AMERICAN NUMISMATIC SOCIETY

75 Varick St (at Canal St), 11th floor   212/571-4470
Mon-Fri: 9:30-4:30   numismatics.org

This location is a museum, library and research institute devoted to the study of coins from all periods and cultures. There are over 800,000 coins, medals, paper currency and other artifacts in the society's vast collection. The small on-site gallery of revolving exhibits is open to the public. Free admission.

AMERICAS SOCIETY GALLERY

680 Park Ave (at 68th St)   212/249-8950
Wed-Sat: noon-6   as-coa.org

Americas Society was founded in 1965 by David Rockefeller with the simple but important goal of furthering understanding between the Americas. The changing exhibitions in its small but elegant gallery space showcase the diverse work of artists from throughout the Americas. Free admission.

ASIA SOCIETY AND MUSEUM

725 Park Ave (at 70th St)   212/288-6400
Tues-Sun: 11-6 (Fri till 9, Sept-June)   asiasociety.org

Drawing upon private collections and its own extensive holdings of art from more than 30 Asia-Pacific nations, the Asia Society mounts changing exhibits of traditional and contemporary art. By all means visit the lovely **Garden Court Cafe** for lunch and a boutique that stocks items by Asian and Asian-American designers. Admission fee charged (reasonable); Fri: 6-9, free.

BARD GRADUATE CENTER GALLERY

18 W 86th St (at Central Park W)   212/501-3023
Tues-Sun: 11-5 (Thurs till 8)   bgc.bard.edu/gallery

The Bard Graduate Center is known around the world for its passionate commitment to the decorative arts, design, history and material culture. Its gallery, located in a beautiful six-story townhouse on the Upper West Side, hosts several changing exhibits each year. Suggested admission fee charged (nominal).

TOURING HARLEM

Harlem is a destination in and of itself deserving a bit of exploration either on your own or via a guided tour with professionals.

Harlem Heritage Tours (212/280-7888; harlemheritage.com): All tours are led by guides who were born, raised and continue to reside in Harlem. Walking tour options include gospel concerts, history, civil rights, hip-hop and jazz.

Harlem One Stop (212/658-9160): Walking and specialty tours highlighting music, culture and jazz.

Harlem Spirituals (212/391-0900, 800/660-2166; harlemspirituals. com): Guided coach tours to Harlem, Manhattan, Brooklyn and the Bronx. Stops may include worship services in a local church, gospel concerts, soul food, jazz and historic sights.

Taste Harlem (212/866-7427, tasteharlem.com): A walking tour with tastings at fine and casual eateries serving flavors of the South, Caribbean, Africa and more. Experience Harlem's history, architecture, entertainment and renaissance.

ANNE FRANK CENTER USA

The **Anne Frank Center USA** (44 Park Place, 212/431-7993, annefrank.com) contains interactive exhibits depicting Anne Frank's life through her diary during the two years she was in hiding with her family during the Nazi occupation of the Netherlands. This small center includes a detailed timeline, a life-sized photography of her bedroom, photos taken by her father, a 26-minute documentary and a bookstore where copies of her diary and other related items are sold. Temporary art exhibits and public programs occur throughout the year.

BRYANT PARK

Ave of the Americas bet 40th and 42nd St   bryantpark.org

Bryant Park is a thriving part of the city's life and is home to the wonderful Le Carrousel, an ice rink and winter village, free movies in summer and chess and backgammon games throughout the year. This urban jewel sits behind the New York Public Library and is built atop the library's archives. Have lunch, attend an event, wander through the formal French gardens or hang out on the Southwest porch. Free Wi-Fi is provided.

CHILDREN'S MUSEUM OF MANHATTAN

212 W 83rd St   212/721-1223
Tues-Sun: 10-5 (Sat till 7)   cmom.org

Five floors of interactive exhibits, programs and diverse cultural experiences focus on early childhood education, creativity in the arts and sciences, healthy lifestyle programs and exploration of world cultures. Admission fee charged (reasonable); first Fri of month: 5-8, free.

CHILDREN'S MUSEUM OF THE ARTS

103 Charlton St   212/274-0986
Mon, Wed: noon-5; Thurs, Fri: noon-6; Sat, Sun: 10-5   cmany.org

Children's art exhibits, artist-in-residence programs and hands-on programs are geared for youngsters between ten months and 15 years. Activities and fee-based classes involve a variety of techniques and mediums. Admission fee charged (reasonable); free to infants under one and seniors.

CHINA INSTITUTE GALLERY

212/744-8181
chinainstitute.org

This not-for-profit gallery, dedicated to showcasing the traditional, modern and contemporary art and culture of China is temporarily closed until it reopens in early 2016 at 104 Washington Street.

DRAWING CENTER

35 Wooster St (bet Grand and Broome St)   212/219-2166
Wed-Sun: noon-6 (Thurs till 8)   drawingcenter.org

Dedicated exclusively to showcasing contemporary and historical drawings, this Soho institution features highly regarded changing exhibitions. Limited edition drawings are sold in the bookstore along with books and catalogs. Admission fee charged (nominal).

DYCKMAN FARMHOUSE MUSEUM

4881 Broadway (at 204th St)   212/304-9422
Fri-Sun: 11-5   dyckmanfarmhouse.org

This is the last surviving example of the sort of farmhouse built all over New York well into the 19th century and is sited on what was once Kingsbridge Road (now known as Broadway). Built around 1784, it has been open to the public for nearly a century. There are some particularly good family programs and a small park. Admission fee charged (nominal).

FEDERAL HALL NATIONAL MEMORIAL

26 Wall St (bet Broad and William St)   212/825-6888
Mon-Fri: 9-5   nps.gov/feha

Everyone knows that Washington, D.C., is the nation's capital, but it didn't start out that way. In fact, George Washington was inaugurated on this spot in the first Federal Hall (torn down in 1812 and rebuilt in 1842), which served briefly as the U.S. Capitol. This National Park Service site hosts a small gallery and an information center featuring the national parks in New York City. Free admission.

FRAUNCES TAVERN MUSEUM

54 Pearl St (at Broad St)   212/425-1778
Daily: noon-5   frauncestavernmuseum.org

Fraunces Tavern was a meeting place for the Sons of Liberty before the Revolutionary War and the site of General George Washington's farewell address to his officers after the war. Its history can be traced back to 1719, and

BROOKLYN AND THE BRONX ATTRACTIONS

Brooklyn Botanic Gardens (990 Washington Ave, 718/623-7200, bbg.org): over a century of gardening

Brooklyn Museum (200 Eastern Parkway, 718/638-5000, brooklynmuseum.org): outstanding Egyptian Collection; 1.5 million works

New York Transit Museum (Boerum Pl at Schermerhorn St, Brooklyn Heights, 718/694-1600, mta.info/mta/museum): public transportation history

Bronx Museum of the Arts (1040 Grand Concourse, 718/681-6000, bronxmuseum.org)

Bronx Zoo (2300 Southern Blvd, 718/367-1010, bronxzoo.org)

New York Botanical Garden (2900 Southern Blvd, 718/817-8700, nybg.org)

Wave Hill (W 249th St and Independence Ave, 718/549-3200, wavehill. org): a well-known public garden along the Hudson River

ORCHARD STREET

Real-estate developers have had their hands in the demise or disfigurement of the Lower East Side tenements ever since immigration slowed in the 1920s. When they haven't been completely replaced by high-rises, drastic renovations have left these vestiges of mass immigration unrecognizable from their previous historical architecture. The National Trust for Historic Preservation has added this area, once one of the most crowded communities on Earth, to its endangered list. Although the colorful shopping area has greatly changed, a visit to Orchard Street is still an experience.

Blue Ribbon Sushi Izakaya (187 Orchard St, 212/466-0404): Bromberg brothers' Japanese tavern

Cafe Katja (79 Orchard St, 212/219-9545): Austrian eats, Bavarian beers

Coming Soon (37 Orchard St, 212/226-4548): home goods, furniture

Project No. 8 (38 Orchard St, 212/925-5599): accessories, books, magazines

Russ & Daughters Cafe (127 Orchard St, 212/475-4881): caviar and more

Sweet Buttons Desserts (145 Orchard St, 212/253-8484): bite-sized cupcakes

it is the oldest surviving structure in Manhattan. The first floor still operates as a restaurant (call 212/968-1776 for reservations), while the second floor is dedicated to a museum with exhibitions of art and artifacts related to the Revolutionary War period. Admission fee charged (nominal).

HISPANIC SOCIETY OF AMERICA

Audubon Terrace
613 W 155th St (Broadway bet 155th and 156th St)   212/926-2234
Tues-Sat: 10-4:30; Sun: 1-4   hispanicsociety.org

The former farm of naturalist John James Audubon is an unlikely place for the Hispanic Society of America, and a man named Archer Milton Huntington sounds like an unlikely founder and benefactor. But North America's most significant collection of paintings, textiles, ceramics, photographs and other items from Spain, Portugal and Latin America sits atop Audubon's farm and was largely assembled by Huntington. If you're interested in the subject, a trek up to this out-of-the-way spot will be well worth your time. An exceptional reference library is also housed here and there are numerous Spanish and Latin American restaurants in the area. Free admission.

INTERNATIONAL CENTER OF PHOTOGRAPHY

Relocating Fall 2015   212/857-0000
                                                        icp.org

If you like photography, this center for the study, preservation and exhibition of photographic art is a "must-see." Beautiful gallery spaces and exceptionally well-conceived shows combine to make visiting here a real treat; the well-stocked museum store is a good source for cameras and accessories, books, prints and posters. Visit the website for details pertaining to the gallery's new location. Admission fee charged (reasonable). Classes geared to photographers, students, artists and scholars are offered at the center's school (1114 Ave of the Americas, 212/857-0001); facilities include photo labs, a library and loaner equipment.

INTREPID SEA, AIR & SPACE MUSEUM

Pier 86 (Twelfth Ave at 46th St)   212/245-0072, 877/957-7447
Mon-Fri: 10-5; Sat, Sun: 10-6 (Daily: 10-5, Nov-Mar)   intrepidmuseum.org

The Intrepid Sea, Air & Space Museum is a nonprofit, educational institution featuring the legendary aircraft carrier *Intrepid*, the space shuttle *Enterprise*, the world's fastest jets and a guided missile submarine. Through exhibitions, educational programming and the foremost collection of technologically groundbreaking aircraft and vessels, visitors of all ages and abilities are taken on an interactive journey through history to learn about American innovation and bravery. The Intrepid Museum fulfills its mission to honor heroes, educate the public and inspire youth by connecting them to history through hands-on exploration while bridging the future by inspiring innovation. Admission fee charged (expensive).

SET SAIL FROM CHELSEA PIERS

Here are a couple of options for getting out on the Hudson River and enjoying the breathtaking Manhattan skyline and surroundings.

Schooner Adirondack (Pier 62 at W 23rd St, 212/627-1825, sail-nyc.com): An 80-foot 1890s-style pilot schooner available for both public cruises and charters from mid-April through October. **Classic Harbor Lines** operates two other vessels from Pier 62: *Yacht Manhattan* (80 feet) and *Schooner America 2.0* (105 feet) for fun and interesting cruises.

Bateaux New York (Pier 61 at W 23rd St, 866/817-3463, bateauxnewyork.com): This elegant glass-enclosed sightseeing boat operates lunch and dinner cruises all year long.

JAPAN SOCIETY GALLERY

333 E 47th St (bet First and Second Ave)
212/832-1155
Tues-Thurs: 11-6; Fri: 11-9; Sat, Sun: 11-5
japansociety.org

Founded in 1907, the Japan Society is a remarkable institution dedicated to furthering understanding between the United States and Japan. The tranquil setting features an indoor garden, bamboo grove, reflecting pool and waterfall. In addition to language classes, lecture series, films and other programs, the society has a small but elegant gallery space that presents three exhibitions every year. Admission fee charged (reasonable).

MERCHANT'S HOUSE MUSEUM

29 E 4th St (bet Lafayette St and Bowery)   212/777-1089
Thurs-Mon: noon-5   merchantshouse.org

Step back in time to an era when this part of town was considered the

TWEED COURTHOUSE

The Old New York County Courthouse, better known as the **Tweed Courthouse** (52 Chambers St, 212/788-2656; nyc.gov/cityhalltours), is architecturally one of New York's greatest civic monuments. Built between 1861 and 1881, it is the product of two of New York's most prominent 19th century architects, John Kellum and Leopold Eidlitz. Today it is home to the Department of Education. The architecture is fascinating and so is the story of "Boss" Tweed who served prison time for embezzling millions of dollars from the city's coffers. Free tours are conducted on Friday at noon (call or register online).

suburbs and New York was the country's leading port city. Built in 1832, this townhouse is a real time capsule, full of the furniture, clothes and other items used by one of New York's wealthy merchant families. The servant call bells, elegant four-poster beds and gas chandeliers are just a few of the 3,000 or so period details you'll see as you wander through inside and out of the beautifully preserved Tredwell family home. This is the only home of its type from this period in New York City, and it is a National Historic Landmark. The backyard is a replica of a 19th-century garden that includes varietals from the era. Check the schedule for museum-hosted events. Admission fee charged (reasonable). Rumor has it that a ghostly spirit of the Tredwells maintains watch over their home.

MORRIS-JUMEL MANSION

65 Jumel Terrace (bet 160th and 162nd St)   212/923-8008
Wed-Sun: 10-4   morrisjumel.org

George Washington used this mansion—located on a hill overlooking the Harlem River, Long Island Sound, the Hudson River and the Palisades—as his headquarters at the beginning of the Revolutionary War. Built in 1765, its commanding views offered an important strategic position, first to Washington and later to the British. When the British finally left, General Washington returned in 1790 for a dinner with some of the country's founding fathers, including John Adams, Thomas Jefferson and Alexander Hamilton. Several owners and much more history passed through these rooms in subsequent years. Most of the furniture (including a bed said to have belonged to Napoleon) dates from the 19th century. The property's gardens have been carefully renovated and the mansion also holds a community arts center. Admission fee charged (nominal).

MOUNT VERNON HOTEL MUSEUM AND GARDEN

421 E 61st St (bet First and York Ave)   212/838-6878
Tues-Sun: 11-4   mvhm.org

Another time machine that's survived into the 21st century, this amazing little spot started life as a carriage house for a large estate. It served as a day hotel in the early 19th century and eventually became a private home. Now owned and lovingly preserved by the Colonial Dames of America, it's full of period pieces reflecting its years as a destination for day-trippers coming out to the country by boat or by carriage from Lower Manhattan. The Mount Vernon Hotel Museum and Garden (formerly known as the Abigail Adams Smith Museum) will transport you back 200 years. Tours are provided on request by wonderfully knowledgeable docents. Admission fee charged (nominal).

MUSEUM AT ELDRIDGE STREET

12 Eldridge St (bet Canal and Division St)   212/219-0302
Sun-Thurs: 10-5; Fri: 10-3   eldridgestreet.org

For decades after opening in 1887, the Eldridge Street Synagogue was a central part of the life of thousands of Eastern European Jewish immigrants on the Lower East Side. Interactive displays, tours and public programs tell some of the stories that passed through these doors. Admission fee charged for tour (reasonable); Mon: free.

THE MUSEUM AT FIT

Seventh Ave at 27th St
                                   212/217-4530
Tues-Fri: noon-8; Sat: 10-5
                                   fitnyc.edu/museum

The Museum at FIT (Fashion Institute of Technology), which is accredited by the American Alliance of Museums, is the only museum in New York City dedicated solely to the art of fashion. This gem of a museum is best known for its innovative, beautiful and informative exhibitions and is an integral part of the Fashion Institute of Technology, a State University of New York college of art, design, business and technology that has been at the crossroads of commerce and creativity for 70 years. FIT offers career education in nearly 50 areas and grants associate's, bachelor's and master's degrees. Free admission.

THRILLING SPEEDBOAT TOURS

If you're a thrill seeker and feel the need for speed, check out these options. Tours operate in spring and summer.

The Beast (Pier 83 at W 42nd St, 212/563-3200, circleline42.com): Boats reach speeds of up to 45 m.p.h. in New York Harbor; plenty of landmark photo ops. Be sure to hang onto your hat!

The Shark (Pier 16 at South Street Seaport, 212/742-1969, nywatertaxi.com): This is a high-energy, 30-minute ride with lots of exciting wakes and turns. It is definitely not like a carriage ride in Central Park!

MUSEUM OF AMERICAN FINANCE

48 Wall St (at William St)   212/908-4110
Tues-Sat: 10-4   moaf.org

This museum is appropriately sited in the building that once housed the Bank of New York, which was founded by Alexander Hamilton (who went on to become our nation's first Secretary of the Treasury). The largest exhibit focuses on New York's financial markets, which are located only a block or so away. Visitors explore the routes of check and credit card transactions, differences between financial institutions and the Federal Reserve System. There's also a piggybank display! Various forms of money are exhibited, from the earliest tender to the latest currency with hidden anti-counterfeiting technology. Special events having to do with current economic issues are often scheduled. Replica historical coins and currency and many other items are sold in the gift shop. Admission fee charged (reasonable).

MUSEUM OF AMERICAN ILLUSTRATION
MUSEUM OF COMIC AND CARTOON ART

128 E 63rd St (bet Park and Lexington Ave)   212/838-2560
Tues: 10-8; Wed-Fri: 10-5; Sat: noon-4   societyillustrators.org

Changing exhibitions, including some from the Society of Illustrators' and the Museum of Comic and Cartoon Art's permanent collections, are housed in an elegant 1875 carriage house that today serves as the society's headquarters. Books, magazines and posters are among the items for sale in the museum shop. Admission fee charged (reasonable); Tues: 5-8, free. **The Hall of Fame Dining Room** is open for lunch to society members and their guests or to non-members who purchase the Museum Experience package.

MUSEUM OF ARTS AND DESIGN

2 Columbus Circle (at Eighth Ave)   212/299-7777
Tues-Sun: 10-6 (Thurs, Fri till 9)   madmuseum.org

The museum, also known as MAD, occupies a recently redesigned building located in the revived Columbus Circle. The concave exterior, covered with small, glazed terra-cotta tiles, seemingly glitters at dusk. Collections and exhibitions are comprised of contemporary objects created in clay, glass, wood, metal and fiber from the mid-20th century to the present; the permanent collection includes more than 2,000 objects. Elsewhere in the building, an attractive store sells useful and decorative items and a restaurant, **Robert**, serves a Mediterranean menu and has gorgeous Central Park views. Admission fee charged (reasonable); Thurs: 6-9, pay what you wish.

MUSEUM OF BIBLICAL ART

1865 Broadway (at 61st St)   212/408-1500
Tues-Sun: 10-6   mobia.org

MOBIA celebrates and interprets art inspired and influenced by the Bible and its cultural legacy in Jewish and Christian traditions through special exhibitions, education and scholarships. Free admission.

MUSEUM OF CHINESE IN AMERICA

215 Centre St (bet Howard and Grand St)   212/619-4785
Tues-Sun: 11-6 (Thurs till 9)   mocanyc.org

This fine museum is dedicated to telling and preserving the stories of Chinese immigrants through its main exhibition which traces over 160 years of Chinese American history, historical exhibits and walking tours. The sizable collection includes business, family and community artifacts, documents, newspapers, photographs and oral histories. Admission fee charged (reasonable).

MUSEUM OF SEX

233 Fifth Ave (at 27th St)   212/689-6337
Sun-Thurs: 10-8; Fri, Sat: 10-9   museumofsex.com

One might call this the most stimulating museum in New York! Revolving exhibitions address a broad range of sexuality topics. New Play cafe/den/bar serves beverages and bites, while the museum store has all sorts of exciting merchandise. Admission fee charged (expensive); ages 18+.

NATIONAL ACADEMY MUSEUM & SCHOOL

1083 Fifth Ave (bet 89th and 90th St)   212/369-4880
Wed-Sun: 11-6   nationalacademy.org

The National Academy is the only institution of its kind that integrates a museum, art school and association of artists and architects dedicated to creating and preserving a living history of American art. The museum houses one of the largest collections of 19th- and 20th-century American art in the country. Admission is pay what you wish.

NATIONAL MUSEUM OF THE AMERICAN INDIAN

1 Bowling Green (foot of Broadway)   212/514-3700
Daily: 10-5 (Thurs till 8)   nmai.si.edu

The National Museum of the American Indian in New York is located with the Alexander Hamilton U.S. Custom House. The museum has two other locations in Washington, D.C. and Suitland, MD. Opened in 1994, this branch in Lower Manhattan offers changing exhibitions featuring both contemporary art and historic objects, as well as a stunning permanent exhibition, *Infinity of Nations*. Its terrific gift shop is well worth a visit, as is the building itself. Take time to look up at the intricate details in the ceilings, especially in the rotunda, and to descend the exquisite staircase. Free admission.

A CHANCE OF A GHOST!

October 31st isn't the only day to look for ghostly apparitions. You may witness spirited occurrences at any time—friendly or otherwise!

■ The headless ghost of actor George Frederick has been spotted at St. Paul's Chapel burial ground.

■ The Palace Theatre supposedly harbors over 100 ghosts.

■ Aaron Burr reputedly haunts the restaurant One if by Land, Two if by Sea (once his carriage house); flying dishes have been observed.

■ The ghost of Bishop Dubois frequents the Old St. Patrick's Cathedral.

■ Unexplained noises, voices and footsteps occur at Beth Israel Hospital.

■ The Hotel Chelsea gained notoriety from some of its guests and their activities. Eugene O'Neill, Thomas Wolfe and Sid Vicious are still making the unearthly scene. Beware of the elevator!

■ Hotel des Artistes' resident ghost allegedly touches people.

■ Even though she killed herself, a Ziegfeld Follies chorus girl still appears at the New Amsterdam Theatre.

■ The fireplace at The Ear Inn Irish tavern is mysteriously lit by the ghost of a sailor named Mickey.

To learn more about these and other mysteries join a tour with **Ghosts of New York Walking Tours** (646/493-7092, ghostsofny. com). The 90-minute walking tours are held rain or shine.

NEUE GALERIE NEW YORK

1048 Fifth Ave (at 86th St)   212/628-6200
Thurs-Mon: 11-6   neuegalerie.org

Ronald Lauder and his longtime friend, the late Serge Sabarsky, loved German and Austrian art and design from the early 20th century and dreamed of opening a museum to showcase it. In 1994 Lauder purchased this amazing building, once home to Mrs. Cornelius Vanderbilt III, and transformed their dream into this first-class museum. Public tours are offered at 2 p.m. on Saturday and Sunday. Children under 12 are not admitted, and children from 12 to 16 must be accompanied by an adult. **Café Sabarsky** and **Café Fledermaus** are beautiful places to enjoy the ambience and Kurt Gutenbrunner's authentic Austrian cuisine. Admission fee charged (reasonable); first Fri of month: 6-8, free.

NEW YORK CITY FIRE MUSEUM

278 Spring St (bet Hudson and Varick St)   212/691-1303
Daily: 10-5   nycfiremuseum.org

In a renovated 1904 firehouse, this fun museum is a "must-see" for anyone interested in firefighting. With hundreds of artifacts dating from the late 18th century, the collection is among the most extensive of its kind in the country. Highlights include leather fire buckets, hand-pumped fire engines and a FDNY 9/11 memorial. Admission fee charged (reasonable).

THE NEW YORK CITY POLICE MUSEUM

100 Old Slip (bet Water and South St)   212/480-3100
                                                 nycpm.org

The museum sustained major damage from Hurricane Sandy and was undergoing extensive repairs at time of this book's printing; consult the website for re-opening information.

NEW-YORK HISTORICAL SOCIETY

170 Central Park W (bet 76th and 77th St)   212/873-3400
Tues-Sun: 10-6 (Fri till 8)   nyhistory.org

Through artwork, historical artifacts, film and other media, the New-York Historical Society paints a layered picture of not just New York City's history, but that of America as a whole as the city's first and oldest museum. John James Audubon's watercolors for *Birds of America*, Thomas Cole's *The Course of Empire* and more Tiffany lamps than you can imagine are just a few highlights of the New-York Historical Society. A visit to this grande dame is a great way to glimpse the city's past. The DiMenna Children's History Museum and a permanent exhibition that takes visitors on an interactive journey from Colonial times through the September 11, 2001, attacks were added after a 2011 renovation. The Henry Luce III Center for the Study of American Culture, located on the fourth floor, will be closed for renovation until December 2016. Admission fee charged (reasonable).

NICHOLAS ROERICH MUSEUM

319 W 107th St (bet Broadway and Riverside Dr) 212/864-7752
Tues-Fri: noon-5; Sat, Sun: 2-5   roerich.org

The late Nicholas Roerich was Russian, but in many ways he was a citizen of the world. He dedicated much of his life to convincing governments to protect art even in times of conflict. His own paintings, many done in (and of) the Himalayas, are on display at this unassuming townhouse near Columbia University. Free admission; donations suggested.

THE PALEY CENTER FOR MEDIA

> 25 W 52nd St (bet Fifth Ave and Ave of the Americas)   212/621-6800
>
> Wed-Sun: noon-6 (Thurs till 8)   paleycenter.org

Is there an episode of *The Brady Bunch* you've always wanted to show your kids? A segment of *The Ed Sullivan Show* you're dying to see again? What about the Nixon-Kennedy debates? Or the Mean Joe Greene Coca-Cola commercial? For folks who love television, this place is Nirvana. In addition to scheduled screenings, you can select from the library's more than 160,000 programs which span the history of television, radio, web programming and commercials. There's no memorabilia here, just thousands of hours of programming and personalized research assistance. Admission fee charged (reasonable).

RADIO CITY MUSIC HALL

> 1260 Ave of the Americas (at 50th St)   212/247-4777 (tour information)
>
> Tours: Daily: 10-5   radiocity.com

This art deco wonder was opened in 1932 and seats nearly 6,000. It's home to America's number one holiday production, the *Radio City Christmas Spectacular*. Countless entertainers have performed here over the years, and you can soak up some of its storied history by taking the Stage Door Tour. Admission fee charged (reasonable).

ROCKEFELLER CENTER

> Bounded by Fifth Ave, Ave of the Americas, 48th St and 51st St   212/332-6868
>
> Daily: 6:30 a.m.-midnight   rockefellercenter.com

A sprawling 12-acre complex built in the midst of the Great Depression in the 1930s, Rockefeller Center is in some ways the anchor of midtown Manhattan. Tenants, owners and even technologies have come and gone, as radio gave way to television at NBC Studios, but this amazing complex is one of the few constants in this ever-changing city. In addition to NBC's famous sets, Rockefeller Center is home to Radio City Music Hall, the beautifully manicured Channel Gardens, the world-famous ice-skating rink, a two-floor Metropolitan Museum of Art store, a U. S. Post Office and seven major subway stops. A hub of commerce, culture and community, world-class shopping is available at over 100 retailers throughout the center. For entertainment, wave to your friends at home outside *The Today Show's* windows, or enjoy dinner while people watching at one of the numerous restaurant options. Visit the **Top of the Rock Observation Deck** (topoftherocknyc.com), towering 70 floors above the sidewalks and take in the 360 degree panoramic view atop 30 Rockefeller Plaza. Guided tours of Rockefeller Center's art and architecture are also available (for schedules and prices call 212/698-2000 or visit rockefellercenter.com). What I like to do at Rockefeller Center, however, is simply walk around. It's like visiting an old friend! Fee charged for tours (reasonable).

CONTEMPORARY ART

The New Museum of Contemporary Art (235 Bowery, 212/219-1222, newmuseum.org) is the first art museum constructed in downtown Manhattan. Nestled among restaurant-supply businesses, this contemporary art museum is uniquely built as seven off-axis stacked rectangles. It features the stimulating works of artists from around the globe in all media, including performance and technology art.

ROSE MUSEUM AT CARNEGIE HALL

154 W 57th St (at Seventh Ave)   212/903-9629
Daily: 11-4:30 (closed June-Sept)   carnegiehall.org/museum

If you're interested in the history of music in New York, this little upstairs museum is the place to go. Its permanent exhibit traces the history of Carnegie Hall from 1891. It's open to the public during the day and to evening concertgoers during intermission. Tours of Carnegie Hall, including the Isaac Stern Auditorium, are offered fall through spring; call or check their website for details. Free admission to museum; admission fee charged for tours (reasonable).

RUBIN MUSEUM OF ART

150 W 17th St (at Seventh Ave)   212/620-5000
Mon: 11-5; Wed: 11-9; Thurs: 11-5; Fri: 11-10; Sat, Sun: 11-6

rubinmuseum.org

The Rubin Museum creates an immersive environment for experiencing the art and culture of the Himalayas, India and neighboring regions, and develops programming that enables visitors to make personal connections to their contemporary lives. Exhibitions (including the Tibetan Buddhist Shrine Room), tours, films, concerts and talks further understanding of this region. Himalayan-inspired cuisine is served in **Cafe Serai** and handcrafted items are sold in the gift shop. Admission fee charged (reasonable); Fri: 6-10, free.

SCANDINAVIA HOUSE: THE NORDIC CENTER IN AMERICA

58 Park Ave (at 38th St)   212/779-3587
Mon-Sat: 11-10; Sun: 11-5; Gallery: Tues-Sat: noon-6 (Wed till 7)

scandinaviahouse.org

Scandinavia House, home of the American-Scandinavian Foundation, offers a wide range of programs presenting contemporary Nordic culture that encompasses the visual arts, music and literature, along with public policy, business, finance and technology. These programs include art, design and historical exhibitions, as well as films, concerts, readings, lectures, symposia, language courses and kid's and family programs that illustrate and illuminate the modern-day vitality of the Nordic countries. **Smörgås Chef @ Scandinavia House** and **The Shop @ Scandinavia House** enhance a visit with contemporary and classic Scandinavian menus and design. Admission varies by program.

SOUTH STREET SEAPORT MUSEUM

12 Fulton St (bet Water and South St)   212/748-8600
Call for days and times   seany.org

Two centuries ago, New York was one of the world's most active ports. Even as recently as 1967, when the Seaport Museum was founded, Fulton Street was synonymous with the Fulton Fish Market (which moved to The Bronx in 2005). Little is left today except the history, and that's what you'll find as you explore **Bowne Printers and Stationers** and ships while wandering around South Street Seaport. With its cobblestone streets, beautiful old boats and salty breezes, it's easy to imagine that you've been transported to a different era. At publication time, the galleries were closed due to significant damages to the building's electrical system resulting from Hurricane Sandy.

SKYSCRAPER MUSEUM

39 Battery Pl (and First Pl), 1st floor   212/968-1961
Wed-Sun: noon-6   skyscraper.org

Where better to have a museum dedicated to the history and future of skyscrapers than New York City? Founded in 1996, this ironically small museum offers various programs, lectures and exhibitions feting the towering buildings. Admission fee charged (nominal).

THE STUDIO MUSEUM IN HARLEM

144 W 125th St (bet Malcolm X and Adam Clayton Powell, Jr. Blvd)
Thurs, Fri: noon-9; Sat: 10-6; Sun: noon-6   212/864-4500
                                                      studiomuseum.org

Like the Museum of Chinese in the Americas, this wonderful place is both a museum and a vibrant part of the community. Including gallery space and an auditorium, The Studio Museum in Harlem displays the work of black artists from around the block and around the world. An artist-in-residence program, a wide range of programs for families and children and film screenings are just a few ways The Studio Museum engages its audience and reaches into the community. Suggested admission fee charged (reasonable); Sun: free.

THEODORE ROOSEVELT BIRTHPLACE
NATIONAL HISTORIC SITE

28 E 20th St (bet Broadway and Park Ave)   212/260-1616
Tues-Sat: 9-5   nps.gov/thrb

This wonderful brownstone is a reconstruction of Theodore Roosevelt's childhood home. Operated by the National Park Service, it houses a small museum and various period rooms in the living quarters. Guided tours are offered hourly from 10 to 4, except at noon. Free admission.

TIBET HOUSE

22 W 15th St (bet Fifth Ave and Ave of the Americas)   212/807-0563
Mon-Fri: 11-5; Sun: 11-4   tibethouse.org

Founded at the request of the Dalai Lama, Tibet House U.S. is the center of efforts in this country to present and preserve Tibetan culture. It has a permanent display of Tibetan artifacts and art and a gallery space that offers changing exhibits which showcase contemporary and classical Buddhist-inspired art. Free admission; donations welcome.

SCOTT'S PIZZA TOURS

Scott Wiener runs **Scott's Pizza Tours** (212/913-9903, scottspizzatours.com) where he and his enthusiastic pizza compadres conduct fun- and pun-filled guided tours of some of New York's most significant pizzerias. You'll view pizza ovens and kitchens, learn why New York pizza is legendary and get the skinny on the history, science, technology and economics of the Italian pies. Walking tours cover Little Italy, Greenwich Village, Soho and the Lower East Side; a Sunday tour via a big yellow school bus goes to four pizzerias in the outer boroughs. By the way, Scott lives and breathes pizza; he has amassed a private collection of over 850 unique pizza boxes from around the world; a Guinness World Record.

THE UKRAINIAN MUSEUM

222 E 6th St (bet Second and Third Ave)   212/228-0110
Wed-Sun: 11:30-5   ukrainianmuseum.org

This museum in the heart of the East Village invites visitors to "discover the wonderful heritage of your parents and grandparents." Changing exhibitions display at various times folk art, fine arts, costumes, paintings and an amazing seasonal collection of *pysanky* (Ukrainian Easter eggs). This museum is a terrific cultural resource for anyone who wants to learn more about Ukrainian heritage — yours or otherwise. Admission fee charged (reasonable).

UNION SQUARE PARK

Bounded by Broadway, Park Ave S, 14th St and 17th St   nycgovparks.org

Union Square Park is home to the city's best-known and largest Greenmarket (which is open all year on Monday, Wednesday, Friday and Saturday). It's full of New Yorkers and tourists enjoying the beautifully renovated pavilion and grounds with statues of George Washington and Mohandas Gandhi. The popular Tot Lot is one area of the well-equipped playground. Nearby, there are dozens and dozens of great restaurants and interesting businesses.

WEST SIDE JEWISH CENTER

347 W 34th Street (bet Eighth and Ninth Ave)   212/502-5291
Mon-Thurs: 9-5   westsidejewishcenter.org

In the early 1900s, New York claimed the largest Jewish population in the world, with immigrants from Germany, Russia and Eastern Europe. Founded in 1890, the West Side Jewish Center synagogue and social center has been at this location since 1925 where it is adjacent to Pennsylvania Station, Madison Square Garden and the Jacob Javits Convention Center. People of all ages engage in interesting classes, lectures and social programs. Services are offered daily, as well as for Shabbat and holidays, and visitors of any denomination are welcome to attend services or visit the synagogue. Sabbath meals can be arranged in advance. It is truly a sanctuary with heart in the heart of the city. Free admission.

YANKEE STADIUM

1 E 161st St (at Jerome Ave)   646/977-8687
                                                yankees.com

The "House That Ruth Built" — that's Babe Ruth, the baseball legend — has been replaced with the billion-dollar Yankee Stadium. Field dimensions remain the same, seats and legroom are more spacious, there are more eateries and team stores, more luxury and party suites and the main scoreboard is seven times larger. The classic tour includes visits to the museum, Monument Park, dugouts and batting cages and clubhouse when the team is on the road. The Party City Birthday Bash and Twilight tours include food and beverages. There are different hours for individual and small and large groups, depending on game-day schedules; therefore it is best to check the website or call for details. Admission fee charged (reasonable to expensive, depending on tour).

YESHIVA UNIVERSITY MUSEUM

15 W 16th St (at Fifth Ave)   212/294-8330
Sun, Tues, Thurs: 11-5; Mon: 5-8; Wed: 11-8; Fri: 11-2:30   yumuseum.org

Part of the Center for Jewish History, this large and vibrant museum provides a window into Jewish culture around the world and throughout history through its acclaimed multi-disciplinary exhibitions and award-winning publications. By educating audiences of all ages with dynamic interpretations of Jewish life, past and present, along with wide-ranging cultural offerings and programs, the YU Museum attracts young and old, Jewish and non-Jewish audiences. Admission fee charged (reasonable); Mon, Wed: 5-8 and Fri: 11-2:30, free.

GALLERIES

When people think of viewing art, they often think only of museums. While the art museums in New York are exceptional, anyone interested in art ought to visit some commercial galleries, too. Galleries are places where potential buyers and admirers alike can look at the work of contemporary and 20th-century artists at their own pace and without charge. (A few galleries specialize in older works, too.) Let me stress "admirers alike." A lot of people are afraid to go into galleries because they think they'll be expected to buy something or be treated poorly if they don't know everything there is to know about art. That just isn't true, and an afternoon of gallery hopping can be a lot of fun. Many galleries close on Sunday.

First decide what kind of art you want to see. New York has long been considered the center of the contemporary art world, and it follows that the city is home to literally hundreds of galleries of all sizes and styles. In general, the more formal and conventional galleries are on or close to Madison Avenue on the Upper East Side and along 57th Street. (You'll need to look up to find a lot of them, particularly on 57th Street.) Some of the less formal, avant-garde galleries tend to be in Soho: on West Broadway, between Broome and Houston streets; on Greene Street, between Prince and Houston streets; and on Prince Street, between Greene Street and West Broadway. Some of the

HORSE-DRAWN CARRIAGES IN CENTRAL PARK

The future of horse-drawn carriages in Central Park is in limbo. New York Mayor Bill de Blasio has introduced legislation that would ban these vehicles in the city. I, for one, hope that one of the city's greatest attractions will continue.

more offbeat galleries are also found in Tribeca.

As a general rule, artists who have yet to be discovered go where the rents are lower, and then more established artists and galleries follow. Gallery hot spots include the west end of Chelsea, the northwest corner of the West Village (on and around West 14th Street), the Lower East Side (particularly on and around Rivington Street) and several parts of Brooklyn.

If you want to experience the diversity of the New York gallery scene, sample a couple of galleries in each neighborhood. **The Art Dealers Association of America** (212/488-5550, artdealers.org) is a terrific resource if you have particular artists or areas of interest in mind.

Galleries are typically known for the artists they showcase. If you are interested in the work of just one artist, the *New Yorker* and *New York* magazine each contain listings of gallery shows. Be sure to look at the dates, as shows can change quickly. *Time Out New York* has a list of galleries by neighborhood in its "Art" section, complete with descriptions of current shows. The Friday and Sunday editions of *The New York Times* are also good resources.

TOURS AND TOUR OPERATORS

Whether you like to walk or ride, be part of a small group or sightsee with a whole herd, New York has a tour for you. While I definitely advocate getting out and exploring on your own, there are lots of interesting tours that will take you places you either won't go or can't go by yourself.

If you're feeling a little overwhelmed by New York and want to see the sights from the safety and anonymity of a tour bus, **Gray Line** (212/445-0848, 800/669-0051, newyorksightseeing.com) is your best bet. The company offers many packages on its double-decker buses, including trips to the Statue of Liberty and the Empire State Building (over 50 stops in all), on the hop-on and hop-off buses. Prices vary, as do tour lengths. Another great way to get a quick and basic orientation is **Circle Line**'s three-hour cruise around the island of Manhattan. The narration tends toward the corny, but you'll learn a lot, get some great photo opportunities and really acquire a sense of New York as an island. (Call 212/563-3200 or go to circleline42.com for more information.)

If you want a personal orientation tour, try **Our Town New York** (212/754-4500, 866/691-8687; ourtownnewyork.com), an award-winning boutique tour service. The private and customized tours depart from your hotel's front door. The mode of transportation is a comfortable Mercedes Benz SUV for up to six passengers; larger groups are also accommodated in comfort. Choose from a list of tours or create your own personalized adventure.

Many of the museums and sights listed in this chapter offer tours of their collections or of surrounding neighborhoods. Just about any tour offered by the **Central Park Conservancy** (212/360-2726, centralparknyc.org) is a personal favorite.

MORE HOT SPOTS IN NEW YORK

Following are places not mentioned in other parts of this book that offer particularly interesting and popular tours.

CITY HALL

Murray St at Broadway   212/788-2656
Tours: Mon-Thurs: by reservation; Wed: noon   nyc.gov/cityhalltours

One of the oldest continuously used city halls in the nation that still houses its original functions, New York's City Hall is considered one of the finest architectural achievements of its period. Constructed between 1803 and 1812, the building was an early expression of the city's cosmopolitanism and is recognized as a NYC landmark. Its rotunda is a designated interior landmark as well.   Free admission.

FEDERAL RESERVE BANK

33 Liberty St (bet Nassau and William St)   212/720-6130
Tours: Mon-Fri: 1, 2 (reservations necessary)   newyorkfed.org

Billions of dollars of gold belonging to central banks, foreign governments and official international organizations is stashed in the New York Fed's vault which rests on the bedrock of Manhattan Island. Daily tours include an

SPECIALTY TOURS

If you want a particular kind of tour, a guide with special skills or areas of expertise, or a tour led by a multilingual guide (Italian, French, Danish, Spanish, Japanese, German, Dutch, Portuguese, Hebrew and other languages), contact the **Guides Association of New York** (855/574-2692, ganyc.org). The website has information about the city's licensed guides and their specialties, as well as practical details regarding tours and other hospitality services. GANYC is a nonprofit organization whose members are professional licensed guides and independent contractors.

TIPPING TOUR GUIDES

Unless discouraged, a 15% to 20% tip for tour guides is recommended. However, the size of the group, length of tour and additional personalized attention may influence the amount of tip.

Small group tour (under 15 participants): $15 to $25 per person
Medium group tour (up to 30 participants): $10 per person
Large group tour (over 30 participants): $5 per person
Tour bus driver: $5 to $10 person

overview of the Federal Reserve System, discussion about New York Fed's role in setting monetary policy and a glimpse into the gold vault. Reservations must be made at least a week in advance. Free admission.

GRACIE MANSION

88th St at East End Ave   212/570-4751 or 311 (in New York)
Call for current schedule   nyc.gov

Thanks to Fiorello LaGuardia and Robert Moses, New York is one of the few cities in the U.S. with an official mayoral residence. Built in 1799, the house is located in Carl Schurz Park and overlooks the East River. Admission fee charged (reasonable).

MADISON SQUARE GARDEN

4 Pennsylvania Plaza (32nd St at Seventh Ave)   212/465-5800
                                                          thegarden.com

"The World's Most Famous Arena" is back and better than ever! The best way to see the results of a three-year, billion dollar transformation is on a tour where guests go behind the scenes to view the state-of-the-art arena. Improvements include a GardenVision Multi-Media Display, spectacular "Chase Bridges" suspended from the Garden's iconic concave ceiling to allow spectators to watch the games on the court or ice below, new seating, interactive kiosks, expanded food and shopping options and redesigned traffic flow. The Knicks' and Rangers' locker rooms are part of the tour, unless the teams are playing at home. The multi-purpose arena is legendary for sell-out concerts, premier sporting events and more; the luxury suites are topnotch. Fee charged: reasonable and up.

METROPOLITAN OPERA

Lincoln Center (Columbus Ave at 64th St)   212/769-7028
Tours: Select weekday and Sun afternoons (Oct-May)   metoperafamily.org

Even folks who are not opera enthusiasts will be wowed by this behind-the-scenes look at this country's most famous opera company. Visit the stage area and get an up-close look at some of the costumes and sets. These popular tours are offered by the Metropolitan Opera Guild during opera season, October through May. Check the calendar on the guild's website and plan well in advance, as tours often sell out. Admission fee charged (reasonable).

WALKING TOURS

Walking tours are another great way to get to know parts of New York you otherwise might overlook. Here are some tour guides. Note that days and times of tours vary so check in advance for tour times, meeting places and prices.

BIG APPLE GREETER

1 Centre St (at Chambers St)   212/669-8159
                                                          bigapplegreeter.org

Big Apple Greeter is like having a new friend show you the wonders of the city! Volunteers from all five boroughs meet individuals or groups of up to six to show them New York City through the eyes of a native. On visits lasting from two to four hours, Greeters use public transportation or travel on foot to introduce visitors to neighborhoods and the city's hidden treasures. There are over 300 volunteer Greeters, and they speak some 25 languages among them. They are matched with visitors by language, interest and neighborhoods. This service is free of charge, and while tipping is not permitted, voluntary donations are accepted. At least four weeks advance notice is required.

BIG ONION WALKING TOURS

                                           212/439-1090, 888/606-9255
                                                              bigonion.com

Seth Kamil and his band of guides—most of them graduate students in American history—share their vast knowledge of New York through a wide array of walking tours. There are over two dozen different tours offered seven days a week. The Multi-Ethnic Eating Tour is the most popular followed by tours to Historic Harlem, Brooklyn Bridge and Heights, Historic Lower

MORE NEW YORK TOURS

New York's first family of tour guides operates **Levy's Unique New York**! (877/692-5869, levysuniqueny.com).The clan, led by dad Mark, conducts educational and enlightening tours that are thoroughly entertaining and sometimes zany! The half-day City Highlights tour is the most popular. Other excursions are New York by Land and Sea, Bohemians and Beats of Greenwich Village, Graffiti, Ethnic Eats and a narrated stroll across the Brooklyn Bridge. Tour times and costs vary; custom tours are also available.

Cliff Strome, **Custom & Private New York Tours** (212/222-1441, customandprivate.com), has a passion for New York. Guests are transported in a chauffeured vehicle (sedan, exotic car, limousine or bus) to locations which target guests' schedules, interests, preferences and whims. These tours are laced with humor, folklore, historical drama and tall tales.

FASHION WINDOW WALKING TOUR

You don't need to be a shopaholic to be interested in this tour, but it sure helps! Enthusiastic **WindowsWear Fashion Window Walking Tour** (646/827-2288, windowswear.com/tours) guides take groups on a fashion tour like no other. Visit big name retailers and their stunning window displays and get the inside scoop as to how they design their windows to feature the latest fashions. A history of the stores and their legendary window displays are part of the guide's dialogue.

Manhattan, Greenwich Village, Chelsea and the High Line. Fee charged: reasonable and up.

JOYCE GOLD HISTORY TOURS OF NEW YORK

212/242-5762
joycegoldhistorytours.com

Nowhere in the United States are past and present so closely quartered as in New York, and few people are better able to convey that simultaneous sense of timelessness and modernity than historian Joyce Gold. Her scheduled tours, which include Crimes of the Fifth Avenue Gold Coast, Grand Central Terminal, High Line Park and other colorful neighborhoods and topics, are usually given on weekends. Joyce personally leads all of her public tours and is available for private tours as well. Reservations for her scheduled tours are not required. Fee charged (reasonable).

MANHATTAN WALKING TOUR

914/564-0461
manhattanwalkingtour.com

These guides are akin to a good friend showing you around their beloved hometown imparting behind-the-scenes tales of what makes the neighborhood really tick. Walking tours are scheduled or custom-designed and part of the charm is a limit of eight guests per tour. Choose from several destinations highlighting historic areas and food, or a combination of both. Private tours feature the patrons of the arts (and gossip from that era) and better beer and wine bars on the night tour. Don your walking shoes and join a small group! Prices vary.

MUNICIPAL ART SOCIETY OF NEW YORK

212/935-3960
mas.org

This terrific advocacy group offers a wide array of thematic and area-specific walking tours for people interested in the city's architecture and history. Most tours are led by historians. The diverse topics include art deco midtown, Chelsea art galleries, Harlem and many other interesting areas and neighborhoods and their famous or infamous residents. Allow several hours for your tour. Fee charged (reasonable).

NEW YORK CITY HIKING TOURS

718/263-4102

nychikingtours.com

Bruce Bernstein leads private tours given on request to individuals and groups. Fun treks are between two and seven miles and designed for participants who are in reasonably good shape and able to keep a steady pace. Areas covered are Central Park, lower Manhattan waterfront, the West Village, the High Line, Riverside Park and the East Village. Prices vary.

URBAN PARK RANGERS

212/360-2774 or 311 (in New York)

nyc.gov/parks/rangers

The city's Department of Parks and Recreation employs NYC Urban Park Rangers who give wonderful weekend walking tours throughout the city. Many are designed for children or families. Free admission.

CHAPTER 4

WHERE TO FIND IT

NEW YORK'S BEST FOOD SHOPS

The greatest collection of fine food shops in the world is in New York City. You can find an unsurpassed assortment of quality provisions and any type of ethnic food by doing a bit of investigating. You'll be amazed at what you can discover in some off-the-beaten-path shops, and oftentimes prices are lower than the fancier shops (but be sure to assess the quality before you purchase). Around any corner could be the very best bagels, smoked fish or whatever your heart (and stomach) may desire.

Meanwhile, the big names remain nothing less than spectacular; they have been in business for a long time for good reason! Zabar's oozes tradition, fine aromas and great ambience. Grace's Marketplace, a family operation, offers top-quality produce and foodstuffs in every category. Dean & Deluca, one of the greatest food emporiums in the country, tempts customers at every turn. Whole Foods Market at the Time Warner Center (Columbus Circle) is a behemoth with a huge selection. Eataly, a spectacular food complex, specializes in everything Italian.

These places are just a sampling of some of the better-known names. Lastly, don't be afraid to experiment with new types of cuisine!

ASIAN

ASIA MARKET

71½ Mulberry St (bet Canal and Bayard St)   212/962-2020
Daily: 8-7; Sun: 9-7

The main attractions are fresh fruit and vegetables, plus exotic herbs and spices from all over Asia, more specifically Southeastern Asia. You'll find items from Thailand, Indonesia, Malaysia, the Philippines, Vietnam, Japan and China, and a staff ready to explain how to prepare dishes from these countries. Asia Market provides produce to some of New York's best restaurants, hotels and institutions.

GOLDEN FUNG WONG BAKERY

41 Mott St (at Pell St)   212/267-4037
Daily: 7-7

Golden Fung Wong is the real thing. Pastries, cookies and baked goods are traditional and delicious and flavor is not compromised in order to appeal to Western tastes. The bakery features a tremendous variety of baked goods, and it has the distinction of being New York's oldest and largest authentic Chinese bakery.

KATAGIRI & COMPANY

224 E 59th St (bet Second and Third Ave)   212/755-3566
Daily: 10-8   katagiri.com

Katagiri & Company is this country's oldest Japanese grocery and the store is looking great thanks to a recent renovation. In addition to Japanese foods, sushi, lunches and side dishes, Katagiri has an expanded fresh fish selection and a separate section for Japanese Premium Beef. Specialists are on hand to offer advice, answer questions and demonstrate

NATURAL FOODS

The selection of high-quality merchandise is huge (and expensive) at **Whole Foods Market**, but in my opinion, it is the best place to go for natural foods. The personnel are knowledgeable, customer service is topnotch, prepared foods are outstanding and convenient locations can be found around town.

Additional quality food emporiums include:

Commodities Natural Market (165 First Ave, 212/260-2600): cheeses, good prices

Gary Null's Uptown Whole Foods (2421 Broadway, 212/874-4000): juice bar and kosher items

The Health Nuts (2611 Broadway, 212/678-0054; 1208 Second Ave, 212/593-0116 and 835 Second Ave, 212/490-2979): juice bar

Integral Yoga Natural Foods (229 W 13th St, 212/243-2642): organic produce and baked items, vegetarian; yoga classes offered in the same building

LifeThyme Natural Market (410 Ave of the Americas, 212/420-9099): salad bar, produce

Westerly Natural Market (911 Eighth Ave, 212/586-5262): large selection, knowledgeable staff

products. Delivery is available in Manhattan, Brooklyn and Queens and throughout the country via UPS.

LUCKY KING BAKERY

280 Grand St (bet Eldridge and Forsyth St) 212/219-8438
Daily: 7-7

Unless you are fluent in the Chinese language, you may find yourself ordering sesame balls, breads and other pastries by pointing to the selection. Rice-flour balls are filled with red bean paste and liberally rolled in sesame seeds before a plunge in the deep-fryer. For maximum taste and texture, you'll want to eat the sesame balls while they are hot.

NEW KAM MAN

200 Canal St (bet Mott and Mulberry St) 212/571-0330
Daily: 9-8 newkamman.com

New Kam Man has evolved from an Oriental grocery store into a source for all things Asian. In addition to Chinese foodstuffs, they carry Japanese, Thai, Vietnamese, Malaysian and Filipino products. All types of traditional condiments and specialty snacks are available as well as all of the necessities for the preparation and presentation of Asian foods. The stock includes sauces and spices, utensils, cookware, tableware, gifts, teas, Chinese herbal medicines and beauty products. Prices are reasonable at this Canal Street market.

SUNRISE MART

4 Stuyvesant St (at Third Ave), 2nd floor 212/598-3040
Sun-Thurs: 10 a.m.-11 p.m.; Fri, Sat: 10 a.m.-midnight
494 Broome St (bet West Broadway and Wooster St) 212/219-0033
Daily: 10-9
12 E 41st St (bet Fifth and Madison Ave) 646/380-9280
Mon-Fri: 8 a.m.-9 p.m.; Sat, Sun: 11-8 sunrisemart-ny.com

These Japanese specialty food marts do a bustling business. Japanese is spoken more often than English, and many package descriptions are in Japanese only. In addition to snack foods and candy, they sell fruits, vegetables, meats, fish, dry goods, tofu, seasonings, sauces and other groceries. They also carry bowls, chopsticks and items for the home and the Broome Street location stocks hard-to-find Japanese beauty products. A Japanese bake shop and deli, **Panya Bakery** (8 Stuyvesant St, 212/777-1930), is next door to the Stuyvesant Street location and features breads, sweet and savory treats and delicious noodle soups.

TONGIN MART

91 Mulberry St (at Canal St) 212/962-6622
Daily: 9-8

If you are planning a home-cooked Oriental dinner, there's no better source than this store in Chinatown. They have an open and friendly attitude, and care is taken to introduce customers to the wide variety of imported Oriental foods, including Japanese, Chinese, Thai and Filipino products. Sushi and sashimi are available at reasonable prices.

BAKERY GOODS

AMY'S BREAD

672 Ninth Ave (bet 46th and 47th St)   212/977-2670
Mon, Tues: 7:30 a.m.-10 p.m., Wed-Fri: 7:30 a.m.-11 p.m.; Sat: 8 a.m.-11 p.m.; Sun: 8 a.m.-10 p.m.
75 Ninth Ave (bet 15th and 16th St)   212/462-4338
Mon-Fri: 7:30 a.m.-8 p.m.; Sat: 8-8; Sun: 8-7
250 Bleecker St (bet Ave of the Americas and Seventh Ave)   212/675-7802
Mon-Thurs: 7:30 a.m.-8 p.m.; Fri: 7:30 a.m.-9 p.m.; Sat: 8 a.m.-9 p.m.; Sun: 8-8
                                                        amysbread.com

The aroma of freshly baked bread and sweets lures customers to line up outside Amy's Bread to sample the many treats for sale. These oases are a cross between a Parisian *boulangerie* and a cozy Midwestern kitchen. Of course, you should come for the hearth-baked bread — Amy's signature semolina with golden raisins and fennel, green-olive *picholine* or a simple French baguette. Other goodies include grilled sandwiches, sticky buns, decadent brownies and nearly a dozen flavors of old-fashioned double layer cakes. The staff provides consistent, friendly service.

BILLY'S BAKERY

Plaza Food Hall
The Plaza, 1 W 59th St, concourse   646/755-3237
Mon-Sat: 11-8; Sun: 11-6
184 Ninth Ave (bet 21st and 22nd St)   212/647-9956
Mon-Thurs: 8:30 a.m.-11 p.m.; Fri, Sat: 8:30 a.m.-midnight; Sun: 9-9
75 Franklin St (bet Broadway and Church St)   212/647-9958
Mon-Fri: 9-8; Sat, Sun: noon-5   billysbakerynyc.com

You simply cannot leave this place without some of the delicacies offered: wonderful layer cakes (like red velvet), cheesecakes, icebox cakes and pies, cupcakes, bars, cookies, muffins, breakfast breads and more. Children's cakes, known as Little Billy's, are decorated to fit any party theme and will definitely "wow" little celebrants. Items are made on-premises at this very clean and professional operation; call to inquire about wedding cakes and baked goods for special occasions.

BIRDBATH

160 Prince St (bet West Broadway and Thompson St)   646/556-7720
Mon-Fri: 8-8; Sat: 9-8; Sun: 9-7
200 Church St (bet Thomas and Duane St)   212/309-7555
Mon-Fri: 8-6   birdbathbakery.com

Birdbath, the little sister of City Bakery, is described as organic, seasonal, recycled, sustainable and eco-friendly, with really good food emphasizing regional ingredients. Customers arriving via bike, scooter or skateboard receive a discount; food from the main kitchen is delivered by bicycle-powered rickshaws and the business is wind-powered. Breakfast and lunch are offered to go (only a couple of stools are available on-site). The menu consists of croissants, muffins, cookies, veggie burgers, mini pizzas, mac and cheese, desserts and specialty drinks.

GROCERY DELIVERY

There is a way to stock up on groceries without setting foot in a grocery store. **FreshDirect** (212/796-8002, freshdirect.com) carries an expansive list of over 3,000 organic and prepared food items to be ordered online. Even better, you can arrange for a specific delivery time for dairy products, meats, fish, bakery items, produce, flowers, beverages, wine and spirits, pet food and other goods. They also provide prepared foods, four-minute meals, heat-and-eat dishes, recipes and cooking information. Prices are competitive, as they do not have a storefront or deal with middle men; delivery charges are reasonable. What a great service!

CAKES 'N SHAPES

466 W 51st St (at Tenth Ave)   212/629-5512
By appointment   cakesnshapes.com

For one-of-a-kind decorated cookies and cookies, furnish owner Edie Connolly with a picture of a person, place, book cover, company logo or other image, and she'll impose an edible likeness on a shortbread/sugar cookie, cupcake or cake. Free-form, 3D works of art start with chocolate and vanilla pound cakes which are formed into edible purses and clothing items, sports equipment, bodies, critters and consumer products. Cookies are shippable and are individually wrapped in a clear bag, tied with a satin ribbon and suitable for invitations and Christmas cards. If you are a do-it-yourselfer, order edible frosting-sheet images to apply to your own cake or cupcakes. And for those who are allergic, this is a nut-free bakery.

CORRADO BREAD AND PASTRY

1361 Lexington Ave (at 90th St)   212/348-8943
Mon-Fri: 7 a.m.-8 p.m.; Sat: 8-7; Sun: 8-5
833 Lexington Ave (at 63rd St)   212/355-9600
Mon-Fri: 7 a.m.-8 p.m.; Sat: 8 a.m.-9 p.m.; Sun: 9-7 corradobreadandpastry.com

The aromas are enticing at these good-looking bakeries. There are about 30 kinds of breads, muffins and rolls, plus yummy desserts, salads and made-to-order sandwiches. The assortment of sandwiches includes smoked turkey on brioche, egg salad on seven grain bread and petite sandwiches which are also big on flavor. For a sweet treat, perhaps try a decadent chocolate-mousse raspberry tart or cake, cheesecake (by the slice or whole), brownie, eclair, cannoli or cookie accompanied by a hot or cold beverage. Outdoor cafe tables are a nice touch.

CREATIVE CAKES

400 E 74th St (at First Ave)   212/794-9811
Mon-Fri: 8-4:30; Sat: 9 a.m.-11 a.m.   creativecakesny.com

Creative Cakes knows how to have fun using fine ingredients and ingenious designs. Cake lovers are fans of the fudgy chocolate cake with buttercream icing and sensational artwork. Since 1979 Bill Schutz has replicated Yankee

Stadium, movie posters, a six-pack of beer and other cute or off-the-wall conversation pieces for bar and bat mitzvahs, showers and birthdays for any age and any theme. Prices are reasonable, and these edible creations are sure to be a huge hit at any party.

CRUMBS BAKE SHOP

1385 Broadway (bet 37th and 38th St)	646/780-0454
420 Lexington Ave (bet 43rd and 44th St)	212/297-0500
880 Third Ave (at 53rd St)	212/355-6500
40 Broad St (bet Beaver St and Exchange Pl)	646/844-1325
775 Columbus Ave (at 97th St)	917/410-5896
2 Park Ave (bet 32nd and 33rd St)	917/410-5719
261 W 42nd St (Eighth Ave)	212/938-0400
1675 Broadway (at 53rd St)	212/399-3100
1418 Lexington Ave (at 93rd St)	917/410-5776
124 University Pl (at W 13th St)	212/206-8011
Hours vary by store	crumbs.com

Crumbs! Just the name evokes visions of decadent little cakes with mounds of frosting and sprinkles or bits of candy on top. The flavor options are unending: S'mores, Black Forest, cotton candy, Butterfinger, Twinkie and "The Elvis." Each Monday brings a new cupcake of the week. If you can't make it to one of their locations, delivery is offered.

DOMINIQUE ANSEL BAKERY

189 Spring St (bet Sullivan and Thompson St)	212/219-2773
Mon-Sat: 8-7; Sun: 9-7	dominiqueansel.com

Dominique Ansel is an award-winning pastry chef who has a way with croissants. Dominique's Kouign Amann (aka DKA) is a tender, caramelized version made with croissant-like dough. The Cronut are an edible phenom best described as a cross between a croissant and a doughnut. The flaky dough is shaped like a doughnut, fried in grape seed oil and finished with a roll in sugar, cream filling and sweet glaze. Each month brings a new flavor sensation. Other temptations include miniature meringues, macaroons, cakes, tarts and French pastries; savories are served for breakfast and lunch. A word to the wise: The Cronut, created by chef Ansel, sell out early in the morning and DKAs are gone in the afternoon (they are so popular that in-store customers are imposed a limit of two per person).

DOUGHNUT PLANT

379 Grand St (at Norfolk St)	212/505-3700
Sun-Thurs: 6:30 a.m.-8 p.m.; Fri, Sat: 6:30 a.m.-9 p.m.	
Hotel Chelsea	
220 W 23rd St (bet Seventh and Eighth Ave)	212/675-9100
Sun-Wed: 7 a.m.-10 p.m.; Thurs-Sat: 7 a.m.-midnight	doughnutplant.com

Mark Isreal presides over an establishment that is truly unique, concocting fluffy, fresh, organic doughnuts made with spring water. He's come a long way since delivering doughnuts on his bicycle. There are more than 35 flavors, including PB&J, blackout, banana with pecans, "Yankee" (blueberry pinstripes) and rosewater (yes, with edible rose petals!). Their best-selling and most

GRAND CENTRAL MARKET

Located in the heart of midtown, **Grand Central Market** (Grand Central Terminal, 43rd St at Lexington Ave; grandcentralterminal.com) has some of Manhattan's finest quality food retailers, including **Ceriello Fine Foods**, **Dishes at Home**, **Eli's Bread and Pastry**, **Eli's Farm to Table**, **Li-Lac Chocolates**, **Murray's Cheese Shop**, **Oren's Daily Roast**, **Pescatore Seafood Company**, **Spices and Tease**, **Wild Edibles Seafood Market** and **Zaro's Bread Basket**.

popular creation is the crème brûlée doughnut which is filled with vanilla bean custard and individually torched to caramelize the sugar topping. Doughnuts are not just round, square jelly doughnuts are available, too, and unusual glazes from pistachios or fresh raspberries are frequently used. The sugary treats are handmade daily from the highest quality all-natural ingredients; organic whenever possible. There are also cinnamon buns and carrot-cake doughnuts, as well as hot chocolate, chai tea, organic coffee and other beverages.

FERRARA BAKERY AND CAFE

195 Grand St (bet Mulberry and Mott St)   212/226-6150
Daily: 8 a.m.-midnight (Sat until 1 a.m.)   ferraracafe.com

Five generations have tended this store in Little Italy, one of the biggest little *pasticcerias* (pastry shops) in the world. Open since 1892, Ferrara is reputedly America's first espresso bar. The business deals in wholesale imports and other ventures, but their edible goodies could support the whole operation. This efficiently run Italian bakery makes delicious cannoli, cream puffs, fresh fruit tartlets, cheesecakes, wedding and special occasion cakes and more, to enjoy with your espresso, cappuccino, soda or other specialty drink. And don't forget about the rainbow cookies!

GLASER'S BAKE SHOP

1670 First Ave (bet 87th and 88th St)   212/289-2562
Tues-Fri: 7-7; Sat: 8-7; Sun: 8-3   glasersbakeshop.com
Closed July and part of Aug

It won't be hard to find Glaser's Bake Shop on a Sunday. The line frequently spills outside as people queue up to buy fresh cakes and baked goods. Since 1902, the Glasers have run their shop as a family business at this same location, and they're justifiably proud of their brownies, cakes, cookies (try the chocolate chip!), doughnuts, muffins, turnovers, buns, rolls, whoopee pies and a long list of other confections.

KOSSAR'S BAGELS AND BIALYS

367 Grand St (at Essex St)   212/473-4810
Daily: 6 a.m.-8 p.m.   kossars.com

The bialy derives its name from Bialystok, Poland, where they were first made. Kossar's brought the recipe over from Europe almost a century ago. Their delicious bialys, kettle-boiled bagels (some of the best in the city), *bulkas* and *pletzels* (onion disks) are sold fresh from the oven and are shipped throughout the country. The taste is Old World and authentic; prices can't be beat.

LADY M CAKE BOUTIQUE

41 E 78th St (at Madison Ave)	212/452-2222 (all locations)
Mon-Fri: 10-7; Sat: 11-7; Sun: 11-6	
Plaza Food Hall (The Plaza, 1 W 59th St)	
Mon-Sat: 11-8; Sun: 11-6	
36 W 40th St (bet Fifth Ave and Ave of the Americas)	
Mon-Thurs: 9-8; Fri: 9 a.m.-10 p.m.; Sat: 11-10; Sun: 11-6	ladym.com

For some of the area's most outstanding cakes (and they should be, at the prices charged) a visit to this house is a must. Multi-layered Mille crepe cakes in a variety of flavors are unique creations and the checkerboard cake is very appealing. You'll find a dazzling selection of over a dozen handmade cakes, which can be enjoyed in the small boutiques (salads and sandwiches till about 3 p.m.) or taken home. Customers can enjoy tea while sampling goodies by the slice.

LE PAIN QUOTIDIEN

1131 Madison Ave (bet 84th and 85th St)	212/327-4900
81 West Broadway (at Warren St)	646/652-8186
1270 First Ave (bet 68th and 69th St)	212/988-5001
Numerous other locations	lepainquotidien.com
Hours vary by store	

Le Pain Quotidien traces its roots to Brussels, Belgium. It is a country-style bakery specializing in European breads and pastries sold at the counter with breakfast, lunch and light afternoon meals served at long communal tables. The meals offered are simple and the service refined. You'll find delicious croissants, pain au chocolate, brioche, heaping bread baskets, Belgian sugar waffles, an unusual Tuscan platter, crisp salads and a splendid board of French cheeses. Wonderful tartines (open-faced sandwiches) are the house specialty; try Scottish smoked salmon with dill or Parisian ham with three mustards. Vegan and vegetarian options are available with a nod to organic ingredients whenever possible. Don't pass up the Belgian-chocolate brownies!

SOMETHING'S STINKY

Stinky (107 W 20th St, 212/243-2873) is a gourmet store that specializes in cheese; many are aged to perfection and develop quite a pungent aroma. Artisanal candies, pickles, charcuterie, breads and craft beers (both in bottles and on-tap) are also featured. Put all the ingredients together for delicious gift baskets or build a sandwich that would impress Dagwood. Next door, owners Michelle and Patrick Watson operate **Black Label Wine Merchants** (111 W 20th St, 212/229-9463), a wine and liquor store. This is a winning combination of food and drink plus fun, informative classes.

THE MODERN DAY MILKMAN

Manhattan Milk Co. (917/388-2713, manhattanmilk.com) sells fresh bottled organic milk (chocolate, too!), organic eggs, cases of water, juices and other products. They'll deliver to your door anywhere in Manhattan (if you're home between 4 a.m. and 10 a.m. to accept the order) or leave it with your doorman at any time. It's possible to receive bacon, eggs and bagels delivered with your milk in time for breakfast; these folks bring convenience to a whole new level.

LEVAIN BAKERY

167 W 74th St	212/874-6080
2167 Frederick Douglass Blvd	646/455-0952
Mon-Sat: 8-7; Sun: 9-7	levainbakery.com

Legendary six-ounce chocolate chip walnut cookies are just one reason to visit Levain Bakery! Other cookie varieties include oatmeal with raisins and dark chocolate with chocolate or peanut butter chips. Raisin sticky buns are fantastic, but so are the muffins, breads, scones, coffee cakes and rustic fruit tarts. A seasonal outpost is in the Hamptons and gift boxes full of cookies can be ordered on the website. These, and all baked goods, are fresh every single day; if any product remains at close of business it is generously shared with agencies to help feed the hungry.

LITTLE PIE COMPANY

424 W 43rd St (bet Ninth and Tenth Ave)	212/736-4780
Mon-Fri: 8-8; Sat: 10-8; Sun: 10-6	littlepiecompany.com

Arnold Wilkerson started baking apple pastries for private orders in his own kitchen and now operates a unique shop that makes handmade pies and cakes using fresh seasonal fruits. Although they specialize in apple pie, they also make fresh peach, cherry, blueberry and other fruit-pie favorites, along with cream, meringue and crumb pies. Delicious brownies, bars, muffins, cupcakes, fruit Danishes, applesauce carrot cakes, white coconut cakes, chocolate cream pies and cheesecakes with wild blueberry, cherry and orange toppings are also available. Stop by anytime for a slice of warm pie a la mode and a cup of cider, or if you really love pie, order savory chicken pot pie for dinner followed by a slice of Mississippi mud pie.

MAGNOLIA BAKERY

401 Bleecker St (at 11th St)	212/462-2572
Grand Central Terminal (42nd St at Vanderbilt Ave), lower level	212/682-3588
1240 Ave of the Americas (at 49th St)	212/767-1123
Bloomingdales, 1000 Third Ave (at 59th St)	212/265-5320
200 Columbus Ave (at 69th St)	212/724-8101
Hours vary by store	magnoliabakery.com

Magnolia Bakery opened in 1996 on a quiet corner in the heart of Greenwich Village. It has expanded to several locations throughout the city. Fashioned as a cozy, old-fashioned bake shop, people come for coffee and something sweet or for the bakery's famous banana pudding made with layers of vanilla wafers, fresh bananas and creamy vanilla pudding (order a single serving or enough to satisfy 20). With its vintage American desserts (layer cakes, cookies, icebox desserts) and homey decor, walking into Magnolia is like taking a step back in time. Locations are now spread around the world!

MOISHE'S BAKE SHOP

115 Second Ave (bet 6th and 7th St)   212/505-8555
Sun-Thurs: 7 a.m.-9 p.m.; Fri: 7 to one hour before sunset

Everything is done to perfection at Moishe's Bake Shop where Jewish bakery specialties are legendary. The cornbread, available only on Sunday, is prepared exactly as it was in the Old Country. The pumpernickel is dark and moist and the rye and whole wheat are simply scrumptious. The pies, cakes, Danish, babka, hamantash, rugelach and other pastries are special, too! The charming owners run one of the best bakeries in the city. By all means try one of the challah breads.

HOT DOG!

At my restaurant (**Gerry Frank's Konditorei**, 310 Kearney St, Salem, OR, 503/585-7070, gerryfrankskonditorei.com), we serve OregonGrassFed beef hot dogs and we call them "Gerry's Franks!" For the best frankfurters in Manhattan try:

2nd Ave Deli (162 E 33rd St, 212/689-9000 and 1442 First Ave, 212/737-1700)

Artie's Delicatessen (2290 Broadway, 212/579-5959)

Asiadog (66 Kenmare St, 212/226-8861)

Brooklyn Diner USA (212 W 57th St, 212/977-1957 and 155 W 43rd St, 212/265-5400)

The Cannibal (Gotham West Market, 600 Eleventh Ave, 212/582-7947 and 113 E 29th St, 212/686-5480)

Crif Dogs (113 St. Mark's Pl, 212/614-2728)

DBGB Kitchen and Bar (299 Bowery, 212/933-5300)

Gray's Papaya (2090 Broadway, 212/799-0243): inexpensive

Hallo Berlin (626 Tenth Ave, 212/977-1944)

Katz's Delicatessen (205 E Houston St, 212/254-2246)

Nathan's Famous Hot Dogs (705 Eighth Ave, 212/956-3400 and 761 Seventh Ave, 212/767-8347)

Old Town Bar and Restaurant (45 E 18th St, 212/529-6732)

Papaya King (179 E 86th St, 212/369-0648 and 3 St. Mark's Pl, 646/692-8482)

Please Don't Tell (PDT) (113 St. Mark's Pl, 212/614-0386): cocktail lounge attached to Crif Dogs; out-of-the-ordinary dogs

Shake Shack (Madison Square Park, Madison Ave at 23rd St, 212/889-6600; 366 Columbus Ave, 646/747-8770; 154 E 86th St, 646/237-5035 and 691 Eighth Ave, 646/435-1035): Madison Square Park location is seasonal.

Westville (210 W 10th St, 212/741-7971; 246 W 18th St, 212/924-2223; 333 Hudson St, 646/561-5233 and 173 Ave A, 212/677-2033): vegan

MURRAY'S BAGELS

500 Ave of the Americas (bet 12th and 13th St)   212/462-2830
Mon-Fri: 6 a.m.-9 p.m.; Sat, Sun: 6 a.m.-8 p.m.   murraysbagels.com

MURRAY'S BAGELS CHELSEA

242 Eighth Ave (bet 22nd and 23rd St)   646/638-1335
Mon-Fri: 6 a.m.-8 p.m.; Sat, Sun: 6-6   murraysbagelschelsea.com

More than a dozen varieties of delicious hand-rolled, kettle-boiled and oven-baked bagels are featured at Murray's. You'll also find smoked fish, spreads and schmears, pastries, breakfast omelets, soups, homemade and classic salads, sandwiches and deli items for sandwiches. Free local delivery.

ORWASHER'S BAKERY

308 E 78th St (bet First and Second Ave)   212/288-6569
Mon-Sat: 7:30 a.m.-8 p.m.; Sun: 8-6   orwashers.com

For nearly a century, New York's original artisan bakery, Orwasher's Bakery, has served Manhattan's Upper East Side. They bake about 30 varieties of all-natural breads every day. Originally famous for its classic New York breads — rye, cinnamon raisin and pumpernickel — Orwasher's offers a complete line of classic European breads, such as Irish soda and ciabatta. Health-conscious customers will enjoy the hearth-baked whole wheat and multigrain breads. A line of artisan wine breads is made with a natural starter created from fermenting wine grapes. Shaped by hand and baked downstairs in an ancient brick oven, these breads have a slightly sour flavor and are extra crusty. They pair perfectly with farm-stand vegetables, stews, cured or braised meats and fine cheeses. The bakery also carries a full line of classic pastries, as well as cupcakes, artisan cheeses and superb coffee.

PASTICCERIA ROCCO

243 Bleecker St (bet Carmine and Leroy St)   212/242-6031
Sun-Thurs: 7:30 a.m.-midnight; Fri: 7:30 a.m.-1 a.m.; Sat: 7:30 a.m.-1:30 a.m.
     pasticceriarocco.com

Pasticceria Rocco is a family-owned pastry and espresso cafe now run by Rocco Generoso's children, using the same recipes and offering the same great tastes. Tempting homemade Italian goodies include biscotti, panettone, cannoli (cream- and fruit-filled pastries), cookies, decadent cakes, pies, cheesecakes (almost a dozen flavors), gelati, ices and beautiful holiday indulgences. There are choices for any time of the day: pastries for breakfast, lunch or break treats; desserts for lunch, dinner or late night and seasonal gelato and Italian ices for any reason. Enjoy your selection with one of the specialty drinks — perhaps a latte or cappuccino. Don't overlook their menus for specialty pancakes, egg sandwiches, focaccia, soups, wraps, paninis and so much more.

POSEIDON BAKERY

629 Ninth Ave (bet 44th and 45th St)   212/757-6173
Tues-Sat: 9-7   poseidonbakery.com

Founded in 1923 by Greek baker Demetrios Anagnostou, Poseidon Bakery is now run by his great-grandson, Paul, to the same exacting standards. When a customer peers over the counter and asks about something, the response is usually a long description and sometimes an invitation to taste. This tiny bakery serves up savory and sweet creations like homemade baklava, strudel, *kataIf, trigona, tiropita* (cheese pie), spanakopita and saragli. Understandably, Poseidon's handmade phyllo is world renowned. They also have cocktail-size frozen spinach, cheese, vegetable and meat pies for home consumption or parties. Plan ahead as they are closed Sunday and Monday.

SIGMUND PRETZEL SHOP

29 Ave B (bet 2nd and 3rd St)   646/410-0333
Tues-Fri: 5 p.m.-midnight; Sat, Sun: 11 a.m.-midnight   sigmundnyc.com

Soft pretzels are one of my favorite snack foods, and Sigmund's handmade twisted treats are delicious. The warm, salt-encrusted pretzels are exceptional either plain or with flavor options such as cinnamon raisin, sesame seed, poppy seed, sunflower seed, pumpkin seed and truffle-cheddar with sweet and savory dips. In 2013 Sigmund's combined a perfect mix of good beer, fresh bread and bar food at the pretzel shop. The menu consists of pretzels, sliders, hot sandwiches on pretzel buns, a New York Reuben like you've not had before, beer cheese fondue, warm German potato salad and more. In addition to a few brunch standards, Sigmund's offers pretzel Benedicts, mimosas and sangria made with red and white wines. This is not just a bakery!

SILVER MOON BAKERY

2740 Broadway (at 105th St)   212/866-4717
Mon-Fri: 7:30 a.m.-8 p.m.; Sat, Sun: 8-7; open some holidays   silvermoonbakery.com

In a tiny, busy space, Silver Moon turns out delicious artisan breads (French, German and Italian), French pastries and cakes, tarts, macaroons, challah, brioche (fresh fruit, raspberry, raisin and chocolate chip), muffins, scones and more. *Speculaas* cookies are molded into interesting designs and range from five inches up to two feet! Not only are they delicious, but they make great gifts. You can also enjoy a sandwich, soup or quiche and watch the neighborhood activity from an outdoor seat. Birthday and wedding cakes, presentation challahs, gigantic gift *Speculaas* and special holiday treats are made to order.

SULLIVAN ST BAKERY

533 W 47th St (bet Tenth and Eleventh Ave)   212/265-5580
Mon-Sat: 7-7; Sun: 7-5
236 Ninth Ave (bet 24th and 25th St)   212/929-5900
Mon-Fri: 7 a.m.-8 p.m.; Sat, Sun: 7:30-7   sullivanstreetbakery.com

Known for its crusty bread, Roman-style pizzas and decadent pastries, Sullivan St Bakery has been a NYC staple for 20 years. Founder Jim Lahey learned the art of bread baking in small-town Italy and started the bakery with little more than hand-cultivated wild yeast and a desire to bring the art of small-batch bread baking to America. Look for ethereal ciabatta, toasty sesamo loaves and dark and crusty *truccio sare* (whole wheat sourdough) year round, and specialty items like *colomba* (Italian Easter bread in the shape of a cross) or chocolate-cherry panettone (traditional Italian Christmas dessert) around the holidays.

SYLVIA WEINSTOCK CAKES

273 Church St (bet Franklin and White St) 212/925-6698
Mon-Fri: 9-5 sylviaweinstock.com

In the special occasion cake business since the 1980s, Sylvia Weinstock knows how to satisfy customers who want the very best. She has been described as the Leonardo da Vinci of elaborate wedding cakes with lifelike floral decorations a stunning trademark. Although weddings are a specialty (two months' notice is suggested), she will produce masterpieces — including hand-molded sugar figures and exquisitely carved cakes — for any occasion.

TAKAHACHI BAKERY

25 Murray St (bet Church St and Broadway) 212/791-5550
Mon-Fri: 7-7; Sat: 8-7; Sun: 9-6
takahachibakery.com

You'll find a mouthwatering assortment of Japanese pastries, desserts and sweets on the constantly changing menu at Takahachi. Green-tea cookies and cake, red-bean buns, berry mousse or truffle cake may be among the tasty selections on any given day. The eating area is a nice place to relax with your cup of tea, coffee, soup, salad or dessert.

TU-LU'S GLUTEN-FREE BAKERY

338 E 11th St (bet First and Second Ave) 212/777-2227
Sun-Thurs: 10:30-10; Fri, Sat: 10:30-10:30 tu-lusbakery.com

Tully Phillips' personal need for a change in diet resulted in this gluten-free bakery. Cookies, brownies, muffins and cupcakes are preservative-free and made with rice and tapioca flour, potato starch and soy ingredients. Coffee cake (regular and mini-size), red velvet cake and cupcakes with choice of icing (including dairy-free and vegan options) are very good. Dozens of gluten-free flavor combinations are available for wedding and other special occasion cakes; they are delicious, too. Enjoy a panini with homemade whole grain sunflower seed bread or indulge in a delicious quiche.

TWO LITTLE RED HENS

1652 Second Ave (bet 85th and 86th St) 212/452-0476
Mon-Thurs: 7:30 a.m.-9 p.m.; Fri: 7:30 a.m.-10 p.m.; Sat: 8 a.m.-10 p.m.; Sun: 8-8
twolittleredhens.com

No counting calories here! The only things you should count at Two Little

Red Hens are the number of luscious fillings (16), about a dozen frostings and icings to go with a half dozen or so regular cake flavors. Classic or specialty cakes (and cupcakes) can be ordered in advance or stop by and choose from their ready-to-eat goodies like delicious pies, cheesecakes, muffins and other morning items and cookies. The assortment includes seasonal favorites such as pumpkin cake with pumpkin apricot cream cheese frosting and filling in autumn and coconut cream and key lime pies on weekends. Everything is delicious and decadent!

VENIERO'S PASTICCERIA AND CAFFE

342 E 11th St (bet First and Second Ave)   212/674-7070
Sun-Thurs: 8 a.m.-midnight; Fri, Sat: 8 a.m.-1 a.m.   venierospastry.com

Veniero's has been serving appealing Italian pastries, cakes, cheesecakes, tarts and gelati to satisfied customers at moderate prices since 1894. Cannolis, with their creamy filling and crisp shells dipped in chocolate, may be difficult to resist, but frozen canolli and *sfogliatella* kits are available to assemble these goodies anytime at home. Cookie trays are filled with crunchy *quaresimali*, *spumenti*, jelly-filled butter cookies, rainbow cookies and other Italian treats; these and other desserts may also be available gluten-free. Cheesecakes are prepared New York style with cream cheese, Italian style with ricotta cheese or Sicilian style also made with ricotta cheese, chocolate chips and glazed cherries. Orders for special occasion cakes, including beautiful wedding cakes, should be made in advance. In addition to busy counter service for takeout, there is a seating area that serves hot and cold drinks and alcoholic beverages with a long list of sweets. Take a look around the building as many of the building's original details, including hand-stamped copper ceilings and etched glass doors, have survived in this appealing shop.

YONAH SCHIMMEL KNISH BAKERY

137 E Houston St (bet First and Second Ave)   212/477-2858
Sun-Thurs: 9:30-7; Fri, Sat: 9:30-9   knishery.com

In 1890 the namesake founder started out dispensing knishes among the pushcarts of the Lower East Side. A Yonah Schimmel knish is a unique experience. It neither looks nor tastes anything like the mass-produced things sold at supermarkets and lunch stands. Yonah's knishes have a thin, flaky crust — almost like strudel dough — surrounding a hot, moist filling, and they are kosher. The best-selling filling is potato, but kasha (buckwheat), spinach, red cabbage and other mixtures are also terrific. No two knishes come out exactly alike, since each is handmade. You can order online or by fax (212/477-2858) for delivery anywhere in the continental U.S.

ZUCKER'S BAGELS & SMOKED FISH

146 Chambers St (between West Broadway and Greenwich St)   212/608-5844
Mon-Fri: 6:30 a.m.-7 p.m.; Sat, Sun: 7-6
370 Lexington Ave (bet 40th and 41st St)   212/661-1080
Mon-Fri: 6:30-6; Sat, Sun: 7-3   zuckersbagels.com

Here are two classic New York City bagel shops featuring Old World, hand-rolled bagels with spreads and schmears, a great assortment of smoked fish, classic deli sandwiches and salads. La Colombe coffee is the featured brew.

FAVORITE CHOCOLATE SHOPS
OF A SERIOUS CHOCOHOLIC (ME!)

5th Avenue Chocolatiere (693 Third Ave, 212/935-5454)

Chocolate Bar (19 Eighth Ave, 917/388-3761)

Chocolat—Michel Cluizel (584 Fifth Ave, 646/415-9126)

Jacques Torres Chocolate (350 Hudson St, 212/414-2462; 285 Amsterdam Ave, 212/787-3256; 30 Rockefeller Plaza, 212/664-1804 and other locations)

Kee's Chocolates (80 Thompson St, 212/334-3284; HSBC Bank, 452 Fifth Ave, 212/525-6099 and 315 W 39th St, 212/967-8088)

L.A. Burdick Handmade Chocolates (5 E 20th St, 212/796-0143)

L'atelier du Chocolat (59 W 22nd St, 212/243-0033)

La Bergamote (177 Ninth Ave, 212/627-9010)

La Maison du Chocolat (1018 Madison Ave, 212/744-7117; 30 Rockefeller Plaza, 212/265-9404; 63 Wall St, 212/952-1123 and Plaza Food Hall, The Plaza, 1 W 59th St, 212/355-3436)

Leonidas (485 Madison Ave, 212/980-2608 and 3 Hanover Sq, 212/422-9600)

MarieBelle New York (484 Broome St, 212/925-6999)

Max Brenner, Chocolate by the Bald Man (841 Broadway, 646/467-8803)

Neuchatel Chocolates (55 E 52nd St, 212/759-1388)

Tache Artisan Chocolate (254 Broome St, 212/473-3200)

Teuscher Chocolates of Switzerland (25 E 61st St, 212/751-8482 and Rockefeller Center, 620 Fifth Ave, 212/246-4416)

Varsano's Chocolates (172 W 4th St, 212/352-1171): hand-dipped

Vosges Haut-Chocolat (132 Spring St, 212/625-2929 and 1100 Madison Ave, 212/717-2929)

BRITISH

MYERS OF KESWICK

634 Hudson St (bet Horatio and Jane St) 212/691-4194
Mon-Fri: 10-7; Sat: 10-6; Sun: noon-5 myersofkeswick.com

Myers of Keswick is your traditional neat-as-a-pin British grocery store, except it is in New York City! The second generation now runs the Big Apple's version of "the village grocer" for imported staples and fresh, home-baked items you'd swear came from a kitchen in Soho — the London neighborhood, that is. Among the tins, a shopper can find Heinz treacle sponge pudding, trifle mix, ribena, mushy peas, steak and kidney pie, Smarties, lemon barley water, chutneys, jams, preserves and all the major English teas. Fresh goods, handmade daily, include sausage rolls, Myers' pork pie, Scotch eggs, British bangers and Cumberland sausages. Delivery, for a nominal fee, is available from 72nd Street and south to the tip of Manhattan. For Anglophiles and expatriates alike, Myers of Keswick is a luverly treat.

CANDY

CHOCOLATE BAR

19 Eighth Ave (bet Jane and 12th St)
Daily: 7:30 a.m.-10 p.m.

212/366-1541
chocolatebarnyc.com

This is my kind of bar! Chocolate in all forms is sold all day long. Superb hot chocolate is made with ground dark chocolate and steamed with milk or soy. A variety of delicious chocolate bars includes milk, bittersweet and dark chocolate, corn flakes, sea salt, molé, salted almonds, fruits and nuts. In fact, everything is delicious: brownies of assorted varieties, bonbons, hand-poured chocolate suckers, almond toffee and over-the-top truffles that are decorated with colorful, seasonally-changing artwork. Chocolate also enrobes such favorites as popcorn, pretzels, s'mores and nuts. What a great shop!

> ## WOOD-FIRED BAGELS
>
> Got a quick need for a bagel? Hurry to **Black Seed Bagels** (170 Elizabeth St, 212/730-1950) where the selection and quality are first rate. These bagels are hand-rolled and wood-fired with standard and fancy spreads; for a big splurge, order Tobiko caviar, salmon and butter lettuce.

DYLAN'S CANDY BAR

1011 Third Ave (at 60th St)
646/735-0078
Mon-Thurs: 10-9; Fri, Sat: 10 a.m.-11 p.m.; Sun: 11-9   dylanscandybar.com

Dylan's Candy Bar is three floors of fun and sweetness. Visit the third-floor cafe for meals, fountain drinks, cocktails and custom-made ice cream flavors. The menu features appetizers, pizzas (including dessert pizzas), sandwiches, salads, sundaes and ooey-gooey cakes and other treats. The retail sections feature at least 5,000 candies from around the world where anyone's sweet tooth can be appeased. There are Belgian chocolate bars, chocolate-covered pretzels, popcorn and nuts; nostalgic, novelty and holiday candies and seemingly everything chocolate; you'll find virtually every sugar treat, some offered in bulk (or order online). There are plenty of items in the non-edible category as well — accessories, jewelry, T-shirts, candy-themed pajamas and more. Dylan's Candy Bar is also party central for children, adult and corporate events.

ECONOMY CANDY

108 Rivington St (bet Essex and Ludlow St)
Mon: 10-6; Tues-Fri, Sun: 9-6; Sat: 10-6

212/254-1531
economycandy.com

The third generation now runs this family business, selling everything from penny candies to beautiful gourmet gift stacks and themed confections for holidays and almost any occasion or special interest. The selection at Economy Candy includes over 2,000 varieties of dried fruits, candies, cookies, nuts, chocolates and sugar-free goodies for any age or sweet tooth! Favorite old-time candies include Skybars, Mary Janes, candy buttons and Ice Cubes. Those who bake will appreciate the selection of cocoas, baking chocolate and glazed fruits, but the second best part of this business is the price. It's easy to replenish your candy jar – place an online order and have your favorite sweets delivered to your door.

JACQUES TORRES CHOCOLATE

350 Hudson St (at King St)	212/414-2462
285 Amsterdam Ave (bet 73rd and 74th St)	212/787-3256
30 Rockefeller Plaza, concourse level	212/664-1804
Grand Central Terminal (43rd St at Lexington Ave)	212/922-3620
327 Lafayette St (bet Bleecker and Houston St)	646/370-4719
1186 Third Ave (bet 69th and 70th St)	212/204-7040
110 E 57th St (bet Park and Lexington Ave)	646/852-6624
Hours vary by store	mrchocolate.com

Jacques Torres will send the chocoholic in you to heaven! Jacques specializes in fresh, handcrafted chocolates that are free of preservatives and artificial flavors — from bonbons and truffles to chocolate bars and chocolate-covered Cheerios. You'll also find ice cream, cookies, pastries, hot chocolate, espresso and other divine delights. The shops are beautifully decorated with crystal chandeliers, mahogany wood counters and mirrored walls. A state-of-the-art chocolate manufacturing plant lets you view production from start to finish at the 8,000-square-foot Hudson Street store.

LA MAISON DU CHOCOLAT

1018 Madison Ave (bet 78th and 79th St)	212/744-7117
Mon-Sat: 10-7; Sun: 11-6	
30 Rockefeller Plaza (49th St bet Fifth Ave and Ave of the Americas)	
Mon-Sat: 9:30-7; Sun: 11-6	212/265-9404
63 Wall St (bet Pearl and Hanover St)	212/952-1123
Mon-Fri: 10-7; Sat: 10-6; Sun: 11-6	
Plaza Food Hall (The Plaza, 1 W 59th St)	212/355-3436
Mon-Sat: 11-8; Sun: 11-6	lamaisonduchocolat.com

La Maison du Chocolat is quite a place! They carry light and dark chocolates, French bonbons (plain or fancy with fine champagne cognac), orangettes, chocolate-covered almonds, caramels, candied chestnuts (seasonal) and fruit paste. Everything is made in Paris, and prices are a cut above the candy-counter norm. There is also a tea salon that serves pastries and drinks (except at The Plaza).

LEONIDAS

485 Madison Ave (bet 51st and 52nd St)	212/980-2608
Mon-Fri: 9-7; Sat: 10-7; Sun: noon-6	
3 Hanover Sq	212/422-9600
Mon-Fri: 7-6	leonidas-chocolate.com

The famous Leonidas' Belgian confections are flown in fresh every week and sold at these exquisite stores. There are over 100 varieties of milk, white and bittersweet chocolate pieces, plus chocolate orange peels, solid chocolate medallions, fabulous fresh-cream fillings, truffle fillings and marzipan; the pralines are particularly sumptuous. Jacques Bergier, the genial general manager, can make the mouth water just describing this treasure trove and best of all, prices are reasonable. Leonidas' chocolates are also available at **Manon Cafe** (120 Broadway, 212/766-6100) as well as coffee, espresso, cappuccino, sandwiches and salads.

LI-LAC CHOCOLATES

40 Eighth Ave (at Jane St)   212/924-2280
Mon-Thurs: 11-8; Fri, Sat: 11-9; Sun: 11-7
Grand Central Market (43rd St at Lexington Ave)   212/924-2280
Mon-Fri: 7 a.m.-9 p.m.; Sat: 10-7; Sun: 11-6   li-lacchocolates.com

Since 1923 Li-Lac Chocolates has been making Old World artisan chocolates in small batches using the founder's original recipes. The time-honored production and fine quality ingredients result in delicious fresh chocolates, walnut fudge, pralines, mousses, French rolls, nuts, glacé fruits and hand-dipped chocolates. Molds are used to create specialty treats for holidays, occasions and wedding favors.

MARIEBELLE NEW YORK

484 Broome St (bet West Broadway and Wooster St)   212/925-6999
Mon-Thurs: 11-7; Fri-Sun: 11-8   mariebelle.com

Forget about the diet when you visit MarieBelle. What awaits you is thick, European-style hot chocolate, homemade cookies, biscuits and French pastries. The exotic chocolate flavors are packed with class and are a great gift for chocoholics! The popular pin-up girl collection of chocolate bars gives new meaning to "eye candy." Crepes, fondues, sandwiches, salads and other light fare are available at the Cacao Bar, which is also an intimate venue for small private events.

MONDEL CHOCOLATES

2913 Broadway (at 114th St)   212/864-2111
Mon-Sat: 11-7; Sun: 11-4   mondelchocolates.com

Mondel has been a tasty gem in Morningside Heights since owner Florence Mondel's father founded the store in 1943. Chocolate-covered ginger, orange peel, nut barks, truffles, creams, cordials and turtles are all excellent, but my all-time favorites are dark chocolate nonpareils crowned with white sprinkles. You'll be pleased to know that Mondel's sugar-free candies are so good, you might not know they are made sans sugar.

PAPABUBBLE NEW YORK

380 Broome St (bet Mott and Mulberry St)   212/966-2599
Thurs-Sat: noon-9; Sun-Wed: noon-6   papabubbleny.com

This artisan candy-making workshop produces sweet treats featuring seasonal flavors in traditional shapes or formed into finger rings, whimsies and lollipops of different sizes and shapes. Personalized candies are a specialty at Papabubble with words, designs, business names and logos hand-sculpted into the candies.

TEUSCHER CHOCOLATES OF SWITZERLAND

25 E 61st St (at Madison Ave)   212/751-8482
Mon-Fri: 10-6:30; Sat: 11-6; Sun: noon-5
Rockefeller Center
620 Fifth Ave (bet 49th and 50th St)   212/246-4416
Mon-Sat: 10-6 (Thurs till 7); Sun: noon-6   teuscher-newyork.com

The Swiss chocolates at Teuscher are not just chocolates, they are imported works of art, shipped weekly from Switzerland and packed into stunning handmade boxes. Truffles are almost obscenely good. Superb champagne truffles have a tiny dot of Dom Pérignon cream in the center and cocoa, nougat, butter-crunch, muscat, orange and almond truffles all have their own little surprises. Truffles may be the stars, but Teuscher's marzipan and praline chocolates are of similar high quality. Fantasy figures and flowers as well as wedding and party favors will make any occasion very special. If there was an award for "most elegant chocolate shop," it would have to go to Teuscher!

CATERING, DELIS AND FOOD TO GO

ABIGAIL KIRSCH

71 W 23rd St (nr Ave of the Americas)   212/696-4076
By appointment   abigailkirsch.com

Abigail Kirsch's creative and delicious menus, service and venues are of the highest quality. Pricing is also high, but you will get your money's worth if you are hosting a class event, wedding, corporate function or intimate cocktail party. You will not have to worry about a single detail as their team draws on over four decades of experience. In addition to your favorite location, Kirsch has exclusive venues for memorable events at Chelsea Piers (Pier Sixty, The Lighthouse and Current) and at The Skylark.

AGATA & VALENTINA

1505 First Ave (at 79th St)   212/452-0690
Daily: 8 a.m.-9 p.m.
64 University Pl (bet 10th and 11th St)   212/452-0690
Daily: 8 a.m.-10 p.m.   agatavalentina.com

These very classy gourmet shops will make you think you're in Sicily. There are good things to eat at every counter, with each one more tempting than the next. The Italian product line, handpicked by Agata and her daughter, Valentina, is extraordinary; you'll love the great selection of gourmet dishes, bakery items, appetizers, magnificent fresh vegetables, meats, cheeses, seafood, candies and gelato. These quality foods are used in preparation of catered meals and gift baskets for any occasion!

BANGKOK CENTER GROCERY

104 Mosco St (bet Mott and Mulberry St)   212/349-1979
Daily: 10-8   bangkokcentergrocery.com

You'll find a complete selection of Thai ingredients in this amazing, one-stop store, including teas, sticky rice, rice noodles, lemon grass, curry paste and all manner of Thai herbs and spices. Bangkok Center also has convenient frozen and prepared foods you can take home for dinner plus snacks, candies, beverages, movies and magazines.

BARNEY GREENGRASS

541 Amsterdam Ave (bet 86th and 87th St)   212/724-4707
Tues-Sun: 8-6 (takeout)   barneygreengrass.com
Tues-Fri: 8:30-4; Sat, Sun: 8:30-5 (restaurant)

This family enterprise, in business since 1908, has occupied the same location since 1929. Barney Greengrass lays claim to the title of "Sturgeon King," but it also carries other regal smoked-fish delicacies, including Nova

CAKE, CAKE AND MORE CAKE

You won't go wrong when you have cake at these bakeries; but for special occasion cakes, they are over the top!

BabyCakes NYC (248 Broome St, 212/677-5047): vegan, dairy-, egg- and gluten-free cakes and pastries

Billy's Bakery (184 Ninth Ave, 212/647-9956; 75 Franklin St, 212/647-9958 and Plaza Food Hall, The Plaza, 1 W 59th St, 646/755-3237): icebox cake

Cafe Lalo (201 W 83rd St, 212/496-6031): impressive selection

Carlo's Bakery (625 Eighth Ave, 646/590-3783): featured on *Cake Boss*

Carrot Top Pastries (3931 Broadway, 212/927-4800 and 5025 Broadway, 212/569-1532): carrot cake, of course

City Cakes (251 W 18th St, 646/688-2286): call ahead to order a cake

Clinton St Baking Company & Restaurant (4 Clinton St, 646/602-6263): black and white cake

Duane Park Patisserie (179 Duane St, 212/274-8447): blackout cake

Francois Payard Bakery (1293 Third Ave, 212/717-5252; 116 W Houston, 212/995-0888 and 210 Murray St, 212/566-8300): wonderful creations

Lady M Cake Boutique (41 E 78th St, 212/452-2222 and Plaza Food Hall, The Plaza, 1 W 59th St, 646/755-3225): alternating layers of handmade crepes and pastry cream

Magnolia Bakery (401 Bleecker St, 212/462-2572; 200 Columbus Ave, 212/724-8101; 1240 Ave of the Americas, 212/767-1123; Bloomingdale's, 1000 Third Ave, 212/265-5320 and Grand Central Terminal, 42nd St at Vanderbilt Ave, lower level, 212/682-3588): white coconut and meringue cake

Moishe's Bake Shop (115 Second Ave, 212/505-8555): kosher

Momofuku Milk Bar (251 E 13th St; Chambers Hotel, 15 W 56th St and 561 Columbus Ave, 347/577-9504 all locations): cake truffles

Two Little Red Hens (1652 Second Ave, 212/452-0476): red velvet cake

Yura on Madison (1292 Madison Ave, 212/860-1598): chocolate cake

Scotia salmon, belly lox, whitefish caviar, pickled herring, pastrami salmon and kippered-salmon salad. The world-renowned dairy and deli line includes vegetable cream cheese, great homemade cheese blintzes, homemade salads, borscht and other soups, sandwiches, desserts and delicious deli items. If you only order one thing, make it the house specialty: Nova Scotia salmon with scrambled eggs and onions. Delicious!

BARRAUD CATERERS LTD.

405 Broome St (at Centre St)   212/925-1334
Mon-Fri. 10-6   barraudcaterers.com

Chef/owner Rosemary Howe was born in India and grew up British. She is very familiar with Indian and Anglo-Indian food and her training in developing recipes is on the French side. Because she was raised in the tradition of afternoon tea, she knows finger sandwiches and all that goes with them. With this varied background, her bespoke menus are unique; all breads are menu-specific, and every meal is customized from a lengthy list. A wine consultant is available for dinners focusing on cheese and wine and tasting menus paired with wines. A specialty is multicourse (degustation) small plate dinners in the style of high-end restaurants. This is a real hands-on operation, with Rosemary taking care of every detail of your brunch, tea, lunch or dinner and, should the need arise, Barraud offers consultations on table etiquette.

BUTTERFIELD MARKET

1114 Lexington Ave (bet 77th and 78th St)   212/288-7800
Mon-Fri: 7a.m.-8 p.m.; Sat: 7:30-5:30; Sun: 8-5   butterfieldmarket.com

Since 1915 Upper East Siders have enjoyed the goodies at Butterfield. Highlights of this popular market include an excellent prepared-foods section, sandwiches, produce, a good selection of quality specialty items, breads, tasty pastries, frozen yogurt, charcuterie, attractive gift baskets, a terrific cheese selection and a diet-busting candy and sweets section. A cafe with the same great prepared food menu and frozen yogurt is located at **Butterfield Kitchen** (346 E 92nd, 212/772-8782) which is also the catering center for the organization.

CHELSEA MARKET

75 Ninth Ave (bet 15th and 16th St)   212/243-6005
Hours vary by store   chelseamarket.com

One of the most unusual marketplaces in the city is housed in a complex of 19 former industrial buildings, including the old National Biscuit Company (Nabisco) of the late 1800s. The 1,800-square-foot space is innovative, including a waterfall fed by an underground spring. Among over 40 shops you'll find **Amy's Bread** (big selection, plus a cafe); **Bowery Kitchen Supply** (kitchen buffs will go wild!); **Chelsea Market Baskets**; **Chelsea Wine Vault** (climate-controlled); **Cull & Pistol** (seafood and raw bar); **Ronnybrook Farm Dairy at Chelsea Market** (fresh milk and eggs); **Buon Italia** (great Italian basics); **Friedman's Lunch** (loaded baked potatoes); **Hale and Hearty Soups** (dozens of varieties); **Imports from Marrakesh**; **The Lobster Place** (takeout seafood); **Sarabeth's**; **Manhattan Fruit Exchange** (for buying in bulk); **Chelsea Thai** (wholesale and takeout); **Morimoto** (Japanese fine dining); **Fat Witch Bakery** (brownies, goodies and gifts) and **Eleni's** (artfully iced sugar cookies, bagels, ice cream and more). A visit to Chelsea Market and a walk along the High Line go hand in hand.

CITARELLA

2135 Broadway (at 75th St)   212/874-0383 (all locations)
1313 Third Ave (at 75th St)
424 Ave of the Americas (at 9th St)
Mon-Sat: 7 a.m.-11 p.m.; Sun: 9-9   citarella.com

Citarella gourmet market started out as a fish market and has been serving customers since 1912. They claim to carry the largest selection of fresh domestic and international seafood in the country. The shelves and cases are stocked with gourmet foods to appease finicky chefs and home cooks. From the take-away section, choose from an extensive selection of steamed lobster, salads, pastas, soups and delicious entrees or charcuterie, antipasti and smoked fish from the deli. Citarella also stocks their own brand of housemade pastas, sauces, oils, vinegars and chocolates. Fully-prepared meals are convenient for everyday dining or for impressive dinner parties; the assortment of foods is staggering. You can count on them for superb customer service and exceptional ingredients for your special meals; or leave the catering for business or social events to them. Three stores are also located in the Hamptons.

DEAN & DELUCA

560 Broadway (at Prince St)   212/226-6800
1150 Madison Ave (at 85th St)   212/717-0800
Mon-Fri: 7 a.m.-8 p.m.; Sat, Sun: 8-8   deandeluca.com

Dean & Deluca is one of the most recognizable names on the American epicurean scene. Don't miss it! The flagship store in Soho offers an extraordinary array of local, national and international culinary selections. Among the many temptations are fresh produce and flowers, fresh-from-the-oven breads and pastries, prepared dishes, a good showing of cheeses and charcuterie; a selection of meats, poultry, seafood and beer. A bustling espresso bar serves coffee and cappuccino, as well as sweets and savories. This part of the business has been expanded into smaller cafes at City Spire, Rockefeller Center and *The New York Times* building. To complete the gourmet adventure, Dean & Deluca offers an assortment of housewares and gourmet gifts.

HEALTHY TREATS

This operation is a new spin on a childhood favorite. **Treat House** (452 Amsterdam Ave, 212/799-7779) is devoted entirely to the snack bars, the foundation being crispy rice cereal and homemade marshmallows. Most treats are gluten- and dairy-free, and high-fructose corn syrup is not used in the recipes. Tempting flavors include chocolate raspberry, bubble gum, caramel sea salt, chocolate mint, chocolate covered cherries and other options with or without nuts. These little treats are only about three bites; bet you can eat more than one!

THE SPICES OF LIFE

Some folks settle for salt and pepper to season their food, whereas others wouldn't think of eating anything without a pinch of this, a dash of that and a smidgeon of something else. Gourmet and international grocers often carry a nice selection of plain or fancy salts and peppers and basic spices, but for a larger selection of exotic spices, check out the offerings at these specialty shops:

Kalustyan's (123 Lexington Ave, 212/685-3451)

La Boite (724 Eleventh Ave, 212/247-4407)

Spice Corner (135 Lexington Ave, 212/689-5182)

Spices and Tease (Grand Central Terminal, 43rd St at Lexington Ave and Chelsea Market, 75 Ninth Ave, 347/470-8327 for both locations)

DELMONICO GOURMET FOOD MARKET

55 E 59th St (bet Madison and Park Ave)   212/751-5559

Daily: 24 hours   delmonicogourmetnyc.com

Delmonico Gourmet Food Market has gourmet groceries, fresh produce, delicious pastries from their bakery, a huge selection of cheeses and sushi, salad and charcuterie bars. I like the clean surroundings and accommodating help, but if you can't make the trip there, order online and request delivery.

EATALY

200 Fifth Ave (bet 23rd and 24th St)   212/229-2560

Market: Daily: 10 a.m.-11 p.m.; Restaurants: hours vary   eataly.com

Moderate (restaurant)

Forget about Little Italy! Instead, visit a one-of-a-kind New York experience you will never forget. This 50,000-square-foot operation is part restaurant, part grocery store, part street fair and part eating circus. Eataly is an inspired venture combining the genius of Mario Batali, Lidia Bastianich and Joe Bastianich (in New York) and Adam and Alex Saper. This complex comprises several boutique restaurants, a fishmonger, butcher, espresso bar, wine store, cheese store, produce stand, cooking school, lunch-dedicated restaurant, gelato stand, kitchenware and so much more. It is assembled to evoke the atmosphere of a refined country fair, with hundreds of folks shopping, grazing, browsing and loving every minute of this unique hot spot. Eataly has excellent, reasonably priced restaurants (which are positioned near the related section of the market), an incredible assortment of edibles, good informational signage and superb eye appeal. The mixture of foodstuffs is part Italian (mostly dry goods) and part high-quality American. The wine selection is awesome, and the pastries are addictive.

Manzo, Pranzo and **Birreria** take reservations, Birreria is a substantial rooftop brewery (which brews cask ales) and a restaurant with a top-quality meat selection. **La Pizza & La Pasta** is worth a visit for the delicious ten-inch pizzas and **Il Pesce** has a raw bar and more in the seafood category.

ELI'S MANHATTAN

1411 Third Ave (at 80th St)   212/717-8100
Daily: 7 a.m.-9 p.m.   elizabar.com

You know that quality is foremost whenever Eli Zabar is involved. This is true at Eli's Manhattan, which carries pristine produce, dairy items, pastries and breads, flowers, prepared foods, appetizers, smoked fish, coffee, wine and spirits, as well as one of the most extensive salad bar selections. The catering department will expertly execute your party instructions with panache. Prices can be high, but so is quality. A market-to-table restaurant called **Eli's Table** (1413 Third Ave, 212/717-9798) serves dinner nightly starting at 5:30, as well as weekend brunch between 8 and 3. The boutique wine portion of the business is called **Eli's List Wine & Spirits** and offers daily tastings. Gift baskets, designed for any occasion, feature Eli's best products and will delight any recipient.

ELI'S VINEGAR FACTORY

431 E 91st St (at York Ave)   212/987-0885
Daily: 7 a.m.-9 p.m.; Brunch: Sat, Sun: 8-4   elizabar.com

Located on the site of what used to be a working vinegar factory, this Eli Zabar operation offers bearable prices on fresh produce, pizzas, fish, meats, desserts, seafood, cheeses, baked goods (including Eli's great breads), coffee, deli items and select groceries. An informal cafe is open during store hours for breakfast, pizza, sandwiches, soups and pastries; popular weekend brunch is available on the balcony. It is interesting to note that Eli's heirloom tomatoes, greens and herbs are grown in the five rooftop greenhouses. This is one of the most intriguing food factories around!

FAIRWAY MARKET

2127 Broadway (at 74th St)   212/595-1888
240 E 86th St (bet Second and Third Ave)   212/327-2008
2328 Twelfth Ave (at 133rd St)   212/234-3883
766 Ave of the Americas (bet 25th and 26th St)   646/676-4550
550 Second Ave (at 31st St)   646/720-9420
Hours vary by store   fairwaymarket.com

Fairway Market is a very busy place! This popular institution made its name with an incredible selection of fruits and vegetables and continues to offer produce in huge quantities at reasonable prices. Each store offers a wonderful array of cheeses, bakery items, organically grown produce, expanded fish and meat departments and catering services. Fairway operates its own farm on Long Island and has developed relationships with area produce dealers; all stores offer a full line of organic and natural grocery, health and beauty items. In-store cafes at both the Broadway and 86th Street locations are convenient and reasonable. As you make your shopping rounds on the Upper East or West Side, you can't go wrong with a Fairway bag on one arm and a Zabar's bag on the other!

FINE & SCHAPIRO

138 W 72nd St (bet Broadway and Columbus Ave)   212/877-2874
Daily: 10-10   fineandschapiro.com

Fine & Schapiro dispenses a full line of cold cuts, hot and cold hors

MEAT MARKETS

Make friends with your local butcher and you'll be rewarded with cooking tips from a professional. They will also fill you in on their best deals and accommodate requests for special cuts and orders. If you're in the neighborhood, check out these places:

Harlem Shambles (2141 Frederick Douglass Blvd, 646/476-4650): locally-sourced beef, pork and poultry; house-made sausages and Cornish pasties

Honest Chops (319 E 9th St, 212/388-0762): halal establishment

Japanese Premium Beef, Inc. (57 Great Jones St, 212/260-2333): domestically-bred Wagyu beef; premium prices, too

Pino Prime Meats (149 Sullivan St, 212/475-8134): fresh meats and game; homemade sausage

d'oeuvres, catering platters and magnificent sandwiches.   Everything that issues from Fine & Schapiro is perfectly cooked and artistically arranged. The sandwiches are masterpieces; the aroma and taste are irresistible and pastrami and hot brisket are sure winners. Chicken-in-a-pot, pirogis, cocktail knishes and stuffed cabbage are among their best items. Complete kosher dinners are a specialty, especially for Jewish holidays, and are available for takeout, delivery or in the restaurant.

GARDEN OF EDEN

162 W 23rd St (bet Ave of the Americas and Seventh Ave)	212/675-6300
7 E 14th St (bet University Pl and Fifth Ave)	212/255-4200
2780 Broadway (bet 106th and 107th St)	212/222-7300
Mon-Sat: 7 a.m.-10 p.m.; Sun: 7 a.m.-9:30 p.m.	edengourmet.com

These stores are both farmers markets and gourmet shops! The food items are fresh, appetizing and priced to please. Moreover, the stores are immaculate and well organized and the personnel are very helpful. You'll find breads and bakery items, cheeses, veggies, frozen foods, household supplies, meats, seafood, pastas, desserts, paté, breakfast items and a wide array of imported goods. Beautiful, generously-filled gift baskets are composed to fit any budget and all manner of catering services are available, too.

GLORIOUS FOOD

522 E 74th St (bet East River and York Ave)	212/628-2320
Mon-Fri: 9-5 (by appointment)	gloriousfood.com

When it comes to catering, Glorious Food is at the top of many New Yorkers' lists. They are a full-service outfit, expertly taking care of every detail of any event including customizing menus to fit any casual or tony occasion. Co-owner Sean Driscoll and crew have met most every challenge since 1972. Give 'em a try!

GOURMET GARAGE

489 Broome St (at Wooster St)	212/941-5850
1245 Park Ave (at 96th St)	212/348-5850
155 W 66th St (bet Broadway and Amsterdam Ave)	212/595-5850
301 E 64th St (at Second Ave)	212/535-5880
117 Seventh Ave S (at 10th St)	212/699-5980
Hours vary by store	gourmetgarage.com

Gourmet Garage, once a food importer/distributor, is now a working-class gourmet food shop which carries a good selection of in-demand items, including fruits and veggies, dairy products, cheeses, breads, pastries, coffees, fresh meats and seafood, olive oils and organic foods at reasonable prices. The award-winning catering department is always eager to make any event extra special and attempts to accommodate last minute emergency jobs. As an added convenience, turn your shopping list over to the store's personal shopper and arrange for delivery at a nominal fee. All locations offer prepared foods, rotisserie chicken and a sushi bar.

GRACE'S MARKETPLACE

1299 Second Ave (at 68th St)	212/737-0600
1735 Park Ave (at 121st St)	212/876-0200
Mon-Sat: 7 a.m.-9 p.m.; Sun: 8-8	gracesmarketplacenyc.com

Grace's Marketplace is another of the city's finest and most popular food emporiums. Members of the Doria family still preside over this operation and they can be seen helping customers on the floor at their new locations where products, service and ambience are all top of the line. You'll find fresh and smoked meats and fish, caviar, cheeses, fresh pastas, homemade sauces, produce, a full range of baked goods, candy, coffees and teas, dried fruits, pastries, gourmet and international groceries, prepared foods, prime meats, sushi and seafood. Quality gift baskets and catering are specialties. **Grace's Trattoria** has an attractive look; it is open daily for breakfast, lunch, dinner and great Italian fare.

GREAT PERFORMANCES

304 Hudson St (at Spring St)	212/727-2424
By appointment	greatperformances.com

Since 1979 Great Performances has been creating spectacular events in the New York area with the help of folks from the city's artistic community. Each division of this full-service catering company has a team of expert staff and

SWEET BASKETS

Manhattan Fruitier (Long Island City, 212/686-0404) makes and delivers tasty, beautiful gift baskets using fresh seasonal and exotic fruits for all occasions. Sweet or savory treats include locally handmade truffles, fine foods, baked goods, fresh flowers, caviar and organic, gluten-free, vegan and kosher products. If you have something specific in mind, build your own basket; otherwise leave it to the experts to create a unique gift. Expect to pay for the dazzling results!

they take pride in recruiting the best and brightest the industry has to offer. From intimate dinner parties to galas for thousands, Great Performances is a complete catering and event-planning resource. They are the first catering company to operate an organic farm, Katchkie Farm, in Kinderhook. Meats, fish and dairy products are sourced from local suppliers. Great Performances is the exclusive caterer at select venues and operates cafes in some of the city's cultural institutions. The interesting settings, gorgeous displays, delicious food and masterful execution make an impressive statement.

H&H MIDTOWN BAGELS EAST

1551 Second Ave (bet 80th and 81st St)   212/734-7441
Daily: 24/7   hhmidtownbagels.com

Delicious bagels are made right on the premises, and if you're lucky, you'll get 'em warm! The shop carries all sorts of good things to pair with your bagel: delicious spreads, jams, honey and smoked fish. If you're not in the mood for bagels, try homemade croissants, pastries, muffins, assorted cookies, soups, knishes, deli meats, sandwiches or salads. The emphasis is on carryout, but tables are available for those who can't wait. Catering, shipping and wholesale sales are offered as well.

HAN AH REUM

25 W 32nd St (bet Broadway and Fifth Ave)   212/695-3283
Daily: 9 a.m.-11:30 p.m.

Korean (also Japanese and Chinese) food items are the specialties at Han ah Reum in Murray Hill on a street surrounded by Korean restaurants. This tightly packed ethnic grocery store has everything from Korean pears, Japanese cucumbers, kalbi, sashimi, acorn flour and rice cakes to a good selection of fresh fish and meat (some pre-marinated). You'll find many brands of items at this central supermarket location. Note the late hours!

INTERNATIONAL GROCERY

543 Ninth Ave (at 40th St)   212/279-1000
Mon-Fri: 7:30-6:30; Sat: 7:30-6

Ninth Avenue is a great wholesale market for international cookery. Accordingly, International Grocery is both a spice emporium and an excellent source of Greek staples for adventurous home cooks. Loose herbs, honey, pastas, olives, pitas and some cooking utensils and pans create a bazaar-like atmosphere. For eats, opt for one of the housemade platters of baklava, spanikopita, halvah, yogurt, feta cheese or other Greek specialty. You will sacrifice frills for some of the best prices and freshest foodstuffs in town in this compact store.

KELLEY AND PING

127 Greene St (at Prince St)   212/228-1212
Daily: 11:30 a.m.-5:p.m.; 5:30 p.m.-11 p.m.   kelleyandping.com

The exotic cuisines of Asia are popular in restaurants and at home. Kelley and Ping specialize in groceries from Thailand, China, Vietnam, Japan, Malaysia and Korea and helpful employees will answer questions regarding the preparation of Asian dishes. The popular on-premises restaurant has become a major part of the operation, serving afternoon tea, lunch and dinner, as well as offering catering services. You'll find lunch boxes, noodle soups, curry, wok items, salads and rolls. Dinner items expand to include chicken, fish and meat entrees along with small Asian dishes and sides like jasmine rice or vegetable dumplings. Free delivery is available to nearby neighborhoods.

RUSS & DAUGHTERS

179 E Houston St (bet Allen and Orchard St)   212/475-4880
Mon-Fri: 8-8; Sat: 8-7; Sun: 8-5:30   russanddaughters.com

With a reputation for serving only the best, Russ & Daughters has been a renowned New York shop for four generations and more than a century. A sample of their merchandise includes the finest caviar, smoked fish (including salmon, sturgeon, sable, whitefish and salt-cured belly lox), herring and other specialty smoked fish. They also sell nuts, dried fruits, bagels, rugelach and salads. Sweets, such as hand-dipped chocolates and chocolate-covered jelly rings and bars, are premium quality. Without exception, platters of cheese, fish, salad or sweets are always beautifully arranged. Russ & Daughters sells over the counter, and will ship anywhere in this country. A Lower East Side shopping trip should definitely include a stop here or at their new cafe (**Russ & Daughters Cafe**, 127 Orchard St). Another cafe, Russ & Daughters at the Jewish Museum (1109 Fifth Ave), will open spring 2015.

SABLE'S SMOKED FISH

1489 Second Ave (bet 77th and 78th St)   212/249-6177
Mon-Fri: 8-7; Sat: 7-7; Sun: 7-5   sablesnyc.com

Kenny and Danny Sze bring their experience and knowledge (learned at Zabar's) to the Upper East Side. The shop offers wonderful smoked salmon, lobster salad, Alaskan crab salad, caviar (good prices), deli meats, cheeses, coffees, salads, chicken soup, fresh breads and prepared foods. Sable's catering service provides platters (smoked fish, cold cuts and cheese), jumbo sandwiches and other items. Limited seating is available for eat-in customers; most products are carried away or shipped locally and nationally.

SALUMERIA BIELLESE

378 Eighth Ave (at 29th St)   212/736-7376
Mon-Fri: 6:30-6; Sat: 9-5   salumeriabiellese.com

In 1925, Ugo Buzzio and Joseph Nello immigrated from the Piedmontese city of Biella. They opened a Chelsea shop a block away from the current one and began producing Italian-style cured meats and delicious fresh sausage. Word spread among the city's chefs that Salumeria Biellese was producing a quality product, and now they supply many fine restaurants in the city. Still a family-run business, Buzzio's son Marc, along with partners Paul and Fouad, are in charge today. The meat case includes artisinally-crafted sausages (pork, game, beef, lamb and poultry), cured meats, fresh pork and specialty patés. Breakfast and lunch are prepared in the deli; there are daily specials, hot heros and cold cut sandwiches, prepared foods and assorted breakfast entrees from the grill. **Biricchino** (260 W 29th St, 212/695-6690), the family's restaurant offering Northern Italian cuisine, is located in back.

SONNIER & CASTLE

554 W 48th St (bet Tenth and Eleventh Ave)   212/957-6481
By appointment   sonnier-castle.com

Sonnier & Castle has brought finesse and style to the table for special events of any size since 1997. From playful to sophisticated, their creativity, presentation, service and innovative cooking will transform any gathering into a memorable one. Special gifts such as housemade caramels, cookies and savory nibbles are attractively packaged and available in their shop.

SPOONBREAD CATERING

Catering at specified sites   212/865-0700

MISS MAMIE'S SPOONBREAD TOO

366 W 110th St (between Columbus and Manhattan Ave)   212/865-6744
Mon-Thurs: noon-10; Fri, Sat: noon-11; Sun: 11-9:30   spoonbreadinc.com

For authentic soul food, go to these Harlem standouts under the direction of Norma Jean Darden. Pork chops, spoonbread (a pudding-like cornmeal bread eaten with a spoon or fork), chicken (fried, smothered, roasted and barbecued), fried catfish and classic sides like collard greens are prepared fresh daily. Prices are moderate, and bargain-priced lunches with one side dish are served weekdays until 3 p.m. Plan to splurge on banana pudding, pecan pie, sweet potato pie or fruit cobbler with ice cream. These down-South favorites, along with more upscale selections, are offered by the catering arm of the business, Spoonbread Catering. Some of the multi-cultural cuisines exhibit Asian, Italian and Mexican influences. Try them for wedding receptions, corporate events or any other occasion and wow your guests.

SHOP LIKE A CHEF

Do you know where to find black garlic extract, dried orange blossoms or hard-to-find spices and exotic ingredients? Shop like a chef and visit **S.O.S. Chefs** (104 Ave B, 212/505-5813). Among the interesting finds are numerous types of preserves, exotic spices, molecular ingredients, oils, chocolates, truffles, mushrooms, foie gras, flavored salts, nuts, vanilla beans, saffron, fennel pollen and much more. There are drawers full of interesting specialty items at reasonable prices at this high-end discovery center!

TODARO BROS.

555 Second Ave (bet 30th and 31st St)   212/532-0633
Mon-Sat: 6:30 a.m.-10 p.m.; Sun: 6:30 a.m.-9 p.m.   todarobros.com

Todaro Bros. carries the very best in specialty foods, great lunch sandwiches, fresh mozzarella, sausages, olives and prepared foods. Customers have come to expect high-quality fresh fish and meats and a huge variety of imported cheeses. The shelves are well stocked with artisanal oils, vinegars, pasta, condiments, coffee, fresh produce and exquisite pastries. These and other Mediterranean products are served in **Todaro Bros. Enoteca**, a very nice addition to the compact scene. The wine bar fare includes small plates, salads, pastas and delicious brunches that are best when accompanied by Italian wines and beers from near and far.

WESTSIDE MARKET NYC

77 Seventh Ave (at 15th St)	212/807-7771
Daily: 7 a.m.-midnight	
2171 Broadway (at 77th St)	212/595-2536
2840 Broadway (at 110th St)	212/222-3367
84 Third Ave (at 12th St)	212/253-8400
2589 Broadway (at 97th St)	212/316-0222
Daily: 24/7	wmarketnyc.com

For grocery shopping, don't overlook Westside Market with first-class locations only on the westside. The stores are immaculately clean, merchandise is well priced and there are many items from which to choose. Catering, free delivery within a ten-block radius and wonderful prepared foods are additional features. You will be very pleasantly surprised! Discover tempting Greek recipes on their website, compliments of the Zoitas family.

WHOLE FOODS MARKET

808 Columbus Ave (at 97th St)	212/222-6160
Time Warner Center, 10 Columbus Cir	212/823-9600
226 E 57th St (bet Second and Third Ave)	646/497-1222
4 Union Square S	212/673-5388
250 Seventh Ave (at 24th St)	212/924-5969
95 E Houston (at Bowery)	212/420-1320
270 Greenwich St (bet Murray and Warren St)	212/349-6555
Hours vary by store	wholefoodsmarket.com

If you can't find a particular food item at Whole Foods Market, it probably doesn't exist. These grocery superstores (approaching eight locations in Manhattan) promote healthy lifestyles and have huge deli, bakery, produce and floral sections, as well as sushi, seafood, fresh juices and all kinds of prepared foods. The big, beautiful and busy markets feature interesting, tasty and educational special events and cooking classes; online ordering also.

ZABAR'S

2245 Broadway (at 80th St)	212/787-2000
Mon-Fri: 8-7:30; Sat: 8-8; Sun: 9-6	zabars.com

No trip to Manhattan is complete without a visit to this fabulous emporium. True New York shoppers swear by this place! You will find enormous selections of bread, smoked fish, coffee, prepared foods, cheeses, olives, deli items, gift baskets, candy and much more. All are of the highest quality and affordably priced. A cafe next door provides snacks all day at bargain prices. Their fresh-from-the-oven rye bread is the best in Manhattan. One important reason for Zabar's success is veteran employees; roughly 50 of them have been with the store for 18 years or more. Upstairs is one of the best housewares departments in America, with a huge selection and good prices. (It opens an hour later than the rest of Zabar's every day except Sunday.) Owner Saul Zabar comes from a legendary food

LOWER EAST SIDE MARKET

Essex Street Market (120 Essex St, essexstreetmarket.com) has been an historic Lower East Side shopping destination since 1947. You'll find vendors of seafood, meats, ethnic groceries, baked goods, cheese, chocolate, produce, coffee, tea, juices and bulk-food items. The market also features restaurants and specialty stores. No matter what you are looking for, Essex Street Market will deliver a unique shopping experience.

family in Manhattan. You will often see him wandering the aisles to make sure everything is topnotch. General Manager Scott Goldshine and Store Manager David Tait provide the extra-special service for which Zabar's is renowned. And some Saturdays you will find your author at Zabar's autographing this book!

CHEESE

ALLEVA DAIRY

188 Grand St (at Mulberry St)
Mon-Sat: 9-6; Sun: 9-3

212/226-7990
allevadairy.com

Alleva is the oldest Italian cheese store in America. The Alleva family has operated the business since 1892, always maintaining meticulous standards of quality and service. Robert Alleva oversees the production of over 4,000 pounds of fresh cheese a week, including *parmigiano, fraschi, manteche, scamoize* and *provoleaffumicale*. The ricotta is superb and the mozzarella tastes like it was made on a side street in Florence. Quality Italian meats, an olive bar, antipasto, grocery items and gift baskets are also offered and online orders are welcome. No meal would be complete without pasta and Alleva makes a fresh assortment daily using durum wheat, seminola flour and eggs. This is a real gem!

DI PALO FINE FOODS

200 Grand St (at Mott St)
Mon-Sat: 9-7; Sun: 9-5

212/226-1033
dipaloselects.com

The authentic cheeses and pastas offered at family-owned Di Palo Fine Foods are simply superb. Olive oils, cured meats and all manner of traditional products to fill a pantry are hand selected from Northern, Southern and Central Italy. It's worth a trip to Little Italy to visit this well-stocked and attractive specialty market.

EAST VILLAGE CHEESE

40 Third Ave (bet 9th and 10th St)
Daily: 8:30-6:30

212/477-2601

Value is the name of the game. For years this store has prided itself on selling cheese at some of the lowest prices in town; just check out the ads plastered on the windows around the front door. They claim similar savings for whole-bean coffees, fresh pastas, extra-virgin olive oils, spreads, quiches, patés and a wide selection of fresh breads. They also have a deli counter and olive bar. Good service, including a knowledgeable staff, is another reason to shop here. This is a cash-only operation.

IDEAL CHEESE SHOP

942 First Ave (at 52nd St)   212/688-7579
Mon-Fri: 8:30-6; Sat: 8:30-5   idealcheese.com

Ideal Cheese Shop has been in operation since 1954, and many Upper East Siders swear by its quality and service. Over 250 types of cheese from 17 countries are sold here, and the owners are constantly looking for new items. They carry gourmet items: olives, olive oils, vinegars, mustards, coffees, biscuits, preserves, specialty and cured meats, pantry items and a small line of specialty beers. The Cheese-of-the-Month Club is an excellent way to sample a variety of cheeses and is offered in three-, six- and 12-month plans; these make great gifts, too. Order online or by phone and they will ship anywhere in the U.S.

MURRAY'S CHEESE SHOP

254 Bleecker St (bet Ave of Americas and Seventh Ave)   212/243-3289
Mon-Sat: 8 a.m.-9 p.m.; Sun: 9-7
Grand Central Terminal (43rd St at Lexington Ave)   212/922-1540
Mon-Fri: 7 a.m.-9 p.m.; Sat: 10-7; Sun: 11-6   murrayscheese.com

Not only does this place smell good, but it is one of the best cheese shops in Manhattan. Founded in 1940, Murray's offers international and domestic cheeses of every description along with a fine selection of cold cuts, prepared foods, antipasto, breads, sandwiches and specialty items, including party platters and gift baskets. Behind the counter, helpful and knowledgeable servers are known for accommodating customers when asked for a cheese sample. Sign up for an evening cheese course with tastings, pairings and useful information. Their underground cheese-aging caves are in Long Island City.

COFFEE AND TEA

EMPIRE COFFEE & TEA CO.

568 Ninth Ave (bet 41st and 42nd St)   212/268-1220
Mon-Fri: 7:30-7; Sat: 9-6:30; Sun: 10-6   empirecoffeetea.com

Empire Coffee & Tea carries an enormous selection of coffee (75 types of beans!), tea and herbs. Because of the aroma and array of the bins, choosing is almost impossible; but helpful personnel will guide you through your decision. Bins are brimming with fresh coffee beans and tea leaves; everything is sold loose and can be ground. Empire also carries a selection of gourmet foods, mugs, coffeemakers (including percolators), grinders, filters and teapots.

HARNEY & SONS

433 Broome St (bet Broadway and Crosby St)   212/933-4853
Mon-Sat: 10-7; Sun: 11-7   harney.com

CHEESECAKE!

New York is famous for great cheesecakes. These are among the best:

Eileen's Special Cheesecake (17 Cleveland Pl, 212/966-5585, 800/521-CAKE)

Junior's (1515 Broadway, 212/302-2000 and Grand Central Terminal, 42nd St at Vanderbilt Ave, 212/586-4677): The restaurant is on the lower level, and the bakery is on the main concourse, near Track 36.

Lady M Cake Boutique (41 E 78th St, 212/452-2222)

Ruthy's Bakery & Cafe (Chelsea Market, 75 Ninth Ave, 212/463-8800)

Two Little Red Hens (1652 Second Ave, 212/452-0476)

Veniero's Pasticceria and Caffe (342 E 11th St, 212/674-7070): New York, Italian and Sicilian styles

There's something comforting about a cup of tea in cozy environs. Harney & Sons meets that expectation in spades at their Soho shop with a tasting bar and tea flights. In addition to having a spot to take a cup of tea and a sweet, they proffer samples of some of their 250+ teas (hot or iced depending on the season). The staff graciously shares their knowledge about the seemingly endless varieties of tea, brewing tips and tasting. In addition to tea (loose, bags and sachets), Harney carries a nice selection of teaware, accessories, books, tasty treats and related gifts.

JACK'S STIR BREW COFFEE

Rag & Bone, 425 W 13th St (at Washington St)	212/647-0900
138 W 10th St (bet Greenwich Ave and Waverly Pl)	212/929-0821
10 Downing St (at Ave of the Americas)	212/929-6011
South Street Seaport, 222 Front St (at Beekman St)	212/227-7631
Hours vary by store	jacksstirbrew.com

Jack's Stir Brew Coffee claims to serve the perfect cup of joe. Behind this claim is the stir-brew process, which oxygenates the coffee, eliminating unpleasant bitterness. Each attractive store lists your favorite preparations on a chalkboard. Certified organic and fair-trade coffees are staples, as are organic milk, brown sugar and granola. The menu includes doughnuts, muffins, scones, soups, salads and sandwiches; the selection varies by location.

JAVA GIRL

348 E 66th St (bet First and Second Ave)	212/737-3490
Mon-Fri: 6:30 a.m.-7 p.m.; Sat, Sun: 8:30-6	

The aroma of fresh coffee in this tiny hideout is overwhelming where fine coffees are flavored by hand without the use of chemicals and include regular and decaf flavors such as toasted praline and red velvet cupcake. There are also teas, pastries, salads and sandwiches to enjoy inside, out front on the tree-lined street or to go. Java Girl describes itself as "indescribably exotic and sometimes nutty."

MCNULTY'S TEA & COFFEE COMPANY

109 Christopher St (bet Bleecker and Hudson St)   212/242-5351
Mon-Sat: 10-9 (closed Tues in July, Aug); Sun: 1-7   mcnultys.com

Since 1895 McNulty's has been supplying discerning New Yorkers with coffee and tea. They carry a complete line of quality spiced and herbal teas and coffee and tea accessories. Coffee beans are sourced from Africa, Arabia, Asia, the Americas and the Pacific and blends are ground to order. Their blends are unique and McNulty's maintains an extensive file of customers' special blend choices. They are also known for their welcoming atmosphere and personal service.

PORTO RICO IMPORTING CO.

201 Bleecker St (bet MacDougal St and Ave of the Americas)   212/477-5421
40½ St. Mark's Pl (bet First and Second Ave)   212/533-1982
Essex Street Market, 120 Essex St (at Delancey St)   212/677-1210
Hours vary by store   portorico.com

Peter Longo's family started a small coffee business in the Village in 1907. Primarily importers and wholesalers, they were soon pressured to open a small storefront as well. That operation gained a reputation for the best and freshest coffee available. Since much of the surrounding neighborhood consisted of Italians, the Longo family reciprocated their loyalty by specializing in Italian espressos and cappuccinos. The list of health, medicinal, green, black and other teas is staggering with some exotic teas priced well over $100 per pound. Dispensed along with such teas are folk remedies and advice to mend whatever ails you. Peter has added coffee bars, making it possible to sit and sip from a selection of 150 coffees and 225 loose teas while listening to folklore or trying to select the best from the bins. All coffees are roasted daily at Porto Rico's Bleecker Street location.

SENSUOUS BEAN

66 W 70th St (at Columbus Ave)   212/724-7725
Mon-Sat: 8-5:30; Sun: 9:30-5:30   sensuousbean.com

The Sensuous Bean was in business long before the coffee craze started. This legendary coffee and teahouse carries roughly 70 varieties of coffee and 50 teas. The bulk bean coffees and loose teas come from all around the world; featured teas originate from England, France, Germany, Ireland and Taiwan.

KOREAN FOODSTUFFS

For a taste of Korea's cuisine and culture, amble down 32nd Street between Fifth Avenue and Broadway. This colorful area is the heart of the Korean business district and is home to restaurants, bakeries, retail shops and other businesses. The best selection of groceries is at **Han ah Reum** (25 W 32nd St, 212/695-3283). **m2m** (55 Third Ave, 212/353-2698 and 2935 Broadway, 212/280-4600) and **New KC Market** (301 Amsterdam Ave, 212/877-2253) are additional sources for Korean foods. **Tous les Jours** (31 W 32nd St, 212/967-9661) is a branch of the Korean pastry chain where pastries are not too sweet, but just right.

A large variety of green, white, chai, herbal, rooibos and blended loose teas, along with many organic and fair-trade coffees are among the offerings. Lattes, cappuccinos, espressos and chais are made to order and loose tea is steeped to order. Sweets, biscottis and chocolates accompany these beverages while you sip your savory cup with neighborhood loyals in the small, cluttered space. Here's an idea, sign up for a monthly shipment of coffee or tea delivered to your door.

T SALON

230 Fifth Ave (at 27th St), Suite 1511   212/358-0506
Mon-Fri: 10:30-6; Sat, Sun: by appointment   tsalon.com

Miriam Novalle, the tea guru at T Salon, has brewed up a wonderful selection of tea and tea accessories. She offers more than 450 custom blends of tea for retail and wholesale purchase. There are green, oolong and black teas, as well as white and red teas. Tea blending is Miriam's specialty and she has created blends for special events, causes and fine establishments throughout the world. You will be happy to hear that afternoon tea is still available by appointment.

TEN REN TEA & GINSENG

75 Mott St (at Canal St)   212/349-2286
Daily: 10-8   tenrenusa.com

A tea lover's paradise! Founded in 1953, this Taiwanese company is the largest tea grower and manufacturer in East Asia. They sell green, oolong, jasmine, black and white teas, plus tea sets, all manner of accessories and American-cultivated ginseng root. Ten Ren means "heavenly love," and you will likely fall in love with one of their flavors. Some of the rarer teas go for more than $100 a pound! Stop in next door for a relaxing spot to sample teas.

FOREIGN FOODSTUFFS (THE BEST)

Craving a specific foreign food item? The following shops feature specialty items from various countries. Each shop is also mentioned within this Food Shops chapter.

ASIAN (Chinese, Korean, Malaysian, Taiwan, Thai, Vietnamese)
Asia Market (71½ Mulberry St)
Bangkok Center Grocery (104 Mosco St)
Golden Fung Wong Bakery (41 Mott St)
Han ah Reum (25 W 32nd St)
Katagiri & Company (224 E 59th St)
Kelley and Ping (127 Greene St)
New Kam Man (200 Canal St)
New KC Market (301 Amsterdam Ave)
Sunrise Mart (4 Stuyvesant St, 494 Broome St and 12 E 41st St)
Takahachi Bakery (25 Murray St)
Ten Ren Tea & Ginseng (75 Mott St)
Tongin Mart (91 Mulberry St)

BRITISH
Myers of Keswick (634 Hudson St)

GREEK
Poseidon Bakery (629 Ninth Ave)

INDIAN
Kalustyan's (123 Lexington Ave)

ITALIAN
Di Palo Fine Foods (200 Grand St)
Eataly (200 Fifth Ave)
Faicco's Pork Store (260 Bleecker St)
Raffetto's (144 W Houston St)
Salumeria Biellese (378 Eighth Ave)

POLISH
Kossar's Bagels and Bialys (367 Grand St)

SPANISH
Despaña Fine Foods and Tapas Cafe (408 Broome St)

FRUITS AND VEGETABLES

GREENMARKET

51 Chambers St (bet Broadway and Centre St), Room 228   212/788-7476
grownyc.org

Note: The following Greenmarkets are arranged from uptown to downtown.
Inwood (Isham St bet Seaman and Cooper St)
175th St (175th St at Broadway)
Fort Washington (168th St at Fort Washington Ave)
Columbia (114th St at Broadway)
Mount Sinai Hospital (99th St at Madison Ave)
97th St (97th St bet Columbus Ave and Amsterdam)
92nd St (92nd St at First Ave)
82nd St (82nd St bet First and York Ave)
79th St (78th St at Columbus Ave)
Tucker Square (66th St at Columbus Ave)

FEAST ON FROZEN FRENCH FARE
Healthy frozen foods and meals are featured at a unique store on the Upper East Side where only frozen foods are sold. The freezers at **Babeth's Feast** (1422 Third Ave, 646/759-7949, babethsfeast.com) are laden with French pastries, appetizers, desserts, veggies, sauces, main and side dishes, meats, fish, appetizers and other treats. From this selection you can assemble a restaurant-worthy dinner for one in quick order or combine various packages for a delicious buffet spread. Weekday delivery in Manhattan and nationwide shipping.

57th St (57th St at Ninth Ave)
Rockefeller Center (Rockefeller Plaza at 50th St)
Dag Hammarskjöld Plaza (47th St at Second Ave)
Union Square (17th St at Broadway)
Abingdon Square (12th St at Eighth Ave)
Stuyvesant Town (Stuyvesant Loop at Ave A; in the Oval)
St. Mark's Church (10th St at Second Ave)
Tompkins Square (7th St at Ave A)
Lower East Side YM (Grand St bet Pitt and Abraham Pl)
Tribeca (Greenwich St at Chambers)
City Hall Park (Broadway at Chambers)
Bowling Green (Broadway at Battery Pl)
Staten Island Ferry/Whitehall (inside South Street Terminal Building)

Starting in 1976 with just one location and 12 farmers, these unique producer-only open-air markets have now sprung up all over town and are overseen by the nonprofit GrowNYC. Bypassing the middle man enables Greenmarkets to provide small family farms in the region with a profitable outlet for their produce. All produce (over 600 varieties), baked goods, flowers, meat, poultry, cheeses, herbs, preserves, honey, candy, handmade items (like candles and wreaths) and fish come straight from the sources. Call the office number or go online to find out the hours and address of the Greenmarket nearest you; many are open year-round while others are open seasonally. The usual operating hours are from 8 to 3, although these vary, too. Come early for the best selection.

GIFT BASKETS

CHELSEA MARKET BASKETS

Chelsea Market
75 Ninth Ave (bet 15th and 16th St)   212/727-1111, 888/727-7887
Mon-Sat: 9-8:30; Sun: 10-7:30   chelseamarketbaskets.com

This retail shop is dedicated to the creation of unique gift baskets. Whether it's for a birthday, housewarming, baby, business gift, thank you or any special occasion, the helpful staff will assist you in creating a truly one-of-a-kind gift. First choose an interesting container (basket, hamper or bag) and then select from a quality assortment of fudge, cheese, candy, nuts, jams, sauces, pastas, beers, ciders, teas and other food items. Or fill your basket with toys, books, spa products, stationery and many other goods (individual items are also for sale). Delivery is available across town or across the country. By the way, you can bring your own items to include in the basket.

HEALTH FOODS

COMMODITIES NATURAL MARKET

165 First Ave (bet 10th and 11th St)   212/260-2600
Daily: 9-9   commoditiesnaturalmarket.com

This small, independently-owned East Village health-food store is just like the vitamins and supplements they sell: full of things that are good for you. They are really more like a gourmet marketplace with a wide range of natural and organic meats, cheeses, produce, dairy products, bulk dry goods, canned foods and even beauty and health aids, pet food and cleaning products. The helpful staff will answer questions, make suggestions and offer samples of great tasting products.

GARY NULL'S UPTOWN WHOLE FOODS

2421 Broadway (at 89th St)   212/874-4000
Daily: 8 a.m.-11 p.m.

Lots of interesting items in this tiny space! Gary Null's Uptown Whole Foods is perhaps Manhattan's premier health-food supermarket. Organic produce, fresh juices, discounted vitamins and a full line of healthy products are featured. They will deliver in Manhattan and ship anywhere in the country.

HEALTH & HARMONY

470 Hudson St (bet Barrow and Grove St)   212/691-3036
Mon-Fri: 8 a.m.-8:30 p.m.; Sat: 9-7:30; Sun: 9-7

This is a great find for the health-conscious! Health & Harmony stocks organic produce, cheeses, baked items and plenty of other good things to eat. Vitamins and herbs, herbal remedies and all manner of natural grocery items are available. They will also deliver and ship.

INTEGRAL YOGA NATURAL FOODS

229 W 13th St (bet Seventh and Eighth Ave)   212/243-2642
Mon-Fri: 8 a.m.-9:30 p.m.; Sat: 8 a.m.-8:30 p.m.; Sun: 9-8:30
                                                  integralyoganaturalfoods.com

Selection and quality abound in this clean, attractive shop which proclaims that "natural food is healthy food." Vegetarian items, packaged groceries, organic produce, bulk foods and baked items are available at reasonable prices. A juice bar, hot and cold salad bar and deli are also on-premises. They occupy the same building as a center that offers classes in yoga, meditation and philosophy and operate **Integral Yoga Natural Apothecary** (234 W 13th St, 212/645-3051), a vegetarian, vitamin and herb shop across the street; a nutritional consultant is on staff.

JUICE GENERATION

171 W 4th St (bet Ave of the Americas and Seventh Ave)   212/242-0440
644 Ninth Ave (bet 45th and 46th St)   212/541-5600
117 W 72nd St (bet Broadway and Columbus Ave)   212/579-0400
122 E 42nd St (bet Park and Lexington Ave)   212/661-1300
1486 Third Ave (bet 83rd and 84th St)   212/249-4071
Numerous other locations   juicegeneration.com
Hours vary by store

Juice Generation is a healthy choice for quick, delicious food and beverage. Fresh and local are the key concepts here. Whenever possible, area farmers provide fresh fruits, vegetables and wheatgrass products for Juice Generation's smoothies, acai bowls, salads and organic soups — all of which are vegetarian.

ICE CREAM, SORBET, GELATO!

40 Carrots (Bloomingdale's, 1000 Third Ave, 7th floor, 212/705-3085)

ABC Cocina (ABC Carpet & Home, 38 E 19th St, 212/677-2233): ice pops, seasonal flavors

Amorino (60 University Pl, 212/253-5599)

Chinatown Ice Cream Factory (65 Bayard St, 212/608-4170)

Cones Ice Cream Artisans (272 Bleecker St, 212/414-1795): Try Johnnie Walker Black Label with macerated kumquats!

E.A.T. (1064 Madison Ave, 212/772-0022): summer only

Emack & Bolio's (389 Amsterdam Ave, 212/362-2747 and 1564 First Ave, 212/734-0105): ice cream, yogurt and sorbet

Fresco Gelateria (138 Second Ave, 212/677-6320): unique flavors

Grom (233 Bleecker St, 212/206-1738 and 1796 Broadway, 212/974-3444): real gelato, excellent hot chocolate; branches in Italy

Il Laboratorio del Gelato (188 Ludlow St, 212/343-9922)

L'Arte del Gelato (Chelsea Market, 75 Ninth Ave, 212/366-0570): Rent their party cart for a special event.

La Maison du Chocolat (1018 Madison Ave, 212/744-7117; 63 Wall St, 212/952-1123; 30 Rockefeller Plaza, 212/265-9404 and Plaza Food Hall, The Plaza, 1 W 59th St, 212/355-3436)

Morgenstern's Finest Ice Cream (2 Rivington St, 212/209-7684): small-batch ice creams and sorbets

Pinkberry (7 W 32nd St, 212/695-9631; 1577 Second Ave, 212/861-0574; 596 Ninth Ave, 212/957-8440; 245 E 54th St, 212/223-0240 and 2873 Broadway, 212/222-0191)

Popbar (5 Carmine St, 212/255-4874): gelato on a stick, dipped in chocolate

Ronnybrook Farm Dairy at Chelsea Market (Chelsea Market, 75 Ninth Ave, 212/741-6455): great flavors

Sant Ambroeus (259 W 4th St, 212/604-9254; 265 Lafayette St, 212/966-2770 and 1000 Madison Ave, 212/570-2211)

Sundaes & Cones (95 E 10th St, 212/979-9398): cones, floats; beautifully decorated ice-cream cakes

For added benefit, choose a refreshing drink that will boost energy, immunity and help promote weight loss.

LIFETHYME NATURAL MARKET

410 Ave of the Americas (bet 8th and 9th St)   212/420-9099

Mon-Fri: 8 a.m.-10 p.m.; Sat, Sun: 9 a.m.-10 p.m.   lifethymemarket.com

At this busy supermarket you'll find organic produce, dairy products, frozen foods and raw and dehydrated foods. In addition, there is an organic-salad table, health-related books, a "natural cosmetics" boutique, a complete vegan bakery and an organic juice bar. Many delicious meals are prepared in their kitchen and available in the deli — baked chicken and turkey, tofu lasagna, wraps, salads and healthy side dishes. Occupying renovated 1839 brownstones in the heart of the Village, LifeThyme also sells discounted vitamins, does catering and offers custom-baked goods for any dietary needs.

ICE CREAM AND OTHER GOODIES

For more choices in this category, see the box on page 257.

AMORINO

60 University Pl (bet 10th and 11th St)   212/253-5599
Sun-Thurs: 11-11; Fri, Sat: 11 a.m.-midnight   amorino.com

Amorino is the first stateside location of this Italian franchise. Icy, creamy gelato varieties are made with all natural ingredients resulting in a superb product. There are over 20 flavors from which to choose, plus a flavor of the month. Each gelato tray looks like a work of art with seductive swirls of chocolate, fruits, nuts and other enticing additions. If you order a cone, dippers artistically fill the sugary holders to resemble a flower in bloom and luscious gelato cakes are beautifully formed and embellished as well. Amorino also serves hot drinks, waffles, milkshakes, chocolates and other fabulous treats.

EASY AS PIE

If you are searching for the perfect Thanksgiving pumpkin or pecan pie, a savory meat pie for dinner or a refreshing cream pie, here are a few sweet and savory suggestions for a pastry-enrobed meal or dessert.

The Breslin (Ace Hotel, 16 W 29th St, 212/679-1939): beef and Stilton pie

Bubby's (120 Hudson St, 212/219-0666 and 71 Gansevoort St, 212/206-6200): mile-high apple pie

Ceci-Cela (55 Spring St, 212/274-9179): raspberry kiwi tart

E.A.T. (1064 Madison Ave, 212/772-0022): cherry pie

Highlands (150 W 10th St, 212/229-2670): shepherd's pie

Jones Wood Foundry (401 E 76th St, 212/249-2700): steak and kidney pie

Little Pie Co. (424 W 43rd St, 212/736-4780): key lime pie

Maison Kayser (921 Broadway, 212/979-1600 and other locations): chocolate cream; apple tart

Momofuku Milk Bar (251 E 13th St; Chambers Hotel, 15 W 56th St and 561 Columbus Ave, 347/577-9504 all locations): candy bar pie

Poseidon Bakery (629 Ninth Ave, 212/757-6173): Greek spinach pie

Sarabeth's (423 Amsterdam Ave, 212/496-6280; Hotel Wales, 1295 Madison Ave, 212/410-7335; 40 Central Park S, 212/826-5959; 381 Park Ave S, 212/335-0093; 339 Greenwich St, 212-966-0421; **Sarabeth's at Lord & Taylor**, 424 Fifth Ave, 212/827-5068 and **Sarabeth's Bakery** (Chelsea Market, 75 Ninth Ave, 212/989-2424): banana cream pie

CHINATOWN ICE CREAM FACTORY

65 Bayard St (bet Elizabeth and Mott St)   212/608-4170
Daily: 11-11   chinatownicecreamfactory.com

Since 1978 this family-run ice cream shop has been churning out frozen,
creamy goodness. With dozens of regular and exotic ice cream and sorbet
flavors to choose from, you may find it hard to decide what to order. Definitely
ask for a taste before you order a bowl or cone! The most popular choice
is lychee or you might also enjoy red bean, taro, Zen butter or green tea. Of
course, there's always chocolate in the freezer!

CONES ICE CREAM ARTISANS

272 Bleecker St (at Seventh Ave)   212/414-1795
Sun-Thurs: 1-11; Fri, Sat: 1-1 (winter: Mon-Fri: 4-11; Sat, Sun: 1-11)

The D'Aloisio family brought their original Italian ice cream recipes to
Manhattan . . . and boy, are they good, especially the coffee mocha chocolate
chip! Cones specializes in creamy gelato made with fresh ingredients. Every
day they offer 32 flavors, including fat-free fruit choices, and every season they
add a couple of new flavors. All are made on-premises and can be packed
for takeout. For an extra special treat, made-to-order ice-cream cakes are
available, too.

INDIAN

KALUSTYAN'S

123 Lexington Ave (bet 28th and 29th St)   212/685-3451
Mon-Sat: 10-8; Sun: 11-7   kalustyans.com

Since 1944 Kalustyan's has operated as an Indian spice store at its
present location. After all this time, it is still a great spot only now they
stock ingredients from over 75 countries. There is a truly global selection of
beans, rice, grains, lentils, honey, oils and vinegars, sauces, olives and pickles,
teas, herbs, noodles, condiments, cookware, Middle Eastern baked goods
and candies and more. Along with over 4,000 packaged items, nuts and
dried fruits are sold in serve-yourself bins. The difference in cost, flavor
and freshness is extraordinary. The best indication of freshness and flavor
is the store's aroma! There is also a Middle Eastern deli upstairs featuring
sandwiches, platters and soups.

ITALIAN

RAFFETTO'S

144 W Houston St (bet Sullivan and MacDougal St)   212/777-1261
Tues-Fri: 9-6:30 (Thurs till 7:30); Sat: 9-6   raffettospasta.com

Raffetto's has been producing fresh-cut noodles and stuffed pastas since
1906. Fresh products include noodles, ravioli (and fresh dough for making
your own ravioli), tortellini, manicotti, gnocchi and fettuccine. Variations
include oodles of ravioli stuffed with meat, spinach, seafood, cheese and other

ingredients. More than a dozen homemade sauces are personally prepared by Mrs. Raffetto. The retail store also stocks dry pasta, cheeses, prepared foods, breads and other Italian groceries and dry goods.

LIQUOR AND WINE

ACKER, MERRALL & CONDIT

160 W 72nd St (bet Broadway and Columbus Ave) 212/787-1700
Mon-Sat: 9 a.m.-10 p.m.; Sun: noon-8 ackerwines.com

Acker, Merrall & Condit (AMC, for short) is the oldest wine and liquor store in America, having opened in 1820. This service-oriented firm stocks an outstanding and diverse global inventory in every price range of popular, fine and rare vintages. The Wine Workshop (Acker, Merrall & Condit's special-events affiliate) offers wine-tasting classes, luxury dinners and private events for companies and individuals. AMC is the largest fine-wine auction house in the world and offers consignments, appraisals, packing and shipping; check their website for live and monthly online auctions.

ASTOR WINES & SPIRITS

399 Lafayette St (at 4th St) 212/674-7500
Mon-Sat: 9-9; Sun: noon-6 astorwines.com

Astor has one of the city's largest selections of French and Italian wines. They also carry wines from every other grape-growing region in the world, along with numerous sakés, sparkling wines and hard liquors. Of special interest to oenophiles is the store's unique "cool room," which holds hundreds of delicate, rare and organic wines at a constant 57 degrees. Astor also features new arrivals, wine clubs and a selection of their top 12 wines priced under $12 per bottle. Inquire about the **Astor Center** (astorcenternyc.com), an upstairs space where four unique venues are available for cooking and wine classes, special events and private functions.

BOTTLEROCKET WINE & SPIRIT

5 W 19th St (at Fifth Ave) 212/929-2323
Mon-Sat: 11-9; Sun: noon-8 bottlerocket.com

Quite a place! Wines are organized by regions and themes, such as takeout food, beef, chicken, seafood, desserts, "green," etc. These folks feature classes, special events, a children's play area and more. A fact sheet about the wine is included with your bottle and friendly, informed service is a plus. If you're looking for a special gift, they have gift baskets with wines and accessories, wine club memberships and packages with the fixings for favorite cocktails.

BURGUNDY WINE COMPANY

143 W 26th St (bet Ave of the Americas and Seventh Ave) 212/691-9092
Tues-Fri: 10-7; Sat: 10-6 burgundywinecompany.com

Burgundy Wine Company, a compact and attractive store in Chelsea, specializes in fine Burgundies, Rhones, Oregon wines and small-grower champagnes, all specially selected. With over 2,000 labels to choose from, there are some great treasures in their cellars; just ask the expert personnel.

CHEERS!

However you prefer your beer — bottles, cans, kegs or on draft — these outfits offer what seems to be an unending assortment. Some have regular tastings and other beer-related events.

Alphabet City Beer Co. (96 Ave C, 646/422-7103): around 350 varieties of craft beers

City Swiggers (320 E 86th St, 212/570-2000): tasting room and store

Flair Beverages, Inc. (3857 Ninth Ave, 212/569-8713): cash only, low prices

Good Beer (422 E 9th St, 212/677-4836): 625 beers; American craft beers; charcuterie and sausages

Malt & Mold (221 E Broadway, 212/227-2242 and 362 Second Ave, 646/896-1341): beer, cheese and other artisanal foods and drinks

New Beer Distributors (167 Chrystie St, 212/473-8757): 800-plus brews; domestic and imported

Noble Grains (313 E 95th St, 212/996-2337): growler station taps

Whole Foods Market Bowery Beer Room (95 E Houston St, 212/420-1320): 1,000 beers; home-brew needs

CRUSH WINE & SPIRITS

153 E 57th St (bet Third Ave and Lexington Ave)   212/980-9463
Mon-Fri: noon-9; Sat: noon-8; Sun: 1-7   crushwineco.com

The focus at Crush Wine & Spirits is on small artisanal producers. In the elegant space, they offer weekly free tastings, cocktail happy hour on Friday nights, personal wine consultations and a stock of rare and collectible bottles at reasonable prices. The inventory is impressive and so is the sophisticated tasting room.

GARNET WINES & LIQUORS

929 Lexington Ave (bet 68th and 69th St)   212/772-3211
Mon-Sat: 9-9; Sun: noon-6   garnetwine.com

You'll love Garnet's prices, which are among the most competitive in the city, for wines, champagnes and liquors. If you're in the market for Champagne, Bordeaux, Burgundy, Italian or other imported wines, check this U.E.S. supplier first, as selections are impressive — over 6,000 choices of wines and spirits.

ITALIAN WINE MERCHANTS

108 E 16th St (bet Union Square E and Irving Pl)   212/473-2323
Mon-Sat: 10-7   italianwinemerchants.com

This place is class personified! Italian Wine Merchants is the leading authority for Italian wines, but their cellar has expanded to carry other artisanal international wines, with specialties in cult and tightly allocated wines, many from undiscovered producers. Take advantage of their personal wine-portfolio manager, tastings, wine clubs, collections and special offers.

K&D FINE WINES AND SPIRITS

1343 Madison Ave (at 94th St)   212/289-1818
Mon-Sat: 9:30-8:30   kdwine.com

K&D is an excellent wine and spirits market on the Upper East Side with hundreds of top wines from regions around the world. There are discounts on 12-bottle mixed cases and free delivery within Manhattan with no minimum. Consult the experts when you are planning a wedding or party; they will help calculate your needs for a well-stocked bar.

MISTER WRIGHT FINE WINES & SPIRITS

1593 Third Ave (bet 89th and 90th St)   212/722-4564
Mon-Sat: 9 a.m.-9:30 p.m.; Sun: 1-7   misterwrightfinewines.com

Since 1976 this neighborhood store has specialized in unique and hard-to-find bottles from a long list of liquors, wines and sakés. Mister Wright has a reputation for amazing global vintages at comfortable prices and extra-friendly Aussie service.

MORRELL & COMPANY

1 Rockefeller Plaza (49th St bet Fifth Ave and Ave of the Americas)212/981-1106
Mon-Sat: 10-7   morrellwine.com

Everyone is a wine expert who works at this small, jam-packed store, which carries all kinds of wine and liquor — 5,000 bottles strong. The Morrell staff will help you find the right bottle of spirits, including brandies and liqueurs and wine vintages ranging from old and valuable to young and inexpensive. Check out the inviting lunch and dinner menu next door at **Morrell Wine Bar & Cafe** (212/262-7700).

QUALITY HOUSE WINES & SPIRITS

2 Park Ave (at 33rd St)   212/532-2944
Mon-Fri: 10-7, Sat: 11-4   qualityhousewines.com

Since 1934 Quality House has boasted one of the most extensive stocks of French wine in the city, with equally fine domestic and Italian offerings and selections from Germany, Spain and Portugal. True to their name, this is a quality house, where wines are well-balanced and exhibit characteristics of their distinctive regions. Delivery is available and usually free within the city.

SHERRY-LEHMANN

505 Park Ave (at 59th St)   212/838-7500
Mon-Sat: 9-7   sherry-lehmann.com

Sherry-Lehmann is one of New York's best-known wine and liquor shops, with an inventory of over 6,500 high-end wines from all over the world. Prices run the gamut from $5 to $75,000 a bottle! A wide selection of glassware and accessories, wine sampler boxes and gift baskets is available at this attractive store. Sherry-Lehmann has been in business since 1932 and offers exemplary, informed service for its customers.

WINE SHOPS WORTH A VISIT

Boutique bottle shops tend to offer limited selections of wines in trendy environs. Most specialize in good values for the price, with a few premium budget-busters for good measure.

Appellation Wine & Spirits (156 Tenth Ave, 212/741-9474): organic and biodynamic wines

Bottlerocket Wine & Spirit (5 W 19th St, 212/929-2323): fun and shopper-friendly

Chambers Street Wines (148 Chambers St, 212/227-1434): European artisanal wines

Embassy Wines & Spirits (796 Lexington Ave, 212/838-6551): a hundred kosher vintages

Landmark Wine & Saké (167 W 23rd St, 212/242-2323): large saké selection

Pasanella and Son Vintners (115 South St, 212/233-8383): Sunday afternoon tastings

September Wines & Spirits (100 Stanton St, 212/388-0770): artisanal wines

Union Square Wines & Spirits (140 Fourth Ave, 212/675-8100): Samples are poured from an Enomatic automatic wine dispenser.

SOHO WINES & SPIRITS

461 West Broadway (bet Prince and Houston St)　　　212/777-4332
Mon-Sat: 10-8　　　　　　　　　　　　　　　　　　sohowines.com

Soho Wines & Spirits is family-run and offers domestic and imported wines and spirits. The shop is lofty; in fact, it looks more like an art gallery than a wine shop. Bottles are tastefully displayed, and classical music plays in the background. Soho Wines also has a large selection of single-malt Scotch whiskeys. Services include party planning and advice on setting up and maintaining a wine cellar.

VINO FINE WINE & SPIRITS

121 E 27th St (bet Lexington Ave and Park Ave S)　　212/725-6516
Mon-Sat: 11-10; Sun: noon-9　　　　　　　　　　　vinosite.com

Come to Vino if you're looking for unusual varietals from around Italy. Small-production and other global vintners are represented, and many offerings are reasonably priced. The staff is extra friendly, and conducts periodic wine-tasting classes and free tastings on Thursday and Friday evenings. Free delivery is offered within the neighborhood.

WAREHOUSE WINES & SPIRITS

735 Broadway (bet 8th St and Waverly Pl)　　　　　212/982-7770
Mon-Thurs: 9-8:45; Fri, Sat: 9 a.m.-9:45 p.m.; Sun: noon-6:45
　　　　　　　　　　　　　　　　　warehousewinesandspirits.com

If you are looking to save on wine and liquor, especially for a party, Warehouse Wines & Spirits is a good place. This large space has miles and miles of bottles at appealing prices and free delivery up to 86th Street (minimums apply, moderate fee for delivery to other areas).

MEAT AND POULTRY

ESPOSITO MEAT MARKET

500 Ninth Ave (at 38th St)   212/279-3298
Mon-Sat: 8-6:30   espositomeatmarket.com

Family members still preside over an operation that has been at the same location since 1932. They specialize in homemade Italian sausages such as breakfast, sage, garlic, smoked and hot dogs. The cold-cuts selection includes bologna, liverwurst, pepperoni, salami, ham and turkey breast to go along with domestic and imported cheeses and much more. Hosting a dinner? You'll find pork roasts, crown roasts, pork chops, spare ribs, slab bacon, tenderloins, sirloin steaks, short ribs, filet mignon, London broil, corned beef brisket, leg of lamb, pheasant, quail and venison. Free home delivery is available in midtown for modestly minimum orders.

FAICCO'S PORK STORE

260 Bleecker St (bet Ave of the Americas and Seventh Ave)   212/243-1974
Mon: 10-6; Tues-Fri: 9-7; Sat: 8:30-6; Sun: 9-3

Take a number! Step up to the counter at this Italian institution and order delicious sausages (dried, hot or sweet). They also sell cuts of pork, veal (cutlets, chops and ground), pork loin, equally good meat cuts for barbecue and an oven-ready rolled leg of stuffed pork. Pick up excellent olive oils, cheeses, vinegars, housemade sauces and ingredients for antipasto. If you like Italian-style deli, try Faicco's first. And if you're pressed for time, take home their heat-and-eat chicken rollettes or other prepared foods including lasagna, baby back ribs and eggplant parmesan. The best snack in the neighborhood is Faicco's *arancini* — fried balls of risotto. Bet you can't eat just one!

FLORENCE PRIME MEAT MARKET

5 Jones St (bet Bleecker and 4th St)   212/242-6531
Tues-Fri: 8:30-6:30; Sat: 8-6

At Florence Prime Meat Market everything is hand cut to order. Since 1936 Florence has been supplying high-quality meats in a rustic setting.

GANSEVOORT MARKET

Various markets have existed in a former storage space now home to **Gansevoort Market** (52 Gansevoort St) and produce vendors have returned with fresh fruits, vegetables and flowers. The food hall in the latest incarnation includes a broad range of flavors: pig roast and barbecue from **Pig Guy NYC**, a booth with lobster rolls from **Ed's Lobster**, 16 flavors of brioche muffins from **The Bruffin Cafe** and sushi, sandwiches, coffee and more from other food vendors. There is limited seating in the market, but takeout is always an option.

FOOD EMPORIUMS

There's good eating at **Gotham West Market** (600 Eleventh Ave, 212/582-7940), a street-level food court in the Gotham West apartment tower in Hell's Kitchen. Popular eateries include **Ample Hills Creamery**, **Blue Bottle Coffee**, **Ivan Ramen Slurp Shop**, **Court Street Grocers Sandwich Shop** and others. Lucky are the folks who live in the building and meander down for breakfast, lunch or dinner; shop hours vary.

Aptly named **Hudson Eats** (230 Vesey Pl), in upscale Brookfield Place, has over a dozen food shops and restaurants. You'll find the likes of **Black Seed Bagels**, **Dig Inn Seasonal Market**, **Nam Pung Sandwich Shop**, **Sprinkles Cupcakes** and other stops for food and drink.

Countermen prepare your order of sausages, poultry, steak and game at good prices. Their "Newport steak" is so delicious that many folks have it shipped to them overnight!

L. SIMCHICK MEAT

988 First Ave (at 54th St)   212/888-2299
Mon-Fri: 8-6:30; Sat: 8-5:30   lsimchick.com

This old-fashioned neighborhood butcher shop sells high-end meats. You'll find domestic game, prime meats (veal, pork, lamb), poultry products, wonderful homemade pork sausage and a wide selection of prepared foods and Saturday entree specials. Sides, soups and ready-to-cook prepared meats will impress your tablemates. Delivery is provided on the East Side.

LOBEL'S PRIME MEATS

1096 Madison Ave (bet 82nd and 83rd St)   212/737-1373
Mon-Sat: 8-6 (closed Sat in July, Aug)   lobels.com

Through five generations of operation and because of their excellent service and reasonable prices, few in Manhattan haven't heard of this shop. The Lobels have published nine cookbooks, and they are always willing to explain the best uses for each cut. It's hard to go wrong, since Lobel's carries only the best quality beef, pork, lamb, veal and poultry. In addition to prime cuts, you'll find great ready-to-cook hot dogs and hamburgers, extreme indulgences, black tie gift boxes and other packages of bacon, sausage, steaks, roasts and more.

OTTOMANELLI & SONS

285 Bleecker St (bet Seventh Ave and Jones St)   212/675-4217
Mon-Sat: 8-6

This three-brother operation gained its reputation by offering full butcher services with a smile. They offer a topnotch selection of prime meats (common and exotic), wild game (venison and kangaroo), dry-aged beef and milk-fed veal. The latter is cut into Italian roasts, chops, steaks and homemade sausages, and the preparation is unique. Best of all, they will sell it by the piece for a quick meal at home.

PARK EAST KOSHER BUTCHERS & FINE FOODS

1623 Second Ave (bet 84th and 85th St)   212/737-9800
Mon-Wed: 8-7:30; Thurs: 7 a.m.-9 p.m.; Fri: 6 a.m. till two hours before Sabbath;
Sun: 8-6   parkeastkosher.com

This is a one-stop kosher shop that carries butcher items (meat, poultry, game), packaged meats, cured and smoked fish, bakery goods, candy, sauces and dressings, pickled products, salads and dips, frozen foods and cheeses. Prepared foods include stuffed cabbage, meatballs, potato kugel, salads and delicious cakes. Park East stocks over 700 items in all and promises delivery within three hours throughout Manhattan. Delivery to nearby areas and shipping throughout the U.S. are also available.

SCHALLER & WEBER

1654 Second Ave (bet 85th and 86th St)   212/879-3047
Mon-Sat: 10-7   schallerweber.com

Once you've been in this store, the image will linger because of the sheer magnitude of cold cuts and hard-to-find imported items on display. There is nary a wall or nook that is not covered with deli meats. Besides offering a complete line of deli items, Schaller & Weber stocks a wide range of wieners, wursts, smoked meats, game and poultry; try their sausage and pork items, which they will prepare, bake, smoke or roll to your preference. Discriminating grocers across the country carry their specialty products.

SCHATZIE'S PRIME MEATS

2665 Broadway (bet 101st and 102nd St)   212/410-1555
Mon-Sat: 8-7; Sun: 10-6   schatziethebutcher.com

Fifth-generation butcher Tony Schatz (the meat man of Manhattan) and his crew offer cut-to-order lamb, veal, poultry, game and prime beef. Schatzie's carries a great selection of prepared foods, including complete turkey, meatloaf and pork loin dinners; with plenty of side dishes, too! A specialty is heat-and-eat dirty brisket (with smoky barbecue sauce) and two side dishes. Call in the morning and they will prepare dinner to your specifications! A recent move to new quarters on Broadway included the addition of Richie's Burger Joint next door.

PICKLES

PICKLES, OLIVES, ETC.

1240 Lexington Ave (bet 83rd and 84th St)   212/717-8966
Daily: 10-8   picklesandolives.com

This one-of-a-kind shop on the Upper East Side is dedicated to pickles and olives. Pickles are sold the old-fashioned way — out of barrels — and in any quantity. You can buy a single pickle or a whole gallon of them. There are ten varieties of pickles (sweet, hot, sour) and 20 types of olives (garlic-stuffed, cheese-stuffed, lemon-stuffed) — you get the idea. If you can't make up your mind, ask for a sample before you buy. You may also encounter this pickle purveyor at local farmers markets.

CAVIAR FACTS AND SOURCES

Caviar is traditionally the roe of sturgeon from the Caspian and Black seas. It is a delicacy, and a pricey one at that. Look for caviar at raw bars, on appetizer menus at high-end restaurants and at trusted stores. Since many restaurants have aligned themselves with sources that pledge sustainability; roe is often cultivated from farmed sturgeon to reduce the threat to declining wild stocks.

The main caviar types are:

Beluga: large, firm and well-defined roe with a smooth, creamy texture
Osetra: strong with a sweet, fruity flavor
Sevruga: subtle, clean taste with a crunchy texture
Sterlet: intense flavor, small- to-medium-size grains

Excellent quality caviar is available at these establishments:

Barney Greengrass (541 Amsterdam Ave, 212/724-4707)

Calvisius Caviar (Four Seasons Hotel, 58 E 58th St, 212/207-8222)

Caviar Russe (538 Madison Ave, 212/980-5908): retail and a luxury restaurant

Dean & Deluca (1150 Madison Ave, 212/717-0800 and 560 Broadway, 212/226-6800)

Murray's Sturgeon Shop (2429 Broadway, 212/724-2650)

Olma Caviar Boutique & Bar (Plaza Food Hall, The Plaza, 1 W 59th St, 212/371-8525)

Petrossian Restaurant (182 W 58th St, 212/245-2214): Providing ambience befitting the caviar set, this is a spectacular place to dine.

Russ & Daughters (179 E Houston St, 212/475-4880)

Sable's Smoked Fish (1489 Second Ave, 212/249-6177)

Zabar's (2245 Broadway, 212/787-2000): If price is important, then make this your first stop.

SEAFOOD

LEONARD'S MARKET

1437 Second Ave (bet 74th and 75th St)   212/744-2600
Mon-Fri: 8-7; Sat: 8-6; Sun: 11-6   leonardsnyc.com

A family-owned business since 1910, Leonard's is a reliable source for fresh seafood. You'll find oysters, crabs, striped bass, tilapia, halibut, salmon, live lobsters and squid. Their takeout seafood department sells lobster and crab cakes; hand-sliced Irish smoked salmon; and some of the tastiest clam chowder and soups in Manhattan. There's more — barbecued poultry, cooked and prepared foods and cut-to-order aged prime meats (beef, lamb and veal) round out Leonard's selection. Their homemade turkey chili and poached salmon are customer favorites. Beautiful party platters of boiled shrimp, crabmeat and smoked salmon can be requested. This service-oriented establishment provides fast, free delivery.

THE LOBSTER PLACE

75 Ninth Ave (bet 15th and 16th St)   212/255-5672
Mon-Sat: 9:30-9; Sun: 10-8   lobsterplace.com

Imagine distributing one million pounds of lobster every year! The Lobster Place does just that, and they have a full line of fish, shrimp and shellfish, too. A selection of prepared foods and sushi are an added bonus to your visit. These folks have a reputation for great service and reasonable prices; an even greater selection is available thanks to a recent expansion. Pick up a lobster roll or crab club at C&P Gallery in the store. Their more formal restaurant, **Cull & Pistol** (212/568-1223), is next door.

MURRAY'S STURGEON SHOP

2429 Broadway (bet 89th and 90th St)   212/724-2650
Daily: 8-7 (Sat till 7:30)   murrayssturgeon.com

Murray's is *the* stop for fancy smoked fish, fine appetizers and caviar. Choose from sturgeon, Eastern and Scottish salmon, whitefish, kippered salmon, sable, pickled and schmaltz herring, trout and lox. The quality is excellent and prices are fair. Murray's also offers kosher soups, salads, deli meats and cheeses, dried fruits, nuts, bagels and other gourmet foodstuffs.

WILD EDIBLES SEAFOOD MARKET

Grand Central Market
43rd St at Lexington Ave   212/687-4255
Mon-Fri: 7 a.m.-9 p.m., Sat: 11-7; Sun: 11-6 wildedibles.com

Wild Edibles specializes in fresh, high-quality seafood and many of the same foods served at Manhattan's top restaurants. Shrimp. Clams. Mussels. Lobster. Crab. Caviar. Smoked fish. Some of it is unique and imported, but no matter the source, they strive to source fish that has been harvested responsibly. The Murray Hill location includes **Wild Edibles Oyster Bar** (535 Third Ave, 212/213-8552) with a fine assortment of wine and beer. Delivery is available throughout the city.

SPANISH

DESPAÑA FINE FOODS & TAPAS CAFÉ

408 Broome St (bet Lafayette St and Cleveland Pl)   212/219-5050
Mon-Fri: 10-7; Sat: 11-7; Sun: 11-6   despanabrandfoods.com

This gourmet boutique is dedicated to bringing you authentic Spanish foodstuffs such as Serrano ham, blood sausage, chorizo, all-natural game products, cheeses, chestnuts in syrup, chocolate, specialty drinks, cookbooks and cookware, preserves, spreads and much more. When you finish shopping, stop at the Tapas Café for a delicious *bocadillo*, tapas, soups, salads and other

JAPANESE SWEETS

To some people, Japanese candies are more flavorful than their American counterparts. Whether your sweet tooth leans toward hard, chewy, crunchy or chocolate, these stores have the Asian goodies to satisfy your craving.

Dianobu (129 E 47th St, 212/755-7380)

Handsome Dan's (186 First Ave, 917/965-2499)

Katagiri & Company (224 E 59th St, 212/755-3566)

m2m (55 Third Ave, 212/353-2698 and 2935 Broadway, 212/280-4600)

Minamoto Kitchoan (509 Madison Ave, 212/489-3747)

Sunrise Mart (4 Stuyvesant St, 212/598-3040; 494 Broome St, 212/219-0033 and 12 E 41st St, 646/380-9280)

Tongin Mart (91 Mulberry St, 212/962-6622)

specialties. Their next door wine store features a large selection of Spanish wines to pair with their Spanish flavors.

SPECIALTY SHOPS

THE MEADOW

523 Hudson St (bet W 10th and Charles St)   212/645-4633
Mon-Thurs: 11-9; Fri, Sat: 11-10; Sun: 11-8   atthemeadow.com

The Meadow is a place where the beautiful, the delicious and the unexpected are brought together. They specialize in artisan salt, the world's great chocolate bars, fresh-cut flowers, bitters and other gourmet items for the bar and kitchen. In addition, they hold a variety of tasting events including finishing salts, chocolates and wines in sometimes unexpected combinations, plus art openings and occasional dinner parties. Please pass the salt!

SPICES AND OILS

SPICE CORNER

135 Lexington Ave (at 29th St)   212/689-5182
Mon-Sat: 10-9; Sun: 10-7   spicecorner29.com

Spice Corner is an Indian food market where shelves are packed with beans, rice, grains, nuts, chutneys and more. The pungent assortment of spices includes essentials for Middle Eastern and South Asian cooking. There is a good selection of reasonably priced specialty foods (fresh and frozen), organic meats and cookware. You'll enter feeling welcome and leave feeling happy about the prices — they are definitely in your "corner."

NOTES

CHAPTER 5

WHERE TO FIND IT
NEW YORK'S BEST SERVICES

New Yorkers can lead very busy lives, so sometimes it may be desirable to get specialized help for specific things related to the home, office or personal needs. The businesses listed here have been carefully checked and provide great help (at mostly reasonable prices). Before entering into an agreement, it may be beneficial to check references, online reviews or with the Better Business Bureau. The hotel section encompasses hostels, alternative housing and large and small hotels — a handy reference for travelers and when accommodating visiting relatives.

AIR CONDITIONING

AIR-WAVE AIR CONDITIONING COMPANY

Mon-Sat: 8-5

212/545-1122
airwaveac.com

Air-Wave has been in business since 1953, and air conditioning is their *only* business. They have sold, serviced, overhauled, installed and delivered over one million units over the years, including top brands like Friedrich, McQuay and Frigidaire. They will also deliver, install and store portable air conditioning units.

ANIMAL SERVICES

ANIMAL MEDICAL CENTER

510 E 62nd St (bet FDR Dr and York Ave)   212/838-8100
By appointment; 24 hour emergency   amcny.org

If your pet gets sick or has an emergency – go to Animal Medical Center first – open 24/7, 365 days a year. Nearly 100 veterinarians on staff care for 44,000 patient cases each year, including 18,000 emergency visits. AMC treats dogs, cats and exotic pets, like birds, ferrets and reptiles; the care is among the best in the city. Call ahead for an appointment (212/838-7053) unless it is an emergency.

BISCUITS & BATH

41 W 13th St (at Fifth Ave)   212/419-2500 (for all locations)
1535 First Ave (at 80th St)
1035 Third Ave (bet 61st and 62nd St)
1067 Park Ave (bet 87th and 88th St)   biscuitsandbath.com
Numerous other locations; hours vary

Biscuits & Bath offers over 22 years of dog experience – grooming, training, workshops and seminars, vet care, dog walking, day and overnight care, adoption, a retail boutique and transportation services. The place is dog- and pocketbook-friendly.

CAROLE WILBOURN

Consultation by appointment   212/741-0397
Mon-Sat: 9-6   thecattherapist.com

Carole Wilbourn is an internationally known cat preventive and corrective therapist who has the answers to most cat problems. Carole makes house calls, phone consults and Skypes from coast to coast. She has also added Reiki to her behavioral program. As a Reiki practitioner, she gives Reiki treatments to cats and their guardians when appropriate. Carole can take care of many feline issues with just one session and a follow-up phone call. She does international consultations, takes on-site appointments at Westside Veterinary Center and is available for speaking engagements. Wilbourn is the author of six cat psychology books.

PET TAXIS

Arrange a ride for your dog to the vet, groomer, airport, boarding kennel or a long-distance destination.

Canine Car Pet Transportation (212/353-2271, caninecar.com): comfortable SUVs, with a courteous, caring driver at the wheel

Pet Taxi New York (718/355-9665, pettaxinewyork.com): minivans; guardians welcome on the ride

CITY PETS

212/581-7387
citypetsvets.com

Since 1992, City Pets has been providing veterinary care to dogs and cats in their own homes or their owner's offices. Dr. Amy Attas and her qualified team offer physical exams, treatments, vaccinations and more. Their website is a great source for medical information and all sorts of tips. When necessary, they will compassionately perform euthanasia at a pet's home.

NEW YORK DOG SPA & HOTEL

32 W 25th St (bet Ave of the Americas and Broadway)   212/243-1199
Daily: 7 a.m.-10 p.m.   dogspa.com

This is a full-service hotel for dogs! They are staffed 24 hours for boarding and also offer day care and grooming services. Fido will get at least one walk every day.

ANTIQUE REPAIR AND RESTORATION

CENTER ART STUDIO

307 W 38th St (bet Eighth and Ninth Ave)   212/247-3550
By appointment   centerart.com

For nearly a hundred years the motto has been "fine art restoration and display design." The word fine should really be emphasized, as owners of fine paintings, sculpture and ceramics have made Center Art Studio the place to go for restoration. The house specialty is art conservation. They will clean and restore paintings, lacquer, terra cotta, scagliola and plaster. Their craftsmen also restore antique furniture and decorative objects and design and install picture frames, display bases and mounts for sculpture. Among the oldest and most diverse restoration studios in the city, Center Art offers a multitude of special services for the art collector, dealer and designer.

MICHAEL DOTZEL & SON

402 E 63rd St (at York Ave)   212/838-2890
Mon-Fri: 8-4

Michael Dotzel & Son specializes in the repair and maintenance of metal antiques and precious heirlooms. They will polish, rewire, replate and cast your objects of brass, copper, tin, iron and silver. Close attention to detail is given, and if an antique has lost a part or if you want a duplication, they can re-create it.

ART APPRAISALS

ABIGAIL HARTMANN ASSOCIATES

415 Central Park W (at 101st St), Room 5-C   212/316-5406
Mon-Fri: 9-5 (by appointment; also available on weekends)   abigailhartmann.com

This respected firm specializes in fine- and decorative-art appraisals whether it be for insurance, donation, damage, tax or other reasons. Their highly principled and experienced staff does not buy, sell or receive kickbacks (a common practice with some auction houses, insurance companies and galleries). Fees are by the hour, and consultations are available. The friendly personnel can also provide restoration, framing, storage and estate disposition.

ART SERVICES

A.I. FRIEDMAN

44 W 18th St (bet Fifth Ave and Ave of the Americas)   212/243-9000
Mon-Fri: 9-8; Sat: 10-7; Sun: 11-6   aifriedman.com

A.I. Friedman has one of the largest stocks of ready-made frames in the city for those who want to frame it themselves, and nearly all are sold at discount. In addition to fully-assembled frames, they sell do-it-yourself frames that come equipped with glass and/or mats. Custom framing is also available. They are really a department store for creative people, providing a large assortment of tools, furniture, paints, easels, books and other supplies and materials for the graphic artist.

ELI WILNER & COMPANY

1525 York Ave (bet 80th and 81st St)   212/744-6521
Mon-Fri: 9:30-5:30   eliwilner.com

The primary business of Eli Wilner is selling and restoring period frames and mirrors. Eli keeps thousands of 19th- and early 20th-century American and European frames in stock and can locate any size or style, or he can create an exact replica of a frame to your specifications. Over 25 skilled craftsmen do expert restoration and replication of frames; also frame appraisals. Boasting such clients as the Metropolitan Museum of Art and the White House, Wilner's expertise speaks for itself.

J. POCKER & SON

135 E 63rd St (bet Park and Lexington Ave)   212/838-5488
Mon-Sat: 9-5:30   jpocker.com

The Pocker family has been in the custom framing business since 1926, so rest assured that you will receive expert advice from a superbly trained staff. All framing is conservation-quality. Also look to them for custom mirrors, decorative prints, custom plaques, gallery rods and picture lights. They can handle pickup and delivery and will recommend professional installation services.

JULIUS LOWY FRAME AND RESTORING COMPANY

223 E 80th St (bet Second and Third Ave)   212/861-8585
Mon-Fri: 9-5:30   lowy1907.com

Lowy is the nation's oldest, largest and most highly regarded firm for the conservation and framing of fine art. Serving New York City since 1907, services include painting and paper conservation, professional photography, conservation framing and curatorial work. They sell antique and authentic reproduction frames, claiming to have the largest inventory and best selection. In addition, Lowy provides mat-making and fitting services. Their client base includes art dealers, private collectors, auction houses, corporations and museums.

LET'S DANCE!

When you need to learn how to gracefully hold your own on the dance floor, contact these studios. Most classes are geared for couples.

Dance with Me (466 Broome St, 212/840-3262): co-founded by dance professional Maksim Chmerkovskiy

DanceSport (22 W 34th St, 212/307-1111): group and private lessons, ballroom and Latin

Fred Astaire Dance Studios (201 E 34th St, 212/697-6535; 328 E 61st St, 212/209-2410 and 174 W 72nd St, 212/595-3200): private lessons; ballroom, Latin, swing, salsa, the Hustle

NY Wedding and Partner Dance (1261 Broadway, Suite 309, 646/742-1520): private lessons only, all genres of dance, three private rooms

You Should be Dancing (412 Eighth Ave, 4th floor, 212/244-0011): group and private lessons, wedding-dance specialists

KING DAVID GALLERY

128 W 23rd St (bet Ave of the Americas and Seventh Ave)   212/727-9700
Mon-Thurs: 10-7; Sat: 10-5; Sun: 11-5   kingdavidgallery.com

King David Gallery provides very professional service in a number of areas: design consulting and custom framing for fine art and mirrors, canvas stretching, glass cutting and 24K gold-leaf framing. They can design and build shadow boxes, glass panels for shower doors and framed TV mirrors to cover a flat-screen TV. Custom glass work is their primary specialty, but they can do almost anything in this field, beginning with designer sketches and measurements and finishing with expert installation.

LEITH RUTHERFURD TALAMO

By appointment   212/396-0399
leithtalamo.com

Leith Rutherfurd Talamo has run a full-service art restoration business since 1985. Her training included stays in France, Belgium and Italy. Whether it be an oil painting, mural, frame or sculpture, she can restore your art to its original state. Well-trained in classical restoration techniques, she is well qualified in the cleaning, relining, reframing, rehanging and lighting of your artwork, as well as in gilding and polishing of frames — all done with expertise and class.

BABYSITTERS

BABY SITTERS' GUILD

477 Madison Ave (bet 51st and 52nd St)   212/682-0227
Daily: 9-9 (office)   babysittersguild.com

The Baby Sitters' Guild has provided TLC for babies and children since 1940. They charge high rates, but their professional reputation commands them. All of their sitters have passed rigorous scrutiny — thorough background checks and fingerprinting. Many have teaching, nursing or nanny backgrounds, all are CPR certified and only the most capable are enlisted. A four-hour minimum is enforced and any travel expenses are reimbursed. Sitters are available 24/7 and some have traveled to New Jersey, Connecticut and even abroad upon request.

BARNARD BABYSITTING AGENCY

Columbia University, Elliott Hall
49 Claremont Ave (at 119th St), 2nd floor   212/854-2035
Mon: 11:30-4; Tues-Fri: 10-4   barnardbabysitting.com

Barnard Babysitting Agency is a nonprofit organization run by students at the undergraduate women's college affiliated with Columbia University. The service is a clearinghouse between parents and sitters to provide affordable child care in the New York metropolitan area. At the same time, it allows students to seek regular or sporadic employment. Parents hire the sitter of their choice. An hourly wage, cab fare and food (or money for food) are required for each job. A minimum registration fee is required to post babysitting requests.

BEAUTY SERVICES

BOTOX TREATMENT

Verve Laser and Medical Spa (240 E 60th St, 212/888-3003)

CELLULITE TREATMENT

Wellpath (903 Madison Ave, 212/737-9604): up-to-date equipment

EYEBROW STYLING

Benefit Boutique Soho (454 West Broadway, 212/769-1111): waxing, tinting

Borja Color Studio (118 E 57th St, 212/308-3232)

Ramy Spa (343 E 30th St, Suite 19-J, 212/684-9500): complimentary makeup consultation; skin-care products

Shobha (594 Broadway, Suite 403, 212/931-8363; 41 E 57th St, Suite 1304, 212/223-2872; 1790 Broadway, 212/977-7771; 65 Broadway, 212/425-4900): shaping

EYELASHES

Ebenezer Eyelash (2 W 32nd St, 4th floor, 212/947-5503; 474 Seventh Ave, 6th floor, 212/967-1301 and 41 W 35th St, 2nd floor, 212/967-1308): extensions

HAIR CARE | BEST IN MANHATTAN, BY AREA

CHELSEA

Antonio Prieto Salon (127 W 20th St, 212/255-3741): popular styling

Chris Chase Salon (182 Ninth Ave, 212/206-7991): Japanese conditioning treatment

BABYSITTING SERVICE

At **Not Just Baby Sitters** (917/523-0065, notjustbabysitters.com), owner Zee Miller Smith strives to make sure the person providing child care in your home is a perfect match for you and your family. She imposes a very strict application and interview process for prospective sitters and conducts home interviews with employers to match suitable caregivers with infants, older children and the elderly. Members pay an annual fee for unlimited use of placements (short- or long-term, or as needed). Rates vary by the number of children, responsibilities, sitter's experience and qualifications.

Gemini 14 (135 W 14th St, 212/675-4546): "Opti-Smooth" straightening treatment

Rudy's (Ace Hotel, 14 W 29th St, 212/532-7200): retro

EAST VILLAGE

Astor Place Hairstylists (2 Astor Pl, 212/475-9854): one of the world's largest barber shops; inexpensive

FLATIRON DISTRICT

Sacha and Olivier (6 W 18th St, 212/255-1100): Parisian-inspired salon

Salon 02 (20 W 22nd St, 212/675-7274): Japanese and Brazilian procedures and treatments

GREENWICH VILLAGE

Red Market (13 E 13th St, 212/929-9600): late night, libations

Shampoo Avenue B (42 Ave B, 212/777-2031): Wella hair color, reasonable prices

LOWER EAST SIDE

Tease Salon (137 Rivington St, 212/979-8327): color

MIDTOWN

Bumble & Bumble (146 E 56th St and 415 W 13th St, 212/521-6500 for both locations): no-nonsense establishment

Elji Salon (601 Madison Ave, Suite 5, 212/838-3454): dry cut

Frederic Fekkai Salon (Henri Bendel, 712 Fifth Ave, 4th floor, 212/753-9500): elegant

Halcyon Days Salons and Spas at Saks Fifth Avenue (611 Fifth Ave, concourse level, 212/940-4000; entrance on 50th St): top-grade, full-service

Julien Farel Restore Salon & Spa (540 Park Ave, 2nd floor, 212/888-8988): upscale, private hair parties

Kenneth Salon (Waldorf Astoria New York, 301 Park Ave, lobby floor, 212/752-1800): full-service with an able staff

Mark Garrison Salon (108 E 60th St, 212/400-8000): popular

Oscar Blandi Salon (545 Madison Ave, 212/421-9800): reliable

Ouidad Salon (37 W 57th St, 4th floor, 212/888-3288): curly- and frizzy-hair specialists

Phyto Universe (715 Lexington Ave, 212/308-0270): private treatment cabins

Pierre Michel (135 E 57th St, 3rd floor, 212/593-1460): full-service, wedding specialists

Salon A· K· S (689 Fifth Ave, 10th floor, 212/888-0707)

Salon Ishi (70 E 55th St, 212/888-4744): shiatsu scalp massages for men and women

Stephen Knoll Salon (625 Madison Ave, 2nd floor, 212/421-0100): highly recommended by celebrities

Vidal Sassoon (7 W 56th St, 212/535-9200): popular with men and women

Warren-Tricomi Salon (The Plaza, Fifth Ave at Central Park S, 2nd floor, 212/262-8899)

SOHO

Frederic Fekkai Salon (394 West Broadway, 2nd floor, 212/888-2600): complimentary Wi-Fi and espresso

Ion Studio (41 Wooster St, 212/343-9060): ecologically sound

Laicale Salon (129 Grand St, 212/219-2424): all services, cutting-edge style

Pas de Deux Salon (79 Worth St, 212/274-0079): hair reconstruction

UPPER EAST SIDE

John Barrett Salon (Bergdorf Goodman, 754 Fifth Ave, penthouse, 212/872-2700): braids and blond highlights

Rita Hazan Salon (720 Fifth Ave, 212/586-4343): very good

Serge Normant at John Frieda (30 E 76th St, 212/879-1000): very "in"

Yves Durif (Carlyle Hotel, 35 E 76th St, 212/452-0954): reliable

UPPER WEST SIDE

Salon Above (2641 Broadway, 2nd floor, 212/665-7149)

WEST VILLAGE

Bumble & Bumble (415 W 13th St, 8th floor, 212/521-6500)

Snip 'n Sip (204 Waverly Pl, 212/242-3880): retro soda shop

HAIR COLORING

Bloom Beauty Lounge (140 W 19th St, 212/255-9355): organic hair care line

Borja Color Studio (118 E 57th St, 212/308-3232): ammonia-free color

Louis Licari Salon (693 Fifth Ave, 212/758-2090): full-service

Q Hair (19 Bleecker St, 212/614-8729): brunettes

Salon A· K· S (689 Fifth Ave, 10th floor, 212/888-0707)

TRAINING SCHOOLS WITH DISCOUNT BEAUTY SERVICES

Inexpensive prices on beauty services are available if you are willing to patronize training schools. Here are some of the better ones:

DENTISTRY

New York University College of Dentistry (345 E 24th St, 212/998-9800): initial visit and X-rays, all for $95!

FACIALS

Christine Valmy International School (261 Fifth Ave, 24th floor, 212/779-7800): Facials start at $27 to $38.

HAIRSTYLING

Bumble & Bumble (415 W 13th St, 212/521-6500, 866/728-6253): model project

HAIRSTYLING AND MANICURES

Empire Beauty Schools (22 W 34th St, 212/695-4555): an old-fashioned learning institute; reasonable prices

MASSAGE

The Aveda Institute (233 Spring St, 212/807-1492): 90-minute therapeutic facial for $50

Swedish Institute (226 W 26th St, 212/924-5900): 12 one-hour Swedish or shiatsu massages for $360

Warren-Tricomi Salon (The Plaza, Fifth Ave at Central Park S, 2nd floor, 212/262-8899 and 1117 Madison Ave, 212/262-8899)

HAIR-LOSS TREATMENT

Le Metric Hair Center for Women (124 E 40th St, Suite 601, 212/986-5620)

Philip Kingsley Trichological Clinic (16 E 52nd St, 212/753-9600)

HAIR REMOVAL

J. Sisters Salon (41 W 57th St, 2nd floor, 212/750-2485): Brazilian bikini-wax specialists

Strip Ministry of Waxing (56 Spring St, 212/431-1121): waxing and laser hair removal

Verve Laser and Medical Spa (240 E 60th St, 212/888-3003): other medical treatments

HAIRSTYLING | BY SPECIALTY

BLOW-STYLING

Amy's Hair Salon (20 Pell St, 212/406-2746): cash only, appointments suggested

Encore Beauty Salon (3 Claremont Ave, 212/222-1241): old-school

Jean Louis David (2146 Broadway, 212/873-1850): good work at reasonable prices

Salon A· K· S (689 Fifth Ave, 10th floor, 212/888-0707): Mika Rummo; house calls, too

Salon de Tops (76 Elizabeth St, 212/219-0728): Asian

Warren-Tricomi Salon (The Plaza, Fifth Ave at Central Park S, 2nd floor, 212/262-8899 and 1117 Madison Ave, 212/262-8899): for work that lasts

DISCOUNT HAIRCUTS

Parlor (102 Ave B, 212/673-5520): check out Apprentice Monday—prices start at $20!

Tease Salon (199 Second Ave, 212/725-7088): $50 and up for a wash and cut

FAMILY HAIRCUTS

Feature Trim (1108 Lexington Ave, 212/650-9746)

Men's Haircuts

3 Aces Barber Shop (664 Ninth Ave, 212/664-9807): inexpensive

Barbiere (246 E 5th St, 646/649-2640): $40 textured scissor cuts, cash only

Blind Barber (339 E 10th St, 212/228-2123): adjacent lounge (open late)

Chelsea Barber (465 W 23rd St, 212/741-2254): inexpensive

Corner Shop (64 MacDougal St, 646/964-5193): two chairs; $35 haircuts, $30 shaves

Frank's Chop Shop (19 Essex St, 212/228-7442): cuts for clients from bankers to rap artists

Martial Vivot (39 W 54th St, 212/956-2990): stylish, up-to-the-moment cuts from $125

Neighborhood Barbers (439 E 9th St, 212/777-0798): bargain haircuts at $14

Salon A· K· S (689 Fifth Ave, 10th floor, 212/888-0707): hair coloring

Truman's Gentlemen's Groomers (120 E 56th St, 212/759-5015 and 121 Madison Ave, 212/683-9400): top-quality gentlemen's groomers

HOME (OR OFFICE) SERVICES

Eastside Massage Therapy Center (351 E 78th St, 212/249-2927)

Gotham Glow (646/397-4438): tans

Harper Monroe Salon and Spa (347/460-3228): spa services, all five boroughs

Miguel Lopez Salon and Spa (458 West Broadway, 2nd floor, 212/343-2643): home, office or hotel

Paul Podlucky (25 E 67th St, 14E, 212/717-6622): hair, his place or yours

Primp In-Home (212/217-6038): full-service and wardrobe consultation

Styled by Jen (917/660-3420): hair, makeup

INTEGRATIVE MEDICINE

Continuum Center for Health & Healing (245 Fifth Ave, 2nd floor, 646/935-2220): East Asian treatments

JEWELRY REPAIR

For minor or major jewelry repairs, try these:

Donna Distefano (37 W 20th St, Suite 1106, 212/594-3757): will also replace lost stones; by appointment

Murrey's Jewelers (1395 Third Ave, 212/879-3690)

MAKEUP

Kimara Ahnert Makeup Studio (1113 Madison Ave, 212/452-4252): applications, lessons and products

MANICURES AND PEDICURES

Angel Nails (151 E 71st St, 212/535-5333): nail-wrapping, massages, waxing

Jin Soon Natural Hand & Foot Spa (56 E 4th St, 212/473-2047; 23 Jones St, 212/229-1070 and 421 E 73rd St, 212/249-9144)

Ohm Spa (260 Fifth Ave, 5th floor, 212/845-9812): eco-friendly, organic, vegan

Paul Labrecque Salon and Spa (171 E 65th St, 66 E 55th St and Chelsea Piers at Pier 60; 212/988-7816 for all locations)

Pierre Michel (135 E 57th St, 3rd floor, 212/593-1460): old-school

Relax Foot Spa (202 Hester St, 212/226-8288 and 193 Centre St, 212/226-5635): reflexology

Spa Martier (1014 Second Ave, 646/781-9758): mesmerizing nail-art

Sweet Lily Natural Nail Spa and Boutique (222 West Broadway, 212/925-5441): seasonal treatments

Think Pink Nails & Spa (41 W 58th St, 212/371-4141)

Touch of East Nail Salon and Spa (11 W 20th St, 212/366-6333)

Townhouse Spa (39 W 56th St, 212/245-8006): enlivening, soothing and nourishing pedicures and manicures

Valley NYC (198 Elizabeth St, 212/274-8985): nail-art

MASSAGE

Angel Feet (77 Perry St, 212/924-3576): reflexology

Asia Tui-Na Wholeness (37 E 28th St, 8th floor, 212/686-8082): traditional Chinese

Expecting (NYC) (80 E 11th St, Suite 407, 212/475-0709): prenatal and postpartum

Graceful Services (1095 Second Ave, 2nd floor, 212/593-9904): facials, too

Relax (716 Greenwich St, 212/206-9714): deep tissue

SPA at Andaz Wall Street (75 Wall St, 212/699-1830): hand and arm massages

MEN'S GROOMING

Bedford Barbers (322 E 59th St, 212/308-0333): bargain-priced cuts and shaves

Ben's Barbers (217 Ave A, 718/644-6701): low-key, inexpensive

Blind Barber (339 E 10th St, 212/228-2123): straight-razor shave or haircut, plus complimentary cocktail

Decatur & Sons (Chelsea Market, 75 Ninth Ave, 646/470-7288): drop-ins welcome

Esquires of Wall St (14 Wall St, 212/349-5064): since 1932

Frederic Fekkai Salon (Henri Bendel, 712 Fifth Ave, 4th floor, 212/753-9500): men's lounge, L'Atelier de Frederic

Geno's Barberia (48 Greenwich Ave, 212/929-9029): immaculate

Hey Man Day Spa (226 W 4th St, 212/929-0838): waxing, massages, nails

John Allan's (95 Trinity Pl, 212/406-3000; 46 E 46th St, 212/922-0361 and 418 Washington St, 212/334-5358): full-service

Kiehl's (109 Third Ave, 212/677-3171 and 157 E 64th St, 917/432-2503): toiletries

La Boîte à Coupe (57 W 57th St, 8th floor, 212/246-2097): cuts, color, manicures, pedicures, waxing

Patrick Melville (Equinox, 45 Rockefeller Plaza, 3rd floor, 212/218-8650): pedicures

Paul Labrecque Salon and Spa (171 E 65th St, 66 E 55th St and Chelsea Piers at Pier 60, 212/988-7816 for all locations): straight-razor shave

Peninsula Spa (The Peninsula New York, 700 Fifth Ave, 21st floor, 212/903-3910): massages created for men

Pierre Michel (135 E 57th St, 3rd floor, 212/593-1460): manicures

Season Spa (165 Hester St, 212/966-7416): aromatherapy

SkinCareLab (568 Broadway, Suite 303, 212/334-3142): full-service for men and women

Spiff for Men (750 Third Ave, 212/983-3240): post-shave facials and hot-oil scalp treatment, Wi-Fi, coffee and select beverages

Truman's Gentlemen's Groomers (120 E 56th St, 212/759-5015 and 121 Madison Ave, 212/683-9400): upscale men's spa

Yasmine Djerradine (30 E 60th St, 212/588-1771): men and women, spa and medi-spa

York Barber Shop (981 Lexington Ave, 212/988-6136): old-time

SAUNA

Russian and Turkish Baths (268 E 10th St, 212/674-9250): since 1892, sauna and steam rooms, ice-cold pool

SKIN CARE

Advanced Skin Care Day Spa (140 W 57th St, 212/758-8867): full-service

Bluemercury (2305 Broadway, 212/799-0500; 131 Third Ave, 212/396-1500 and 865 Broadway, 212/243-8100): makeup, skin care and facials

Christine Chin Spa (82 Orchard St, 212/353-0503): facials, waxing

Euphoria Spa (18 Harrison St, 212/925-5925): full-service

Face to Face (20 W 20th St, 6th floor, 212/633-0404): back and chest treatments

Joean Beauty Salon (80 Lafayette St, 718/333-0313): inexpensive

Lia Schorr (57 W 57th St, Suite 1409, 212/486-9670)

Ling Skin Care Salons (105 W 77th St, 212/877-2883 and 12 E 16th St, 212/989-8833): facials, waxing

Mario Badescu Skin Care Salon (320 E 52nd St, 212/758-1065): European facials

Miano Viel (16 E 52nd St, 2nd floor, 212/980-3222): great facials by Alla Katkov

Oasis Day Spa (1 Park Ave, 212/254-7722 and Affinia Dumont, 150 E 34th St, 212/545-5254): facials a specialty

Paul Labrecque Salon and Spa (171 E 65th St, 66 E 55th St and Chelsea Piers at Pier 60, 212/988-7816 for all locations): full- service

Shizuka New York Day Spa (7 W 51st St, 6th floor, 212/644-7400): anti-aging facial with intense pulsed light

Smooth Synergy (139 E 57th St, 8th floor, 212/397-0111): medi-spa with a resident physician

Tamago Skin Care (236 E 13th St, 212/505-1599): seaweed facial

Tracie Martyn (101 Fifth Ave, 212/206-9333): resculpting facial

SPAS | BY NEIGHBORHOOD

Includes day spas with full or limited services, medi-spas and body treatments.

CHELSEA

Acqua Beauty Bar (7 E 14th St, 212/620-4329): full-service, pedicures

Graceful Spa (205 W 14th St, 2nd floor, 212/675-5145): budget-friendly

Paul Labrecque Salon and Spa (Chelsea Piers at Pier 60, 212/988-7816): Thai massage, facials

FINANCIAL DISTRICT

Setai Spa Wall Street (40 Broad St, 3rd floor, 212/792-6193): full-service, June Jacobs products

FLATIRON DISTRICT

Spruce and Bond (103 Fifth Ave, 3rd floor, 212/366-6060): one of the best laser hair-removal treatments in town; dewrinkling facials

GRAMERCY

Gloria Cabrera Salon and Spa (309 E 23rd St, 212/689-6815): full-service

GREENWICH VILLAGE

Silk Day Spa (47 W 13th St, 212/255-6457): "Silk Supreme Eastern Indulgence Body Scrub and Polish," skin care, waxing

Spruce and Bond (25 Bond St, 212/366-6060)

KIPS BAY

Essential Therapy (122 E 25th St, 212/777-2325): spa services with a healing bent, co-ed

Oasis Day Spa (1 Park Ave, 212/254-7722): full-service

LOWER EAST SIDE
Takamichi Hair (263 Bowery, 212/420-7979): stylist Takamichi Saeki

MEATPACKING DISTRICT
Exhale Spa (Gansevoort Meatpacking NYC, 18 Ninth Ave, 212/660-6733): full-service

MIDTOWN
Bliss 49 (W New York, 541 Lexington Ave, 877/862-5477): full-service

Bliss 57 (12 W 57th St, 877/862-5477)

Bloomie Nails (44 W 55th St, 212/664-1662): nails, massages, facials

Dorit Baxter Skin Care, Beauty & Health Spa (47 W 57th St, 3rd floor, 212/371-4542): salt scrub, lymphatic drainage massage

Elizabeth Arden Red Door Salon (663 Fifth Ave, 212/546-0200): full-service

Exhale Spa (150 Central Park S, 212/249-3000): full-service

Faina European Skin Care Center and Day Spa (330 W 58th St, Suite 402, 212/245-6557): full-service

Frederic Fekkai Salon (Henri Bendel, 712 Fifth Ave, 4th floor, 212/753-9500): the ultimate services; waxing, manicures, pedicures, facials

Halcyon Days Salons and Spas at Saks Fifth Avenue (611 Fifth Ave, concourse level, 212/940-4000; entrance on 50th St): full-service

Ido Holistic Center (22 E 49th St, 212/599-5300): immune-system boost, Japanese massage

Juva Skin and Laser and Plastic Surgery Center (60 E 56th St, 2nd floor, 212/688-5882): microdermabrasion, massages and facials

Juvenex (25 W 32nd St, 646/733-1330): 24-hour Korean oasis, body scrub

La Prairie at the Ritz-Carlton Spa (50 Central Park S, 2nd floor, 212/521-6135): top-drawer

Lia Schorr (57 W 57th St, Suite 1409, 212/486-9670): efficient and reasonably priced, hot-stone foot massage

Metamorphosis (127 E 56th St, 5th floor, 212/751-6051): small but good, men and women

Paul Labrecque Salon and Spa (171 E 65th St and 66 E 55th St, 212/988-7816 for both locations): Thai massage, facials

Peninsula Spa (The Peninsula New York, 700 Fifth Ave, 21st floor, 212/903-3910)

Remède Spa (St. Regis New York, 2 E 55th St, 19th floor, 212/339-6715): massages, facials, waxing, body treatments

Salon de Tokyo (200 W 57th St, Room 1308, 212/582-2132): shiatsu parlor, massages, sauna, open till midnight

Spa at Mandarin Oriental (Time Warner Center, 80 Columbus Cir, 35th floor, 212/805-8880): deep-tissue massage, holistic foot ritual

STORAGE STRATEGY

If you have limited space for storing seasonal clothes and equipment, think outsourcing. These storage-pickup services will remove your boxes, store them and return them again when needed.

Box Butler (888/881-0810, boxbutler.com)

MakeSpace (800/920-9440, makespace.com)

Spa at the Four Seasons Hotel New York (57 E 57th St, 212/350-6420): exclusive

Susan Ciminelli Beauty Clinic (118 E 57th St, 3rd floor, 212/750-4441): full-service, men and women

Townhouse Spa (39 W 56th St, 212/245-8006): full-service

Yasmine Djerradine (30 E 60th St, 212/588-1771): skin care, remodeling facials, eyebrows, men's facials

MURRAY HILL

Elite Day Spa (24 W 39th St, 212/730-2100): "Sugar Daddy" brown-sugar scrub

Hair Party (450 Park Ave S, 212/213-0056): open 24 hours a day

Murray Hill Skin Care (567 Third Ave, 2nd floor, 212/661-0777): full-service, "backcials"—i.e., a facial for the back

Yi Pak Spa (325 Fifth Ave, 212/594-1025): massages, body scrub

SOHO

Bliss Soho (568 Broadway, 2nd floor, 877/862-5477): oxygen facials, laser hair removal

Haven Spa (150 Mercer St, 212/343-3515): full-service, calm and refreshing, open weekends

La Alegria (196 Prince St, 212/966-1445): full-service, facials, skin care, waxing, massages, manicures, pedicures

SkinCareLab (568 Broadway, Suite 303, 212/334-3142): full-service, body treatments, facials, men welcome

Soho Sanctuary (119 Mercer St, 212/334-5550): full-service, facials

TRIBECA

Aire Ancient Baths (88 Franklin St, 212/274-3777): ancient Roman bathing traditions

Euphoria Spa (18 Harrison St, 2nd floor, 212/925-5925): "Fresh Air Facial," laser, waxing, massages

Shibui Spa (The Greenwich Hotel, 377 Greenwich St, 212/941-8900): gorgeous, Japanese-style

TriBeCa MedSpa (114 Hudson St, 212/925-9500): exfoliation, skin care, laser, facials

UPPER EAST SIDE

Ajune (853 Fifth Ave Ave, 212/628-0044): medi-spa, full-service, Botox, facials
Equinox Spa (817 Lexington Ave, 212/750-4671): facials, sports massage
Institute Beauté (885 Park Ave, 212/535-0229): foot facial
Spruce and Bond (764 Madison Ave, 3rd floor, 212/717-9300): sunspot removal

UPPER WEST SIDE

All Seasons Nails & Spa (2566 Broadway, 212/666-8822): manicures, pedicures, massages, facials
Ettia Holistic Day Spa (239 W 72nd St, 212/362-7109): massages, waxing, facials, men and women
Prenatal Massage Center of Manhattan (123 W 79th St, 917/359-8176): postpartum, too

TANNING

Brazil Bronze Glow Bar (580 Broadway, Suite 501, 212/431-0077): spray body bronzing
City Sun Tanning (50 E 13th St, 212/353-9700): spray, sunbeds
Paul Labrecque Salon and Spa (171 E 65th St and 66 E 55th St, 212/988-7816 for both locations): exfoliation, self-tanning moisturizing lotion
Spa at Equinox (203 E 85th St, 212/396-9611): body bronzing

CABINETRY

HARMONY WOODWORKING

153 W 27th St (bet Ave of the Americas and Seventh Ave), Room 902

212/366-7221

By appointment   harmonywoodworking.org

With 30 years of experience, expert woodworker Ron Rubin devotes his time to one-of-a-kind custom projects.   Kitchens, bookcases, wall units, entertainment centers, desks and tables are just a few of the handcrafted designs at Harmony Woodworking.

JIM NICKEL

By appointment   718/963-2138

Jim Nickel is an expert at projects that use wood: cabinets, bookcases, wall sculptures and much more. He prefers small- to medium-sized jobs and can do an entire project — from consultation and design to installation — all by himself. He has decades of experience and is budget conscious. Call in the afternoon or evening for an appointment.

MANHATTAN CABINETRY

Showroom: 227 E 59th St (bet Second and Third Ave)   212/750-9800
Mon-Thurs: 10-7; Fri: 10-6; Sat: 10-5:30; Sun: noon-5:30 manhattancabinetry.com

The motto at Manhattan Cabinetry is "If you can imagine it, we can build it."

BEAUTY APPS

With these phone apps, you can request prompt and professional style in the comfort of your home, office or hotel; hair stylists and makeup artists are screened to very high standards. This is a great idea solution for a bachelorette or sweet sixteen party, baby or bridal shower, new mom and a good old-fashioned girls' night out. You'll also find beauty and wellness tips.

City Mani   **Priv**
Get Beautified   **StyleBee**
Glamsquad   **Uber Beauty**

Do you need a custom piece for a special nook or have a unique design in mind? Visit the showroom to see product samples, from French Deco reproductions to contemporary designs. They will work with you from design to finish to build bars, credenzas, desks, storage, tables, kitchen cabinets or whatever your particular need.   Check their website periodically to view discounted floor samples.

CARPENTRY

NOTJUSTHANDYMEN.COM

By appointment   212/257-2132, 718/857-1381
notjusthandymen.com

Everyone needs a guy like Kellam Clark at some time or another. Major renovations, minor handy work and even last-minute jobs are no problem for his friendly, resourceful crew. They'll do carpentry and sheetrock work; air-conditioning installation, cleaning and storage; bathroom and kitchen repairs and remodeling; wallpapering; window treatments and installation; door and lock replacement and repairs; furniture assembly; painting and TV mounting. Other services include moving, domestic cleaning, light fixture installation and tile work. For emergencies, their 24-hour contact number is 917/399-0583. All five boroughs are serviced.

CARPET CLEANING

STEAMPRO CARPET CLEANING

24-hour customer-service line   718/606-0549
steampronyc.com

Routine carpet cleaning, carpet and upholstery emergencies, fine-textile cleaning — it's all in a day's work at Steampro Carpet Cleaning. You begin with a free estimate. A typical carpet job starts with an analysis of the problem; then on to pretreatment, agitation and allowing time for the elements to work, neutralization, steam cleaning, post-grooming and speed drying. Optional finishing services include deodorizing and Scotchgarding. They'll even leave a spot-cleaning bottle for touchups until their next visit; their product line is eco-friendly and green.

CARRIAGES

CHATEAU STABLES/CHATEAU WEDDING CARRIAGES

608 W 48th St (bet Eleventh and Twelfth Ave)   212/246-0520
Call for reservations   chateaustables.net
                                          chateauweddingcarriages.com

If you want to arrive at a big event in a horse-drawn carriage, Chateau is the place to call. They have the largest working collection of antique, horse-drawn vehicles in the U.S. — carriages, surreys, wagons, sleighs and royal coaches are all available. Although they prefer advance notice, requests for weddings, group rides, hayrides, sleigh rides, tours, funerals, movies and overseas visitors can generally be handled at any time. This family business has been in operation for nearly half a century.

CARS FOR HIRE

ABC NYC LIMO

Daily: 7 a.m. to 11 p.m. (customer service)   718/429-5285
                                                      abcnyclimo.com

This limousine service was founded by a group of experienced chauffeurs in order to offer elegance, dependability and first-class service at competitive rates; all drivers have extensive city knowledge. ABC will drive you from airport to city and from hotel to theater, but their specialty is guided tours of New York City. They offer topnotch service for shopping trips, corporate clients and social occasions.

CARMEL CAR AND LIMOUSINE SERVICE

2642 Broadway (at 100th St)   212/666-6666
Daily: 24 hours   carmellimo.com

These people are highly commended for quality service and fair prices. Full-size and luxury sedans, minivans, passenger vans, SUVs, Lincoln Town cars and limos are available. Prices are by the hour and set fees apply for airport transportation.

COMPANY II LIMOUSINE SERVICE

Daily: 24 hours   718/430-6482 (718/409-9129, fax)

This is a good choice! Steve Betancourt provides responsible, efficient chauffeur service at reasonable prices. I can personally vouch that Steve's reputation for reliability is well-earned.

DMC LIMOUSINE

10 Waterside Plaza   212/481-6365
Daily: 24 hours   watersideplaza.com/limo

Since 1988 this limousine company has housed a fleet of meticulously-maintained luxury vehicles in Manhattan. Chauffeurs are knowledgeable, professional and discreet; trained private security specialists are also available.

CHAIR CANING

VETERAN'S CHAIR CANING AND REPAIR

442 Tenth Ave (bet 34th and 35th St)   212/564-4560
Mon-Thurs: 7:30-4:30; Fri: 7:30-4; Sat: 8-1   veteranscaning.com

Veteran's Chair Caning and Repair has been family-owned and -operated since 1899. The crafts of hand- and machine-caning along with wicker repair are still available here. John Bausert, a third-generation chair caner, has even written a book about his craft. His prices and craftsmanship are among the best in town. Bausert believes in passing along his knowledge and encourages customers to repair their own chairs, and the necessary materials are sold in the shop. If you don't want to try it yourself, Veteran's will repair your chair (cane, wicker and wooden). For a charge, they will pick up and deliver.

CLOCK AND WATCH REPAIR

FANELLI ANTIQUE TIMEPIECES

790 Madison Ave (bet 66th and 67th St), 2nd floor   212/517-2300
Mon-Fri: 11:30-6 (Sat by appointment)   fanelliantiquetimepiecesltd.com

Cindy Fanelli specializes in the care of high-quality "investment-type" timepieces, especially carriage clocks, in this beautiful clock gallery. Her store has one of the nation's largest collections of rare and unusual Early American grandfather clocks and vintage wristwatches. She does sales and restoration, makes house calls, gives free estimates, rents timepieces and purchases single pieces or entire collections.

J&P TIMEPIECES

1057 Second Ave (at 56th St)   212/980-1099
Mon-Fri: 10-5   jptimepieces.com

Fine-watch repair is a family tradition in Europe, but this craft is being forgotten in our country. Fortunately for Manhattan, the Fossners have passed down this talent for four generations. You can be confident of their work on any kind of mechanical watch or clock. They guarantee repairs for six months and generally turn around jobs within ten days.

SUTTON CLOCK SHOP

218 E 82nd St (bet Second and Third Ave)   212/758-2260
Tues-Fri: 11-4 (call ahead)   suttonclocks.com

Sutton's forte is selling and acquiring unusual timepieces, but this operation also maintains and repairs antique clocks. Some of the timepieces they sell, even the contemporary ones, are truly outstanding. They also sell and repair barometers and will make house calls.

TIME PIECES, INC.

115 Greenwich Ave (at 13th St)   212/929-8011
Tues-Fri: 10-6; Sat: 11-5   timepiecesrepair.com

Time Pieces, Inc. has been in business on Greenwich Avenue since 1978. Grace Szuwala services, restores, repairs and sells antique timepieces; a two-year guarantee is offered on all clock repairs. Her European training has made her a recognized expert.

CLOTHING REPAIR

FRENCH-AMERICAN REWEAVING COMPANY

119 W 57th St (bet Ave of the Americas and Seventh Ave), Room 1406
Mon-Fri: 10-4; Sat: 11-2 (closed in July and Aug)   212/765-4670

Has a tear, burn or stain ruined a favorite outfit? Head to French-American Reweaving Company where Ronald Moore's team will work wonders on almost any garment in nearly every fabric. Often a repaired item will look just like new!

METRO DYEING

306 W 38th St (at Eighth Ave), 7th floor

212/391-1001
Mon-Fri: 9-5   metrodyeing.com

Designers and fashionistas know the merits of custom fabric-dyeing by the experts at Metro Dyeing. You might use them to dye a garment to cover a stain or create a new look. Metro has perfected their system to color a yard of fabric, an entire line of garments, a wedding dress, a jacket or a favorite pair of jeans. Dyes are organic, and no chemicals are used in the intricate process. Cotton, silk and nylon fibers are more dye-friendly than other fabrics, each fiber requiring a different formula for best results. Consultation with these experts will identify the chances of a successful result. Their client list reads like a who's who in the fashion industry and boasts numerous celebrities.

COMPUTER SERVICE AND INSTRUCTION

ABC COMPUTER SERVICES

15 E 40th St (bet Fifth and Madison Ave), Suite 903   212/725-3511
Mon-Fri: 9-5   abccomputerservices.com

ABC Computer provides service, sales and supplies for desktop and laptop computers, as well as all kinds of printers. They'll work on Apple, Microsoft

CARPET PLUS

There's nothing like a clean, plush carpet to enhance the beauty of your home or office. The main carpeting problems come from dirt, food, pets and red-wine spills.

Flat Rate Carpet (212/777-9277, 866/466-4576, flatratecarpet.com): They will clean up a mess, re-stretch and Scotchgard carpeting, or clean mattresses, drapes, blinds and air ducts. Only organic cleaning products are used; emergency situations can be handled any time of day or night.

Rug Renovating (800/252-7738, rugrenovating.com): Since 1896 they have been cleaning, restoring and protecting fine rugs, carpets and furniture.

and Novell-based systems, and they are an authorized Hewlett-Packard service center. They have been around since 1988 which is a good recommendation in itself.

TEKSERVE

119 W 23rd St (bet Ave of the Americas and Seventh Ave)   212/929-3645
Mon-Fri: 9-8; Sat: 11-6   tekserve.com

Founded in 1987 as a service provider and retailer to support the Apple brand, Tekserve is proud of their roots. They are the largest single-site Apple premium service provider in North America. They assist customers with Mac repairs, honoring all in-warranty, AppleCare and out-of-warranty service issues. Tekserve also sells Apple products from OS X to iOS.

DELIVERY, COURIER AND MESSENGER SERVICES

AVANT BUSINESS SERVICES

60 E 42nd St (bet Park and Madison Ave)   212/687-5145
Daily: 24 hours   avantservices.com

Avant Business Services was doing round-the-clock local and long-distance deliveries even before the big shipping companies got in the business. If you have time-sensitive material, give them a call. They'll promptly pick up your item, even in the middle of the night or during a snowstorm.

SERVICE YOUR FIRE EXTINGUISHER

Every home should have at least one working fire extinguisher for emergency preparedness. **Able Fire Prevention** (241 W 26th St, 212/675-7777) sells new fire extinguishers and recharges old ones. Able offers pickup, delivery and installation, and sells cabinets and hardware for mounting extinguishers.

CLEMENTINE COURIER

Mon-Fri: 9-6:30   917/681-3936
clementinecourier.com

The foundation of this delivery service is quick service and cheap rates. Base rates start at $7 for an envelope delivery. Charges increase for special handling, time of day, zone, wait time, weight over ten pounds, larger packages and flights of stairs. In addition to urgent envelopes, Clementine's friendly couriers will deliver lunch or items provided by their personal shopping service. Someone is on duty 24/7 to handle the delivery needs of all five boroughs and surrounding states.

NEED IT NOW

153 W 27th St (bet Ave of the Americas and Seventh Ave), 1st floor
212/989-1919
Daily: 24 hours   needitnowcourier.com

Need It Now provides any and all courier services via walking, vans and trucks. They can handle everything from a crosstown rush letter (delivery completed within an hour) or a pre-scheduled service, to delivering nearly anything worldwide.

DRY CLEANERS AND LAUNDRIES

CLEANTEX

2335 Twelfth Ave (at 133rd St)   212/283-1200
Mon-Fri: 8-4   cleantexny.com

In business since 1928, Cleantex specializes in cleaning draperies, upholstered pieces, shades (Austrian, balloon and Roman), vertical blinds, Oriental and area rugs and wall-to-wall carpeting. They provide free estimates and will pick up and deliver. Museums, restaurants, churches and rug dealers are among their satisfied clients.

HALLAK CLEANERS

1232 Second Ave (at 65th St)   212/832-0750
Mon-Fri: 7-6:30; Sat: 8-5   hallak.com

Hallak Cleaners will celebrate their 50th anniversary in 2016. This family business is recognized as one of the country's premiere couture dry cleaners, shipping all over the country. All work is done in their 22,000-square-foot state-of-the-art plant – dry cleaning, bespoke shirt laundry and treatments for leather, draperies and rugs. They also specialize in cleaning and preservation of wedding gowns and antique pieces and offer museum-quality archival preservation. For those (like your author) who have trouble with stains on ties, Hallak is the place to go. Their skilled work takes time, though rush service is available at no additional cost. Free pickup and delivery is offered in New York City.

MADAME PAULETTE CUSTOM COUTURE CLEANERS

1255 Second Ave (bet 65th and 66th St)   347/689-7010
Mon-Fri: 7:30-7; Sat: 8-5; Sun: 10-3   madamepaulette.com

This full-service establishment has been in business since 1959. And what a clientele! Christian Dior, Vera Wang, Chanel, Givenchy, Louis Vuitton and Burberry. Madame Paulette does dry cleaning (including knits, suedes and

DEPENDABLE CLEANERS

Chris French Cleaners (57 Fourth Ave, 212/475-5444): an East Village favorite

Fashion Award Cleaners (383 Amsterdam Ave, 212/289-5623): full-service

G-G Cleaners (46 Grand St, 212/966-9813): legendary among fashion editors and boutique owners

Hallak Cleaners (1232 Second Ave, 212/832-0750): museum-quality cleaning

Jeeves New York (39 E 65th St, 212/570-9130): extra-special care for an extra price; pickups from 3 a.m.

leathers), tailoring (including reweaving and alterations), laundry and household and rug cleaning. Additionally, they provide seasonal storage of furs. Care of wedding dresses is a specialty, and they do superior hand-cleaning of cashmere, making sure that each item's shape is maintained. Other specialties include expert repair of garments damaged by water, bleach and fire, plus wet cleaning and hand-cleaning of upholstery and tapestry. Madame Paulette offers free pickup and delivery throughout Manhattan; one-day service is available upon request.

MEURICE GARMENT CARE

31 University Pl (bet 8th and 9th St) 212/475-2778
Mon-Fri: 7:30-6; Sat: 9-6; Sun: 10-3
245 E 57th St (bet Second and Third Ave) 212/759-9057
Mon-Fri: 7:30-6; Sat: 9-5 garmentcare.com

Meurice specializes in cleaning and restoring fine garments. Their Eco-Care process is environmentally friendly. They handle each piece individually, taking care of details like loose buttons and tears. Special services include exquisite hand-finishing; expert stain removal; museum-quality preservation, cleaning and restoration of wedding gowns; careful handling of fragile and chemically sensitive garments; on-site leather cleaning and repair and smoke, fire and water restoration. Pick up, delivery and shipping are available.

TIECRAFTERS

252 W 29th St (bet Seventh and Eighth Ave) 212/629-5800
Mon-Fri: 9-4:45; Sat: 10-2 tiecrafters.com

At Tiecrafters, old ties never fade away, instead they're dyed, widened, narrowed, straightened and cleaned. Since 1952 this business has acted on the belief that a well-made tie can live forever, and they provide services to make longevity possible. They restore soiled or stained ties and clean and repair all kinds of neckwear. Owner Andy Tarshis gives pointers on tie maintenance. (Hint: if you hang a tie at night, wrinkles will be gone by morning.) Tiecrafters offers several pamphlets on the subject, including one that tells how to remove spots at home. Their cleaning charge is reasonable, and they also make custom neckwear, bow ties, braces, scarves, vests and cummerbunds.

VILLAGE TAILOR & CLEANERS

125 Sullivan St (at Prince St) 212/925-9667
Mon-Fri: 7-7; Sat: 8-6 villagetailor.com

This Soho dry cleaner has been in business since 1977. Wash-and-fold shirt service is available, as is same-day turnaround. Village Tailor & Cleaners also make custom men's and ladies' apparel, including leather and suede garments. Alterations are performed, with tailoring of Nicole Miller gowns and designs a specialty.

ELECTRICIANS

ALTMAN ELECTRIC

94 E 4th St (bet First and Second Ave), 4th floor 212/924-0400
Daily: 24 hours altmanelectric.com

Family-owned and -operated for two generations, the licensed crew at this reliable outfit is available day and night for small or large jobs at home or office. Rates are reasonable for jobs such as increased power, showcase lighting or emergency repairs.

ELECTRONICS REPAIR

NYCIPODDOCTOR

By appointment   646/202-3935

nycipoddoctor.com

Drop your portable electronic device? Don't toss it out until you check with these doctors. The techs at NYCiPodDoctor provide on-site repairs at homes and businesses throughout Manhattan, replacing screens and making repairs to extend the life of your iPod, iMac, iPhone, laptop or other electronic gadget. If you're not in Manhattan, call to arrange for mail-in service. Free diagnostics are offered.

PORTATRONICS

2 W 46th St (at Fifth Ave), 16th floor   646/797-2838 (both locations)
Mon-Fri: 11-7
307 W 38th St (at Eighth Ave), 8th floor
Mon-Fri: 10:30-7; Sat: 11-7   portatronics.com

Portatronics provides on-the-spot repair of iPods, iPads, iPhones, laptops, smartphones, cameras, GPS, game consoles and more. Work on portable electronics may be done while a customer waits or the item is returned by mail. You'll find replacement hard drives, LCD screens, motherboards, headphone jacks and touch panels.

EMBROIDERY

JONATHAN EMBROIDERY PLUS

256 W 38th St (bet Seventh and Eighth Ave)   212/398-3538
Mon-Fri: 9-6; Sat: 9-4   jeplus.com

Any kind of custom embroidery work can be done at this classy workshop. Bring a photo or sketch or just give them an idea, and Jonathan Embroidery Plus (aka JE Plus) will produce a design you can amend or approve. They specialize in fashion embroidery on all types of fabrics, as well as embellishments with sequins, rhinestones, studs, beads and grommets. All kinds of garment printing (screen, digital and heat transfer) are also offered.

MONOGRAMS BY EMILY

224 W 30th St (bet Seventh and Eighth Ave), Suite 606   212/924-4486
By appointment only

Emily is one of the few still doing fine, detailed work on a hand-guided monogram machine. With over 30 years of experience, she guarantees that each monogram is stitched to your exact specification on items such as wedding-dress labels, men's shirts, handkerchiefs and other delicate items. She'll make suggestions on thread color and style to ensure perfect results.

EXTERMINATORS

ACME EXTERMINATING

365 W 36th St (at Ninth Ave)
Mon-Fri: 7-5

212/594-9230
acmeexterminating.com

Got uninvited guests? Acme provides pest extermination services to homes, offices, stores, museums and hospitals. They employ state-of-the-art pest-management technology.

FASHION SCHOOLS

FASHION INSTITUTE OF TECHNOLOGY

Seventh Ave at 27th St

212/217-7999
fitnyc.edu

In operation since 1944, the Fashion Institute of Technology is an internationally renowned college of art, design, fashion, business and communication. Part of the State University of New York system, FIT blends liberal arts with a real-world curriculum. Its graduates are successful in fashion, design and business. The college offers associate, bachelor's and master's degrees in advertising and marketing, fashion merchandising, fine arts, jewelry design, illustration, photography, production management, technical design, textiles and toy design. Industry leaders such as Jhane Barnes, Calvin Klein and Norma Kamali are among its distinguished alumni.

FORMAL WEAR

BALDWIN FORMALS

1156 Ave of the Americas (at 45th St), 2nd floor
Mon-Fri: 9-7; Sat: 10-5

212/245-8190
nyctuxedos.com

Going to an event? Baldwin has been taking care of style details since 1946. They rent and sell all types of formal attire: suits, overcoats, top hats, shoes and more. They will pick up and deliver for free in midtown and for a slight charge to other Manhattan addresses. Prompt alteration service (from two hours to several days) is available for an additional charge.

FUNERAL SERVICE

FRANK E. CAMPBELL THE FUNERAL CHAPEL

1076 Madison Ave (at 81st St)
Daily: 24 hours

212/288-3500
frankecampbell.com

In time of need, it is good to know of a highly professional funeral home. These folks have been providing superior service since 1898.

FURNITURE RENTAL

CHURCHILL FURNITURE RENTAL

44 W 24th St (bet Fifth Ave and Ave of the Americas)
Mon-Fri: 9:30-5:30 (by appointment)

212/686-0444
furniturerent.com

Churchill Furniture Rental carries a wide range of furnishing styles, from traditional to contemporary, to help you furnish any size residence or business.

They will rent anything from a single chair to equipping an entire home; free interior decorating advice as well. Churchill also offers help in staging for a home sale.

CORT FURNITURE RENTAL

140 E 45th St (bet Lexington and Third Ave), 5th floor   212/867-2800
Mon-Fri: 9-6; Sat: 10-4 (by appointment)   cort.com

CORT rents furnishings and accessories for a single room, an apartment or an entire office. The showroom, near Grand Central Terminal, shows all furnishings (including electronics and housewares) available for rental, with an option to purchase. The stock is large and varied, and delivery and setup can often be done within 48 hours. Check out their clearance items for purchase.

FURNITURE REPAIR

ALL FURNITURE SERVICES

Call for service   888/575-6757
furnitureservices.com

All Furniture will repair, restore and clean all parts of your furniture, from leather, fabric, caning and vinyl to wood and metal (including the innermost mechanisms). The same thoroughness holds true for rugs and carpets. Perhaps the most intriguing part of this business is their "take apart" service. If you're trying to move a ten-foot armoire through an eight-foot door frame, these experts will disassemble the oversized piece, transport it to the new spot and proceed with reassembly. They work with moving companies to tackle the most difficult pieces of furniture. Same-day and 24/7 emergency services are offered.

GARDENING

GROWNYC

51 Chambers St (bet Broadway and Centre St), Room 228   212/788-7900
Mon-Fri: 9-5   grownyc.org

GrowNYC's Grow Truck program lends and delivers garden tools, plants and horticultural advice to community greening efforts. Schools, community gardens, block associations and any new garden efforts are eligible to borrow tools. Loans are limited to one week, but the waiting period is not long and the price (nothing!) is right. You can borrow the same tools several times a season. This outfit is a huge resource for recycling information, too.

LONG-TERM HOME HEALTH CARE

When it becomes necessary to look into long-term home health care, call **Priority Home Care** (866/263-5074, priorityhomecare.com). Since 1992 they have provided professional and courteous live-in aides, respite relief care and home visits. Employees specialize in Russian, Asian, Spanish, Polish, Portuguese, Italian, Yiddish and French languages and customs.

RUSH DELIVERY

For quick and inexpensive same-day delivery of documents or small items in Manhattan, call **Elite Couriers** (212/696-4000) to dispatch a bicycle messenger (or motorcycle, van or truck). Rates are calculated on a base fee and by zone. This company has been in business since 1981 and serves many clients in the fashion and film industries.

HAIRCUTS

See additional Hair Care listings in Beauty Services beginning on page 276.

CHILDREN

COZY'S CUTS FOR KIDS

1416 Second Ave (at 74th St)   212/585-2699

COZY'S CUTS FOR KIDS WEST

448 Amsterdam Ave (at 81st St)   212/579-2600
Mon-Fri: 10-6; Sat: 9-6; Sun: 10-5   socozy.com

Cozy's takes care of kids of all ages, including the offspring of some famous personalities. What an experience: videos and videogames, themed barber chairs and balloons. They issue a "first-time" diploma with a keepsake lock of hair! Besides providing professional styling services, Cozy's is a toy boutique. "Glamour parties" for girls, makeup and glamour art projects, ear-piercing and mini-manicures are other services. Their own "So Cozy" hair-care products for children are available in-shop and online. Appointments are strongly suggested.

FAMILY

ASTOR PLACE HAIRSTYLISTS

2 Astor Pl (at Broadway)   212/475-9854
Mon: 8-8; Tues-Fri: 8 a.m.-9 p.m.; Sat: 8-8; Sun: 9-6   astorplacehairnyc.com

What started in 1947 as a neighborhood barbershop has become an East Village institution, giving some of New York's trendiest and most far-out haircuts. It all started when the Vezza brothers inherited their father's barbershop at a time when "not even cops were getting haircuts." Now over 35 stylists offer stylish haircuts at affordable prices.

FEATURE TRIM

1108 Lexington Ave (bet 77th and 78th St)   212/650-9746
Mon-Fri: 10:30-7; Sat: 10:30-6   featuretrim.com

Feature Trim specializes in highlights and coloring for men and women, hairstyling for women and natural haircuts for men. Easy care, reasonable prices, friendly faces and more than 60 years of experience have helped them maintain an impressive clientele. Appointments are encouraged, but walk-ins are welcome.

NEIGHBORHOOD BARBERS

439 E 9th St (bet First Ave and Ave A)   212/777-0798
Mon-Sat: 8-8; Sun: 10-7   neighborhoodbarbers.com

Neighborhood Barbers is a place to keep a clean-cut look while saving some dough. Owner Eric Uvaydov runs this no-frills East Village barbershop with only three chairs. Services include shampoo, shave and haircut, chest-hair trim, back shave and beard trims. You'll like the old-school prices and treatment; $24 for a haircut and shave.

PAUL MOLE BARBER SHOP

1034-A Lexington Ave (bet 73rd and 74th St)   212/535-8461
Mon-Fri: 7:30-8; Sat: 7:30-5:30; Sun: 9-4   Facebook

Paul Mole Barber Shop is a family business, and they have been around since 1913. This is a true gentlemen's barbershop, but they employ two children's barbers, too. Hours are customer-friendly and prices are affordable. Men can still get a straight-edged razor shave, manicure and shoeshine. You can even sit in one of the original chairs (refurbished, of course) that such notables as General George Patton or Joseph Pulitzer once occupied. The place is packed after school and on weekends, so appointments are strongly recommended.

HEALTH AND FITNESS CLUBS

Manhattan has a great variety of athletic facilities, and if you're considering joining a club, check newspapers or websites for membership enticements. Be sure to investigate a club thoroughly (staff, cleanliness, equipment, price and policies) before signing on the dotted line.

Visitors might have reciprocal arrangements through their "home" fitness centers, so check before you travel. Otherwise, most hotels offer some type of exercise equipment; some even have full-fledged facilities with personal trainers. And if you forgot to pack your workout gear or clothes conducive for exercising, they may be sold at some of the listed gyms. The better clubs often carry major brands and boutique fashions, as well as bodycare products and more.

24 Hour Fitness (225 Fifth Ave, 212/271-1002; 153 E 53rd St, 212/401-0660 and 136 Crosby St, 212/918-9811)

Bally Sports Club and Bally Total Fitness (multiple locations, 800/515-2582)

BFX Studio (555 Ave of the Americas, 917/382-5573): Fit 3D technology

Clay (25 W 14th St, 212/206-9200): fitness concierge service

Complete Body & Spa (10 Hanover Sq, 212/777-7702; 301 E 57th St, 212/777-7703 and 22 W 19th St, 217/777-7719)

David Barton Gym (656 W 6th St, 212/414-2022; 30 E 85th St, 212/517-7577 and 4 Astor Pl, 212/505-6800)

Dolphin Fitness Club (94 E 4th St, 212/387-9500)

Equinox Sports Club (160 Columbus Ave, 212/362-6800 and 330 E 61st St, 212/355-5100)

Hanson Fitness (42 Wooster St, 212/431-7682; 795 Broadway, 212/982-2233 and 132 Perry St, 212/741-2000)

REPAIR SERVICES

Here is a listing of some special services to be found in Manhattan:

CERAMICS

Ceramic Restorations (224 W 29th St, 12th floor, 212/564-8669): by appointment

CHIMNEY CLEANING AND REPAIRS

Homestead Chimney (800/242-7668): Tues-Fri: 8-4, by appointment

CLOTHING REPAIRS

Ban's Custom Tailor Shop (1544 First Ave, 212/570-0444)

LEATHER

Falotico Studio (315 E 91st St, 212/369-1217)

WATCH REPAIR

Master of Time (15 W 47th St, Booth 8, 212/354-8463)

WOODWORK RESTORATION

Traditional Line (212/627-3555): by appointment

Manhattan Plaza Health Club (482 W 43rd St, 212/563-7001)

The Movement (32 W 18th St, 646/491-9131)

New York Health & Racquet Club (multiple locations, 800/472-2378)

New York Sports Club (multiple locations, 800/666-0808)

Pablo Fitness (226 E 54th St, 212/308-0077): small classes

Paris Fitness (752 West End Ave, 212/749-3500)

Sal Anthony's Movement Salon (190 Third Ave, 212/420-7242): pay by the class or service for Pilates, massage, yoga and one-on-one sessions

Sports Center at Chelsea Piers (Pier 60, Twelfth Ave at Hudson River, 212/336-6000)

Uplift Studios (24 W 23rd St, 2nd floor, 212/242-3103): cardio drills and strength-training followed by a glass of wine; women only

Clubs with Child Care

Equinox Sports Club (multiple locations, 212/774-6363): all locations

New York Health & Racquet Club (800/472-2378): some locations

HEALTH AND FITNESS CLUBS | BY SPECIALTY

BARRE

The Bar Method (155 Spring St, 212/431-5720): ballet-inspired workout

Pure Barre (1841 Broadway, Suite 330, 917/344-9175 and 78 Fifth Ave, 4th floor, 917/675-1528)

BOOT CAMP

Barry's Bootcamp (135 W 20th St, 646/559-2721 and 1 York St, 646/569-5310): cardio and strength training

Circuit of Change (57 W 16th St, 4th floor, 212/255-0053): holistic workout
Warrior Fitness Boot Camp (29 W 35th St, 3rd floor, 212/967-7977): Train like a Marine.

PERSONAL TRAINERS

The Bodysmith Co. (212/249-1824): in-home training for women
FOCUS Integrated Fitness (115 W 27th St, 11th floor, 212/319-3816)
LA PALESTRA (11 W 67th St, 212/799-8900): training and wellness center
Madison Square Club (210 Fifth Ave, 212/683-1836)
Mike Creamer (142 Wooster St, 212/353-8834)
Nimble Fitness (42 E 12th St, 212/633-9030): complimentary assessment
Sitaras Fitness (150 E 58th St, 212/702-9700): a dozen personal trainers

PILATES

Power Pilates (920 Third Ave, 6th floor, 855/670-2897)
Real Pilates, Alycea Ungaro's Studio (177 Duane St, 212/625-0777)
Soho Sanctuary (119 Mercer St, 3rd floor, 212/334-5550): individual sessions

POMFIT

Pearl Studios (500-519 Eighth Ave, 212/904-1850): cheerleader-like fitness workout

PRENATAL

Maternal Massage and More (73 Spring St, 212/533-3188): pre- and postnatal, during labor and with baby, too
Patricia Durbin-Ruiz (349 E 82nd St, 646/643-8369): pre- and postnatal, yoga and Pilates
Physique 57 (24 W 57th St, Suite 805, 212/399-0570 and 161 Ave of the Americas, 212/463-0570): prenatal workout system and more

SPINNING

Flywheel Sports (39 W 21st St, 212/242-9433; 470 Columbus Ave, 212/242-5161 and 201 E 67th St, 212/327-1217)
Pedal NYC (33 West End Ave, 212/561-5435): spinning and more
SoulCycle (103 Warren St, 212/406-1300 and other locations): SoulBands class — spinning plus upper-body-strengthening resistance bands (at select studios)

SWIMMING

Asphalt Green Fitness (555 E 90th St, 212/369-8890): 50-meter indoor Olympic-standard swimming pool
Asser Levy Recreation Center (392 Asser Levy Pl, 212/447-2020): year-round indoor and two seasonal outdoor pools
Chelsea Recreation Center Pool (430 W 25th St, 212/255-3705): indoor pool, water-aerobics classes

FITNESS CONCIERGE

No more excuses! Vanessa Martin's fitness-concierge business, **SIN Workouts** (48 W 21st St, Suite 908, 212/488-6277), will do most anything to help keep you on track with your fitness goals and workouts; both at home and in the gym. SIN employees will recommend and book fitness classes, show up at 5 a.m. with coffee or your favorite green juice and arrange for car service. They will help you get acquainted with your fitness center, whether it be locating equipment, help with your lock or even picking out comfortable gym attire. Staff will set up your treadmill or bike and if needed, stand beside you to make sure you complete every last lunge or sprint. Services are tailored to your specific needs, and with all this encouragement you'll be in peak form in no time.

Manhattan Plaza Health Club (482 W 43rd St, 212/563-7001): atrium pool with retractable roof

YOGA

Asphalt Green Fitness (212 North End Ave, 212/369-8890): anti-gravity aerial yoga

Atmananda Yoga Sequence (67 Irving Pl, 2nd floor, 212/625-1511)

Bikram Yoga (143 W 72nd St, 212/724-7303; 182 Fifth Ave, 212/206-9400; 797 Eighth Ave, 212/245-2525 and 173 E 83rd St, 212/288-9642): based on hatha yoga postures, heated room

Integral Yoga Institute (227 W 13th St, 212/929-0585): ashram

Jivamukti Yoga School (841 Broadway, 2nd floor, 212/353-0214)

Joschi (163 W 23rd St, 5th floor, 212/399-6307)

Kula Yoga Project (28 Warren St, 4th floor, 212/945-4460): Vinyasa classes

Laughing Lotus Yoga Center (59 W 19th St, 3rd floor, 212/414-2903)

Pure Yoga (204 W 77th St, 212/877-2025 and 203 E 86th St, 212/360-1888)

YogaWorks (1319 Third Ave, 2nd floor, 212/650-9642; 138 Fifth Ave, 4th floor, 212/647-9642; 37 W 65th St, 4th floor, 212/769-9642 and 459 Broadway, 212/965-0801)

HOTELS

Today's unlimited access to travel planning information gives travelers a better–than-ever understanding of what to expect while on the road, including some of the more recent hotel trends. Renovations are huge, whether it is a major overhaul or just refreshing rooms and reimagining a lobby. Some hotels are opting out of traditional services like room service, and most now offer free Wi-Fi connection. Mini-bars are being replaced by mini-fridges with the option of ordering groceries to be stocked prior to arrival.

Hotel rates can be budget-breaking, particularly during holiday periods. If you are an intrepid traveler, you might try taking your chances by calling the front desk (rather than the toll-free reservation number) before departing. Room rates are usually better on weekends, when there are fewer business travelers. Sign up for loyalty or frequent-traveler programs, as regular guests may get special deals.

We list some hotels with very good accommodations for the money. Remember that during your stay you are (or ought to be) "out on the town" a good deal of the time, so rooms need not be fancy! The big things to watch for are cleanliness, security and service.

EXTENDED STAYS

If you are planning to be in Manhattan for awhile, check out these extended-stay facilities. Some require a 30-day minimum stay. Amenities may include kitchens, maid service, fitness and laundry facilities, business centers and planned activities.

59th Street Bridge Suites (351 E 60th St, 212/221-8300)

The Bowery House (220 Bowery, 212/837-2373): rooms with or without windows, shared baths

Bristol Plaza (210 E 65th St, 212/826-9000)

Marmara Manhattan (301 E 94th St, 212/427-3100): single night stays also

Off Soho Suites (11 Rivington St, 212/979-9815): no minimum requirement

Phillips Club (155 W 66th St, 212/835-8800)

Residence Inn New York (Times Square, 1033 Ave of the Americas, 212/768-0007)

Webster Apartments (419 W 34th St, 212/967-9000): women only

HOSTELS

American Dream Hostel (168 E 24th St, 212/260-9779): family-run and -owned; private and dormitory rooms ($59 and up)

Chelsea International Hostel (251 W 20th St, 212/647-0010): private and dormitory rooms; passport required for check-in

Hostelling International New York (891 Amsterdam Ave, 212/932-2300): one of the world's largest; dorm rooms start at $49

INEXPENSIVE

Belvedere Hotel (319 W 48th St, 212/245-7000)

Carlton Arms (160 E 25th St, 212/679-0680)

Chelsea Savoy Hotel (204 W 23rd St, 212/929-9353)

Chelsea Star Hotel (300 W 30th St, 212/244-7827): $99 and up; single with shared bath

The Evelyn (7 E 27th St, 212/545-8000)

Excelsior Hotel (45 W 81st St, 212/362-9200)

Holiday Inn Express Madison Square Garden (232 W 29th St, 212/695-7200)

HOTEL PRICE RANGES

I have categorized hotels by nightly room tariff (without taxes or surcharges) as follows:

Inexpensive	$199 and under
Moderate	$200-$399
Expensive	$400-$599
Very expensive	$600 and up

Keep in mind that approximately 15% will be added to your final bill for state and local sales taxes plus a "bed tax."

Holiday Inn Soho (138 Lafayette St, 212/966-8898)
Hotel 31 (120 E 31st St, 212/685-3060)
Hotel Grand Union (34 E 32nd St, 212/683-5890)
Hotel Metro (45 W 35th St, 212/947-2500)
Hotel Newton (2528 Broadway, 212/678-6500)
Hotel Stanford (43 W 32nd St, 212/563-1500)
The Wolcott Hotel (4 W 31st St, 212/268-2900)
Hudson New York (356 W 58th St, 212/554-6000)
La Quinta Inn Manhattan Midtown (17 W 32nd St, 212/736-1600)
Larchmont Hotel (27 W 11th St, 212/989-9333)
Manhattan Broadway Hotel (273 W 38th St, 212/921-9791)
Milburn Hotel (242 W 76th St, 212/362-1006)
Park Central New York (870 Seventh Ave, 212/247-8000)
Ramada Inn Eastside (161 Lexington Ave, 212/545-1800)

HOTELS NEAR AIRPORTS

The following hotels are conveniently located to three major airports. Most provide airport transportation and have restaurants, meeting facilities, business centers and Wi-Fi. Facilities such as fitness rooms and pools may also be offered.

JOHN F. KENNEDY INTERNATIONAL AIRPORT

Comfort Inn JFK Airport (144-36 153rd Lane, Jamaica, Queens, NY; 718/977-0001): complimentary breakfast, inexpensive

Fairfield Inn by Marriott JFK Airport (156-08 Rockaway Blvd, Jamaica, Queens, NY; 718/977-3300): complimentary continental breakfast, inexpensive

Hampton Inn JFK Airport (144-10 135th Ave, Jamaica, Queens, NY; 718/322-7500): complimentary breakfast, inexpensive

Sheraton JFK Airport Hotel (132-26 S Conduit Ave, Jamaica, Queens, NY; 718/322-7190): free Wi-Fi; moderate

LAGUARDIA INTERNATIONAL AIRPORT

Courtyard by Marriott New York LaGuardia Airport (90-10 Ditmars Blvd, East Elmhurst, Queens, NY; 718/446-4800):   outdoor pool and sundeck, moderate

Hampton Inn LaGuardia Airport (102-40 Ditmars Blvd, East Elmhurst, Queens, NY; 718/672-6600): complimentary breakfast and all-day beverages, inexpensive

LaGuardia Airport Hotel (100-15 Ditmars Blvd, East Elmhurst, Queens, NY; 718/426-1500): free Wi-Fi

LaGuardia Marriott (102-05 Ditmars Blvd, East Elmhurst, Queens, NY; 718/565-8900): 432 rooms, inexpensive to moderate

LaGuardia Plaza Hotel (104-04 Ditmars Blvd, East Elmhurst, Queens, NY; 718/457-6300): restaurant and lounge, inexpensive

NEWARK LIBERTY INTERNATIONAL AIRPORT

Crowne Plaza Hotel Newark Airport (901 Spring St, Elizabeth, NJ; 908/527-1600): nice indoor pool, inexpensive

DoubleTree by Hilton Newark Airport (128 Frontage Rd, Newark, NJ; 973/690-5500): indoor pool, inexpensive

Hilton Newark Airport (1170 Spring St, Elizabeth, NJ; 908/351-3900): inexpensive

Newark Liberty International Airport Marriott (1 Hotel Rd, Newark, NJ; 973/623-0006): on airport property, inexpensive

Wyndham Garden Hotel Newark Airport (550 U.S. Route 1 and 9 S, Newark, NJ; 973/824-4000): inexpensive

THE BEST HOTELS
IN EVERY PRICE CATEGORY

6 COLUMBUS

6 Columbus Cir (58th St bet Eighth and Ninth Ave)   212/204-3000
Moderate to expensive   sixtyhotels.com

Location is key at 6 Columbus with its close proximity to Central Park, the Theater District and many Michelin-starred restaurants. As you enter you are greeted by cheery 60s-era modernist design and decor. The 88 rooms (including 16 suites) in this extensively renovated 1903 building feature custom linens and furnishings and state-of-the-art technology. Just off the lobby is the popular Japanese restaurant, **Blue Ribbon Sushi Bar & Grill**, or perch awhile at popular **Above 6**, the indoor/outdoor rooftop lounge. The hotel is pet-friendly.

ACE HOTEL

20 W 29th St (bet Broadway and Fifth Ave)   212/679-2222
Inexpensive to moderate   acehotel.com

Ace Hotel is among the most original of the newer hotels in New York. It has something for everyone: affordable accommodations, fabulous restaurants, travel shops and nightly music in the lobby. The lowest room category is a bunk-bedded room for two. The next category has queen or full beds and a garment rack in lieu of a closet. Spend a bit more and rooms are larger with more amenities. All rooms have private baths, mini-refrigerators and minibars. Many rooms feature vintage or repurposed furnishings, turntables and records and original art from local and international artists. You can't go wrong with the hotel dining options: Michelin-starred **The Breslin** (English-style gastropub, with 24/7 room service), **The John Dory Oyster Bar** (seafood) and **Stumptown Coffee Roasters** (from my hometown of Portland, OR).

THE ALGONQUIN HOTEL

59 W 44th St (bet Fifth Ave and Ave of the Americas)   212/840-6800
Expensive   algonquinhotel.com

The Algonquin is legendary and was designated a historic landmark by the City of New York in 1987. This home of the famous Round Table — where Dorothy Parker, Alexander Woollcott, Harpo Marx, Tallulah Bankhead, Robert Benchley and other literary wits sparred and dined regularly — exudes the same charm and character as it did in the Roaring Twenties! There are 181 rooms, including 25 suites (some named after well-known personalities), with an intimate, friendly atmosphere. The busy lobby is an excellent spot for people watching. Amenities include comfy furnishings, a 24-hour fitness center, complimentary Wi-Fi and a business center. Enjoy a meal at **Round Table** or rendezvous at **Blue Bar**, the hotel's classic New York watering hole.

THE BENJAMIN

125 E 50th St (at Lexington Ave)   212/715-2500
Moderate to expensive   thebenjamin.com

In a restored 1927 building, The Benjamin has the ambience of a private club. The 209 rooms offer varying options, from a guest room with kitchenette to a one-bedroom terrace suite. Of note are the popular sleep offerings that include pillow choices, sleep masks, blackout drapes, lavender turn down, white noise machine and sleep-inducing spa treatments. For additional pampering, **Federico Hair & Spa** is on-site and a fitness concierge is on-call. For all day dining, a major dining plus is chef Geoffrey Zakarian's restaurant, **The National**, offering chef's signature modern bistro cuisine. A new pet program, **goodDOG**, has recently been launched.

THE BENTLEY HOTEL

500 E 62nd St (at York Ave)   212/644-6000
Moderate to expensive   bentleyhotelnyc.com

This 197-room Upper East Side hotel is situated in the shadow of Rockefeller University and affords views of the East River and skyline. The location is convenient to Central Park, renowned shopping areas and public transportation. Spacious rooms feature premium bedding, designer toilets and on-site parking. Beyond the gleaming façade is the sleek **Lobby Bar and Cafe** and **Prime**, which features a panoramic view and an eclectic, kosher menu.

THE BOWERY HOTEL

335 Bowery (bet 2nd and 3rd St)   212/505-9100
Expensive to very expensive   theboweryhotel.com

The Bowery is a posh and reliable destination with every amenity one would expect at a luxury hostelry. All guest rooms are classically designed for comfort and timeless elegance, with hardwood floors, large windows, upscale linens and toiletries and marble bathrooms (some of which include tubs with a view). The one-bedroom suites open onto private terraces, as does the **Lobby Bar**. Room service is available 24 hours a day from **Gemma**, the adjoining restaurant; hotel guests may make dinner reservations at this otherwise no-reservations restaurant.

THE BROOME

431 Broome St (bet Broadway and Crosby St)   212/431-2929
Moderate   thebroomenyc.com

You'll find a bit of French charm at this boutique hotel in Soho. The Broome has 14 rooms that are smallish, but clean and cozy, and all look out onto a beautiful courtyard with iron railings. Amenities in these modish spaces include a workspace, marble bathrooms, luxurious bathrobes and a complimentary continental breakfast. If you book five nights you'll enjoy a complimentary sixth night. A five-story atrium cafe and wine bar are located downstairs.

BRYANT PARK HOTEL

40 W 40th St (bet Fifth Ave and Ave of the Americas)   212/869-0100
Moderate to expensive   bryantparkhotel.com

Right across the street from Bryant Park, this contemporary hotel is situated in the historic American Radiator Building. It is favored by hip fashion and media types. Some suites have terraces to enjoy a birdseye view of the park, while the upper-floor suites have views of both the park and the Empire State Building. Amenities include Tibetan rugs and spacious marble bathrooms with soaking tubs. The property boasts a 62-seat private theater with plush seats, which is often used for press conferences and screenings. There are also two lofts of 1,100 square feet with ten foot ceilings, hardwood floors, natural light and city and park views. **Koi**, a Japanese fusion restaurant, and the **Cellar Bar** are on-premises.

THE CARLTON HOTEL

88 Madison Ave (bet 28th and 29th St)   212/532-4100
Moderate to expensive   carltonhotelny.com

Built in 1904 as the Seville Hotel, The Carlton blends modern comfort with historic preservation. In addition to 317 non-smoking rooms and suites there is a dramatic three-story lobby, a lobby bar and fine meeting facilities. For those doing business in the Madison Park, Gramercy Park or Murray Hill neighborhoods, the Carlton's urban setting is a convenient choice. Their excellent French restaurant, **Millesime**, is a dining plus.

HOTELS WITH EXCEPTIONAL SWIMMING POOLS

Crowne Plaza Times Square Manhattan (1605 Broadway, 212/977-4000): 15th-floor indoor lap pool in the New York Sports Club

Empire Hotel (44 W 63rd St, 212/265-7400): rooftop pool with Pool Deck menu and spa services (in summer only)

Gansevoort Meatpacking NYC (18 Ninth Ave, 212/206-6700): in the Meatpacking District; heated outdoor, year-round pool and great views; awesome "Renewal Day Package"

Holiday Inn Downtown (440 W 57th St, 212/581-8100): unheated pool on the 11th-floor deck (in summer only); nonguest passes available for minimal charge

Hotel Americano (518 W 27th St, 212/525-0000): outdoor pool on 10th floor with cozy cabanas (in summer only)

The James (27 Grand St, 212/465-2000): rooftop open-air plunge pool

Le Parker Meridien New York (118 W 57th St, 212/245-5000): penthouse year-round pool with sundeck (Central Park views); nonguests may purchase user passes

Mandarin Oriental New York (80 Columbus Cir, 212/805-8800): 75-foot year-round indoor lap pool in a dramatic setting on the 36th floor, with floor-to-ceiling windows

Millennium U.N. Plaza Hotel (1 United Nations Plaza, 212/758-1234): heated indoor pool (undergoing extensive renovation at press time)

The Peninsula New York (700 Fifth Ave, 212/956-2888): luxurious glass-enclosed facility with sundeck dining

Skyline Hotel (725 Tenth Ave, 212/586-3400): heated indoor pool

Thompson LES (190 Allen St, 212/460-5300): outdoor rooftop pool with Andy Warhol image (in summer only)

Trump International Hotel and Tower (1 Central Park W, 212/299-1000): 55-foot lap pool

Trump SoHo New York (246 Spring St, 212/842-5500): outdoor pool on 7th floor surrounded by deck chairs and lounge seating

CASABLANCA HOTEL

147 W 43rd St (bet Broadway and Ave of the Americas)   212/869-1212
Moderate   casablancahotel.com

The Casablanca Hotel is a hidden gem close to Times Square. It is a boutique hotel with Moroccan glamour and hospitality, small (48 rooms and suites) and family-owned. Free European-style continental breakfasts, afternoon tea and evening wine and cheese receptions are served in **Rick's Cafe**. Wi-Fi is available in all guest rooms, and you will pleased with the comfortable rates.

CITIZENM

216-218 W 50th St (bet Broadway and Eighth Ave)   212/461-3638
Moderate   citizenm.com

At citizenM you'll step into an art-filled lobby for self-check-in at welcome kiosks. This trendy but affordable hotel in Times Square has 230 compact double rooms. More spacious common areas include a lively lobby bar, a homey mezzanine library and guests-only rooftop lounge. citizenM stands for "citizen mobility" and in keeping with the high-tech concept, reservations are accepted only online; Wi-Fi and use of Apple computers in the library is free. Trim rooms with wall-to-wall windows make efficient use of the space; bedside Samsung tablets control everything from TV to room lighting and video art projection on the otherwise bare walls. In lieu of room service, the 24-hour lobby cafeteria, **canteenM**, offers snacks, sandwiches, salads and some hot items should you decide to dine in.

CROSBY STREET HOTEL

79 Crosby St (bet Prince and Spring St)   212/226-6400
Expensive   thecrosbystreethotel.com

This luxury boutique hotel is located on a quiet cobbled street in Soho. High ceilings and full-length windows provide city and courtyard views from 86 rooms, each individually decorated. Linens, technology and amenities are all top-drawer; the property also offers a state-of-the-art screening room, valet parking and event space. It is family-friendly with games, menus, toiletries and necessary items geared to kids; breakfast, lunch, afternoon tea and dinner are served in the **Crosby Bar**. The Meadow Suite comes with its own garden to enjoy. It's difficult to imagine that this space was a car park in its previous life.

DREAM MIDTOWN

210 W 55th St (bet Broadway and Seventh Ave)   212/247-2000
Moderate   dreamhotels.com

If you're dreaming of a trendy, modern boutique hotel, then the Dream Midtown is for you. There are an exotic two-story aquarium and artwork-covered vaulted ceilings. With 220 modern guest rooms and suites that have been floor-to-ceiling redesigned, it offers all the comforts of home and then some. You'll enjoy luxurious sheets and bathrobes, the latest in-room technology and complimentary overnight shoeshine. Try their Italian restaurant, **Serafina**; a bi-level rooftop lounge is set to open summer 2015.

FOUR SEASONS HOTEL NEW YORK

57 E 57th St (bet Madison and Park Ave)   212/758-5700
Expensive to very expensive   fourseasons.com

Fewer hotel names elicit higher praise or win more awards than Four Seasons. Upscale visitors to the Big Apple have an elegant, 52-story Four Seasons designed by I. M. Pei. This palatial establishment provides 368 generously-sized rooms and suites (some with terraces), several eating areas and a lobby lounge for light snacks and tea. There's also a fully-equipped business center, with freestanding computer terminals and modem hookups; a 5,000-square-foot fitness center and full-service spa; and numerous meeting rooms. The principal

HOTELS MOVE INTO GARMENT DISTRICT

For those who want a hotel away from the noise of Times Square, Manhattan's Garment District offers a growing number of lodging options. Traditionally home to the fashion industry, the area is bounded by Fifth and Ninth avenues from 34th to 42nd streets, within walking distance of Broadway theaters. These are some of the newer options, complete with Empire State Building views:

Archer Hotel (45 W 38th St, 212/719-4100): 180 rooms; David Burke's restaurant, **fabrick**; rooftop bar, **Spyglass**

Hyatt Herald Square (30-32 W 31st St, 212/330-1234): 122 rooms; reclaimed redwood paneling; **The Den** dining; rooftop lounge with views of midtown

Refinery Hotel (63 W 38th St, 646/664-0310): 197 rooms; 1912 former hat factory; restaurant **Parker & Quinn**; rooftop bar with retro decor

appeal, however, is the size of certain guest rooms, which run to 600 square feet, offer spectacular city views and feature luxurious marble bathrooms with separate dressing areas. The Ty Warner Penthouse Suite, one of the most expensive hotel rooms in the world, soars 800 feet above the city and offers 360 degree views.

GANSEVOORT MEATPACKING NYC

18 Ninth Ave (at 13th St)   212/206-6700
Moderate to expensive   gansevoorthotelgroup.com

Sleek and stylish, Gansevoort Meatpacking NYC is the first luxury full-service hotel in Manhattan's vibrant Meatpacking District. Chic design blends with hi-tech amenities in the 186 generously appointed guest rooms; featherbeds, Bluetooth sound systems and complimentary high speed Wi-Fi. Located on Ninth Avenue, the signature rooftop offers stunning views of the city and the Hudson River, and a 45-foot heated outdoor pool, **Plunge** bar and a rooftop garden are also featured. Eateries include several lounge areas and an American eatery, **The Chester**; pamper yourself at **Exhale Spa** or **Prieto Select Hair Studio**.

GRAMERCY PARK HOTEL

2 Lexington Ave (bet 21st and 22nd St)   212/920-3300
Expensive   gramercyparkhotel.com

This one-of-a-kind, eclectic hotel can best be described as antiestablishment. Each of the 185 rooms, six suites and penthouse is different. The Bohemian look of the place and its guests combine to make a stay here both fun and unusual. A rotating art collection of prominent 20th-century masters is an unexpected bonus. Old World-luxury, accented with contemporary touches, is found everywhere. Set aside time to relax at the unique **Rose Bar** or dine at Danny Meyer's Italian trattoria, **Maialino**; reservations required at these popular venues. An added bonus is guest access to private Gramercy Park.

THE GREENWICH HOTEL

377 Greenwich St (at N Moore St)   212/941-8900
Expensive   thegreenwichhotel.com

Owner Robert De Niro should be very proud! Each of the unique 88 rooms and suites at the Greenwich is individually decked out with Moroccan tiles, Tibetan rugs, reclaimed wood floors, English-leather settees, Swedish DUX beds, soaking tubs and small libraries. A lantern-lit swimming pool is the focal point of the exclusive **Shibui Spa**. Here services include massages, manicures, specialty soaks and facials. If you really want to splurge, check into the two-level, three-bedroom and two-and-a-half bath Tribeca Penthouse. The space offers an open floor plan with a full-sized chef's kitchen, four fireplaces (including one outdoor wood-burning fireplace on the upper level), private outdoor gardens and heated spa pool. For leisurely all-day dining, chef Andrew Carmellini's enticing Italian menu at **Locanda Verde** is a winner.

HILTON NEW YORK FASHION DISTRICT

152 W 26th St (bet Ave of the Americas and Seventh Ave)   212/858-5888
Moderate   newyorkfashiondistrict.hilton.com

With a nod to its Garment District locale, fashion-themed guest rooms feature tailored decor of pinstripe, herringbone, polka dot and silk-tie patterns. Furnishings throughout the ultra-modern boutique hotel are evocative of the iconic cutting and sewing rooms. Amenities include 37-inch flat-screen TVs, laptop-sized safes, cordless phones, Keurig coffeemakers and plush bedding and towels. Known for their burgers, the **Rare Bar & Grill** serves breakfast,

PET-FRIENDLY HOTELS

It seems that more people are travelling with their pets these days. Many hotels in Manhattan are pet-friendly, but you may be charged some additional fees. Here are a few locations to consider:

Archer Hotel (45 W 38th St, 212/719-4100)

The Bowery Hotel (335 Bowery, 212/505-9100)

Crosby Street Hotel (79 Crosby St, 212/226-6400)

Gramercy Park Hotel (2 Lexington Ave, 212/920-3300)

Langham Place, Fifth Avenue (400 Fifth Ave, 212/695-4005)

Loews Regency Hotel (540 Park Ave, 212/759-4100)

The Quin (101 W 57th St, 212/245-7846)

Refinery Hotel (63 W 38th St, 646/664-0310)

The Surrey (20 E 76th St, 212/288-3700)

Trump International Hotel and Tower (1 Central Park W, 212/299-1000)

HOTELS WITH PARADE VIEWS

Looking for a room with a view of the **Macy's Thanksgiving Day Parade**? This much-anticipated annual parade serpentines down Central Park West to Columbus Circle, takes a short jaunt on Central Park South before heading down Avenue of the Americas to 34th Street and the famed Macy's department store. Some hotels offer parade packages and specials. Make your reservations well in advance, but before plunking down a deposit, check on cancellation policies and occupancy limits and make sure your room is positioned to see this great holiday tradition.

6 Columbus (6 Columbus Cir, 212/204-3000)

JW Marriott Essex House New York (160 Central Park S, 212/247-0300)

Mandarin Oriental New York (80 Columbus Cir, 212/805-8800)

New York Hilton (1335 Avenue of the Americas, 212/586-7000)

Residence Inn New York (1033 Ave of the Americas, 212/768-0007): event spaces, too

The Ritz-Carlton New York, Central Park (50 Central Park S, 212/308-9100)

Trump International Hotel and Tower (1 Central Park W, 212/299-1000)

Warwick New York (65 W 54th Street, 212/247-2700)

lunch and dinner; the **Rare View Rooftop Bar** offers spectacular birdseye views and tasty libations.

HOTEL ON RIVINGTON

107 Rivington St (bet Essex and Ludlow St)   212/475-2600
Moderate   hotelonrivington.com

The sleek rooms at this upscale 21-story glass tower hotel have floor-to-ceiling glass walls that afford sweeping views of the city and the rivers; some rooms also have balconies. Luxurious furnishings and oversized closets enhance the larger-than-usual rooms. Some bathrooms have steam showers, Japanese soaking tubs or showers with a skyline view. Try **CO-OP Food & Drink** for new American offerings or the full bar at **Viktor and Spoils**.

HUDSON NEW YORK

356 W 58th St (bet Eighth and Ninth Ave)   212/554-6000
Inexpensive to moderate   hudsonhotel.com

Want a cool and stylish hotel? Hudson New York is an affordable hotel in an often unaffordable area. A lushly landscaped courtyard garden is open to the sky. You will find abundant amenities, including walk-in closets and a plush lounging sofa in some rooms. The 800 guest rooms and 13 suites reveal modern decor and furniture and attractive wood paneling. The scene is the big thing here, especially **Hudson Common**, a popular beer hall and burger joint.

INK48

653 Eleventh Ave (at 48th St)   212/757-0088
Expensive   ink48.com

The unlikely setting for this Kimpton hotel is a former printing house, explaining the names given **PRINT** restaurant, **Press Lounge** and **InkSpa**. The contemporary loft design of the 222 rooms and suites is accented by colorful accessories and furnishings, and the magnificent city and river views are framed by large windows. Guests are treated to complimentary morning coffee and tea service and loaner bicycles for pedaling Manhattan. Room service is available any time of the day. Pets are welcome; walking or sitting arrangements for your animal companion may be made through the concierge.

IROQUOIS NEW YORK

49 W 44th St (bet Fifth Ave and Ave of the Americas)   212/840-3080
Moderate   iroquoisny.com

This stylish luxury-boutique hotel certainly fulfills the meaning of location… location…location.   Classy and low-key Iroquois New York is conveniently close to Times Square, Radio City Music Hall, Fifth Avenue shopping, the Theater District and more.   The well-appointed 114 rooms and nine suites are furnished with plush Frette linens; amenities include complimentary Wi-Fi, overnight shoeshine, turndown service and daily room delivery of *The New York Times*.   Breakfast, lunch and dinner are served at **Triomphe**, the hotel's restaurant, where seasonal French dishes are featured. A cocktail salon, **Lantern's Keep**, is a popular gathering place just off the lobby. The concierge service at Iroquois is reported to be both well-informed and friendly.

THE JANE

113 Jane St (bet West and Washington St)   212/924-6700
Inexpensive to moderate   thejanenyc.com

The Jane hotel, once home to everyone from survivors of the Titanic to RuPaul, offers stylish and thoughtful accommodations for plucky travelers. All of the rooms at this former sailors' haven are designed like luxury train cabins with a single bed, built-in drawers, luggage rack, personal television, river views or a balcony. The famous 50-square-foot Standard room has communal bathrooms down the hall, while the larger Captain's Cabins feature en suites. Each room comes with an iPod-docking clock radio, free Wi-Fi, flat-screen TV with DVD player and complimentary bottled water.   There are several bar/lounge areas and the rooftop is open to the public for enjoying sunsets over the Hudson River. Do some two-wheel exploring on a complimentary cruiser.

JW MARRIOTT ESSEX HOUSE NEW YORK

160 Central Park S (bet Ave of the Americas and Seventh Ave)   212/247-0300
Moderately expensive to expensive   marriott.com

You'll love the superb location right on Central Park! The Essex House, a JW Marriott property, remains one of the prized resting places in Manhattan. The tastefully decorated rooms and suites are very comfortable and equipped with every modern amenity. A very attractive lobby and all-marble bathrooms add a classy flavor and a health spa and a club lounge with business center

HOTELS RACE TO ATTRACT SUPER-RICH

A trend that actually started in Europe is getting stronger in New York; a major push by hotels to outdo each other in attracting the super-rich. High-net individuals, generally foreign travelers, are accustomed to opulence, and this luxury lure has stimulated the creation of over-the-top, super suites. Hotels want bragging rights for these high-end offerings. One example is the Jewel Suite at **The New York Palace** (455 Madison Ave). This three-story, 5,000-square-foot space resembles a jewel box with crystals and marble, private rooftop hot tub, private elevator and an unequaled view of the Empire State and Chrysler buildings. At **Mandarin Oriental New York** (Time Warner Center, 80 Columbus Cir), a 3,300-square-foot space features floor-to-ceiling windows and a dining room that seats ten. And following a yearlong renovation, **Loews Regency Hotel** (540 Park Ave) now has six one-of-a-kind super suites. One can only imagine how far this trend will go!

add to the attractions. **South Gate** is a modern tavern that serves up an inventive American menu in glam quarters.

KIMBERLY HOTEL

145 E 50th St (bet Lexington and Third Ave)   212/702-1600
Moderate   kimberlyhotel.com

This charming and hospitable boutique hotel offers guests the kind of personal attention that is a rarity in today's world. There are 192 luxury rooms with marble bathrooms and in-room safes. One- and two-bedroom suites are fully equipped with executive kitchenettes, and private terraces come with most suites, some with spectacular Chrysler Building views. Dining options include **Bistango** for Italian offerings or visit **Ibis** for Mediterranean-inspired dishes. The penthouse-level bar and lounge, **Upstairs**, serves breakfast and small plates at night. There are on-site fitness facilities and access to the **New York Health & Racquet Club** is complimentary; there is a complimentary wine hour in the evening for all guests. Ask about the summer Kimberly yacht excursions, at special rates to hotel guests.

THE KITANO NEW YORK

66 Park Ave (at 38th St)   212/885-7000
Moderate   kitano.com

A tranquil hotel with Zen-like hospitality describes this Japanese-owned hotel in Manhattan. Rooms are clean, comfortable and uncluttered, with down comforters and spacious, marble bathrooms. Premium television channels and American and Japanese newspapers are complimentary. Many rooms offer views of Grand Central Terminal, the Empire State Building or Murray Hill. On-premises you can enjoy Japanese cuisine at **Habukai**, then move to **Jazz at Kitano** for a nightcap and world-class jazz.

THE KNICKBOCKER HOTEL

6 Times Square (at 42nd St)   212/204-4980
Expensive   theknickerbocker.com

Steeped in history, this hotel was built in 1906 by John Jacob Astor IV, only to close in 1920 largely due to prohibition. For years the building was used predominately as office space; it was placed on the National Register of Historic Places in 1980. With new owners and a $240 million restructure, the Knickerbocker Hotel reopened in February 2015. Many of the original exterior features were preserved, like the copper lion heads on the rooftop terrace, but the interior was completely redone. There are 299 rooms (including 31 suites) all in sleek, international style; of course you'll find all the tech bells and whistles. Many of the suites are named for previous residents like legendary tenor Enrico Caruso and renowned American playwright George Cohan. There's a lot going for this location just blocks from Broadway, MoMa, Fifth Avenue and Central Park. Chef Charlie Palmer's progressive American cooking is showcased at **Charlie Palmer at the Knick** on the fourth floor; a 7,500-square-foot rooftop bar overlooks the lights of Times Square and Broadway.

LANGHAM PLACE, FIFTH AVENUE

400 Fifth Ave (at 36th St)   212/695-4005
Expensive   newyork.langhamplacehotels.com

This contemporary beauty on Fifth Avenue is housed in a soaring 60-story skyscraper. Each of the 157 larger-than-usual guest rooms and 57 suites are impeccably appointed with fresh orchids, Pratesi linens, an espresso maker and a bathroom mirror which doubles as a television. Guests have 24/7 access to personal assistants and a fitness center. Michael White's popular and rustic Italian restaurant, **Ai Fiori**, serves three meals a day; the **Measure** lobby lounge is open nightly and hosts live jazz performances. Of course, such opulence comes with a price, so expect to pay big bucks for luxury with a view of the Empire State Building.

LE PARKER MERIDIEN NEW YORK

119 W 56th St (bet Ave of the Americas and Seventh Ave)   212/245-5000
Moderate to expensive   starwoodhotels.com/lemeridien

Lots going on with this large midtown hotel: great location, 721 ergonomically-designed rooms, atrium pool, junior suites with separate sitting

RENOVATIONS AT INTERCONTINENTAL NEW YORK BARCLAY

The **InterContinental New York Barclay** is currently undergoing a year-long $175 million renovation. This grande dame property is located at East 48th Street along a stretch of hotels that includes the Waldorf Astoria New York. The intent of the extensive renovation is to restore the 1926 hotel to its original federal-style elegance; 17 rooms will be added for a total of 702. Hopes are for a reopening in fall 2015.

MAXIMIZE YOUR LODGING DOLLARS

■ Rates may go down closer to your stay. Call before your cancellation deadline to see if that is the case, and then book again at the lower rate. Rather than have a glut of empty rooms, many hotels will drastically lower rates. Bargain with the hotel's desk clerk, not with whoever answers the hotel's off-site 800 number.

■ What is a high-demand night at one hotel may be a low-demand night at another. Depending on the timing, you may be able to stay in a more luxurious hotel.

■ Rates are typically lowest in January, February, late April and May.

■ Try the large chains' more budget-friendly brands, such as Hampton Inn (by Hilton), Fairfield Inn (by Marriott), Four Points (by Sheraton) and Holiday Inn Express. These outfits are significantly less expensive than the upscale names in the chain.

■ Stay in less expensive neighborhoods. The subway is likely just a few minutes away and often the money saved is well worth the short trip.

areas and oversized baths and showers. There are several excellent on-site eateries: **Norma's**, one of New York's top breakfast rooms; and one of the best burgers in town at street-level **Burger Joint at Le Parker Meridien New York**. **Knave** is an elegant espresso bar by day and alcohol bar at night. You can complete your daily workout in the 15,000-square-foot total wellness center. Note: If you are driving, the entrance to the hotel is on 56th Street.

LIBRARY HOTEL

299 Madison Ave (at 41st St)   212/983-4500
Moderate   libraryhotel.com

Travelers who are avid readers should check out the Library Hotel with its excellent midtown location. Sixty rooms are individually appointed with artwork and books, room numbers are ingeniously based on the Dewey decimal system and floors are organized by its ten major categories. Guests can enjoy glimpses of the New York Public Library from the 14th-floor Poetry Terrace. Continental breakfast and a three-hour wine-and-cheese reception are complimentary. Additionally, you'll find **Madison and Vine** (American bistro and wine bar) and **Bookmarks** (rooftop lounge) on-premises.

LOEWS REGENCY HOTEL

540 Park Ave (at 61st St)   212/759-4100
Expensive to very expensive   loewshotels.com

Following a recent $100 million renovation, the Loews Regency Hotel welcomes midtown guests to modern classic accommodations. Luxury abounds in 379 guest rooms (including 58 suites) with upgraded amenities in soothing neutral-hued rooms and stunning Park Avenue views. You'll find sleek, classic furnishings, Frette linens and bathrobes, smart TVs, free Wi-Fi and state-of-the-art technology. Services include turndown service, complimentary shoeshine, valet parking and **Julien Farel Restore Salon & Spa. Regency Bar & Grill** serves up American dishes with an emphasis on locally-sourced ingredients; the Power Breakfast presents the perfect opportunity for people watching.

THE LONDON NYC

151 W 54th St (bet Ave of the Americas and Seventh Ave)   212/307-5000
Expensive   thelondonnyc.com

This 54-floor midtown suites hotel boasts of being the tallest place to stay in Manhattan. First-class furnishings in 562 rooms offer views of Central Park and the city skyline, and the service is very personal. The luxury hotel offers a 24-hour business center, fitness facility and complimentary newspapers. **The London Bar** (small bites) and **Maze** (casual, French) provide excellent eating facilities and room service.

THE LOWELL

28 E 63rd St (bet Park and Madison Ave)   212/838-1400
Moderately expensive   lowellhotel.com

Like an attractive English townhouse, The Lowell is a well-located boutique hotel which features 74 guest rooms. The service and attention to detail are outstanding. Amenities include a 24-hour multilingual concierge service, at least two phones per room, complimentary Wi-Fi, DVRs, marble bathrooms, complimentary shoeshines and a fitness center. Wood-burning fireplaces warm 33 suites, some of which have private terraces and most include a full kitchen. Try the **Pembroke Room** for breakfast, brunch, pre-theater dinner (5 to 7) or their well-known afternoon tea.

MANDARIN ORIENTAL NEW YORK

Time Warner Center
80 Columbus Cir (at 60th St)   212/805-8800
Expensive to very expensive   mandarinoriental.com/newyork

Boasting a superior location at the Time Warner Center, Mandarin Oriental New York offers great views of Central Park from the 35th floor up. In its usual classy (and pricey) style, the Mandarin Oriental provides New York visitors 244 elegant rooms and suites, all beautifully furnished and equipped with state-of-the-art technology. The 35th-floor eateries include **Asiate**, which features modern American cuisine and room service, as well as **MObar**, a popular spot for drinks. A beautiful ballroom is available, and a two-story spa features "holistic rejuvenation." The 75-foot lap pool has a spectacular setting with views of the Hudson River.

THE MARITIME HOTEL

363 W 16th St (at Ninth Ave)   212/242-4300
Moderate   themaritimehotel.com

Located in an area with few modern hotels, The Maritime is making it convenient for those doing business in Chelsea. Amenities include a 24-hour fitness center, in-room safes, goose down duvets and oversized towels. The 126 cabin-inspired rooms and bathrooms are small, but all rooms face the Hudson River and feature five-foot porthole-style windows to enjoy the view.

REAL SMALL HOTEL ROOMS

Just when you thought New York hotel rooms couldn't get any smaller, they have! As you read the following, consider that the average hotel room is 320 square feet.

Ace Hotel (20 W 29th St, 212/679-2222): 140 square feet, twin bunk beds; moderate

The Jane (113 Jane St, 212/924-6700): 50 square feet, bunk-bed cabin with communal bathroom; inexpensive

The Pod Hotel (230 E 51st St, 212/355-0300): 70 square feet, bunk pod with shared bath or 120 square feet with double bed; inexpensive

The Standard High Line (848 Washington St, 212/645-4646): 250 square feet, standard queen; moderately expensive

Yotel (570 Tenth Ave, 646/449-7700): 167 square feet, premium cabin with overhead bunk; moderate

Dramatic Asian restaurant, **Tao Downtown**, is quite a party scene; and word has it that a Mario Batali restaurant is in the works as well.

THE MARK

25 E 77th St (at Madison Ave)   212/744-4300
Very expensive   themarkhotel.com

In a landmark building dating back to 1927, this beautiful retreat is reminiscent of a luxurious 1930s Parisian hotel — with a modern twist. There are 150 rooms and suites, outfitted with advanced technologies and specially designed Italian linens for bed and bath. Some studios and suites include custom kitchens. **The Mark Restaurant by Jean-Georges** is an exemplary elegant dining venue. The handcrafted signature cocktails at the **Mark Bar** are similarly superior. Service and personal attention at this exclusive address are topnotch. Additional features are a gym, Frederic Fekkai salon, daily newspaper delivery and complimentary shoeshine.

THE MARLTON HOTEL

5 W 8th St (bet Fifth Ave and Ave of the Americas)   212/321-0100
Moderate   marltonhotel.com

A $10 million transformation of this 1900s building marks the revival of the Village's 8th Street, culminating with The Marlton Hotel. The lobby is welcoming with weathered marble floors and wood-burning fireplace. Within the nine floors, 102 snug rooms feature crown molding, mahogany closets, hand-shaped light fixtures and French accents; luxury bath products, free Wi-Fi and complimentary breakfast, too. Chic and clubby **Margaux** restaurant offers a seasonally-driven French/Mediterranean menu and seems to have attracted the attention of stylistas for afterwork drinks, dinner and weekend brunch. The room is charming with a spectacular skylight and floral tiles; there is also a vibrant bar.

MONDRIAN SOHO

9 Crosby St (bet Grand and Howard St)   212/389-1000
Moderate   mondriansoho.com

Mondrian Soho is a charming member of the Morgans Hotel Group. The 270 "sleeping chambers" (guest rooms) are decorated in a romantic blue-and-white color scheme. Benjamin Noriega-Ortiz used "La Belle et la Bête" as a theme throughout. Elegant foyers, mirrors, crystal sconces and jewel-toned doors add sparkle inside the property. Each comfortable room affords a view of Manhattan and is outfitted with an iPod docking station, spa bathroom and chrome desk. Optional in-room spa services are a relaxing treat. Italian restaurant **Isola Trattoria & Crudo Bar** is inspired by the Italian coast and serves breakfast, lunch and dinner. A seasonal rooftop bar is an excellent summer destination offering panoramic views of the city.

MORGANS HOTEL

237 Madison Ave (bet 37th and 38th St)   212/686-0300
Inexpensive to expensive   morganshotel.com

Exceptional attention, lush amenities and a fabulous location make this 114-room beauty a welcome stop for discriminating travelers. Andrée Putman designed the signature black, white and gray interiors of this boutique hotel. Soothing Malin+Goetz toiletries are a luxurious touch. Rooms are equipped with desks, flat-screen HDTV and Wi-Fi and there is a state-of-the-art fitness center. Continental breakfast and daily newspaper are complimentary.

NEW YORK HILTON

1335 Ave of the Americas (bet 53rd and 54th St)   212/586-7000
Moderate to moderately expensive   newyorkhiltonhotel.com

For leisure travelers interested in shopping, theater, Radio City Music Hall and other midtown attractions, the New York Hilton midtown location is highly desirable. A popular business and convention hotel, the Hilton outfits its rooms with the most up-to-date communications equipment. Special features include an outstanding art collection, upscale executive floors with a private lounge and large luxury suites, dozens of rooms equipped for the disabled, a highly trained international staff and an 8,000-square-foot state-of-the-art fitness club and spa. The New York Hilton features several eating and drinking spaces, including **Herb N' Kitchen** (seasonal salads, sandwiches and pizzas) and **minus5** ice bar.

NEW YORK MARRIOTT DOWNTOWN

85 West St (at Battery Park)   212/385-4900
Moderate   nymarriottdowntown.com

Close to Lady Liberty! For those doing business in the Wall Street area, this 497-room hotel (490 rooms and 7 suites) is ideal. Contemporary and deluxe rooms offer quality amenities including restful Revive beds with down comforters, marble bathrooms, a great fitness center and spectacular views of the harbor and Statue of Liberty. The newly renovated concierge lounge offers complimentary breakfast and hors d' oeuvres. Be sure to check out the popular **Bill's Bar & Burger**, now serving delicious burgers, fries and shakes.

NEW YORK MARRIOTT MARQUIS

1535 Broadway (bet 45th and 46th St)   212/398-1900
Moderate to expensive   nymarriottmarquis.com

This one puts you in the hustle and bustle of Times Square! The New York Marriott Marquis has nearly 2,000 guest rooms and suites, sizable meeting and convention facilities and one of the largest hotel atriums in the world. Visitors can enjoy the two-story revolving rooftop restaurant and lounge, **The View**, or visit **Crossroads American Kitchen & Bar** for more casual breakfast, lunch or dinner. In addition, a legitimate Broadway theater, a fully-equipped health club and a special concierge level are on the property.

THE NEW YORK PALACE

455 Madison Ave (bet 50th and 51st St)   212/888-7000
Expensive   newyorkpalace.com

Since its recent multi-million dollar renovation, The New York Palace has a stunning redesign and much improved technology. Located close to Rockefeller Center, the 899-room hotel offers commanding views of the city skyline. The public rooms encompass the 1882 Villard Mansion, a legendary New York landmark. Amenities include The Towers, Tower Club and a spa and fitness center. A multilingual concierge staff is ready to serve guests, and function space and a business center are offered. Be sure to visit **Pomme Palais**, a delightful bakery that also serves lunch items like tarts, crab cake sandwiches and French onion soup; several inviting lounge areas are located within the hotel. A complimentary shuttle goes to Wall Street and the Theater District.

NH JOLLY MADISON TOWERS

22 E 38th St (at Madison Ave)   212/802-0600
Moderate   jollymadison.com

Located right in the heart of Manhattan, this charming European-style hotel has 242 tastefully decorated rooms, just blocks from the best shopping and attractions. Nothing fancy here, but everything is clean and comfortable, and some rooms on the top floor have views of the Empire State Building. The **Whaler Bar**, a breakfast room and meeting rooms are among the amenities. For a minimal fee, small pets (defined as up to 20 pounds) are welcome.

NYLO NEW YORK CITY

2178 Broadway (at 77th St)   212/362-1100
Moderate to expensive   nylo-nyc.com

On the Upper West Side this is a great place for those who plan to visit the legendary Zabar's, the American Museum of Natural History, Columbus Circle and other attractions in the area. With a roaring 20s theme, there are vintage accents throughout, including a beautiful lobby library with fireplace. Room choices include lofts and apartment-style suites, with amenities like beautiful bed linens and towels, Italian black-marble bathrooms, private balconies, concierge and business center. Open balconies on the 14th and 16th floors offer super views and comfortable chairs to all guests. Great pizzas, pasta and small plates can be enjoyed at rustic Italian restaurant, **Serafina**.

THE PENINSULA NEW YORK

700 Fifth Ave (at 55th St)
Expensive

212/956-2888
newyork.peninsula.com

When the name "Peninsula" is mentioned, the words quality and class immediately come to mind. The Manhattan property is certainly no exception. This 1905 landmark offers 239 luxurious rooms, including the palatial Peninsula Suite (3,300 square feet at $24,000 per night!). Room features include oversize marble bathrooms with numerous amenities, printers, large work desks and audiovisual systems with cable. Features of the 21st-floor Peninsula Spa include an enclosed pool, sun terrace, modern fitness equipment and spa services. Newly-renovated **Gotham Lounge** provides afternoon tea, light lunch and dinner; rooftop hot spot **Salon de Ning** lists Chinese-inspired dishes and cocktails amid dramatic views from its east and west terraces and newcomer **Clement** offers all-day dining plus afternoon tea service.

THE PIERRE

2 E 61st St (at Fifth Ave)
212/838-8000
Very expensive

tajhotels.com

Overlooking Central Park, The Pierre is the U.S. flagship property of the Taj Hotels. The 189 elegant guest rooms (49 are suites) are in luxurious residential-style with rich woods, silk and brocade fabrics and bathrooms that incorporate floor-to-ceiling, glass-walled showers and soaking tubs. The in-room entertainment and electronics are first-class. Function rooms remain a popular venue for Manhattan's glitziest events. The well-loved Sirio Maccioni offers traditional Italian dishes at **Sirio Ristorante**. Lobby lounge **Two E Bar** is a grand watering hole and an option for light meals and coveted afternoon tea. A 24-hour fitness center and beauty salon are on-site. With a ratio of three staff members per guest, impeccable and attentive service is assured.

WITHOUT A ROOM?

You'll want to download this helpful (and free) phone app. **Hotel Tonight** lists unsold rooms each morning at 9 for the town you're in, and the same-night rates are sometimes impressively low; sometimes up to 70% off standard rack rates.

THE PLAZA

Fifth Ave at Central Park S
Expensive to very expensive

212/759-3000
theplazany.com

The Plaza has been a focal point for New York residents and visitors for decades as it possesses one of Manhattan's most prized and well-known landmark locations. Besides privately-owned residential suites on Fifth Avenue and Central Park South, there are currently 282 guest rooms (102 are suites) on 58th Street which continue to welcome New York guests; 24-hour butler service is offered to guests in suites. Under the culinary direction of chef Geoffrey Zakarian, legendary **Palm Court** is still an unforgettable choice for afternoon tea or evening snacks and cocktails; the **Plaza Food Hall** and

Todd English Food Hall bring additional exciting dining options. Top-notch amenities include the world-class **Shops at The Plaza** and health and wellness facilities **Caudalie Vinothérapie Spa, Warren-Tricomi Salon** and **LA PALESTRA** training and wellness center.

THE QUIN

101 W 57th St (at Ave of the Americas)   212/245-7846
Expensive   thequinhotel.com

Just a block from Central Park and iconic Fifth Avenue shopping, the former Buckingham Hotel was re-christened as the Quin after massive renovations. It now embodies everything that is quintessential New York: renowned architecture with contemporary finishes, progressive art at every turn and professional and all-inclusive resources. This address was home away from home to many musicians, artists and actors through the years. Luxury abounds in the 208 guest rooms (including suites) which are furnished with plush, clean lines and special touches like Nespresso machines; Bergdorf Goodman's personal shoppers are on speed-dial. Hotel attachés deliver personalized care by arranging shopping trips, booking gallery tours and acquiring coveted restaurant reservations. If you are staying in for the night, you'll find classic American fare at **Wayfarer.**

REFINERY HOTEL

63 W 38th St (bet Fifth Ave and Ave of the Americas)   646/664-0310
Moderate   refineryhotelnewyork.com

This former hat factory turned luxury hotel is conveniently located in the Garment District. The neo-gothic 12-story building offers 197 guest rooms just blocks from Bryant Park, the theater district, Times Square and the Empire State Building. Chic rooms feature 12-foot ceilings and large windows that open (providing lots of natural daylight), dark oak hardwood floors, handmade wool rugs and original artwork, much of which is locally created. There are several onsite eateries: signature restaurant **Parker & Quinn** offers all meals, plus weekend brunch and the **Refinery Hotel Rooftop** is a popular cocktail bar with retro decor, live entertainment and views of the Empire State Building.

THE RITZ-CARLTON NEW YORK, BATTERY PARK

2 West St (at Battery Park)   212/344-0800
Expensive

THE RITZ-CARLTON NEW YORK, CENTRAL PARK

50 Central Park S (at Ave of the Americas)   212/308-9100
Expensive   ritzcarlton.com

These two properties provide the outstanding service, comfort and amenities identified with The Ritz-Carlton name. At both locations you'll find great views, top-grade lobby-level restaurants, gym and spa services, luxurious rooms and bathrooms and business centers. Club Level guests get special treatment, which may include unpacking and packing services, a library of children's DVDs and an assortment of snacks and beverages.

ROYALTON

44 W 44th St (bet Fifth Ave and Ave of the Americas)   212/869-4400
Expensive   royaltonhotel.com

When you step into the Royalton lobby, you are greeted by a sophisticated environment with a vintage feel. A combination of glass, brass, wood and leather make up the brilliant designer interior. The midtown location provides proximity to Rockefeller Center, Broadway and Times Square. The hotel's 168 rooms feature banquette seating, work areas and slate bathrooms, some include wood-burning fireplaces and round soaking tubs. For breakfast, lunch and dinner, guests can enjoy American fare at **Forty Four;** or grab a cocktail at the buzzing neighborhood bar, a gem for those who like to see and be seen. Royalton also offers a 24-hour fitness center and valet parking.

ST. REGIS NEW YORK

2 E 55th St (at Fifth Ave)   212/753-4500
Expensive   starwoodhotels.com/stregis

The St. Regis, a historic landmark in the heart of Manhattan, is rightfully one of the crown jewels of Starwood Hotels & Resorts. The hotel's 171 guest rooms and 67 suites have been dramatically redesigned with luxurious accommodations. All rooms feature marble baths, sumptuous linens, silk wall coverings and round-the-clock butler service (including free pressing of two garments upon arrival). Dine at the newly renovated **King Cole Bar & Salon**, providing breakfast, lunch and dinner; or enjoy afternoon tea and harpist Wednesday through Sunday.

SALISBURY HOTEL

123 W 57th St (bet Ave of the Americas and Seventh Ave)   212/246-1300
Moderate   nycsalisbury.com

I highly recommend the Salisbury as one of New York's best hotel deals near Carnegie Hall and other midtown attractions! Capably run by Edward Oliva, it has nearly 200 rooms and suites with walk-in closets and safes; many rooms are outfitted with butler's pantries and refrigerators. Suites are large, comfortable and reasonably priced; the thick walls really are soundproof! If you've waited until the last minute for reservations, the Salisbury is less well-known among out-of-towners, and therefore may have available rooms. A continental breakfast buffet and Wi-Fi are available for a nominal charge; nearby parking is discounted for hotel guests with cars. I'm sure that you will agree that folks here are exceedingly friendly.

SHERATON NEW YORK TIMES SQUARE HOTEL

811 Seventh Ave (at 53rd St)   212/581-1000
Moderate to moderately expensive   sheratonnewyork.com

With an outstanding location in central Manhattan, the Sheraton New York Times Square is an excellent choice for tourists and business travelers. Polished, contemporary upgrades include pillowtop mattresses, ergonomic desk chairs and extra storage. Club Room guests have exclusive access to the Club Lounge on the 44th floor which provides breathtaking views, complimentary continental breakfast, evening hors d'oeuvres and beverages and other privileges. Take advantage of the state-of-the-art fitness center by Core Performance and the large selection of equipment, classes, trainers and saunas. Several in-house eateries include **Hudson Market** (breakfast, brunch and dinner) and **Hudson Market Bistro** (dinner).

THE STANDARD HIGH LINE

848 Washington St (at 13th St)   212/645-4646
Moderately expensive   standardhotels.com/high-line

This ultramodern Meatpacking District hotel straddles the High Line — a defunct elevated freight railway that is now a linear park. Wall-to-wall and floor-to-ceiling windows in the 338 guest rooms and suites provide views of the Hudson River and dramatic skyline. Rooms have see-through bathrooms with soaking tubs and walk-in rain showers, extra-large-sized towels and cozy robes. Wi-Fi is complimentary and you can work out while taking in the amazing views from the 17th-floor gym. Food and beverage options are plentiful. **The Standard Grill** and **The Biergarten** are under the High Line, and **Top of the Standard** is rooftop for small plates and Sunday brunch.

TRAVEL EXPERTS

If you wish to use a travel agency for assistance with complicated bookings, group tours or emergencies, here are some established choices:

AAA Travel (1881 Broadway, 212/586-1723): discounted rates on travel bookings with AAA membership

Liberty Travel (86 Nassau St, 212/608-0073): locations around Manhattan and the outer boroughs

THE STRAND HOTEL

33 W 37th St (bet Fifth Ave and Ave of the Americas)   212/448-1024
Moderate   thestrandnyc.com

The Strand Hotel NYC is located just off Fifth Avenue in midtown Manhattan, in the heart of the Fashion District. The 176 rooms are adorned in distinctive upholstered pieces, neutral shades and light textures. Warm mahoganies and rich walnuts complement soft-paletted walls that display vintage prints culled from *Condé Nast* archives. Relax in the whimsical **Strand Restaurant** for contemporary American dining or enjoy breathtaking views of the Empire State Building and skyline from **Top of the Strand,** a year-round rooftop lounge. Turn-down service, early morning coffee and tea available to go, a complimentary wine hour, 24-hour fitness center access and free Wi-Fi all add to your stay.

THE SURREY

20 E 76th St (bet Madison and Fifth Ave)   212/288-3700
Expensive   thesurrey.com

Built in 1926 as a residence hotel, the original Surrey was home to many celebrities. It is now modernized and yet maintains its classic integrity. Each of the 189 rooms is tastefully appointed and serenely elegant. Salons include handpainted wardrobes; some rooms are enhanced with fireplaces and terraces. Elsewhere on the property is a private, seasonal roof garden for guests and a fitness center that never closes. **Bar Pleiades** and **Café Boulud**, under the direction of chef Daniel Boulud, are delightful cocktail and dining destinations; or you can enjoy their French fare in your room. Pets are welcome and pampered in style.

TRUMP INTERNATIONAL HOTEL AND TOWER

1 Central Park W (at 60th St)   212/299-1000
Expensive   trumphotelcollection.com

Trump International is everything you'd expect from a place with The Donald's name attached — handcrafted chandeliers, gold-leaf mirrors, rich wood and plush seating in the 176 luxury suites and guest rooms. Rooms have fully-equipped kitchens and many rooms have wonderful views of Central Park. Besides 24-hour room service, complete office facilities, entertainment centers in every room, a state-of-the-art fitness center, a swimming pool and marble bathrooms, there are special amenities like fresh flowers, umbrellas and garment bags. One of Manhattan's best (and more expensive) restaurants, **Jean Georges**, will pamper your taste buds; like the hotel, it has a five-star, five diamond rating.

TRUMP SOHO NEW YORK

246 Spring St (at Varick St)   212/842-5500
Expensive   trumphotelcollection.com

The legendary Trump hospitality and opulence is also available downtown at Trump SoHo New York. This newer high-rise hotel boasts 391 guest rooms, of which 132 are one-bedroom suites, eight are penthouse suites and three are spa suites connecting to **The Spa at Trump**. Each luxurious room is custom furnished by Fendi Casa with Bellino bed linens creating serene, contemporary elegance. The TV remote also controls lights, drapes and room temperature. All rooms include spacious bathrooms with large soaking tubs and separate showers, Nespresso machines, microwaves and minibars. Privacy is optimized, with only 12 guest rooms per floor. Views of the city from the rooms are exceptional. Try contemporary Japanese cuisine at fabulous **Koi** restaurant and good eats at seasonal **Bar d'Eau** adjacent to the outdoor pool deck.

VICEROY NEW YORK

120 W 57th St (bet Ave of the Americas and Seventh Ave)   212/830-8000
Expensive   viceroyhotelsandresorts.com

Viceroy New York is a striking property with an excellent midtown location close to Manhattan's most popular attractions. The hotel boasts a double-height lobby accented by marble and vintage elements. Every one of the 240 guest rooms (including 42 luxury suites) feature floor-to-ceiling windows, many with sprawling panoramas of Central Park. Exotic woods, leather and metal accents and handmade lighting fixtures decorate each space. Service is paramount at Viceroy with both 24-hour room service and personal concierge, complimentary newspapers and magazines upon request, twice-daily housekeeping and available babysitting and translation services. Street-level restaurant, **Kingside**, features chef Marc Murphy's new American cuisine. Capping it all is **The Roof,** an alluring lounge and outdoor terrace serving

BEWARE ILLEGAL HOTELS

Over the years, complaints of illegal hotels have garnered little effort to identify and crackdown on responsible parties, but in 2014, numerous lawsuits and thousands of dollars in penalties have been issued against owners. These are opportunistic entrepreneurs trying to capitalize on record-high tourism and the demand for hotel rooms by illegally renting out apartment rooms. One such known property is **The Branson** (15 and 19 W 55th St), with no concierge, bellhop or front desk. Apartment keys are handed out by a doorman who checks your name off a list; no proof of reservation or photo ID is required. If that doesn't make you suspicious, perhaps the dirty looks from the building tenants will tell you this is not a hotel. Illegal hotel reservations are unknowingly found on such websites as **booking.com** and **hotels.com** where they are advertised as suites or luxury rooms. Do your research before committing to lesser known real estate for your NYC stay!

handcrafted cocktails, regionally-brewed craft beers and small-batch spirits; the extraordinary views will complete your visit!

W NEW YORK

541 Lexington Ave (bet 49th and 50th St)   212/755-1200
Moderately expensive   wnewyork.com

Located in midtown, this Starwood property has 688 rooms (including 62 spacious suites), a large ballroom, Bliss49 Spa, FIT gym for private and semi-private training and 24-hour room service. The look is strictly modern. Dining options include casual American at **Heartbeat** or an upbeat cocktail lounge with small bites at **Whiskey Blue**. Pets (dogs and cats) are pampered with the P.A.W. program (Pets Are Welcome).

W NEW YORK TIMES SQUARE

1567 Broadway (at 47th St)   212/930-7400
Moderately expensive   wnewyorktimessquare.com

This 57-story W flagship features 509 guest rooms and 43 suites in the heart of Times Square. The modern, high-energy space offers a classy retail store, FIT gym, 24-hour room service, pillowtop mattresses and feather beds, comfy robes and other quality amenities. Ask to stay on the highest floor possible, as the views of Times Square and the Hudson River are dramatic. If you just want to stay in, **Blue Fin** restaurant offers savory seafood and **The Living Room** bar is open until the wee hours. The hotel is pet-friendly.

WALDORF ASTORIA NEW YORK

301 Park Ave (at 50th St)   212/355-3000
Moderate to expensive   waldorfnewyork.com

The Waldorf Astoria New York has been world-renowned for over a century as one of the first "grand hotels" to combine elegance, luxurious amenities and personal service. The rich, impressive lobby is bedecked with magnificent mahogany wall panels, hand-woven carpets and a 148,000-tile mosaic floor. The upper floors house the Waldorf Towers, home to celebrities, royalty and every American president since Herbert Hoover. The more than 1,400 stately guest rooms and select suites are spacious and richly appointed. Forty meeting venues and ballrooms accommodate special events of most any size. The Grand Ballroom is the only two-tiered, four-story ballroom with a full Broadway stage in New York. Guerlain Spa and the hotel's on-site fitness center are available 24/7. The famed Waldorf Astoria Sunday brunch is served at **Peacock Alley**, just off the elegant lobby. You'll also find **Bull & Bear** (steaks, seafood and bar) and the more casual **Oscar's American Brasserie** (breakfast and lunch).

WASHINGTON SQUARE HOTEL

103 Waverly Place (at MacDougal St)   212/777-9515
Inexpensive to moderate   washingtonsquarehotel.com

Located in historic Washington Square Park, this hotel offers good value in rooms, a capable staff and a nice restaurant. Since 1902 this location has been handy for many artists and writers, for those with business at New York University or visitors who want to explore the Village. The 152 guest rooms are art deco in style and are comfortably equipped with pillowtop mattresses, Keurig coffeemakers, granite-top vanities; complimentary Wi-Fi and continental breakfast are available. **North Square** is a classy on-site venue for cocktails or dining or visit the Deco Room for formal tea service. And for a meal in the park, request a picnic lunchbox.

THE WOLCOTT HOTEL

4 W 31st St (bet Fifth Ave and Broadway)   212/268-2900
Inexpensive to moderate   wolcott.com

Perhaps one of Manhattan's better hotel bargains, The Wolcott Hotel offers a good location (just south of midtown) with views of the Empire State Building. The 200 rooms offer private baths, good security, direct-dial phones, TVs with pay-per-view movies and games, Wi-Fi, in-room safes, irons and ironing boards, clock radios, laundry facilities and a small fitness and business centers. No wonder students, foreign travelers and savvy business people are regular patrons!

HOUSING ALTERNATIVES

Many travelers and families visiting New York City prefer to stay someplace other than a hotel. This Alternative Housing section presents options such as apartments, bed and breakfasts, townhouses and dormitory housing.

92Y RESIDENCE

1395 Lexington Ave (at 92nd St)   212/415-5660, 800-858-4692
Moderate   92y.org/residence

The 92Y Residence offers unique social, cultural and recreational student housing for 18 and older students, interns and young professionals from around the globe. Upper East Side housing is offered on a first-come, first-served

SHORT-TERM APARTMENT RENTALS

Many travelers and families find that staying in an apartment while visiting New York City can save money, since more guests can be accommodated and meals can be prepared there.

Abode (212/472-2000, abodenyc.com): discounts on stays of a month or longer

Affordable New York City (212/533-4001, affordablenewyorkcity. com): B&Bs and furnished apartments; four-night minimum stay for B&Bs, five nights for apartments

At Home in New York (212/956-3125, athomeny.com): hosted and nonhosted properties

City Sonnet (212/614-3034, citysonnet.com): hosted rooms, apartments, lofts; minimum five-night stay

Ivy Terrace B&B (516/662-6862, ivyterrace.com): studio apartments in charming townhouse; call for address

Radio City Apartments (142 W 49th St, 877/921-9321, radiocityapartments.com): apartment-style lodging; no minimum stay

basis by application only; stays can range from 30 days or more. Single and double furnished rooms include Wi-Fi, weekly linen service, 24-hour doormen, communal kitchens, dining rooms with cable TVs, communal baths on each floor, on-premises cafe, free health club membership and discounted access to an array of art, dance and music classes, workshops, programs, talks and readings.

ABODE

Mailing address: 520 E 76th St, Suite 3-E, New York, NY 10021
Mon-Fri: 9-5   212/472-2000, 800/835-8880 (outside tri-state area)
Moderate to expensive   abodenyc.com

Would you like to stay in a delightful old brownstone? How about a contemporary luxury apartment in the heart of Manhattan? Abode selects apartments with great care, personally inspecting them to ensure the highest standards of cleanliness, attractiveness and hospitality; all are nicely furnished. Nightly rates begin at $200 for a studio and rise to $550 and up for a three-bedroom apartment. Extended stays of a month or longer receive discount rates.

AKA CENTRAL PARK

42 W 58th St (bet Fifth Ave and Ave of the Americas)   646/744-3100

AKA SUTTON PLACE

330 E 56th St (bet First and Second Ave)   212/752-8888

AKA TIMES SQUARE

123 W 44th St (bet Ave of the Americas and Broadway)   212/764-5700

AKA UNITED NATIONS

234 E 46th St (bet Second and Third Ave)   646/291-4200

AKA WALL STREET

84 William St (bet Platt St and Maiden Lane) *target opening date summer 2015
stayaka.com

Specializing in stays of a week or longer, AKA offers prime locations for business and leisure travelers visiting Manhattan. Each apartment-hotel location offers something different in the way of accommodations. There are studios and suites, some with kitchens; others offer outdoor dining areas with unsurpassed city views and all offer meticulous housekeeping. The 56th street location offers one- and two-bedroom apartments. AKA is a great option if you're looking for a bit more comfort and privacy than your standard hotel room.

AT HOME IN NEW YORK

P.O. Box 407, New York, NY 10185   212/956-3125, 800/692-4262
Inexpensive to expensive   athomeny.com

For most people, the words "bed and breakfast" connote quaint country inns, but B&Bs can also be found throughout the city. Accommodations are available in various settings — apartments, co-ops, artists' lofts and condos — and rates are a fraction of those at higher-priced hotels. At Home in New York carefully screens hosted and nonhosted properties to fit every need and budget. In addition to breakfasts, hosts often dish out favorite tips for a true local experience.

CHELSEA PINES INN

317 W 14th St (bet Eighth and Ninth Ave)   212/929-1023
Moderate to expensive   chelseapinesinn.com

This isn't your typical inn; it is a 19th-century five-story walk-up with 23 movie-themed guest rooms and common areas that include a lounge and recently expanded business center. All rooms have private bathrooms, refrigerators, flat-screen TVs and iPod docks (alas, there's no elevator). Local calls, Wi-Fi, an expanded continental breakfast and 24/7 snacks are free. As befits the eclectic Chelsea locale, the inn is gay- and lesbian-friendly.

BEFORE TRAVELING OVERSEAS

Overseas travelers can find valuable information and obtain immunizations at these places:

Travel Health Services (50 E 69th St, 212/734-3000): Mon-Fri, by appointment

Traveler's Medical Service of New York (595 Madison Ave, Suite 1200, 212/230-1020): Mon-Fri: 9-4, by appointment

Travelers' Wellness Center (952 Fifth Ave, Room 1-D, 212/737-1212): by appointment, hours vary

HOSTELLING INTERNATIONAL NEW YORK

891 Amsterdam Ave (at 103rd St)   212/932-2300
Inexpensive   hinewyork.org

Hostelling International New York provides inexpensive overnight accommodations for travelers of all ages. This renovated century-old landmark has over 672 beds. They offer meeting spaces, Wi-Fi, a coffee bar, complimentary continental breakfast, self-service kitchens, lockers, a TV and game room and laundry facilities to individuals and groups. Guests under 18 must be accompanied by a parent, or in groups, by a chaperone. There is a strict rule forbidding alcohol on the premises; smoking must be confined to outdoor areas. And, the price is certainly right!

INN NEW YORK CITY

266 W 71st St (bet West End Ave and Broadway)   212/580-1900
Expensive   innnewyorkcity.com

For a secluded, civilized stay, Inn New York City offers four suites behind a discreet exterior in a restored 19th-century townhouse. Depending on the suite chosen, you may find a double Jacuzzi, extensive library, leaded glass skylights, fireplaces, baby grand piano, private terrace or a fully-equipped kitchen stocked with hearty delights for breakfast, snacks and beverages. Additional services include high-speed Internet, cable TV, daily newspapers, maid service and a 24-hour concierge. Personal laundry is done on request at no additional charge — a real plus.

IVY TERRACE B&B

230 E 58th St (bet Second and Third Ave)   516/662-6862
Moderate   ivyterrace.com

There are six studio apartments with private baths in this charming century-old townhouse, two with outdoor terraces. Kitchens are stocked with breakfast goodies. Hardwood floors, ceiling fans and 15-foot ceilings are very inviting. Innkeeper Vinessa promises special care, including tips of where to eat and explore. There is a three-night minimum, and weekly rates are available; local calls and Wi-Fi are free.

THE PHILLIPS CLUB

Lincoln Square
155 W 66th St (at Broadway)   212/835-8800
Moderate to expensive   phillipsclub.com

This 162-unit residential hotel near Lincoln Center is designed for long-term visitors but will also take short-stay customers. Studios and suites come with fully-equipped kitchens, flat-screen TVs and Bose sound systems. Other features include 24-hour concierge, laundry and valet services, in-room safes, a handy conference room and preferential access to the nearby Equinox Sports Club NY.

SOLDIERS', SAILORS', MARINES', COAST GUARD & AIRMEN'S CLUB

283 Lexington Ave (at 37th St)   212/683-4353, 800/678-8443
Inexpensive   ssmaclub.org

Since 1919 this organization has been providing friendly, safe, affordable accommodations for our military personnel and their families visiting Manhattan. American and allied servicemen and women — active, retired, veterans, reservists, military cadets, NYFD, NYPD, EMS and Coast Guard personnel — are welcomed at this convenient Murray Hill location; proof of eligibility must be shown. Rates are extremely low (with no tax); if you're traveling solo, you may be assigned a roommate. Twenty-one rooms on five floors have two, three, four and six beds. Communal bathroom facilities are on each floor; there is no elevator but a stair chair is available on each floor. Two lounges, TVs with DVD players and a lobby canteen with refrigerator, microwave and coffee are additional conveniences.

WEBSTER APARTMENTS

419 W 34th St (at Ninth Ave)   212/967-9000, 800/242-7909
Inexpensive   websterapartments.org

This is one of the best deals in the city for working women with moderate incomes. The hotel operates on a policy developed by Charles B. Webster, a first cousin of Rowland Macy (of the department-store family). Webster left an endowment to found these apartments, which opened in 1923. Residents include working college students, interns, designers, actresses, secretaries and other business and professional women. Facilities include dining rooms, recreation areas, a library, lounges and laundry rooms. The Webster has private gardens for guests, and meals can be taken outdoors. Rates are on a sliding scale based on income and range from $335 to $360 per week for a furnished room; this includes two meals a day and maid service. Women visiting New York on business can stay for a daily rate of $100 which includes a full breakfast; three-day minimum.

INTERIOR DESIGNERS

AERO STUDIOS

419 Broome St (bet Lafayette and Crosby St)   212/966-1500
Mon-Sat: 11-6   aerostudios.com

Thomas O'Brien and his staff are well equipped to handle everything from a major commercial interior design project to a minor residential one. Modernism with a warm, livable style is his signature, along with elegant, vintage touches. Be sure to visit his home boutique, Aero, for a collection of home furnishings, tableware, decor and lighting — beautiful items with both meaning and style.

BERCELI INTERIOR REMODELLING

1402 Lexington Ave (bet 92nd and 93rd St)   212/722-8811
Mon-Fri: 9-6:30; Sat: 10-6   berceli.com

Give Berceli a call if you're ready to redo your kitchen or bathroom. For over two decades they have worked with homeowners to bring function and beauty to home interiors. Whether the style is contemporary or traditional, they use only the finest American and European products and appliances. They'll do the whole job (consult, design, install and finish), or you can choose to do portions of the work in order to save costs. Projects might include removing or adding a wall or creating new architectural features.

BEST FOR DESIGN

Looking for an architect or decorator? Here are some of the very best:

Ashley Whittaker Design (191 E 76th St, Suite 5-A, 212/650-0024): neotraditionalist

Bella Mancini Design (41 Union Square W, Room 827, 212/741-3380): Bella Zakarian Mancini is mindful of budgets.

Bilhuber and Associates (330 E 59th St, 6th floor, 212/308-4888): Jeffrey Bilhuber has contemporary ideas.

Miles Redd (77 Bleecker St, Suite C-111, 212/674-0902): color expert

MR Architecture & Decor (245 W 29th St, 10th floor, 212/989-9300): David Mann is very practical.

S.R. Gambrel (15 Watt St, 212/925-3380): You can't beat Steven Gambrel for detailing.

Sara Story Design (54 Thompson St, 212/228-6007): contemporary, eclectic

Shamir Shah Design (10 Greene St, 212/274-7476): interior and architectural design

Specht Harpman Architects (338 W 39th St, 10th floor, 212/239-1150): Scott Specht and Louise Harpman are pocketbook-conscious.

Steven Holl Architects (450 W 31st St, 11th floor, 212/629-7262): residential and commercial, worldwide

MARTIN ALBERT INTERIORS

257 W 39th St (bet Seventh and Eighth Ave), 12th floor   212/673-8000
Mon-Thurs: 9-5:30; Fri: 9-5   martinalbert.com

Since 1980 Martin Albert Interiors has been specializing in custom furniture design and upholstery and window treatments. You can choose from thousands of fabric samples for your project. Services include custom upholstery and slipcovers, a furniture shop (bring a photo and they will re-create the piece), custom draperies, motorized shades and a large selection of drapery hardware.

RICHARD'S INTERIOR DESIGN

1390 Lexington Ave (bet 91st and 92nd St)   212/831-9000
Mon-Fri: 10-6; Sat: 10:30-3   richardsinteriordesign.net

Richard's offers interior design services, in-home consultation and installation. Reupholstery and refinishing, slipcovers, window treatments, custom bedding, bedroom ensembles, custom cabinetry, high-end furniture, carpeting and wall coverings are available. You'll find thousands of imported decorator fabrics, including tapestries, damasks, stripes, plaids, silks, velvets and floral chintzes; these are all first-quality goods at competitive prices.

JEWELRY SERVICES

GEM APPRAISERS & CONSULTANTS

589 Fifth Ave (at 48th St), Suite 1309   212/333-3122

By appointment (Mon-Thurs)   robaretz.com

Rob Aretz is a graduate gemologist and certified member of the Appraisers Association of America. With over 35 years in the industry he has provided appraisals for major insurance companies, banks and jewelry stores through Gem Appraisers & Consultants. His specialty is antique jewelry, colored stones, diamonds, natural pearls and watches. Aretz also does private appraisals and/ or consultations for estate, insurance, tax, equitable distribution, charitable donations and other purposes.

RISSIN'S JEWELRY CLINIC

10 W 47th St (bet Fifth Ave and Ave of the Americas), Suite 902   212/575-1098

Mon, Tues, Thurs: 9:30-5   rissinsjewelryclinic.com

Rissin's is indeed a clinic! The assortment of services is staggering: jewelry repair and design, antique and museum restorations, supplying diamonds and other stones, eyeglass repair, pearl and bead stringing, restringing of old necklaces, stone identification and appraisals. Joe and Toby Rissin run the place, carrying on the tradition started by Joe's father, a master engraver. Estimates are gladly given and all work is guaranteed; honesty and quality are their bywords. Due to a possible move, be sure to call ahead before you visit!

LAMP REPAIR

THE LAMP SURGEON

On location   917/414-0426

Daily: 8:30-8:30   lampsurgeon.com

Since 1975 Roy Schneit has been working as the lamp surgeon — repairing, restoring, refinishing and re-wiring at customers' homes, offices and apartments. Services include work on table and floor lamps, halogen lamps, chandeliers, wall sconces, antiques and custom lampshades.   He gives accurate quotes over the phone.

LANDSCAPE DESIGN

AMERICAN FOLIAGE & DESIGN GROUP

122 W 22nd St (bet Ave of the Americas and Seventh Ave)   212/741-5555

Mon-Fri: 8:30-5:00   americanfoliagedesign.com

Planning a special event? The focus at American Foliage is on concepts and designs for anything to do with gardens and exteriors for theater, film and corporate or private special events. These folks sell or rent live and artificial plants, props, lighting and special-effects items and party supplies. Full-service is provided, including trucking and installation. Drop by to browse the impressive inventory; they have an imposing list of clients!

LEATHER REPAIR

FORDHAM REPAIR

39 W 32nd St (bet Fifth Ave and Broadway), Suite 1201   212/889-4553
Mon-Fri: 8:30-5:30   fordhamrepair.com

Fordham Repair is a business you will want to note. They repair, clean and refurbish leather luggage, handbags, wallets, briefcases and totes — even your great-grandmother's old trunk. Ripped stitching and bindings, broken zippers and locks, missing wheels and damaged handles receive careful attention to bring goods back to useful life. They will also repair designer shoes and leather garments; turn-around time is quick.

MODERN LEATHER GOODS

2 W 32nd St (bet Fifth Ave and Broadway), 4th floor   212/279-3263
Mon-Fri: 8:30-4:45; Sat: 8:30-1   modernleathergoods.com

Modern Leather Goods, a family business since 1944, is the place to go for repairs, reconditioning and cleaning. They are authorized with all major luggage manufacturers and recommended by top leather companies and department stores. They also reglaze alligator bags, clean leather and suede and repair shoes and leather clothing; usually a one week turn-around. Ask for owner Tony Pecorella.

SUPERIOR LEATHER RESTORERS

383 Fifth Ave (bet 35th and 36th St), 2nd floor   212/889-7211
Mon-Fri: 9:30-5:30   superiorleathernyc.com

Leather repair is the highlight of the services offered at Superior Leather Restorers and they seem to have the answer to all leather-related problems. They are experts at cleaning leather (suede, shearling and reptile) and repairing or replacing zippers on leather items. They can make alterations and even remove ink spots. Many major stores in the city use this family-owned business for luggage and handbag work; just ask Gucci, Calvin Klein, Bergdorf Goodman and Prada!

LOCKSMITHS

AAA ARCHITECTURAL HARDWARE

44 W 46th St (at Ave of the Americas)   212/840-3939
Mon-Thurs: 8-5:30; Fri: 8-5   aaahardware.com

Do not call them with a flat tire! This "AAA" began as a locksmith business. It has been a family-operation for over 60 years, and that says a lot. Services have expanded to keying systems, designing and installing electronic security and architectural hardware.

MEDICAL SERVICES

CENTER FOR HEARING AND COMMUNICATION

50 Broadway (bet Morris St and Exchange Pl), 6th floor   917/305-7700
917/305-7999 (TTY)
Mon, Wed, Fri: 8-5; Tues, Thurs: 8-7 (by appointment)   chchearing.org

These folks come highly recommended. People of all ages with any degree of hearing loss have been served by this not-for-profit organization since 1910. They test hearing, evaluate and dispense hearing aids and provide speech and language therapy, as well as emotional health and wellness services. Support groups are conducted to assist people with hearing loss (and their families) in all aspects of their lives. They will do their best to accommodate walk-ins with emergency or last minute needs, but otherwise appointments are required.

DOCS 'R US

The task of finding a good doctor in Manhattan has gotten easier, thanks to **Top Doctors, New York Metro Area**. It identifies over 6,000 primary and specialty doctors. Only the top docs are included in this helpful resource, available at book outlets and online at castleconnolly.com.

DR WALK-IN MEDICAL CARE

1627 Broadway (at 50th St)
212/245-2943
125 E 86th St (at Lexington Ave)
212/828-8060
131 Eighth Ave (at 17th St)
212/675-4800
40 Wall St (bet Nassau and William St)
212/785-0284

Hours vary by store
Numerous other locations in
Manhattan   drwalkin.com

Take note: if you find yourself ill in New York, these convenient locations inside Duane Reade drugstores may be able to help you feel better. Licensed physicians and medical assistants are on duty to perform screenings, provide basic care for common ailments, tend to minor sprains and lacerations, administer vaccinations, write prescriptions and make referrals to appropriate specialists. (However, you should head for the emergency room for any life-threatening condition or broken bones.) Appointments are not necessary, and they will bill most major insurance companies for you.

N.Y. HOTEL URGENT MEDICAL SERVICES

Urgent Care Center of New York   212/737-1212
Daily: by appointment   travelmd.com

Keep this information handy; this is one of the most valuable services in Manhattan! Dr. Ronald Primas, the CEO and medical director, is tops in his field as a concierge doctor. This outfit is locally based and has been in operation over 15 years. All manner of health care is available on a 24/7 basis: internists, pediatricians, obstetricians, surgeons, dentists, chiropractors, physicians on call and more. Doctors will come to your hotel, workplace or apartment, arrange

EMERGENCY DENTIST

An evening or weekend dental emergency is both inconvenient and painful, especially if you are away from home. **Dr. Isaac Datikashvili, Emergency Dentist NYC** (8 Gramercy Park S, 212/486-9458, emergencydentistnyc.com) — Dr. Isaac, for short — will come to the rescue! He is available during normal business hours, weekends, evenings and holidays to treat toothaches, perform emergency extractions and root canals and re-cement crowns.

IN CASE OF ILLNESS

New York City's largest hospitals offer world-class treatment by top doctors.

Beth Israel Medical Center (10 Nathan D. Perlman Place, 212/420-2000)

Memorial Sloan-Kettering Cancer Center (1275 York Ave, 212/639-2000)

The Mount Sinai Hospital (1 Gustave L. Levy Place, 212/241-6500)

New York-Presbyterian Hospital/Weill Cornell Medical Center (525 E 68th St, 212/746-5454)

NYU Langone Medical Center (550 First Ave, 212/263-7300)

for tests, prescribe medications, admit patients to hospitals and provide nurses. They also give travel immunizations and consultations and they are an official WHO-designated yellow-fever vaccination site. The urgent-care center is also available around the clock by appointment for patients not requiring a house call. Payment is expected at time of service; credit cards are accepted. All physicians are board-certified and have an exemplary bedside manner.

PASSPORT HEALTH

1001 Ave of the Americas (bet 37th and 38th St), Suite 1215   516/626-2004

By appointment   passporthealthusa.com

Travel to certain out-of-the-country destinations may require immunizations and/or vaccinations. Passport Health has competent, professional physicians and nurses with up-to-date health information from the Centers for Disease Control and World Health Organization. Travel-related products and conveniences are available as well as international health tips.

MOVERS

BIG APPLE MOVING & STORAGE

83 Third Ave (bet Bergen and Dean St), Brooklyn   212/505-1861, 718/768-7818

Mon-Fri: 9-5   bigapplemoving.com

Big Apple Moving & Storage has a sterling reputation and even though they are located in downtown Brooklyn, they do 80% of their moving business in Manhattan. They are experts with antiques, art and high-end moves, yet manage to keep rates reasonable. You'll find moving supplies at their "do-it-yourself" moving store where every size of box, container and wood crate for moving or storage is stocked. They also have bubble pack, plate dividers, custom paper and "French wraps" for crystal and delicate breakables. For those who need overnight or short-term storage, Big Apple will keep your entire truckload of furniture inside their high-security, heated warehouse. Interstate and international moving is also provided, and every item is fully wrapped and padded before leaving your residence.

BOX BUTLER

On location Daily: Delivery and pick up   888/881-0810
                                                        boxbutler.com

So where can you store seasonal clothes, sports equipment, suitcases and Christmas decorations? Box Butler offers short- or long-term storage options. They deliver empty containers and locks to your residence or business. You box the items and inventory the contents. The containers are then transported to their secure warehouse for storage. When you need your items, contact them for delivery. The monthly rate is based upon the size of your container. Box Butler is a great option for stowing trade-show displays, client records and furniture and household items during a remodeling job.

BROWNSTONE BROS. MOVING

321 Rider Ave (at 140th St), The Bronx   718/665-5000
Mon-Fri: 9-5   brownstonebros.com

Brownstone Bros. has been offering packing, moving, unpacking and storage services with a very personal touch since 1977; they are highly rated by customers. Most of their business is high-end residential moving, but they also do commercial moves. Their storage facility is fire proof and has 24-hour surveillance. Here's a good tip from them: to avoid the inconvenience of temporary loss, personally move your medicines, remote-control devices and other important small items to your next location.

FLATRATE MOVING

27 Bruckner Blvd, The Bronx   212/509-0512
Mon-Fri: 8-8; Sat, Sun: 9-5

If you are planning a move of any kind, FlatRate Moving has some of the most experienced and well-trained movers in the business. For fragile items and collections that require special handling, they take extreme care in packing (and unpacking), padding and labeling items. Items are inventoried, photographed and carefully transported in secure vans; additional services include custom crating, disposal and cleaning.

MOVING RIGHT ALONG

101-21 101st St, Ozone Park, NY   718/738-2468
Mon-Fri: 8-5; Sat: 8-1:30   movingrightalong.com

With over three decades of service and a top-quality reputation, Moving Right Along is an excellent choice if you have a move ahead of you. Moving,

MAGIC SHOP AND MUSEUM

Fantasma Magic (421 Seventh Ave, 2nd floor, 212/244-3633) is the largest manufacturer of magic kits in the world. The midtown shop includes two stages, flat screens, a 3D video display, magic props and a Houdini museum with a huge collection of his original props. A secret VIP room can accommodate 250 to 300 guests for birthday parties and special events, or 75 seated guests for professional magic shows.

MEDICAL HOUSE CALLS

Remember when doctors made house calls? Well, in New York, some of them still do! In addition to office appointments, house calls are routine with **New York House Call Physicians** (20 Park Ave, Suite 1-A, 646/957-5444, doctorinthefamily.com). They will cater to patients' schedules and location of choice. The doctor's black bag has been expanded to include mobile medical equipment, allowing them to perform numerous procedures. They carry suture equipment, digital electrocardiogram machines and ophthalmoscopes. When necessary, the doctors have admitting privileges at Beth Israel Medical Center. Costs are flat-fee based and include most testing, medication dispensing and procedures. They do not bill insurance companies, Medicare or Medicaid, so plan on using a credit card or cash. Available services include family medicine, hospice, pain management, pediatric care, psychotherapy, ultrasound and addiction treatment. Patients of all ages are welcome to call or visit.

storage, packing and crating are offered. Their handy home-cleaning and junk-removal service will help get your residence ready for quick occupancy. Be sure to check out their 10,000-square-foot Furniture Depot for pre-owned furniture, antiques and imports; they also buy furniture and estates.

WEST SIDE MOVERS

963 Columbus Ave (bet 107th and 108th St)   212/874-3800
Mon-Fri: 8-6; Sat: 9-3; Sun: 10-3   westsidemovers.com

This well-respected moving company is a family-run business that started in the kitchen of a studio apartment back in 1972. From its Upper West Side location, West Side Movers continues to offer dependable residential and office moving, including disassembly, reassembly, crating and short-term storage. They are experts in the handling of fine art and antiques. Close attention is paid to efficiency, promptness and courtesy. Packing consultants will help do-it-yourselfers select moving boxes and other supplies; boxes come in a multitude of sizes, including four different options for mirrors alone.

OFFICE SERVICES

PURGATORY PIE PRESS

19 Hudson St (bet Duane and Reade St), Room 403   212/274-8228
Mon-Fri: by appointment   purgatorypiepress.com

Purgatory Pie Press is ideal for small printing jobs. They do graphic design and handset typography, hand letterpress printing, die-cutting and hand bookbinding. They'll also create envelopes, logos and other identity designs. They can even design handmade paper with unique watermarks. Specialties include printing and calligraphy for weddings and parties. They also make limited-edition postcards and artists' books. Private lessons and small group classes are offered in letterpress printing, handmade books, paper toys and the like.

WORLD-WIDE BUSINESS CENTRES

575 Madison Ave (at 57th St), 10th floor   212/605-0200
Mon-Fri: 9-5   wwbcn.com

World-Wide Business Centres caters to executives who need more than a hotel room and to companies that need a conference room or fully-equipped, furnished and staffed office or conference room in New York on short notice. A full range of well-trained office staff and telecommunication services are available; evening and weekend help can be arranged at additional rates. Desk space, private offices and conference rooms may be rented on a temporary (hourly, daily, weekly or monthly) basis.

OPTICIANS

E.B. MEYROWITZ & DELL OPTICIANS

19 W 44th St (at Fifth Ave)   212/575-1686
Mon-Fri: 9-5:45; Sat: 10-4   ebmeyrowitz-dell.com

E.B. Meyrowitz has been a leader in the optical field since 1875. A leader in optical needs since 1875, their large, eclectic frame selection includes materials ranging from 18K gold to buffalo horn to titanium. Just bring your prescription; opticians are ready and waiting. They also do on-the-spot eyeglass repairs.

PAINTING

GARVEY PAINTING COMPANY

By appointment   718/894-8272

Bernie Garvey is a meticulous, reliable painter who can also do plastering and decorative finishes. His team serves residential clients, and customers tout the reasonable prices, positive attitude and terrific work.

GOTHAM PAINTING COMPANY

336 E 94th St (bet First and Second Ave), basement level   212/427-5752
Mon-Fri: 9-5

If you need interior painting or wallpapering for your home, Gotham is a good resource. For over two decades they have done spray work, restoration, faux painting and plastering. There is a large staff of full-time painters and the company is fully licensed and bonded.

PARENTING RESOURCES

92ND STREET Y PARENTING CENTER

1395 Lexington Ave (at 92nd St)   212/415-5611
Mon-Fri: 9-5 (office hours may fluctuate)   92y.org/parenting-center

Just about everything the 92nd Street Y does is impressive, and its Parenting Center is no exception. It offers every kind of class you can imagine: parents-to-be classes, pre- and postnatal yoga, boot camp for dads, parents of twins, sibling rivalry and so on. Workshops and seminars are offered on a wide range of topics, from sleep problems to setting limits. They host drop-in sessions such as parent get-togethers. Perhaps most important, they act as a parenting resource and support center for members and the general public.

PARENTS LEAGUE

115 E 82nd St (bet Lexington and Park Ave)   212/737-7385
Mon-Thurs: 9-4; Fri: 9-noon   parentsleague.org

Beginning in 1913, this nonprofit organization is a gold mine for parents in New York. They provide advisory services to families applying to preschools, private K-12 schools in the city, boarding schools and for special-needs and summer camps and programs. In addition to putting together a calendar of events for parents of children of all ages, the Parents League maintains extensive files on early-childhood programs, private schools throughout the city, nannies and tutoring resources. For a membership fee of $235 per academic year, you can access all of these resources, talk to advisors and attend workshops, forums and other events.

SOHO PARENTING

568 Broadway (at Prince St), Suite 402   212/334-3744
Mon-Fri: 9-5 (by appointment)   sohoparenting.com

Soho Parenting is dedicated to helping parents move through the changing stages of parenthood with support and guidance. It conducts workshops and group discussions for parents of newborns, toddlers and older children. Topics might include discipline, anger management and sibling relationships. They are available for individual therapy and couples counseling.

PARTY SERVICES

BUBBY GRAM

Mon-Thurs: 11-7; Fri: 11-5   212/353-3886
          bubbygram.com

If creating fun and laughter is on your mind, then call this number. These folks have outrageous and humorous acts that run the gamut from simple singing telegrams to complete shows for gags, parties or business meetings. They'll provide celebrity impersonators, roasts, magicians, psychics, belly dancers, wedding officiants, game shows and much more. Contact them after hours via their website; seasonal gigs as well.

EXPRESSWAY MUSIC DJ'S

10 E 39th St (bet Fifth and Madison Ave), Suite 1126   212/953-9367
By appointment   expresswaymusic.com

Expressway Music DJ's will furnish stylish DJs and live music to your wedding, corporate party or other special event. DJs and musicians are chosen according to your specifications for music style. All performers are professional and polished — soloists, trios and specialty bands – to make your event both unique and memorable.

LINDA KAYE'S PARTYMAKERS

23 E 69th St (bet Madison and Park Ave)   212/288-7112
Mon-Fri: 10-5 (parties available 7 days a week)   partymakers.com

Linda Kaye's Partymakers will handle every detail of your party, from invitations, menus and favors to cleanup. Over 40 themed children's birthday parties are offered at several locations. A safari-themed birthday party uses restaurant Serafina as a base camp and then moves on to the Central Park Zoo. Parties at the American Museum of Natural History have such themes as Dinosaur Discovery and Cosmic Blast Off. Partymakers also offers Linda Kaye's signature Bake-a-Cake party for ages four and up. The adult division of Partymakers specializes in corporate picnics and holiday parties, as well as grand openings. The website is a resource for birthday-party ideas, entertainers and locations. Their blog, Party Times, provides a steady stream of celebration ideas.

MARCY BLUM ASSOCIATES

55 Fifth Ave (bet 12th and 13th St), 19th floor   212/929-9814
By appointment   marcyblum.com

Marcy Blum is a great lady, and she is so well organized that no matter what the event — wedding, reception, corporate event, birthday party, bar and bat mitzvah or dinner for the boss — she will execute it to perfection. As anyone knows, it's the details that count, and Marcy is superb at the nitty-gritty. Her events are beautiful, stylish and oftentimes surprising. Many celebrity weddings have been created by this talented "eventista."

PARTY POOPERS

By appointment   212/274-9955
                                                        partypoopers.com

Performance artist Marla Mase began Party Poopers in 1991; it is now highly regarded in Manhattan's event-organizing world. This full-service party-planning company can handle a job as simple as booking entertainment all the way to designing and implementing an entire event. Party Poopers' roster of top entertainers, caterers, designers, DJs and specialty acts will ensure that you have the best possible party. Although their niche is whimsical, interactive kids' parties (pirates, princesses, puppies, pony rides and dance), they have launched an adult division called party-SWANK.

DRIVING INSTRUCTION

Whether your teen is preparing for his or her driver's license or you are mandated to attend driving classes, these schools provide instruction. Hours vary, as do the slate of services offered, which include defensive driving and parallel parking lessons, as well as instruction for obtaining special licenses.

Attila School of Driving (1690 Second Ave, 212/410-6363): private lessons

Driving Center of New York (1551 Second Ave, 212/752-9250): customized lessons; early and late appointments

Professional Driving School of the Americas (40 E 23rd St, 212/375-1111): prep for the written test

PEN REPAIR

FOUNTAIN PEN HOSPITAL

10 Warren St (bet Broadway and Church St)   212/964-0580, 800/253-7367
Mon-Fri: 7:30-5:30   fountainpenhospital.com

Since 1946 this experienced establishment has been selling and repairing fountain pens of all types. A knowledgeable staff is at-the-ready with advice on an extensive parts and tools inventory for "do-it-yourselfers." Fountain Pen Hospital also carries one of the world's largest selections of modern and vintage writing tools.

PERSONAL SERVICES

ACK! ORGANIZING

By appointment   646/831-9625
                                                        ackorganizing.com

Want to get and stay organized? Alison Kero is an expert in organization, time management and productivity, whether it be for home or office. She will teach you the tools to get rid of unwanted clutter and move to a freer, organized future, one area at a time. Help is also available for relocations and home staging in preparation for a move. Pricing is by the hour with a three-hour minimum.

AL MARTINO AGENCY

60 E 42nd St (bet Park and Madison Ave), Suite 2227   212/867-1910
Mon-Fri: 9:30-5:30   martinodom.com

Since 1972, Al Martino Agency has been providing clientele with qualified domestic staffing such as private chefs, butlers, housekeepers, gardeners, personal assistants and chauffeurs. Look to them for party and seasonal help as well. A free consultation determines your exact needs; fees are competitive and incorporate a long-term replacement service guarantee. Rest assured that the agency is completely licensed, bonded and insured.

CELEBRITIES CONCIERGE & STAFFING SERVICES

20 Vesey St (bet Church St and Broadway), Suite 510   212/227-3877
Mon-Fri: 9-5   celebrities-staffing.com

Turn to Celebrities Concierge & Staffing Services when you are looking to hire top-of-the-line staffing for estates, mansions and corporations – baby nurses, governesses, nannies, "mannies" (male nannies), housekeepers, ladies' maids, butlers, housemen, chefs and cooks, couples, laundresses, house managers, estate managers, personal assistants, personal shoppers, chauffeurs, bodyguards, caregivers, companions and other types of household personnel. With 25 years of experience, their services extend across the U.S. and internationally with clients who include royalty, celebrities, dignitaries, top executives and families who are simply looking to hire the best. 24/7 concierge service is now offered.

CROSS IT OFF YOUR LIST

60 W 22nd St (bet Fifth Ave and Ave of the Americas)   212/725-0122
Mon-Fri: 9-6   crossitoffyourlist.com

The staff at Cross It Off Your list will do virtually anything to help busy people manage their lives: organize closets, bathrooms, garages, file cabinets and desks; oversee a move; help with daily chores; pack bags; pick up or hold your mail and even provide on-call personal assistants. In tackling any general disorder, they will literally help you do just that – cross it off your list!

FLATIRON CLEANING COMPANY

231 W 29th St (bet Seventh and Eighth Ave), Suite 304   212/876-1000
Mon-Fri: 7-4   flatironcleaning.com

These people have cleaned many homes and apartments since opening in 1893. Whether it be a routine visit or one-time job, expert services include residential house and window cleaning, installing, repairing and refinishing wood floors, maid service, party help, laundry service and carpet and upholstery cleaning. They can expertly clean crime scenes, too.

INTREPID RELOCATION

220 E 57th St (bet Second and Third Ave), Suite 2-D   212/750-0400
Mon-Fri: 9-5   intrepidny.com

Beginning as a concierge service, Sylvia Ehrlich and her team provide one of the most complete relocation-consulting services in this area. They will help with your home search; arrange temporary housing, furniture rental and storage; set up bank accounts or whatever your needs. They maintain an ongoing hotline of resources.

LINDQUIST GROUP

708 Third Ave (at 44th St), Suite 3000   212/644-0990
Mon-Fri: 8:30-5   thelindquistgroup.com

With more than a hundred years experience, the Lindquist Group specializes in providing household staffing for an affluent clientele. You can be sure of highly-qualified butlers, cooks, housekeepers, chauffeurs, nannies, personal assistants and estate couples. Temporary and permanent workers are

AIRLINE TRAVEL SITES

These are some of the best sites for booking flights:

Pintrips.com: compares flights from multiple airline sites and provides up-to-date fares

GetGoing.com: allows flexible travelers to choose itineraries for two destinations; the site then selects where they go; up to 40% discounts; tickets are nonrefundable and no changes are allowed

RouteHappy.com: scores routes based on the type and age of planes, in-flight entertainment options, legroom, traveler feedback and more

PAWNBROKERS

Looking for a short-term loan or to sell some of your goods for quick cash? Try these pawnshops:

Gem Pawnbrokers (3513 Broadway, 212/283-3333)
Lincoln Square Pawnbrokers (724 Amsterdam Ave, 212/865-8860)
New York Pawnbrokers (177 Rivington St, 212/228-7177)

available, many on a moment's notice. Employment references, criminal records and drivers' licenses are checked independently.

MAID FOR YOU NEW YORK

718/433-1499
maidforyounewyork.com

Maid for You claims to be one of the largest residential and commercial cleaning services in Manhattan. They provide free estimates and will customize a program for your specific needs — daily, weekly, monthly or upon moving in or moving out. They do windows, floors and carpets; pick up dry cleaning and remove and dispose of unwanted items (one room or an entire building). The highly-trained and uniformed employees provide quality "green" cleaning services at competitive rates.

NEW YORK'S LITTLE ELVES

151 First Ave (bet 8th and 9th St), Suite 204   212/673-5507
Mon-Fri: 8:30-6; Sat: 9-1 (call for appointment)   nyelves.com

No need to worry about cleaning up! These folks will do the job, whether it is a normal dusting or cleaning up after a big party — even post-construction jobs. New York's Little Elves can do window, chandelier, carpet and upholstery cleaning; assist with packing and unpacking and aid in housekeeper training. They provide free estimates, employ screened personnel, carry liability insurance and are fully bonded.

PAVILLION AGENCY

15 E 40th St (bet Fifth and Madison Ave), Suite 400   212/889-6609
Mon-Fri: 9-5   pavillionagency.com

Pavillion has been a family business since 1962. If you are in need of nannies, baby nurses, housekeepers, laundresses, domestic couples, butlers, chefs, chauffeurs, caretakers, gardeners, property managers or personal assistants, call and ask for Keith or Clifford Greenhouse. They can also assist with payroll processing and on-site training. Applicants are screened by a reputable private firm.

TALK POWER, A PANIC CLINIC FOR PUBLIC SPEAKING

333 E 23rd St (bet First and Second Ave)   212/684-1711
By appointment   talkpowerinc.com

Need to speak to a group but experience intense anxiety? Talk Power will help you overcome the phobia. They are true professionals whose niche is training clients via a "panic clinic" for public speaking. Individual or group training as well as workshops are available; the success rate is very high. Check the website for scheduled seminars.

UNAME IT ORGANIZERS

226 E 10th St (bet First and Second Ave), Suite 222   212/598-9868
By appointment   masterorganizers.com

Call uName It to do those tasks you've been putting off. They can, they do and they will. This company has been freeing up time for people who can't get certain jobs done themselves. They perform over 200 services, including uncluttering, providing personal assistants or clergy, special editing, event planning, handling a traffic ticket and even finding a soulmate. In the crowded field of organizers, uName It has been in business for over 27 years with many kudos from customers, so they must be doing something right.

WHITE GLOVE ELITE

39 W 32nd St (bet Fifth Ave and Broadway), Suite 504   212/684-4460
Mon-Fri: 9-6 (cleaners available anytime)   whitegloveelite.org

Actor Jim Ireland started this business in 1992 as an adjunct to his stage career. The company provides trained cleaners for apartments in Manhattan, The Bronx, Brooklyn and Queens, whether it be daily, weekly or monthly. They also provide party and bar servers as needed. About half of the personnel are actors between jobs.

ZOE INTERNATIONAL HOMECARE

20 Vesey St (bet Church St and Broadway), Suite 510   212/227-3880
Mon-Fri: 9-5 (24-hour emergency service)   zoehomecare.com

Zoe International Homecare specializes in the placement of private-pay caregivers — nurses and nurses' aides, home health- and personal-care aides, companions and housekeepers to work for the elderly, sick and chronically ill. The agency also has newborn specialists. They work closely with doctors, hospitals, health-care organizations, family members, friends, attorneys, estate planners and others involved in a patient's life. Caregivers are available for live-in or live-out and they can work day or night shifts or provide 24-hour service. Specially priced packages are available for families on fixed incomes.

PHOTOGRAPHIC SERVICES

CLASSIC KIDS

1182 Lexington Ave (at 81st St)   212/396-1160
395 Amsterdam Ave (at 79th St)   212/799-3730
Tues-Sat: 8:30-5:30 (by appointment)   classickidsphotography.com

Julie Floyd began Classic Kids as a one-woman show some 20 years ago. Today it is part of a consortium of child photographers who produce black-and-white and hand-tinted photographs of kids and families. No stuffy formal sittings are allowed; it's strictly fun for everyone involved. Belly laughs, mischievous grins and playful poses are captured as a treasured pictorial memory. The end products are heirloom pieces created the old-fashioned way: with film and handmade prints.

DEMETRIAD STUDIOS

1674 Broadway (at 52nd St), 4th floor
Mon-Fri: 10:30-6:30 (by appointment)

212/315-3400
demetriad.com

Since 1985, Dan Demetriad and his energetic team have parlayed their expertise into commercial portraiture and head-shot photography, as well as digital imaging and restoration of old and damaged photographs. They are pros at image retouching and high-end portrait and editorial photography. They also design blogs, individual and small-business websites and corporate branding.

HAND HELD FILMS

129 W 27th St (bet Ave of the Americas and Seventh Ave)
Mon-Fri: 9-6

212/502-0900
handheldfilms.com

Founded in 1987 as a camera rental boutique, Hand Held Films rents motion picture equipment for feature films, commercials, music videos and documentaries, both for large and small productions. Digital high-definition cameras, lenses and accessories and lighting are available. They have an impressive list of equipment — even a 20-foot truck to haul everything to your set.

PLUMBING AND HEATING

KAPNAG HEATING AND PLUMBING

109 W 38th St (bet Ave of the Americas and Seventh Ave), Suite 801

212/929-7111

24-hour emergency service

kapnagplumbing.com

In business since 1925, Kapnag reliably provides licensed heating and plumbing to New Yorkers. Two dozen professional workers handle plumbing repairs and renovations for kitchens and bathrooms, replace toilets, repair pipes and heating equipment, expertly diagnose plumbing system problems, install and repair sprinkler systems and more.

SCISSORS AND KNIFE SHARPENING

HENRY WESTPFAL & CO.

115 W 25th St (bet Ave of the Americas and Seventh Ave)
Mon-Fri: 9:30-6

212/563-5990
nysharpeningservice.com

The same family has been running Henry Westpfal since 1874. This premier knife-sharpening company does all kinds of sharpening and repair, from barber scissors and pruning shears to cuticle scissors; they'll also work on light tools. Cutlery, shears, scissors and tools for leather workers are sold here; even lefthanded scissors!

SHIPPING AND PACKAGING

UNITED SHIPPING & PACKAGING

200 E 10th St (at Second Ave)
Mon-Fri: 10:30-8; Sat: 11-6

212/475-2214
uspnyc.com

Known for their great service, United Shipping has been shipping anything and everything anywhere in the world – since 1988! Some of their regular customers include bakeries and other businesses with products that require special care. Additional skills include packing, faxing, copying, binding and messenger service. Rent a mailbox or order office and packaging supplies, including bubble wrap and all sizes of boxes.

SHOE REPAIR

CESAR'S SHOE REPAIR

180 Seventh Ave (bet 20th and 21st St)   212/961-6119
Mon-Fri: 7:30-7; Sat: 9-6   cesarsshoerepair.com

Third-generation cobbler Edward Andrade and his skilled craftsmen implement the latest technologies to repair and refurbish shoes, boots, handbags and other leather items. Besides the usual sole and heel repairs, Cesar's Shoe Repair can customize boots with calf extensions and stretching, zipper replacement, ankle tapering and shortening the height of a boot.

HECTOR'S SHOE REPAIR

11 Greenwich Ave (bet Christopher and 10th St)   212/727-1237
Mon-Fri: 7:30-7; Sat: 9-6

For 20 years owner Hector Sanchez has been offering a variety of repair and reconstruction services, including leather resoling ($80), restitching loose or broken seams ($10 to $40) and leather conditioning ($6). The customer service could be warmer, but Hector is a reliable choice for durable fixes.

JIM'S SHOE REPAIRING

50 E 59th St (bet Madison and Park Ave)   212/355-8259
Mon-Fri: 8-6; Sat: 9-4   jimsshoerepair.com

This family operation has been offering first-rate shoe repair, shoeshines and shoe supplies since 1932. The shoe-repair field has steadily been losing its

CUSTOM TAILORS

Bespoke (custom) tailoring is available from these folks. Most work by appointment only.

Alton Lane (11 W 25th St, 5th floor, 646/896-1212): a 3D body scanner records 300 measurements; 25 lining choices

Bespoke Tailors (509 Madison Ave, 212/888-6887)

Cameo Cleaners of Gramercy Park (284 Third Ave, 212/677-3949)

Domenico Vacca (781 Fifth Ave, 212/759-6333): He will do good things for your figure.

Dynasty Custom Tailors (6 E 38th St, 212/679-1075): dresses and wedding gowns

Ghost Tailor (153 W 27th St, 11th floor, 212/253-9727): dressmaker; one-of-a-kind wedding gowns and heirloom-dress reconstruction

Nino Corvato (420 Madison Ave, Suite 406, 212/980-4980)

craftsmen, and this is one of the few shops that upholds the tradition. Owner Jim Rocco specializes in orthopedic shoe and boot alterations; bags, belts and straps receive superior treatment, too.

LEATHER SPA

55 W 55th St (bet Fifth Ave and Ave of the Americas)   212/262-4823
Mon-Fri: 8-7; Sat: 10-6
Plaza Hotel Retail Boutiques
Fifth Ave at Central Park S   212/527-9944
Mon-Fri: 10-7; Sat: 10-6; Sun: 11-5
Grand Central Terminal (42nd St at Vanderbilt Ave), lower level   212/661-0307
Mon-Fri: 7-6:30; Sat: 9-4   leatherspa.com

Quality work is done here — shoe and handbag repair and reconditioning and custom work — and you will pay well for it. Notable luxury stores using their service include Manolo Blahnik, Jimmy Choo and Gucci, to name a few. Leather Spa also offers delivery; top quality leather care products are available.

NANNIES ON CALL

If you need a nanny at the last minute, call **A Choice Nanny** (850 Seventh Ave, Suite 706, 212/246-5437, achoicenanny/nyc.com). Alan and Joan Friedman carefully screen personnel and offer several search options. Another recommended source for nannies is **Pavillion Agency** (15 E 40th St, Suite 400, 212/889-6609), which is very reliable.

MINA'S SHOE REPAIR

63 Wall St (at Hanover St)
212/938-0199
Mon-Fri: 7-6; Sat: 10-4

This family-run shop gets high marks for prompt turn-around, reasonable prices and quality repairs. Mina Polychronakis and staff will do repairs like sole replacements ($8 to $65), recoloring ($30 to $150) or a shoe shine ($3 to $10).

PAVLOS SHOE REPAIR

125 E 88th St (bet Lexington and Park Ave)   212/876-8569
Mon-Fri: 7-6; Sat: 8-5   Facebook

Pavlos performs such customary tasks as repairing, cleaning, dyeing and stretching shoes. They also shorten or lengthen heels or alter calf lengths on boots. Most leather items — boots, purses, luggage, jackets and briefcases — can be rejuvenated here. A full range of shoe-care, shoe-fitting and shoe-comfort products are for sale. Many repeat customers attest to the friendly and quality service at Pavlos, which has been around for four decades.

SILVERSMITHS

BRANDT & OPIS

46 W 46th St (bet Fifth Ave and Ave of the Americas), 5th floor   212/302-0294
Mon-Fri: 8:30-5

For anything silver, Brandt & Opis can handle it. This includes silver repair and polishing, buying and selling estate silver, repairing and replating silver-plated items and fixing silver tea and coffee services. They restore combs and brushes (dresser sets) and replace old knife blades. Other services include gold-plating, lacquering, lamp restoration and plating antique bath and door hardware. In short, Brandt & Opis is a complete metal-restoration specialist.

TAILORS

BHAMBI'S CUSTOM TAILORS

14 E 60th St (bet Madison and Fifth Ave), Suite 610   212/935-5379
By appointment   bhambis.com

At Bhambi's Custom Tailors you'll discover the incomparable luxury of a bespoke suit in the best British tradition. This long-standing family business (since 1968) combines style, quality, tradition and skill to make suits, jackets, slacks, tuxedos and shirts that will flatter the successful businessman or professional. A distinguished list of satisfied clients attests to Bhambi's superior merchandise, excellent customer service and fair prices.

CEGO CUSTOM SHIRTMAKER

254 Fifth Ave (at 28th St), 3rd floor   212/620-4512
Mon-Fri: 9:30-6; Sat: 10-3:30 (by appointment)   cego.com

For over 25 years, owner Carl Goldberg and his team have been making quality shirts for both media types and regular people. Shirts are patterned, cut and tailored and usually take two to three weeks. For out-of-town visitors or if time is important, shirts can be produced in as little as two days. Full custom shirts start at $225 and go up, depending on fabric selection. The five-shirt minimum can be waived for weddings, gift certificates and students. Monograms, too!

MOHAN'S CUSTOM TAILORS

60 E 42nd St (bet Park and Madison Ave), Suite 1432   212/697-0050
Mon-Sat: 10-7:30   mohantailors.com

Mohan Ramchandani left India to open Mohan's Custom Tailors in 1972. Since then he has created over 150,000 custom suits at reasonable prices. The shop claims to offer 40% to 50% savings from that of overpriced designers. To achieve the best-fitting suits, 25 meticulous measurements are taken. Over 10,000 fabric samples and a myriad of colors and styles are available; your custom suit will be delivered to your door in just four to five weeks. Mohan's also makes coats, sports jackets, slacks, shirts and formal wear.

PEPPINO TAILORS

138 E 61st St (at Lexington Ave), Suite 205   212/832-3844
Mon-Fri: 8:30-6; Sat: 8:30-4   peppinotailors.com

The fine craftsmen at Peppino Tailors have been tailoring clothes since 1973. Expert attention to alterations is given to all types of garments, including evening and bridal wear, suits, jackets and pants (for men and women). Services include lengthening or shortening hems, repairing pockets and replacing zippers and linings. Delivery is offered.

CONCIERGE SERVICES

ABC NYC Concierge (800/429-5285, abcnycconcierge.com) started as a limousine service, and owner Russell Figaredo expanded the offerings over time. Here's a sampling of their services: concierge, personal assistant, personal chef, travel planning, senior care and the ever-reliable limousine service. Contact this amazing crew when you need assistance with business or domestic errands, pet sitting or care, special-event tickets and restaurant reservations, personalized shopping and returns, a special night on the town or planning for out-of-town guests. I'd keep this number handy for just about anything!

TRANSLATION SERVICES

TRANSLINGUA

211 E 43rd St (bet Second and Third Ave), Suite 1404   212/697-2020
Mon-Fri: 9-5   translingua.com

TransLingua is a total language solution by a team of business professionals. They provide a full complement of linguistic services in over 80 languages and dialects. Services include cultural branding, translation, interpretation, graphic services and audio and video production with subtitles and voiceovers.

TRAVEL SERVICES

PASSPORT PLUS.NET

20 E 49th St (bet Fifth and Madison Ave), 3rd floor   212/759-5540
Mon-Fri: 9:30-5   passportplus.net

Getting a passport and the proper visas can be difficult and time-consuming. Passport Plus takes care of these chores by securing business and tourist travel documents; renewing and amending U.S. passports; obtaining duplicate marriage certificates and obtaining international drivers' licenses. They work closely with the U.S. Passport Agency and foreign consulates and embassies. Passport Plus offers assistance in case of rush, damaged, lost or stolen passports, serving customers all over the country.

UMBRELLA REPAIR

GILBERT CENTER

917/692-2078

If your favorite umbrella has a broken rib, runner, tube or stretcher, or if the fabric is ripped or worn, call umbrella repairman extraordinaire Gilbert Center. A fine craftsman, he takes great care to bring designer and vintage umbrellas back to life; people contact him from all over the country.

UNIFORM RENTAL

I. BUSS & ALLAN UNIFORM

142 W 36th St (bet Ave of the Americas and Seventh Ave), 2nd floor
Mon-Fri: 9-5   212/529-4655
                                                    ibuss-allan.com

I. Buss & Allan Uniform has been dressing four generations of doormen, concierges, police and security personnel, firemen, maintenance and housekeeping staffs, chefs and others. The company creates custom uniforms and branding and offers full-service sales and rentals to those in real estate, hospitality or entertainment industries; government agencies and other businesses. Uniform cleaning and delivery are also available.

WINDOW CLEANING

EXPERT WINDOW CLEANERS

212/831-1115
expertwindowcleaners.com

Yes, they do windows! Brent Weingard's window cleaning team assesses each job before they start; different types of glass and grunge require various products and methods. Their expertise in residential window cleaning includes glass restoration and renewal, waterproofing and caulking. Other high–rise applications include banner and flag placement or removal.

FRANK'S WINDOW CLEANING COMPANY

450 E 81st St (bet First and York Ave)   212/288-4631
By appointment   frankswindowcleaningnyc.com

Are your home's windows or mirrors dirty? If so, then call Frank's to put the sparkle and shine back on your glass surfaces. The experienced crew for this family-owned and –operated business has been in operation since 1929; prices are reasonable.

RED BALL WINDOW CLEANING

221 E 85th St (bet Second and Third Ave), Suite 4   212/861-7686
Mon-Sat: 7:30-5   Facebook

The people at Red Ball have cleaned a lot of windows since opening in 1928! Still a family business, they specialize in residential window cleaning, inside and out. The higher the windows, the happier they are; the work is guaranteed.

CHAPTER 6

WHERE TO FIND IT
NEW YORK'S BEST STORES

No city on earth has more shopping opportunities than New York City. Giant department stores offer huge selections for men, women, children and the home. Specialty outlets feature every well-known or obscure item you might be seeking. There are more shopping options: street peddlers, marketplaces, e-commerce and at special events. How can one possibly make sense of it all? For starters, I suggest carefully reading this entire chapter. You will find all of the information you need for shopping in Manhattan, with the most useful and complete array of information available anywhere. Discovering a real treasure is still possible, so good luck and have fun!

GERRY'S EXCLUSIVE LIST

THE BEST PLACES TO SHOP FOR SPECIFIC ITEMS IN NEW YORK

THINGS FOR THE PERSON (MEN, WOMEN, CHILDREN)

ACCESSORIES, FASHION, VINTAGE AND CONTEMPORARY | **Eye Candy Store** (225 W 23rd St, 212/343-4275)

ACCESSORIES, MEN'S AND WOMEN'S LEATHER | **Will Leather Goods** (29 Prince St, 212/925-2824)

ACCESSORIES, WOMEN'S | **La Crasia** (Grand Central Terminal, 42nd St at Lexington Ave, 212/370-0310) and **Marc Jacobs** (385 Bleecker St, 212/924-6126)

BACKPACKS | **Bag House** (797 Broadway, 212/260-0940)

BRIEFCASES | **Brooks Brothers** (1270 Ave of the Americas, 212/247-9374 and 346 Madison Ave, 212/309-7765) and **Per Tutti** (49 Greenwich Ave, 212/675-0113)

CANES, WALKING | **Rain or Shine** (45 E 45th St, 212/741-9650)

CLOTHING, CASUAL | **Mr. Joe** (500 Eighth Ave, 212/279-1090)

CLOTHING, CHILDREN'S (infants through teens) | **Lester's** (1534 Second Ave, 212/734-9292)

CLOTHING, CHILDREN'S FRENCH | **Catimini** (1125 Madison Ave, 212/987-0688) and **Jacadi** (1242 Madison Ave, 212/369-1616)

CLOTHING, CHILDREN'S, FUNKY AND FUN | **Space Kiddets** (26 E 22nd St, 212/420-9878)

CLOTHING, CHILDREN'S PARTY DRESSES AND SUITS | **Prince and Princess** (41 E 78th St, 212/879-8989)

CLOTHING, CONTEMPORARY | **Theory** (40 Gansevoort St, 212/524-6790; flagship store)

CLOTHING, CUSTOM-MADE | **Saint Laurie Merchant Tailors** (22 W 32nd St, 5th floor, 212/643-1916; by appointment)

CLOTHING, DESIGNER, SAMPLES | **Showroom Seven** (263 Eleventh Ave, 3rd floor, 212/643-4810)

CLOTHING, FAMILY | **American Apparel** (429 Broadway, 212/925-0560; 140 West Broadway, 212/393-3489 and 1030 Third Ave, 212/207-3239)

CLOTHING, GIRLS' (tweens) | **Infinity** (1116 Madison Ave, 212/734-0077)

CLOTHING, GIRLS' SOCKS | **LittleMissMatched** (565 Fifth Ave, 212/297-2570)

CLOTHING, JEANS, CUSTOM-FINISH | **Jean Shop** (37 Crosby St, 212/366-5326)

CLOTHING, JEANS, DISCOUNTED | **Buffalo Exchange** (332 E 11th St, 212/260-9340 and 114 W 26th St, 212/675-3535) and **Quiksilver** (3 Times Square, 212/888-7526; 519 Broadway, 212/226-1193 and 403 W 14th St, 212/337-1089)

CLOTHING, JEANS, FAMILY | **Unlimited Jeans** (850 Second Ave, 212/661-6495; 61 W 23rd St, 212/675-2872 and 492 Sixth Ave, 212/645-4021)

CLOTHING, JEANS, GOOD QUALITY | **G-Star** (270 Lafayette St, 212/219-2744),

Madewell (115 Fifth Ave, 212/228-5172), **Paige Premium Denim** (869 Washington St, 212/807-1400; 245 Columbus Ave, 212/769-1500 and 71 Mercer St, 212/625-0800) and **Uniqlo** (666 Fifth Ave, 31 W 34th St and 546 Broadway; 877/486-4756 for all locations)

CLOTHING, LINGERIE, DISCOUNTED | **Orchard Corset** (157 Orchard St, 212/674-0786)

CLOTHING, LINGERIE, FANTASY | **Agent Provocateur** (133 Mercer St, 212/965-0229 and 675 Madison Ave, 212/840-2436)

CLOTHING, LINGERIE, FINE | **Bra Smyth** (905 Madison Ave, 212/772-9400 and 2177 Broadway, 212/721-5111) and **Peress** (1070 Madison Ave, 212/861-6336)

CLOTHING, LINGERIE, POST-BREAST SURGERY | **Underneath It All** (320 Fifth Ave, 10th floor, 212/717-1976; by appointment)

CLOTHING, MEN'S AND WOMEN'S GENERAL | **Scotch & Soda** (273 Lafayette St, 212/966-3300 and 866 Broadway, 646/561-9679)

CLOTHING, MEN'S AND WOMEN'S SHIRTS, SOPHISTICATED | **Kamakura Shirts** (400 Madison Ave, 212/308-5266)

CLOTHING, MEN'S AND WOMEN'S SOCKS (all colors) | **Sock Man** (27 St. Mark's Pl, 212/529-0300)

CLOTHING, MEN'S, BIG AND TALL | **DXL** (703 Sixth Ave, 212/242-3189)

CLOTHING, MEN'S BOUTIQUE | **Odin** (199 Lafayette St, 212/966-0026 and 328 E 11th St, 212/475-0666)

CLOTHING, MEN'S BRAND-NAME, DISCOUNTED | **Century 21** (22 Cortlandt St, 212/227-9092) and **L.S. Men's Clothing** (49 W 45th St, 3rd floor, 212/575-0933)

CLOTHING, MEN'S CLASSIC | **Carson Street Clothiers** (63 Crosby St, 212/925-2627), **FrankStella** (921 Seventh Ave, 212/957-1600 and 440 Columbus Ave, 212/877-5566) and **Peter Elliot** (997 Lexington Ave, 212/570-2301)

CLOTHING, MEN'S CONTEMPORARY | **Jay Kos** (55 Houston St, 212/319-2770) and **Topman** (608 Fifth Ave, 212/757-8240)

CLOTHING, MEN'S CUSTOM-MADE | **Alan Flusser** (3 E 48th St, 3rd floor, 212/888-4500), **Ascot Chang** (110 Central Park S, 212/759-3333) and **Bhambi's Custom Tailors** (14 E 60th St, Suite 610, 212/935-5379)

CLOTHING, MEN'S EUROPEAN SUITS | **Jodamo International** (321 Grand St, 212/219-1039)

CLOTHING, MEN'S BESPOKE SHIRTS | **20 Peacocks** (99 Madison Ave, 718/674-5873; by appointment)

CLOTHING, MEN'S SURFER | **Saturdays Surf** (17 Perry St, 347/246-5830)

CLOTHING, MEN'S UNDERWEAR | **Pengallan** (123 E 7th St, 212/777-7211)

CLOTHING, MEN'S VINTAGE | **Stock** (143 E 13th St, 212/505-2505)

CLOTHING, OUTDOOR WEAR | **Eastern Mountain Sports** (530 Broadway, 212/966-8730 and 2152 Broadway, 212/873-4001)

CLOTHING, SPORTSWEAR | **Atrium** (644 Broadway, 212/473-9200), **Filson NYC** (40 Great Jones St, 212/547-3121) and **Paul & Shark** (667 Madison Ave, 212/452-9868)

CLOTHING, VINTAGE | **Reminiscence** (74 Fifth Ave, 212/243-2292) and **Resurrection** (217 Mott St, 212/625-1374)

CLOTHING, VINTAGE, DESIGNER | **New York Vintage** (117 W 25th St, 212/647-1107)

CLOTHING, WOMEN'S BRIDAL AND SPECIAL OCCASION | **Kleinfeld** (110 W 20th St, 646/633-4300), **Mary Adams The Dress** (31 E 32nd St, Room 604, 212/473-0237; by appointment), **Monique Lhuillier** (19 E 71st St, 212/683-3332) and **Reem Acra** (730 Fifth Ave, Suite 205, 212/308-8760; by appointment)

CLOTHING, WOMEN'S BRIDAL AND SPECIAL-OCCASION, CUSTOM-MADE | **Jane Wilson-Marquis** (42 E 76th St, 212/452-5335; by appointment)

CLOTHING, WOMEN'S CLASSIC DESIGNER | **Nina McLemore** (135 E 55th St, 7th floor, 212/319-7700) and **Yigal Azrouël** (1011 Madison Ave, 212/929-7525)

CLOTHING, WOMEN'S DESIGNER, RESALE | **Ina** (101 Thompson St, 212/941-4757 and other locations) and **New & Almost New** (171 Mott St, 212/226-6677)

CLOTHING, WOMEN'S EASTERN-INSPIRED | **Vivienne Tam** (40 Mercer St, 212/966-2398)

CLOTHING, WOMEN'S IMPORTED | **Creatures of Comfort** (205 Mulberry St, 212/925-1005) and **Roberta Roller Rabbit** (1019 Lexington Ave, 212/772-7200 and 176 Duane St, 212/966-0076)

CLOTHING, WOMEN'S MATERNITY, CONSIGNMENT | **Clementine** (39½ Washington Sq S, 212/228-9333)

CLOTHING, WOMEN'S PANTS | **Theory** (201 Columbus Ave, 212/362-3676)

CLOTHING, WOMEN'S PLUS-SIZE | **Curvaceous K** (179 Stanton St, 374/294-4404)

CLOTHING, WOMEN'S SPORTSWEAR | **Giselle** (143 Orchard St, 212/673-1900)

CLOTHING, WOMEN'S TAILORED | **Judith & Charles** (1355 Third Ave, 212/988-4611 and 188 Columbus Ave, 212/877-2250)

CLOTHING, WOMEN'S TIGHTS | **Club Monaco** (121 Prince St, 212/533-8930)

CLOTHING AND ACCESSORIES, MEN'S AND WOMEN'S | **Etro** (720 Madison Ave, 212/317-9096)

CLOTHING AND ACCESSORIES, WOMEN'S | **Derek Lam** (764 Madison Ave, 212/966-1616)

COSMETICS, BESPOKE AND ECO-FRIENDLY | **Bite** (174 Prince St, 646/484-6111)

COSMETICS, MEN'S AND WOMEN'S LUXURY | **Space NK** (99 Greene St, 212/941-4200)

COSMETICS AND SOAPS, NATURAL | **Lush Cosmetics** (1293 Broadway, 212/564-9120)

EYEWEAR, ELEGANT | **Morgenthal-Frederics** (944 Madison Ave, 212/744-9444; 399 West Broadway, 212/966-0099 and 699 Madison Ave, 212/838-3090) and **Oliver Peoples** (812 Madison Ave, 212/585-3433 and 366 West Broadway, 212/925-5400)

FABRICS, DESIGNER | **B&J Fabrics** (525 Seventh Ave, 2nd floor, 212/354-8150)

FABRICS AND PATTERNS | **P&S Fabrics and Crafts** (359 Broadway, 212/226-1534)

FRAGRANCES | **Aedes de Venustas** (9 Christopher St, 212/206-8674), **Azmere** (1220 Broadway, 212/868-0181) and **Osswald** (311 West Broadway, 212/625-3111)

GLOVES, CASHMERE KNIT | **Meg Cohen Design Shop** (59 Thompson St, 212/966-3733)

GLOVES, ITALIAN | **Sermoneta Gloves** (609-611 Madison Ave, 212/319-5946)

HANDBAGS, DESIGNER | **Ghurka** (65 Prince St, 212/334-4000 and 781 Fifth Ave, 212/ 826-8300), **Lulu Guinness** (394 Bleecker St, 212/367-2120) and **Sigerson Morrison** (28 Prince St, 212/219-3893)

HANDBAGS, MAGNIFICENT, VERY EXPENSIVE, EXOTIC SKINS | **Devi Kroell** (717 Madison Ave, 212/644-4499)

HANDBAGS, MEN'S AND WOMEN'S | **Club Monaco** (160 Fifth Ave, 212/352-0936) and **Longchamp** (132 Spring St, 212/343-7444 and 713 Madison Ave, 212/223-1500)

HATS, CUSTOM-MADE FUR | **Lenore Marshall** (231 W 29th St, 212/947-5945)

HATS, MEN'S | **J.J. Hat Center** (310 Fifth Ave, 212/239-4368) and **Rod Keenan** (202 W 122nd St, 212/678-9275; by appointment)

JEWELRY, 14K AND 18K | **Hernandez Jewelry** (1427 Ave of the Americas, 212/265-4071)

JEWELRY, CHARMS | **Aaron Basha** (685 Madison Ave, 212/935-1960)

JEWELRY, COSTUME | **Lanciani** (922 Madison Ave, 212/717-2759; 826 Lexington Ave, 212/832-2092 and 510 Madison Ave, 212/759-4415) and **Lord & Taylor** (424 Fifth Ave, 212/391-3344)

JEWELRY, CUFF LINKS | **Links of London** (535 Madison Ave, 212/588-1177 and MetLife Building, 200 Park Ave, 212/867-0258) and **The Missing Link** (Showplace Antiques and Design Center, 40 W 25th St, Room 108, 212/645-6928)

JEWELRY, CUFF LINKS, VINTAGE | **Deco Jewels** (131 Thompson St, 212/253-1222)

JEWELRY, CUSTOM-DESIGNED | **Karen Karch** (38 Gramercy Park N, 212/965-9699) and **Ted Muehling** (52 White St, 212/431-3825)

JEWELRY, FINE | **S.J. Shrubsole** (104 E 57th St, 212/753-8920) and **Stuart Moore** (411 West Broadway, 212/941-1023)

JEWELRY, HANDMADE | **Ten Thousand Things** (423 W 14th St, 212/352-1333) and **Wendy Mink Jewelry** (72 Orchard St, 212/260-5298)

JEWELRY, PEARLS| **Mikimoto** (730 Fifth Ave, 212/457-4600)

JEWELRY, VINTAGE | **Deco Jewels** (131 Thompson St, 212/253-1222) and **Doyle & Doyle** (412 W 13th St, 212/677-9991)

JEWELRY, WEDDING RINGS | **Wedding Ring Originals** (608 Fifth Ave, Suite 509, 212/751-3940; call ahead)

LEATHER GOODS | **Il Bisonte** (120 Sullivan St, 212/966-8773) and **M0851** (415 West Broadway, 212/431-3069)

MASSAGE OILS | **Fragrance Shop** (65 E 4th St, 212/254-8950)

MILLINERY, VINTAGE | **Ellen Christine** (99 Vandam St, Room 4-E, 212/242-2457; by appointment)

SHAVING PRODUCTS | **The Art of Shaving** (141 E 62nd St, 212/317-8436; 373 Madison Ave, 212/986-2905 and other locations) and **C.O. Bigelow Chemists** (414 Ave of the Americas, 212/533-2700)

SHOES, ADULT | **David Z** (556 Broadway, 212/431-5450; 384 Fifth Ave, 917/351-1484 and other locations), **Dr. Martens** (148 Spring St, 212/226-8500) and **Rag & Bone** (182 Columbus Ave, 212/362-7138; 100 Christopher St, 212/727-2999 and other locations)

SHOES, ATHLETIC | **JackRabbit** (42 W 14th St, 212/727-2980)

SHOES, BRITISH BRAND | **Crockett and Jones** (7 W 56th St, 212/582-3800)

SHOES, CHILDREN'S, UPSCALE | **Harry's Shoes for Kids** (2315 Broadway, 212/874-2034) and **Shoofly** (42 Hudson St, 212/406-3270)

SHOES, DISCOUNTED | **DSW** (40 E 14th St, 212/674-2146) and **Stapleton Shoe Company** (1 Rector St, 212/964-6329)

SHOES, FAMILY, COMFORT | **Tip Top Shoes** (155 W 72nd St, 212/787-4960)

SHOES, MEN'S AND WOMEN'S CUSTOM-MADE | **Eneslow** (470 Park Ave S, 212/477-2300) and **Oberle Custom Shoes/Mathias Bootmaker** (1502 First Ave, 212/717-4023)

SHOES, NON-LEATHER | **MooShoes** (78 Orchard St, 212/254-6512)

SHOES, SANDALS, HANDMADE | **Jutta Neumann** (355 E 4th St, 212/982-7048)

SHOES, WOMEN'S DESIGNER | **Sigerson Morrison** (28 Prince St, 212/219-3893) and **United Nude** (25 Bond St, 212/420-6000)

SHOES, WOMEN'S CASUAL | **Matt Bernson** (20 Harrison St, 212/941-7634)

SKIWEAR | **Bogner** (380 West Broadway, 212/219-2757; seasonal)

SOAPS | **Fresh** (57 Spring St, 212/925-0099 and other locations)

SUNGLASSES, AVIATOR AND RETRO | **Fossil** (38 W 34th St, 212/594-5850; 1585 Broadway, 212/445-1021 and 530 Fifth Ave, 212/997-3978)

SUNGLASSES, CUSTOM AND VINTAGE | **Fabulous Fanny's** (335 E 9th St, 212/533-0637)

SUNGLASSES, FASHION | **Sunglass Hut** (1313 Broadway, 212/947-7789; 496 Broadway, 212/966-6501 and other locations)

SWIMWEAR, MEN'S AND BOYS' | **Vilebrequin** (1007 Madison Ave, 212/650-0353 and 436 West Broadway, 212/431-0673)

SWIMWEAR, WOMEN'S | **Canyon Beachwear** (1136 Third Ave, 917/432-0732), **Malia Mills Swimwear** (199 Mulberry St, 212/625-2311; 1015 Lexington Ave, 212/517-7485 and 220 Columbus Ave, 212/874-7200) and **Wolford** (619 Madison Ave, 212/688-4850 and other locations; seasonal)

TIES | **Andrew's Ties** (30 Rockefeller Center, 212/245-4563) and **Tie Coon** (400 Seventh Ave, 212/904-1433)

TIES, CUSTOM-MADE AND LIMITED-EDITION | **Seigo** (1248 Madison Ave, 212/987-0191)

UMBRELLAS | **Rain or Shine** (45 E 45th St, 212/741-9650)

WATCHBANDS | **Central Watch** (Grand Central Terminal, 45th St passageway, 212/685-1689)

WATCHES | **Fossil** (38 W 34th St, 212/594-5850; 1585 Broadway, 212/445-1021 and 530 Fifth Ave, 212/997-3978) and **Swatch** (640 Broadway, 212/777-1002; 1528 Broadway, 212/764-5541 and other locations)

WATCHES, DISCOUNTED | **Sandy Yaeger Watch** (578 Fifth Ave, 212/819-0088)

WATCHES, SWISS ARMY | **Victorinox Swiss Army Soho** (99 Wooster St, 212/431-4950)

WEDDING BANDS | **Wedding Ring Originals** (608 Fifth Ave, Suite 509, 212/751-3940)

ZIPPERS | **ZipperStop** (27 Allen St, 212/226-3964)

THINGS FOR THE HOME AND OFFICE

AIR CONDITIONERS | **Elgot Sales** (937 Lexington Ave, 212/879-1200)

APPLIANCES, DISCOUNTED | **Price Watchers** (800/336-6694)

APPLIANCES, KITCHEN | **Gringer & Sons** (29 First Ave, 212/475-0600) and **Zabar's** (2245 Broadway, 212/787-2000)

ART, ANCIENT GREEK, ROMAN, EGYPTIAN AND NEAR EASTERN | **Royal Athena Galleries** (153 E 57th St, 212/355-2033)

ART, EROTIC | **Erotics Gallery** (41 Union Sq W, Room 635, 212/633-2241; by appointment)

ART, 19TH- AND 20TH-CENTURY WESTERN | **J.N. Bartfield Galleries** (60 W 55th St, 5th floor, 212/245-8890)

ART, 20TH-CENTURY DADAIST AND SURREALIST | **Timothy Baum** (40 E 18th St, 212/879-4512; by appointment)

ART DECO, FRENCH | **Maison Gérard** (53 E 10th St, 212/674-7611)

AXES, HANDMADE | **Best Made Co.** (36 White St, 646/478-7092)

BABY EQUIPMENT | **Schneider's** (41 W 25th St, 212/228-3540)

BASKETS | **Bill's Flower Market** (816 Ave of the Americas, 212/889-8154)

BATH AND BED ITEMS | **Bed Bath & Beyond** (620 Ave of the Americas, 212/255-3550; 410 E 61st St, 646/215-4702; 1932 Broadway, 917/441-9391 and 270 Greenwich St, 212/233-8450)

BATH FIXTURES, EXPENSIVE | **Boffi Soffi** (31½ Greene St, 212/431-8282)

BEDDING AND PILLOWS | **Ankasa** (1200 Madison Ave, 212/996-5200 and 424 Broome St, 212/226-8002)

BEDS, HEADBOARDS AND FOOTBOARDS | **Charles P. Rogers** (26 W 17th St, 212/675-4400)

BEDS, MURPHY | **Murphy Bed Center** (113 W 25th St, 1st floor, 212/645-7079)

BEDS, SWEDISH HANDMADE | **Hästens** (75 Grand St, 212/219-8022; 876 Broadway, 212/505-8022 and 1100 Madison Ave, 212/628-8022)

BOXES, WOODEN | **An American Craftsman Galleries** (790 Seventh Ave, 212/399-2555)

CANDLE AND AROMATICS, CUSTOMIZED | **Le Labo** (233 Elizabeth St, 212/219-2230 and 14 W 29th St, 212/532-7206)

CHANDELIERS | **Foundry Lighting** (225 E 58th St, 212/759-9332) and **Le Fanion** (299 W 4th St, 212/463-8760)

CHINA, BARGAIN PIECES | **Fishs Eddy** (889 Broadway, 212/420-9020)

CHINA, ENGLISH IMARI | **Bardith, Ltd** (901 Madison Ave, 212/737-3775)

CHINA, PORCELAIN | **Porcelain Room** (13 Christopher St, 212/367-8206)

CHRISTMAS DECOR | **Christmas Cottage** (871 Seventh Ave, 212/333-7380)

CHRISTMAS DECORATIONS, DISCOUNTED | **Kurt S. Adler Santa's World** (7 W 34th St, 212/924-0900; opens around Thanksgiving for sample sale)

CLOCKS, CUCKOO | **Time Pieces, Inc.** (115 Greenwich Ave, 212/929-8011)

CLOSET FIXTURES | **California Closets** (26 Varick St, 646/486-3905)

COOKBOOKS, USED | **Bonnie Slotnick Cookbooks** (163 W 10th St, 212/989-8962) and **Joanne Hendricks Cookbooks** (488 Greenwich St, 212/226-5731)

DECOUPAGE ITEMS | **Kaas Glassworks** (117 Perry St, 212/366-0322) and **John Derian Company** (6 E 2nd St, 212/677-3917)

DINNERWARE, FIESTA (individual pieces) | **Mood Indigo** (Showplace Antiques and Design Center, 40 W 25th St, Gallery 222, 212/254-1176)

DINNERWARE, PORCELAIN | **Bernardaud** (499 Park Ave, 212/371-4300)

ELECTRONICS, HIGH-END | **Audioarts** (210 Fifth Ave, 212/260-2939; by appointment)

ELECTRONICS, VINTAGE | **Waves** (Showplace Antiques and Design Center, 40 W 25th St, Gallery 107, 212/273-9616)

FABRICS, DECORATOR, DISCOUNTED | **Zarin Fabrics** (69 Orchard St, 212/925-6112)

FDNY MERCHANDISE | **FDNY Fire Zone** (34 W 51st St, 212/698-4529)

FLAGS AND BANNERS | **Art Flag Co.** (8 Jay St, 212/334-1890)

FLOOR COVERINGS | **ABC Carpet & Home** (881and 888 Broadway, 212/473-3000)

FLOOR COVERINGS, VINTAGE | **Doris Leslie Blau** (306 E 61st St, 212/586-5511; by appointment) and **Secondhand Rose** (230 Fifth Ave, 5th floor, 212/393-9002)

FLORAL DESIGNS | **L. Becker Flowers** (217 E 83rd St, 212/439-6001)

FLOWER BOUQUETS | **Posies** (366 Amsterdam Ave, 212/721-2260)

FLOWERS, FRESH-CUT (from Europe) | **VSF** (204 W 10th St, 212/206-7236)

FLOWERS, ORCHIDS | **Judy's Plant World** (1384 Lexington Ave, 212/860-0055)

FLOWERS, SILK | **Pany Silk Flowers** (146 W 28th St, 212/645-9526)

FOLIAGE, LIVE AND ARTIFICIAL | **American Foliage & Design Group** (122 W 22nd St, 212/741-5555)

FRAMES, PICTURE | **A.I. Friedman** (44 W 18th St, 212/243-9000) and **Framed on Madison** (976 Lexington Ave, 212/734-4680)

FURNITURE | **Design Within Reach** (110 Green St, 212/475-0001; 408 W 14th St, 212/242-9449 and other locations)

FURNITURE AND MATTRESSES, FOAM | **Dixie Foam** (113 W 25th St, 212/645-8999)

FURNITURE, ANTIQUE | **H.M. Luther Antiques** (35 E 76th St, 212/439-7919 and 61 E 11th St, 212/505-1485)

FURNITURE, CLASSIC HAND-CARVED | **Devon Shops** (111 E 27th St, 212/686-1760)

FURNITURE, CONTEMPORARY | **DwellStudio** (77 Wooster St, 646/442-6000)

FURNITURE, HANDCRAFTED, EXPENSIVE | **Thomas Moser Cabinetmakers** (699 Madison Ave, 2nd floor, 212/753-7005)

FURNITURE, HARDWOOD | **Pompanoosuc Mills** (124 Hudson St, 212/226-5960)

FURNITURE, HOME AND OFFICE | **Knoll** (1330 Ave of the Americas, 212/343-4000)

FURNITURE, INFANTS' | **Albee Baby** (715 Amsterdam Ave, 212/662-5740) and **Schneider's** (41 W 25th St, 212/228-3540)

FURNITURE, MODERN-DESIGN | **Cassina USA** (155 E 56th St, 212/245-2121)

FURNITURE, SOFABEDS | **Avery-Boardman** (Decoration & Design Building, 979 Third Ave, 4th floor, 212/688-6611)

FURNITURE, VINTAGE | **Regeneration Furniture** (38 Renwick St, 212/741-2102)

GARDEN ACCESSORIES | **Lexington Gardens** (1011 Lexington Ave, 212/861-4390)

GLASS, VENETIAN | **End of History** (548½ Hudson St, 212/647-7598) and **Gardner & Barr** (444 W 55th St, 212/752-0555; by appointment)

GLASSWARE, STEUBEN, USED | **Lillian Nassau** (220 E 57th St, 212/759-6062)

HARDWARE, DOORKNOBS | **Simon's Hardware & Bath** (421 Third Ave, 212/532-9220)

HARDWARE AND ACCESSORIES, BRASS | **The Brass Center** (248 E 58th St, 212/421-0090)

HOME ACCESSORIES | **Aedes de Venustas** (9 Christopher St, 212/206-8674) and **Scent Elate** (313 W 48th St, 212/258-3043)

HOME ACCESSORIES, MADE FROM NATURE | **Creel and Gow** (131 E 70th St, 212/327-4281)

HOUSEPLANTS | **The Sill** (84 Hester St, 646/450-7455)

HOUSEWARES | **Dinosaur Designs** (211 Elizabeth St, 212/680-3523) and **Gracious Home** (1201 and 1220 Third Ave, 212/517-6300 and 1992 Broadway, 212/231-7800)

HOUSEWARES, DESIGNER | **Jung Lee** (25 W 29th St, 212/257-5655)

HOUSEWARES, UPSCALE | **Lancelotti** (66 Ave A, 212/475-6851)

KITCHEN CABINETRY | **Effeti** (645 W 27th St, 212/502-8916)

KITCHENWARE (best all-around store) | **Zabar's** (2245 Broadway, 212/787-2000)

KITCHENWARE, BAKEWARE, DISCOUNTED | **Broadway Panhandler** (65 E 8th St, 212/966-3434)

KITCHENWARE, COOKWARE | **Bed Bath & Beyond** (620 Ave of the Americas, 212/255-3550; 410 E 61st St, 646/215-4702; 1932 Broadway, 917/441-9391 and 270 Greenwich St, 212/233-8450), **Korin** (57 Warren St, 212/587-7021) and **Zabar's** (2245 Broadway, 212/787-2000)

KITCHENWARE, KNIVES | **Roger & Sons** (268 Bowery, 212/226-4734)

KITCHENWARE, PROFESSIONAL | **Hung Chong Imports** (14 Bowery, 212/349-3392) and **J.B. Prince** (36 E 31st St, 11th floor, 212/683-3553)

LAMPSHADES | **Just Shades** (21 Spring St, 212/966-2757) and **Oriental Lampshade Co.** (223 W 79th St, 212/873-0812)

LIGHTBULBS | **Just Bulbs** (220 E 60th St, 212/228-7820)

LIGHTING, CHANDELIERS | **The Lively Set** (33 Bedford St, 212/807-8417)

LIGHTING, CUSTOM-MADE AND ANTIQUE | **Lampworks** (New York Design Center, 200 Lexington Ave, Suite 903, 212/750-1500)

LIGHTING FIXTURES | **City Knickerbocker** (665 Eleventh Ave, 212/586-3939) and **Lighting by Gregory** (158 Bowery, 212/226-1276)

LIGHTING FIXTURES, ANTIQUE | **Olde Good Things** (124 W 24th St, 212/989-8401; 5 E 16th St, 212/989-8814; 149 Madison Ave, 212/362-8025 and other locations)

LIGHTING, PHOTOGRAPHIC (purchase or rental) | **Flash Clinic** (164 W 25th St, 212/337-0447)

LINENS | **Bed Bath & Beyond** (620 Ave of the Americas, 212/255-3550; 410 E 61st St, 646/215-4702; 1932 Broadway, 917/441-9391 and 270 Greenwich St, 212/233-8450) and **Layther's Linen & Home** (2270 Broadway, 212/724-0180 and 237 E 86th St, 212/996-4439)

OFFICE SUPPLIES, MUJI | **Muji** (455 Broadway, 212/334-2002; 620 Eighth Ave, 212/382-2300; 16 W 19th St, 212/414-9024 and 52 Cooper Sq, 212/358-8693)

PERFUME BOTTLES, VINTAGE | **Kenneth James Collection** (1050 Second Ave, 212/888-0165)

PLUMBING FIXTURES | **Blackman** (85 Fifth Ave, 2nd floor, 212/337-1000)

PORCELAIN ITEMS | **Lladro** (500 Madison Ave, 212/838-9356)

PORTFOLIOS, CUSTOM | **House of Portfolios** (133 W 25th St, 7th floor, 212/206-7323)

POSTERS, AMERICAN AND INTERNATIONAL MOVIE | **Jerry Ohlinger's Movie Materials Store** (216 W 30th St, 2nd floor, 212/989-0869)

POSTERS, BROADWAY THEATER | **Triton Gallery** (630 Ninth Ave, Suite 808, 212/765-2472)

POSTERS, ORIGINAL, 1880 TO PRESENT | **Philip Williams Posters** (122 Chambers St, 212/513-0313)

POSTERS, VINTAGE | **La Belle Epoque Vintage Posters** (115-A Greenwich Ave, 212/362-1770) and **Ross Art Group** (532 Madison Ave, 4th floor, 212/223-1525)

POTTERY, HANDMADE | **Mugi Studio and Gallery** (993 Amsterdam Ave, 212/866-6202)

PRINTS, BOTANICAL | **W. Graham Arader** (29 E 72nd St, 212/628-3668 and 1016 Madison Ave, 212/628-7625)

QUILTS | **Down and Quilt Shop** (527 Amsterdam Ave, 212/496-8980)

RUGS | **Rahmanan Antique & Decorative Rugs** (36 E 31st St, 9th floor, 212/683-0167) and **Stepevi** (147 Wooster St, 212/466-0400)

SAFES | **Empire Safe** (6 E 39th St, 212/684-2255)

SCREENS, SHOJI | **Miya Shoji** (228 W 18th St, 212/243-6774)

SHOWER CURTAINS | **Delphinium Home** (353 W 47th St, 212/333-7732)

SILVER ITEMS, UNUSUAL | **Christofle** (846 Madison Ave, 212/308-9390) and **Jean's Silversmiths** (16 W 45th St, 212/575-0723)

SLIPCOVERS | **Joe's Fabrics Warehouse** (102 Orchard St, 212/674-7089)

TABLEWARE, METAL, HANDMADE | **Michael Aram** (136 W 18th St, 212/461-6903)

TILES | **Mosaic House** (32 W 22nd St, 212/414-2525)

TILES, CERAMIC AND MARBLE | **Complete Tile Collection** (42 W 15th St, 212/255-4450) and **Quarry Tiles, Marble & Granite** (129 W 22nd St, 212/679-8889)

TOOLS | **Best Made Company** (36 White St, 646/478-7092) and **Nuthouse Hardware** (202 E 29th St, 212/545-1447)

TRAYS | **Extraordinary** (247 E 57th St, 212/223-9151)

TYPEWRITER RIBBONS | **Abalon Business Machines & Service** (22 W 38th St, 7th floor, 212/682-1653)

VACUUM CLEANERS | **Desco** (131 W 14th St, 212/989-1800)

WALLPAPER, VINTAGE | **Secondhand Rose** (230 Fifth Ave, 5th floor, 212/393-9002)

WROUGHT-IRON ITEMS | **Morgik Metal Design** (145 Hudson St, 212/463-0304)

THINGS FOR LEISURE TIME

ATHLETIC GEAR | **Modell's Sporting Goods** (41 E 42nd St, 212/661-4242 and other locations)

ATHLETIC GEAR, TEAM | **New York Mets Clubhouse** (11 W 42nd St, 212/768-9534) and **Yankee Clubhouse** (110 E 59th St, 212/758-7844; 393 Fifth Ave, 212/685-4693; 245 W 42nd St, 212/768-9555 and 8 Fulton St, 212/514-7182)

BACKGAMMON SETS | **Clare V.** (239 Elizabeth St, 646/484-5757)

BALLOONS | **Balloon Saloon** (133 West Broadway, 212/227-3838)

BEADS | **Beads of Paradise** (16 E 17th St, 212/620-0642) and **Beads World** (57 W 38th St, 212/302-1199)

BICYCLES | **Bicycle Habitat** (244 and 250 Lafayette St, 212/625-1347 and 228 Seventh Ave, 212/206-6949)

BICYCLES, FOLDING | **Frank's Bike Shop** (553 Grand St, 212/533-6332)

BINOCULARS | **Clairmont-Nichols** (1016 First Ave, 212/758-2346)

BOOKS, AFRICAN AND AFRICAN-AMERICAN | **Jumel Terrace Books** (426 W 160th St, 212/928-9525; by appointment)

BOOKS, CHILDREN'S, EDUCATORS' AND PARENTS' | **Bank Street Bookstore** (2875 Broadway, 212/678-1654)

BOOKS, COMIC | **Forbidden Planet NYC** (832 Broadway, 212/473-1576) and **Midtown Comics** (200 W 40th St, 459 Lexington Ave and 64 Fulton St; 212/302-8192 for all locations)

BOOKS, COMIC, VINTAGE | **Metropolis Collectibles** (36 W 37th St, 6th floor, 212/260-4147; by appointment)

BOOKS, EXAM-STUDY AND SCIENCE-FICTION | **Civil Service Book Shop** (38 Lispenard St, 212/226-9506)

BOOKS, FASHION DESIGN | **Fashion Design Bookstore** (250 W 27th St, 212/633-9646)

BOOKS, METAPHYSICAL AND RELIGIOUS | **Quest Bookshop** (240 E 53rd St, 212/758-5521)

BOOKS, NEW, USED AND REVIEW COPIES | **Strand Book Store** (828 Broadway, 212/473-1452)

BOOKS, PROGRESSIVE POLITICAL | **Revolution Books** (146 W 26th St, 212/691-3345)

BOOKS, PUBLICATIONS BY ARTISTS | **Printed Matter** (195 Tenth Ave, 212/925-0325)

BOOKS, RARE | **Imperial Fine Books** (790 Madison Ave, 2nd floor, 212/861-6620), **Martayan Lan** (70 E 55th St, 6th floor, 212/308-0018) and **Strand Book Store** (828 Broadway, 212/473-1452)

BOOKS, SCHOLARLY | **Book Culture** (536 W 112th St, 212/865-1588)

CAMERA, VIDEO | **AC Gears** (69 E 8th St, 212/375-1700)

CAMPING AND OUTDOOR EQUIPMENT | **Tent and Trails** (21 Park Pl, 212/227-1761)

CIGARETTES, LUXURY | **Nat Sherman** (489 Fifth Ave, 212/764-5000)

CIGARS | **Davidoff of Geneva** (515 Madison Ave, 212/751-9060), **DP Cigars** (265 W 30th St, 212/367-8949) and **Mulberry Street Cigars** (140 Mulberry St, 212/941-7400)

COMPACT DISCS, NEW AND USED | **Disc-O-Rama** (44 W 8th St, 212/206-8417)

COMPUTERS, APPLE | **Apple Store** (103 Prince St, 212/226-3126; 767 Fifth Ave, 212/336-1440; 401 W 14th St, 212/444-3400 and 1981 Broadway, 212/209-3400)

COSTUMES AND MAKEUP | **New York Costumes/Halloween Adventure** (104 Fourth Ave, 212/673-4546)

DANCE ITEMS | **World Tone Dance** (580 Eighth Ave, 2nd floor, 212/691-1934)

DOLLHOUSES | **Tiny Doll House** (314 E 78th St, 212/744-3719)

ELECTRONICS, TRAVEL | **Tumi** (Rockefeller Center, 53 W 49th St, 212/245-7460)

EMBROIDERY, CUSTOM-DESIGNED | **Jonathan Embroidery Plus** (256 W 38th St, 212/398-3538)

FISHING TACKLE, FLY | **Orvis** (489 Fifth Ave, 212/827-0698)

GAMES | **Compleat Strategist** (11 E 33rd St, 212/685-3880)

GAMES, CHESS SETS | **Chess Forum** (219 Thompson St, 212/475-2369)

GAMES, WARHAMMER | **Games Workshop** (54 E 8th St, 212/982-6314)

GIFTS | **Exit 9** (51 Ave A, 212/228-0145), **Greenwich Letterpress** (39 Christopher St, 212/989-7464), **House of Cards and Curiosities** (23 Eighth Ave, 212/675-6178) and **Pylones** (Grand Central Terminal, 42nd St at Vanderbilt Ave, 212/867-0969 and Rockefeller Center, 74 W 50th St, 212/227-9273)

GOLF EQUIPMENT (best selection) | **New York Golf Center** (131 W 35th St, 212/564-2255 and other locations)

GUNS | **Beretta Gallery** (718 Madison Ave, 212/319-3235) and **Holland & Holland** (10 E 40th St, 19th floor, 212/752-7755)

HARLEY-DAVIDSON GEAR | **Harley-Davidson of New York** (686 Lexington Ave, 212/355-3003)

HOLOGRAPHS | **Holographic Studio** (240 E 26th St, 212/686-9397)

HORSEBACK-RIDING EQUIPMENT | **Manhattan Saddlery** (117 E 24th St, 212/673-1400)

KNITTING | **Gotta Knit!** (14 E 34th St, 5th floor, 212/989-3030), **Knitty City** (208 W 79th St, 212/787-5896), **String** (33 E 65th St, 212/288-9276) and **The Yarn Company** (2274 Broadway, 212/787-7878)

LUGGAGE AND TRAVEL ACCESSORIES | **Altman Luggage** (135 Orchard St, 212/254-7275), **Bag House** (797 Broadway, 212/260-0940), **Flight 001** (96 Greenwich Ave, 212/989-0001), **Pertutti** (49 Greenwich Ave, 212/675-0113) and **Tumi** (Rockefeller Center, 53 W 49th St, 212/245-7460; 520 Madison Ave, 212/813-0545 and other locations)

MAGIC TRICKS | **Tannen's Magic** (45 W 34th St, 6th floor, 212/929-4500)

MAPS AND PRINTS, ANTIQUARIAN | **Argosy Book Store** (116 E 59th St, 212/753-4455)

MAPS, GLOBES AND ATLASES, ANTIQUE | **George Glazer Gallery** (308 E 94th St, 212/535-5706) and **Martayan Lan** (70 E 55th St, 6th floor, 212/308-0018)

MARINE SUPPLIES | **West Marine** (12 W 37th St, 212/594-6065)

MEMORABILIA | **American Icon NYC** (360 Broadway, 212/334-3600), **Firestore** (17 Greenwich Ave, 212/226-3142) and **Museum of the City of New York** (1220 Fifth Ave, 917/492-3330)

MUSICAL INSTRUMENTS | **Music Inn World Instruments** (169 W 4th St, 212/243-5715), **Roberto's Winds** (149 W 46th St, 212/391-1315), **Rogue Music** (220 W 30th St, 212/629-5073), **Sam Ash Music Store** (333 W 34th St, 212/719-2299 and other locations) and **Universal Musical Instrument Co.** (732 Broadway, 212/254-6917)

MUSICAL INSTRUMENTS, ACCORDIONS | **Alex & Bell Accordions** (165 W 48th St, 212/819-0072)

MUSICAL INSTRUMENTS, GUITARS | **Carmine Street Guitars** (42 Carmine St, 212/691-8400), **Dan's Chelsea Guitars** (224 W 23rd St, 212/675-4993), **The Guitar Salon** (212/675-3236; by appointment), **Ludlow Guitars** (172 Ludlow St, 212/353-1775), **Matt Umanov Guitars** (273 Bleecker St, 212/675-2157) and **Rudy's Music Stop** (169 W 48th St, 212/391-1699)

NOVELTIES | **Gordon Novelty** (52 W 29th St, 212/696-9664)

PET SUPPLIES, DISCOUNTED | **Petland Discounts** (314 W 23rd St, 212/366-0512 and other locations)

PET SUPPLIES, HOLISTIC | **Spoiled Brats** (340 W 49th St, 212/459-1615)

PETS, DOGS AND CATS | **Le Petit Puppy** (18 Christopher St, 212/727-8111) and **Pets-on-Lex** (1109 Lexington Ave, 212/426-0766)

PHOTOGRAPHIC EQUIPMENT, RENTAL AND SALES | **Adorama Camera** (42 W 18th St, 212/741-0063)

POOL TABLES | **Blatt Billiards** (330 W 38th St, 212/674-8855)

RECORDS, RARE | **House of Oldies** (35 Carmine St, 212/243-0500)

SCUBA-DIVING AND SNORKELING EQUIPMENT | **Pan Aqua Diving** (460 W 43rd St, 212/736-3483) and **Scuba Network** (43 W 21st St, 212/243-2988)

SEWING AND CRAFTS, BUTTONS, RARE AND UNUSUAL | **Tender Buttons** (143 E 62nd St, 212/758-7004)

SEWING AND CRAFTS, QUILTING SUPPLIES | **The City Quilter** (133 W 25th St, 212/807-0390)

SKATEBOARDS | **Supreme** (274 Lafayette St, 212/966-7799)

SKATING EQUIPMENT | **Blades** (156 W 72nd St, 212/787-3911 and 659 Broadway, 212/477-7350)

SNOWBOARDS | **Burton Snowboard Company** (106 Spring St, 212/966-8068)

SPORTS CARDS | **Alex's MVP Cards** (1577 York Ave, 212/831-2273)

STATIONERY | **Il Papiro** (1021 Lexington Ave, 212/288-9330), **JAM Paper & Envelope** (135 Third Ave, 212/473-6666; 1282 Third Ave, 212/737-0037 and 466 Lexington Ave, 212/687-6666), **Kate's Paperie** (435 Broome St, 212/941-9816) and **Paper Presentation** (23 W 18th St, 212/463-7035)

TENNIS EQUIPMENT | **Mason's Tennis** (56 E 53rd St, 212/755-5805)

THEATRICAL ITEMS | **One Shubert Alley** (1 Shubert Alley, 212/944-4133)

TOYS, DESIGNER ART | **myplasticheart** (210 Forsyth St, 646/290-8866)

TOYS, GOOD SELECTION | **Kidding Around** (60 W 15th St, 212/645-6337 and 107 E 42nd St, 212/972-8697)

TOYS, JAPANESE | **Image Anime** (242 W 30th St, 212/631-0966)

TOYS, LEGO | **LEGO Store** (Rockefeller Center, 620 Fifth Ave, 212/245- 5973)

TOYS, NOVELTIES AND PARTY SUPPLIES | **E.A.T. Gifts** (1062 Madison Ave, 212/861-2544)

THINGS FROM FAR AWAY

AFRICAN CLOTHING, CUSTOM-MADE | **Bébénoir** (2164 Frederick Douglass Blvd, 212/828-5775)

AROUND-THE-WORLD CURIOSITIES | **Creel and Gow** (131 E 70th St, 212/327-4281)

AUSTRALIAN, LUXURY FOOTWEAR, HANDMADE | **Feit** (2 Prince St, 646/308-1700)

BUDDHAS | **Leekan Designs** (4 Rivington St, 212/226-7226)

CHINESE DINNERWARE | **Wing On Wo & Co.** (26 Mott St, 212/962-3577)

CHINESE GOODS | **Chinese American Trading Company** (91 Mulberry St, 212/267-5224), **Pearl River Mart** (477 Broadway, 212/431-4770) and **Ting's Gift Shop** (18 Doyer St, 212/962-1081)

EUROPEAN POTTERY (Italian, French, Portuguese) | **La Terrine** (1024 Lexington Ave, 212/988-3366)

FRENCH HANDMADE POTTERY, CHANDELIERS, FURNITURE | **Le Fanion** (299 W 4th St, 212/463-8760)

GERMAN GIFTS | **Liebeskind Berlin** (276 Lafayette St, 212/993-7894)

HIMALAYAN IMPORTS | **Himalayan Crafts** (2007 Broadway, 212/787-8500)

INDIAN IMPORTS | **Bharatiya Dress Shoppe** (83 Second Ave, 212/228-1463) and **Soigne K** (717 Madison Ave, 212/486-2890)

INDONESIAN HOME FURNISHINGS | **Andrianna Shamaris** (261 Spring St, 212/388-9898)

ITALIAN CLOTHING, MEN AND WOMEN | **Moncler** (90 Prince St, 646/350-3620)

ITALIAN SHOES, EXOTIC SKINS | **Cellini Uomo** (59 Orchard St, 212/219-8657)

JAPANESE CLOTHING, HIGH-END | **Uniqlo** (666 Fifth Ave, 31 W 34th St and 546 Broadway; 877/486-4756 for all locations)

KOREAN ART, TRADITIONAL | **Kang Collection** (9 E 82nd St, 212/734-1490)

MEXICAN IMPORTS | **La Sirena** (27 E 3rd St, 212/780-9113) and **Pan American Phoenix** (857 Lexington Ave, 212/570-0300)

NEW ZEALAND CLOTHING | **Icebreaker** (102 Wooster St, 646/861-2523; by appointment)

NORDIC TEXTILES AND WOMENSWEAR | **Gudrun Sjödén** (50 Greene St, 212/219-2510)

SWEDISH OUTERWEAR | **Fjällräven** (262 Mott St, 212/226-7846)

TIBETAN HANDICRAFTS | **Do Kham** (51 Prince St, 212/966-2404) and **Vajra** (146 Sullivan St, 212/529-4344)

UKRAINIAN CLOTHING, NEWSPAPERS, BOOKS, CDS AND TAPES | **Surma — The Ukrainian Shop** (11 E 7th St, 212/477-0729)

NEW YORK STORES
THE BEST OF THE LOT

In this section you'll find dozens of descriptions for new stores; perennial favorites have been updated to reflect their efforts to bring shoppers the best possible deals and merchandise.

ANATOMICAL SUPPLIES

THE EVOLUTION STORE

120 Spring St (bet Greene and Mercer St)　　　　212/343-1114
Daily: 11-7　　　　　　　　　　　　theevolutionstore.com

The Evolution Store offers a unique presentation of both science and art. It is an authorized dealer selling unique science and natural-history collectibles, including insects, fossils, skulls and skeletons, anatomical models, minerals, posters, seashells and decorative antique taxidermy. Unusual gifts and home furnishings are the norm here. Some merchandise is available for rental by the day, week or month. Shopping is rarely this educational and fascinating, and kids will love the lollipops with edible bugs inside!

ANIMATION

ANIMAZING GALLERY

54 Greene St (at Broome St)　　　　　　　212/226-7374
Mon-Sat: 10-7; Sun: 11-6　　　　　　　　　animazing.com

A landmark in Soho since 1984, Animazing Gallery exhibits a unique collection of original and limited-edition animation and illustration artworks. Exclusive collections include art and sculpture by American illustrators like Maurice Sendak, Ted Geisel and Charles M. Schulz. The gallery also showcases original vintage animation art and whimsical fine art, including The Peanuts Paintings, by Tom Everhart. They also appraise vintage animation pieces. Check the website for current exhibitions, upcoming events and opening receptions.

ANTIQUES

CHELSEA

David Stypmann Company (Showplace Antiques and Design Center, 40 W 25th St, Gallery 112, 212/226-5717): art pottery, art glass objects, mirrors and lighting

EAST VILLAGE

Alan Moss (436 Lafayette St, 212/473-1310): 20th-century furniture, art, jewelry

FLATIRON DISTRICT

Secondhand Rose (230 Fifth Ave, 5th floor, 212/393-9002)

GREENWICH VILLAGE

End of History (548½ Hudson St, 212/647-7598): vintage glass

Hyde Park Antiques (836 Broadway, 212/477-0033): 18th- and 19th-century English furniture

Karl Kemp & Associates (36 E 10th St, 212/254-1877): art deco and Beidermeier furniture

Kentshire Galleries (700 Madison Ave, 212/673-6644): antique and costume jewelry

La Belle Epoque Vintage Posters (115 Greenwich Ave, 212/362-1770): advertising posters

Le Fanion (299 W 4th St, 212/463-8760): French handmade pottery, chandeliers, furniture

Maison Gérard (53 E 10th St, 212/674-7611): French art deco

Ritter-Antik (35 E 10th St, 212/673-2213): early first-period Beidermeier

MIDTOWN

A la Vielle Russie (781 Fifth Ave, 212/752-1727): Russian art

Chameleon (223 E 59th St, 212/355-6300): lighting

Evergreen Antiques (200 Lexington Ave, 10th floor, 212/744-5664): European and Scandinavian furniture

George N. Antiques (227 E 59th St, 212/935-4005): mirrors, lighting, furniture, jewelry

Gotta Have It! (153 E 57th St, 212/750-7900): celebrity memorabilia

Gray & Davis (15 W 47th St, 212/719-4698): vintage engagement rings and other jewelry

NEW YORK CITY SOUVENIRS

CityStore (Manhattan Municipal Building, 1 Centre St, 212/386-0007): official City of New York merchandise

FDNY Fire Zone (34 W 51st St, 212/698-4520): officially licensed FDNY products

Harlem Underground (20 E 125th St, 212/987-9385): mugs and T-shirts with Harlem logos and uptown attitude

Macy's Herald Square Arcade (151 W 34th St, 212/695-4400): unique and classy items

The Metropolitan Museum of Art (1000 Fifth Ave, 212/535-7710): posters of recent art exhibits

Museum of the City of New York (1220 Fifth Ave, 212/534-1672): ties, scarves and umbrellas with New York-themed designs

New York Gifts (729 Seventh Ave, lobby, 212/391-7570)

New-York Historical Society (170 Central Park W, 212/873-3400): posters, prints and holiday cards featuring scenes of old New York

Statue of Liberty Gift Shop (Liberty and Ellis Islands, 212/363-3180): mini statues, books, postcards, glassware and holiday ornaments

J.J. Lally (41 E 57th St, 212/371-3380): Chinese art

James Robinson (480 Park Ave, 212/752-6166): silver flatware

Lars Bolander N.Y. (232 E 59th St, 3rd floor, 212/924-1000): 17th- and 18th-century Swedish and French antiques and reproductions

Leo Kaplan, Ltd. (114 E 57th St, 212/249-6766): ceramics and glass

Manhattan Art & Antiques Center (1050 Second Ave, 212/355-4400): 60 galleries

Martayan Lan (70 E 55th St, 6th floor, 212/308-0018): 16th- and 17th-century maps and books

Newel LLC (425 E 53rd St, 212/758-1970): all styles and periods

Philip Colleck (311 E 58th St, 212/486-7600): 18th- and early 19th-century English furniture

Ralph M. Chait Galleries (730 Fifth Ave, 10th floor, 212/758-0937): ancient Chinese art

S.J. Shrubsole (104 E 57th St, 212/753-8920): English silver and jewelry

Stephen Herdemian (78 W 47th St, 212/944-2534): antique and estate jewelry

NOHO/SOHO/TRIBECA

Donzella (17 White St, 212/965-8919): furnishings from the 1940s through the 1970s

Gill & Lagodich Gallery (108 Reade St, 212/619-0631; by appointment): period frames and restoration

Hostler Burrows Antik (51 E 10th St, mezzanine, 212/343-0471): mid-century Scandinavian, contemporary designs

Urban Archaeology (143 Franklin St, 212/431-4646): lighting, wash stands, accessories, reproductions

Wyeth (315 Spring St, 212/243-3661): early-to-mid-20th century antiques and custom furniture from Denmark, Italy and the U.S.

UPPER EAST SIDE

Antiquarium (948 Madison Ave, 212/734-9776): jewelry, classical Near Eastern and Egyptian antiquities

Arader Gallery (29 E 72nd St, 212/628-3668 and 1016 Madison Ave, 212/628-7625): rare prints and furniture

Art of the Past (1242 Madison Ave, 212/860-7070): South and Southeast Asia

Bernard & S. Dean Levy (24 E 84th St, 212/628-7088): American furniture and paintings

Bizarre Bazaar (130¼ E 65th St, 212/517-2100; appointment suggested): 20th-century industrial design

Cora Ginsburg (19 E 74th St, 3rd floor, 212/744-1352; by appointment): antique textiles

Dalva Brothers (53 E 77th St, 212/717-6600): 18th-century French furniture and porcelain

Didier Aaron (32 E 67th St, 212/988-5248): 18th- and 19th-century furniture; 17th-, 18th- and 19th-century masters' paintings

Doris Leslie Blau (306 E 61st St, 212/586-5511; by appointment): rugs

Fanelli Antique Timepieces (790 Madison Ave, Suite 202, 212/517-2300): antique timepieces (and repairs)

Florian Papp (962 Madison Ave, 212/288-6770): European furniture

Friedman & Vallois (27 E 67th St, 212/517-3820): high-end French art deco furniture, objects and lighting

Gardner & Barr (444 W 55th St, 212/752-0555; by appointment): vintage Murano glass

George Glazer Gallery (308 E 94th St, 212/327-2598): maps, globes

Greene Street Interiors (210 E 60th St, 212/274-1076): Scandinavian and Beidermeier

Hayko Rugs (857 Lexington Ave, 212/717-5400): kilims

Karl Kemp & Associates (833 Madison Ave, 212/288-3838): art deco and Biedermeier furniture

Kentshire Antiques (700 Madison Ave, 212/421-1100): English antiques, jewelry

L'Antiquaire & the Connoisseur (36 E 73rd St, 212/517-9176): 18th-century French and Italian furniture

Linda Horn Antiques (1327 Madison Ave, 212/772-1122): late 19th- and 20th-century English and French

Macklowe Gallery (667 Madison Ave, 212/644-6400): Tiffany and art nouveau

Naga Antiques (145 E 61st St, 212/593-2788): antique Japanese screens, fine Asian and European furniture

Sotheby's (1334 York Ave, 212/606-7000): art

Sylvia Pines Uniquities (1102 Lexington Ave, 212/744-5141): jewelry and handbags

Ursus Books and Prints (699 Madison Ave, 212/772-8787): books

THE LIVELY SET

33 Bedford St (bet Carmine and Downing St)   212/807-8417
Mon-Fri: 11-7; Sat, Sun: 11-6   Facebook

This charming and diminutive West Village antique home and garden shop is chock-full of vintage furniture for living rooms and gardens and decorative accents for the entire home. The eclectic inventory, including lamps, chandeliers, sconces, accent tables and Murano glass bowls changes frequently, adding to the store's allure. It is a reflection of Marcelo Soriano's love of antiques.

MANTIQUES MODERN

146 W 22nd St (bet Ave of the Americas and Seventh Ave)   212/206-1494
Mon-Fri: 10:30-6:30; Sat, Sun: 11-7   mantiquesmodern.com

No dainty antiques here! What an amazing collection of objects from the 18th, 19th and 20th centuries. A journey through the crowded store might reveal mannequins, serveware, a Gucci sculpture, industrial or building equipment suitable for home use, garden elements and an assortment of furniture, lighting and wall decor. Be sure to look under, atop and between

SHOPPING ABBREVIATIONS

Be sure to read the fine print in sales ads and in-store promotions. Some are sprinkled with abbreviations. Here are a few common ones:

AR: after rebate

BOGO: buy one, get one

CPN: coupon

MIR: mail-in rebate

RTW: ready-to-wear

S&H: shipping and handling

all the items. Some of them may require a bit of imagination to fit into your scheme.

ARCHITECTURAL ANTIQUES

DEMOLITION DEPOT & IRREPLACEABLE ARTIFACTS

216 E 125th St (bet Second and Third Ave)   212/860-1138
Mon-Fri: 10-6; Sat: 11-6   demolitiondepot.com

Look inside this shabby building and you'll be immersed in a treasure trove of vintage pieces for interior and exterior use. There is a large assortment of fixtures, lighting pieces, doors, windows, bars, mantels, shutters, gates, railings and even kitchen sinks, all in a variety of styles (art deco, French country, etc.). Services include demolition, reclamation and on-site liquidation. The idea is to preserve architectural history by reclaiming building elements; it may take some creativity to come up with all the possibilities.

OLDE GOOD THINGS

5 E 16th St (bet Fifth Ave and Union Sq W)   212/989-8814
149 Madison Ave (at 32nd St)   212/321-0770
124 W 24th St (bet Ave of the Americas and Seventh Ave)   212/989-8401
Mon-Sat: 10-7; Sun: 11-7
302 Bowery (at Houston St)   212/498-9922
Mon-Thurs: 10-7; Fri: 10-8; Sat, Sun: 11-7   oldegoodthings.com

What a fascinating business this is! Olde Good Things salvages significant artifacts from old buildings, offering one of the largest showings of architectural antiques and salvaged items in the country. You'll find mantels, irons, doors, stone and terra cotta, hardware, garden items, tables and other furniture, tin pieces, floorings, mirrors, lighting and an assortment of altered antiques.

ART SUPPLIES

LEE'S ART SHOP

220 W 57th St (bet Broadway and Seventh Ave)   212/247-0110
Mon-Fri: 9-7:30; Sat: 10-7; Sun: 11-6   leesartshop.com

Lee's Art Shop is a midtown landmark offering four stories of materials for amateur and professional artists and kids. There are art supplies, as well as lamps, silk screens, paper goods, party supplies, stationery, fine pens, cards, picture frames, calendars, crafts, creative gifts and much more. Custom printing and custom framing are available.

NEW YORK CENTRAL ART SUPPLY

62 Third Ave (at 11th St)   212/473-7705
Mon-Sat: 8:30-6:15   nycentralart.com

Artists have looked to this firm for fine-art materials, especially unique and custom-made items since 1905. There are two floors of fine-art papers, including one-of-a-kind decorative papers and over a thousand Oriental papers from Europe, Bhutan, India and Nepal. Amateur and skilled artisans will find a full range of decorative paints and painting materials; their brush selection is outstanding. A framing annex offers custom–cut glass, mats and frames as well as ready-made frames.

ARTWORKS

J.N. BARTFIELD GALLERIES

60 55th St (bet Fifth Ave and Ave of the Americas), 5th floor   212/245-8890
Mon-Fri: 10-5   bartfield.com

Founded in 1937, J. N. Bartfield Galleries is the oldest gallery in the nation that specializes in artworks by the masters of the American West — to purchase, sell or consign. Their works include Western, sporting and wildlife paintings and bronzes. Featured works include early Western artists like George Catlin, Karl Bodmer, Albert Bierstadt and Alfred Jacob Miller as well as Western masters like Frederic Remington, Charles M. Russell, W. R. Leigh, Frank Tenney Johnson and Maynard Dixon. In addition to these, Bartfield's also deals in classic American paintings from Thomas Cole to Thomas Hart Benton and Norman Rockwell to Rockwell Kent.

BARGAIN STORES

GABAY'S OUTLET

195 Ave of the Americas (bet 12th and 13th St)   212/254-3180
Mon-Wed, Sun: 11-7; Thurs-Sat: 11-8   gabaysoutlet.com

The third generation of this family-run business offers designer overstocks from 50% to 80% off retail. You'll find handbags, shoes, sunglasses and wallets with designer names like Chanel, Chloe, Emporio Arman, Fendi, Gucci, Manolo Blahnik, Marc Jacobs and Prada.   Goods for men and women come from

STORES FOR CRAFTS

If you want to try your hand at a craft project, then check out these shops, where you'll likely find everything that's needed — and then some.

Beads of Paradise (16 E 17th St, 212/620-0642): beads and antiques

City Quilter (133 W 25th St, 212/807-0390): fabrics, patterns, supplies, quilting machines, notions, lessons

M&J Trimming (1008 Ave of the Americas, 800/965-8746): notions

Purl Soho (459 Broome St, 212/420-8796): yarns and notions, quilting supplies, needlework supplies and kits

Rita's Needlepoint (150 E 79th St, 212/737-8613): mainly needlepoint supplies; lessons by appointment

some of Manhattan's exclusive department stores, boutiques and showrooms. Merchandise is sourced from overstocks, samples, seasonal liquidations and customer returns. Check out their online product index for current inventory.

JACK'S WORLD

110 W 32nd St (bet Ave of the Americas and Seventh Ave)   212/268-9962
45 W 45th St (bet Ave of the Americas and Fifth Ave)   212/354-6888

JACK'S 99¢ STORE

16 E 40th St (bet Madison and Fifth Ave)   212/696-5767
Hours vary by store   jacksnyc.com

This is closeout central! Jack's is constantly working with manufacturers with excessive inventory or making packaging changes, and the amazing values are funneled to bargain-hunting customers. The results — great values on paper goods, housewares, food items, cleaning supplies, toiletries and other everyday items. Jack's 99¢ Store has inexpensive (99 cents!) values while Jack's World has more of the same, plus electronics, domestics, gifts, toys and goods of a higher quality. You never know what will turn up at these discount stores; there's always something new!

BATHROOM ACCESSORIES

A.F. SUPPLY CORPORATION

22 W 21st St (bet Fifth Ave and Ave of the Americas)   212/243-5400
Mon-Fri: 8-5   afsupply.com

For nearly thirty years A.F. Supply has been offering a great selection of mid- to high-end bath (some kitchen) products; fixtures, whirlpools, faucets, bath accessories, lighting, door and cabinet hardware, saunas, steam showers, shower doors, medicine cabinets and spas from top architectural and decorative suppliers. Access to the showroom is by appointment only.

SHERLE WAGNER INTERNATIONAL

300 E 62nd St (at Second Ave)   212/758-3300
Mon-Fri: 9:30-5:30   sherlewagner.com

If you desire elegance and originality and price is no object, then come to Sherle Wagner for luxury hardware, fixtures and accessories for the bathroom. The showroom displays all kinds of bed, bath and bar items, including lighting and wall coverings, from classic to contemporary designs. They've been around since 1945 and are happy to work with architects, designers and clients on projects of any scale.

WATERWORKS

215 E 58th St (bet Second and Third Ave)   212/371-9266
7 E 20th St (bet Fifth Ave and Broadway)   212/254-6025
Mon-Fri: 8:30-6   waterworks.com

If it is for the bathroom, then Waterworks will likely have it! You'll find faucets and shower heads, tubs and sinks; ceramic, glass and stone surfaces;

towels, rugs, mirrors and lighting. There is also a selection of small furniture, including hampers, stools, etageres and small tables.

BOOKS

ART

PRINTED MATTER

195 Tenth Ave (bet 21st and 22nd St)   212/925-0325
Mon-Wed, Sat: 11-7; Thurs, Fri: 11-8   printedmatter.org

Appropriately located in the Chelsea art district, this store is devoted exclusively to artists' books — a trade term for portfolios of artwork in book form. They stock 15,000 titles by over 6,000 contemporary artists for viewing and purchase. The store is a nonprofit operation to promote public awareness of artists' projects and ideas. The idea is carried further with a selection of periodicals and audio-works in a similar vein. Nearly all featured artists are contemporary (from 1960), so just browsing the store will bring you up to date on the art world.

CHILDREN'S

BANK STREET BOOKSTORE

2780 Broadway (at 107th St)   212/678-1654
Sat-Wed: 10-7; Thurs, Fri: 9-8   bankstreetbooks.com

This store has been a Manhattan icon for years and is a marvelous source of books for and about children and books about education and parenting. Located adjacent to the Bank Street College, a progressive graduate school for teachers and a lab school for children, it's a treasure trove of educational toys, activity books and New York City-themed books and gifts. The staff really knows its stock (30,000 titles in stock) and cares enormously about quality children's literature. Check the website for a schedule of story hours, puppet shows, workshops, author events and literary talks.

BOOKS OF WONDER

18 W 18th St (bet Fifth Ave and Ave of the Americas)   212/989-3270
Mon-Sat: 10-7; Sun: 11-6   booksofwonder.com

Since 1980 this enchanting spot has had a special place in the hearts of New York children and parents. Books of Wonder stocks the newest children's titles along with endearing classics. There is a section of rare, collectible children's books as well. In addition to their world-famous Oz section (as in *The Wizard of Oz*), this store is known for frequent "Meet the Author" events, beautiful used and often signed classics and weekly story hours for young children.

COMICS

CHAMELEON COMICS & CARDS

3 Maiden Lane (at Broadway)   212/587-3411
Mon-Fri: 9-7; Sat: 10-5   chameleoncomics.com

Chameleon Comics & Cards is a full-service collectibles store specializing in comic books, graphic novels and trading cards (sports and non-sports); new comics arrive every Wednesday. You'll also find much more in this tiny shop: statues and busts of comic characters, comic-themed toys and action figures. The staff is friendly and informed, and you can order books up to two months prior to publication from the preview catalog.

ST. MARK'S COMICS

11 St. Mark's Pl (bet Second and Third Ave)   212/598-9439
Mon, Tues: 10 a.m.-11 p.m.; Wed: 9 a.m.-1 a.m.;   Facebook
Thurs-Sat: 10 a.m.-1 a.m.; Sun: 11-11

This unique store carries mainstream and licensed products, as well as hard-to-find small-press and underground comics. They have a large selection of back issues and claim, "If it's published, we carry it." Comic-related toys, T-shirts, statues, posters and cards are stocked, and they also carry TV- and movie-related products. These service-oriented folks will hold selections for you and will buy comics and related collectibles.

COOKBOOKS
KITCHEN ARTS & LETTERS

1435 Lexington Ave (at 94th St)   212/876-5550
Mon: 1-6; Tues-Fri: 10-6:30; Sat: 11-6   kitchenartsandletters.com

Cookbooks are more popular than ever with all the interest in health, fitness and natural foods. It should come as no surprise that Nach Waxman's Kitchen Arts & Letters found immediate success as a store specializing in food- and drink-related books and literature. A former cookbook editor, he identified a demand for out-of-print cookbooks. So while his cozy shop stocks more than 13,000 current titles, much of the business consists of tracking down a book nobody else has; the search service is free.

FOREIGN
KINOKUNIYA BOOKSTORE

1073 Ave of the Americas (bet 40th and 41st St)   212/869-1700
Mon-Sat: 10-8; Sun: 11-7:30   kinokuniya.com

At Kinokuniya Bookstore, Japanese, English and Chinese reading materials coexist, with the purpose of creating harmony between cultures. There are books, CDs, DVDs, comics, hard-to-find magazines, beautiful stationery and pictorial books; new stock arrives about three times a week. Subjects cover all aspects of Japanese culture: art, cooking, travel, language, literature, history, business, economics, martial arts, comic books and more. The multilingual staff is a big plus.

GENERAL
BARNES & NOBLE

97 Warren St (at Greenwich Ave)   212/587-5389
555 Fifth Ave (at 46th St)   212/697-3048
2289 Broadway (at 82nd St)   212/362-8835
Numerous other locations
Hours vary by store   barnesandnoble.com

Barnes & Noble stores continue to offer deep discounts on best sellers and other pop titles and are beloved by book buyers and browsers alike. Besides carrying an excellent selection of books (including bargain-priced remainders), they stock CDs, DVDs, audio books, video games, toys, digital pocket dictionaries, e-book readers, magazines and many gift items.

MCNALLY JACKSON BOOKS

52 Prince St (bet Lafayette and Mulberry St)   212/274-1160
Mon-Sat: 10-10; Sun: 10-9   mcnallyjackson.com

McNally Jackson Books is a unique, independent bookstore, the inspiration of owner Sarah McNally. The store is chock-full of titles in every category, organized by geographic area. Free Wi-Fi, comfortable sitting areas, a cafe and personal, informed service are part of the big draw here. McNally's print-right-now "Espresso Book Machine" can download, bind and trim a paperback in minutes. A cloud library of four million titles is available for about the same price as a typical paperback. Budding authors can use it to print their own works; pretty amazing and gratifying to a new writer!

STRAND BOOK STORE

828 Broadway (at 12th St)   212/473-1452
Mon-Sat: 9:30 a.m.-10:30 p.m.; Sun: 11-10:30

STRAND BOOK KIOSK

Central Park, Fifth Ave at 60th St
Daily: 10 a.m. — dusk, April-Dec (weather permitting)   strandbooks.com

Strand Book Store is the largest and best secondhand bookstore in the world. Family-owned since 1927, it is a fascinating place to visit and shop. The store has over 2.5 million titles in stock — that's 18 miles of books — tagged at up to 85% off list prices. They sell secondhand, out-of-print and rare books. Thousands of new books and quality remainders are sold at 50% off publisher's prices. An outstanding rare-book department is located on the third floor. You'll find 20th-century first editions, limited signed editions, fine bindings and much more. Be sure to browse the paperbacks on the famous dollar carts outside.

THREE LIVES & CO.

154 W 10th St (at Waverly Pl)   212/741-2069
Mon, Tues: noon-8; Wed-Sat: 11-8:30; Sun: noon-7   threelives.com

Founded in 1978, Three Lives is one of New York's top remaining independent bookstores. It specializes in literary fiction and nonfiction and has

RIZZOLI BOOKSTORE GRAND RE-OPENING SPRING 2015

Rizzoli Bookstore has announced a spring 2015 grand re-opening at their new location (1133 Broadway, 212/759-2424, rizzolibookstore.com). The new site is just three blocks north of Madison Square Park in the NoMad neighborhood. For updates, check their website or Facebook.

become a neighborhood gathering place. The helpful staff are knowledgeable as well as avid readers. Take note of the abbreviated hours.

UNOPPRESSIVE NON-IMPERIALIST BARGAIN BOOKS

34 Carmine St (bet Bedford and Bleecker St)   212/229-0079
Sun-Thurs: 11-10; Fri, Sat: 11 a.m.-midnight   unoppressivebooks.blogspot.com

Beyond the intriguing name and teal awning are scads of unique, eclectic books in all genres. The inventory at this family-owned store is constantly changing, as it is carefully chosen from publisher overstock. The shelves are loaded with art, fiction, poetry, philosophy, spirituality, music, children's titles, food books and more, all new and unused. Tables flanking the front door are piled with some of the best deals, some books for only a few dollars. This is a great neighborhood spot with liberatingly low prices.

MUSIC

THE JUILLIARD STORE

144 W 66th St (bet Broadway and Amsterdam Ave)   212/799-5000, ext 237
Mon-Fri: 10-7; Sat: 10-6; Sun: noon-5   thejuilliardstore.com

The Juilliard Store is one of the few remaining brick-and-mortar sheet music stores. With an extensive selection of sheet music and scores and hard-to-find books on classical music, this bookstore claims to carry every classical-music book in print! You will also find general interest and specialty books, CDs, DVDs, musical accessories and Juilliard apparel and gifts. As a bonus, there are many talented classical musicians employed here, and they are ready to share their musical passions.

MYSTERY

MYSTERIOUS BOOKSHOP

58 Warren St (bet West Broadway and Church St)   212/587-1011
Mon-Sat: 11-7   mysteriousbookshop.com

Now in its 35th year, Mysterious Bookshop is one of the country's oldest bookstores specializing in mysteries. The shop stocks all types of new mystery books in hardcover and paperback, as well as periodicals. It is also filled from floor to ceiling with out-of-print, used and rare books. Amazingly, the staff seems to know exactly what is in stock. If it is not on the shelves, they will order it. There is as much talk as business conducted here, and you can even converse with authors who sign their works from time to time. Mysterious carries thousands of autographed books, and over recent years has published some limited, signed editions by some of the most popular mystery authors.

NEW YORK

CITYSTORE

1 Centre St (at Chambers St), north plaza of Municipal Bldg
Mon-Fri: 10-5   212/386-0007 (both locations)
141 Worth St (at Hamill Pl)
Mon-Fri: 8:30-3:45   a856-citystore.nyc.gov

CityStore is the official store of the city of New York, the "museum store" for the city. It is the retail entity for gifts, collectibles and research materials.

From classic to fun, a variety of items includes authentic NYC memorabilia, sterling silver jewelry, city seal silk ties and scarves, cuff links, charms, pins, taxi medallions, posters and official merchandise for the NYPD, FDNY, DSNY, NYC Parks, NYC Taxi, NYC Subway and more. Book topics include biking and walking in New York, guides and maps, history, sports and cookbooks. Note that the City Clerk's location on Worth Street has a much more limited inventory.

RARE AND OUT-OF-PRINT
ALABASTER BOOKSHOP

122 Fourth Ave (bet 12th and 13th St)   212/982-3550
Mon-Sat: 10-10; Sun: 11-10

Alabaster Bookshop remains the lone holdout on Fourth Avenue, once known as "Bookshop Row." Owner Steve Crowley offers a great selection of used and rare books in all categories while focusing on literature and the arts. Prices at this tiny outpost range from $2 paperbacks to a $1,000 first edition. Among the stacks of books, specialties include New York City, photography and the arts, or check out bargains on the rolling carts just outside on the sidewalk.

INDEPENDENT BOOKSTORES

Independent bookstores offer personalized services, special events and new, used and sometimes rare editions.

Books of Wonder (18 W 18th St, 212/989-3270): children's

Crawford Doyle Booksellers (1082 Madison Ave, 212/288-6300): great neighborhood bookstore

Drama Book Shop (250 W 40th St, 212/944-0595): plays, musicals, theater; since 1917

Forbidden Planet NYC (832 Broadway, 212/473-1576): sci-fi, fantasy, Japanese animation, comics

McNally Jackson Books (52 Prince St, 212/274-1160): general bookstore with a cafe, too

Mysterious Bookshop (58 Warren St, 212/587-1011): thrillers and killers

Posman Books (Chelsea Market, 75 Ninth Ave, 212/627-0304 and 30 Rockefeller Center, 212/489-9100): cookbooks at Chelsea Market location

Quest Bookshop (240 E 53rd St, 212/758-5521): spirituality and esoterica

St. Mark's Bookshop (136 E 3rd St, 212/260-7853): eclectic stock with books on culture and foreign and domestic periodicals

Strand Book Store (828 Broadway, 212/473-1452): 18 miles of new and used books; something for everyone

Three Lives & Co. (154 W 10th St, 212/741-2069): specializes in literary fiction and nonfiction

ARGOSY BOOK STORE

116 E 59th St (bet Park and Lexington Ave)   212/753-4455
Mon-Fri: 10-6; Sat: 10-5 (closed Sat in summer)   argosybooks.com

Since 1925 and now in its third generation of ownership, Argosy Book Store houses six stories of antiquarian and out-of-print items. They specialize in Americana, modern first editions, autographs, art, antique maps and prints and the history of science and medicine. Beyond that, there are also thousands of books in other fields of interest; a specialty service is finding unusual gifts for the unusual people in your life.

BAUMAN RARE BOOKS

535 Madison Ave (bet 54th and 55th St)   212/751-0011
Mon-Sat: 10-6   baumanrarebooks.com

In their Madison Avenue gallery, Bauman Rare Books displays a fine collection of rare books and autographs, maps and prints dating from the 15th through the 20th centuries. Included are works of literature, history, economics, law, science, medicine, nature, travel and exploration; first editions and children's books are a specialty. Whether you are an advanced collector, novice or just looking for a unique gift, Bauman is an excellent source with over 4,000 books and documents in a wide range of subjects.

IMPERIAL FINE BOOKS

790 Madison Ave (bet 66th and 67th St), 2nd floor   212/861-6620
Mon-Fri: 10:30-6; Sat: 11-5   imperialfinebooks.com

If you are in the market for books that look as great as they read, Imperial is the place to visit. You will find fine leather, jeweled and exhibition bindings, illustrated books, vintage children's books, unique first editions and magnificent sets of prized volumes; the inventory includes literature, history and children's books. Services include complete restoration, binding and cleaning of damaged or aged books, as well as custom bookbinding and library projects.

RELIGIOUS

J. LEVINE BOOKS & JUDAICA

5 W 30th St (bet Fifth Ave and Broadway)   212/695-6888
Mon-Wed: 9-6; Thurs: 9-7; Fri: 9-2; Sun: 10-5   levinejudaica.com

Guided by five generations of the Levine family, this is one of the oldest Jewish bookstores in the city and a leader in the market. Though the emphasis is still on the written word, they also carry many gift items, coffee-table books, novels, thousands of Judaica items and one of the largest selections of Jewish marriage ketubahs.

ST. PATRICK'S CATHEDRAL GIFT SHOPS

Inside the cathedral (Fifth Ave bet 50th and 51st St)   212/355-2749
Daily: 8:30-8
15 E 51st St (bet Fifth and Madison Ave); across the street from the cathedral
Daily: 10-6   stpatscathedralgiftshop.com

With lovely music playing in the background, these shops are an oasis of calm in midtown. You can browse hundreds of religious and spiritual items, including books on Catholicism, displays of rosary beads, statues of saints, music, music boxes, wall decor, medals, prayer cards and children's and keepsake gifts. Proceeds go toward the social outreach and ministry of the church and the cathedral's maintenance.

THEATER

THE DRAMA BOOK SHOP

250 W 40th St (bet Seventh and Eighth Ave)   212/944-0595
Mon-Sat: 11-7 (Thurs till 8); Sun: noon-6   dramabookshop.com

This shop has been providing a valuable service to the performing-arts community since 1917. Its stock includes publications dealing with musical theater, TV, radio, film, Shakespeare, directing, writing, stagecraft, makeup and costumes. It is the premiere shop for screenplays and scripts, and keeps current listings of agents, producers, managers and casting directors that are updated monthly. Check online for a schedule of in-store scene readings.

RICHARD STODDARD — PERFORMING ARTS BOOKS

43 E 10th St (bet University Pl and Broadway), Room 6-D   212/598-9421
By appointment   richardstoddard.com

Richard Stoddard runs a one-man operation dedicated to rare and out-of-print books, autographs and memorabilia relating to the performing arts. Equipped with a Ph.D. from Yale in Theater History and 35 years of experience as a dealer and appraiser of performing-arts materials, Stoddard offers a broad range of items. He has the largest collection of New York playbills (about 20,000) for sale in the U.S., as well as books, autographs, souvenir programs and original stage designs, including hundreds of Broadway costume designs.

USED

HOUSING WORKS BOOKSTORE CAFE

126 Crosby St (bet Houston and Prince St)   212/334-3324
Mon-Fri: 9-9; Sat, Sun: 10-5   housingworks.org

Housing Works Bookstore Cafe is a great spot to relax, shop and meet with friends. It's also an affordable source for books, movies and music; all merchandise has been donated. You'll find new and rare used books, collectibles, out-of-print titles, first editions, DVDs, CDs, vinyl records and audiobooks. Ask about their "Books by the Foot" offer. The cafe features baked goods, seasonal soups, sandwiches, salads, soft drinks, beer and wine and catering services; all workers are volunteers. Proceeds go to Housing Works to provide services for homeless and low-income men and women living with HIV/AIDS.

BUTTONS

TENDER BUTTONS

143 E 62nd St (bet Lexington and Third Ave)   212/758-7004
Mon-Fri: 10:30-6; Sat: 10:30-5:30   tenderbuttons-nyc.com

Inside a tiny brick townhouse, Tender Buttons could be considered a lesson in the history of buttons. Millicent Safro shows some of the most unusual examples discovered in world travels in floor-to-ceiling displays. One antique wooden display cabinet shows off a selection of original buttons, many imported or made exclusively for the store. There are buttons of pearl, wood, horn, silver, leather, ceramic, bone, ivory, pewter and semiprecious stones; many are antiques. Some are as highly valued as artwork; for instance, a French enamel button can cost almost as much as a painting! Unique pieces can be made into special cuff links — real conversation pieces for the lucky owner. Blazer buttons are a specialty and they also have a fine collection of antique and period cuff links and men's stud sets. I am a cuff link buff and have purchased some of my best pieces from this shop. It is impressive to think of the efforts someone took to make something so small!

CHINA AND GLASSWARE

CRATE & BARREL

650 Madison Ave (at 59th St)   212/308-0011
Mon-Fri: 10-8; Sat: 10-7; Sun: noon-6
611 Broadway (at Houston St)   212/780-0004
Mon-Sat: 10-9; Sun: 11-7   crateandbarrel.com

Named for their original display pieces, Crate & Barrel stores are loaded with attractive quality merchandise at sensible prices. Even if you aren't in the market for china, glassware, cookware, cutlery, home accessories, bed and bath furnishings, storage pieces or casual furniture (indoor and outdoor), the creative displays will make shopping hard to resist.

FISHS EDDY

889 Broadway (at 19th St)   212/420-9020
Mon-Thurs: 9-9; Fri, Sat: 9 a.m.-10 p.m.; Sun: 10-8   fishseddy.com

This shop is fun to browse for some of the most unusual and durable-strength china and glassware items available anywhere. Nearly everything at Fishs Eddy is made in America; the stock of dinnerware, flatware, glassware, serveware and kitchenware changes regularly. Check out their own unique patterns including New York, Brooklynese (shuguh) and American history or random vintage pieces. This is a treasure trove for bargain hunters; you'll find interesting accessory selections of linens, T-shirts, coasters and more.

CLOTHING AND ACCESSORIES

ANTIQUE AND VINTAGE

FAMILY JEWELS VINTAGE CLOTHING

130 W 23rd St (bet Ave of the Americas and Seventh Ave)   212/633-6020
Sun-Tues: 11-7; Wed-Sat: 11-8   familyjewelsnyc.com

Family Jewels has an impressive following as the place to go for American vintage clothing, shoes, accessories and beautiful costume jewelry from the Victorian era through the 1980s. The men's and women's stock in the 2,000-square-foot shop is carefully selected, well organized, the service is excellent and prices are reasonable! The 1940s shop decor and retro background music add to the pleasantness of a visit. Ask about costume and styling services.

LEGACY

109 Thompson St (between Prince and Spring St)   212/966-4827
Daily: noon-7   legacy-nyc.com

In keeping with their credo "it's in the mix," Legacy carries vintage women's fashions alongside the Legacy label and that of emerging designers, some made with vintage fabrics. Big-name designers like Gucci, Chanel and Ungaro are represented in this eclectic Soho shop, which shows an assortment of suits, dresses, separates, outerwear, shoes, handbags and accessories. Legacy's owner, Rita Brookoff, will help pair a vintage blouse with a current fashion suit or select the perfect black dress for a timelessly chic look.

REMINISCENCE

74 Fifth Ave (bet 13th and 14th St)   212/243-2292
Mon-Sat: 10-8; Sun: noon-7   reminiscence.com

Visit this quirky emporium in Greenwich Village to revisit the decades from the 1960s through the 1980s. Founder Stewart Richer is a product of this era, and his finds are unusual and wearable. Large selections of colorful vintage clothing and costumes, attractive displays of jewelry, hats, gifts and accessories are featured, for both men and women. Richer's own brand of goods, although vintage in style, is inexpensive and varied, with Hawaiian prints one of the most popular choices. You'll also find a unique selection of toys and housewares.

SCREAMING MIMI'S

382 Lafayette St (bet 4th and Great Jones St)   212/677-6464
Mon-Sat: noon-8; Sun: 1-7   screamingmimis.com

Founded in 1978, Screaming Mimi's is a landmark vintage emporium, well-known for its excellent selection of men's and women's clothing and accessories from the 1920s through the 1990s. There is a treasure trove of handbags, shoes, jewelry, sunglasses and hats; an excellent source for authentic costumes. A private penthouse houses high-end vintage designer and specialty couture.

TRASH & VAUDEVILLE

4 St. Mark's Pl (bet Second and Third Ave)   212/982-3590
Mon-Thurs: noon-8; Fri: 11:30-8:30; Sat: 11:30-9; Sun: 1-7:30
                                          trashandvaudeville.com

Trash & Vaudeville is an energetic shop with stock that changes constantly and seems to have no boundaries. Its inventory for men and women is geared toward outrageous rock, punk, mod and goth clothing; footwear and accessories, including original designs. They are an excellent source for rock and roll styles from the 1950s to the present and you'll find a few items for kids as well.

ATHLETIC

LULULEMON ATHLETICA

1146 Madison Ave (at 85th St)   212/452-1909
1127 Third Ave (at 66th St)   212/755-5019

1928 Broadway (at 64th St)   212/712-1767
15 Union Sq W (bet 14th and 15th St)   212/675-5286
Numerous other locations
Hours vary by store   lululemon.com

Founded in Canada, these yoga-inspired clothing stores show attractive and offbeat wear for active people. You'll find clothing and gear for yoga, dancing, running, swimming and other athletic pursuits; stink-free clothing, too! Check out in-store events, including self-defense, goal-setting and yoga classes.

LUXURY DESIGNER

Michael Kors (The Shops at Columbus Circle, 10 Columbus Cir, ground floor, 212/896-2037; Rockefeller Center, 610 Fifth Ave, 212/582-2444; 520 Broadway, 212/336-4501 and numerous other locations) is a world-renowned, award-winning designer of luxury accessories and ready-to-wear. His namesake company, established in 1981, currently produces a range of products under his signature Michael Kors Collection and MICHAEL Michael Kors labels. Accessories, footwear, watches, jewelry, women's ready-to-wear, eyewear and a full line of fragrance products are glamourous and timelessly chic. Note that only the flagship store on Broadway carries menswear.

NIKE RUNNING

156 Fifth Ave (at 20th St)
                                212/243-8560
1131 Third Ave (67th St)
                                212/535-1530

NIKELAB 21M

21 Mercer St (at Grand St)
                                212/226-5433

NIKETOWN NEW YORK

6 E 57th St (bet Fifth and Madison Ave)   212/891-6453
Hours vary by location   nike.com

Within these entities Nike showcases the creative product innovation and sports heritage by which their empire is known. Cutting-edge athletic and workout apparel, including a zillion footwear choices, fill these flashy spaces. You'll find colorful sports-specific clothing in the newest designs and materials for basketball, baseball, football, golf, soccer, running, tennis and training; exactly what you'd expect from Nike. In the newest retail space, NikeLab 21M, product presentation in a traditional retail space has been reinvented, and in the process, building materials from the former space at 21 Mercer Street were reused. Another example of Nike's goal to elevate performance along with exceptional form!

BRIDAL
HERE COMES THE BRIDESMAID

213 W 35th St (bet Seventh and Eighth Ave), Room 403   212/647-9686
Tues-Sat by appointment   bridesmaids.com

This store is just for bridesmaids! Here Comes the Bridesmaid carries one of the largest selections of designer bridesmaid gowns available in every size from After Six, Bari Jay, Bill Levkoff, Dessy, Lazaro and others. They now carry accessories like shoes, clutches, shawls, jewelry and hair accents. Peruse their website for your top picks by design and color before your scheduled appointment.

KLEINFELD

110 W 20th St (bet Ave of the Americas and Seventh Ave)   646/633-4300
Tues, Thurs: 10:30-7; Fri: 11-5:30; Sat, Sun: 9:30-5:30   kleinfeldbridal.com
By appointment only

From beginning to end, the Kleinfeld experience sets the standard for all brides-to-be. A 35,000-square-foot location features the most exclusive bridal fashions, including plus-size gowns and all bridal accessories. Tops in the business, the Manhattan salon is a wonder to experience. Brides will enjoy a private dressing room with an experienced consultant to choose from 1,500 styles of American and European designer bridal gowns, including Amsale, Carol Hannah, Dennis Basso, Pnina Tornai and Temperley London. The perfect Kleinfeld fit is achieved with an experienced team of professional stylists, bridal consultants, custom fitters, seamstresses, beaders, embroiderers and pressers.

MONIQUE LHUILLIER

19 E 71st St (bet Fifth and Madison Ave)   212/683-3332
Mon-Sat: 10-6 (Thurs till 7)   moniquelhuillier.com

At this designer-owned boutique you'll find the feminine, sophisticated creations of Monique Lhuillier. The second floor holds racks of five-figure bridal gowns along with glamorous footwear and detailed hairpieces for the big day. High-end evening and ready-to-wear (day dresses, trousers, silk blouses) are displayed on the first floor. Shoppers are welcome to browse, but brides need to make an appointment for try-ons. Check online for one-day sample sales at 40% to 90% markdowns.

SHOPPING THE LOWER EAST SIDE

Over the last decade the Lower East Side has been gentrifying at a fast pace. Thankfully there are still shops on Orchard Street that honor the neighborhood's long enjoyed shopping history.

A.W. Kaufman (73 Orchard St, 212/226-1629): European designer lingerie

Altman Luggage (135 Orchard St, 212/254-7275): luggage and travel accessories

Cellini Uomo (59 Orchard St, 212/219-8657): Italian shoes of exotic skins

Giselle (143 Orchard St, 212/673-1900): women's sportswear

Joe's Fabrics Warehouse (102 Orchard St, 212/674-7089): decorator designer fabrics

Sheherazade Home (121 Orchard St, 212/539-1771): handcrafted home decor from the Middle East and Central Asia

Wendy Mink Jewelry (72 Orchard St, 212/260-5298): handmade jewelry

Zarin Fabrics (69 Orchard St, 212/925-6112): discounted decorator fabrics

CHILDREN'S

Before describing what I consider to be the best children's clothing stores in New York, let me be clear about what I'm not including: big chains and the haughty "just so" boutiques that line Madison Avenue. That is not to say some of the chains don't have great stores here. GapKids and babyGap, The Children's Place and Gymboree all have good selections, as does the cavernous "big-box" buybuy Baby. But unlike the stores listed below, they sell very little that isn't available in any other city. As for the haughty boutiques, I see no reason to patronize these wildly overpriced and unwelcoming places.

BONNE NUIT

1193 Lexington Ave (at 81st St)   212/472-7300
Mon-Fri: 9-7; Sat: 10-7; Sun: noon-5   bonnienuitnewyork.com

What a fun place to shop! You'll find European children's wear for boys and girls (up to preteen sizes); all have timeless details, some with smocking and hand embroidery. There are also old-fashioned children's books, wool and cashmere blankets, baby gifts and women's pajamas, robes and slippers. Very personal service is another plus.

CLEMENTINE

39½ Washington Sq S (bet Ave of the Americas and MacDougal St)
                                                       212/228-9333
Mon-Sat: 11-7; Sun: 11-5   clementineconsignment.com

You can dress your little darlings at this adorable consignment shop, which specializes in infant and toddler fashions (up to size 4T), at exceptional prices. The mother-daughter owners select luxury kids' brands such as Bonpoint, Isabella Oliver, Liz Lange, Oilily and Petit Bateau. There is an amazing selection of top-name maternity wear as well.

ESTELLA

27 W 20th St (bet Fifth Ave and Ave of the Americas), Room 304 212/255-3553
Mon-Fri: 9-5   estella-nyc.com

Estella is a popular and sophisticated children's boutique created by the husband-and-wife team of Jean Polsky and Chike Chukwolozie. Clothing of unusual colors and fabrics may include bamboo and organic cotton under labels like Amelia, Bon Bon, Bobo Choses, Munster, Muny and Soft Gallery. Stock includes unique toys, gear and furniture, as well as special and unusual gifts for youngsters six and under.

GIGGLE

120 Wooster St (bet Spring and Prince St)   212/334-5817
Mon-Sat: 10-7; Sun: noon-6
1033 Lexington Ave (at 74th St)   212/249-4249
352 Amsterdam Ave (bet 76th and 77th St)   212/362-8680
Mon-Sat: 10-7; Sun: 11-6   giggle.com

giggle is a godsend for parents and soon-to-be parents! You'll find most every baby item needed to take care of little ones, including furniture for the nursery. There are clothing items, toys, books, music, bath and spa items, strollers, car seats, baby monitors and information on keeping baby healthy and happy. Helpful personal shoppers and a baby registry are available.

LUCKY WANG

799 Broadway (bet 10th and 11th St)	212/353-2850
82 Seventh Ave (bet 15th and 16th St)	212/229-2900
Mon-Sat: 11-7; Sun: noon-6	luckywang.com

For something unusual or unique in children's wear, these sister stores showcase colorful contemporary kimonos and karate pants for babies and kids; they are as fashionable as they are practical. A few more labels are featured as well, as are dresses, pants, shirts, shoes, blankets, toys and other items.

SPACE KIDDETS

26 E 22nd St (bet Park Ave S and Broadway)	212/420-9878
Mon-Sat: 10:30-6 (Wed, Thurs till 7); Sun: 11-5	spacekiddets.com

This cheerful store is overflowing with funky children's clothes, shoes and accessories for newborns to preteens. The eclectic selection at Space Kiddets is always fresh and fun, with hundreds of brands represented; check out the vintage rock T-shirts from Angel Blue label. There is also a wide assortment of one-of-a-kind toys.

COSTUMES

ABRACADABRA

19 W 21st St (bet Fifth Ave and Ave of the Americas)	212/627-5194
Mon-Sat: 11-7; Sun: noon-5 (extended hours in Halloween season)	
	abracadabrasuperstore.com

Abracadabra is a gagster's heaven! They rent and sell costumes and costume accessories, wigs, hats, masks, magician's supplies, theatrical makeup and props for magic tricks. You can be transformed into almost anything! On-site magicians will show you magic tricks for free!

NEW YORK COSTUMES/HALLOWEEN ADVENTURE

104 Fourth Ave (bet 11th and 12th St)	212/673-4546
Mon-Sat: 11-8; Sun: noon-7 (extended hours in Halloween season and holidays)	
	newyorkcostumes.com

You and your family will be the talk of the neighborhood after a visit here. You'll find an extensive inventory of retail and rental costumes for adults, kids and pets. Rave party gear and decor, wigs, hats, gags, magic items, props and all manner of games and novelties are showcased. In addition, makeup artists are on hand most of the time.

RICKY'S NYC

375 Broadway (bet Franklin and White St)	212/925-5490
383 Fifth Ave (bet 35th and 36th St)	212/481-6701
111 Third Ave (bet 13th and 14th St)	212/674-9640
112 First Ave (at 7th St)	212/539-1015

Numerous other locations
Hours vary by location   rickyshalloween.com

Ricky's may be best known for their Halloween paraphernalia: costumes and masks for the whole family, including pets and every scary accessory under the full moon. With expanded locations throughout the city, they also stock crazy, funky, historical and seasonal costumes for other holidays and events, plus everyday fashion accessories, cosmetics and wigs.

FAMILY

AMERICAN APPAREL

429 Broadway (bet Canal and Hood St)	212/925-0560
140 West Broadway (at Thomas St)	212/393-3489
1030 Third Ave (at 61st St)	212/207-3239
Numerous other locations	
Hours vary by store	americanapparel.net

American Apparel is touted for their made-in-the-USA label. The company proudly employs thousands of American workers in the fashion industry; designers, cutters, dyers, sewers, pressers and technology experts. The clothing line features fun styles of solid-color cotton basics; T-shirts, dresses, pants, denim, underwear and accessories for the entire family, including the family dog. You may want to check out the brand's factory outlet (285 Lafayette St, 212/675-2360).

FOREVER 21

640 Fifth Ave (bet 51st and 52nd St)	212/757-1896
50 W 34th St (bet Broadway and Fifth Ave)	212/564-2346
4 Union Sq S (at 14th St)	212/228-0598
568 Broadway (at Prince St)	212/941-5949
Hours vary by store	forever21.com

Just follow the well-dressed younger crowd to these stores where merchandise is trendy, bright and fun and moderately priced for men, women and girls. Apparel choices include casual, business, occasion, maternity and swimwear. There is also a line of good-looking plus-size clothing. Beauty products, shoes and up-to-the-minute accessories complete the look.

MARC JACOBS

163 Mercer St (bet Prince and Houston St), women's, men's	212/343-1490
298 W 4th St (at Bank St), Little Marc	212/206-6644
301 W 4th St (at Bank St), women's accessories	212/929-9455
382 Bleecker St (at Perry St), men's	212/929-0304
385 Bleecker St (at Perry St), men's and women's accessories	212/924-6126
400 Bleecker St (at 11th St), Bookmarc (books, stationery, accessories)	
	212/620-4021
403 Bleecker St (at 11th St), women's	212/924-0026
Hours vary by store	marcjacobs.com

Walk around Bleecker Street and before long, you are sure to encounter a Marc Jacobs store! Each entity is a specialty shop, with offerings of very stylish ready-to-wear women's clothes and accessories, adorable children's togs, men's attire and accessories, eyeglasses, footwear, handbags and books. This popular American designer has certainly made his mark in the West Village and Soho.

FURS AND LEATHER

BARBARA SHAUM

60 E 4th St (bet Bowery and Second Ave)   212/254-4250
Wed-Sat: 1-6

Barbara Shaum has been doing magical things with leather since 1963. She's a wonder with sandals, bags, sterling-silver buckles and belts (with handmade brass, nickel-silver, inlaid wood and copper buckles). Everything is designed on-site in the tiny shop, and each item is meticulously crafted using only the finest materials.

GOODMAN COUTURE FURS

224 W 30th St, Room 402   212/244-7422
Mon-Fri: 9-5; Sat: by appointment

The Goodman family has been creating fine fur styles since 1918. Third-generation furrier David Goodman is famous for high-quality fur-lined and reversible fur coats and jackets. He carries a beautiful collection of the world's finest furs, including the latest fashions in minks, sheared minks, fine sables and other unique furs, plus a luxurious selection of custom-made shearlings. Goodman is a trailblazer in restyling furs and restoring life to an out-of-style or unused fur coat. Another specialty is converting unused furs into fur-lined all-weather coats. A "must-have" item and the perfect town-and-travel coat for women on the go is Goodman's featherweight fur-lined reversible coat.

HOSIERY

FOGAL

611 Madison Ave (at 58th St)   212/207-3080
Mon-Fri: 10-6:30; Sat: 10-8; Sun: noon-5   fogal.com

For luxurious and fashionable legwear, Fogal is an excellent source. Plain hosiery comes in nearly a hundred hues; the elegant designs and patterns make the number of choices almost incalculable. Fogal also carries tights, socks, bodywear and fine knitwear.

MEN'S AND WOMEN'S ACCESSORIES

FOSSIL

38 W 34th St (bet Fifth Ave and Ave of the Americas)   212/594-5850
Mon-Sat: 9 a.m.-10 p.m.; Sun: 10-9
1585 Broadway (bet 47th and 48th St)   212/445-1021
Sun-Thurs: 9 a.m.-midnight; Fri, Sat: 9 a.m.-1 a.m.
530 Fifth Ave (bet 44th and 45th St)   212/997-3978
Daily: 9-9   fossil.com

Fossil has been creating high-quality products for men and women since 1984. Besides a rainbow of traditional watches in tin cases, these shopping destinations offer bags, sunglasses, fragrances and a full line of accessories. Many watches are water-resistant and come with a formidable 11-year warranty. Bags come in a wide range of size and purpose from compact cross

APPAREL BARGAINS IN NEW YORK!

Baby gear: **buybuy Baby** (270 Seventh Ave, 917/344-1555)

Clothing: **Old Navy** (150 W 34th St, 212/594-0115; 610 Ave of the Americas, 212/645-0663; 503-511 Broadway, 212/226-0838 and 300 W 125th St, 212/531-1544)

Clothing for the family: **H&M** (1328 Broadway, 646/473-1164 and other locations) and **Loehmann's** (101 Seventh Ave, 212/352-0856 and 2101 Broadway, 212/882-9990)

Clothing, men's and women's: **Zara** (101 Fifth Ave, 212/741-0555; 39 W 34th St, 212/868-6551; 500 Fifth Ave, 212/302-2551; 750 Lexington Ave, 212/754-1120; 580 Broadway, 212/343-1725 and 1963 Broadway, 212/362-4272)

Discount department store: **Century 21** (22 Cortlandt St, 212/227-9092 and 1972 Broadway, 212/518-2121)

Shoes: **DSW** (40 E 14th St, 212/674-2146; 213 W 34th St, 967-9703 and 2220 Broadway, 917/746-9422)

Shoes, running: **Super Runners Shop** (745 Seventh Ave, 212/398-2449 and other locations): apparel and accessories, too!

Shoes, athletic: **Sprint Sports** (2511 Broadway, 212/866-8077)

bodies to large book-toting work bags and backpacks. The brand shows off timeless American design in its collections, and at reasonable, mid-range price points. Note the late hours for the Times Square store on Broadway!

SUNGLASS HUT

1313 Broadway (at 34th St)	212/947-7789
496 Broadway (bet Broome and Spring St)	212/966-6501
157 Spring St (at Broadway)	212/966-7293
351 Bleecker St (at 10th St)	212/924-4769
Numerous other locations	sunglasshut.com
Hours vary by store	

Sunglass Hut is a premier shopping destination for high quality men's and women's fashion sunglasses — top brands, the latest trends and exclusive styles. Brands shown include Michael Kors, Ray-Ban, Dolce & Gabbana, Burberry, Oakley, Maui Jim, Tom Ford and more. Styles range from retro to a modern take on vintage; from low profile rimless to bold, oversized butterfly to classic aviator. Frames and lenses are offered in a range of colors and in your choice of polarized, non-polarized and photo-polarized. There is also a substantial selection for kids.

WILL LEATHER GOODS

29 Prince St (bet Mott and Elizabeth St)	212/925-2824
Daily: 11-8	willleathergoods.com

The Nolita outpost for Will Leather Goods is truly an ocean of leather.

Founded in 1981 in Eugene, Oregon, the family-owned operation looks to be a sort of tannery swap meet with every surface space covered by mostly leather products for men and women: belts, bracelets, duffel bags, backpacks, handbags, totes, briefcases, wallets, leather travel kits and even huaraches. Great attention is given to craftsmanship and detailing, including monogramming. There are additional textile items of cotton, silk and canvas with beautiful woven designs.

NOTABLE CONSIGNMENT AND THRIFT SHOPS IN MANHATTAN

CHELSEA
Angel Street Thrift Shop (118 W 17th St, 212/229-0546)
Fisch for the Hip (90 Seventh Ave, 212/633-6965): high-end consignment
Goodwill (103 W 25th St, 646/638-1725)
Housing Works Thrift Shop (143 W 17th St, 718/838-5050): additional locations
New York Vintage (117 W 25th St, 212/647-1107): women's designer evening wear
Second Time Around (94 Seventh Ave, 212/255-9455)
Shareen Vintage (13 W 17th St, 2nd floor, 212/206-1644)

EAST 20s
City Opera Thrift Shop (222 E 23rd St, 212/684-5344)
Goodwill (220 E 23rd St, 212/447-7270)
Salvation Army Thrift Shop (208 E 23rd St, 212/532-8115)
Vintage Thrift (286 Third Ave, 212/871-0777)

EAST VILLAGE
Jane's Exchange (191 E 3rd St, 212/677-0380): children's, maternity fashions
Tokio 7 (83 E 7th St, 212/353-8443)

GREENWICH VILLAGE
Fisch for the Hip (88½ Seventh Ave), 212/633-9053)

NOLITA
Second Time Around (262 Mott St, 212/965-8415)

SOHO
A Second Chance Designer Resale (155 Prince St, 212/673-6155): trendy clothing
Ina (101 Thompson St, 212/941-4757)
Second Time Around (111 Thompson St, 212/925-3919)
V.I.A. Vintage Intelligence Agency (611 Broadway, Suite 534, 212/673-0703): women's clothing and accessories; by appointment only

UPPER EAST SIDE
A Second Chance Designer Resale (1111 Lexington Ave, 2nd floor, 212/744-6041): designer handbags

Arthritis Foundation Thrift Shop (1430 Third Ave, 212/772-8816)
Bis Designer Resale (1134 Madison Ave, 2nd floor, 212/396-2760)
Cancer Care Thrift Shop (1480 Third Ave, 212/879-9868)
Council Thrift Shop (246 E 84th St, 212/439-8373)
Memorial Sloan-Kettering Thrift Shop (1440 Third Ave, 212/535-1250)
Michael's, The Consignment Shop for Women (1041 Madison Ave, 212/737-7273)
Second Time Around (1040 Lexington Ave, 212/628-0980)

UPPER WEST SIDE
Off Broadway Boutique (139 W 72nd St, 212/724-6713)

MEN'S AND WOMEN'S GENERAL
BAPE

91 Greene St (bet Spring and Prince St)	212/925-0222
Mon-Fri: 11-7; Sat: 11-7:30; Sun: 11:30-6:30	us.bape.com

A Bathing Ape is a Japanese clothing label created by designer Nigo. Lovers of the brand will find the recognizable camo and star-and-lightning-bolt on urban streetwear at BAPE. Offerings include digital printed T-shirts and unusual clothing (jackets, pants and sweatshirts), shoes and accessories (hats, belts, gloves, backpacks and more). Fans of rock-star couture will be blown away.

BILLY REID

54 Bond St (at Bowery), Suite 2	212/598-9355
Mon-Sat: 11-8; Sun: 11-7	
94 Charles St (at 4th St)	646/461-6427
Mon-Sat: 1-8; Sun: noon-7	billyreid.com

Billy Reid sells clothes that might best be described as "Southern comfort." An Alabama gentleman, William "Billy" Reid designs tailored apparel in easy-to-wear moleskin, hopsack, tweeds and plaids. Men and women will find outerwear, jackets, sweaters, pants, shirts, dresses and tops. A custom-tailoring department will make you look extra sharp. It's worth a trip to Reid to see the decor alone, as recommissioned heirloom items from down South have taken on creative uses up North at both locations.

CHRISTOPHER FISCHER

80 Wooster St (bet Broome and Spring St)	212/965-9009
1225 Madison Ave (bet 88th and 89th St)	212/831-8880
Mon-Sat: 10-6; Sun: noon-6	christopherfischer.com

Christopher Fischer collections represent the opulence of the Hampton's lifestyle. Items are created from the finest of knits in superfine and baby cashmere, to unique chunky and hand-knitted pieces of alpaca or fine wools. There are luxurious cashmere and leather goods for men, women and children, including sweaters, shawls, scarves, blankets, bags and cushions; there's even a cashmere line for babies. Soft cotton and cool linen creations more suitable for summer can also be found.

THE DRESSING ROOM BOUTIQUE & BAR

75-A Orchard St (bet Broome and Grand St)   212/966-7330
Tues-Wed: 1 p.m.-midnight; Thurs-Sat: 1 p.m.-2 a.m.; Sun: 1:30-8
                                                        thedressingroomnyc.com

Shoppers at this hybrid boutique are treated to a wide assortment of both new and consigned accessories, jewelry and clothing, with emerging independent fashion and accessory designers being featured. The full-service bar on the first level is a welcome resting spot for the weary shopper — Wi-Fi, movies shown on a large screen and live DJ events are additional draws. On the lower level customers have the chance to shop or consign carefully selected vintage and secondhand items for cash or store credit.

FAÇONNABLE

Rockefeller Center
636 Fifth Ave (at 51st St)   212/319-0111
Mon-Sat: 10-8; Sun: 11-6   faconnable.com

French company Façonnable has made a name for itself in the fashion world with tailored Euro-clothes that appeal to conservative dressers. The 21,000-square-foot Rockefeller Center store shows two floors of men's and women's sportswear, tailored clothing, suits and shoes, all rich in style and color; new items in the collection take inspiration from the French Riviera. You'll find that your tab can add up quickly here.

HARLEM UNDERGROUND

20 E 125th St (bet Fifth and Madison Ave)   212/987-9385
Mon-Thurs: 10-7; Fri, Sat: 10-8; Sun: noon-6   harlemunderground.com

This shop is a great source for comfortable, reasonably-priced and "cool" urban wear. The merchandise has the feel of the historic neighborhood it represents; guys will like the Harlem-themed T-shirts. Personal or corporate embroidery is available for denim shirts and jackets, T-shirts, sweats and caps.

RACHEL COMEY LABEL

At her Soho flagship, **Rachel Comey** (95 Crosby St, 212/334-0455) shows a complete collection of vintage-inspired women's clothing, with a touch of rock 'n roll. Some of the items, like jumpsuits and coveralls, are somewhat utilitarian with forgiving shapes. This independent NYC designer launched her label in 2000, but the store did not open until 2014. Arguably her shoes are her most popular offerings and take center stage under a skylight in the shop. The collection also includes accessories such as tote bags, cross-body bags and sunglasses. Dressing rooms are enormous and beautiful.

SHOPPING SAMPLE SALES

As I've said elsewhere, shopping in New York can be expensive. However, with a little legwork, dressing fashionably or outfitting your home with designer goods does not necessarily mean paying full retail prices. Designer sample sales are held in retail stores and temporary locations on a regular basis with deep discounts.

Here are a few tips:

■ Know your size, as dressing rooms are not always available.

■ Bring cash, since checks and plastic are not always accepted.

■ Scrutinize your intended purchases, as all sales are final.

■ Be prepared for disarray; many locations are temporary sales rooms located up several flights of stairs.

■ Scout out shopping sections of *New York* and *Time Out New York* or be on the lookout for flyers and billboards.

JEAN SHOP

37 Crosby St (bet Broome and Grand St)   212/366-5326
Mon-Sat: 11-7; Sun: noon-6   jean-shop.com

These are no ordinary jeans. Each pair is created to a customer's specifications using high-quality Japanese selvedge denim (custom woven on projectile looms in Japan or the U.S.A.) and then constructed stateside. Choose from classic and relaxed fit or rocker styles in short, medium and long lengths and show your personality with custom distressing and dyeing. Create a one-of-a-kind denim outfit from a selection of jackets, shirts, belts and accessories; some leather clothing, too. These are quality goods, so expect to pay accordingly.

JEFFREY — NEW YORK

449 W 14th St (bet Ninth and Tenth Ave)   212/206-1272
Mon-Fri: 10-8 (Thurs till 9); Sat: 10-7; Sun: 12:30-6   jeffreynewyork.com

Look to Jeffrey Kalinsky's store for chic and high-end men's and women's clothing in the Meatpacking District. Besides ready-to-wear, there are innovative accessories and an excellent selection of shoes. With fashion names like Prada, Gucci, Missoni, Nina Ricci and Valentino, expect matching price tags.

LOUIS VUITTON

1 E 57th St (at Fifth Ave)   212/758-8877
Mon-Sat: 10-7 (Thurs till 8); Sun: noon-6   louisvuitton.com

In spectacular quarters, this shop has nearly everything you might expect with the Louis Vuitton name: a dramatic exterior, compelling windows, a tasteful assortment of merchandise, service with an attitude and inflated prices. Classic brown leather travel goods and Marc Jacobs-designed luxury apparel fill these exclusive spaces. If the LV signature is important to you, then this is the place to shop.

OPENING CEREMONY

33 and 35 Howard St (bet Broadway and Crosby St)   212/219-2688
Mon-Sat: 11-8; Sun: noon-7   openingceremony.us

Opening Ceremony is actually a multinational retail store, showroom and gallery. Each year, men's and women's fashions by emerging designers and artists from a visiting country are added to the existing lines of brand-name designers and retailers. Lines from Brazil, Germany, the United Kingdom, Sweden, Japan, France and others have been introduced, sometimes springboarding a designer into the American retail market. Many styles are avant-garde, and you'll find special lines from established brands like Pendleton, Rodarte and Topshop. Constantly changing displays make this an interesting place to revisit.

RALPH LAUREN

867 Madison Ave (at 72nd St), men's flagship   212/606-2100
888 Madison Ave (at 72nd St), women's and home flagship   212/434-8000
872 Madison Ave (bet 71st and 72nd St), baby store   212/434-8083
878 Madison Ave (bet 71st and 72nd St), children's store   212/606-3376
109 Prince St (at Mott St), men's and women's store   212/625-1660

RRL

381 Bleecker St (at Perry St), men's tailored clothing   212/625-3480
383 Bleecker St (bet Charles and Perry St), men's sportswear   212/645-5513

POLO

711 Fifth Ave (at 55th St), men's, women's and children's flagship   646/774-3900

DENIM & SUPPLY

99 University Pl (at 12th St), men's and women's denim   212/677-1895
Hours vary by store   ralphlauren.com

The story of Ralph Lauren is the epitome of the American dream. With a vision that began close to 50 years ago with a collection of ties, Lauren has redefined American style. His outstanding collection of clothing for men, women and children, plus a top-flight line of home goods and accessories, are available at the above listed locations. The Ralph Lauren brand stands for class, quality and unparalleled service. **RRL** and **Denim & Supply** are extensions of the brand that feature rugged, Western-inspired clothing (RRL) and youthful, free-spirited denim (Denim & Supply).

The lines are always beautifully showcased in amazing, one-of-a-kind environments as described below:

RALPH LAUREN MEN'S FLAGSHIP

Opened in 1986, this iconic store revolutionized the shopping experience by creating a retail space in an authentic residential environment. Spanning nearly 16,000 square feet, the Rhinelander Mansion is the first location to showcase Ralph Lauren's finest menswear collections. Originally designed in the 1890s by Kimball & Thompson, the mansion is an architectural treasure and one of the few remaining turn-of-the-century great homes in Manhattan. Unrivaled in terms of preservation, architecture and design, the former home is the perfect showcase for the timeless style of Ralph Lauren.

RALPH LAUREN WOMEN'S AND HOME FLAGSHIP

At nearly 22,000 square feet, this store stands as the feminine counterpart to the company's men's flagship across the avenue. Reminiscent of the grand Beaux-Arts architecture of the early 20th century, the exterior's neoclassical French design is inspired by the rich architectural heritage of the Upper East Side. The stately four-story building's scale and detailing are an elegant complement to the Rhinelander Mansion.

POLO RALPH LAUREN FLAGSHIP

Opened in September 2014 and spanning nearly 38,000 square feet over three floors, the Polo flagship is the first store to unveil a new world of Polo for women, and the first store to showcase women's Polo alongside the Polo men's collection. Located in a historic building at the corner of Fifth Avenue and 55th Street, in the center of one of the world's most legendary shopping districts, the stunning Polo flagship transports shoppers to a world that is contemporary, youthful and cool. Drawing on authentic American inspirations, from the rich woods of an Adirondack boathouse to the whitewashed bricks of a Brooklyn loft, vibrant collections are showcased throughout the store alongside custom bikes, kayaks and vintage guitars. Beautiful fixtures, rare art and two custom-cut river-rock stone fireplaces complete the landmark setting. The store also introduces Ralph Lauren's first-ever coffee shop, **Ralph's Coffee**, on the second floor. An antique oak library table and bistro-style marble-top tables offer a place to enjoy the private coffee blends. Adjacent to the store is Ralph Lauren's first New York restaurant, **The Polo Bar** (1 E 55th St, 212/207-8562), which opened January 2015. Classic American cuisine inspired by some of Lauren's personal favorites is presented in a comfortable and luxurious equestrian setting.

SCOTCH & SODA

273 Lafayette St (at Prince St)	212/966-3300
Mon-Thurs: 11-8; Fri-Sun: 10-8	
866 Broadway (bet 17th and 18th St)	646/561-9679
Mon-Sat: 11-8; Sun: 11-7	scotch-soda.com

Scotch & Soda, the Amsterdam-based fashion brand, has landed in Manhattan. Two Dutch-chic shops with wooden floors and antique carpets showcase casual basics for both men and women. On the feminine side are shorts, T-shirts, skirts, cable-knit sweaters, sundresses and swimwear. Items for men include comfy chinos, polos, jeans, parkas and swimwear. A few accessories like cosmetic and shopping bags, scarves, bowties, suspenders and fun socks round out the collegiate-style clothing.

STEVEN ALAN

229 Elizabeth St (bet Prince and Houston St), men's	212/226-7482
230 Elizabeth St (bet Prince and Houston St), women's	212/343/7974
103 Franklin St (bet Church St and West Broadway)	212/343-0692
158 Franklin St (bet Varick and Hudson St), home shop	646/402-9661
Hours vary by store	stevenalan.com

Steven Alan has gathered an eclectic group of more than 20 emerging designers and showcases their creations in his stores. You'll find men's and women's casual essentials, outerwear, handbags, accessories and toiletries — all unique.   A home shop was recently added which features an assortment of bed, bath, kitchen and tabletop items; books; food items and even a line of bicycles.

TOPSHOP

608 Fifth Ave (at 49th St)   212/757-8240
478 Broadway (bet Broome and Grand St)   212/966-9555
Mon-Sat: 10-9; Sun: 11-8   topshop.com

This U.S. affiliate of the trendy British retail chain offers floor upon floor of the latest style-setting apparel for "cool" girls (sizes zero to 12); accessories and shoes, too. Personal stylists are on hand to help customers pull together the right look. The experience is spread over an amazing 40,000-square-foot megastore on Fifth Avenue. Guys will find plenty of modern shirts, pants, sweaters, coats and hoodies for their wardrobes at **Topman**, housed within the same buildings.

UNIQLO

546 Broadway (at Spring St)   877/386-4756 (all stores)
31 W 34th St (bet Fifth Ave and Ave of the Americas)
666 Fifth Ave (at 53rd St)
Mon-Sat: 10-9; Sun: 11-8   uniqlo.com

These Uniqlo locations are branches of one of Japan's largest retailers, started in 1984 in Hiroshima, Japan. Their motto is "made for all." You'll find high-quality casual wear for men, women and children in a wide range of fabrics and prices. Denim and cashmere items with matching accessories are featured. The ultra-modern midtown location has over 100 dressing rooms in the 89,000-square-foot space, the biggest retail location on Fifth Avenue.

MEN'S AND WOMEN'S HATS
WORTH & WORTH

45 W 57th St (bet Fifth Ave and Ave of the Americas), 6th floor   212/265-2887
Mon, Tues: 10-6; Wed-Sat: 10-7   hatshop.com

Worth & Worth is one of the few remaining custom hat makers in the U.S. where hat master, Orlando Palacios, works on-site. Men and women can shop for hats from the current collection of fedoras, panamas, felts, caps and berets, all available for purchase at reasonable prices. Custom hat orders can be ready in two to three weeks and begin at $250 for straw and $350 for felt.

SALES ALERT!

Top Button is a web-based company (topbutton.com) that informs consumers about sample, warehouse, outlet, clearance and promotional sales. Categories include apparel, housewares, accessories, food, beauty and many more. Information can be accessed by company name, product type and date. It's a great resource and the service is free.

MEN'S FORMAL WEAR

CUSTOM MEN

140 W 57th St (bet Ave of the Americas and Seventh Ave), Suite 4-C
212/767-0545
Mon-Fri: 10-8; Sat: 10-5; Sun: by appointment
14 Maiden Lane (bet Broadway and Nassau St)   646/559-4065
Mon-Fri: 9-6; Sat: 10-5; Sun: by appointment   custommen.com

The choices at Custom Men are almost limitless! Men's suits, sport coats, slacks, tuxedos, topcoats, vests and shirts are individually tailored. There are about 15,000 luxury fabrics to peruse, including Wain Shiell, Holland & Sherry, Armani and Ermenegildo Zegna for suits; French pique, Italian tessitura and pinpoint Oxford shirtings and a wide variety of linings. Choose from double- or single-breasted jackets. Pants can be made in any style to fit all shapes and sizes. There are dozens of shirt-collar, cuff and monogram style options. Prices are competitive (especially sale prices) and free alterations are offered within one year of purchase. The company is family-owned and -operated and all articles are crafted by experienced, skilled tailors with 100% guaranteed satisfaction.

MEN'S GENERAL

BILLIONAIRE BOYS CLUB & ICECREAM

456 West Broadway (at Houston St)   212/777-2225
Mon-Sat: noon-7; Sun: noon-6   bbcicecream.com

At Billionaire Boys Club & Icecream the young-at-heart will find a novel collection of men's clothing with equally unique branding. The vision of musician Pharrell Williams and Japanese designer Nigo resulted in two floors of edgy, haute clothing and shoes. Lots of colors and patterns; unique shirts, T-shirts, jackets, pants, shorts and accessories are yours for a pretty price. By the way, Icecream is a brand, not the frozen treat!

CARSON STREET CLOTHIERS

63 Crosby St (at Spring St)   212/925-2627
Mon-Sat: 11-7; Sun: noon-6   carsonstreetclothiers.com

Since opening its doors in spring 2013, Carson Street Clothiers has become one of the leaders in American menswear taste-making. Located in Soho, CSC prides itself on its ability to appeal to men of all demographics by blending classic tailoring with more progressive, contemporary sportswear. Clothing includes outerwear, sweaters, dress and sports shirts, T-shirts and tanks, suiting, trousers, sweats, swimwear, denim and shorts. You'll also find footwear and accessories in the sophisticated industrial space where leisurely shopping is encouraged; enjoy a beer (on them, of course) in the lounge or while perusing the numerous racks, tables and shelves.

DAVE'S NEW YORK

581 Ave of the Americas (bet 16th and 17th St)   212/989-6444
Mon-Fri: 9-7; Sat: 10-6; Sun: 11-5   davesnewyork.com

Dave's New York is family-run and has been in business since 1963. Branded "Americana" work clothes and military wear fill these shelves. Reasonably-priced clothing and boots with such iconic names as Dickies, Levi's, Carhartt, Woolrich, Timberland Pro and Red Wing are neatly arranged. These rugged clothes have stood the test of time and are favorites of construction workers and those looking for solid, long-wearing casual apparel.

FREEMANS SPORTING CLUB

Freeman Alley
8 Rivington St (bet Bowery and Chrystie St)   212/673-3209
Mon-Fri: 11-8; Sat: 11-7; Sun: noon-6   freemanssportingclub.com

Here's a good source for classic work shirts, pants, custom suiting and high-quality outerwear. The majority of their products are made within ten miles of their shop, the kind of local sourcing of clothing that is pretty much unheard of these days! The entire F.S.C. brand is built around the vanishing trade of handmade clothing for stylish guys; pieces are durable and meant to be worn day in and day out. Next door is **F.S.C. Barber** (212/256-1309), an old-school barbershop to keep men looking ruggedly handsome.

JOHN VARVATOS

122 Spring St (at Greene St)   212/965-0700
Mon-Sat: 11-7; Sun: noon-6
315 Bowery (at Bleecker St)   212/358-0315
Mon-Fri: noon-8; Sat: 11-8; Sun: noon-6   johnvarvatos.com

The John Varvatos brand offers refined tailoring with a modern edge. The outstanding menswear collection shows off leather and shearling outerwear, sportswear, footwear, belts and other accessories and fragrance items. Men of all ages will feel comfortable with the Old World detailing of a line that exudes class. The Bowery location shows an edgier mixture of retro clothing and accessories, as well as vintage and contemporary vinyls (Varvatos is a music buff); live rock music concerts as well. The stores reek of atmosphere, and the salespeople couldn't be more helpful. An additional boutique will open in 2015 at the World Trade Center.

L.S. MEN'S CLOTHING

49 W 45th St (bet Fifth Ave and Ave of the Americas), 3rd floor   212/575-0933
Mon-Thurs: 9-6:30; Fri: 9-3; Sun: 10-4   lsmensclothing.com

L.S. Men's is known for discounting American-made, high-end custom suits. The main attraction, though, is the tremendous selection of ready-to-wear executive-class styles (sizes from 36 short to 60 extra-long) by name designers; plus ready-made shirts, pants and sport coats at 40% to 60% savings. The custom-order department stocks an amazing number of Italian and English fabrics. Custom-made suits take two to four weeks and sell from $645 to $1,295. Ask for Izzy!

PAUL STUART

Madison Ave at 45th St   212/682-0320
Mon-Fri: 9-7; Sat: 9-6; Sun: noon-6   paulstuart.com

Paul Stuart has been supplying luxury menswear since 1938. Preppy made-to-measure and bespoke menswear are of the utmost quality; and worth the

NO-STOCK SHOPS

One of the newest trends in retail shopping is the guide shop — retail outlets that do not carry inventory. Instead of purchasable merchandise, shops carry one or two of each item in each size. You get the look and feel without having to guess at fit, quality or color. Once you've decided what you want to buy, the clerk orders it for delivery to your door. For the retailer this means no storeroom full of inventory; for the customer, no toting around shopping bags. **Bonobos** (45 W 25th St, 5th floor, 646/738-3314 and 35 Crosby St, 212/343-4235) is a front-runner in this new class of New York fashion and retail that skips wholesalers, middlemen and traditional distributors. Also called "omnichannel retail," these are generally e-commerce companies that find that the internet by itself is not sufficient, so wherever people shop, the merchandise is offered for inspection. It will be interesting to see where this trend goes from here.

price! A great selection of sweaters, ties (bowties, too!), socks, shirts and more is shown, with a small offering of ready-to-wear for women, too. Check out Phineas Cole, the new men's luxury brand with a slimmer cut.

ROTHMAN'S

222 Park Ave S (at 18th St)   212/777-7400
Mon-Sat: 10-7 (Thurs, Fri till 8); Sun: noon-6   rothmansny.com

Harry Rothman's grandsons, Ken and Jim Giddon, reinvented this family-run men's clothing store. They made a conscious decision to move away from the "discount store" mantra. "Clothes for real men" is their tag today, with their goal to find the best designer names, but still at a great value. Classic suits, coats, sportswear and accessories fill the modern, 11,000-square-foot space. Let the family help you find exactly what you're looking for!

SAINT LAURIE MERCHANT TAILORS

22 W 32nd St (bet Fifth Ave and Ave of the Americas), 5th floor   212/643-1916
Mon-Fri: 9-6; Sat: 9-4 (closed Sat in summer)   saintlaurie.com

With a long history of creating many items for Broadway shows, TV and movies, you know these folks must be good! For four generations Saint Laurie has provided quality made-to-order handmade clothing including tuxedos, suits and shirts for men (and women) at rack prices; they buy fabric directly from weavers, resulting in price savings for customers. Their showroom and manufacturing facility occupy the same location. A fine selection of accessories is also offered; check out the Mimi Fong neckwear!

SEIZE SUR VINGT

78 Greene St (bet Spring and Broome St)   212/625-1620
Mon-Sat: 11-7; Sun: noon-6   16sur20.com

Everything about this store is first-class: the elegant materials, the quality craftsmanship and styles and the faultless fit. The translation of their name, seize sur vingt, is "16 out of 20," as in a test score. Ready-made shirts, suits and sportswear are proportioned for the lean, well-toned man or woman. If you want to splurge, order a bespoke suit of the finest imported wool, linen or cashmere. Shirts, sportswear and accessories are also custom-made. Be sure to check out the colorful buck sneakers!

TOPMAN

608 Fifth Ave	212/757-8240
478 Broadway	212/966-9555
Mon-Sat: 10-9; Sun: 11-8	us.topman.com

What began as a British phenomenon now has hundreds of international locations featuring the collections of over 50 U.K. and U.S. designers. Topman houses the hottest trend-driven pieces for men; inventory is refreshed on a monthly basis. The sleek Broadway store boasts such details as raw brick, floor-to-ceiling windows on every level, glossy finishes and an army of mannequins dressed to impress. The Fifth Avenue shop is a basement bazaar of higher-end fast fashion with an outfit for any occasion, from signature logo T-shirts and jeans to beautiful suits and accessories. Students will like the standing student discount of 10%. **Topshop** for women is housed within these same buildings.

MEN'S HATS

J.J. HAT CENTER

310 Fifth Ave (at 32nd St)	212/239-4368
Mon-Fri: 9-6; Sat: 9:30-5:30	jjhatcenter.com

This renowned hat shop stocks thousands of brand-name hats and caps (to size 8) alongside its own brand. Founded in 1911, it is New York's oldest hat shop, creating hats from blacktie fedoras to Greek fisherman caps from felt, straw, wool, leather and linen. Special services include free brush-up, hat stretching or tightening. A satellite location called **Pork Pie Hatters** is located in the East Village (440 E 9th St, 212/260-0408).

MEN'S SHIRTS

NEPENTHES

307 W 38th St (bet Eighth and Ninth Ave)	212/643-9540
Mon-Sat: noon-7; Sun: noon-5	nepenthesny.com

Forego boring white button-down Oxford shirts in favor of Nepenthes' vibrant and unique patterned shirts. This store is the first U.S. location of this Japanese retailer. This men's store has an eclectic mix of great looking jackets, vests, wraps, backpacks and other bags, accessories and boat shoes. Expect a hefty price!

SHIRT STORE

51 E 44th St (bet Vanderbilt and Madison Ave)	212/557-8040
Mon-Fri: 9-6:30; Sat: noon-6	justwhiteshirts.com

The appeal of the Shirt Store is that you're buying directly from the manufacturer, so there's no middle man to hike prices. The Shirt Store offers 100% cotton dress shirts for men in sizes from 14½x32 to 18½x37, plus sport shirts, blazers and sport coats, ties and accessories have been added. Although the ready-made stock is great, they also do custom work; an office visit with swatches is not unusual. Additional services include mail order, alterations and monogramming.

MEN'S TIES

ANDREW'S TIES

30 Rockefeller Plaza (bet 48th and 49th St), south concourse   212/245-4563
Mon-Fri: 8:30-7; Sat: noon-7; Sun: noon-5   andrewstiesusa.com

There are very few really good tie stores left in New York. It's certainly not like it used to be, when one could find great selections and bargains on the Lower East Side. But Andrew's Ties has some classic handmade Italian ties made of silk and cashmere, along with some trendier options, in a wide range of style, color and cut; prices are reasonable. Also displayed are ascots, bowties, pocket squares, cuff links, belts, men's and women's scarves and the like.

RESALE CLOTHING

ALLAN & SUZI

237 Centre St (bet Grand and Broome St)   212/724-7445
Mon-Fri: 12:30-6:30; Sat: noon-7; Sun: noon-6   allanandsuzi.net

Allan & Suzi's retro clothing store is quite an operation. Under one roof you'll find a real mix of both new clothing from current designers and vintage clothing for men and women, along with old and new shoes and accessories, most sold on consignment. There are big names like Chanel, Donna Karan, Marc Jacobs, Prada, Roberto Cavalli and Versace. And to impress you further, note that proprietors Allan Pollack and Suzi Kandel dress a number of Hollywood and TV personalities. Check the website for some of their newest arrivals!

DESIGNER RESALE

324 E 81st St (bet First and Second Ave)   212/734-3639
Mon-Fri: 11-7 (Thurs till 8); Sat: 10-6; Sun: noon-5
                                        designerresaleconsignment.com

Designer Resale offers previously-owned ladies' designer clothing, shoes and accessories at moderate prices. The shop carries one of the largest collections of American and European designer brands in the area. You might find Chanel, Armani, Donna Karan, Gucci, Hermes, Prada, Louis Vuitton and hundreds of others. Prices on many items are marked down 20% to 50% at the first of each month. Call Myrna Skoller to inquire about the latest bargains or possible consignment of your own luxury items. Just next door is the companion store, **Gentlemen's Resale** (see write-up next page).

ENCORE

1132 Madison Ave (bet 84th and 85th St), upstairs   212/879-2850
Mon-Sat: 10:30-6:30 (Thurs till 7:30); Sun: noon-6   encoreresale.com

Encore has offered new and almost new clothing of designer/couture quality since 1954. It is a consignment boutique (not a charity thrift shop) presently owned and operated by Carol Selig. Its donors receive a portion of the sales price, and many of them are socialites and other luminaries who don't want to be seen in the same outfit twice. The fashions are up to date and sold at 50% to 70% off original retail prices. There are over 6,000 items in stock, including a small selection for men. Prices range from reasonable to astronomical — but just think about the numbers on the original tags!

GENTLEMEN'S RESALE

322 E 81st St (bet First and Second Ave)   212/734-2739
Mon-Fri: 11-7; Sat: 10-6; Sun: noon-5   gentlemensresaleclothing.com

Gentlemen interested in top-quality designer suits, jackets, sportswear, shoes and accessories can save a bundle at this resale operation. Gentlemen's Resale is the men's version of **Designer Resale**. Shopping here is like a treasure hunt, and that is half the fun. Imagine picking up a $1,000 Armani suit for $200! Call Gary Scheiner to learn about earning some extra bucks by consigning fine quality items from your own wardrobe.

INA

101 Thompson St (bet Prince and Spring St), women	212/941-4757
19 Prince St (bet Mott and Elizabeth St), men	212/334-2210
21 Prince St (bet Mott and Elizabeth St), women	212/334-9048
15 Bleecker St (bet Lafayette St and Bowery), men and women	212/228-8511
207 W 18th St (bet Seventh and Eighth Ave), men and women	212/334-6572
110 E 13th St (bet Third and Fourth Ave), men and women	212/254-8400
Hours vary by store	inanyc.com

INA offers the latest designer clothing, shoes, handbags and accessories (plus selected vintage) at a fraction of the original cost. The constantly changing consignment inventory routinely features labels like Gucci, Halston, Louis Vuitton and Vera Wang, for both men and women. Some items are new and have been creatively acquired through networking with stylists, models and manufacturers; others have been gently worn. Get a heads up on special sales and fashion trends by checking their online blogs, and contact them about consigning your still-stylish luxury fashions, as they are always looking for more great merchandise.

MICHAEL'S, THE CONSIGNMENT SHOP FOR WOMEN

1041 Madison Ave (at 79th St), 2nd floor   212/737-7273
Mon-Sat: 9:30-6 (Thurs till 8); Sun: noon-5   michaelsconsignment.com

Since 1954, Michael's has been the source for pieces from high-end designers. If you are dying to own one of those fabulous haute couture gowns you have seen in the magazines or on TV, visit this family-run consignment store. Chanel, Chloe, Gucci, Missoni, Prada and YSL — all amazing labels! Along with evening wear you'll also find furs, pantsuits, skirts, suits, jewelry, bags, shoes and more. Personal attention is assured, and prices are right.

ROUNDABOUT

1100 Madison Ave (bet 82nd and 83rd St)   212/472-3625
31 E 72nd St (bet Madison and Park Ave), ground floor   646/755-8009
Mon-Sat: 10-6; Sun: noon-6   roundaboutcouture.com

Roundabout is a new and resale women's clothing boutique offering high-end clothing, shoes, handbags and accessories. The owners started

SHOPPING SAMPLE SALES

You can find some great deals at discount designer stores like Century 21, but these stores are oftentimes packed with shoppers and tourists, have long lines and picked-over inventory. A better idea is visiting some of the amazing sample sales in NYC. For a good rundown of these sales events, check in with **Racked NY** (ny.racked.com) where you'll also find fashion trends and some of the season's best deals.

their business in Connecticut in 1989 and then successfully branched out to Manhattan. Some of the items bear brand names like Pucci, Prada, Gucci, Hermes and Chanel, with savings up to 70% off retail. You can add a little green to your wallet by consigning your own designer couture with Roundabout.

TATIANA DESIGNER RESALE

767 Lexington Ave (bet 60th and 61st St), 2nd floor   212/755-7744
Mon-Fri: 11-7; Sat: noon-6   tatianaresale.com

High fashion at low cost! Since 1998, famous models and high-society trendsetters have consigned their barely used haute couture garments at Tatiana Designer Resale. The shop also has samples from Italy, showroom pieces and a vintage collection of designer couture. Designers represented include Chanel, Dior, Fendi, Gucci, Hermes, Lanvin and Prada. You'll find top label clothing, shoes, jewelry and handbags at amazing markdowns. Call them if you are interested in consigning; they make housecalls!

SHOES — CHILDREN'S

HARRY'S SHOES FOR KIDS

2315 Broadway (bet 83rd and 84th St)   212/874-2034
Mon-Sat: 10-6:45 (Mon, Thurs till 7:45); Sun: 11-6   harrys-shoes.com

Though there's nothing fancy here, this Upper West Side shoe store is often wildly busy; the terrific inventory makes a visit worthwhile. Every single person working here knows how to fit shoes. There are lots of big-name brands, and prices are often more reasonable than at other Manhattan shoe stores. Just bring along some patience, particularly on weekends and in summer. Down the street, **Harry's Shoes** (2299 Broadway, 212/874-2035) offers quality footwear for the rest of the family.

LITTLE ERIC SHOES

1118 Madison Ave (bet 83rd and 84th St)   212/717-1513
Mon-Sat: 10-6; Sun: noon-6

Little Eric Shoes is not just a shoe store, they are foremost an Italian shoemaker. Everything in this shop is designed and manufactured by them for their private label. They specialize in dressy and casual shoes, boots and sandals for infants and children in a multitude of colors. Knowledgeable staff will fit children's fast-growing feet; they also indulge adults with women's and men's sizes to 12. Parents will love the welcoming family atmosphere and outstanding customer service.

SHOOFLY

42 Hudson St (bet Duane and Thomas St)   212/406-3270
Mon-Sat: 10-7; Sun: noon-6   shooflynyc.com

Shoofly will take care of your children's shoewear needs with styles that are both classic and funky. Attractive and reasonably-priced European shoes for infants to 14-year-olds are displayed. Women with tiny feet will appreciate the chic selection of footwear, as well. Amazing colors and detailing adorn most styles, and a selection of hats, tights, socks and accessories is impressive, too.

SHOES — FAMILY

KENNETH COLE

595 Broadway (at Houston St)   212/965-0283
Mon-Wed: 10-8; Thurs-Sat: 10-9; Sun: 11-7
107 E 42nd St (bet Vanderbilt and Park Ave)   212/949-8079
Mon-Fri: 10-9; Sat: 10-8; Sun: 11-7   kennethcole.com

American clothing designer Kenneth Cole started selling shoes from a production trailer on Avenue of the Americas, but he didn't stop there. Now two outposts in Manhattan (and scores across the country) offer his quality shoes at sensible prices. Other trendy staples include belts, handbags, scarves, watches, sportswear, outerwear and accessories for men and women.

T.O. DEY CUSTOM MADE SHOES

151 W 46th St (bet Ave of the Americas and Seventh Ave)   929/999-1866
Mon-Fri: 9-5; Sat: 9-1   todeyshoes.com

Needing a pair of comfortable shoes (or boots)? Visit this midtown shop for a pair of custom-made shoes. T.O. Dey welcomes a wide spectrum of customers, from individuals to Broadway shows. Choose from finished samples, bring a style to copy or confer with staff to design your own footwear. Whether you need orthopedic shoes or simply want a comfortable, perfect fit for fashion, dancing, running, walking or whatever, this experienced team of shoemakers can help.

DRINK AND SHOP

You may be more inclined to buy if you are relaxed and happy, whether it be the buzz from caffeine or alcohol. These stores offer liquid refreshment while you shop:

Dressing Room Boutique & Bar (75-A Orchard St, 212/966-7330): beer, wine and cocktails

Saturdays Surf (31 Crosby St, 212/966-7875 and 17 Perry St, 347/246-5830): coffee bar

Sustainable NYC (139 Ave A, 212/254-5400): coffee bar plus sandwiches and other light bites

Tiffany & Co. (727 Fifth Ave, 212/755-8000): champagne

SHOES — MEN'S
STAPLETON SHOE COMPANY

1 Rector St (bet Broadway and Trinity Pl)   212/964-6329
Mon-Fri: 8:45-5

For over 60 years Stapleton Shoe Company has provided "better shoes for less," but there is much more to this superlative operation. Gentlemen, these stores offer Alden, Allen-Edmonds, Cole Haan, Florsheim, Timberland, Rockport, Johnston & Murphy and a slew of other top names at discount. There isn't a better source for quality shoes. They are size specialists, carrying expanded men's sizes from 5 to 17 in widths A to EEE.

SPORTSWEAR
FILSON NYC

40 Great Jones St (bet Lafayette St and Bowery)   212/547-3121
Mon-Sat: 10-7; Sun: noon-6   filson.com

Veteran outdoorsman's outfitter for the Pacific Northwest, Filson has expanded Eastward to Noho. This store is for the outdoors-obsessed customer wanting apparel, accessories and leather goods, all of which are still made in the U.S.A. The space exudes history with touches like a vintage leather couch and a working shuffleboard table. Clothing items of wool, leather and mole skin include an iconic multipocketed field jacket (Mackinaw Cruiser), flannel shirts, weathered vests, sweaters, boots, travel and professional-grade camera bags, luggage, watches and other accessories. Most products are appropriate for rugged outdoor activities, like hunting and fishing, with emphasis on quality and durability. There are a handful of women's items as well.

PATAGONIA

426 Columbus Ave (bet 80th and 81st St)   917/441-0011
414 W 14th St (bet Ninth Ave and Washington St)   212/929-6512
72 Greene St (bet Broome and Spring St)   212/334-5213
313 Bowery (bet 1st and 2nd St)   212/228-2514
Mon-Sat: 11-7; Sun: noon-6   patagonia.com

Patagonia is a popular source for outdoors enthusiasts in need of clothing and gear for hiking, climbing, surfing or skiing. This green-minded company designs family clothing, packs and bags; even books to inspire your next adventure! The company takes pains to assure that their clothing allows freedom of movement, is durable and looks and feels good. Even those who don't spend much time in the great outdoors appreciate Patagonia attire.

SURPLUS
KAUFMAN'S ARMY & NAVY

319 W 42nd St (bet Eighth and Ninth Ave)   212/757-5670
Mon-Fri: 11-6 (Thurs till 7); Sat: noon-6   kaufmansarmynavy.com

Kaufman's has long been a favorite destination for its extensive selection of genuine military surplus from around the globe. Since 1938 they have outfitted dozens of Broadway and TV shows and supplied a number of major movie productions with military garb. The store is a treasure trove of military collectibles, hats, helmets, uniforms and insignias. You'll also find peacoats, parkas, outdoor gear, bags and maps. The inventory is constantly in flux, with great bargains just waiting to be discovered.

UNCLE SAM'S ARMY NAVY OUTFITTERS

37 W 8th St (bet Fifth Ave and Ave of the Americas)   212/674-2222
Mon-Thurs: 10-8; Fri-Sat: 10-9; Sun: 11-7   armynavydeals.com

For authentic military surplus, Uncle Sam's stocks apparel and products from 26 countries around the world. The store lays claim to getting their stock straight from military branches. The randomly displayed merchandise includes an excellent selection of pants, shirts, flight jackets, headwear, watches, flags, bags, pins, patches and more. You might find yourself shopping next to one of their celebrity customers like Kelly Osbourne or P. Diddy.

SWIMWEAR

CANYON BEACHWEAR

1136 Third Ave (bet 66th and 67th St)   917/432-0732
Mon-Fri: 10-8; Sat: 10-7; Sun: 11-6   canyonbeachwear.com

Come to this store before you dive into a pool, visit a beach or take a cruise. Canyon Beachwear is the ultimate in swim, sun and vacation wear. You'll find over a thousand swimsuits, with most major manufacturers represented; cover-ups and accessories and great salespeople, also!

PARKE & RONEN

176 Ninth Ave (at 21st St)
212/989-4245
Mon-Sat: 11-7; Sun: 1-6
parkeandronen.com

For men's swimsuits, come to Parke & Ronen. Styles include briefs and trunks (two-, four-, six- and eight-inch lengths). All are folded neatly in an array of stripes, plaids and paisley patterns. Designers Ronen Jehezkel and Parke Lutter feature their unique creations in this store, although Parke & Ronen designs are also sold in other

LUXURY SAMPLE SALES

Since 1982, **Soiffer Haskin** (317 W 33rd St, 917/562-2140, soifferhaskin.com) has organized private sales for luxury brand companies offering samples and excess inventory at deep discounts. Designers might include Armani, Escada, Ralph Lauren, Roger Vivier, Yves Saint Laurent and others. The varied stock includes clothing, silver, gifts, housewares, linens, shoes and the like. It's a good idea to get on their mailing list for notification of private sale events.

retailers. You will also find shirts, T-shirts, tanks, jeans, shorts, sweaters and trousers, all with refined details, quality fabrics and exquisite fit.

UNIFORMS

O.K. UNIFORM CO.

253 Church St (bet Franklin and Leonard St)   212/791-9789
Mon-Thurs: 9:30-6:30; Fri: 9-3; Sun: 11-3   okuniform.com

Since 1938, this fourth-generation company has been in the business of affordable uniforms. O.K. Uniform Co. manufactures and distributes apparel for doctors, nurses and technicians, as well as the finest domestic uniforms, chef's apparel and industrial wear. They enhance the offerings with additional items from Dickies, Red Kap, Chefswear, White Swan, Clogs, Crocs and more. Embroidery and screen printing are available.

WOMEN'S ACCESSORIES

ARTBAG

1130 Madison Ave (at 84th St)	212/744-2720
Mon-Fri: 9:30-5; Sat: 10-4	artbag.com

At Artbag, European-trained artisans craft purses, wallets, totes and briefcases from a large selection of exotic skins, leathers and fine fabrics. Choose from a profusion of ready-made, beautifully beaded bags and handsome wallets or supply your own quality materials for a unique accessory. They also clean and repair all types of luggage and handbags, from minor stitching to total renovations.

FOLLI FOLLIE

575 Madison Ave (bet 56th and 57th St)	212/421-3155
133 Prince St (bet Wooster St and West Broadway)	212/780-5555
Mon-Fri: 10-7; Sat: 10-6; Sun: noon-5	follifollie.com

Quality accessories at Folli Follie feature jewelry, watches and handbags. The handbags are colorful and stylish. Trendy, fun jewelry collections include necklaces, bracelets, rings, earrings and pendants. Chic watches make a glam fashion statement. Guys will appreciate the fine assortment of fashion and sport watches, too. All pieces are sold individually, and though they look expensive, shopping here won't break the bank.

JIMMY CHOO

716 Madison Ave (bet 63rd and 64th St)	212/759-7078
Mon-Sat: 10-7; Sun: noon-6	
645 Fifth Ave (at 51st St)	212/593-0800
Mon-Sat: 10-6 (Thurs till 7); Sun: noon-6	jimmychoo.com

Just follow the celebrities to a Jimmy Choo boutique, where you can find classic boots, daytime and evening bags, small leather goods, scarves, belts, fabulous designer footwear, jeweled sandals and fragrances. The designs are ultra-chic, but bring your "goldest" credit card!

MZ WALLACE NEW YORK

93 Crosby St (bet Prince and Spring St)	212/431-8252
Mon-Sat: 11-7; Sun: noon-6	
993 Lexington Ave (bet 71st and 72nd St)	212/737-0347
Mon-Sat: 10-6; Sun: noon-5	mzwallace.com

The enterprising ladies behind this company have developed a quality line of functional luxury handbags. Plain or fancy, the colorful bags are meant for everyday use, like the lightweight Bedford Nylon collection with Italian leather trim and custom hardware. Purses in all sizes, along with computer cases, wallets, totes and other designs, are displayed meticulously and uncluttered in the gallery-like boutiques.

RAIN OR SHINE

45 E 45th St (bet Madison and Vanderbilt Ave)   212/741-9650
Mon-Sat: 10-6:30 (Thurs till 7); Sun: only when raining   rainorshine.biz

There are run-of-the-mill unisex umbrellas, and then there are umbrellas and parasols which make a stylish statement — open or closed. Enter Rain or Shine under the umbrella-shaped awning to peruse a full array of bumbershoots for men and women in myriad shapes, sizes, colors, designs and accouterments, including hard-to-find styles and brands. The selection of walking canes is impressive: plain to fancy; ergonomic, telescopic and folding and with handsome decorative handles of wood, marble, sterling silver and other materials. Conveniently, they will repair umbrellas purchased here.

SUAREZ

5 W 56th St (bet Fifth Ave and Ave of the Americas)   212/315-3870
Mon-Sat: 10-6; Sun: noon-5 (closed Sun in summer)   suarezny.com

Women-in-the-know look to Suarez as their resource for fine leather handbags, belts and accessories. Since its start in 1938, the company has developed a reputation for quality merchandise, good service, an excellent selection and luxury prices. City chic leather goods are available in a variety of colors and exotic designs; some pieces are hand-painted.

WOMEN'S GENERAL

ANNELORE

636 Hudson St (at Horatio St)   212/255-5574
18 Jay St (bet Greenwich and Hudson St)   212/775-0077
Mon-Sat: 11-7; Sun: 11-6   annelorenyc.com

The clothes at Annelore can best be described as timeless fashion, which explains in part why the shops have become somewhat of a celebrity magnet. The well-edited, original designs of Juliana Cho are inspired by the city and

PLUS-SIZE SHOPPING

There's no need to forego fashionable styles if you wear larger sizes of clothing, especially if you buy from these shops:

Ashley Stewart (216 W 125th St, 212/531-0800)

HotSexyFit (35 W 125th St, 212/369-1979): Brazilian jeans

Imparali Custom Tailors (555 Fifth Ave, Suite 703, 212/245-5555): larger sizes at no additional charge, alterations

Marina Rinaldi (13 E 69th St, 212/734-4333): classy women's clothes, cashmere, boots, accessories

Monif C. Plus Sizes (325 W 38th St, Room 207, 212/842-1641): swimwear, cocktail dresses

Orchard Corset (157 Orchard St, 212/674-0786): sexy and affordable undergarments

Rochester Big & Tall (1301 Ave of the Americas, 212/247-7500): full selection of brand-name menswear

handmade in New York. These shops also highlight locally-crafted one-of-a-kind jewelry and accessories.

BOUTIQUE OFF BROADWAY

139 W 72nd St (bet Amsterdam and Columbus Ave)   212/724-6713
Mon-Fri: 10:30-8; Sat: 10:30-7; Sun: 1-7   boutiqueoffbroadway.com

Want to make a statement? Vivacious owner Lynn Dell travels the world to acquire dramatic clothing and accessories for her customers. There's a little bit of everything to appeal to women of varying sizes and age. New merchandise is in the front with day and evening wear, sportswear and exciting hats and accessories. Vintage and consigned items are in the back; all are dramatic and new or gently worn. Alterations can be done in-house.

CALYPSO ST. BARTH

900 Madison Ave (bet 72nd and 73rd St)   212/535-4100
137 West Broadway (bet Duane and Thomas St)   212/608-2222
191 Lafayette St (at Broome St)   212/941-6512
654 Hudson St (at Gansevoort St)   646/638-3000
Hours vary by store   calypsostbarth.com

Casual, trendy and colorful resort-like flirty women's attire and accessories are featured at this chain of upscale stores. You will understand the bohemian-chic merchandise when you realize that the store started in the West Indies and the designer was born in the south of France. Shopping the amazing sales may help keep your budget on track or visit their outlet, **Calypso Au Marché** (426 Broome St, 212/941-9700).

EILEEN FISHER

341 Columbus Ave (bet 76th and 77th St)   212/362-3000
521 Madison Ave (bet 53rd and 54th St)   212/759-9888
166 Fifth Ave (bet 21st and 22nd St)   212/924-4777
395 West Broadway (bet Spring and Broome St)   212/431-4567
Numerous other locations
Hours vary by store   eileenfisher.com

From a 1984 start in the East Village to more than 60 outlets scattered throughout Manhattan, Eileen Fisher has assembled a collection of easy-care, mostly washable natural-fiber outfits in earthy colors. This talented designer's clothes are cool, loose and casual; they travel well and are admired for their simple and attractive lines. Accessories, sleepwear, outerwear and shoes will round out your wardrobe.

GEMINOLA

41 Perry St (bet Seventh Ave and 4th St)   212/675-1994
Mon-Wed: noon-7; Thurs-Sat: noon-8; Sun: 11-7   geminola.com

This unique store shows an eclectic assortment of handmade and one-of-a-kind dresses, skirts and tops for women. The pricey clothing is made from vintage (pre-1950) fabrics, ribbons and lace. Home items include unusual curtains, napkins and bed linens. Geminola also has a few original selections for little girls.

GISELLE

143 Orchard St (bet Delancey and Rivington St)   212/673-1900
Sun-Thurs: 9-5:30; Fri: 9-3   gisellenny.com

Giselle is a popular shopping boutique on the Lower East Side for many reasons. They offer women's top European designers, current-season goods, a large selection (sizes 4 to 20) and discount prices. Etro, Escada, Basler, Lafayette and Laurel are just a few of the coveted names. All merchandise is first-quality. Factor in excellent service and four floors of merchandise, and Giselle is well worth a trip.

KIRNA ZABÊTE

477 Broome St (bet Greene and Wooster St)   212/941-9656
Mon-Sat: 11-7; Sun: noon-6   kirnazabete.com

Two friends (nicknamed Kirna and Zabête) brainstormed this unique shop. All manner of women's clothing, from swimwear to casual to evening wear is shown, with well over 60 designers represented. Amedeo, Celine, Fendi, Mua Mua and Sacai are just a sampling. And there is a mixture of other quality items — jewelry, shoes, bags and more — with *inspiration* the byword.

LANVIN

815 Madison Ave (bet 68th and 69th St)   646/439-0381
Mon-Sat: 10-6; Sun: noon-5   lanvin.com

This women's couture and ready-to-wear boutique is nestled in a glamorous, renovated five-story townhouse on the Upper East Side. Seasonal collections, shoes, handbags, fragrances and accessories are lavishly displayed; steep prices come with the famous name. When you venture into the store, browse the display of vintage photos of Lanvin models. Just a few doors down there is a location with men's ready-to-wear (807 Madison Ave, 212/812-2866).

PRADA

575 Broadway (at Prince St)   212/334-8888
841 Madison Ave (at 70th St)   212/327-4200
45 E 57th St (bet Park and Madison Ave)   212/308-2332
724 Fifth Ave (bet 56th and 57th St)   212/664-0010
160 Lexington Ave (at 30th St)   646/837-7750
Hours vary by store   prada.com

Prada locations are glamorous destinations that attract well-heeled fashionistas as well as tourists. The distinctive, coveted label embellishes chic clothing, knockout shoes and trendy leather goods and accessories (including fragrances) for men and women. Many ladies consider a Prada handbag an essential fashion statement, and there is certainly an ample assortment of sizes, shapes and colors. Be sure to mark your calendar for the July and December end-of-season sales.

REALLY GREAT THINGS

284 Columbus Ave (bet 73rd and 74th St)   212/787-5354
Tues-Sat: 11-7; appointments recommended

At this store featuring high couture merchandise, you will indeed find some *really great things.* The boutique is gallery-like with what seems like very few items displayed; the bulk of the inventory is secured out of sight. Clothing, bags, shoes and accessories are featured from four to five select designers at a time. Best to make an appointment for assistance with your selections.

REBECCA TAYLOR

34 Gansevoort St (bet Greenwich and Hudson St)	212/243-2600
260 Mott St (bet Houston and Prince St)	212/966-0406
980 Madison Ave (bet 76th and 77th St)	646/560-2515
Hours vary by store	rebeccataylor.com

Rebecca Taylor designs clothing, shoes, handbags, hosiery, jewelry and accessories. This is a popular stop for the young (and young-at-heart) who are looking for whimsical merchandise. Lots of unconventional color combinations and prints show off this very fresh, feminine fashion.

ROBERTA ROLLER RABBIT

1019 Lexington Ave (bet 73rd and 74th St)	212/772-7200
Mon-Sat: 10-6; Sun: noon-5	
176 Duane St (bet Greenwich and Hudson St)	212/966-0076
Mon-Sat: 11-7; Sun: noon-5	

The vibrant clothing and accessories at these shops are inspired by Roberta Freymann's world travels. A sea of colorful prints permeates the beach and resort wear along with home furnishings, unique furniture, linens and gift items. Visiting these shops is like going to an international bazaar!

SAN FRANCISCO CLOTHING

975 Lexington Ave (at 71st St)	212/472-8740
Mon-Sat: 11-6	sanfranciscoclothing.com

Looking like an old-world emporium, San Francisco Clothing sells women's items that are perfect for a casual weekend. The mature woman will find an interesting collection of comfortable, colorful classics. A full selection of white shirtings is their specialty, but there are also great pieces of traditional outerwear, including a nautical collection.

WOMEN'S MILLINERY

BARBARA FEINMAN MILLINERY

66 E 7th St (bet First and Second Ave)	212/358-7092
Tues-Sat: 12:30-8; Sun: 12:30-7	feinmanhats.com

The big draw in this tiny, romantic space is the couture hats, made on-premises from original designs. If you are looking for something really funky or, by contrast, very classy, try this spot first. Handcrafted jewelry is also a specialty and custom orders are welcome.

THE HAT SHOP

120 Thompson St (at Prince St)	212/219-1445
Mon-Sat: noon-7; Sun: 1-6	thehatshopnyc.com

The owner of The Hat Shop, Linda Pagan, has quite a background as a former Wall Street broker, bartender and world traveler. The shop's stock reflects her diverse history, with showings from 30 local milliners. Sewn, knit and blocked hats are available in many colors and trims. Special orders are accepted.

SUZANNE COUTURE MILLINERY

136 E 61st St (bet Park and Lexington Ave) 212/593-3232
Mon-Fri: 10-6; Sat: 11-6 suzannehats.com

For over 25 years Suzanne and her talented staff have been creating stunning bridal headpieces and high-fashion hats. Exotic feathers, Austrian crystals, gleaming pearls and quality trims embellish classic and contemporary hat shapes resulting in one-of-a-kind designs. A Suzanne bridal headpiece is a work of art, be it a simple tiara or a long, flowing veil with a fresh-flower band. No matter the occasion, visit Suzanne for the perfect ready-to-wear or custom-order hat. Customers include overseas royalty!

WOMEN'S UNDERGARMENTS

A.W. KAUFMAN

73 Orchard St (bet Broome and Grand St) 212/226-1629
Sun-Thurs: 10:30-5; Fri: 10:30-2 awkaufman.com

For three generations A.W. Kaufman has combined excellent merchandise with quality customer service. They specialize in European designer lingerie, in all fabrics, for women. Among the wonderful labels you will find are Bonsoir, Hanro, Chantelle, Wolford, La Perla, Louis Feraud, Pluto and Zimmerli. Items include bras, panties, pantyhose, bodywear, camisoles, nightgowns, pajamas, robes and more.

LA PETITE COQUETTE

51 University Pl (bet 9th and 10th St) 212/473-2478
Mon-Sat: 11-7; Sun: noon-6 thelittleflirt.com

La Petite Coquette offers a large, eclectic mix of sexy lingerie from around the world in a diverse price range. The atmosphere is described as: "Flirtatious!" You'll find bras, panties, sexy lingerie and sleepwear in everything from classic La Perla to edgy designers like Aubade. There are also old standbys like Cosabella, Hanky Panky, Marie Jo, On Gossamer and Eberjey.

LINDA'S BRA SALON

552 Third Ave (bet 36th and 37th St) 646/736-1949
Mon-Fri: 10-8; Sat: 10-7; Sun: 11-6 lindasonline.com

Linda's carries dozens of brands and hundreds of sizes of bras for petite to full-figured gals, nursing mothers, post-surgery and athletes. Though not required, reservations are suggested for a fitting consultation with trained experts. Fitters are sensitive to clients' needs and give the same attention to customers whether buying mastectomy bras, shapewear or swimwear.

ONLY HEARTS

386 Columbus Ave (bet 78th and 79th St) 212/724-5608
Mon-Sat: 11-7:30; Sun: 11-6:30

FACTORY OUTLET MALLS IN THE TRI-STATE REGION AND PENNSYLVANIA

Shop for deeply discounted merchandise at these outlet malls. Look for special events and coupon books to maximize your savings!

CONNECTICUT

Clinton Crossing Premium Outlets (20 Killingworth Turnpike, Clinton, CT; 860/664-0700, premiumoutlets.com): 70 upscale outlet stores

NEW JERSEY

Atlantic City Outlets (2014 Baltic Ave, Atlantic City, NJ; 609/344-0095): 100 Shops

Jackson Premium Outlets (537 Monmouth Rd, Jackson, NJ; 732/833-0503, premiumoutlets.com): 70 stores, top retailers

Jersey Gardens (651 Kapkowski Rd, Elizabeth, NJ; 908/354-5900, jerseygardens.com): over 200 stores, New Jersey's largest outlet center

Jersey Shore Premium Outlets (1 Premium Outlets Blvd, Tinton Falls, NJ; 732/918-1700, premiumoutlets.com): 120 stores, designer clothes and shoes

Liberty Village Premium Outlets (1 Church St, Flemington, NJ; 908/782-8550, premiumoutlets.com): 40 outlets, family shopping

NEW YORK

Tanger Outlet Center I & II (200 Tanger Mall Dr, Riverhead, NY; 631/369-2732, tangeroutlet.com): 165 shopping choices

Tanger Outlets at The Arches (152 The Arches Cir, Deer Park, NY; 631/667-0600, tangeroutlet.com): over 95 shops and services

Woodbury Common Premium Outlets (498 Red Apple Court, Central Valley, NY; 845/928-4000, premiumoutlets.com): 220 upscale outlet stores

PENNSYLVANIA

The Crossings Premium Outlets (1000 Premium Outlets Dr, Tannersville, PA; 570/629-4650, premiumoutlets.com): over 100 stores

Philadelphia Mills (1455 Franklin Mills Cir, Philadelphia, PA; 215/632-1500): nearly 200 manufacturers' and retail outlet stores

Closer to the city, an outlet mall is under construction in The Bronx.

230 Mott St (bet Prince and Spring St)   212/431-3694
Mon-Sat: 11:30-7:30; Sun: 11:30-6:30   onlyhearts.com

Helena Stuart offers romantics a beguiling array of "inner outwear," all designed and sewn in the Garment District of Manhattan. Feminine bras, panties, camis, tanks, slips, leggings, skirts and slip dresses are stylishly sexy. An organic line with a commitment to sustainability is currently one of the brand's most popular.

TOWN SHOP

2270 Broadway (bet 81st and 82nd St)   212/724-8160
Mon-Fri: 10-7; Sat: 9:30-6; Sun: 11-6   townshop.com

For four generations this Upper West Side store has maintained a reputation for superior customer service, over 60 designer brands of intimate apparel and expert bra-fitting. Merchandise includes activewear, sleepwear, shapewear, slips, hosiery, bras and panties in brands like Wacoal, Chantelle, Natori, Spanx and PrimaDonna. Specialties include bridal and sexy lingerie, maternity and nursing bras and mastectomy bras and breast prostheses.

UNDERNEATH IT ALL

320 Fifth Ave (bet 32nd and 33rd St), Suite 1009   212/717-1976
Mon-Thurs: 9-5 by appointment   underneathitallnyc.com

The staff at Underneath It All works hard to give attentive, informed and personal service to women who have had breast surgery. The store carries a large selection of breast forms in light and dark skin tones and in a variety of shapes, sizes and contours. They specialize in breast equalizers and enhancers to create body symmetry. There is a complete line of mastectomy and brand-name bras; mastectomy and designer swimwear; sleepwear, loungewear and body suits and wigs and fashionable head accessories.

COINS AND STAMPS

STACK'S BOWERS GALLERIES

123 W 57th St (at Ave of the Americas)   212/582-2580
Mon-Fri: 10-7; Sat: 10-3   stacksbowers.com

Specializing in coins, medals, bullion and paper money of interest to collectors, Stack's Bowers has a solid reputation for individual service, integrity and knowledge of the numismatic field. In addition to walk-in business, a number of public auctions are conducted each year; check for dates online. Visit the gallery to add to your collection, sell items outright or consign for auction.

COSMETICS, DRUGS AND PERFUMES

C.O. BIGELOW CHEMISTS

414 Ave of the Americas (bet 8th and 9th St)   212/533-2700
Mon-Fri: 7:30 a.m.-9 p.m.; Sat: 8:30-7; Sun: 8:30-5:30   bigelowchemists.com

Bigelow touts itself as the oldest apothecary in America, and the old-school approach to customer service helps explain its longevity. The selection of signature Bigelow products and other brand names is vast, with treatments for almost any condition from acne to sleeplessness. Cruise the aisles for beauty and health-care products, plus carefully selected gifts and fragrances. They are open 365 days a year.

KIEHL'S

154 Columbus Ave (bet 66th and 67th St)   212/799-3438
157 E 64th St (at Lexington Ave)   917/432-2503
841 Lexington Ave (at 64th St)   917/432-2511

678 Ninth Ave (at 47th St)   212/956-2891
400 W 14th St (at Ninth Ave)   212/337-0406
109 Third Ave (bet 13th and 14th St)   212/677-3171
233 Mulberry St (bet Spring and Prince St)   212/219-2369
Hours vary by store   kiehls.com

Kiehl's has been a New York institution since 1851. Their special treatments and preparations are made by hand with natural ingredients. Peruse the myriad of cleansers, toners, moisturizers, bath and shower products, shampoos, conditioners and treatments for blemishes, age spots, fine lines and more. Express an interest in a particular product and you'll receive a decent-size sample and advice about using it.

MIN NEW YORK

117 Crosby St (bet Prince and Houston St)   212/206-6366
Sun, Mon: noon-6; Tues-Sat: 11-7   min.com

Rare fragrances and grooming products from around the world for men and women are attractively displayed in this relaxing Soho shop. Testing and smelling the personal indulgences is encouraged. MiN New York stocks many luxury brands, such as Amouage and Sospiros, and equally luxurious gifts and home accessories fill this Crosby Street charmer.

CRAFTS

ALLCRAFT

35 W 29th St (bet Ave of the Americas and Seventh Ave), Suite 205
                                                             212/279-7077
Mon-Fri: 9:15-5:30 (open late some evenings)   allcraftusa.com

Allcraft is the metalsmith and jewelry-making supply store. Their catalog includes a complete line of tools and supplies for jewelry making, silver- and metal-smithing, lost-wax casting and much more. Crafters shouldn't miss the opportunity to visit this gleaming cornucopia.

THE CITY QUILTER

133 W 25th St (bet Ave of the Americas and Seventh Ave)   212/807-0390
Mon: noon-6; Tues-Fri: 11-7; Sat: 10-6; Sun: 11-5   cityquilter.com

The City Quilter is the only shop in Manhattan that's completely devoted to quilting. They serve everyone from beginners to professionals with classes, books, notions, thread, gifts, New York-themed fabrics, patterns and kits and more than 4,000 bolts of 100% cotton fabrics. The selection includes an extensive collection of batiks, hand-dyed and Japanese fabrics. Some 150 classes include hand- and machine-quilting, embroidery, photo transfers and much more.

CLAYWORKS POTTERY

332 E 9th St (bet First and Second Ave)   212/677-8311
Tues: 3:30-7; Wed: 1:30-7; Thurs-Sun: 1:30-8:30 (Fri beginning at 3:30);
Mon: by appointment   clayworkspottery.com

If you are interested in stoneware and fine porcelain, then you will love Clayworks, run by talented Helaine Sorgen since 1974. It has a wide range of handcrafted items for tabletop and home decor. All of Clayworks' pottery is lead-free and dishwasher- and microwave-safe, and everything is individually produced, from teapots to casseroles, mugs and saké sets. One-of-a-kind decorative pieces include honey pots, garlic jars, pitchers, cream and sugar sets, butter and cheese domes, oil bottles, vases, candleholders, goblets, platters and bowls. Small classes in wheel-throwing are given for adults.

GOTTA KNIT!

14 E 34th St (bet Fifth and Madison Ave), 5th floor   212/989-3030
Mon-Wed: noon-6; Thurs: noon-7; Sun: 11-4; Fri, Sat: by appointment
gottaknit.net

In this colorful and inviting store you'll find luxury hand-dyed cashmere and specialty yarns for hand-knitting and crocheting. Browse the equally fine selection of buttons, accessories and books. For beginners, the staff will willingly walk you through, step-by-step, and group knitting classes are offered, too. If you can't find the pattern you want, custom pattern-writing is available.

KNITTY CITY

208 W 79th St (bet Broadway and Amsterdam Ave)   212/787-5896
Mon, Tues, Fri, Sat: 11-6; Wed, Thurs: 11-8; Sun: noon-5   knittycity.com
Knitty City stocks a fine selection of beautiful yarn for knitting and crocheting. There are also needle art books and magazines, notions, patterns and a sampling of finished items. Classes for every level are offered, including a weekly class for children.

THE YARN COMPANY

2274 Broadway (bet 81st and 82nd St), 2nd floor   212/787-7878
Mon: 11-6; Tues: 11-8; Wed, Thurs: 11-7; Fri-Sun: 11-6   theyarnco.com
A brother-sister team head up The Yarn Company which is said to have the largest selection of high-end and basic knitting yarns in the city; you'll find cashmeres, merino wools, silks, linens, rayons and more. Spinning fibers come in an array of textures, types and color combinations. Guest workshops and classes in knitting, crocheting, quilting, embroidery, spinning, weaving and hand-sewing will teach you to purling, casting-on, binding-off, carding or whatever techniques are necessary to your new favorite hobby.

LOOKING FORWARD

Over the next few years there are big plans for several super-megatowers to rise up on West 57th Street. One of these will be the Nordstrom Tower (225 W 57th St). Ninety-four floors will rise to 1,776 feet, second only to One World Trade Center. The building will be anchored by **Nordstrom** department store on seven floors; a hotel will occupy the next five floors. This will be the first location in NYC for this classy store.

DANCE ITEMS

CAPEZIO

1650 Broadway (at 51st St), 2nd floor   212/245-2130
Mon-Sat: 10-7; Sun: noon-6   capeziodance.com

Capezio offers one-stop shopping for all of your dance, theater and fitness needs. This dance emporium stocks the Capezio brand's full line including sections for men and a variety of leotards, dresses, shoes and accessories for ballroom, ballet, tap, jazz and more. The 7,000-square-foot store overlooks the Theatre District; you don't have to be a performer to appreciate the wares.

ON STAGE DANCEWEAR

197 Madison Ave (bet 34th and 35th St)   212/725-1174
Mon-Sat: 11-7; Mon-Fri: 10-6:30; Sat: 11-6   onstagedancewear.com

On Stage serves professional ballet and theater companies across the world, including the New York City Ballet. Individuals are welcome, too! You'll find everything in dancewear for ballet, tap, flamenco and ballroom. They specialize in discount dancewear and are an authorized dealer for Capezio. This is also a good source for bodywear for yoga and cheerleading, skatewear and warm-ups. If you don't find what you are looking for, ask about their custom-made dancewear services.

DEPARTMENT STORE SCENE
IN MANHATTAN

The current scene for New York department stores is quite healthy; the trend away from crowded and yuppie suburban malls has been a plus for these stores. At the top of the scale (price-wise) is Bergdorf Goodman (both the men's and women's stores); at the bottom end with some good values are the two Century 21 stores. In between, while Lord & Taylor and Saks Fifth Avenue have had some uneven spells, Macy's and Bloomingdale's are doing very well. Smart shoppers watch the advertised (and emailed) sales events, particularly at the end of each season.

Barneys New York (660 Madison Ave, at 61st St, 212/826-8900 and 2151 Broadway, at 75th St, 646/335-0978; barneys.com): Over the last several years Barneys has been working towards a reinvention of their brand, back to that which folks remember as a label that spells class. Luxury designers offer women's and men's ready-to-wear, accessories, shoes, jewelry, cosmetics, fragrances and home gifts. New partnerships with artists and designers are bringing a fresh look to the store, like the limited edition collection inspired by the city. And there is great food and people watching at **Freds at Barneys New York** on the ninth floor. Things seem to be moving in the right direction!

Bergdorf Goodman (754 Fifth Ave, at 58th St, 212/753-7300; bergdorfgoodman.com): One cannot get more upscale than at this stylish emporium, where practically every top label can be found in their many clothing departments. The store is noted for its personalized service. There is nothing the salespeople won't do to be of service. BGs windows are always avant-garde; check them out when you stroll down Fifth Avenue. Several convenient restaurants are available, as well as some very interesting gift sections. Bring along as gold a credit card as you can find.

Bergdorf Goodman Mens (745 Fifth Ave, at 58th St, 212/753-7300; bergdorfgoodman.com): The male members of your family who like to shop, and who are very fashion-savvy, love this store, where (like the sister store for women) nearly every world-famous label in men's furnishings and clothing is featured. Of course, you pay the price, but you probably will not see the same suit on your friends at the country club. Custom-made suits are a specialty, as well as the latest in formal wear. I find the sportswear sections particularly well stocked.

Bloomingdale's (1000 Third Ave, at 59th St, 212/705-2000 and 504 Broadway, at Broome St, 212/729-5900; bloomingdales.com): The Upper East Side shopper can find a tremendous selection of better merchandise at this famous store; its cosmetics department must be among the largest in the world. A fine selection of men's and women's clothing and home furnishings, gifts, luggage and china and glassware also are featured. A number of handy refreshment stops are located throughout the store; I particularly like the delicious frozen yogurt at **40 Carrots** on the seventh floor; very good burgers are available at **Flip** on the lower level. One could happily spend full days and much cash going from one floor to another in this well-merchandised store where service is vastly improved. The downtown Bloomies is a convenient place for young-nesters to shop, what with more wallet-friendly products and designers being featured. However, this smaller store does not carry the vast assortments of its uptown sister store.

Century 21 (22 Cortlandt St, at Church St, 212/227-9092 and 1972 Broadway at 66th St, 212/518-2121; c21stores.com):   For decades lower Manhattan shoppers have found great bargains at this mainly discount department store. Three additional shopping floors and upgrades to the once small fitting rooms improve the experience. Upper West Siders can enjoy some of the great finds at the newer Lincoln Square location. There are good selections of moderately-priced clothing for the family, especially for the youngsters; shoes are another specialty. For men working in lower Manhattan, this is a very good place to find clothing and furnishings for work or play at good prices.

H&M (589 Fifth Ave, at 48th St, 855/466-7467; hm.com): This global fashion company is known to inspire creativity. It appeals mostly to younger shoppers, but their selection has something for everyone. The wide range of collections include women's, men's, juniors and children's clothing as well as home interiors, cosmetics and jewelry. They are highly influenced by social media and blogging which assures that their designers and buyers continue with an unerring eye for what's next in fashion. When walking into H&M you might find your next vintage treasure, functional basics or something more lavish for a night out. They take pride in having more sustainable choices and selling quality fashion at the very best price.

Henri Bendel (712 Fifth Ave, at 56th St, 212/247-1100; henribendel. com): With a great Fifth Avenue location, this specialty store is touted as the "ultimate girl's playground." Henri Bendel was the first luxury retailer with an

APPLE SOURCE

No outfit is better at merchandising than Apple! One of New York's most exciting shopping destinations is the **Apple Store** (767 Fifth Ave, 212/336-1440). Located in a unique setting just off Central Park, the place never closes and is always crowded. Just look for the General Motors building and the magnificent illuminated glass cube in front. Other Apple Stores can be found around town (401 West 14th St, 212/444-3400; 1981 Broadway, 212/209-3400; Grand Central Terminal at 42nd St, 212/284-1800 and 103 Prince St, 212/226-3126), but only the flagship Fifth Avenue location is open 24/7.

upper Fifth Avenue address and became well known for its legendary brown-and-white striped shopping bag and hat box. The store offers the Henri Bendel brand of handbags, jewelry, luxury fashion accessories, home fragrances and gifts. Make sure you look at the great Lalique art glass windows on the upper floors.

Lord & Taylor (424 Fifth Ave, at 38th St, 212/391-3344; lordandtaylor. com): Under the ownership of Canada's Hudson's Bay Company, Lord & Taylor has been modernizing its departments, making shopping here easier and more attractive. The store lost much of its traffic to nearby Macy's in recent years, but it still does a very good job of featuring American fashion labels. At one time, New York matrons swore by this store; that was in the days of legendary CEO Dorothy Shaver, a top merchandiser in her day. Perhaps with renewed energy and big bucks, the glory days will return. Two things you will still find at L&T: good food at **Sarabeth's** (on the fifth and sixth floors) and great window displays (especially at holiday time). Personnel are especially helpful and well trained.

Macy's Herald Square (151 W 34th St, 212/695-4400; macys.com): It is said that no visit to the Big Apple is complete without a visit to the "World's Largest Store!" Encompassing an entire New York City block, it's one of Manhattan's most-visited tourist destinations, second only to the Empire State Building. Under the dynamic leadership of Terry Lundgren, considered the number one retail executive in the country, the store has clearly become the industry leader in innovation. With over two million square feet of shops spanning ten floors, Macy's Herald Square is an ever-changing environment filled with fashion, fun, food and fresh ideas to inspire and delight. You'll discover excitement and newness at every turn, all staged within the historical framework of iconic architectural grandeur, and a host of services and luxury brands you'll only find at this historic flagship location. Looking for a special dining experience with a one-of-a-kind view? Visit the sixth floor's award-winning **Stella 34 Trattoria** (see restaurant section). Stop first at Macy's Visitor Center on the balcony and they'll make sure your NYC visit is magical from the moment you join them to the moment you leave.

Saks Fifth Avenue (611 Fifth Ave, at 50th St, 212/753-4000; saks. com): Dreaming of a unique specialty store synonymous with fashionable and gracious living, Horace Saks and Bernard Gimbel opened the first Saks Fifth Avenue in 1924 in what was then a primarily residential district on upper Fifth Avenue, between 49th and 50th streets. As the store expanded, new and innovative brands were introduced, cementing Saks' status as a key American icon in luxury retailing. New leadership in 2014 revitalized the spirit of its heritage with a modern relevance by introducing a new merchant and creative direction. President Marigay McKee increased luxury offerings and designer edits. Today, Saks Fifth Avenue offers a fine assortment of women's and men's designer ready-to-wear, luxury handbag shops, attractive jewelry, a large beauty and cosmetics section and a shoe floor that boasts its own zip code — 10022-SHOE.

DOMESTIC GOODS

BED BATH & BEYOND

620 Ave of the Americas (bet 18th and 19th St)	212/255-3550
410 E 61st St (at First Ave)	646/215-4702
1932 Broadway (at 65th St)	917/441-9391
270 Greenwich St (bet Warren and Murray St)	212/233-8450
Hours vary by store	bedbathandbeyond.com

The name says it all! At Bed Bath & Beyond you'll find most everything you could need for your home, in every possible category. The selection is huge, the quality is unquestioned and prices are discounted. The service is prompt and informed. The store on Avenue of the Americas has over 103,000 square feet stuffed floor to ceiling with sheets, blankets, rugs, kitchen gadgets, towels, dinnerware, hampers, window treatments, furniture, cookware, kid's items, pillows, paper goods and appliances. The fine china and giftware department is superb. Several locations now have health and beauty departments. Unique seasonal items and a wedding/baby registry are added bonuses at Bed Bath & Beyond.

BOUTIQUE D. PORTHAULT

470 Park Ave (at 58th St)	212/688-1660
Mon-Sat: 10-6 (closed Sat in Aug)	dporthault.com

Wherever the name Porthault appears — for instance, on linens at some fancy hotels — you know you're at a topnotch operation. Their printed sheets seem to last forever and are handed down from one generation to another. Custom-made linens are available in a wide range of designs, scores of colors and weaves of luxurious density. Porthault can handle custom work of an intricate nature for odd-sized beds, baths and showers. Specialties include signature prints (hearts, four-leaf clovers, stars and mille fleurs), printed terry towels, table linens, children's items and unique gift items.

ELECTRONICS AND APPLIANCES

AC GEARS

69 E 8th St (bet Broadway and Mercer St)	212/375-1700
Mon-Sat: 11-8; Sun: noon-7	acgears.com

Attention gadget lovers! AC Gears features Japanese and European electronic design and ingenuity at its best. The latest electronic products are

DIGITAL RETAIL

You'll experience the future of retail at the New York flagship store of **Rebecca Minkoff** (96 Greene St, 212/677-7883). Shop the latest collection of handbags, clothing, accessories and shoes via an interactive video wall. Try on your favorite styles in personalized fitting rooms featuring mood lighting, and via a tap of the mirror, swap out colors and sizes. Another smart mirror offers styling tips based on your selections. Minkoff's app for mobile phones saves your browsing history for your next visit in case you're feeling a bit indecisive.

displayed in a gallery-like setting. There are wireless speakers and headphones, amplifiers, keyboards (musical and computer), synthesizers, computer mice and other related tools, accessories and gadgets, including watches, clocks and toys.

DALE PRO AUDIO

22 W 19th St (bet Fifth Ave and Ave of the Americas), 9th floor   212/475-1124
Mon-Fri: 9:30-5:30   daleproaudio.com

Visit Dale Pro Audio for the largest selection of audio merchandise for recording, broadcast, DJ and sound contracting in the country, including hundreds of brands from A Designs to Zoom. Dale has been a family business since 1956, offering superior technical expertise. Topnotch demo rooms and an event space are available; prices are competitive.

GRINGER & SONS

29 First Ave (at 2nd St)   212/475-0600
Mon-Fri: 8:30-5:30; Sat: 8:30-4:30   gringerandsons.com

For brand-name major appliances (and some you may have never heard of) at discount prices, come to family-owned Gringer & Sons. Bosch, Frigidaire, Kitchen Aid, Maytag, Whirlpool and others. Gringer's informed personnel sell refrigerators, microwaves, ranges, air conditioners and other appliances to both residential and commercial customers. If it plugs in for cooking or cleaning, they likely sell it!

P.C. RICHARD & SON

205 E 86th St (bet Second and Third Ave)   212/289-1700
2372 Broadway (at 86th St)   212/579-5200
53 W 23rd St (bet Fifth Ave and Ave of the Americas)   212/924-0200
120 E 14th St (bet Third and Fourth Ave)   212/979-2600
Mon-Fri: 9 a.m.-9:30 p.m.; Sat: 9-9; Sun: 10-7   pcrichard.com

P.C. Richard started as a hardware business, and the dedication to personalized service has successfully been passed down from one generation to the next. Since 1909 this family-owned and -operated store has been selling appliances, electronics, TVs, cameras, car audio, computers and air conditioners. They offer a large inventory, good prices, delivery seven days a week and in-house repair service; they also get high marks for friendliness.

SONY STORE

Sony Plaza
550 Madison Ave (bet 55th and 56th St)   212/833-8800
Mon-Sat: 10-7; Sun: 11-6   sony.com

Inside Sony's expansive flagship store you'll find the latest computers, cameras, TV and home theater equipment, portable electronics, iPods, PlayStations and games and all types of accessories. Be forewarned that these items are tagged to fetch top dollar. This mecca appeals to technophiles of all ages. The adjacent **Sony Wonder Technology Lab** (212/833-8100, sonywondertechlab.com) offers four floors of more than 60 interactive exhibits, plus workshops and special event space. It's open Tuesday through Saturday with advance tickets (free); check their website for details.

STEREO EXCHANGE

627 Broadway (bet Bleecker and Houston St)   212/505-1111
Mon-Fri: 11-7:30; Sat: 10:30-7; Sun: noon-7   stereoexchange.com

For high-end audio-video products, visit this outfit! Since 1984 Stereo Exchange has been carrying top names like Integra, McIntosh and B&W. Trained, certified engineers will work with architects and designers on home installations. Before you make your decision, check out the sound quality in one of their listening rooms. They also buy and sell previously-loved high-end audio equipment.

WAVES

Showplace Antiques and Design Center
40 W 25th St (bet Fifth Ave and Ave of the Americas), Gallery 107   212/273-9616
Wed-Sun: 11-5; Mon, Tues: by appointment   wavesradios.com

Searching for a vintage radio or record player? Waves has a collection of vintage record players, radios, telephones, speakers and televisions. They favor the age of radio over the high-tech present; the shop is a virtual shrine to the 1930s and before. At Waves you'll find the earliest radios (still operative!) and artifacts. There are promotional pieces, such as a radio-shaped cigarette lighter, gramophones and virtually anything dealing with the radio age. Waves will rent phonographs, telephones and neon clocks, and they also buy, appraise and repair items.

EYEWEAR AND ACCESSORIES

20/20 EYEWEAR

57 E 8th St (bet Broadway and University Pl)   212/228-2192
Mon-Fri: 10-7; Sat: 10-6

Whether you see glasses as a simple necessity, a statement of style or both, the large selection at 20/20 will likely suit your needs. For over 35 years 20/20 has offered trendsetting eyewear in a wide range of price points. Besides the 20/20 label there are unique frames by Chanel, Paul Smith, Ralph Lauren and Oliver Peoples. They provide eye exams, prescription fulfillment and overnight delivery.

THE EYE MAN

2264 Broadway (bet 81st and 82nd St)   212/873-4114
Mon, Wed: 10-7; Tues: 10-7:30; Thurs: 10-8; Fri, Sat: 10-6

Dozens of stores in Manhattan carry eyeglasses, but few take special care with children. Family-owned and -operated, The Eye Man carries a great selection of frames for young people, as well as specialty eyewear and contact lenses. They have been providing eye exams since 1976.

FABULOUS FANNY'S

335 E 9th St (bet First and Second Ave)   212/533-0637
Daily: noon-8   fabulousfannys.com

"If you have to wear them, make it fun!" That is the slogan of Fabulous Fanny's, and what they are referring to are glasses. This store may have the largest and best selection of antique and vintage eyewear in the country. Both men and women will be dazzled by the stock which includes modern and avante-garde frames.

ILORI

138 Spring St (bet Greene and Wooster St)   212/226-8276
Mon-Sat: 10-8; Sun: 11-7   iloristyle.com

Ilori displays hundreds of luxury eyeglass frames and sunglasses from fashion luminaries in exclusive and limited-edition designs. Chrome Hearts, Dolce & Gabbana, Gucci, Maui Jim and Tiffany are just a few. All are temptingly displayed gallery-style at this Soho boutique. The staff can recommend the ideal shape and color of frames to best play up your facial features. You may want to spring for a couple of unusual pairs to change your persona.

MORGENTHAL-FREDERICS

944 Madison Ave (bet 74th and 75th St)   212/744-9444
699 Madison Ave (bet 62nd and 63rd St)   212/838-3090
Shops at Columbus Circle
10 Columbus Cir (Time Warner Center)   212/956-6402
399 West Broadway (at Spring St)   212/966-0099
Hours vary by store   morgenthalfrederics.com

If you are looking for unique eyewear and accessories, put Morgenthal-Frederics high on your list. Since 1986 they have been displaying high-end innovative styles and exclusive designs of eyewear and sunglasses. With their various locations and attentive staff, clients are truly well serviced.

OPTYX

2384 Broadway (at 87th St)   212/724-0850
1225 Lexington Ave (bet 82nd and 83rd St)   212/628-2493
1076 Third Ave (bet 63rd and 64th St)   212/751-6177
599 Lexington Ave (bet 52nd and 53rd St)   212/688-3580
Numerous other locations
Hours vary by store   optyx.com

Optyx enjoys a reputation for excellent service. They carry a superb selection of specialty eyewear: sunglasses, theater glasses, sports spectacles and party eyewear. Ask about emergency fittings and one-day turnaround.

FABRICS AND TRIMMINGS

B&J FABRICS

525 Seventh Ave (at 38th St), 2nd floor   212/354-8150
Mon-Fri: 8-5:45; Sat: 9-4:45   bandjfabrics.com

Appropriately located in the Garment District, B&J started its fabric business in 1940. In this well-organized space, they carry high-quality fashion fabrics, many imported from all over the world. Specialties of the house are the best of the best of ladies' fashion textiles; high-end cottons, laces, silks (over a thousand in stock!) and suedes. You will also find a wonderful selection of hand-dyed batiks, brocades, tweeds and faux furs.

BECKENSTEIN FABRIC AND INTERIORS

32 W 20th St (bet Fifth Ave and Ave of the Americas)   212/366-5142
Mon-Sat: 10-6 (Thurs till 8); Sun: noon-5   beckensteinfabrics.com

Beckenstein has a rich history as purveyors of designer fabrics for window treatments, bedding, pillows, slipcovers and home accessories. There are hundreds of top decorative fabrics, some with exclusive designs. Custom upholstery work is their specialty — restoration, restyling or reupholstering to spruce up a new decor. There is a wallpaper department and select finished furniture pieces are also displayed. Impressive selections, reliable service and excellent workmanship have kept them in business since 1918.

HYMAN HENDLER AND SONS

142 W 38th St (bet Ave of the Americas and Seventh Ave)   212/840-8393
Mon-Fri: 9-5   hymanhendler.com

In the trimmings world, Hyman Hendler is one of the oldest, and it is considered the crown head of the ribbon field. Begun by Hyman Hendler in 1900, it is now proudly run by his capable son-in-law. Used by dressmakers, milliners and crafters alike, the company manufactures, retails, imports and acts as a wholesaler for every kind of ribbon imaginable: basic, vintage and novelty ribbon. It's hard to believe the many variations that are jammed into this store — thousands and thousands!

JOE'S FABRICS WAREHOUSE

102 Orchard St (at Delancey St), 2nd floor   212/674-7089
Sun-Thurs: 9-6; Fri: 9-4   joesfabrics.com

Enter this Orchard Street establishment and you'll find an extensive assortment of top-quality designer and imported fabrics for upholstery, drapery and window treatments. They claim to have the largest such inventory of velvet, damask, linen, canvas, silk, lace, mohair and other opulent fabrics and trims. Decorating professionals, Broadway set designers and do-it-yourselfers are given a warm welcome to select from the thousands of choices; there is no minimum order. An experienced custom-furniture department will design a new piece to your specs or reupholster and transform your worn piece that has seen better days. They also excel with slipcovers and window coverings.

DESIGNER SHOWROOMS

It used to be that only those holding designer's cards were admitted to some trade buildings. These days, a number of design outfits will take care of individual customers, even if the signs on their doors say "Trade Only." Listed below are some of the trade buildings worth checking out. Each has a multitude of shops where you can find just about anything you need to fix up an apartment or home.

Architects & Designers Building (150 E 58th St, 212/644-2766; Mon-Fri: 9-5): 35 showrooms

Decoration & Design Building (979 Third Ave, 212/759-5408; Mon-Fri: 8:30-5:30): 18 floors

Manhattan Art & Antiques Center (1050 Second Ave, 212/355-4400; Mon-Sat: 10:30-6, Sun: noon-6): over 130 galleries

NY Design Center (200 Lexington Ave, 212/679-9500; Mon-Fri: 9-5): 90 showrooms

LES TOILES DU SOLEIL

261 W 19th St (bet Seventh and Eighth Ave)   212/229-4730
Mon-Sat: noon-7:30; Sun: noon-6   lestoilesdusoleilnyc.com

Walking into this sunny boutique will brighten any day! Fabulous striped cotton fabrics associated with the French Riviera are sold by the yard. Most are 100% cotton and a generous 72 inches wide. Many colorful items are made in-store from this cloth, including throw pillows, computer cases, tote bags, aprons, deck chairs, espadrilles and other useful items. Les Toiles also sells Sunbrella fabrics that are sun-, stain- and water-resistant, making them ideal for outdoor use and as custom-made goods (window or shower curtains, cushions, etc.). The translation of the store name — the "cloth of the sun" — sums up their product line!

M&J TRIMMING

1008 Ave of the Americas (bet 37th and 38th St)   212/391-6200
Mon-Fri: 9-8; Sat: 10-7; Sun: 11-7   mjtrim.com

M&J Trimming claims to have the largest selection of high-quality trims at one location, and I'm inclined to believe them! You will find everything from imported trims, buckles, buttons and decorator trims to various jewelry-making tools and findings. One area specializes in clothing and fashion trims, like ribbons, lace, sequins, bridal beading, Swarovski crystals and rhinestone appliqués; another features interior decor trim.

PARON FABRICS

257 W 39th St (bet Seventh and Eighth Ave)   212/768-3266
Mon-Thurs: 8:30-7; Fri: 8:30-6; Sat: 9-5; Sun: 11-4   paronfabrics.com

Paron Fabrics carries an excellent selection of contemporary designer fabrics suitable for clothing, home decor, theatrical set design, costumes and banners, all at discount prices; many of the goods are available only in this store.

A full line of patterns is also stocked. This is a family operation, so personal attention is assured. Check the back room for some real bargains!

ROSEN & CHADICK FABRICS

561 Seventh Ave (at 40th St), 2nd floor   212/869-0142
Mon-Fri: 8:30-5:45; Sat: 11-4:30   rosenandchadickfabrics.com

For over a half-century this family-owned business has been offering customers (including the theatrical trade) a huge selection of designer fabrics: silks, wools, cashmeres, linens, cottons, laces, velvets, brocades and more. The selection of cashmere is particularly impressive. You can be assured of personal, attentive service at this showroom; ask for David Chadick, the hands-on owner.

SPANDEX HOUSE, INC.

263 W 38th St (bet Seventh and Eighth Ave)   212/354-6711
Mon-Fri: 9-6; Sat: 10-5   spandexhouse.com

This firm claims to have one of the largest Spandex and Lycra offerings in the world. The assortment of stretch fabrics is amazing, including animal prints, meshs, lamés, laces, metallics, velvets and mattes. You can buy it plain or embellished with glitter, beads and sequins. These fabrics are widely used by costume designers for ice- and figure-skaters; gymnasts, dancers, wrestlers and other athletes and circus performers. They're also perfect for anyone who just wants really comfortable clothes that move easily with you. The minimum cut for wholesale or retail orders is one yard of material and $20.

TOHO SHOJI

990 Ave of the Americas (bet 36th and 37th St)   212/868-7465
Mon-Fri: 9-7; Sat: 10-6; Sun: 10-5   tohoshoji-ny.com

Only in New York will you find an establishment like Toho Shoji, which stocks all manner of items for designing and making custom jewelry: earring parts, metal findings, chains, charms and every type of jewelry component. Beads are made of ceramic, shell, CZ (cubic zirconia), wood, glass and more. Items are well displayed for easy selection at this "bead supermarket."

ZARIN FABRICS

69 Orchard St (bet Grand and Broome St)   212/925-6112
Mon-Fri: 9-6 (Fri till 5); Sun: 10-5   zarinfabrics.com

Founded in 1936, Zarin is the largest and oldest drapery and upholstery fabric warehouse in Manhattan. This three-floor fabric wonderland stocks thousands of bolts of designer fabrics and trims at below wholesale prices. It is a favorite source for decorators, set designers and celebrity clientele. The drapery hardware department, located on the lower level, closes at 6 p.m. sharp daily. Full decorating services are also available.

ZIPPERSTOP

27 Allen St (bet Hester and Canal St)   212/226-3964
Mon-Fri: 9-4:30; Sun: 9-3   zipperstop.com

Eddie Feibusch is the man behind ZipperStop, and one could say that his business has literally been going up and down since 1941! The company sells YKK zippers of every color and description imaginable: rainbow-colored teeth, leather tapes and studded with Swarovski crystals. There are zippers for every purpose, including handbags, clothing, sleeping bags, upholstery, tents and even hot-air balloons. Additionally, numerous other sewing essentials, including elastic, bias tape, cleaning fluid and lubricating wax for zippers, fill three floors.

FIREPLACE ACCESSORIES

WILLIAM H. JACKSON COMPANY

18 E 17th St (bet Fifth Ave and Broadway)   212/753-9400
Mon-Thurs: 9:30-4:30; Fri: 9:30-3:30   wmhjacksoncompany.com

Surprisingly, wood-burning fireplaces are hugely popular in New York. In business since 1827, William H. Jackson is familiar with the city's various types of fireplaces; in fact, the company originally installed many of those fireplaces. Jackson has hundreds of mantels on display in its showroom, ranging from antiques and reproductions (in wood or marble combinations) to starkly modern pieces. There are also beautiful andirons, fire tools, grates and screens. Repair work (removing and installing mantels) is a specialty, but they're better known for crafting and selling custom fireplace accessories.

FLAGS

ACE BANNER FLAG AND GRAPHICS

107 W 27th St (at Ave of the Americas)   212/620-9111
Mon-Fri: 8:30-4   acebanner.com

If you need a flag, Ace is the place. Established in 1916, Ace prides itself on carrying the flags of every nation, as well as New York City and New York State flags in all sizes. Custom fabric displays of any size can be made to order; from small desk flags to bridge-spanning banners. Portable trade-show graphics and large-format digital prints are available on a quick turnaround. They will ship anywhere.

FLOOR COVERINGS

COUNTRY FLOORS

15 E 16th St (bet Fifth Ave and Union Sq W)   212/627-8300
Mon-Fri: 9-6 (Thurs till 7); Sat: 10-5   countryfloors.com

Country Floors began in 1964 in a tiny, cramped basement under the owner's photography studio. It has grown to include huge stores in New York, California, Virginia and other locations. The finest floor, wall and outdoor tiles made of stone, glass, porcelain, metal and terra cotta are shown. Sources include artisans from all over the world. A visit (or at least a look at their website) is necessary to appreciate the quality and intricacy of each design; even the simplest solid-color tiles are exquisite.

ELIZABETH EAKINS

654 Madison Ave (bet 60th and 61st St), 14th floor   212/628-1950
Mon-Fri: 10-5:30   elizabetheakins.com

This is a first-class source for custom, high-end wool, cotton and linen rugs.

Elizabeth Eakins designs and makes hand-woven and hand-hooked natural fiber rugs in standard and hand-dyed colors. The yarn is dyed and then woven at the 22,000-square-foot Connecticut studio. Designs are amazing! And since this is a small shop, it is recommended to call ahead for an appointment.

JANOS P. SPITZER FLOORING COMPANY

131 W 24th St (bet Ave of the Americas and Seventh Ave)   212/627-1818
Mon-Fri: 8:30-4:30   janosspitzerflooring.com

This topnotch hardwood flooring company features installation of high-end (read: pricey) wooden floors in residences, as well as expert restoration and repair. You'll find many unusual finishes, as they source wood from around the world: domestic, imported and exotic tree species. The selection ranges from simple to elegant, with unique borders, medallions and parquets. Janos Spitzer brings the best in craftsmanship and service with over 50 years of experience.

PASARGAD CARPETS

180 Madison Ave (bet 33rd and 34th St)   212/684-4477
Mon-Fri: 9-6; Sat: 11-5   pasargadcarpets.com

This fifth-generation family business was established in 1904. Pasargad Carpets has one of the largest collections of new and antique decorative rugs in the country. Persian and Oriental rugs are their specialty, showing traditional, tribal, antique, silk and more. In-house cleaning and restoration are available.

FLOWERS, PLANTS AND GARDENING ITEMS

BELLE FLEUR

134 Fifth Ave (bet 18th and 19th St), 4th floor   212/254-8703
Mon-Fri: 8:45-5:45   bellefleurny.com

This mother-daughter team's floral style is refined, abundant and luxurious. (I would add "expensive" to that description.) Their gift bouquets and wedding/event displays are absolutely gorgeous works of art, using exotic blooms from around the globe. If you'd like to make your own floral arrangement, hands-on private classes and workshops are scheduled.

BLOOM

255 Murray St (at Vesey St)   212/832-8094
Mon-Fri: 10-7; Sat: 9-6   bloomflowers.com

When price is no object, you can do no better in the floral department than Bloom. Come here for a superb bouquet or arrangement when you have a special occasion to celebrate. If you're fortunate enough to have an outdoor space, their landscape-architecture experts do wonders with rooftop gardens, poolside areas and country estates for any event.

CHELSEA GARDEN CENTER HOME

580 Eleventh Ave (at 44th St)   212/727-7100
Mon-Sat: 9-5; Sun: 10-5   chelseagardencenter.com

For the urban gardener this place is a dream, offering a wide selection of

THE SHOPS AT COLUMBUS CIRCLE

Time Warner Center (10 Columbus Cir, 212/823-6300) is a vertical mall in a dramatic setting on the corner of Central Park West and Central Park South. The Shops at Columbus Circle is a mall that compares with the very best in America. Assembled under one roof are **bebe, Bose, Coach, Cole Haan, Davidoff of Geneva, Equinox Fitness Club, Godiva Chocolatier, L'Occitane, Microsoft, Montmartre, Stuart Weitzman, Swarovski, Thomas Pink, Whole Foods Market, Williams-Sonoma** and more. The magnificent **Mandarin Oriental New York** (see Services) is among the city's most luxurious hotels.

indoor and outdoor plants and flowers, as well as other garden items from fertilizers to fountains. The knowledgeable crew can give gardening and landscaping advice or can expertly complete your next outdoor project — decking, patio or stonework. You'll find other items at the garden center like candles, holiday decor, garden books and more.

FLORISITY

I W 19th St (bet Fifth Ave and Ave of the Americas)   212/366-0891
Mon-Fri: 10-6; Sat: 10-3   florisity.com

Each exotic arrangement and centerpiece from Florisity is custom-designed and made especially for the recipient. Expect to pay handsomely for the breathtaking floral art. If you are looking for a special vase, Florisity has a great selection, some antique.

JAMALI GARDEN SUPPLIES

149 W 28th St (bet Ave of the Americas and Seventh Ave)   212/244-4025
Mon-Sat: 6:30-5   jamaligarden.com

This store in the Flower Market carries just about everything except live plants and fresh flowers. The stock includes colorful accouterments to create stunning arrangements for any occasion. Creative event planners, brides and floral designers shop here for party lights, candles and holders, seashells, river stones, tabletop items, curtains, pillows, baskets, ribbons, floral picks and all sorts of other objects.

JONATHAN COUTURE

224 W 29th St (bet Seventh and Eighth Ave)   212/586-8414
Mon-Sat: 9-6   jonathantabletop.com

Jonathan's boasts one of the most beautiful Christmas floral displays in the city. The designers use top-quality, exotic fresh flowers and gifts and accessories from private collections to create one-of-a-kind artistic arrangements. Birthdays, weddings, anniversaries and other occasions are more spectacular and memorable with florals from Jonathan. Major events with distinctive themes and elegant styles are a specialty.

ROSA ROSA

831-A Lexington Ave (bet 63rd and 64th St)   212/935-4706
Mon-Fri: 8-8; Sat: 9-7; Sun: 11-5   rosarosaflowers.com

Rosa Rosa specializes in high-quality roses at low prices. The fragrant beauties arrive daily from Ecuador in a rainbow of colors and varieties and in five different sizes. Other specialties are fresh-daily seasonal Dutch flowers and orchid plants. All are used in classic bouquets and dramatic floral arrangements for every occasion, as well as budget-pleasing daily specials. Same-day local delivery is offered weekdays, and overnight delivery of roses and tulips is available nationally.

SIMPSON & CO.

457 W 56th St (at Tenth Ave), 2nd floor   212/765-6929
Mon-Fri: 9-6; Sat: 9-5   simpsonandco.net

This flower shop features cut flowers, plants and orchids. Baskets of wicker and wrought-iron and a good selection of fine glass containers are available for their floral creations. They will decorate for gatherings of all sizes, and their prices are very competitive. One of their specialties is creating custom gift baskets.

TREILLAGE

418 E 75th St (at York Ave)   212/535-2288
Mon-Fri: 10-6   treillageonline.com

New Yorkers have garden areas, too, although they are necessarily small. Many times they are just potted patio blooms placed in a small outside area, but still they add special charm to city living. Treillage can help make an ordinary space into something special. They carry furniture and accessories for indoors and out, with a great selection of unusual pieces to set your place apart, including many one-of-a-kind antiques and textiles. They sell everything except plants and flowers! Prices are not inexpensive, but why not splurge to enhance your little corner of the world?

VSF

204 W 10th St (at Bleecker St)   212/206-7236
Mon-Fri: 10-5; Sat: 11-4   vsfnyc.com

When it comes to fresh-cut flowers and dried or silk creations, you'll be happy with VSF. Colorful, voluptuous and unique. Unusual fresh flowers are shipped in daily from flower markets around the world. Their top-drawer list of clients attests to their talents for weddings and other special events. Ask for owners Jack Follmer or Todd Rigby.

ZEZÉ FLOWERS

938 First Ave (at 52nd St)   212/753-7767
Mon-Fri: 8-6; Sat: 9-3   zezeflowers.com

With roots in Rio de Janeiro, Zezé came to New York bringing a bit of drama to Manhattan's flower business. Zezé's romantic windows reflect his unique talent. The exotic orchid selection is outstanding. You'll find premium fresh-cut flowers, topiaries, ceramics and glassware, furniture, gift items and

FURNITURE CONSIGNMENT STORE

Furnish your home or apartment with high-end furniture and accessories from **Décor NYC** (159 W 25th St, 212/488-4977) and it won't cost you an arm and a leg. The goods are consigned by decorators, customers and showrooms to bring you sizable savings. One day you may find a dining room table and chairs to seat all your Thanksgiving dinner guests and another day you may come across the perfect sculpture to place on the buffet. The unpredictable merchandise mix may include antiques and uniques, fine art, sculptures, lighting, rugs and more for every room in your home — large or small.

antiques. They offer the ultimate in personalized service, including same-day delivery and special requests. A small, skylit venue space around the corner on 52nd Street is a delightful setting for a small catered affair.

FRAMES

HOUSE OF HEYDENRYK

601 W 26th St (bet Eleventh and Twelfth Ave), Suite 305   212/206-9611
Mon-Fri: 10-6; Sat: by appointment   heydenryk.com

House of Heydenryk has been crafting frame reproductions of the highest quality since 1845 in Amsterdam; and since 1936 in Manhattan. In this showroom/factory they stock reproductions, contemporary moldings and an extensive collection of European and American antique frames dating from the 15th through the 20th centuries. They also feature exclusive original frame designs created over the years for such artists as Picasso, Dali, Hopper, O'Keeffe and Wyeth. A team of master finishers, gilders, carvers and carpenters continue to carry on this art of custom frame-making.

FURNITURE

GENERAL

CHARLES P. ROGERS

26 W 17th St (bet Fifth Ave and Ave of the Americas)   212/675-4400
Mon-Fri: 9-8; Sat: 10-7; Sun: noon-6   charlesprogers.com

Rogers has been making comfortable, handcrafted beds since 1885! Brass beds made from heavy-gauge brass tubing with solid brass castings, wooden and leather-upholstered beds and hand-forged iron beds are exceptionally heavy and sturdy. Select bed linens are made from the finest materials, including European linen.

FLOU

42 Greene St (bet Broome and Grand St)   212/941-9101
Mon-Sat: 11-7; Sun: noon-5   flou.it

In its U.S. flagship store, the Italian retailer Flou shows everything for the bedroom, from designer beds, mattresses and furniture to bed linens. This outfit is well known in Europe and Japan, where they tout the brand as promoting "the art of sleeping." The furniture designs are sleek and minimal and include beds, dressers and wardrobes.

GRANGE

New York Design Center Building
200 Lexington Ave (at 32nd St), 2nd floor   212/685-9057
Mon-Fri: 9-6   grange.fr

French furniture and accessories fill this stylish showroom. Pieces range from classic period designs to exotic and contemporary styles and are manufactured to emphasize form, function and comfort. Dozens of finishes and levels of antiquing are available on most furniture pieces.

LOST CITY ARTS

18 Cooper Sq (Bowery at 5th St)   212/375-0500
Mon-Fri: 10-6; Sat, Sun: noon-6   lostcityarts.com

Established in 1982, Lost City Arts shows 20th-century design furniture, lighting and accessories. Owner James Elkind travels the world in search of unique pieces. You'll also find some of the company's own production pieces in the same style.

OFFICE FURNITURE HEAVEN

22 W 19th St (bet Fifth Ave and Ave of the Americas), 4th floor   212/989-8600
Mon-Fri: 9-6   officefurnitureheaven.com

If you are setting up an office or upgrading one, visit Office Furniture Heaven. There are great bargains in first-quality contemporary pieces; some are new, while others are brand-name close-outs and discontinued or used items that have been refurbished to look almost new. You'll find a large showroom display of refurbished Knoll and Haworth furniture and new ones by Global and OFS. There are conference tables, chairs, bookcases, file cabinets, accessories and much more.

RESOURCE FURNITURE

969 Third Ave (at 58th St), 4th floor   212/753-2039
Mon-Fri: 9:30-6; Sat: noon-5   resourcefurniture.com

It is possible to squeeze great looking furniture into a wee Manhattan apartment. Resource Furniture is known for its contemporary, space-saving European furniture, including wall beds modeled after the familiar Murphy beds. What's really impressive is a sofa that transforms into a bunk-bed set. Beautiful fabrics and quality structural materials combine good looks with functionality. Resource also stocks tables, seating, lighting, rugs and executive office pieces to complete the look.

INFANTS AND CHILDREN

ALBEE BABY

715 Amsterdam Ave (at 95th St)   212/662-7337
Mon-Fri: 10-7; Sat: 10-6; Sun: 11-6   albeebaby.com

One of the city's best selections of basics for infants and toddlers is to be had at Albee Baby. This longtime (since 1933) family-owned and -operated store has everything from strollers and car seats to cribs and rocking chairs. Furniture for baby's room includes cribs, changing tables, dressers and gliders and moves up to bunk and twin beds. If you can't find what you need, check in with the helpful staff.

FOR THE DOGS

Are you ready to get a dog? If it is a purebred you want, call the **American Kennel Club** (919/233-9767) and tell them the breed you have in mind. Another good bet is **Bide-a-Wee** (410 E 38th St, 212/532-4455). If you need to train your dog, try **Follow My Lead** (212/873-5511).

SCHNEIDER'S

41 W 25th St (bet Broadway and Ave of the Americas)   212/228-3540
Mon-Sat: 10-6 (Tues till 8)

schneidersbaby.com

This Chelsea store is a find for those interested in children's furniture at comfortable prices. Bedroom suites are fit for a princess or young gent. You'll also find car seats, strollers, diaper bags, bedding, backpacks and much more for infants through teens.

GAMES

COMPLEAT STRATEGIST

11 E 33rd St (at Fifth Ave)   212/685-3880
Mon-Sat: 10:30-6 (Thurs till 9)   thecompleatstrategist.com

Touting itself as the "true gamers strategic choice," Compleat Strategist started up over 25 years ago. It began as an armory of sorts for military games and equipment, but as time went on, the store branched out: science fiction, fantasy and murder-mystery games, as well as adventure games, DVDs and books. The stock is more than ample and the personnel are knowledgeable and friendly. They now have chess and backgammon sets, board games and cards!

GIFTS AND ACCESSORIES

BIZARRE BAZAAR

130¼ E 65th St (bet Lexington and Park Ave)   212/517-2100
Mon-Fri: by appointment   bzrbzr.com

Bizarre Bazaar is a great stop if you are looking for a unique gift. You'll find aviation and automotive memorabilia, industrial-inspired curiosities, architectural miniatures, jewelry and all sorts of art deco objects. A unique, one-of-a-kind gift is sure to be found at this bazaar.

BLUE TREE

1283 Madison Ave (at 91st St)   212/369-2583
Mon-Fri: 10-6; Sat, Sun: 11-6   bluetreenyc.com

You never know what you will find at this unusual boutique! The street floor has gifts and trinkets for almost any occasion, while the second floor displays a rather exclusive collection of clothing, fragrances and accessories for men and women. A number of big-name clothing designers are represented at Blue Tree. One-of-a-kind jewelry, eclectic music, home items, kids' toys and fragrances can also be found.

DE VERA

1 Crosby St (at Howard St)	212/625-0838
26 E 81st St (at Madison Ave)	212/288-2288
Tues-Sat: 11-7	deveraobjects.com

As he travels the world, Federico de Vera purchases whatever catches his eye. The result is a unique operation, with decorative arts, antiques, Japanese lacquerware, Venetian glass, ivory carvings and other unusual items. There's an emphasis on jewelry (vintage, one-of-a-kind and some designed by Federico). Both a craftsman and a merchant, he does wonders with the most unusual vintage elements.

DELPHINIUM HOME

353 W 47th St (bet Eighth and Ninth Ave)	212/333-7732
Mon-Sat: 11-8; Sun: noon-7	delphiniumhome.com

Whimsical and practical would describe many of the gift items sold here. Pan Am bags, shower curtains printed with a map of the New York subway system and art deco replicas of New York monuments are some favorites. Less quirky decor and accessories for the kitchen, bath and home are attractively displayed. The kids' line features similarly whimsical items, including beautiful pop-up books. You'll also find cards, candles, jewelry, clocks and wine caddies, all unique in design and perfect for that surprise gift.

DOMUS

413 W 44th St (at Ninth Ave)	212/581-8099
Tues-Sat: noon-8; Sun: noon-6	domusnewyork.com

Shopping at this eclectic Hell's Kitchen housewares store is fun! Luisa Cerutti and Nicki Lindheimer have excellent taste. On their travels they select one-of-a-kind European and Asian imports (many handcrafted), including jewelry, pottery, tabletop, linens and unusual, eye-catching pieces. By working directly with international artisans, they are able to trim costs by eliminating middle men. Domus (which is Latin for home) is a super place to shop for wedding gifts; consider a hand-woven runner from Guatemala, an inlaid wood box from Morocco or a handquilted coverlet from India. Take advantage of free gift wrapping.

EXTRAORDINARY

247 E 57th St (bet Second and Third Ave)	212/223-9151
Daily: 11-9	extraordinaryny.com

An international gift selection is the draw at Extraordinary. With a background in museum exhibition design, owner J.R. Sanders hand picks each item. You'll find hand-painted boxes, hand-carved bowls, lacquered trays, metal candle holders, unique lamps, jewelry and other items for the home. The round-the-world theme includes merchandise from the Philippines, Japan,

NICHE PERFUMES

There is an area of Lower Manhattan that has been dubbed the "Fragrance District." The area starts on the east at Elizabeth Street (just south of Houston) and continues through Lafayette Street and Crosby Street to West Broadway. Boutique studios in the area offer *niche* perfumes (non-existent in mainstream retail stores and therefore less common, more individual scents). At **Osswald** (311 West Broadway, 212/625-3111) you'll find a carefully-chosen portfolio of niche perfume brands and luxury skin-care products. The family-owned and -operated Swiss business now pampers Manhattan customers with a highly knowledgeable and customer service-oriented staff. Spritz to your heart's content!

Thailand, China, Vietnam, India, Morocco, Ghana, Peru and other stops; local artists are also featured. No matter your budget, you'll have no trouble finding something "extraordinary" from a wide range of price points.

GLOBAL TABLE

107 Sullivan St (bet Prince and Spring St)	212/431-5839
Mon-Sat: noon-7; Sun: noon-6	
471 Amsterdam Ave (bet 82nd and 83rd St)	646/657-0318
Daily: 11:30-6:30	globaltable.com

Looking for a thoughtful surprise for mom or a hostess gift for a dinner party? Make a stop at Global Table. The carefully edited inventory at this crowded tabletop and home accessory store is affordable, different, fun and worldwide in scope. Mix-and-match pieces are popular, or scan the one-of-a-kind dishes, glassware and accessories, most with simple lines and vivid colors. All sure to please!

MICHAEL C. FINA

500 Park Ave (at 59th St)	212/557-2500
Mon-Thurs: 10-7; Fri, Sat: 10-6	michaelcfina.com

Michael C. Fina has been a New York tradition since 1935. This popular bridal-gift registry firm has an extensive selection (over 200 brand names) of sterling silver, china, crystal, barware and home decor. Frames, vases, bowls, decorative accents and vintage silver are all of superior quality. Besides its own Michael C. Fina line, designers include Anna Weatherley, Ashanti, Gorham, Lenox and Mariposa. It is renowned for an exquisite selection of wedding and engagement rings. Prices are attractive, quality is topnotch and the store is well organized.

RANDOM ACCESSORIES

77 E 4th St (bet Bowery and Second Ave)	212/358-0650
Mon-Sat: noon-8; Sun: noon-7	

At this small East Village shop, an amazing assortment of lighthearted, must-have merchandise packs the shelves. Cute, clever and frivolous (and sometimes tacky) best describe the mix of baby gifts, books, kitchen gadgets, frames, vases, decor items, personal accessories and greeting cards. There are also cuff links and other jewelry. It is a great place to shop for that random gift that is sure to raise a smile.

SUSTAINABLE NYC

139 Ave A (bet St. Mark's Pl and 9th St)   212/254-5400
Mon-Fri: 8 a.m.-10 p.m.; Sat, Sun: 9 a.m.-10 p.m.   sustainable-nyc.com

In trying to be a responsible steward of our planet, this store offers local, organic, recycled, fair-trade, repurposed and biodegradable products and gifts. The shop itself is built from reclaimed 300-year-old lumber from New York City buildings; even the sign is solar-powered. There is a variety of cards, stationery, jewelry, T-shirts, shoes, bags, beauty products and solar backpacks and chargers. You'll want to take a break from your shopping at the in-store cafe offering snacks and organic Ethiopian coffee.

WORKS GALLERY

1250 Madison Ave (bet 89th and 90th St)   212/996-0300
Mon-Thurs: 10-6:30; Fri, Sat: 10-6   worksgallery.com

At Works Gallery you will find one-of-a-kind jewelry, art-glass items and wall art handmade by talented artists. Owner, Frank Pereira oversees the gallery which presents 30 studio jewelers, glassmakers, woodworkers and fine artists. You can also have a personal piece made from your own stones or have an item redesigned, repaired or resized. Check online for special events featuring new artists.

GREETING CARDS

UNICEF CARDS & GIFTS

3 United Nations Plaza (44th St bet First and Second Ave)   212/326-7054
Mon-Fri: 10-6   shop.unicefusa.org

Improving the lives of the world's children has been the mission of the United Nations Children's Emergency Fund (UNICEF) for over 60 years. One way this tremendous organization raises money for its lifesaving projects and programs is through the sale of cards and gifts. If you've never seen UNICEF products before, then you're in for a treat at this well-planned and friendly store, which carries fabulous calendars, greeting cards, stationery, books and puzzles for children, home decor, jewelry, scarves, bags and other accessories — all for a good cause.

HOBBIES

JAN'S HOBBY SHOP

1435 Lexington Ave (bet 93rd and 94th St)   212/987-4765
Mon-Sat: 10-6:30; Sun: 11-5

Jan's stocks everything a serious model builder could possibly want. The store has a superb stock of plastic scale models, model war games and all kinds of model cars, trains, planes, remote-controlled helicopters, ships and tanks. Jan's also carries remote-controlled planes and boats. Owner Fred Hutchins can be found some mornings at the 72nd Street Model Boat Pond in Central Park showing off his remote-controlled boats.

HOME FURNISHINGS

ABC CARPET & HOME

881 and 888 Broadway (at 19th St)   212/473-3000
Mon-Sat: 10-7 (Thurs till 8); Sun: 11-6:30   abchome.com

If you can visit only one home-furnishings store in Manhattan, ABC should be it! Starting in 1897 as a pushcart business, ABC expanded into one of the city's most unique, exciting and well-merchandised emporiums. (It's actually two buildings, located across the street from each other.) ABC is the Bergdorf Goodman of home furnishings. There are floors of great-looking furniture, dinnerware, linens, gifts, home accessories and antiques. You will see many one-of-a-kind pieces as you explore corner after corner, plus an extensive selection of carpets and rugs at reasonable prices. Don't miss their restaurant, **ABC Kitchen** (38 E 18th St, 212/475-5829), a class operation from Jean-Georges Vongerichten that serves brunch, lunch and dinner.

ADELAIDE

702 Greenwich St (at 10th St)   212/627-0508
Wed-Sun: noon-7   adelaideny.com

The elegant interior of this shop belies its former life as a trucking garage. Exceptional furniture, rugs, lighting, interesting decor pieces and artwork from the 1930s to the 1960s are attractively staged. Classy vignettes incorporate gleaming aluminum, glass, brass tables, books and interesting accessories alongside upholstered chairs, settees and sofas. Window displays feature unique design pieces; the stock changes frequently.

CALYPSO SOHO

407 Broome St (at Lafayette St)   212/925-6200
Mon-Sat: 11-6; Sun: noon-6   calypsostbarth.com

Bedrooms will look casual and breezy with high-end merchandise from Calypso. This outfit specializes in beautiful pillows, throws, textiles, furniture, rugs, lighting and other home items, including some designer originals, most from earthy, natural fibers; there is a mix of modern and loungey coastal decor.

MACKENZIE-CHILDS

20 W 57th St (bet Fifth Ave and Ave of the Americas)   212/570-6050
Mon-Sat: 10-6 (Thurs till 7); Sun: 11-5   mackenzie-childs.com

Landscape murals, greenhouse door partitions and red brick paving make this boutique an exciting and inviting space. Mackenzie-Childs is all about style, color and quality. Stripes, checks, plaids, florals and black-and-white patterns adorn the handcrafted and hand-painted tableware, kitchen accessories, gifts, home decor, lighting, unique furniture pieces, garden furniture and outdoor decor and stunning accessories. This same theme carries over to the selection of apparel and holiday items. Check out the whimsical bathroom sinks! A visit here will brighten any day.

RESTORATION HARDWARE

935 Broadway (at 22nd St)   212/260-9479
Mon-Sat: 10-8; Sun: 11-7   restorationhardware.com

Restoration Hardware is a luxury brand that represents more than its name would indicate. Part home furnishings and part hardware, you'll find a large selection of furniture, bed and bath items, textiles, home decor, draperies, outdoor and garden items, lighting, bathware, cabinets and retro hardware. With the belief that old things can be chic, Restoration proudly reproduces a timeless, classic look in its collection; it is among the best in its field.

WEST ELM

112 W 18th St (bet Ave of the Americas and Seventh Ave)   212/929-4464
1870 Broadway (at 62nd St)   212/247-8077
Mon-Sat: 10-9; Sun: 11-7   westelm.com

For home furnishings, West Elm is like a slightly less expensive Crate & Barrel. You'll find minimalist modern furniture, shelving, mirrors, lamps, quilts, bedding, shower curtains, bath accessories, towels, kitchen tools, clocks, room accents, rugs, dinnerware, glassware and flatware. The stores are attractive and merchandise is well-displayed.

HOUSEWARES AND HARDWARE

BASICS PLUS

2315 Broadway (bet 84th and 83rd St)   212/873-7837
845 Second Ave (at 45th St)   212/682-6311
194 Third Ave (at 18th St)   212/432-2230
386 Canal St (at West Broadway)   212/219-7601
Numerous other locations
Mon-Fri: 8 a.m.-10 p.m.; Sat: 9 a.m.-10 p.m.; Sun: 10-10   basicsplusny.com

After starting his first locksmith company on the Upper East Side, Zvi Cohen realized he also needed merchandise on the shelves. He asked his customers what they would buy, and the rest is history. Every Basics Plus location has a New York Locksmith service counter, as well as hardware-store essentials like tools, cleaning supplies, repair items, housewares, paint, fasteners and automotive basics. Oh, and let's not forget the locks!

BROADWAY PANHANDLER

65 E 8th St (bet Broadway and University Pl)   212/966-3434
Mon-Sat: 11-7 (Thurs till 8); Sun: 11-6   broadwaypanhandler.com

Broadway Panhandler maintains a tradition of great assortments and low prices. Family-owned and -operated since 1976, the folks here are a pleasure to deal with. Thousands of cutlery, kitchen tools, bakeware, tabletop items and cookware pieces are available at sizable savings. Guest chefs make periodic appearances, and a fine selection of professional items is offered to walk-in customers and restaurant and hotel buyers.

DICK'S CUT RATE HARDWARE

9 Gold St (at Maiden Lane)   212/425-1070
Mon-Fri: 7:30-6:30; Sat: 9-6; Sun: 10-5   dickshardware.co

Hardware stores like Dick's are a great convenience for shoppers. In a

HARDWARE FOR KITCHEN AND BATH

For bathroom and kitchen fix-ups, these firms stand out:

Krup's Kitchen & Bath (11 W 18th St, 212/243-5787): good source for appliances; custom cabinetry and countertops, too

Simon's Hardware & Bath (421 Third Ave, 212/532-9220): everything for the bathroom and kitchen; fixtures, hardware, even towels

Lower Manhattan location where there are few such stores, Dick's provides good prices, informed service and great selections of electrical and plumbing supplies, tools, cleaning and gardening supplies, housewares, plus much more. They also cut duplicate keys.

GARBER HARDWARE

710 Greenwich St (bet 10th and Charles St)   212/242-9807
Mon-Thurs: 8-8; Fri, Sat: 8-5; Sun: 10-4   garberhardware.com

This unique family business has become a New York institution. The Garbers have been operating their old-style hardware store since 1884 with this appealing motto: "Either we have it or we can get it for you." You will find a complete inventory of paints, hardware, home and garden, plumbing and electrical supplies, locks, tools and building materials. Making custom window shades and cutting keys and pipes are among the many handy services offered.

GEORGE TAYLOR SPECIALTIES

76 Franklin St (bet Church St and Broadway)   212/226-5369
Mon-Thurs: 7:30-5; Fri: 7:30-4

Porcelain and chrome abounds here! Antique-style towel bars, tubs, toilets, pedestal sinks, fixtures and bath accessories are among Taylor's specialties. They offer hard-to-find vintage items and custom designs of fittings for unique installations. Founded in 1869, Taylor remains a friendly, family-run operation. Ask for father Chris, daughter Valerie or son John. Repairs are done in the in-house machine shop and they can also make custom pieces to replace old fixtures.

GRACIOUS HOME

1201 and 1220 Third Ave (at 70th St)   212/517-6300
1992 Broadway (at 67th St)   212/231-7800
45 W 25th St (bet Ave of the Americas and Broadway)   212/414-5710
Hours vary by store   gracioushome.com

Savvy New Yorkers love Gracious Home! These stores are must-visits for anyone interested in fixing up their home, establishing a new one, looking for gifts or just browsing stores that typify the New York lifestyle. The quality, expertise and service are outstanding. You'll find appliances, wall coverings, paint, gifts, hardware, decorative bath accessories, lighting, china, casual furniture, bedding, shelving, pots and pans and heaven knows what else! They install window coverings and large appliances, offer tool rental and repair services, create custom lampshades and provide a gift registry and special-order department. The location in Chelsea (W 25th Street) is a design center limited to decorative and architectural hardware and plumbing supplies.

MANHATTAN WARDROBE SUPPLY

245 W 29th St (bet Seventh and Eighth Ave), 8th floor   212/268-9993
Mon–Fri: 9–7; Sat: 10–6   wardrobesupplies.com

What a unique shop! Manhattan Wardrobe Supply has all sorts of items having to do with making, storing, cleaning and displaying clothes for the home or theater; theatrical makeup and hair and wig accessories; jewelry maintenance and storage and miscellaneous bits and pieces like location-set bags, fabric dyes and distressing kits. If you're a wardrober, you'll definitely want to shop here. If not, you'll learn the secrets of the professionals to maintain your attire in tiptop condition. (Note: clothes are not sold here.)

P.E. GUERIN

23 Jane St (bet Greenwich and Eighth Ave)   212/243-5270
Mon-Fri: 9-5:30 (by appointment)   peguerin.com

Andrew Ward is the fourth generation to run the oldest decorative hardware firm in the country and the only remaining foundry in the city. The company began in 1857 and has been on Jane Street since 1892. In that time, the firm has grown into an impressive worldwide operation. Under this same roof they manufacture and/or import decorative hardware and bath accessories. Artisans craft intricate metalwork in brass, nickel, pewter, verde or bronze, and the foundry can make virtually anything from those materials, including copies and reproductions; they stock 25,000 beautiful items. No job is too small for Guerin, which operates like the hometown firm it still believes itself to be. They offer free estimates and can help with any hardware problem.

S. FELDMAN HOUSEWARES

1304 Madison Ave (at 92nd St)   212/289-7367
Mon-Sat: 9-6; Sun: 11-5   sfeldmanhousewares.com

Sam Feldman opened this store, originally a five-and-dime store, during the Depression. Over the years it has changed dramatically, but it is still family-owned and -operated. Customer service is a top priority; they even provide free espresso to shoppers. With over 12,000 items, from lightbulbs to vacuum cleaners, this is truly a one-stop shopping spot. You'll find housewares, cookware, home decor, gifts, tabletop items, appliances, toys, gift items and more. They repair vacuum cleaners and offer free delivery in New York City. What more could they do?

SAIFEE HARDWARE & GARDEN

114 First Ave (at 7th St)   212/979-6396
Mon-Sat: 8:30-7:30; Sun: 10-6:30   saifeehardware.com

This is your neighborhood hardware store, that is, if you live in the East Village. Saifee has the usual supplies for plumbing, electrical, gardening and small building projects, as well as housewares, decorative items, tools and other gadgets. Although prices are not as low as at big-box stores, the personal attention and expertise you'll find make it worth the stop. Services include key and glass cutting and tool rentals.

SIMON'S HARDWARE & BATH

421 Third Ave (bet 29th and 30th St)   212/532-9220
Mon-Fri: 8-5:30 (Thurs till 7); Sat: 10-5   simonsny.com

Simon's is really a hardware supermarket, offering one of the city's finest selections of quality decorative hardware items, bath and kitchen fixtures and accessories. Woodworkers and plumbers will find myriad tools, supplies and materials. The personnel are patient and helpful, even if you just need something to fix a broken handle on a door or chest of drawers.

SUR LA TABLE

75 Spring St (at Crosby St)   212/966-3375
1320 Third Ave (bet 75th and 76th St)   646/843-7984
306 W 57th St (at Eighth Ave)   212/574-8334
Hours vary by store   surlatable.com

Whether you are outfitting a tiny kitchenette or a sprawling kitchen and dining room, this is the place to shop. You'll find a large and colorful assortment of essentials for cooking and entertaining, with name brands such as All-Clad, Le Creuset, Zoku and more, not to mention Sur la Table's own quality merchandise. Foodies love the frequent cooking demos and classes!

WILLIAMS-SONOMA

1175 Madison Ave (at 86th St)   212/289-6832
110 Seventh Ave (at 17th St)   212/633-2203
121 E 59 St (bet Park and Lexington Ave)   917/369-1131
10 Columbus Cir (Time Warner Center)   212/581-1146
Hours vary by store   williams-sonoma.com

From humble beginnings in the wine country of Sonoma County, California, Williams-Sonoma has expanded across the nation and is referred to as the "Tiffany of cookware stores." The serious cook will find a vast display of quality gourmet cookware, bakeware, cutlery, kitchen linens, specialty foods, cookbooks, small appliances, kitchen furniture, glassware and tableware. Only the Columbus Circle location carries a home-furniture collection. The stores also offer a gift and bridal registry, cooking demonstrations, free recipes, gift baskets and shopping assistance for corporations or individuals. Especially at holiday time, the candy assortment is first-class. Call customer service (877/812-6235) or access William-Sonoma's website to request their attractive catalog, which includes a number of excellent recipes.

IMPORTS

AFGHAN

NUSRATY AFGHAN IMPORTS

85 Christopher St (bet Bleecker and Seventh Ave S)   212/691-1012
Tues-Sun: noon-7

This West Village shop is jam-packed with colorful textiles, carpets and rugs and antique silver and jewelry. Abdul Nusraty has an unerring eye for things unique and of high quality; many items are from Afghanistan, Egypt and Morocco. There are magnificently embroidered native dresses and shirts displayed alongside semiprecious stones mounted in jewelry. Be sure to look up to see the beautiful wall hangings and silk paintings anchored from the ceiling.

CHINESE

CHINESE PORCELAIN COMPANY

475 Park Ave (at 58th St)   212/838-7744
Mon-Fri: 10-6   chineseporcelainco.com

The Chinese Porcelain Company has been offering Asian and European works of art and fine furniture since 1984. Their specialty is Chinese ceramics, but there are also beautiful one-of-a-kind creations in wood, stone, lacquer, jade, glass, enamel and ivory. Chinese, Tibetan, Indian, Khymer and Vietnamese sculptures are represented, along with French and continental furniture.

CQ ASIAN FURNITURE

37 W 20th St (at Ave of the Americas)   212/366-1888
Daily: 10-8   cqasianantiquefurniture.com

Whether you decorate with an Asian theme or need the perfect accent piece, check out the vast selection at CQ. Antiques, reproduction furniture and accessory collections (like vases, ginger jars and bronze carvings) have been imported from Korea, Mongolia, Tibet and Beijing. Choose from a variety of table styles, armoires, buffets, chairs and desks. Talk to store personnel if you don't find exactly what you're looking for, as they have a huge warehouse and take custom orders.

PEARL RIVER MART

477 Broadway (bet Broome and Grand St)   212/431-4770
Daily: 10-7:20   pearlriver.com

Pearl River Mart is a true Chinese department store, presenting items imported from China and other Asian countries. The store is busy, well-organized, and well-stocked with 15,000 items of clothing and accessories, home furnishings, kitchenware, arts and crafts, Chinese brocade and more, most at low prices. A furniture department is located on the upper level.

YUNHONG CHOPSTICKS SHOP

50 Mott St (bet Bayard and Pell St)   212/566-8828
Daily: 10:30-8:30   happychopsticks.com

The name is truly descriptive of the merchandise here. Chopsticks in all manner of materials: plastic, steel, ceramic, porcelain and various woods. Some are elaborately embellished; some are themed. All are priced accordingly, from a couple of dollars to $1,000 for a mahogany/pearl boxed set. For the chopstick-challenged (like me), there are "training sticks" for kids. Associated mealtime merchandise rounds out the selection: spoons, bowls and, of course, chopstick stands. Presenting chopsticks as a gift is considered giving someone happiness.

ESKIMO/NATIVE AMERICAN

ALASKA ON MADISON

1065 Madison Ave (bet 80th and 81st St), 2nd floor   212/879-1782
Tues-Sat: 1:30-6   alaskaonmadison.com

This gallery is New York's most complete collection of Inuit and Northwest Coast ceremonial artifacts and sculptures and objects from the Old Bering Sea cultures. Additionally, there is a collection of small Alaskan ivories. It is run by collectors for collectors and includes museum-quality pieces as well as more modest ones. Periodic shows highlight aspects of these cultures. A number of contemporary artists whose works have been shown here have gained international acclaim.

GENERAL

KATINKA

303 E 9th St (at Second Ave)   212/677-7897
Tues-Sat: 4-7 (call ahead; hours can vary)

This closet-sized shop is an import paradise, with jewelry, natural-fiber clothing, shoes, scarves, belts, hats, musical instruments, incense and artifacts from India, Thailand, Pakistan, Afghanistan and South America. The most popular items are colorful shoes and embroidered wraps, sarongs and bedspreads from India. You'll feel like you've embarked on a worldwide shopping safari! Prices are reasonable.

SHEHERAZADE HOME

121 Orchard St (bet Delancey and Rivington St)   212/539-1771
Mon-Fri: 11-7; Sat: noon-7; Sun: noon-6   sheherazadehome.com

Sheherazade features handcrafted home decor imported from the Middle East and Central Asia. Antique and contemporary furniture, carpets, tapestries, chandeliers, textiles, glassware, lanterns, jewelry and gifts are displayed. Islamic art and Oriental decorative furnishings are also featured. Owner Rachid works with native artisans to bring exotic pieces that are exclusive to his store.

JAPANESE

MUJI

620 Eighth Ave (at 40th St)   212/382-2300
455 Broadway (bet Grand and Canal St)   212/334-2002
52 Cooper Sq (near Astor Place)   212/358-8693
Mon-Sat: 11-9; Sun: 11-8
16 W 19th St (bet Fifth Ave and Ave of the Americas)   212/414-9024
Mon-Sat: 11-8; Sun: 11-6:30   muji.us

Muji's wide array of products share one common theme — simplicity in design. This Japanese department store stocks eye-catching and unique desk, office and stationery items as part of their no-name generic line. They also carry personal accessories, housewares and home accessories and books — even furniture and lighting! Shoppers appreciate the quality goods at low prices.

SARA JAPANESE POTTERY

950 Lexington Ave (bet 69th and 70th St)   212/772-3243
Mon-Fri: 10-7; Sat: noon-6   saranyc.com

If you're looking for something with a Japanese flair, Sara is the place to go for modern Japanese ceramics, glassware, tableware, cast iron and gifts. Check out the colorful lacquerware, textiles, bamboo products and iron sculptures. The works of well-known and up-and-coming artisans are featured. Artist exhibitions and Japanese tea ceremonies are occasionally held at Sara; check the website or call for a schedule of events.

MEXICAN

PAN AMERICAN PHOENIX

857 Lexington Ave (bet 64th and 65th St)   212/570-0300
Mon-Fri: 10:30-6:30; Sat: 11-6   panamphoenix.com

Colorful items made of gleaming silver, vibrant glass, pottery and fabrics from Mexico and Latin America have adorned this East Side locale since 1959. Some items are wearable, including jewelry for men and women and traditional clothing (such as huipiles). Vibrant folk art and decorative and useful home items are also sold: textiles, tabletop and holloware, mirrors, rugs, pillows and lanterns.

MIDDLE EASTERN

PERSIAN SHOP

534 Madison Ave (bet 54th and 55th St)   212/355-4643
Mon-Fri: 10-5:30; Sat: 10-4:30

The Persian Shop is filled with unusual Middle Eastern items: end tables, chairs, frames, mirrors and brocades sold by the yard or made into magnificent neckties. But the jewelry selection is especially noteworthy and is the main

BARGAIN SOURCES
FOR HOME AND OFFICE

Asian goods: **Pearl River Mart** (477 Broadway, 212/431-4770)

Flowers, cut (retail and wholesale): **Wholesale Flower Market** (29th St bet Ave of the Americas and Seventh Ave)

Furniture: **Room & Board** (105 Wooster St, 212/334-4343)

Home furnishings: **Bed Bath & Beyond** (270 Greenwich St, 212/233-8450; 410 E 61st St, 646/215-4702; 620 Ave of the Americas, 212/255-3550 and 1932 Broadway, 917/441-9391)

Kitchenware: **Broadway Panhandler** (65 E 8th St, 212/966-3434)

Photo equipment & supplies: **B&H Photo Video Pro Audio** (420 Ninth Ave, 212/444-6615)

Sewing and upholstering notions: **M&J Trimming** (1008 Ave of the Americas, 212/391-9072)

Stationery and office products: **JAM Paper & Envelope** (135 Third Ave, 212/473-6666)

feature. You'll find precious and semiprecious items, silver and gold cuff links, rings, earrings, bracelets, necklaces and heirloom pieces. A purchase here will add a touch of the exotic.

UKRAINIAN

SURMA — THE UKRAINIAN SHOP

11 E 7th St (at Third Ave)	212/477-0729
Mon-Fri: 11-6; Sat: 11-4	surmastore.com

Surma has functioned as the "general store of the Slavic community in New York City" since 1918. This bastion of Ukrainism makes it difficult to believe you're still in New York. The clothing is pure ethnic opulence: dresses, vests, shirts, blouses and accessories. All are hand-embroidered with authentic detailing. Home items include colorful, hand-woven kilims, porcelains, ceramics, woodcrafts, hand-embroidered linens, hand-painted *pysanky* (Easter eggs) and Surma's own Ukrainian-style honey (different and very good). Above all, Surma is known for its educational tapes and books. Pay particular attention to the artwork and stationery, which depict ancient Ukrainian glass paintings. A visit here is like a walk through the old country.

JEWELRY

ALEXIS BITTAR

1100 Madison Ave (bet 82nd and 83rd St)	212/249-3649
353 Bleecker St (bet 10th and Charles St)	212/727-1093
465 Broome St (bet Mercer and Greene St)	212/625-8340
410 Columbus Ave (at 80th St)	646/590-4142
Hours vary by store	alexisbittar.com

Designer Alexis Bittar is known as one of the greatest jewelry designers of the 21st century. His chic, handcrafted Lucite jewelry is certain to draw attention. Each colorful pin, ring, bracelet, necklace and earring is hand-carved and hand-painted; some are embellished with a sprinkling of semiprecious stones; others are brass with a rhodium or gold coating. Some of the collection has been seen in Paris and New York runway shows.

CATWALK

100 Park Ave (bet 40th and 41st St), 34th floor	212/249-5066
By appointment	catwalk10021.com

Want to make a bold statement with your accessories? Catwalk offers one of the largest selections of vintage couture costume jewelry in the city. Bracelets, earrings and necklaces from featured designers including Chanel, Laquoix, Pucci, YSL and more. Check the website for current "runway" items; if you don't see what you want, contact them and they will try to locate it!

CHRISTOPHER 19

19 Christopher St (bet Ave of the Americas and Seventh Ave)	212/627-9159
Daily: 11:30-7 (Thurs, Fri till 8)	christopher19.com

Artist and designer William Felder handcrafts fashion jewelry in Greenwich Village and sells the collection at Christopher 19. A select group of local and international designers also sell their jewelry and men's and women's accessories at this attractive boutique. You'll find jewelry made of metal, wood, beads, crystals, glass and many types of stones. The price range is as varied as the selection of merchandise.

CHROME HEARTS

870 Madison Ave (bet 70th and 71st St)
Mon-Sat: 10-6

212/794-3100
chromehearts.com

If you're looking for rocker-type accessories, Chrome Hearts is the place to go! They show a broad selection of handmade jewelry (with lots of attitude and studs) in sterling silver, 22K gold, platinum and precious stones. Inventory is across the board with clothing in leather and fabric; gadgets for people who think they have everything; handcrafted furniture in exotic woods; great-looking eyewear and much more. Be sure to bring your biggest wallet.

DOYLE & DOYLE

412 W 13th St (bet Washington St and Ninth Ave)
Daily: noon-7 (Thurs till 8)

212/677-9991
doyledoyle.com

This shop is operated by two creative sisters who specialize in antique and estate jewelry, with an emphasis on treasured engagement rings. You'll find Georgian, Victorian, Edwardian, art deco, art nouveau and retro pieces. The Doyles also show their own design collection. This is a great source for men's vintage cuff links and rings.

HERNANDEZ JEWELRY

1427 Ave of the Americas (bet 58th and 59th St)
Mon-Sat: 10-8; Sun: 10-5

212/265-4071

I highly recommend this jewelry store. You'll find a selection of great watches and Italian jewelry in 14K and 18K gold. Carlos is a superb craftsman and works wonders with repairs, including watches. This is a great place to shop for that special gift for someone.

JENNIFER MILLER JEWELRY

972 Lexington Ave (bet 70th and 71st St)
Mon-Sat: 10:30-6; Sun: noon-5

212/734-8199
jennifermillerjewelry.com

Jennifer Miller is the ultimate jewelry store, and therefore a great place to build on your jewelry wardrobe! Miller specializes in contemporary, classic and estate jewelry, both fine and faux in a wide range of prices. The varied selection changes daily; a wide choice of classically-chic earrings, necklaces, bracelets, rings and watches in yellow or white gold, with man-made or genuine stones. Handbags, shoes and decorative home items round out the mix.

PIPPIN VINTAGE JEWELRY

112 W 17th St (bet Ave of the Americas and Seventh Ave)
Mon-Sat: 11-7; Sun: noon-6

212/505-5159
pippinvintage.com

Get ready for a treasure hunt! At Pippin Vintage Jewelry value-priced rhinestone, Bakelite, crystal, silver, plastic and ceramic vintage baubles are neatly spread out, begging to be tried on. The colorful pieces include such

SOURCES FOR LUMBER

Remodelers and builders, take note! For lumber, plywood, Masonite, bricks, cork, paint and more, try these stores:

Chinatown Lumber (140 East Broadway, 212/608-2055)

Metropolitan Lumber and Hardware (175 Spring St, 212/966-3466)

Prince Lumber (404 W 15th St, 212/777-1150)

---

names as Sarah Coventry, Coro and Trifari. But there's more! A display case full of fine jewelry holds baubles of gold, platinum, diamonds and other genuine stones, from the Victorian age to the 1980s. Continue through the shop to **Pippin Vintage Home** (212/206-0008), where you'll find fine vintage furniture and home furnishings.

LADDERS

PUTNAM ROLLING LADDER COMPANY

32 Howard St (bet Lafayette St and Broadway) 212/226-5147
Mon-Fri: 8:30-4 putnamrollingladder.com

This is certainly an esoteric shop! And why, you might ask, would anyone in New York need those magnificent rolling ladders traditionally used in formal libraries? Could there possibly be enough business to keep a place like this "rolling" since 1905? The answer is that clever New Yorkers turn to Putnam to improve access to their lofts (especially sleeping lofts) and display shelves. Ladders come in 11 woods and 15 hardware finishes and range from rolling ladders (custom made, if necessary) to folding library ladders. The company also makes a variety of stools.

LIGHTING FIXTURES AND ACCESSORIES

CITY KNICKERBOCKER

665 Eleventh Ave (at 48th St), 2nd floor 212/586-3939
Mon-Fri: 8:30-5 cityknickerbocker.com

The fourth generation of the Liroff family operates this outfit, which has been in business since 1906. These folks are reliable when it comes to all aspects of lighting, including quality antique reproductions, glassware and first-rate repairs and restoration. The large sales inventory includes contemporary art-glass lamps; table and floor lamps; ceiling and wall fixtures and shades and globes in a multitude of colors, shapes and sizes from top manufacturers.

JUST BULBS

220 E 60th St (bet Second and Third Ave) 212/888-5707
Mon-Sat: 10-7; Sun: noon-6 justbulbsnyc.com

Just Bulbs stocks almost 25,000 types of bulbs, including some that can be found nowhere else. Incandescent, halogen, fluorescent, mercury, sodium and metal halide — you'll find it all. The shop looks like an oversized dressing-room mirror. Everywhere you turn, bulbs are connected to switches that can be flicked on and off. Besides standard sizes, there are light bulbs for use in old fixtures. They will also make repairs and "refresh" light fixtures, changing bulbs and cleaning fixtures at your home or office.

JUST SHADES

21 Spring St (at Elizabeth St)   212/966-2757
Tues-Fri: 9:30-6 (Thurs till 8); Sat: 9:30-5; Sun: 11-5   justshadesny.com

Just Shades has specialized in custom and ready-made lampshades for over 40 years. They are experts at matching shades to lamps and willingly share their knowledge with retail customers. They have lampshades of silk, hide, parchment, mica and other intriguing materials. You'll also find a large selection of finials. No job, residential or commercial, is too large or small for their full attention.

LAMPWORKS

630 Ninth Ave (bet 44th and 45th St), Suite 215   212/750-1500
Mon-Fri: 9-5   lampworksinc.com

Lampworks' specialty is custom fabrication of lighting and shades. The showroom offers an extensive selection of table lamps, floor lamps, sconces, chandeliers, exterior fixtures and stock shades; over 45 lines are represented. Beautiful antique lighting, all restored and rewired, is definitely worth a look.

LIGHTING BY GREGORY

158 Bowery (bet Delancey and Broome St)   212/226-1276
Mon-Fri: 8:30-6; Sat, Sun: 10-6   lightingbygregory.com

Celebrities, museums and film companies are among the satisfied customers at this full-service designer lighting store. It is the largest contemporary and traditional lighting and ceiling-fan distributor in America. They are major dealers of Lightolier, Tech Lighting, Monte Carlo, Artemide and Murray Feiss. They are packed with a fantastic selection of lamps, sconces, ceiling lights and outdoor lighting, and are also experts in track lighting.

LIGHTING PLUS

680 Broadway (bet Great Jones and Bond St)   212/979-2000
Mon-Sat: 10-6:30; Sun: 11-6:30   lpdlightingplus.com

Lighting Plus is a very handy neighborhood lighting store, featuring floor and table lamps, all manner of bulbs and extension cords. There are dimmers, sockets, electrical cord by the yard, party lights, work lights and more. Prices and service are good, but the selection is even better.

SCHOOLHOUSE ELECTRIC

27 Vestry St (at Hudson St)   212/226-6113
Tues-Sat: 10:30-6   schoolhouseelectric.com

At Schoolhouse Electric you'll find period lighting fixtures and glass shades, all hand-blown in authentic antique molds. They replicate more than a hundred light fixtures from the early 1900s to the late 1940s. Handcrafted solid brass lighting fixtures, historically accurate and made to order in many finishes, are also available. The store has branched out to offer kitchen, bed and bath items and furniture and home accessories, some with period styling.

LUGGAGE AND OTHER LEATHER GOODS

DEAN LEATHER

822 Third Ave (at 50th St)   212/583-0461
Mon-Sati: 9-7:30; Sun: 9-6   Facebook

If it is made of leather, you can probably find it at Dean Leather: briefcases, wallets, luggage, watchbands and gift items. The prices are right on many top names like Hartmann, Swiss Army, Samsonite, Briggs & Riley, Bosca, Tumi and more.

LEXINGTON LUGGAGE

793 Lexington Ave (bet 61st and 62nd St)   212/223-0698
Mon-Sat: 9-6; Sun: 11-5   lexingtonluggage.com

Stop here if you are in the market for luggage. Lexington Luggage has been family-owned and -operated since 1978. They carry nearly every major brand: Samsonite, Delsey, Travelon, American Tourister, Kipling, Rimowa and Briggs & Riley — at deep discounts. You'll also find attaché cases and backpacks. Most luggage and handbag repairs can be done the same day. Other pluses: free same-day delivery, free monograms and friendly personnel.

T. ANTHONY

445 Park Ave (at 56th St)   212/750-9797
Mon-Fri: 9:30-6; Sat: 10-6   tanthony.com

T. Anthony handles luxurious, handcrafted luggage of distinction. Anything purchased here will stand out in a crowd. Luggage ranges from small overnight bags to massive steamer trunks. Their briefcases, jewelry boxes, desk sets, albums, key cases and wallets make terrific gifts, individually or in matched sets. While you won't find discount prices, T. Anthony's high quality and courteous service are established New York traditions. Engraving and repair service on their products are available.

MAGIC

ENCHANTMENTS

424 E 9th St (bet First Ave and Ave A)   212/228-4394
Wed-Mon: 1-9   enchantmentsincnyc.com

Enchantments claims to be the largest and oldest occult store in the city, and one best not argue with them! There is a great selection of essential and fragrance oils, lotions, potions, herbs, resins and incense; many of these items are custom-blended. Hundreds of magical formulas can be mixed upon request. Ask for guidance when purchasing magical candles, talismans and charms with a desired outcome in mind.

TANNEN'S MAGIC

45 W 34th St (bet Fifth Ave and Ave of the Americas), Suite 608 212/929-4500
Mon-Fri: 11-6; Sat, Sun: 10-4   tannens.com

Stocking more than 8,000 magic tricks, books and DVDs, Tannen is one of the world's largest suppliers of magicians' items. It has been patronized by the most accomplished magicians, as well as novices, since 1925. The floor demonstrators are some of the best in the business — always friendly, helpful and eager to share their knowledge of "effects." Tannen's Magic Camp is for budding magicians age 12 to 20, spawning some of today's greatest working magicians. Check the website for upcoming workshops and lectures by some of the best in the magic field.

MEMORABILIA

FIRESTORE

17 Greenwich Ave (bet Christopher and 10th St)   212/226-3142
Mon-Thurs: 11-7; Fri, Sat: 11-8; Sun: noon-6   nyfirestore.com

Firefighters, police and families and fans of these first responders can find everything under the sun relating to them. Patches, pins, T-shirts, sweatshirts, turnout coats, caps, work shirts, FDNY memorial shirts, firefighter jackets, jewelry, calendars and toys are available at this fascinating shop! EMS, EMT and NYC items, too!

GOTTA HAVE IT!

153 E 57th St (bet Lexington and Third Ave)   212/750-7900
Mon-Fri: 10:30-6; Sat: 11-5 (call ahead on Sat)   gottahaveit.com

Do you have a favorite sports star, Hollywood personality, musical entertainer or political figure? Since 1994, Gotta Have It! has been a pop-culture time capsule. The shop features original and unique top-quality collectibles in these categories. There are signed photos, musical instruments, baseball bats, used sports uniforms, trophies, documents and movie props. All items are fully authenticated and guaranteed.

NBC EXPERIENCE STORE

30 Rockefeller Plaza (49th St bet Fifth Ave and Ave of the Americas)
212/664-3700

At press time, the NBC Experience Store is closed for extensive upgrades and restorations at 30 Rock; projected opening date is mid-2015. When it reopens the shop will stock games, DVDs, T-shirts, mugs, key chains and other merchandise with the NBC logo or images from popular TV shows such as *Saturday Night Live*, *The Meredith Viera Show* and *The Tonight Show*, all filmed at this location. The behind-the-scenes NBC studio tours will also resume when the redesign is complete; check for updates online at nbcstudiotour.com.

24-HOUR HARDWARE STORE

You never know what time of day a plumbing or electrical emergency will arise, and for do-it-yourselfers, **Nuthouse Hardware** (202 E 29th St, 212/545-1447) is open all hours. This family-owned neighborhood hardware store offers thousands of items for plumbing, electrical and cleaning needs. If needed, they also offer installation.

MOVIES

VIDEOROOM

1403 Third Ave (bet 79th and 80th St)   212/879-5333
Mon-Thurs: 10-10; Fri, Sat: 10 a.m.-11 p.m.; Sun: noon-10   videoroom.net

As the largest and oldest independent video store in New York City, VideoRoom stocks over 12,000 VHS and DVD titles. They specialize in foreign, classic and hard-to-find films, but there is also an in-depth selection of new releases. The highly competent staff are students of film, motivating them to help inquiring customers. Gold and platinum memberships offer such privileges as advance reservations, free delivery and pick up.

MUSEUM AND LIBRARY SHOPS

For one-of-a-kind gifts that are classy, artistic and well-made, I especially recommend shopping in the following unique and large museums. In most cases, at least some of the wares relate directly to current and past exhibits or the museum's permanent collection. Even at museums that charge an admission fee, you need not pay if you just want to shop. However, you might save money with a museum membership, which generally offers store discounts.

AMERICAN FOLK ART MUSEUM

2 Lincoln Square (Columbus Ave at 66th St)   646/783-5985
Tues-Sat: 11:30-7; Sun: 11:30-6   folkartmuseum.org

Located across from Lincoln Center, the American Folk Art Museum runs an excellent gift shop. Stock includes items such as stationery, jewelry, toys, books and media, clothing and accessories and home decor. Most items are handcrafted in folk tradition. This is a great source for finding quirky and original gifts in a wide range of prices.

AMERICAN MUSEUM OF NATURAL HISTORY

Central Park W at 79th St   212/769-5100
Daily: 10-5:30   amnh.org

This museum's amazing three-level store features a wide selection of unusual merchandise related to the natural world, diverse cultures, exploration and discovery. There is the Space Shop, with items like meteorite specimens, gems, books, movies and iconic museum apparel and memorabilia; the Science Shop, with science kits, toys and games, posters and more; the Dinosaur Shop, which features dinosaur-themed games, puzzles, fossil replicas and models, books, posters and apparel and the Butterfly Shop with all things butterfly. Smaller satellite shops featuring products related to special exhibitions are located near each exhibition's exit doors. Note that the shop closes 15 minutes before the museum.

ASIASTORE

725 Park Ave (at 70th St)   212/327-9217
Tues-Sun: 11-6 (Fri till 9)   asiasociety.org

The fabulous AsiaStore at the Asia Society and Museum showcases the best in Asian design and literature. Offerings include hundreds of unique items from Asia and Asian-American artists: jewelry, apparel and accessories, home accents, stationery, music and gifts. A selection of books includes scores of titles on Asian art, culture, politics, religion and philosophy.

EL MUSEO DEL BARRIO

1230 Fifth Ave (at 104th St)   212/660-7191
Wed-Sat: 11-6   elmuseo.org

La Tienda is the charming museum gift shop at El Museo del Barrio. It is a great source for unique jewelry and handicrafts; art from Latin America, the Caribbean and local artists; children's books in Spanish and English and books for adults about the history, art and culture of Latin America, the Caribbean and immigrants from these regions.

FRICK COLLECTION

1 E 70th St (at Fifth Ave)   212/547-6848
Tues-Sat: 10-5:45; Sun: 11-4:45   frick.org

Making the most of its small space, the Frick's gift shop concentrates on exquisite cards, stationery, prints, posters and art books. You will also find a small collection of paperweights, scarves and other quality museum-inspired gifts. Note that the shop closes 15 minutes before the museum.

INTERNATIONAL CENTER OF PHOTOGRAPHY

212/857-0000
icp.org

The museum and store are moving downtown to an exciting new space on the Bowery and will reopen late 2015. At our press time, details were still being finalized; check the website for updates about the relocation. Keep this store in mind if you are shopping for a photography buff.

THE JEWISH MUSEUM

1109 Fifth Ave (at 92nd St)   212/423-3211
Sun-Fri: 11-5:45 (Thurs till 8)   thejewishmuseum.org

Cooper Shop, a relatively large store located within the museum, is an excellent source for Jewish literature, decorative art and Judaica. Merchandise reflects the current exhibitions as well as the permanent collections; cards and coffee-table books; gifts for men and women, including jewelry and numerous toys and children's books. Located next door is the Jewish Museum's design shop, **Celebrations** (1 E 92nd St, 212/423-3260). It is worth a look if you're interested in finely-crafted ceremonial objects; its selection of menorahs is among the classiest in the city.

MET OPERA SHOP

Metropolitan Opera House
Lincoln Center (Columbus Ave at 65th St)   212/580-4090
Mon-Sat: 10 a.m. to half an hour after last intermission or 8 p.m. if there is no
performance; Sun: noon-6   metoperashop.org

Opera lovers will be in heaven at the Metropolitan Opera Shop. In addition to more than a hundred operas and ballet on CD and DVD, you'll find opera glasses, music boxes, calendars, books, posters, opera-inspired clothing and jewelry and wall art. New collectibles include framed autographs and photos from stars of the Met.

THE METROPOLITAN MUSEUM OF ART

1000 Fifth Ave (bet 80th and 84th St)	212/570-3894
Rockefeller Center	
15 W 49th St (bet Fifth Ave and Ave of the Americas)	212/332-1360
The Cloisters	
799 Fort Washington Ave (Fort Tryon Park)	212/650-2277
Hours vary by store	store.metmuseum.org

The two-floor store inside the Metropolitan Museum of Art is the grandfather of all museum gift shops. It specializes in reproductions of paintings and other pieces in The Met's incredible collection, as well as from museum collections around the world. You can find jewelry; ties, scarves and other clothing; vases, porcelain, rugs and more home items; prints, posters and wall decor; cards, stationery and journals; statues and scores of other beautiful gift items. They also carry books relating to special exhibits, as well as umbrellas, tote bags and other items with the Metropolitan name on them. Prices are reasonable and the salespeople are generally patient and helpful. Satellite shops are located at JFK airport (Terminals 4 and 8), as well as the remote Manhattan locations listed above. Both the main Met store (2nd floor) and the satellite shop in Rockefeller Center have particularly good children's sections.

MOMA DESIGN AND BOOK STORE

11 W 53rd St (bet Fifth Ave and Ave of the Americas)	212/708-9700

MOMA DESIGN STORE/MUJI AT MOMA

44 W 53rd St (bet Fifth Ave and Ave of the Americas)	212/767-1050
Daily: 9:30-6:30 (Fri till 9)	

MOMA DESIGN STORE, SOHO/MUJI AT MOMA

81 Spring St (at Crosby St)	646/613-1367
Mon-Sat: 10-8; Sun: 11-7	momastore.org

These magnificent stores are dedicated to what the curators consider the very best in modern design. Design objects and gifts include art reproductions, furniture, textiles, vases, silverware, frames, watches and lamps, along with unique toys and books for children. An extensive collection of architectural and design books lists more than 2,000 titles. These items are not cheap, but the selection is truly exceptional.

NATIONAL MUSEUM OF THE AMERICAN INDIAN

1 Bowling Green (foot of Broadway)	212/514-3767
Daily: 10-5 (Thurs till 8)	nmai.si.edu

Just like everything else about the National Museum of the American Indian, the Gallery Store is a classy operation. There is a wide selection of beautiful weavings, pottery, jewelry and other handicrafts by skilled Native artisans. A second-level museum shop offers children's books, DVDs, toys and craft kits, along with T-shirts and cards. Because the museum is part of the Smithsonian Institution, associate members receive a discount on every purchase.

NEUE GALERIE BOOK STORE AND DESIGN SHOP

1048 Fifth Ave (at 86th St)   212/628-6200, ext. 2
Wed-Mon: 11-6   neuegalerie.org

The Neue Galerie Book Store is clearly the source for books on fine art, architecture and decorative arts in Germany, Austria and Central European cultures in the 19th and 20th centuries. The Design Shop has a smart selection of beautiful high-end jewelry, lighting, tableware, textiles and other decorative arts based on modern German and Austrian designers like Biedermeier. Additionally, the selection includes pieces by renowned designers inspired by museum objects.

NEW YORK PUBLIC LIBRARY SHOP

476 Fifth Ave (bet 41st and 42nd St), Room 116   212/930-0641
Mon-Sat: 10-6; Sun: 1-5   nypl.org

This is the perfect gift shop for book lovers. Located just off the main lobby of the New York Public Library's main branch, it features a high-quality selection of unusual merchandise. You'll find books about New York and the library's history, catalogs of past library shows, fine stationery and writing tools, bookends, jewelry and whimsical ties, socks, T-shirts and totes. There are children's puzzles and books with themed dolls and puppets. The staff is particularly pleasant and helpful.

NEW YORK TRANSIT MUSEUM STORE

Grand Central Terminal (42nd St at Vanderbilt Ave), Shuttle Passage
                                                                         212/878-0106
Mon-Fri: 8-8; Sat: 10-8; Sun: 10-7   nytransitmuseumstore.com

Train and subway buffs love this little shop and gallery. Items for sale include books about Grand Central Terminal, clever T-shirts, replicas of trains and old station signs, banks for children in the shape of city buses, jewelry made from old tokens, token collections and mosaic and photo tiles. Bus and subway maps, as well as other MTA information, are also available. Note that this shop is a branch of the much larger main store at the New York Transit Museum in Brooklyn Heights (Boerum Pl at Schermerhorn St, 718/694-1600).

PICKMAN MUSEUM SHOP OF THE MUSEUM OF JEWISH HERITAGE

36 Battery Pl (in Battery Park City)   646/437-4213
Sun-Thurs: 10-5:45 (Wed till 8); Fri: 10-3 (till 8 April through Oct)   mjhnyc.org

This shop is a fitting companion to the museum in its celebration of Jewish art, crafts and culture. The selection is diverse, and many items are related to the museum's collection. Everything is high quality; some is quite unusual. One section includes carefully chosen books and gifts for children of various ages. Elegant jewelry, DVDs, music, holiday items and Judaica are also shown; prices are extremely good. Note that the store and the museum are closed on all major Jewish holidays.

THE SHOP AT SCANDINAVIA HOUSE: THE NORDIC CENTER IN AMERICA

58 Park Ave (at 38th St)   212/847-9737
Mon-Sat: 11-7; Sun: 11-5   scandinaviahouse.org

This lifestyle shop is nestled in Scandinavia House: the Nordic Center in America. It showcases leading modern designers alongside the legends of Nordic culture. Luxurious home-design items, tableware, art glass, textiles, handbags, jewelry and accessories range from trendy to classic.

SOLOMON R. GUGGENHEIM MUSEUM STORE

1071 Fifth Ave (at 89th St)   212/423-3615
Sun-Wed, Fri: 9:30-6: 15; Thurs: 11-6; Sat: 9:30-8:30   guggenheimstore.org

Although much for sale here is typical gift shop fare (including scarves, T-shirts, prints and posters, tote bags, note cards and stationery, jewelry and children's toys), the design and craftsmanship are anything but ordinary. If you're looking for an unusual clock, a great wedding present or just the right pair of earrings, try this store. Do be aware, however, that prices are often through the roof. Of course, the store also carries books on modern art and exhibition catalogs. Unlike many other museum stores, this one is actually open before and after the museum itself closes; it is also open on Thursday, when the museum is closed.

THE STORE AT MUSEUM OF ARTS AND DESIGN

2 Columbus Cir (at Eighth Ave)   212/299-7700
Mon-Sat: 10-7 (Thurs, Fri till 9); Sun: 10-6   thestore.madmuseum.org

With its Columbus Circle address, this is one of the most attractive museum stores in town. Craft and design objects by exceptional artisans from around the globe are displayed. Choose from a constantly changing collection of beautifully designed jewelry; wood, glass and metal accessories for the home; blankets and other textiles; women's accessories and more.

THE STUDIO MUSEUM IN HARLEM

144 W 125th St (bet Malcolm X and Adam Clayton Powell, Jr. Blvd)
                                                              212/864-4500, ext. 237
Sun, Wed: noon-6; Thurs: noon-7; Fri: noon-9; Sat: 10-6   studiomuseum.org

Located just inside the museum's entrance, this store sells a wide and generally high-quality selection of jewelry, textiles, crafts, note cards, limited-edition prints and calendars created by African-Americans and artists of African descent. It also carries an unusually broad selection of cookbooks, fiction, biographies, children's books by and about Africans and African-Americans, catalogs of art by artists of African descent, museum logo merchandise plus the usual tourist gift items.

THE UKRAINIAN MUSEUM

222 E 6th St (bet Second and Third Ave)   212/228-0110
Wed-Sun: 11:30-5   ukrainianmuseum.org

Fabulous *pysanka* Ukrainian Easter eggs (premade eggs or kits for do-it-yourselfers) lure customers to this gift shop that honors the cultural heritage of Ukrainians. Art books, exhibition catalogs, music, cards, posters, toys, jewelry, embroidered items and other handicrafts are also waiting to be discovered.

UN BOOKSHOP/UN GIFT SHOP

United Nations Visitor Centre
First Ave at 42nd St   212/963-7680
Mon-Fri: 9-5:30   visit.un.org

The UN Bookshop is located within the new United Nations Visitor Centre. The store carries the latest titles published by the UN and other international publishers, children's books, posters and small souvenirs like UN emblem items (lapel pins, window decals and magnets). Walk over to the UN Gift Shop for traditional handicrafts, gifts, accessories (jewelry and scarves), flags of member nations and NYC souvenirs.

MUSIC

ACADEMY RECORDS & CDS

12 W 18th St (bet Fifth Ave and Ave of the Americas)   212/242-3000
Daily: 11-7   academy-records.com

Academy Records & CDs has Manhattan's largest stock of used, out-of-print and rare classical LPs, CDs and DVDs. They emphasize opera, contemporary classical and early music (through the Baroque period), but jazz and rock can be found as well. Movie genre from classic Hollywood, foreign, silent, documentaries and other movies are available. Academy boasts an international reputation and a knowledgeable staff.

JAZZ RECORD CENTER

236 W 26th St (bet Seventh and Eighth Ave), Room 804   212/675-4480
Mon-Sat: 10-6   jazzrecordcenter.com

Jazz Record Center is run by Fred Cohen, a charming guy who really knows his business. It is the only jazz specialty store in the city. They deal in rare, out-of-print and new jazz records (some blues), CDs, videos, books, posters, photos, concert programs, periodicals, postcards and T-shirts. The store buys collections, fills online orders and offers appraisals. They periodically auction jazz rarities on eBay, too.

SCENTS OF MANHATTAN

Here's a catchy phrase — making scents of New York. And for the first time in fragrance history, a major, full-blown fragrance collection was launched as an homage to a great city. The name of this fragrance collection is **Bond No. 9** (9 Bond St, 212/228-1732; 399 Bleecker St, 212/633-1641; 897 Madison Ave, 212/794-4480 and 863 Washington St, 212/206-9907), which is also the Noho address of its headquarters boutique on Bond Street. The collection of women's and men's perfumes, scented candles and luxury skin-care products restore artistry to perfumery. Every New York neighborhood has a scent of its own and there are new introductions every season.

OTHER MUSIC

15 E 4th St (bet Broadway and Lafayette St) 212/477-8150
Mon-Fri: 11-8 (Thurs, Fri till 9); Sat: noon-8; Sun: noon-7 othermusic.com

Other Music is an independent music store specializing in rare, underground and experimental music. They have an excellent stock of CDs and vinyl and hard-to-find releases; T-shirts and totes emblazoned with the company logo, too. Ask about getting cash or store credit for your used CDs and records. Other Music frequently hosts in-store performances and readings.

> # PIANO ROW
>
> **Faust Harrison Pianos** (207 W 58th St, 212/489-3600) is a prestigious source for the most sought-after brands of pianos (new, used and rebuilt). Additionally, the showroom has a performance area for student recitals and concerts. Fewer shops now make up the famed Piano Row which was once considered the destination for a perfect piano.

WESTSIDER RECORDS

233 W 72nd St (at Broadway)
212/874-1588
Mon-Thurs: 11-7; Fri, Sat: 11-9; Sun: noon-6 westsiderbooks.com

Westsider remains one of the few stores specializing in rare and out-of-print LPs, with 30,000 in stock. CDs have been added to the inventory and you'll also find printed music, scores and books on the performing arts. There are all genres: classical, jazz, rock, pop, blues, country, folk and spoken word. Turntables, amps and speakers (new and used) are sold as well. A short walk away is their sister store, **Westsider Rare & Used Books** (2246 Broadway, 212/362-0706). These places buy, sell and trade records and books, respectively.

MUSICAL INSTRUMENTS

THE GUITAR SALON

212/675-3236
By appointment theguitarsalon.com

The Guitar Salon is known for its outstanding collection of classical and flamenco guitars. Beverly Maher's unique operation is located in an historic brownstone in Greenwich Village. She is an expert in 19th- and 20th-century vintage instruments and offers beautiful, handmade classical and flamenco guitars for students, professionals and collectors. Appraisals are available, and lessons with Virginia Luque can be arranged in the salon or via Skype for all styles of guitars. Celebrity customers who have shopped here include Keith Richards, Paul Simon and the Rolling Stones!

SAM ASH

333 W 34th St (bet Eighth and Ninth Ave) 212/719-22991
Mon-Sat: 10-8; Sun: 11-7 samashmusic.com

Sam Ash offers a full selection of quality musical instruments — guitars, drums, keyboards and wind and string instruments for purchase or rent. In addition, there's recording equipment and software, lighting, sheet music, music books, amplifiers, DJ gear and more. Sam Ash has just about anything that a band, orchestra or solo musician might need. Services include lessons and repairs.

PETS AND ACCESSORIES

BARKING ZOO

172 Ninth Ave (bet 20th and 21st St)   212/255-0658
Mon-Fri: 11-8; Sat: 10-6; Sun: noon-5   barkingzoo.com

Barking Zoo offers quality items for your favorite canine. They stock plenty of healthy, organic food options for dogs (and cats); also toys, beds, blankets, clothes, bowls and other accessories for your barking family member. Read their in-store and online posts for valuable information on the care of dogs and cats and a list of dog runs.

DOGGYSTYLE, NYC

46 University Pl (bet 9th and 10th St)   212/228-5824
Mon-Wed: 10-7; Thurs-Sat: 10-8; Sun: 11-6   doggystylenyc.com

Shop here for practical items for your pet at sensible prices. DoggyStyle features boutique-quality collars, leashes, coats, messenger bags and feeding bowls, plus handy products for traveling with a pet. Dog and cat grooming is available downstairs.

LE PETIT PUPPY

18 Christopher St (bet Waverly Pl and Gay St)   212/727-8111
Mon-Sat: 10:30-8; Sun: 10:30-7   Facebook

This upscale puppy boutique displays some of its small breeds in the storefront "puppy window."   Choose from miniature, toy and teacup puppies: dachshunds, poodles, Chihuahuas, French Bulldogs and Yorkshire Terriers. Adoptions include pet health guarantees and ongoing hotline support. Everything needed to care for and pamper a new puppy is here as well: food and treats, apparel, accessories and beds; services include grooming (cats, too) and day care.

PACIFIC AQUARIUM & PET

46 Delancey St (bet Forsyth and Eldridge St)   212/995-5895
Daily: 10-7   pacificnyc.com

Exotic tropical fish are their specialty! Pacific Aquarium & Pet also carries all types of freshwater and saltwater fish, aquatic plants, dozens of species of fancy goldfish and every kind of aquarium and related supply you could imagine. Custom-made tanks (up to 500 gallons) are designed, built and installed in homes, businesses and restaurants. Tank maintenance packages are available.

PHOTOGRAPHIC EQUIPMENT AND SUPPLIES

ADORAMA CAMERA

42 W 18th St (bet Fifth Ave and Ave of the Americas)   212/741-0063
Mon-Thurs: 9-8; Fri: 9-2; Sun: 9:30-5   adorama.com

Adorama carries a huge stock of new and used photographic, video and imaging equipment and supplies for amateurs to pros. They also showcase astronomy equipment, iPods and cell phones, stockroom accessories, frames, albums and video paraphernalia, all sold at discount. Seminars for all skill levels are frequently offered, and they have an array of rental equipment.

B&H PHOTO VIDEO PRO AUDIO

420 Ninth Ave (at 34th St)   212/444-6615
Mon-Thurs: 9-7; Fri: 9-2; Sun: 10-6   bhphotovideo.com

B&H is a superstore in more ways than one! You'll find departments for photo, video and pro audio, as well as a wide array of home entertainment equipment, computers and accessories. The store has been in operation since 1974 and is staffed by informed personnel. Inventory levels are high (about 235,000 products), prices are reasonable and hands-on demo areas make browsing easy. Trade-ins are considered; quality used equipment is sometimes available.

WILLOUGHBY'S

298 Fifth Ave (at 31st St)   212/564-1600
Mon-Fri: 9:30-7; Sat: 9-6; Sun: 10:30-6:30   willoughbys.com

As New York's oldest camera emporium (started in 1898), Willoughby's has a huge stock, an extensive clientele list and a solid reputation. Cameras and photo equipment for every budget and skill level fill the shelves, plus camcorders, binoculars, telescopes and other high-tech equipment. They service cameras, supply photographic equipment and recycle used items; used cameras are bought and sold.

PICTURES, POSTERS AND PRINTS

JERRY OHLINGER'S MOVIE MATERIALS STORE

216 W 30th St (bet Seventh and Eighth Ave), 2nd floor   212/989-0869
Fri: 11-6; Mon-Thurs: by appointment   moviematerials.com

A perfect stop for movie buffs! Jerry Ohlinger stocks a huge selection of movie posters (current, classic and rare) and photos from film and TV. Lobby cards and press books are also part of the collection. Let Jerry know if you are looking for something specific as he will gladly research these items.

OLD PRINT SHOP

150 Lexington Ave (bet 29th and 30th St)   212/683-3950
Tues-Fri: 9-5; Sat: 9-4 (closed Sat in summer)   oldprintshop.com

Kenneth M. Newman specializes in Americana, including original prints, town views, Currier & Ives prints, atlases and original maps that reflect America's yesteryear. The shop exudes old-fashioned charm and the impression of timelessness. Many of the nostalgic pictures that have adorned calendars and stationery were copies of prints found here. Amateur and professional historians have a field day in this shop. Newman also does correct period framing and also purchases estate and single items.

PHILIP WILLIAMS POSTERS

122 Chambers St (bet Church St and West Broadway)   212/513-0313
Mon-Sat: 10-7   postermuseum.com

This is perhaps the largest vintage poster gallery in the world, with over

100,000 unique posters, from 1870 to the present. Philip Williams features prints in a variety of categories, including travel, food, dance, trains, sports, magic, political and films; also books about posters. The complete inventory of original artifacts includes vintage maps. Inquire about custom framing and poster restoration.

PHYLLIS LUCAS GALLERY — OLD PRINT CENTER

235 E 60th St (bet Second and Third Ave)   212/755-1516
Mon-Fri: 10-5; Sat: 2-5; Sun: by appointment   phyllislucasgallery.com

Inside Phyllis Lucas Gallery — Old Print Center is a treasure trove of antiquarian prints, antique maps and illustrations. Modern engravings, photographs, original paintings and a large selection of New York City scenes are displayed. The Gallery is known for its superior custom framing services and print, painting and frame restoration.

TRITON GALLERY

630 Ninth Ave (at 44th St), Suite 808   212/765-2472
Mon-Fri: 10-6   tritongallery.com

No one presents theatrical art and posters like Triton. Posters of current Broadway and Off-Broadway shows join a stock of rare and highly-collectible show posters. Posters range in size, and as you would expect, are priced according to rarity, age and demand. Window cards for all shows are archived for historical preservation. Triton also has wood and metal poster frames and does custom framing.

RUBBER GOODS

CANAL RUBBER SUPPLY COMPANY

329 Canal St (at Greene St)   212/226-7339
Mon-Fri: 9-4:45; Sat: 9-3:45   canalrubber.com

This wholesale-retail industrial foam and rubber operation has occupied the same location since 1954. There are foam bolsters and cushions and foam

TIPS TO NEGOTIATING THE BEST PRICE

A few tips to help with negotiating the best possible price:

■ **Pay in cash**: Most stores pay the credit-card company for every card transaction; offer to pay cash in exchange for a discount.

■ **Timing**: When you are buying an item that is likely on a commission, go at the end of the quarter when salespeople are scrambling to meet their goals. Best to haggle during slower times.

■ **Draw out the process**: The more time invested, the more likely they will work with you. Before sealing the deal, don't be afraid to ask for a freebie (like a tie or scarf) when making a large purchase.

■ **Pick your battles**: Some smaller-priced items may not be worth the effort.

by the sheet; hydraulic, vacuum and ventilation hoses; floor matting, rubber tiles and stair treads and rubber tubing and sheet-rubber products. Ask about their foam specialty applications if you have a special project in mind.

SAFES

EMPIRE SAFE

6 E 39th St (bet Fifth and Madison Ave)   212/684-2255
Mon-Fri: 9-5 or by appointment   empiresafe.com

Empire shows the city's largest and most complete selection of high-security safes and vault rooms for residences and businesses. They also offer specialized burglary-protection safes with jewelry and watch drawers. Whether you want to protect jewelry and valuables at home or documents in an office building, you can rely on these folks. Delivery and installation are available.

TRAUM SAFE

946 Madison Ave (at 74th St)   212/452-2565
Mon-Sat: 10-6   traumsafe.com

Protect and store your special collection in a luxury vault designed and constructed by Traum Safe. Safes come in contemporary or classic styles, bold or subdued and include interior lighting and electronic locks. From consultation to installation, Traum can analyze your needs and recommend the right size and finish to match your decor. There is even a safe with custom-made drawers to wind your watches!

SECURITY EQUIPMENT

SPY TEC

252 W 38th St (bet Seventh and Eighth Ave), 6th floor   212/957-7400
Mon-Fri: 9:30-6:30   spytecinc.com

If you're looking for high-quality security or surveillance equipment, then look no further than Spy Tec. This outfit offers cell phone recon, video surveillance and countersurveillance items, network cameras, digital and analog recorders, nanny cams, wireless camera detection and location, metal detectors, GPS trackers, infrared sensors and more. All items are available for residential or commercial installation and Spy Tec's trained personnel will discreetly take care of any need.

SIGNS

LET THERE BE NEON

38 White St (bet Broadway and Church St)   212/226-4883
Mon-Fri: 9-5   lettherebeneon.com

Flashing neon signs have become the ultimate urban cliché, but here they are rendered as fine art. Let There Be Neon operates as a gallery with a variety of sizes, shapes, functions and designs to entice the browser. Almost all their sales are custom pieces; some vintage and others stock. Usually a rough sketch is enough for them to create a literal or abstract neon sculpture. You can view their current projects when you visit.

SILVER

JEAN'S SILVERSMITHS

16 W 45th St (at Fifth Ave)   212/575-0723
Mon-Fri: 9-4:45   jeanssilversmiths.com

Want to replace a fork that went down the disposal? Proceed directly to
Jean's Silversmiths, where you will find more than 2,000 discontinued, obsolete
and current flatware patterns. Items also include sterling hollowware, fine
jewelry and giftware. A card catalog keeps track of items — new, estate and
used — from mass market to high end. Unusual pieces include duck shears,
marrow scoops and oyster ladles. Jean's will restore, engrave and polish your
prized silver for you.

TIFFANY & CO.

727 Fifth Ave (at 57th St)   212/755-8000
Mon-Sat: 10-7; Sun: noon-6
97 Greene St (bet Prince and Spring St)   212/226-6136
Mon-Sat: 11-7 (Thurs till 8); Sun: 11-6
37 Wall St (bet William and Broad St)   212/514-8015
Mon-Fri: 10-7; Sat: 11-5; Sun: noon-5   tiffany.com

The Tiffany legacy began in 1837 as a small "fancy goods" store. With the
growing reputation of Tiffany as the "King of Diamonds," it soon became a
magnet for the rich and famous. Yes, there really is a Tiffany diamond; a yellow
diamond that can be viewed on the first floor of the flagship Fifth Avenue
location. That floor also houses the watch and jewelry departments. The stores
are famous for exquisite diamonds, but they carry much more: silver jewelry,
sterling silver items, bar accessories, small leather goods, fragrances, china,
crystal, glassware, flatware and gift items. The real surprise is that Tiffany carries
an excellent selection of reasonably-priced items. Many are emblazoned with
the Tiffany name and wrapped in the signature blue box. Tourists and residents
alike enjoy walking by the beautiful displays in the store's magical windows.

SPORTING GOODS

BICYCLES AND ACCESSORIES

BICYCLE HABITAT

244 and 250 Lafayette St (bet Spring and Prince St) 212/431-3315
Mon-Sat: 10-7 (Thurs, Fri till 8); Sun: 10-6
228 Seventh Ave (bet 23rd and 24th St)   212/206-6949
Mon-Sat: 11-8 (Sat till 7); Sun: 11-6   bicyclehabitat.com

These customer-oriented folks are *geared* toward cycling buffs and they
really want to get more people interested in biking! There's something for
everyone at Bicycle Habitat — tricycles for the little ones, urban commuter
bikes, very expensive racing bikes and all the accessories for riding, transporting
and storing bikes. If you don't find what you want, they will special order it
or have a bike custom-built to your specifications. Attend one of their bike
maintenance classes, including one on roadside repairs. Information on group
rides is posted on their website.

BICYCLE RENAISSANCE

430 Columbus Ave (at 81st St)   212/724-2350
Mon-Fri: 10:30-7; Sat, Sun: 10-6   bicyclerenaissance.com

Biking is a way of life at Bicycle Renaissance. They carry commuter, road, racing, mountain and kids' bikes by Cannondale, Felt, Kuota, Jamis and Specialized, as well as custom frames for Guru and Calfee Design. Services include custom-built bikes and bicycle repair; mechanics aim for same-day service on all makes and models. Prices are on par with so-called discount shops.

CITY BICYCLES

315 W 38th St (bet Eighth and Ninth Ave)   212/563-3373
Mon-Fri: 9-6:30; Sat: 10-5   citybicyclesnyc.com

City Bicycles carry a huge selection of bicycles and also design and construct custom bikes for the ultimate ride. They have commuter, road, mountain and BMX models from manufacturers such as Bianchi, Schwinn, Jamis, Haro and Specialized. The informed staff will help you decide which kind of bike is best for your needs — classic, suspension or hybrid. See them for bike rentals and repairs.

BILLIARDS

BLATT BILLIARDS

330 W 38th St (bet Eighth and Ninth Ave)   212/674-8855
Mon-Fri: 8-6:30; Sat: 10-5   blattbilliards.com

Everything for billiards is on display at Blatt Billiards. You'll see some 65 pool tables, including antique ones made by well-known Brunswick. Skilled craftsmen design, carve, build and polish each new table in the manufacturing shop now located in Wood Ridge, New Jersey; the variety shown is amazing. A large selection of pool cues from the finest makers and beautiful museum-quality lighting fixtures are at the ready for your game room.

EXERCISE EQUIPMENT

GYM SOURCE

40 E 52nd St (bet Park and Madison Ave)   212/688-4222
Mon-Fri: 9-7; Sat: 10-6; Sun: noon-5   gymsource.com

As the largest exercise equipment dealer in the Northeast, Gym Source carries new and pre-owned treadmills, ellipticals, exercise bikes, steppers, home gyms, free weights, rowers and fitness gear. Top brands are available at good prices, and Gym Source's skilled technicians provide competent servicing. They also rent and deliver equipment.

FISHING

CAPITOL FISHING TACKLE COMPANY

132 W 36th St (bet Seventh Ave and Broadway)   212/929-6132
Mon, Tues: 10-6; Wed-Fri: 10-7; Sat: 10-5   capitolfishing.com

Right in the heart of Manhattan, anglers will find the store of their dreams! Established in 1897, Capitol Fishing is the oldest surviving fishing-tackle store in the U.S. For rods, reels, tackle and accessories, these folks carry a full line of fishing gear from names like Penn, Shimano, Newell, Power Pro and Avet.

URBAN ANGLER

381 Fifth Ave (bet 35th and 36th St)   212/689-6400
Mon-Fri: 10-6 (Wed till 7); Sat: 10-5   urbanangler.com

Urban Angler is your Manhattan source for anything that's fly-fishing. You'll find fly-fishing tackle, high-end spin and surf tackle and travel clothing for beginners and avid fishers. Manufacturers include Sage, Simms, Tibor, Hatch, Patagonia and more. Sign up for casting and fly-tying lessons and then have these folks organize your next fishing trip, anywhere you want to go.

GENERAL

EASTERN MOUNTAIN SPORTS (EMS)

530 Broadway (bet Prince and Spring St)   212/966-8730
Mon-Fri: 10-9:30; Sat: 10-9; Sun: 10-8
2152 Broadway (bet 75th and 76th St)   212/873-4001
Mon-Sat: 10-9; Sun: 10-8   ems.com

Active and adventurous people look to EMS as a great place for outdoor clothing and gear. Although prices can be bettered elsewhere, it is an excellent source for one-stop shopping, and the merchandise is top-quality. EMS covers virtually all outdoor sports, including biking, climbing, snowsports, hiking, paddling and camping.

G&S SPORTING GOODS

43 Essex St (at Grand St)   646/213-1100
Mon-Sun: 9-6   gandssportinggoods.com

If you are looking to buy a birthday or Christmas gift for a sports buff, I recommend G&S. They have a large selection of brand-name sneakers, in-line skates, boxing and exercise equipment, balls, bats, gloves, tennis racquets, toys, games, sports clothing and accessory items. Prices reflect a 20% to 25% discount.

MODELL'S SPORTING GOODS

1535 Third Ave (bet 86th and 87th St)   212/996-3800
234 W 42nd St (bet Seventh and Eighth Ave)   212/764-7030
607 Ave of the Americas (bet 17th and 18th St)   212/989-1110
55 Chambers St (bet Broadway and Elk St)   212/732-8484
Numerous other Manhattan locations
Hours vary by store   modells.com

Founded in 1889, Modell's is America's oldest family-owned sporting-goods retailer, with a total of ten stores in Manhattan. They carry a large selection of footwear and apparel for men, women and children, including team apparel and sporting goods for football, baseball, soccer, hockey, basketball, golf, racquet sports and more. Modell's can't be beat for quality and value.

PARAGON SPORTS

867 Broadway (at 18th St)   212/255-8889
Mon-Sat: 10-8:30 (Sat till 8); Sun: 11-7   paragonsports.com

TOBACCONIST

Gentlemen, are you tired of searching for a place where cigar smoking is not only allowed, but encouraged? At **De La Concha** (1390 Ave of the Americas, 212/757-3167), you can enjoy your stogie and good conversation or make use of their Wi-Fi. High quality, imported and domestic cigars, cigarillos, pipes, tobacco, humidors and leather goods are carried here.

Paragon is truly a sporting-goods mecca, with over 100,000 square feet of specialty shops devoted to all kinds of sports and fitness equipment and apparel. There are departments for team equipment, athletic footwear, skateboards, ice skates, in-line skates, racquet sports, running, aerobics, swimming, golf, skiing and snowboarding, hiking, camping, diving, biking, watersports and anything else that can be done in the great outdoors — all top brands.

GOLF

NEW YORK GOLF CENTER

131 W 35th St (bet Seventh Ave and Broadway)	212/564-2255
Chelsea Piers, Pier 59 (West Side Hwy at 18th St)	212/242-8899
100 Park Ave (at 40th St)	212/564-0078
Hours vary by store	nygolfcenter.com

Golfers will find the latest equipment and styles at New York Golf Center from their over 70,000 items. There are clubs, bags, clothing, shoes, accessories and novelties — everything except one's own hard-won golfing expertise. They carry pro-line equipment by such names as Callaway, TaylorMade, Cleveland, Titleist, Odyssey, Tour Edge and Nike. Employees couldn't be more helpful in finding the correct product and fit.

GUNS

JOHN JOVINO GUN SHOP

183 Grand St (at Mulberry St)	212/925-4881
Mon-Sat: 10-6; Sun: 2-6	

Claiming to be the oldest gun shop (and factory) in the country, John Jovino Gun Shop has been in business since 1911. They carry all major brands of handguns, rifles and shotguns, as well as ammunition, holsters, bulletproof vests, knives and scopes. Major brands include Smith & Wesson, Colt, Ruger, Beretta, Browning, Remington, Walther, Glock, Winchester and Sig Sauer. Jovino is an authorized warranty repair station for gun manufacturers.

MARINE

WEST MARINE

12 W 37th St (bet Fifth Ave and Ave of the Americas)	212/594-6065
Mon-Sat: 10-7; Sun: 10-5	westmarine.com

Perhaps a bit of a surprise, West Marine sells marine supplies as if it were situated in the middle of a New England seaport rather than the heart of Manhattan. With a mission to promote boating, they carry marine electronics, sailboat fittings, gamefish tackle, lifesaving gear, ropes, anchors, dock bumpers, compasses, clothing, clocks and barometers. You'll also find foul-weather suits and a line of clothing for yachters.

OUTDOOR EQUIPMENT
TENT AND TRAILS

21 Park Pl (bet Broadway and Church St)   212/227-1760
Mon-Sat: 9:30-6 (Thurs, Fri till 7); Sun: noon-6   tenttrails.com

Before leaving town on that weekend camping trip, head to Tent and Trails. In the urban canyons near City Hall, this 6,000-square-foot store is devoted to camping. The staff is experienced and knowledgeable. There are boots from Asolo, Lowa, Merrell, Hi-Tec and Scarpa. They carry camping gear from top makers like Patagonia, Big Agnes, Canada Goose and Osprey with items like backpacks, sleeping bags, tents, down clothing and much more. Tent and Trails also rents camping equipment.

RUNNING
SUPER RUNNERS SHOP

2543 Broadway (at 95th St)   646/756-5058
1337 Lexington Ave (at 89th St)   212/369-6010
360 Amsterdam Ave (bet 77th and 78th St)   212/787-7665
1244 Third Ave (bet 71st and 72nd St)   212/249-2133
821 Third Ave (bet 50th and 51st St)   212/421-4444
745 Seventh Ave (at 49th St)   212/398-2449
346 W 14th St (bet Eighth and Ninth Ave)   646/852-6500
Hours vary by store   superrunnersshop.com

Gary Muhrcke's passion for running became his livelihood; that was over 33 years ago. (Incidentally, Gary won the first New York City Marathon in 1970.) The stock at the seven Super Runners locations includes a superb selection of state-of-the-art men's and women's running and racing shoes, as well as performance running clothes. The informed staff, themselves runners, know firsthand the importance of proper fit and size. Check with them or online for details on upcoming runs.

SKATING
BLADES

156 W 72nd St (bet Broadway and Columbus Ave)   212/787-3911
Mon-Sat: 10-8; Sun: 10-7
659 Broadway (at Bleecker St)   212/477-7350
Mon-Sat: 10-9; Sun: 11-7   blades.com

Blades embraces the skate/snow/surf lifestyle with carefully selected merchandise. The store has great offerings of snowboarding, skateboarding and in-line skating equipment and a good stock of men's and women's apparel, footwear and accessories. Service is enthusiastic and informed; inline rentals are available.

TENNIS
MASON'S TENNIS

56 E 53rd St (bet Park and Madison Ave)   212/755-5805
Mon-Fri: 10-7; Sat: 10-6; Sun: noon-6   masonstennis.com

Mason's is the oldest tennis specialty store in Manhattan. Mark Mason offers a superb collection of clothing by Adidas, Fila, Lija, Polo Ralph Lauren, Nike, Lucky in Love, Yaffa and more. U.S. Open products are carried from May to December. You will also find ball machines, bags and other tennis paraphernalia. They sell racquets and shoes at the minimum prices allowed by the manufacturers and will special order any tennis product. Same-day stringing is offered. Signed memorabilia by stars of the sport are an added draw.

STATIONERY

JAM PAPER & ENVELOPE

135 Third Ave (bet 14th and 15th St)   212/473-6666
Mon-Fri: 8:30-8 (Fri till 7); Sat, Sun: 10-6   jampaper.com

At 7,500 square feet, JAM Paper is the largest paper and envelope store in the city and perhaps the world! They stock over 150 kinds of paper, with matching card stock and envelopes in every color, size and shape. You will find a vast selection of presentation folders, plastic portfolios, plastic envelopes and folders, cello sleeves, translucents, gift wraps, bags, tissue and raffia — all in matching colors. Close-outs and discounted items provide excellent bargains.

PAPER PRESENTATION

23 W 18th St (bet Fifth Ave and Ave of the Americas)   212/463-7035
Mon-Fri: 9-7:30; Sat, Sun: 11-6   paperpresentation.com

Come here for a huge selection of quality paper goods such as business cards, writing paper, invitations, post cards, place cards, envelopes, folders and portfolios, bags, gift wrap, labels and more. All shapes and sizes of boxes for favors, tin boxes and boxes for mailing are stocked. Select from a rainbow of colors and a multitude of textures and finishes: matte, metallic, parchment, transparent and linen included.

TILES

BISAZZA

43 Greene St (bet Broome and Grand St)   212/334-7130
Mon-Sat: 10-6   bisazzausa.com

This company claims to be the world's leader in glass mosaic, and whether that is true, there is no disputing that Bisazza's Italian mosaic designs are beautiful and colorful. Tiles are made almost entirely by hand in an age-old Venetian technique. There are large stocks of glass mosaic tiles, custom mosaics and tiles for indoor and outdoor use — for kitchens, bathrooms, pool areas or wherever.

COMPLETE TILE COLLECTION

42 W 15th St (bet Fifth Ave and Ave of the Americas)   212/255-4450
Mon-Fri: 10-6:30; Sat: 11-6   completetile.com

If you are shopping for quality tiles, come to Complete Tile Collection. They carry American art tiles; glass, ceramic, concrete, metal, slate, granite and molded tiles; marble and limestone mosaics and a large assortment of handmade tiles. Design services are available and the selection, including 800 distinct varieties of natural stone and 500 ceramic colors, is unmatched. They fabricate stone countertops, too!

IDEAL TILE

405 E 51st St (at First Ave)   212/759-2339
Mon-Fri: 9-5; Sat: 10-3   idealtile.com

Ideal Tile imports porcelain, granite and natural stone from Italy, Spain and Brazil. They also offer marble and granite fabrication for fireplaces, countertops, window sills and tables. Installation of tiles by skilled craftsmen is guaranteed.

TOBACCO AND SMOKING ACCESSORIES

BARCLAY-REX

90 Water St (bet Wall St and Gouverneur Lane)   212/962-3355
Mon-Fri: 8-7; Sat: 10-5
70 E 42nd St (bet Madison and Park Ave)   212/692-9680
Mon-Fri: 8-7; Sat: 10-6   barclayrex.com

Barclay-Rex is the product of three generations of the Nastri family. From 1910 they have catered to devotees of fine cigars, pipes and tobaccos, plus smoking-related gifts and accessories. Their shops are stocked with more than 200 brands of imported and domestic tobaccos. The finest tobaccos from all over the world are hand-blended and packaged under the Barclay-Rex label. Custom blending is one of their specialties. Cigars are housed in walk-in humidors at controlled temperatures; their signature line of pipes are made from beautiful natural woods.

TOYS AND CHILDREN'S ITEMS

GENERAL

DINOSAUR HILL

306 E 9th St (bet First and Second Ave)   212/473-5850
Daily: 11-7   dinosaurhill.com

Dinosaur Hill stocks diverse and consistently high-quality merchandise that they call "wonderments." Items are handmade and include brightly colored toys, solid wood blocks and a wonderful assortment of games, hats, music boxes, stuffed toy animals, puppets and musical instruments. In addition, they carry handmade clothing, quilts, bibs, hats and T-shirts in natural-fiber fabrics, some made locally.

WIGS, HAIRPIECES AND EXTENSIONS

Wigs may be a necessity for some men and women and a convenience for others. Before you shell out big bucks for a new head of hair, research all the options and work with a reputable wig salon.

Helena Collection (120 W 31st St, 212/967-9945): men's and women's ready-made and custom hair pieces

Joseph Fleischer Company (276 Fifth Ave, 212/686-7701): custom made for men and women

Karen's Wigs (1776 Broadway, Suite 1708; 212/977-2555): ready-made pieces

Wigbar (431 W 54th St, 212/233-0908): European or synthetic hair

F.A.O. SCHWARZ

767 Fifth Ave (at 58th St)   212/644-9400
Sun-Thurs: 10-8; Fri, Sat: 10-9   fao.com

Being greeted at the door by a toy soldier is part of the iconic experience here. This New York institution offers pricey merchandise that is over the top and that is not readily available elsewhere. The mere fact that your purchase came from F.A.O. Schwarz makes it special for many youngsters and adults alike. The beautiful store is a lesson in retail presentation.

KIDDING AROUND

60 W 15th St (bet Fifth Ave and Ave of the Americas)   212/645-6337
Mon-Sat: 10-7; Sun: 11-6
Grand Central Terminal
107 E 42nd St (at Vanderbilt Ave)   212/972-8697
Mon-Fri: 8-8; Sat: 10-8; Sun: 11-6   kiddingaroundtoys.com

These independent toy emporiums are arguably some of the city's best toy stores. Books, toys, puzzles, balls, games, dollhouses, craft supplies and birthday party favors are colorful, great finds. In addition to a wide selection of Playmobil, Brio and Corolle dolls, Kidding Around stocks an amazing assortment of quality wooden toys for riding and building. There is a small dress-up clothing section, too. You'll be impressed at how much fun is crammed into these neighborhood shops!

MARY ARNOLD TOYS

1010 Lexington Ave (at 72nd St)   212/744-8510
Mon-Fri: 9-6; Sat: 10-5:30; Sun: 10-5   maryarnoldtoys.com

Mary Arnold Toys is a spacious, well-organized and well-stocked source for the basics. There are separate sections for games, early-development toys, puzzles, books, videos, dolls, stuffed animals and craft kits and supplies. Outdoor toys include trikes, bikes, kites, stilts, goalie sets and more. The dress-up collection deserves a close look.

TOYS "R" US

1514 Broadway (at 44th St)   646/366-8800
Sun-Fri: 10 a.m.-11 p.m.; Sat: 9 a.m.-11 p.m.
901 Ave of America (bet 32nd and 33rd St); outlet store   212/239-7306
Mon-Sat: 9:30-9; Sun: 10-8   toysrus.com

Every square inch of this busy flagship store (Broadway location) is filled with kid-pleasing merchandise. The marketing marvel features a huge stage set with a giant animatronic T-Rex dinosaur and a 60-foot ferris wheel; each car of the ferris wheel models a different toy. A life-size Barbie dollhouse displays two floors of toys and fashions. Interactive displays showcase the hottest electronics. The outlet location on Avenue of the Americas is an express convenience store. **Babies "R" Us** (24-30 Union Sq E, 212/798-9905) is a one-stop baby-supply destination: clothing, toys, baby equipment and other necessities.

SPECIALTY AND NOVELTY

ALPHABETS

64 Ave A (bet 4th and 5th St)   212/353-2201
Sun-Tues: 11-8; Wed-Sat: 11-10   Facebook

Alphabets is a combination toy store and novelty shop where you'll find classic toys from everyone's childhood. You might find funky items like a Slinky, Gumby and Pokey piggybank, kitschy ceramics and a Beatles T-shirt. Alphabets is the place to visit for a baby boomer's trip down memory lane or to purchase the perfect retro gift.

AMERICAN GIRL PLACE

609 Fifth Ave (at 49th St)   877/247-5223
Mon-Thurs: 10-7; Fri: 10-9; Sat: 9-9; Sun: 9-7   americangirl.com

If you have a young girl in your life, you are probably aware of the American Girl doll phenomenon! This store is a restaurant, retail store and giant credit-card bill all wrapped up into one. Birthday-party packages run from $38 to $59 per child; a late night at American Girl gives you and friends private use of the space, with a meal and doll hair-salon time. In addition to dolls and doll clothes, there are accessories for dolls and doll furniture or choose from matching doll-girl outfits. Enjoy a break from shopping at the **American Girl Cafe** for brunch, lunch, afternoon tea and dinner. A doll hospital, doll hair salon, doll ear piercing, exhibits and special events will complete your visit.

DISNEY STORE

1540 Broadway (bet 45th and 46th St)   212/626-2910
Sun-Fri: 9 a.m.-1 a.m.   disneystore.com

This three-floor maze of merchandise in Times Square is filled with Disney-themed items: Mickey Mouse, Winnie the Pooh, Buzz Lightyear, Disney princesses and characters from *Planes* and *Frozen*. Besides the expected toys, games, movies and books, you will find clothing, luggage, backpacks and accessories; just about anything that can be emblazoned with Disney logos, characters and creations. For collectors, their gallery offers authentic pieces of Disney art from past and present. The staff really knows the stock and they are personable as well. Call or check online for frequent in-store events.

FORBIDDEN PLANET NYC

832 Broadway (bet 13th and 14th St)   212/473-1576
Sun-Tues: 9 a.m.-10 p.m.; Wed-Sat: 9 a.m.-12 a.m.   fpnyc.com

This unique shop is a shrine for science-fiction artifacts. Forbidden Planet stocks fantasy-related toys and games, including anime figures, military figures and vehicles, model kits and plush and vinyl toys. There are sci-fi comic books and publications, videos, posters, T-shirts and cards.

IMAGE ANIME

242 W 30th St (bet Seventh and Eighth Ave)   212/631-0966
Mon-Fri: 11-7; Sat, Sun: noon-6   imageanime.com

Since 1992, Image Anime has specialized in imported Japanese toys, models and anime collectibles. If that category interests you — and a great many children and adults are fanatically devoted to it — then this packed little store will thrill you. Lines include Gundam, Naruto, Pokémon, Transformers, Robotech, Zoids and nearly every other popular Japanese line.

LEGO STORE

Rockefeller Center
620 Fifth Avenue (at 50th St)   212/245-5973
Mon-Sat: 10-8; Sun: 11-7
200 Fifth Ave (at 23rd St)   212/25503217
Mon-Sat: 10-8; Sun: 11-6   stores.lego.com

Manhattan is home to two incredible LEGO stores, one at a corner of Rockefeller Center and one in the Flatiron District. The selection of colorful, plastic bricks from Denmark is vast: there are sets to fabricate farms and villages, vehicles and landmarks and collectible kits with action-movie and character themes. Video games with characters from movies like *The Hobbit* are very popular. Large LEGO sculptures, play areas and computer design stations are sure to stimulate the imagination and challenge the dexterity of folks of all ages.

THE RED CABOOSE

23 W 45th St (bet Fifth Ave and Ave of the Americas)   212/575-0155
Mon-Fri: 11-7; Sat: 11-5   theredcaboose.com

Customers at this toy stores are frequently sharp-eyed adults who are dead serious about model railroads. The Red Caboose claims to have 100,000 items on hand, including a line of 300 hand-finished, imported brass locomotives; New York subway cars, too. The five basic sizes (1:22, 1:48, 1:87, 1:161 and 1:220 in a ratio of scale to actual size) allow model railroaders to build layouts sized to fit everything from a desk drawer to an entire room. They stock an extensive line of track, plastic kits, paints, tools, model supplies and related books. Red Caboose also carries die-cast airplanes and vehicles (military and commercial), autos, trucks and ships.

TOY TOKYO

91 Second Ave (at 5th St)   212/673-5424
Sun-Thurs: 1 p.m.-9 p.m.; Fri, Sat: 12:30 p.m.-9 p.m.   toytokyo.com

This store is another great example of why I love New York! Since 2000, Toy Tokyo has been selling toys and collectibles from every genre, including wonderful Japanese anime figures, *Star Wars* collectibles and hard-to-find classics. The pop culture stock changes a bit every week, and many items come straight from Hong Kong, Japan and other points east. If you're a collector or just a curious browser, put this overflowing shop on your list. You must see it to believe it!

TRAVEL ITEMS

FLIGHT 001

96 Greenwich Ave (bet Jane and 12th St)   212/989-0001
Mon-Sat: 11-8; Sun: noon-6   flight001.com

The travel store began as the result of an in-flight brainstorm by two businessmen. Their mission: to procure and develop the best travel products. You will find novel and useful travel aids, including luggage, luggage tags, totes, passport holders, spacepaks, wallets, TSA travel bottles, USB cables, 4-in-1 travel adapters and all manner of bags for cosmetics, lingerie, shoes, laundry and *stuff*. Jetsetters love this place!

WATCHES

SANDY YAEGER WATCH

578 Fifth Ave (at 47th St), Space 54   212/819-0088
Mon-Fri: 10-5   sandyyaegerwatch.com

Family-owned since 1973, Sandy Yaeger Watch carries over 2,000 discounted, name-brand watches. From classics to the latest styles, watches retail from $100 to $150,000. If you don't find what you want, Yaeger will begin a search for you. Repairs and warranties are offered, and prices are quoted over the phone.

TEMPVS FVGIT

Showplace Antiques and Design Center
40 W 25th St (bet Fifth Ave and Ave of the Americas), Gallery 29 212/673-1995
Thurs-Sun: 10-5   tempvsfvgit.com

Tempvs Fvgit could be the place if you are looking for a vintage Rolex! They carry other collectibles and top-brand watches, plus quality watchbands — all at considerable savings. Watch repair and restoration are among the services offered. Before you make the trip, you can view many of the watches at the Tempvs website.

TOURNEAU

510 Madison Ave (bet 52nd and 53rd St)   212/758-5830
Mon-Fri: 10-6:30; Sat: 10-6; Sun: noon-5
1095 Ave of the Americas (at 42nd St)   212/278-8041
Mon-Sat: 9-7 (Thurs till 8); Sun: 11-6

TOURNEAU TIMEMACHINE

12 E 57th St (at Madison Ave)   212/758-7300
Mon-Sat: 10-6 (Thurs till 7); Sun: 11:30-5   tourneau.com

This celebrated watchmaker and luxury watch retailer has been operating for 115 years. As the largest such retailer in the U.S., they carry 100 of the world's top brands, showing over 8,000 styles. Besides their own Tourneau line, select brands include Rolex, Cartier, Longine, Rado and more. A complimentary extended warranty of up to five years, free lifetime battery replacement and excellent in-store service and repair are additional customer benefits. Tourneau has perhaps the greatest selection of certified pre-owned timepieces, all fully restored in-house. Tourneau TimeMachine on 57th and Madison Avenue is an amazing 16,000-square-foot timepiece emporium.

CHAPTER 7

WHERE TO "EXTRAS"

This chapter contains a dozen or so subjects not found elsewhere in this edition. Here you'll find where to purchase tickets, attend music and sporting events, take kids, spend a romantic evening and host a party or special event.

ANNUAL EVENTS

While stores, museums, restaurants and the like are open all year, some special events are held only during certain seasons or once a year. Keep in mind that since some of these events are seasonal, dates and venues frequently change.

JANUARY

Polar Bear Club New Year's Dip (Coney Island)
Ice skating (Rockefeller Center, Central Park, Bryant Park and other venues)
Winter Antiques Show (Park Avenue Armory)
Chinese New Year (January or February)
New York National Boat Show (Jacob K. Javits Convention Center)
Restaurant Week (January/February)

FEBRUARY
Westminster Kennel Club Dog Show (Madison Square Garden)
Empire State Building Run-Up (Empire State Building)
Valentine's Day wedding ceremony (Empire State Building)
Outsider Art Fair (Chelsea)
Fall/Winter Fashion Week

MARCH
St. Patrick's Day Parade (Fifth Ave)
Big East and NIT college basketball tournaments (Madison Square Garden)
Macy's Spring Flower Show
Artexpo New York (Pier 94 on the Hudson River)

APRIL
Major League Baseball season opens (Yankees and Mets)
New York Antiquarian Book Fair (Park Avenue Armory)
New York International Auto Show (Jacob K. Javits Convention Center)
Tribeca Film Festival

MAY
Ninth Avenue International Food Festival (Ninth Ave)
Ukrainian Festival (7th St in the East Village)
Fleet Week for the U.S. Navy and Coast Guard (week before Memorial Day)
River to River Festival (Lower Manhattan)
Washington Square Outdoor Art Exhibit (University Pl)

JUNE
Salute to Israel Parade (Fifth Ave)
Free concerts and performances (Central Park and other city parks)
Lesbian and Gay Pride Week and Parade
Museum Mile Festival (Fifth Ave bet 82nd and 105th St)
Restaurant Week (June/July)
Midsummer Night Swing (Lincoln Center; three weeks in June and July)

JULY
Free concerts and performances (Central Park and other city parks)
Free outdoor movies (Bryant Park and other locations)
Macy's Fourth of July fireworks (East River and other locations)
Mostly Mozart Festival (Avery Fisher Hall, Lincoln Center; July/August)
New York City Triathlon (July/August)

AUGUST
Free concerts and performances (Central Park and other city parks)
Free outdoor movies (Bryant Park and other locations)

Lincoln Center Out-of-Doors Festival (Lincoln Center)

U.S. Open tennis tournament begins (USTA Billie Jean King National Tennis Center in Flushing Meadows, Queens; August/September)

SEPTEMBER

Washington Square Outdoor Art Exhibit (University Pl)

National Football League season opens (Giants and Jets)

Feast of San Gennaro (Little Italy)

New York Film Festival (Lincoln Center)

Spring/Summer Fashion Week

OCTOBER

Columbus Day Parade

National Basketball Association season opens (Knicks and Liberty)

National Hockey League season opens (Rangers and Islanders)

Union Square Autumn Fair (Broadway at 23rd St)

Halloween Parade (Greenwich Village)

The ING New York City Marathon (late October or early November)

NOVEMBER

New York Comedy Festival

Margaret Mead Film Festival (American Museum of Natural History)

Macy's Thanksgiving Day Parade

Christmas tree lighting (Rockefeller Plaza)

DECEMBER

Christmas windows (Saks Fifth Avenue, Macy's, Lord & Taylor and other locations)

Messiah Sing-In (Avery Fisher Hall, Lincoln Center)

Radio City Christmas Spectacular (Radio City Music Hall)

Holiday bazaar and New York Transit Museum Train Show (Grand Central Terminal)

New Year's Eve celebrations (Times Square and other locations)

First Night celebrations (Grand Central Terminal, Central Park and other locations)

WHERE TO PLAY

FILMS

Like any city, New York has a multitude of theaters for first-run movies. Indeed, most movies debut in New York and Los Angeles before opening anywhere else. (Depending on the size of the crowds they draw, some never do open elsewhere.) For information about what movies are showing at virtually every theater in Manhattan and to purchase tickets by credit card at many of those theaters, go to moviefone.com.

If you're looking for an old movie, a foreign film, an unusual documentary, a 3D movie or something out of the ordinary, try calling one of the following theaters. Most numbers connect you with a recording that lists current movies and times, ticket costs (some places accept cash only) and directions.

American Museum of Natural History IMAX Theater (Central Park W at 79th St, 212/769-5100)

Angelika Film Center and Cafe (18 W Houston St, 212/995-2570)

Anthology Film Archives (32 Second Ave, 212/505-5181)

Asia Society and Museum (725 Park Ave, 212/288-6400)

Austrian Cultural Forum (11 E 52nd St, 212/319-5300)

Film Forum (209 W Houston St, 212/727-8110)

Florence Gould Hall at the French Institute (55 E 59th St, 212/355-6160)

Japan Society Gallery (333 E 47th St, 212/715-1258)

Lincoln Plaza Cinema (1886 Broadway, 212/757-0359)

Paley Center for Media (25 W 52nd St, 212/621-6800)

Quad Cinema (34 W 13th St, 212/255-2243)

Symphony Space (2537 Broadway, 212/864-5400)

Walter Reade Theater at Lincoln Center (165 W 65th St, 212/875-5600)

Whitney Museum of American Art (99 Gansevort St, 212/570-3600)

Like everything else, the price of movie tickets in New York tends to be higher than elsewhere in the country. Second-run theaters, film societies and museums usually charge a little less, and Bryant Park, Central Park, South Street Seaport and other parks throughout the city host free movies in summer.

Of course, New York is home to dozens of popular film festivals. The best known is the Film Society of Lincoln Center's New York Film Festival, held in late September and early October. This annual event showcases top international films and special events and gets more popular every year. Call the Walter Reade Theater box office, 212/875-5601, for more information.

NIGHTLIFE

Whether you want an evening of elegant dining and dancing, rocking and rolling till the wee hours, dropping in on a set of jazz or catching some stand-up comedy, New York's club scene offers endless choices. I've listed several popular places in each category to get you started. Most levy a cover charge, many offer at least a light menu and a very few require reservations (dress codes may apply). As with so many other things, it is wise to call in advance.

CABARET ROOMS

54 Below (254 W 54th St, 646/476-3551): dinner shows

Cafe Carlyle, The Carlyle (35 E 76th St, 212/744-1600): closed in summer months

Don't Tell Mama (343 W 46th St, 212/757-0788)

The Duplex (61 Christopher St, 212/255-5438): piano bar, cafe

Metropolitan Room (34 W 22nd St, 212/206-0440)

UP LATE AND LOOKING FOR SOMETHING TO DO?

Bowlmor Lanes (222 W 44th St, 212/680-0012): Friday and Saturday until 2 a.m.

Bowlmor Chelsea Piers (23rd St at Hudson River, 212/835-2695): Friday and Saturday until 3 a.m.

Cafeteria (119 Seventh Ave, 212/414-1717): American classics served 24/7

The Dressing Room Boutique & Bar (75-A Orchard St, 212/966-7330): Thursday through Saturday until 2 a.m.

Forever 21 (1540 Broadway, 212/302-0594): shop until 2 a.m.

Slate Billiards (54 W 21st St, 212/989-0096): Friday and Saturday until 4 a.m.

COMEDY CLUBS

Caroline's on Broadway (1626 Broadway, 212/757-4100)

Comedy Cellar (117 MacDougal St, 212/254-3480)

Dangerfield's (1118 First Ave, 212/593-1650)

Gotham Comedy Club (208 W 23rd St, 212/367-9000)

Greenwich Village Comedy Club (99 MacDougal St, 212/777-5233)

Stand Up New York (236 W 78th St, 212/595-0850)

Tribeca Comedy Lounge (22 Warren St, 646/504-5653): lower level of Brick NYC; great pizza and more

Upright Citizens Brigade Theatre (307 W 26th St, 212/366-9176 and 153 E 3rd St, 212/366-9231): inexpensive; also classes in improvisation and sketch comedy

DANCING

Cielo (18 Little West 12th St, 212/645-5700)

Finale (199 Bowery, 212/980-3011)

Hilo (26 Ninth Ave, 212/837-4700)

LeBain at the Standard (848 Washington St, 212/645-4646)

Marquee (289 Tenth Ave, 646/473-0202)

Pacha (618 W 46th St, 212/209-7500)

Pianos (158 Ludlow St, 212/505-3733)

Provocateur (18 Ninth Ave, 212/929-9036)

SOB's (204 Varick St, 212/243-4940)

GAY AND LESBIAN CLUBS

Boiler Room (86 E 4th St, 212/254-7536): gay

G Lounge (225 W 19th St, 212/929-1085): gay

Henrietta Hudson (438 Hudson St, 212/924-3347): lesbian
Posh (405 W 51st St, 212/957-2222)
The Stonewall Inn (53 Christopher St, 212/488-2705): historic bar

JAZZ CLUBS

Arthur's Tavern (57 Grove St, 212/675-6879): The Grove Street Stompers play every Monday night.

Bill's Place (148 W 133rd St, 212/281-0777): Bill Saxton's Jazz Club and Speakeasy; no alcohol

Birdland (315 W 44th St, 212/581-3080)

Blue Note (131 W 3rd St, 212/475-8592)

Iridium Jazz Club (1650 Broadway, 212/582-2121)

Jazz Standard (116 E 27th St, 212/576-2232): Blue Smoke restaurant is upstairs.

Showman's Jazz Club (375 W 125th St, 212/864-8941)

Smoke Jazz and Supper Club (2751 Broadway, 212/864-6662)

Swing 46 (349 W 46th St, 212/262-9554): jazz and supper club

Village Vanguard (178 Seventh Ave S, 212/255-4037)

ROCK, FOLK AND BLUES CLUBS

B.B. King's Blues Club and Lucille's Grill (237 W 42nd St, 212/997-4144)

Bitter End (147 Bleecker St, 212/673-7030): one of the original Greenwich Village folk clubs; rock and blues as well

Bowery Ballroom (6 Delancey St, 212/533-2111): the city's premier rock (with a bit of everything else) showcase venue

MUSIC IN THE MUSEUMS

Brooklyn Museum (200 Eastern Parkway, Brooklyn, 718/638-5000): free music and entertainment from 5 to 11 on the first Saturday of every month

The Cloisters Museum and Gardens (Fort Tryon Park, 99 Margaret Corbin Drive, 212/923-3700): winter and spring concerts

RUNNING

Central Park may come to mind first if you're looking for a running trail in New York City. There are many other routes, ask your concierge or check at a sporting goods store for suggestions and definitely don't overlook the Brooklyn Bridge.

City Running Tours (877/415-0058, cityrunningtours.com/newyorkcity): organizes group runs throughout the borough and a monthly Brooklyn Brewery run

Fun on Foot (funonfoot.com): maintains a list of running clubs and groups, routes and more

MEMBERSHIPS IN NEW YORK CITY RECREATION CENTERS

For $100 to $150 a year (just $25 for senior citizens over 62 and free for children under 18), you can use the city's wonderful recreation centers with indoor pools and excellent facilities and sign up for all sorts of classes. Go to nycgovparks.org and click on "Facilities" and "Recreation Centers" for descriptions of each center and its offerings.

Frick Collection (1 E 70th St, 212/288-0700): concerts on some Sundays at 5

The Metropolitan Museum of Art (1000 Fifth Ave, 212/535-7710): classical music on Friday and Saturday from 4 to 8:30 in the Great Hall Balcony Bar

The Morgan Library & Museum (225 Madison Ave, 212/685-0008): lots of concerts, mostly classical; tickets required

RECREATION

People who live in Manhattan know that you can do just about anything in New York that can be done anywhere else; and then some! Whether it's batting cages, tennis courts, or bocce ball courts, chances are that New York has it; you just have to know where to look.

BADMINTON

New York Badminton Club (646/271-3228)

BASEBALL

Baseball Center NYC (202 W 74th St, 212/362-0344): 15,000-square-foot training facility

Central Park (212/628-1036): 26 ball fields throughout the park

Field House at Chelsea Piers (23rd St at Hudson River, 212/336-6500): four batting cages

BASKETBALL

BasketBall City (Pier 36, 299 South St, 212/233-5050)

Field House at Chelsea Piers (23rd St at Hudson River, 212/336-6500)

BILLIARDS

Amsterdam Billiards and Bar (110 E 11th St, 212/995-0333)

Slate Billiards (54 W 21st St, 212/989-0096)

BOCCE BALL

Bryant Park (Ave of the Americas bet 40th and 42nd St)

Il Vagabondo (351 E 62nd St, 212/832-9221)
New York City Bocce League (410/952-7436, nycbocce.com)

BOWLING

Bowlmor Chelsea Piers (Chelsea Piers, 23rd St at Hudson River, 212/835-2695)

Bowlmor Times Square (222 W 44th St, 212/680-0012): carnival; Boomer Esiason's Stadium Grill

Frames (Port Authority Bus Terminal, 550 Ninth Ave, 212/268-6909): plus billiards, games, dance clubs, food and cocktails

Lucky Strike (624-660 W 42nd St, 646/829-0170): 26 lanes; LuXe Lounge

CHESS, CHECKERS AND BOARD GAMES

Bryant Park (Ave of the Americas bet 40th and 42nd St)

Chess NYC (82 W 3rd St, 212/475-8130): chess instruction for all ages

The Uncommons (230 Thompson St, 646/543-9215): board-game cafe; games to rent or purchase

Washington Square Park (foot of Fifth Ave, below 8th St)

CLIMBING

Field House at Chelsea Piers (23rd St at Hudson River, 212/336-6500): one of the largest indoor rock climbing gyms in the country

GOLF

Golf Club at Chelsea Piers (Pier 59, 23rd St at Hudson River, 212/336-6400): multi-tiered outdoor driving range; open year round

ICE SKATING

Bryant Park (Ave of the Americas at 42nd St, 212/661-6640): seasonal

Riverbank State Park (679 Riverside Dr, 212/694-3642): state-of-the-art facilities; summer roller skating

Rockefeller Center (Fifth Ave bet 49th and 50th St, 212/632-3975): seasonal

Sky Rink at Chelsea Piers (Pier 61, 23rd St at Hudson River, 212/336-6100): year round

Trump Lasker Rink (Central Park at E 107th St, 917/492-3856): seasonal

Trump Wollman Rink (Central Park, 59th St at Ave of the Americas, 212/439-6900): seasonal

SAILING LESSONS

Have you always wanted to learn how to sail? Strap on a life jacket and head to **Manhattan Sailing School** (375 South End Ave, #20-L, 212/786-0400, sailmanhattan.com). Programs, including hands-on experience, cover basics, coastal cruising and navigation, racing and bareboat chartering. Sailing school grads are eligible to join the Manhattan Sailing Club with access to two seasonal floating clubhouses.

LOCATE A PARK

Nothing can compare to Central Park in size or attractions, but there are several other relaxing spots throughout the city:

Greenacre Park (51st St bet Second and Third Ave): A beautiful 25-foot high waterfall is surrounded by lush greenery.

High Line Park (parallels Tenth Ave bet Gansevoort and 34th St): built along a 1.45-mile-long elevated defunct rail line

Hudson River Park (Battery Park City to W 59th St): biking, skating, rock climbing, water sports and more

Jefferson Market Garden (Greenwich Ave bet 10th St and Ave of the Americas): best viewed from May to October; one-third acre

Paley Park (53rd St bet Fifth and Madison Ave): the former site of the legendary Stork Club with a 20-foot-tall section of the Berlin Wall and an enticing waterfall

Sutton Place Park (57th St at East River): comprised of five tiny parks with a wild boar statue, kids' sandbox and view of the Queensboro Bridge

Teardrop Park (Battery Park City, River Terrace between Murray and Warren St): lots of rocks for sitting, walking and climbing

West Side Community Garden (89th St bet Amsterdam and Columbus Ave): floral amphitheater, massive autumn tulip display

PING-PONG

SPiN (48 E 23rd St, 212/982-8802): craft brews, too

SLEDDING

Carl Schurz Park (88th St at East End Ave): the lawn north of Gracie Mansion

Central Park, Pilgrim Hill (Fifth Ave at 72nd St) and Cedar Hill (Fifth Ave bet 76th and 79th St)

Morningside Park (110th, 113th and 122nd St at Morningside Dr)

Riverside Park (103rd St at Riverside Dr)

SOCCER

Field House at Chelsea Piers (23rd St at Hudson River, 212/336-6500)

SWIMMING

Asphalt Green Aqua Center (1750 York Ave, 212/369-8890)

Asser Levy Recreation Center (392 Asser Levy Place, 212/447-2020): indoor and outdoor pools

Tony Dapolito Recreation Center (1 Clarkson St, 212/242-5418): indoor and outdoor pools

Vanderbilt YMCA (224 E 47th St, 212/912-2500)

TENNIS

Central Park Tennis Center (Central Park W, bet 94th and 96th St, 212/316-0800)

Midtown Tennis Club (341 Eighth Ave, 212/989-8572)

Riverside Clay Tennis Association (96th St and Riverside Dr, 212/978-0277): ten red clay courts

Sutton East Tennis (488 E 60th St, 212/751-3452): red clay; open mid-September to mid-July

USTA Billie Jean King National Tennis Center (Flushing Meadows, Queens, 718/760-6200)

Vanderbilt Tennis and Fitness Club (Grand Central Terminal, 42nd St at Vanderbilt Ave, 212/599-6500): one indoor court, two practice courts

Yorkville Tennis Club (1725 York Ave, 212/987-0301)

SPECTATOR SPORTS

Some people associate New York with fine food and expensive stores, while others link the city with the Yankees, the Mets, the Knicks, the Rangers and other professional sports teams. The New York area is home to more than a half dozen professional sports teams, although only basketball's Knicks and hockey's Rangers actually play in Manhattan. Home field for the city's two pro football teams, the Jets and the Giants, is across the river in New Jersey, while pro baseball's Yankees and Mets play in the New York City boroughs of The Bronx and Queens, respectively.

If you want tickets to a professional sporting event, plan as far in advance as possible. Each team's website has detailed information about schedules, tickets and how to get there.

A word of warning: New York fans are like no others. They are loud, rude and typically very knowledgeable about their teams and sports in general. If you're cheering against the home team, keep your voice down; and your head, too!

BASEBALL

New York Mets (Citi Field, Flushing Meadows, Queens, newyork.mets.mlb.com)

New York Yankees (Yankee Stadium, 1 E 161st St, The Bronx, newyork.yankees.mlb.com)

BASKETBALL

Brooklyn Nets (Barclays Center, Brooklyn, nba.com/nets)

New York Knicks (Madison Square Garden, nba.com/knicks)

New York Liberty (Prudential Center, Newark, NJ, wnba.com/liberty)

FOOTBALL

The Giants and the Jets share a state-of-the-art sports facility across the Hudson River.

New York Giants (MetLife Stadium, East Rutherford, NJ, giants.com)

CIRCUS MOVES

If you'd like to fly through the air with the greatest of ease, like the famed daring young man on the flying trapeze, you can make it happen at **Circus Warehouse** (53-21 Vernon Blvd, Long Island City, NY; 212/751-2174). Weekend and evening professional and recreational classes are taught by pros from Cirque du Soleil and Ringling Brothers; Circus Warehouse also takes their shows on the road to private parties and events.

Trapeze School New York (212/242-8769, newyork. trapezeschool.com) specializes in aerial trapeze, trampoline, silks and other acrobatic sessions at outdoor locales during warm weather months. The indoor space is in Brooklyn—swing on by.

New York Jets (MetLife Stadium, East Rutherford, NJ, newyorkjets.com)

ICE HOCKEY
New York Rangers (Madison Square Garden, rangers.nhl.com)

WHERE TO GO

GREAT VIEWS, PHOTO OPS

There are thousands of great views and photo opportunities in every part of New York. If you're a photographer or just want a memorable "only in New York" photo, then here are some favorite views and backdrops worth checking out.

Battery Park Esplanade (length of Battery Park City along the Hudson River)

Brooklyn Bridge (anywhere along its length)

Central Park rock outcrops (just inside the park's southwest corner)

The Cloisters Museum and Gardens (Fort Tryon Park)

LOVE Sculpture (Ave of the Americas at 55th St)

Morris-Jumel Mansion grounds (65 Jumel Terrace, in Harlem Heights)

New York Harbor (particularly from the Staten Island Ferry)

Patience and Fortitude (lion statues in front of New York Public Library, 455 Fifth Ave)

Prometheus Statue (Rockefeller Plaza, west of Fifth Ave bet 49th and 50th St)

Roosevelt Island (anywhere on the west side, particularly Lighthouse Park)

Statue of Liberty (off Battery Park in New York Harbor)

Wall Street Bull (bronze sculpture, Broadway at Bowling Green)

Washington Arch (Washington Square Park, foot of Fifth Ave in Greenwich Village)

IN THE MIDDLE OF THE NIGHT

New York bills itself as "the city that never sleeps," and many who live here are night people. They include not only actors and artists, but also those who clean and maintain the huge office buildings, put together morning newspapers and newscasts and work the night shift at hospitals and other businesses that never close.

In general, stores and restaurants in Soho, Tribeca and Greenwich Village stay open later than those in the rest of the city. The restaurants and mom-and-pop operations along Broadway on the Upper West Side and on Lexington and Third avenues on the Upper East Side also tend to keep late hours. As with everything else, call before setting out.

WITH KIDS

Remember that New York can be totally overwhelming for children. (The same is true for adults!) Don't push too hard and plan to retreat to quiet spaces from time to time. Remember, too, that New York can be a wonderland for all ages, if you know where to go. Look inside toy stores and bookstores for seasonal calendars.

Big Apple Parent (nymetroparents.com) is an online resource with activities, advice and information geared to kids and families in and around New York City.

I've suggested things to do with kids in several categories. In many cases, these places are described in detail in other parts of this book. Of course, children's interests can vary dramatically, so I've inevitably included places that one child will love and another might find boring. I'll let you be the judge of that!

I also recommend looking at the Children's Books, Children's Clothing Stores and Toy Stores sections in Chapter VI.

ENTERTAINMENT, MUSEUMS AND SIGHTS

BUSY LITTLE ONES

92nd Street Y (Parenting Center, 1395 Lexington Ave, 212/415-5611)

The Carousel at Pier 62 (Hudson River Park at 23rd St, 212/627-2020): 33 hand-carved animals; seasonal

Central Park Zoo and **Tisch Children's Zoo** (behind The Arsenal in Central Park at E 64th St, 212/439-6500)

BRING THE KIDS!

It used to be that everyone dressed up for the theater and nobody would think of bringing a young child. Now the pre-teen set is seen in almost every Broadway theater, especially at performances of *The Lion King, Annie, Aladdin, Matilda* and *Wicked*. Some theaters thoughtfully provide booster seats! Here's some advice from this adult: choose productions your child will appreciate, and leave promptly if your little one behaves disruptively. I know you paid a lot for that ticket, but so did the rest of us!

SAILING, SAILING

Enjoy the waters around Manhattan without having to share the ride with hundreds of others on the 82-foot **Shearwater**, a restored 1929 schooner that holds up to 48 passengers. Scheduled trips and charters begin and end at North Cove Marina in lower Manhattan.

Kids will enjoy the 158-foot topsail schooner **Clipper City**. This 150 passenger tall ship departs from the south end of Battery Park.

Make reservations for either vessel at manhattanbysail.com or call 212/619-6900.

Children's Museum of the Arts (103 Charlton St, 212/274-0986)

Field Station: Dinosaurs (One Dinosaur Way, Secaucus, NJ, 855/999-9010): June through September

Friedsam Memorial Carousel (behind The Arsenal in Central Park at E 64th St)

The Heimbold Family Children's Playing and Learning Center (Scandinavia House: The Nordic Center in America, 58 Park Ave, 212/779-3587)

Le Carrousel (Bryant Park, Ave of the Americas at 42nd St)

LEGO Store (Rockefeller Center, 620 Fifth Ave, 212/245-5973 and 200 Fifth Ave, 212/255-3217)

MUSEUMS WITH A FAMILY FOCUS

American Museum of Natural History (Central Park W at 79th St, 212/769-5100)

Children's Museum of Manhattan (212 W 83rd St, 212/721-1223)

Dyckman Farmhouse Museum (4881 Broadway, 212/304-9422)

Fraunces Tavern Museum (54 Pearl St, 212/425-1778)

Intrepid Sea Air & Space Museum (Pier 86, Twelfth Ave at 46th St, 212/245-0072

Liberty Science Center (Liberty State Park, Jersey City, NJ, 201/200-1000)

Lower East Side Tenement Museum (103 Orchard St, 212/431-0233)

Madame Tussauds (234 W 42nd St, 212/512-9600)

Museum of the City of New York (1220 Fifth Ave, 212/534-1672)

New York City Fire Museum (278 Spring St, 212/691-1303)

New-York Historical Society, DiMenna Children's History Museum (170 Central Park W, 212/873-3400)

Sony Wonder Technology Lab (550 Madison Ave, 212/833-8100)

South Street Seaport Museum (12 Fulton St, 212/748-8600)

FOR TWEENS AND TEENS

Dylan's Candy Bar (1011 Third Ave, 646/735-0078)

Field House at Chelsea Piers (23rd St at Hudson River, 212/336-6500)

Frames (Port Authority Bus Terminal, 550 Ninth Ave, 212/268-6909): bowling, games

Madame Tussauds (234 W 42nd St, 212/512-9600)

Museum of Comic and Cartoon Art (128 E 63rd St, 212/838-2560)

On Location Tours (212/683-2027)

Sony Wonder Technology Lab (550 Madison Ave, 212/833-8100)

NEW YORK CLASSICS

Bronx Zoo (2300 Southern Blvd, The Bronx, 718/367-1010)

Empire State Building (350 Fifth Ave, 212/736-3100)

New York Hall of Science (47-01 111th St, Queens, 718/699-0005)

Statue of Liberty and **Ellis Island** (New York Harbor, 212/363-3200)

United Nations (First Ave bet 42nd and 47th St, 212/963-4440)

Yankee Stadium (1 E 161st St, The Bronx, 212/926-5337)

PLAYS, MOVIES AND TV

American Museum of Natural History IMAX Theater (Central Park W at 79th St, 212/769-5100)

The Lion King (Minskoff Theater, 1515 Broadway)

Paley Center for Media (25 W 52nd St, 212/621-6800)

BOATS AND OTHER TRANSPORTATION

Circle Line Sightseeing Tours (Pier 83, 42nd St at Hudson River, 212/563-3200)

New York Transit Museum (Boerum Pl at Schermerhorn St, Brooklyn, 718/694-1600)

Roosevelt Island Tram (Second Ave bet 59th and 60th St): inexpensive

SEASONAL ACTIVITIES

Some things can only be done in New York if you're in town at the right time.

■ If you are planning a trip in spring or summer, get tickets to a baseball game at **Yankee Stadium** (newyork.yankees.mlb.com) or **Citi Field**, home of the Mets (newyork.mets.mlb.com).

■ If you're in town during the summer, find out what's going on in **Central Park** (centralparknyc.org).

■ In the fall, get tickets to the **Metropolitan Opera** (metoperafamily.org).

■ If you're in town around Christmas, take the family to see the Christmas Spectacular at **Radio City Music Hall** (radiocity.com).

ROLLER-SKATING RINK

Looking for a roller-skating rink in Manhattan? You'll need to look a little further. The last of the hardwood rinks has closed, but head over to Staten Island to **RollerJam USA** (236 Richmond Valley Rd, 718/605-6600) which includes an entertainment center, bounce houses and arcade. Check the schedule for sessions and classes. DJs keep the pace moving with lively tunes. For special events, book the party room, which serves beer and wine to legal-age adults.

The Shark (South Street Seaport, 212/742-1969): speedboat harbor ride

Staten Island Ferry (Whitehall Ferry Terminal, south end of Manhattan): free

RESTAURANTS

Cercle Rouge (241 West Broadway, 212/226-6252): weekend brunch and magic show

Shake Shack (Madison Square Park, Madison Ave at 23rd St, 212/889-6600; 366 Columbus Ave, 646/747-8770; 154 E 86th St, 646/237-5035; 691 Eighth Ave, 646/435-0135; 600 Third Ave, 646/668-4880; Grand Central Terminal, 646/517-5805 and 215 Murray St, 646/545-4600)

Union Square Cafe (21 E 16th St, 212/243-4020)

GREAT BASICS

Jackson Hole Burgers (232 E 64th St, 212/371-7187; 521 Third Ave, 212/679-3264 and 517 Columbus Ave, 212/362-5177)

John's Pizzeria (260 W 44th St, 212/391-7560 and other locations)

Lombardi's (32 Spring St, 212/941-7994)

Two Boots (42 Ave A, 212/254-1919 and other locations)

GREAT DESSERTS

Bubby's (120 Hudson St, 212/219-0666)

Cafe Lalo (201 W 83rd St, 212/496-6031)

ChikaLicious (203 E 10th St, 212/995-9511)

Peanut Butter & Co. (240 Sullivan St, 212/677-3995)

Serendipity 3 (225 E 60th St, 212/838-3531)

Veniero's (342 E 11th St, 212/674-7070)

THEME RESTAURANTS

Alice's Tea Cup (102 W 73rd St, 212/799-3006; 156 E 64th St, 212/486-9200 and 220 E 81st St, 212/734-4832)

Barking Dog Luncheonette (1678 Third Ave, 212/831-1800 and other locations)

Brooklyn Diner USA (212 W 57th St, 212/977-1957 and 155 W 43rd St, 212/265-5400)

Hard Rock Cafe (1501 Broadway, 212/343-3355)

Jekyll and Hyde of Greenwich Village (91 Seventh Ave, 212/989-7701)

Ninja New York (25 Hudson St, 212/274-8500)

BOOKSTORES

Bank Street Bookstore (2875 Broadway, 212/678-1654)

Scholastic Store (557 Broadway, 212/343-6166)

TOY STORES

Boomerang Toys (119 West Broadway, 212/226-7650 and 1 North End Ave, 212/227-7271)

F.A.O. Schwarz (767 Fifth Ave, 212/644-9400)

Kidding Around (60 W 15th St, 212/645-6337 and Grand Central Terminal, 42nd St at Vanderbilt Ave, 212/972-8697)

Toy Tokyo (91 Second Ave, 212/673-5424)

Toys "R" Us (Times Square, 1514 Broadway, 646/366-8800)

West Side Kids (498 Amsterdam Ave, 212/496-7282)

HOT DEALS

Every theater does things differently, so you really need to get accurate, up-to-date information if you want to secure in-demand tickets at lower prices. Some theaters have lotteries a couple of hours before each performance for seats in the first few rows. Some offer Standing Room Only (SRO) tickets. Some give discount tickets only to students, while others have so-called rush tickets available for certain performances.

Just as some things are fun to do with kids, there are other activities that you should not do with them.

Check your destination's age requirement before bringing the kids. If you're going shopping at a perpetually crowded place like Zabar's or Fairway, don't take kids, or keep a firm grip on their hands if you do.

The latter holds true just about everywhere in New York; it's easy for a young one to get lost in a crowd! And remember that kids tire more quickly than adults. Chances are you'll do a lot of walking, and they're taking two or three steps for every one of yours! As the New York Times once put it, "Baby miles are like dog years."

Finally, it's a challenge to tote an infant or toddler in New York. While hundreds of thousands of children are born and raised in the city, visitors who are accustomed to carting children through malls in strollers and around town in car seats may have trouble here.

Many places, including the subway system, are not exactly stroller-accessible.

Taxis with functioning seatbelts have become much easier to find in recent years, but ones with children's car seats are a rarity. Taxi drivers must allow passengers to install car seats.

FATHER DUFFY SQUARE

The focal point of **Father Duffy Square** (Times Square between Broadway and Seventh Ave and 45th and 47th St) is the glowing ruby-red stairs, which are built mostly of structural-strength glass. The 27 wide steps seat 1,500 (if everyone gets cozy) and offer a commanding view down Broadway. It's a great place to meet friends or come solo; don't forget your latte or lunch, as eating and drinking are welcome here. LED lights bring the stairs to life at night and an innovative heating system keeps them snow- and ice-free.

FOR FREE

Even the most frugal and resourceful visitors often feel as if they're bleeding money. ("Didn't we just get $200 out of the ATM!?") Still, you can find some good deals and do a lot of sightseeing for free.

MUSEUMS AND SIGHTS

You can find some free or reduced price museums and sights in New York; and remember, most have days and times with pay-what-you-wish or free admission. They include:

American Folk Art Museum (2 Lincoln Square)

American Numismatic Society (75 Varick St, 11th floor)

The Cathedral Church of Saint John the Divine (1047 Amsterdam Ave)

Drawing Center (35 Wooster St)

Federal Hall National Memorial (26 Wall St)

Federal Reserve Bank (33 Liberty St)

General Grant National Monument (Riverside Park)

Hispanic Society of America (613 W 155th St)

The Museum at FIT (Seventh Ave at 27th St)

Museum of American Illustration and **Museum of Comic and Cartoon Art** (128 E 63rd St)

National Museum of the American Indian (Alexander Hamilton U.S. Custom House, 1 Bowling Green)

New York Public Library (455 Fifth Ave)

New York Transit Museum Gallery Annex (Grand Central Terminal, 42nd St at Vanderbilt Ave)

Sony Wonder Technology Lab (550 Madison Ave)

Staten Island Ferry (Whitehall Ferry Terminal)

Theodore Roosevelt Birthplace (28 E 20th St)

Tibet House (22 W 15th St)

Trinity Church (Broadway at Wall St)

Many places admit children under 12 for free. Active-duty military personnel in uniform are admitted free to the Empire State Building, and Smithsonian Institution members are admitted free to the Cooper Hewitt, Smithsonian Design Museum. Although it definitely isn't free, you can tour both The Cloisters Museum and Gardens and The Metropolitan Museum of Art on the same day for one admission price. You can also get a discount on admission to The Jewish Museum if you show a ticket stub from the Museum of Jewish Heritage (and vice versa). You will find addresses, phone numbers and more information on these and other museums in Chapter 3.

FOR TICKETS

Nowhere else in the world will you find such a wealth of performing arts. And no trip to New York is complete without taking in at least one play, musical, ballet, concert or opera.

The trick, of course, is getting tickets. People have written entire books about how and where to get tickets, while others have made lucrative careers out of procuring them for out-of-towners. I've provided a variety of approaches for getting theater tickets and to find out about other performances. Keep your eye out for student and other discounts, but be aware that good deals for the best shows and performances are few and far between.

BROADWAY

People often have different things in mind when they say they want to see a show. Some may have their hearts set on great seats at a Saturday night performance of the hottest show on Broadway, while others are willing to sit anywhere and see anything. A lot of people fall somewhere between those extremes. In addition, some are willing to pay whatever it takes to see the show they want, while others just won't go if they can't pay less than full price. If the main purpose of your visit to the city is to see a particular show (or shows), make sure you have the tickets you want before leaving home so you're not disappointed.

Box Offices and Phone Orders—If you want to save money and pick your seat, go directly to the theater's box office with cash or a major credit card. Ask to see a diagram of the theater if it isn't posted, although most theaters are small enough to ensure that every seat has a good view. The best time to try is midweek. You can also ask the box office if day-of-performance cancellations or rush tickets will be released. (See "Hot Deals" box.)

If you're willing to spend a little extra money and let a computer pick the "best available" seat, call the number or go to the website listed and have your credit card ready. Most numbers will be for **Telecharge** (212/239-6200 or 800/447-7400, telecharge.com) or **TicketMaster** (800/745-3000,

> ## INFORMATION, PLEASE!
>
> 311 is New York City's all-purpose information number. If you need to know how to rent a baseball field in Central Park, how to sign up for a Gracie Mansion tour, how to pay a parking fine or anything related to New York City (including loud music and noise complaints), operators are standing by. Outside of the local area, call 212/639-9675. Dial 911 for emergencies.

THEATER TICKETS

I'm often asked about reliable ticket brokers. **Americana Tickets** (800/833-3121, 212/581-6660, americanatickets.com) has been recognized for setting the standard. The third generation of the Radler family is outstanding to deal with! Americana offers availability of the specific theater, sports and concert tickets you want at all price points and discounts available for current, next day and later dates. An Americana retail store is located in Times Square (Broadway at 47th St) and their main headquarters is in the New York Marriott Marquis (Broadway at 46th St, 3rd floor). In Times Square, look for Americana's Street Team wearing black shirts printed with the word "tickets." They have been helping people buy tickets since 1927!

ticketmaster.com). Both charge a handling fee in addition to the ticket price.

Be forewarned: full-price tickets to Broadway shows typically cost at least $100 and sometimes fetch well over $300. Moreover, if the play or musical you want to see is hot, it may be sold out the entire time you're in New York. In fact, a few really hot shows may be sold out months in advance.

Care-Tix—If you have your heart set on a particular show and cost is no obstacle, **Broadway Cares/Equity Fights AIDS** sells house seats for sold-out Broadway and off-Broadway shows for twice the face value; premium seats cost the face value plus $150. The extra money goes to a good cause and is a tax-deductible contribution. Call 212/840-0770 and ask for **Care-Tix** or visit broadwaycares.org.

TKTS Outlets—If you want to see a Broadway show, are flexible and have some free time, go to one of the TKTS outlets in Manhattan operated by the not-for-profit Theatre Development Fund. These outlets sell whatever tickets happen to be left for various shows on the day of performance for up to half price (plus a $4 per-ticket charge). The most popular TKTS outlet is easily located as a result of some snazzy construction. Look for the ruby-red glass stairs at Father Duffy Square (47th St and Broadway, 212/912-9770) where 12 ticket windows are tucked underneath the steps.

For matinee performances, tickets are sold Wednesday, Thursday and Saturday from 10 to 2 and Sundays from 11 to 3. For evening performances, tickets are sold Monday through Saturday from 3 to 8 (from 2 on Tuesday) and Sunday from 3 until 7 for same day performances. A less crowded TKTS outlet is located in Lower Manhattan at the intersection of Front and John streets, just below South Street Seaport's main plaza. It's open Monday through Saturday from 11 to 6, and Sunday in summer months from 11 to 4. Matinee tickets at this location go on sale the day before a performance. To see what shows are available at the TKTS locations, you can download their free app which shows in real time what shows are available or see the same information online at tdf.org/tktslive. Tickets may be purchased with major credit cards as well as cash.

The Theatre Development Fund also offers extremely good deals to its members on tickets to theater and other performances. If you're a student, member of the clergy or armed forces (serving or retired), teacher, union member or performing artist, go to the Fund's website for more information. TDF acquires a small number of deeply discounted tickets for people with disabilities and their companion or attendant.

Off-Broadway and off-off-Broadway—In part because staging a Broadway production is almost prohibitively expensive, off-Broadway and off-off-Broadway theaters have really taken off. Thanks to a glut of talented actors and actresses in New York, such theater is typically excellent and often innovative. Tickets for off-Broadway and off-off-Broadway productions tend to be significantly less expensive.

OPERA AND CLASSICAL MUSIC

No other city in the world has as many musical events to choose from as New York! Contact the **92nd Street Y** (1395 Lexington Ave, 212/415-5500, 92y.org) if you're interested in chamber music or recitals by top performers. Otherwise, here's how to find schedule and ticket information at New York's top venues:

Carnegie Hall—Individual musicians, out-of-town orchestras and chamber-music ensembles perform at Carnegie Hall all year. Contact them for detailed information about performances, rush tickets, same-day student, senior and partial-view ticket discounts (154 W 57th St, 212/247-7800, carnegiehall.org). A limited number of partial-view seats are available for $10 on the day of each performance.

Metropolitan Opera—The season for the internationally renowned Met runs from fall through spring, and tickets are available through the box office (212/362-6000, metoperafamily.org) at Lincoln Center (Columbus Ave at 64th St) from 10 to 8 (noon to 6 on Sunday). Be aware that choice seats can cost as much as $375! If you have a little time on your hands, there are bargains to be had for members, subscribers and students. Standing Room Only (SRO) tickets are often available the day of the performance.

LINCOLN CENTER JAZZ

Jazz at Lincoln Center is actually at the Time Warner Center (10 Columbus Circle; take the JAZZ elevator). The managing and artistic director is none other than jazz trumpeter Wynton Marsalis. He and his orchestra are featured regularly; other nights might bring a surprise guest appearance or up and coming musicians. **Dizzy's Club Coca-Cola** (212/258-9595, jazz. org/dizzys) is the venue for it all, with great food to accompany the great music.

The New York Philharmonic—The Philharmonic's season runs from September through June at Avery Fisher Hall in Lincoln Center. For schedule and ticket information, go to the Philharmonic's website (nyphil.org) or call 212/875-5656. If you would rather attend a performance during the day and save a bit, ask about reduced-price tickets to open rehearsals; rush tickets may also be available.

ONLINE TICKETS

Here are some better-known websites for event tickets in the city (and sometimes elsewhere). Check for discount programs associated with Costco, AAA and other memberships. Compare prices from a couple of sites to make sure you are getting the best deal.

Broadway.com: tickets plus comprehensive theatrical information

Broadway.org: information on all New York shows

BroadwayBox.com: discounted theater, sports events and concerts

Kidsnightonbroadway.com: For one week each spring, kids aged six to 18 attend participating shows free with a full-paying adult.

StubHub.com: Buy or sell any tickets to any event, anywhere.

Teens.artsconnection.org: $5 tickets through High 5 Tickets for teens from 13 to 18 to music, dance, theater and visual-arts events

TodayTix is an app for purchasing last-minute theatre tickets at great prices.

DANCE AND BALLET

New York is home to several world-class companies and a great many smaller ones. They include:

Alvin Ailey American Dance Theater (405 W 55th St, 212/405-9000, alvinailey.org)

American Ballet Theatre (212/477-3030, abt.org)

Dance Theatre of Harlem (212/690-2800, dancetheatreofharlem.org)

New York City Ballet (212/496-0600, nycballet.com)

New York Live Arts (212/691-6500, newyorklivearts.org)

Paul Taylor Dance Company (212/431-5562, ptdc.org)

A number of major companies perform at the **New York City Center** (131 W 55th Street). Contact **CityTix** (212/581-1212, nycitycenter.org), or visit an individual dance company's website for information about tickets and upcoming performances.

TELEVISION SHOW TAPINGS

There is one kind of ticket almost everybody wants to get in New York; one that allows you to become part of the studio audience for one of the many TV talk shows filmed here. I've listed some of the most popular shows with a brief description for obtaining tickets; *The Dr. Oz Show, Live! With Kelly and Michael* and other shows have similar policies. Check their websites for particulars.

Saturday Night Live—Year in and year out, these are the hardest tickets of all to get. A lottery is held every August from emails collected during the preceding 12 months, and each winner gets two tickets. If you want to be included in the lottery, send an email to snltickets@nbcuni.com. Standby tickets for the 8 p.m. dress rehearsal and the 11:30 p.m. live show are available at 7 a.m. on the day of the show at the 49th Street entrance to 30 Rockefeller Plaza.

The Tonight Show starring Jimmy Fallon—Tickets to this nightly program are available by visiting showclix.com/event/thetonightshowstarringjimmyfallon. The host entertains millions with comedy, pop culture, music and the unexpected from Studio 6-B, 30 Rockefeller Plaza.

The View—This women's gabfest is taped Monday through Thursday at ABC Studios on Manhattan's Upper West Side (320 W 66th St). Go to abc.go.com/daytime/theview/tickets to request tickets for a specific date at least three months in advance. If you're in town and feel lucky, go by the studio between 8 and 9 on a morning when they're taping and pick up a standby number. You must be at least 16 years old to attend.

FOR A ROMANTIC INTERLUDE

Whether you're falling in love for the first time or celebrating a wedding anniversary, New York can be one of the most romantic places in the world to celebrate. If you're in the mood for love or want to create a mood that's just right for romance, try the following:

- Dinner at **River Café** (1 Water St, Brooklyn)
- A summertime dinner in the garden at **Barbetta** (321 W 46th St)
- Dinner at the discreet and classy **Le Périgord** (405 E 52nd St)
- Drinks at **Campbell Apartment**, an elegant spot tucked away in a corner of Grand Central Terminal (just east of Vanderbilt Ave)
- A late-night visit to the **Empire State Building** Observation Deck (Fifth Ave between 33rd and 34th St)
- A walk across the **Brooklyn Bridge** is a must!
- Watching the sun rise from the **Brooklyn Bridge**, the **Battery Park Esplanade**, **Lighthouse Park** on Roosevelt Island or the deck of the **Staten Island Ferry**
- A visit to the **Winter Garden** (World Financial Center)
- A picnic lunch overlooking the Hudson River from **The Cloisters Museum and Gardens**
- A stroll through the splendid lobby of the **Waldorf Astoria New York**
- An early evening spent listening to classical music from the balcony of the **The Metropolitan Museum of Art**'s Great Hall
- A rowboat or gondola ride on **Central Park Lake** or a nighttime sail around Manhattan

FOR PARTIES AND SPECIAL EVENTS

If you're looking for the perfect place to hold a wedding reception, bar mitzvah or gala event for thousands, New York inevitably has the right place

FOR JAZZ LOVERS

Keep the **Garage Restaurant & Cafe** (99 Seventh Ave S, 212/645-0600) in mind if you're looking for live jazz. You can hear two sets of jazz seven days a week: over a relaxing brunch on the weekends, nightly during dinner and on into the wee morning hours. If you're a people watcher, opt for a table on the balcony or a sidewalk cafe table in the summer.

OPERA CHANGES

The **New York City Opera** was a cultural scene in New York for 70 years before going bankrupt. The good news is that it will relaunch in 2015 at Lincoln Center's Rose Theater in the Time Warner Center. Follow their progress at nycorenaissance.com.

. . . and the people to put it together. The trick, of course, is finding them. The other trick is paying for the event!

If you want to throw a party at your favorite museum, restaurant, hotel or bar, by all means ask. Many museum spaces, including the **Mount Vernon Hotel Museum and Garden**; the **Cooper Hewitt, Smithsonian Design Museum**; and the Theodore Roosevelt Rotunda at the **American Museum of Natural History** (complete with its dinosaur display) can be rented for parties and other events.

Some of my favorite private party rooms in New York are at **Barbetta** (321 W 46th St), **Four Seasons** (99 E 52nd St), **Gramercy Tavern** (42 E 20th St), **Le Périgord** (405 E 52nd St), **One if by Land, Two if by Sea** (17 Barrow St), **Serendipity 3** (225 E 60th St) and **Tribeca Grill** (375 Greenwich St).

Some venues available for special events take care of all the catering, while others simply provide the space. This list should give you an idea of the breadth of spaces available: **New York Public Library** (455 Fifth Ave), **Studio 450** (450 W 31st St), **Astra** (979 Third Ave), the **Loeb Boathouse** (in Central Park), **Pier Sixty** (at Chelsea Piers) and **91** (The Upper Crust, 91 Horatio St). Catering is optional at the **New York Botanical Garden** (in The Bronx) and the **Pratt Mansions** (1027 Fifth Ave).

Before forging ahead with planning a party in New York, be aware that it's going to cost a great deal of money. I'm talking really big bucks. You can save money by avoiding Saturday evening, holding your numbers down and throwing your party in the off months of July and August or between January and early April. Some venues and caterers may negotiate on price, but don't expect any great or even particularly good deals. Make your reservations at least two months and as far as two years in advance.

FOR RESTROOMS

Nothing's more bothersome than not being able to find a bathroom when one is needed. By law, public buildings are required to have public restrooms. They are not, however, required to be clean and safe.

Following is a list of bathrooms that meet at least minimal standards of safety and cleanliness. You may need to ask for directions or a key, but all are free to the public. As a general rule, try hotel lobbies, department stores, schools, theaters, municipal government buildings, churches, libraries and even hospitals. Starbucks, other coffee houses and fast-food locations throughout the city are also good bets. Of course, if you have small children in tow, just about any store or restaurant will likely take pity.

Wherever you end up, be sure to follow a few safety tips. Leaving anything on the floor in a public restroom is a mistake, as purses and packages have a bad habit of disappearing while you're occupied! The same is true of items left hanging on the back of a stall door. Avoid deserted bathrooms, as well as those in parks (unless listed below) and most subway stations.

BELOW 14TH STREET

Castle Clinton National Monument (inside Battery Park)
National Museum of the American Indian (1 Bowling Green)
Trinity Church (Broadway at Wall St)
Federal Hall National Memorial (26 Wall St, at Broad St)
South Street Seaport (Fulton St at Water St)
Hotel on Rivington (107 Rivington St, bet Essex and Ludlow St)
Essex Street Market (120 Essex St, at Delancey St)
New York City Fire Museum (278 Spring St, bet Hudson and Varick St)
Strand Book Store (828 Broadway, at 12th St)

BETWEEN 14TH AND 42ND STREETS

ABC Carpet & Home (888 Broadway, at 19th St)
Macy's (Herald Square, 151 W 34th St, at Broadway)
Science, Industry and Business Library (188 Madison Ave, at 34th St)
New York Public Library (455 Fifth Ave, bet 40th and 42nd St)
Bryant Park (Ave of the Americas bet 40th and 42nd St)
Grand Hyatt New York (109 E 42nd St, bet Park and Lexington Ave)
Grand Central Terminal (42nd St at Vanderbilt Ave)

MIDTOWN

United Nations (First Ave bet 42nd and 47th St)
Waldorf Astoria New York (301 Park Ave, at 50th St)
Saks Fifth Avenue (611 Fifth Ave, bet 49th and 50th St)
Rockefeller Center (concourse level, bet Fifth Ave and Ave of the Americas from 49th to 51st St)
Fendi (677 Fifth Ave, bet 53rd and 54th St)

JOIN THE AUDIENCE!

Look for NBC's *Today Show* crowd on the sidewalk along 49th Street between Fifth Avenue and Avenue of the Americas. People show up before dawn, although cameras don't start rolling until 7 a.m. ABC's *Good Morning America* welcomes audiences Monday through Friday for their 7 to 9 a.m. live show. See their website (abcnews.go.com/gma) for ticket information. A standby line forms outside the Times Square studio (44th St and Broadway), alongside those with tickets. Fans of CBS's *The Early Show* may stop by the Early Show plaza (Fifth Ave and 59th St) before 7:15 a.m. to join the audience. Backstage tours of the studio are conducted after the show. No tickets are needed.

FIELD HOUSE AT CHELSEA PIERS

If you have a child who wants to climb a wall, take batting practice or kick a soccer ball around, then go to the **Field House at Chelsea Piers** (212/336-6500, chelseapiers.com). Located on the far west side of Manhattan, between 17th and 23rd streets, this is a remarkable complex; they also offer camps, scholarships and plenty of sports programs for adults, too.

Park Avenue Plaza (55 E 52nd St, at Madison Ave)
Henri Bendel (712 Fifth Ave, at 56th St)
Park Central New York (870 Seventh Ave, at 56th St)
Sony Wonder Technology Lab (550 Madison Ave, at 56th St)

UPPER EAST SIDE

Bloomingdale's (1000 Third Ave, at 59th St)
Asia Society and Museum (725 Park Ave, at 70th St)
Ralph Lauren (867 Madison Ave, at 72nd St)
Marimekko (1262 Third Ave, at 73rd St)
Niketown New York (6 E 57th St, at Madison Ave)
92nd Street Y (1395 Lexington Ave, at 92nd St)
Charles A. Dana Discovery Center (in Central Park, Fifth Ave at 110th St)

UPPER WEST SIDE

Avery Fisher Hall (Lincoln Center, 65th St at Columbus Ave)
New York Public Library for the Performing Arts (Lincoln Center, 65th St at Broadway)
The Cathedral Church of Saint John the Divine (1047 Amsterdam Ave, at 112th St)

FOR VISITORS WITH SPECIAL NEEDS

If you're coming to New York with a physical challenge, you ought to know about a couple of resources. First, get a copy of an exceptional guide to the city's cultural institutions that describes in detail facilities for people in wheelchairs, as well as the blind and deaf. This invaluable guide is available from **Hospital Audiences, Inc.** (212/284-4100, hainyc.org). Second, the **Metropolitan Transportation Authority** has a very informative website (mta.info/accessibility). The **Mayor's Office for People with Disabilities** (212/639-9675, nyc.gov/html/mopd) is also a great resource. Finally, many Broadway theaters offer deeply discounted tickets for people in wheelchairs and their companions. Call individual theaters for more information.

NOTES

CHAPTER 8

INDEX

The index is in word-by-word alphabetical order. Business names that begin with a number precede the alphabetical list. All-cap entries indicate a main write-up or review for that listing. The main write-up is on the bold pages number.

508   INDEX

N

Q

R

T

NOTES